16e

THE CHALLENGE OF
Effective Speaking

in a Digital Age

Rudolph F. Verderber
University of Cincinnati

Deanna D. Sellnow
University of Kentucky

Kathleen S. Verderber
Northern Kentucky University

CENGAGE
Learning·

Australia • Brazil • Mexico • Singapore • United Kingdom • United States

CENGAGE Learning·

The Challenge of Effective Speaking in a Digital Age, **Sixteenth Edition**

Rudolph F. Verderber, Deanna D. Sellnow, Kathleen S. Verderber

Product Director: Monica Eckman

Senior Product Manager: Nicole Morinon

Managing Developer: Megan Garvey

Content Developer: Kassi Radomski

Content Coordinator: Alicia Landsberg

Product Assistant: Colin Solan

Media Developer: Jessica Badiner

Marketing Manager: Lydia LeStar

Content Project Manager: Corinna Dibble

Art Director: Linda May

Manufacturing Planner: Doug Bertke

Rights Acquisition Specialist: Ann Hoffman

Production Service: Cenveo® Publisher Services

Interior and Cover Designer: Studio Montage

Cover Credits: Audience icon, © Sielan/ Shutterstock; all other icons, © CoraMax/ Shutterstock

Compositor: Cenveo Publisher Services

For product information and technology assistance, contact us at **Cengage Learning Customer & Sales Support, 1-800-354-9706.**

For permission to use material from this text or product, submit all requests online at **www.cengage.com/permission**. Further permissions questions can be emailed to **permissionrequest@cengage.com**.

Library of Congress Control Number: 2013943069

ISBN-13: 978-1-285-09484-7

ISBN-10: 1-285-09484-0

Cengage Learning
200 First Stamford Place, 4th floor
Stamford, CT 06902
USA

Cengage Learning is a leading provider of customized learning solutions with office locations around the globe, including Singapore, the United Kingdom, Australia, Mexico, Brazil and Japan. Locate your local office at **international.cengage.com/region**.

Cengage Learning products are represented in Canada by Nelson Education, Ltd.

For your course and learning solutions, vis**it www.cengage.com**.

Purchase any of our products at your local college store or at our preferred online store **www.cengagebrain.com**.

Instructors: Please visit **login.cengage.com** and log in to access instructor-specific resources.

Printed in the United States of America
1 2 3 4 5 6 7 17 16 15 14 13

Brief Contents

contents

part 1 Orientation

Principles

part ②

Informative and Persuasive Speaking   part ③

Adapting to Other Occasions and Formats   part ④

preface

We are really excited about this sixteenth edition of *The Challenge of Effective Speaking in a Digital Age* and believe you will be too. As you will see, we do several important things to make this revision highly relevant for today's readers.

Most important, we worked hard to highlight throughout the book the role of **digital media and technology** in preparing, presenting, and interpreting public speeches today. We have even revised the title of the book slightly to reflect this important update. In other words, we talk about the role of digital media and technology in topic selection, audience analysis, conducting research and gathering information, preparing and sharing presentational aids, and delivery. Not only do we integrate these updates throughout the chapters, we also include sample student speeches about issues related to technology and social media such as online social networks, cyberbullying, and online identity theft. And we embed actual examples addressing technology-related challenges in public speaking occurring in both face-to-face and online settings.

Likewise, we make a special effort in this edition to highlight the **relevance of public speaking in the real world** through our **Reflect on Ethics** and **Public Speaking in the Real World** features. We focus on ethical issues in our Reflect on Ethics case studies, which include well-known actors, comedians, professional athletes and musicians, such as Kanye West (Chapter 3), Jon Stewart (Chapter 4), Manti Te'o (Chapter 5), Coldplay (Chapter 6), Seth McFarlane (Chapter 8), David Ortiz (Chapter 14), and Steve Carell (Chapter 15). Public Speaking in the Real World examples range from Julia Roberts on stuttering (Chapter 1), Harrison Ford on speech anxiety (Chapter 2), Dale Carnegie on effective listening (Chapter 3), Oprah Winfrey on audience analysis (Chapter 5), Daniel Day Lewis and Sally Field on doing research (Chapter 6), Steve Jobs on organizing (Chapter 7), Lady Gaga on introductions and conclusions (Chapter 8), President Obama on language and oral style (Chapter 10), Anne Hathaway on practicing speech delivery (Chapter 11), and Charlize Theron and Brad Pitt on persuasive speaking (Chapters 13 and 14).

We have also made several revisions that respond directly to reviewer suggestions. For example, **Chapter 2, Your First Speech**, now focuses specifically on getting students up and speaking. Similarly, we now include an **Impromptu Speech Challenge** in each chapter to provide students opportunities to practice this skill throughout the term. We also added many more timely and relevant **sample student outlines** on topics ranging from a eulogy speech about "Grandma Frances"; a self-introduction speech from a first-generation college student; informative speeches about prescription drug abuse, online identity theft, civic engagement, and online social networks; as well as persuasive speeches on "hooking up" and cyberbullying. We also updated the **opening vignettes** to focus on multimodal (integrated oral, written, visual, and digital) communication issues and now thread them as examples throughout the chapters. Finally, to address the assessment-driven world of education today, we now open each chapter with specific **learning outcomes** driving the content and closing with reflective questions readers should be able to answer after reading the chapter and applying it to their speeches.

While we are excited about these new revisions, we have also retained some key features that reviewers appreciate. For example, you will see that we continue to ground public speaking firmly in its roots—**rhetorical theory**—beginning in Chapter 1 and then throughout the book. Doing so reminds readers that public speaking concepts and skills are based on a rhetorical tradition that has stood the test of time for over 2,000 years! And we continue to organize the heart of the book around the six **Speech-Planning Action Steps**, although in a bit more streamlined way than in previous editions. We first discuss each step and then provide a sequence of easy-to-complete activities that readers can use to prepare an effective speech. We hope instructors will assign the activities and encourage students to use the activities even when they are not assigned. Why? Because we know they work, and we want readers to succeed.

New to This Edition

- We made a conscious decision to incorporate an even **stronger emphasis on rhetoric and rhetorical theory** so that students understand why public speaking is a liberal art. We worked hard to make this theory student-friendly through the use of clear definitions and interesting examples.

- In response to faculty requests, we have included even more **sample student speeches**, as well as extended examples based on the opening scenarios described in each chapter.

- **All new Public Speaking in the Real World boxes** highlight how successful people use the public speaking skills we discuss in each chapter. Examples include Julia Roberts on stuttering, Harrison Ford on managing speech anxiety, and Anne Hathaway on practicing speeches in advance.

- New **Impromptu Speech Challenge** boxes in each chapter encourage students to prepare and present impromptu speeches based on some concept or skill discussed in that chapter.

- We include intentional discussions of effective public speaking skills as played out in **virtual settings;** using **technology** and **digital media** to research, prepare, and present public speeches; and the expanding role of technology in preparing and using **presentational aids.**

Chapter-by-Chapter Updates and Revisions

- **Chapter 1, Foundations of Public Speaking**, now begins with a discussion of public speaking as an empowering civic right and our ethical responsibility in being ethical public speakers. Then we explain how public speaking functions as one form of communication whether we do so in a face-to-face or online setting. After discussing the elements in the communication process and the contexts that situate public speaking among intrapersonal, interpersonal, group, and public communication; we describe the foundational theoretical concept of the rhetorical situation as it grounds effective public speaking. Finally, the major principles of effective speechmaking are discussed. The chapter ends with a sample speech outline for a eulogy speech called "My Grandma Frances."

- **Chapter 2, Your First Speech**, begins with a scenario about Kira, a first-generation college student who is terrified about giving her first classroom speech. We then use Kira as an example as we discuss public speaking apprehension, including symptoms, causes, and methods for managing it effectively. From there, we introduce the six-step speech planning process and demonstrate how Kira employed each step to construct an effective public speech. We close with Kira's formal outline for her speech of self-introduction titled "On Being First."

- **Chapter 3, Listening**, begins by addressing why it is important to study listening in a public speaking course and then differentiates hearing from listening. We then talk about some of the reasons effective listening can be difficult and provide specific strategies one can employ to improve our listening skills. The chapter concludes with a comprehensive discussion of how to listen to and constructively critique a speech, including preparing feedback for the speaker.

- **Chapter 4, Speech Topic and Goal,** opens with a conversation between Kameron and Kayla, and they are used as examples throughout the chapter. We begin by reminding readers that a good speech goal is grounded in the rhetorical public speaking situation. In other words, a good speech topic and goal is based on the speaker's interest and expertise, the knowledge and expectations of the audience, and the nature of the occasion. The chapter also focuses specifically on how to collect audience demographic and subject-related data, as well as data about the occasion and how to use that data when preparing a speech. We close the chapter with Kameron's speech on same-sex marriage.

- **Chapter 5, Adapting to Audiences,** has had minor revisions and continues to focus more specifically on tailoring speech ideas to different audiences. In this edition, we open with a scenario about Megan who had decided to do her speech on hurricanes, and J.J. who selected cell phone distracted driving. We use them and their topics as examples throughout the chapter as we discuss why and how to identify the audience's initial disposition, establish common ground, demonstrate relevance, highlight speaker credibility, and be comprehensible and memorable. We continue to highlight important considerations regarding language and cultural differences.

- **Chapter 6, Topic Development,** has been updated to reflect the way we use the Internet to locate and evaluate sources and information. We expanded our discussion on skimming online information to determine what to select for the speech and how to keep track of information in an annotated bibliography, in electronic slide files, or on research cards. Finally, we provide examples for citing sources and information on speech outlines and transcripts, as well as citing them orally during the speech.

- **Chapter 7, Organizing the Speech Body,** features an opening scenario about Katie and Alyssa who are taking their public speaking class online over the summer. An updated version of Katie's speech body outline on the uses and abuses of the prescription drug Adderall is used as an extended example to demonstrate each substep in the organizing process.

- **Chapter 8, The Introduction and Conclusion,** continues to feature Katie and Alyssa in the opening scenario and Katie's Adderall speech outline throughout the chapter. We emphasize the importance of audience-centered introductions and conclusions with specific examples of rhetorical devices that can be used as attention getters and clinchers. Finally, Katie's entire updated speech outline including the introduction and conclusion is offered.

- **Chapter 9, Presentational Aids,** has been updated to reflect the increasingly prominent role of technology-enhanced visual, audio, and audiovisual presentational aids in public speeches today. We begin the chapter by discussing how they not only serve as embellishments, but are actually most effective when they function as a form of supporting material to develop content. We offer the increasingly popular ignite-type speech format to server as an example of this point. After describing the various types of visual, audio, and audiovisual aids that might be used in a speech and offering illustrations that mirror how they might appear in computerized slideshows, we explain how to select, create, and use them effectively.

- **Chapter 10, Language and Oral Style,** continues to focus on how oral style differs from written style, as well as how to choose language that is appropriate, accurate, clear, and vivid. In this edition, however, we deliberately integrate a how-to demonstration of verbal immediacy and linguistic sensitivity when speaking to diverse audiences that may or may not share the same first language as the speaker. We believe this slight perspective shift more accurately reflects the language challenges facing public speakers today.

- **Chapter 11, Delivery**, has been lightly revised in ways that acknowledge how to rehearse effectively using the technology tools available to us. We also now include an entire section on how to deliver speeches effectively to virtual audiences over the Internet. Our opening scenario returns to Katie and Alyssa, this time focusing on Alyssa's concerns about using her voice and body to most effectively convey her great speech content about volunteering and civic engagement. Throughout the chapter, we use Alyssa as an extended example regarding use of voice, body, and presentational aids. The chapter closes with Alyssa's sample speaking notes, formal speech outline, and annotated speech transcript on volunteering and civic engagement.

- **Chapter 12, Informative Speaking**, includes a new chapter opening scenario with sample speeches and how they are introduced, which serves as an extended example throughout the chapter. The chapter continues to include a brief discussion of the nature of informative speaking and the importance of developing material that is suited to different learning styles. The chapter also highlights the important role of using listener relevance links to gain and maintain audience interest throughout the speech. New to this edition is Anna's sample process speech on Internet identity theft and Logan's sample process speech on online social media networks and society.

- **Chapter 13, Persuasive Messages**, which was revised significantly for the 15th edition, continues to focus in this edition on the nature of persuasion, how people process persuasive messages, and the role of logos, ethos, and pathos in persuasion. For this edition, however, we revised our discussion of logos to begin with the general nature of arguments based on Toulmin's model and tightened our discussion of the types of arguments speakers can use to make a case for their position. In the section on ethos, we continue to focus specifically on how conveying good character, goodwill, competence, and credibility function to persuade. Finally, in the section on pathos, we continue to focus on how speakers use specific positive and negative emotions to persuade.

- **Chapter 14, Persuasive Speaking**, builds on the nature of persuasive messages in general as described Chapter 13 by focusing specifically on how to create a persuasive speech. We explain how to use audience analysis data to detect an audience's attitude toward a persuasive topic; how to frame a persuasive speech goal as a proposition of fact, value, or policy; and how to organize speeches to convince and speeches to actuate. We offer two sample speeches in this chapter: a speech to convince focused on hooking up, friends with benefits, and dating and a speech to actuate on cyberbullying. Finally, we emphasize the special duty that persuasive speakers have to maintain high ethical standards, and we provide several ethical guidelines to follow when speaking to persuade.

- **Chapter 15, Ceremonial Speaking**, now includes several impromptu speech challenges students might complete to practice various types of ceremonial speeches they might be called on to make sometime in their life. Our opening scenario points to such an instance for Ben who is working on a eulogy for his grandfather's funeral.

- **Chapter 16, Group Communication and Presentations**, has been revised to focus first on the nature of effective leadership in groups and the shared leadership responsibilities of all group members. We then focus on group conflict as it contributes to successful problem solving when managed effectively. We devote an entire section to communicating effectively in virtual groups before describing the various formats available today for communicating group results. More specifically, we discuss communicating group deliverables in written formats (e.g., written briefs and comprehensive reports), oral formats (e.g., oral briefs, oral reports, panel discussions, symposiums), and virtual formats (e.g., remote access reports, streaming videos). Finally, we explain how to evaluate both group dynamics and formal group presentations using the criteria of effective communication described throughout this book.

Continuing Features

- **Speech-Planning Action Steps** guide students through a step-by-step preparation process that results in significantly better speeches. These Action Step activities are streamlined for this edition and continue to be supplemented by in-text and online examples of each activity prepared by other students.

- **Sample student speeches** continue to be a hallmark in this edition. In fact, we include even more sample student speeches and speech excerpts, which can be found in Chapters 1, 2, 5, 8, 11, 12, and 14. In addition, video of several of these speeches—including an impromptu speech—are featured in this book's online resources.

- **Speech Snippet boxes** throughout the book provide "snippets" of speeches by student speakers working through the myriad issues they must face when preparing a speech. For example, in the Chapter 5 discussions about adapting to an audience, the Speech Snippet boxes highlight how speakers demonstrated personal impact in a speech, addressed timeliness and acknowledged listener attitudes, demonstrated their direct expertise, established their trustworthiness, and more.

- **Reflect on Ethics boxes** in each chapter use contemporary situations to help students think through ethical challenges and the choices people face in public communication settings today.

- End-of-chapter activities including **Impromptu Speech Exercises** and **Assessment Activities**. Although students may only give three or four graded speeches per term, the impromptu speech exercises challenge students to practice speaking more often with short, quickly prepared speeches related to chapter material. Assessment activities are also tied to chapter content so that students and instructors can measure how well students understand and can apply the concepts and skills in each chapter.

- **Two bonus chapters** are available through Cengage Learning's Flex-Text customization program, present a more detailed look at impromptu speaking and a workbook for students who are completing service learning assignments. (For more information about the Flex-Text program, see the Instructor Resources section later in this preface.)

In addition, the sixteenth edition includes the following new and updated technological features:

- **MindTap** from Cengage Learning represents a new approach to a highly personalized, online learning platform. A fully online learning solution, MindTap combines all of a students learning tools – readings, multimedia, activities and assessments into a singular Learning Path that guides the student through the curriculum. Instructors personalize the experience by customizing the presentation of these learning tools to their students; even seamlessly introducing their own content into the Learning Path via "apps" that integrate into the MindTap platform. Additionally, MindTap provides interoperability with major Learning Management Systems (LMS) via support for open industry standards and fosters partnerships with 3rd party educational application providers to provide a highly collaborative, engaging and personalized learning experience. Learn more at www.cengage.com/mindtap.

- The **Speech Communication CourseMate for *The Challenge of Effective Speaking*** provides students with easy access to the integrated technology resources that accompany the book. These resources include learning, study, and exam preparation tools such as *Challenge*'s interactive eBook, flashcards, and the interactive Speech-Planning Action Steps and Applying What You've Learned activities that support the printed textbook. Watch comprehension soar as your class works with the printed textbook and the textbook-specific website. In addition, CourseMate's Engagement Tracker tracking tools allow instructors to monitor the progress of the class as a whole or of individual students. Engagement Tracker helps you identify students at risk early in the course, uncover which concepts are most difficult for your class, monitor time on task, and keep your students engaged. The CourseMate for *Challenge* goes beyond the book to deliver what you need!

- The *Challenge* **Interactive Video Activities** feature videos of all the sample student speeches featured in the text, as well as critical thinking questions for each speech.

- The book's **Web Links** are easily accessed from the MindTap for *Challenge*. These links have been integrated into the text to expand skills practice and learning online—they are highlighted in the text with colored text and icons.

If you want your students to have access to the online resources for *Challenge*, please be sure to order them for your course. These resources can be bundled with every new copy of the text or ordered separately. If you do not order them, your students will not have access to these resources. *Contact your Cengage Learning sales representative for more details.*

Supplementary Materials

In addition to the *Challenge* online textbook resources just described, the sixteenth edition can be packaged with a suite of integrated resources for students and instructors.

Student Resources

- **Online Student Workbook for *The Challenge of Effective Speaking*** by Larry Edmonds, Arizona State University. The student workbook has been updated for the sixteenth edition and offers chapter-by-chapter skill-building exercises, vocabulary lists, quizzes, and copies of the speech evaluation checklists featured in the text. The online Student workbook is available via CourseMate.

- Many of the Speech-Planning Action Steps can be completed with **Speech Builder Express 3.0 organization and outlining program, available in MindTap.** This interactive web-based tool coaches students through the speech organization and outlining process. By completing interactive sessions based on the in-text Action Steps, students can prepare and save their outlines—including a plan for visual aids and a Works Cited section—formatted according to the principles presented in the text. Text models of speech elements reinforce students' interactive practice.

- **MindTap** from Cengage Learning represents a new approach to a highly personalized, online learning platform. A fully online learning solution, MindTap combines all of students' learning tools – readings, multimedia, activities and assessments into a singular Learning Path that guides the student through the curriculum. Learn more at www.cengage.com/mindtap.

- **InfoTrac College Edition with InfoMarks.** Access this virtual library's more than 18 million reliable, full-length articles from 5,000 academic and popular periodicals, and retrieve results almost instantly. They also have access to InfoMarks—stable URLs that can be linked to articles, journals, and searches to save valuable time when doing research—and to the InfoWrite online resource center, where students can access grammar help, critical-thinking guidelines, guides to writing research papers, and much more. InfoTrack College Edition is available via CourseMate.

- **CengageBrain Online Store**. CengageBrain.com is a single destination for more than 15,000 new print textbooks, textbook rentals, eBooks, single eChapters, and print, digital, and audio study tools. CengageBrain.com provides the freedom to purchase Cengage Learning products à-la-carte—exactly what you need, when you need it. Visit www.CengageBrain.com for details.

- *Service Learning in Communication Studies: A Handbook* by Rick Isaacson and Jeff Saperstein. This is an invaluable resource for students in the basic course that integrates, or will soon integrate, a service learning component. This handbook provides guidelines for connecting service-learning work with classroom concepts and advice for working effectively with agencies and organizations. It also provides model forms and reports, as well as a directory of online resources.

- *A Guide to the Basic Course for ESL Students* by Esther Yook, Mary Washington College. This guide for non-native speakers includes strategies for accent management and overcoming speech apprehension, in addition to helpful web addresses and answers to frequently asked questions.

Instructor Resources

- **Electronic Instructor's Resource Manual with Test Bank** This electronic manual features changes from the fifteenth edition to the sixteenth edition, sample syllabi, chapter-by-chapter outlines, summaries, vocabulary lists, suggested lecture and discussion topics, classroom exercises, assignments, and a comprehensive test bank with answer key and rejoinders.

- **The Instructor Companion site** is accessible through an SSO login and contains an electronic version of the Instructor's Resource Manual, Cognero® Computerized Testing, predesigned Microsoft® PowerPoint® presentations, and JoinIn® classroom quizzing. The PowerPoint presentations contain text, images, and videos of the case studies and can be used as they are or customized to suit your course needs.

- **Public Speaking: An Online Approach; Public Speaking: A Problem Based Learning Approach; and Public Speaking: A Service-Learning Approach for Instructors** by Deanna Sellnow, University of Kentucky. Each of these instructor workbooks includes a course syllabus and icebreakers; relevant discussions of basic public speaking topics such as coping with anxiety, learning cycles and styles, outlining, and ethics; and informative, persuasive, and ceremonial (special occasion) speeches.

- **The Teaching Assistant's Guide to the Basic Course** by Katherine G. Hendrix, University of Memphis. Based on leading communication teacher training programs, this guide covers general teaching and course management topics as well as specific strategies for communication instruction—for example, providing effective feedback on performance, managing sensitive class discussions, and conducting mock interviews.

- **Student Speeches for Critique and Analysis**. This multivolume video series offers both imperfect and award-winning sample student speeches.

- **ABC News DVD: Speeches by Barack Obama**. This DVD includes nine famous speeches by President Barack Obama, from 2004 to present day, including his speech at the 2004 Democratic National Convention; his 2008 speech on race, "A More Perfect Union"; and his 2009 inaugural address. Speeches are divided into short video segments for easy, time-efficient viewing. This instructor supplement also features critical thinking questions and answers for each speech, designed to spark class discussion.

- **Videos for Speech Communication 2010: Public Speaking, Human Communication, and Interpersonal Communication**. This DVD provides footage of news stories from BBC and CBS that relate to current topics in communication, such as teamwork and how to interview for jobs, as well as news clips about speaking anxiety and speeches from contemporary public speakers, such as Michelle Obama and Hillary Clinton.

- **Flex-Text Customization Program**. With this program you can create a text as unique as your course: quickly, simply, and affordably. As part of our flex-text program, you can add your personal touch to *Challenge* with a course-specific cover and up to 32 pages of your own content—at no additional cost.

Contact your local Cengage Learning representative or go to http://www.cengage.com/highered/ for more information, user names and passwords, examination copies, or a demonstration of these ancillary products. These items are available to qualified adopters.

Acknowledgments

The book you are holding is the result of a team effort, and we have been privileged to work with the best. First, we want to acknowledge the wonderful students whose speeches appear in this book. We also want to thank our colleagues around the world who have used previous editions of the book and have graciously shared with us their experiences teaching from these texts. We would like to single out the following people who participated in the review process for this edition: Diane Badzinski, Colorado Christian University; Benjamin Cline, Culver-Stockton College; Ginni Jurkowski, State University of New York, Geneseo; Susan Lichtman, Miami Dade College, Kendall Campus; Kimberly Rosenfeld, Cerritos College; Yasmin Shenoy, University of Hartford; Amy Trombley, Collin College; Jamie Ward, University of Michigan, Dearborn; Angelique Wood, Westwood College; Pamela Xanthopoulos, Jackson State Community College; and Wendy Yarberry, Florida State College.

As we prepared this revision, we worked with some familiar faces and welcomed several new editorial, marketing, and production team members. We have enjoyed working with Alicia Landsberg, content coordinator; Colin Solan, product assistant; Julia Schuster, market development manager; Lydia LeStar, marketing manager; Jessica Badiner, media developer; Samantha Ross Miller, production manager; Corinna Dibble, senior content project manager; Nicole Morinon, senior product manager; and Lois Lombardo project manager. Special thank yous are due for two people. First, to Monica Eckman, our product director, whose belief in this book is only outweighed by her enthusiasm and hard work on our behalf. Her responsiveness to our needs as authors is above and beyond. And second, to Kassi Radomski, our content developer, who not only keeps us on task, but also offers great advice to improve the quality of our work. She has been a godsend for us on this project.

Finally, with this edition, Rudy and Kathie Verderber have moved from a primary role in the revision process to an advisory one. As they do so, I (Deanna) would like to pay tribute to Rudy for his innovative vision in conceiving the step-by-step process approach to public speaking that continues to ground this book and for his forty plus years of authoring and refining it. I also want to thank both Rudy and Kathie for entrusting me with the privilege of taking these ideas forward in ways that now also address the digital age we live in today. Lastly, I ask you to keep them both in your thoughts and prayers as Rudy continues his ongoing battle with Alzheimer's. This edition is dedicated to them both. As always, to God be the glory!

The Challenge of Effective Speaking in a Digital Age

1 "foundations of public speaking"

⊙ WHEN YOU'VE FINISHED THIS CHAPTER, YOU WILL BE ABLE TO:

1-1 Describe the nature and purpose of public speaking as a liberal art

1-2 Identify the ethical responsibilities of effective public speaking

1-3 Explain how public speaking fits within the realm of communication

1-4 Define the components of the rhetorical situation

1-5 Examine effective speech components of content, structure, and delivery

🌐 MindTap™

Review the chapter **Learning Objectives** and **Start** with quick warm up activity.

ⓔ **Ethical communicators are honest, fair, responsible, and respectful of others.**

Dominic just returned from a two-day training and development workshop where he learned how to use a new online purchase order requisition submission and tracking program. Dominic's supervisor now wants him to lead a series of training sessions for the other 50 to 60 full- and part-time purchasing clerks at the company where he works.

Chen Chen was awarded "server of the month" three times since she started working at the restaurant. Customers really liked her and several had begun to request that they be seated in her section. Her manager asked her to give her a pep talk to the managers and other servers about "how she does it" at the next company-wide meeting. She felt a bit nervous, but she agreed to do it.

Although her grandmother had been sick for some time, Diana is heartbroken when she learns her grandmother has passed away. She is caught off-guard when her mother asks her to represent the family by delivering the eulogy at the funeral, but of course, Diana graciously agrees.

Jediah landed an interview for his dream job as an electrical engineer. The interview is going to be conducted via videoconference. To prepare for the interview, Jediah was asked to create a 10- to 15-minute webinar explaining why he was the best candidate for the position.

"Her manager asked her to give a pep talk to the managers and other servers about "how she does it" at the next company-wide meeting. She felt a bit nervous, but she agreed to do it."

Which of these situations illustrates someone who will be giving a "speech"? Actually, because the definition of **public speaking** is a sustained formal presentation by a speaker to an audience, each one of them is an example of public speaking. Public speaking today might occur in a face-to-face professional setting, as it will for Dominic and Chen Chen, in a nonprofessional setting as it will for Diana, or in an online environment as it will for Jediah. In this course, you will learn how to give effective speeches; a skill that will actually help you to be more successful in both your personal and professional life.

This chapter provides an overview of the fundamentals of effective public speaking as it pertains to the digital age we live in today. We begin with a discussion of public speaking as a liberal art. Next, we discuss the ethical responsibilities expected of public speakers. Then, we describe public speaking broadly as a form of communication and more specifically as an audience-centered endeavor rooted in the rhetorical situation. By the time you finish reading this chapter and applying what you learn, you will have begun the exciting journey toward becoming an effective audience-centered public speaker in a digital age.

1-1 PUBLIC SPEAKING AS A LIBERAL ART

When we say public speaking is a liberal art, we mean that public speaking knowledge and skills are fundamental to participating effectively in a democratic society regardless of major or profession. So that's why a course devoted to public speaking is often required in a general education curriculum.[1] Public speaking is a powerful right for engaged citizens—a right that also carries with it several important ethical responsibilities. Public speaking has been revered as a civic right in democratic civilizations dating back to ancient Greece. **Civic rights** are the essential conditions for individuals to live happy and successful lives.[2]

public speaking: a sustained formal presentation by a speaker to an audience

civic rights: the essential conditions for individuals to live happy and successful lives

1-1a The Civic Right of Public Speaking

Since ancient times, liberal arts education has been at the center of study for free people in democracies. In fact, the word "liberal" means "free," and in ancient Greece it was the type of general education offered to free men (yes, back then it was restricted to men). Public speaking was central because it was the means by which free men conducted business, made public decisions, and gained and maintained power.[3] Today, effective public speakers continue to reap rewards in personal relationships, the work world, and the public sphere.[4]

Certainly, the formal study of public speaking equips us to give effective presentations; however, the process of preparing these speeches accomplishes something even more important. The study of public speaking teaches us not *what* to think but *how* to think—a central skill for a responsible citizen living in a democracy, especially the sound-bite-saturated, image-managed, political environment we live in today. Essentially, we learn to think critically about what we read, see, and hear. When we choose a topic, we must consider why we are speaking and what we think is important enough to present to others. We must critically evaluate the credibility, validity, and reliability of the information we collect. We must thoughtfully consider how to organize our ideas and choose words that will be both clear and compelling. And we must adjust to the nonverbal reactions of our listeners to ensure they are getting the meaning we intend.

Learning to think critically as we prepare and present our own speeches also equips us to analyze the messages offered by others. We are able to critically evaluate the information and arguments of others, identify reasoning flaws, and realize unethical communication practices. Democracies only thrive in settings where citizens are capable of fulfilling our civic responsibilities to analyze, think about, and eloquently speak out about important issues (Photo 1.1). So public speaking is a liberal art—an essential skill for free, engaged citizens.

AP Photo/The Journal Times, Mark Hertzberg

Photo 1.1 Public speaking is both a civic right and responsibility for free, engaged citizens.

1-1b The Power of Public Speaking

Democratic civilizations throughout history have understood the importance of public speaking as a right. Like them, we know that effective public speaking is empowering in several ways. First, public speaking skills empower us to participate in democratic processes. Free speech is a hallmark of democracy. The policies a democratic government adopts are a direct result of the debates that occur across the nation: in living rooms; over pizza at the local hangout; on blogs and social networking sites; in the media;

as well as in our executive, legislative, and judicial branches of government. Effective public speaking skills give us the confidence to voice our ideas on important public issues.

Second, public speaking skills empower us to communicate our ideas and opinions in ways that all audience members can understand. Most of us have had an unfortunate experience with a teacher who "talked over our heads." The teacher understood the material but was unable to express it clearly to us. When we can express our ideas clearly, we are more likely to share them. When others understand our ideas, they learn from us.

Third, public speaking skills empower us to achieve our career goals. Research shows that, for almost any job, one of the most highly sought-after skills in new hires is oral communication skills.[5] So whether you aspire to a career in business, industry, government, the arts, or education, good communication skills are a prerequisite to your success. Certainly, Dominic, Diana, and Chen Chen will have to draw upon their public speaking skills to prepare their speeches. Jediah will also need to do so as he prepares the "job talk" he will deliver via videoconference.

1-2 ETHICAL RESPONSIBILITIES OF PUBLIC SPEAKERS

Ethics are a set of moral principles held by a society, group, or individual that differentiate right from wrong. In other words, ethics reflect what we believe we "ought to" and "ought not to" think and do. As audience members, we expect speakers to behave ethically. Likewise, as speakers, we expect audience members to behave ethically. What standards should we conform to as ethical communicators? Five generally agreed-upon ethical standards are honesty, integrity, fairness, respect, and responsibility. Let's look at how public speakers meet each of these responsibilities.

ethics: moral principles that a society, group, or individual hold that differentiate right from wrong

1. **Ethical communicators are honest.** In other words, ethical public speakers tell the truth. An audience expects that what you tell them will not be made up, will not be your personal belief presented as fact, and will not be an exaggeration. To make sure that what you say is truthful, you will need to research your topic carefully and present all sides of controversial issues accurately.

    In addition, honest speakers do not **plagiarize** by presenting other's ideas as their own. Instead, they properly credit the ideas of others they use in their speech. Sadly, according to a survey conducted in 2011 by the Pew Research Center in conjunction with the *Chronicle of Higher Education,* plagiarism is commonplace among college students today and has increased dramatically over the past decade.[6] Results of a survey conducted by the Center for Academic Integrity indicate that as many as 80 percent of college students admit to plagiarism.[7] As a result, many colleges and universities now use plagiarism-detection software programs regularly when grading student work. In most colleges, plagiarism can result in failing an assignment or the entire course, and it can even lead to being suspended from school. In the world beyond the classroom, plagiarism has led to lawsuits and has ruined promising careers. Here are some tips to remember so you don't plagiarize unintentionally:

    plagiarize: to pass off the ideas, words, or created works of another as one's own by failing to credit the source

    - If you change a few words at the beginning, in the middle, or at the end of a material, but copy much of the rest and don't cite the source of the information, you are plagiarizing.

    - If you completely paraphrase the unique ideas of another person and do not credit that person, you are plagiarizing.

    - If you purchase, borrow, or use a speech or essay in part or in whole that was prepared by another and present it as original, you are plagiarizing.[8]

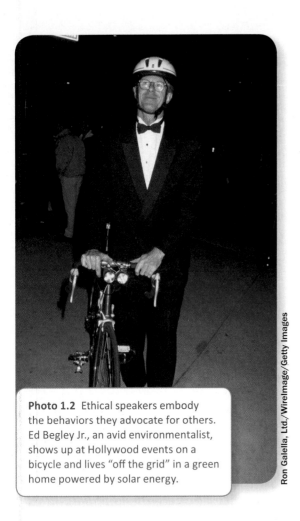

Photo 1.2 Ethical speakers embody the behaviors they advocate for others. Ed Begley Jr., an avid environmentalist, shows up at Hollywood events on a bicycle and lives "off the grid" in a green home powered by solar energy.

Ron Galella, Ltd./WireImage/Getty Images

2. **Ethical communicators act with integrity.** In other words, ethical communicators "practice what they preach." The person who says, "Do what I say, not what I do," lacks integrity. In other words, a speaker who implores listeners to quit smoking and then goes outside and lights up lacks integrity. A listener who espouses the importance of civility but then interrupts and heckles speakers lacks integrity.

3. **Ethical communicators behave fairly.** Fair communicators attempt to act impartially and acknowledge any potential bias they might have regarding a topic. For speakers, behaving fairly means researching and accurately reporting all sides of an issue. For listeners, it means considering all of the evidence a speaker presents, even when that evidence contradicts what they believe.

4. **Ethical communicators demonstrate respect.** Behaving respectfully means showing regard for others, including their point of view, their rights, and their feelings. For example, speakers show respect for their audience by choosing language and humor that is inclusive and inoffensive. Listeners demonstrate respect by giving their undivided attention to the speaker. In other words, it is disrespectful to send or read texts, emails, or Facebook or in any other way "multitask" during a speech.

5. **Ethical communicators are responsible.** Responsible communicators recognize the power of words. So ethical speakers only advocate for things that are in the best interest of audience members. Similarly, ethical listeners critically evaluate the positions that speakers advocate and do not blindly accept positions that are not in their best interest (Photo 1.2).

Throughout this book, we will elaborate on how these ethical communication principles should guide you as you both present and listen to speeches. We will also challenge you to reflect on ethical choices presented in the feature "Reflect on Ethics" like the one on page 7. To learn more about ethics, go to **Web Link 1.1, The Basics of Ethics, and Web Link 1.2, Ethics Connection,** in your MindTap for *Challenge.* The first links to the Internet Encyclopedia of Philosophy, which provides an easy-to-read, thorough discussion about ethics. The second links to the website for the Markkula Center for Applied Ethics at Santa Clara University, a forum for research and discussion on ethical issues in American life.

communication: the process of creating shared meaning

participants: the individuals who assume the roles of senders and receivers during an interaction

senders: participants who form and transmit messages using verbal symbols and nonverbal behaviors

1-3 PUBLIC SPEAKING AS COMMUNICATION

Public speaking is a specialized type of communication. So to become effective public speakers, we need to understand what communication is. **Communication** is the process of creating shared meaning. At its core, communication involves forming and transmitting messages to achieve mutual understanding or to incite action. To understand how the communication process works, let's look at its essential elements: participants, messages, feedback, channels, interference/noise, and contexts/settings.

1-3a Participants

Participants are the individuals who assume the roles of senders and receivers during an interaction (see Exhibit 1.1). As **senders**, participants form and transmit

Reflect on Ethics

CELEBRITY CHEF CONCOCTS IMPRESSIVE PAST

Celebrity chef Robert Irvine came to St. Petersburg in 2007 with a plan to turn it into "the next Monaco." He claimed to be a royal knight and asked to be introduced as Sir Robert Irvine. He said he owned a castle in Scotland and had cooked for presidents and royalty.[9]

Today, however, it's difficult to separate fact from fiction when it comes to Sir Robert Irvine. What is known to be true is that he is an excellent chef and starred on the Food Network's, *Dinner: Impossible*, until July 20, 2008 when he was replaced by *Iron Chef America's* Michael Symon amidst a thick controversy about assertions he had made in his biography posted on the Food Network website. For example, Irvine claimed:

- he had a B.S. degree in food and nutrition from the University of Leeds. Officials from the University of Leeds have no record of Robert Irvine having been a student there.

- to have worked on the wedding cake for Prince Charles and Princess Diana. He was at the school where the cake was made, but did he actually help make it? Does "picking fruit and things like that" count?

- he received several Five Star Diamond Awards from the American Academy of Hospitality Sciences. The "academy" is actually housed in a Manhattan apartment, and recipients pay for the honor.

- he was a royal knight, according to Jenn Stebbing, press officer at Buckingham Palace: "He is not a KCVO Knight Commander of the Royal Victorian Order and he wasn't given a castle by the queen of England." Irvine now admits that was a lie.

- to have trained White House military cooks and served presidents and heads of state. White House spokespersons claim he has never had anything to do with planning, preparing, or serving at any public or private White House food function.

The Food Network rehired Irvine in November of 2008 and continued to host the program through its eighth season, which ended in 2010. While the program continues to air in reruns, Irvine also went on to replace chef Beau MacMillan on *Worst Cooks in America* in 2011 and to appear on other programs such as *Restaurant: Impossible* and *The Next Iron Chef.* Although the controversy regarding the "facts" about Irvine's biography remain unclear, it appears he has landed on his feet and is not suffering any negative consequences from it.

1. What, if any, ethical communication principles did Irvine violate and, if so, how?

2. When, if ever, is it ok to stretch the truth about your qualifications?

3. Is it ok to exaggerate the facts about yourself if you're famous? If "everyone else does it" too? Explain.

4. Do you think The Food Network behaved ethically when it rehired Irvine?

Exhibit 1.1 Model of Communication

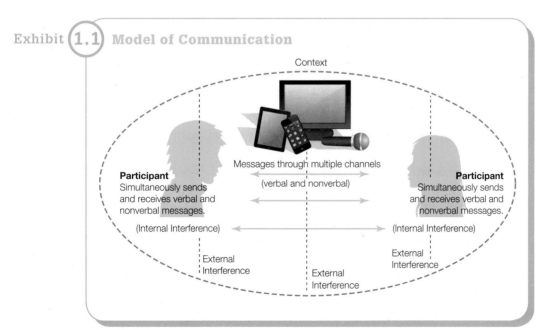

Context

Messages through multiple channels
(verbal and nonverbal)

Participant
Simultaneously sends and receives verbal and nonverbal messages.

Participant
Simultaneously sends and receives verbal and nonverbal messages.

(Internal Interference)

(Internal Interference)

External Interference

External Interference

External Interference

receivers: participants who interpret the messages sent by others

messages: the verbal utterances and nonverbal behaviors to which meaning is attributed during communication

encoding: the process of putting our thoughts and feelings into words and nonverbal behaviors

decoding: the process of interpreting the verbal and nonverbal messages sent by others

feedback: the reactions and responses to messages that indicate whether and how a message was heard, seen, and interpreted

channels: both the route traveled by a message and the means of transportation

mediated channels: technology-enhanced auditory and visual channels

virtual presence: simulated presence made possible through the use of digital technology

interference/noise: any stimulus that interferes with the process of sharing meaning

---

SPEECH SNIPPET

Jediah practiced his videoconference in advance for his mother back in his hometown. He was glad he did because he realized there is sometimes a delay in getting feedback. He made a note to himself where to pause for a moment to try to account for this challenge.

---

messages using verbal symbols (words) and nonverbal behaviors. **Receivers** interpret the messages sent by others. Although all participants serve as both senders and receivers, in public speaking contexts, one participant acts primarily as sender and presents an extended message to which the other participants listen, interpret, and provide mostly nonverbal feedback. So when Dominic presents his training workshop, he will act as the sender and his coworkers will be the receivers. And when Jediah presents his online "job talk," he will act as the sender and the interviewers observing the videoconference will act as the receivers.

1-3b Messages

Messages are the verbal utterances, visual images, and nonverbal behaviors used to convey thoughts and feelings. We refer to the process of creating messages as **encoding** and the process of interpreting them as **decoding**. In public speaking situations, messages are typically speeches that are prepared beforehand and presented by one participant.

1-3c Feedback

Feedback consists of the messages sent by receivers to let the sender know how the message is being interpreted. We can express feedback verbally by telling the sender what we understand or think about a message, or we may indicate our understanding and reaction through nonverbal behavior, like nodding our heads to indicate agreement, raising eyebrows to register our surprise, or cocking our head and furrowing our eyebrows to indicate that we do not understand. When audiences listen to a speech, usually most of their feedback is nonverbal. So as Dominic conducts his workshop, he observes the facial expressions of his coworkers for feedback about whether his message is making sense. He also periodically stops and asks for feedback in the form of actual questions.

1-3d Channels

Channels are both the route traveled by a message and the means of transportation. We send and receive messages primarily through auditory (speaking and hearing) and visual (seeing) channels. Sometimes these channels are enhanced by technology. We call these technology-enhanced auditory and visual (a.k.a. audiovisual) channels or **mediated channels**. Chen Chen, Dominic, and Diana send and receive verbal and nonverbal messages when they speak in a face-to-face setting. Jediah's videoconferencing software allows him and his presentational aids to be both seen and heard, even though he is not physically present in the room with his interviewers. This software also allows him to see his interviewers' feedback on the computer screen as he speaks. We call this phenomenon of simulated presence made possible through the use of digital technology, **virtual presence**.

1-3e Interference/Noise

Interference, also referred to as **noise**, is any stimulus that interferes with the process of achieving shared meaning. Noise can be physical or psychological. Physical noise is any external sight or sound that distracts us from the message. For example, when someone enters the room or someone's cell phone goes off while a speaker is talking, we might not hear the message. Similarly, when we get an email or Facebook update while listening to a speaker online, we might be distracted from the message. Psychological noise refers to the thoughts and feelings we experience that compete with the sender's message for our attention. So when we daydream about what we have to do at work today or feel offended when a speaker uses foul language, we are being distracted by psychological noise.

1-3f Contexts

Communication context refers to the environment in which communication occurs.[10][11] Communication contexts differ by the number of participants and the balance of roles among them.[12] Let's briefly look at four of these.

Intrapersonal communication (a.k.a. self-talk) is communicating with yourself. Usually this is done by thinking through choices, strategies, and the possible consequences of taking action. When you sit in class and consider what you'll have for dinner tonight, you are communicating intrapersonally. Much of our intrapersonal communication occurs subconsciously.[13] When we drive into the driveway "without thinking," we're communicating intrapersonally but at a subconscious level. When we give a speech and notice confused looks on listeners' faces, we might communicate intrapersonally as we recognize the need to rephrase our explanation.

Interpersonal communication is communication between two people who have an identifiable relationship with each other.[14][15] Talking with a friend on the sidewalk between classes, visiting on the phone with your mother, and texting or chatting online with a family member or friend are all examples of interpersonal communication. Interpersonal communication sometimes occurs in a public speech setting when, during a question-and-answer session, a speaker directs remarks to one audience member.

Small group communication typically occurs among approximately three to ten people.[16][17][18] Examples of small groups include a family, a group of friends, a group of classmates working together on a class project, and a management team in the workplace.[19] Some research suggests there are more small groups in the United States than there are people. Small group communication occurs in a public speech setting when a team is asked to work together to research, prepare, and deliver a presentation on a particular topic.

Public communication occurs among more than ten people by one primary sender to multiple receivers. This communication may occur face-to-face or via mediated, technology-driven channels. One form of public communication is **mass communication**, which is communication produced and transmitted via mass media to large segments of the population at the same time. Examples include newspapers, magazines, books, blogs, listservs, television programs, movies, websites, Facebook pages, Twitter tweets, and YouTube posts. Another form is public speaking, which is a sustained, formal, oral presentation delivered to an audience that is typically present at the time. As technology and media become increasingly accessible, however, the lines between mass communication and public speaking are blurring (Photo 1.3). For example, when President Obama gives a State of the Union address, some people are there, others watch on TV or over the Internet as he speaks, and still others view it later in the form of televised snippets or a website video (e.g., YouTube).

1-4 AUDIENCE-CENTERED SPEAKING AND THE RHETORICAL SITUATION

The communication discipline as a formal field of study in colleges and universities is fairly young.[20][21][22] The study and practice of public speaking, however, has a long and rich history dating back more than 2000 years to ancient Greek (e.g., Aristotle and Plato) and Roman (e.g., Cicero and Isocrates) philosophers. They were in fact the ones who coined the terms *rhetoric* and *oratory* to describe the processes of preparing, presenting, and critiquing public speeches.

Fundamental to public speaking then and now is *audience*. The ancient Greek philosopher, teacher, and public speaker, Aristotle, is often credited with claiming, "The audience is the end and object of the speech."[23] What he meant was that the eloquence

communication context: the environment in which communication occurs

intrapersonal communication: communicating with yourself (a.k.a. self-talk)

interpersonal communication: communication between two people

small group communication: the interaction that occurs in a group of approximately three to ten people

public communication: communication that occurs among more than ten people where one message is presented to the participants who function as receivers whose own messages are limited to feedback

mass communication: communication produced and transmitted via media to large audiences

Photo 1.3 As media become more pervasive, the distinction between mass communication and public speaking is becoming blurred.

of your words is irrelevant if the words are not heard by, are not understood by, or do not affect the people to whom you are speaking. Frankly, whether conveyed in written, oral, or visual form, or some combination of them, and whether delivered in a face-to-face setting or via a mediated channel, a message is only effective if it is understood and internalized by the people being addressed. Today, we recognize that the effectiveness of any speech depends not just on understanding the audience but also on how well the message addresses the entire rhetorical situation. Let's turn now to a discussion of the rhetorical situation generally and then to the specific effective speech principles of content, structure, and delivery.

1-4a The Rhetorical Situation

The **rhetorical situation** is the composite of the speaker, audience, and occasion. Exhibit 1.2 illustrates the rhetorical situation in a Venn diagram. As you can see, the rhetorical situation is the place where the speaker, audience, and occasion overlap. Lloyd Bitzer, the rhetorical scholar who introduced the concept of the rhetorical situation, believed that the particular speech given by an individual to an audience on a specific occasion is also the result of some real or perceived specific need that a speech might help to address.[24] Bitzer referred to this as the "**exigence**."[25] According to the Encarta dictionary, exigence is "something that a situation demands or makes urgently necessary and that puts pressure on the people involved."[26]

rhetorical situation: the composite of the occasion, speaker, and the audience that influences the speech that is given.

exigence: some real or perceived need that a speech might help address.

On December 14, 2012, a lone gunman charged into Sandy Hook Elementary School in Newtown, Connecticut and massacred 26 defenseless children and adults before killing himself. This unfathomable heinous mass murder of innocent children created an exigence that led many people to speak out about the dire need to do something ranging from tightening gun control laws to arming teachers to increasing support for mental health care facilities to banning violent video games. In the United States, from President Obama's televised speeches to simple calls to action heard in

Exhibit **1.2** The Rhetorical Public Speaking Situation

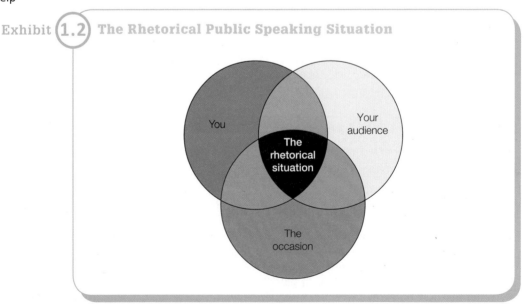

Copyright © Cengage Learning

classrooms across the country to thousands of Facebook posts, Twitter feeds, blogs, vlogs, and YouTube videos, individuals felt compelled to speak out and do something to help the families of the victims and to stop school violence.

The massacre created an exigence that motivated speakers to seek an occasion and audience where a speech they would give could help accomplish positive change. For example, high school senior, Perry Rockwood, gave a 10-minute speech at a school-wide assembly urging fellow classmates to purchase bracelets for $1 that would then be donated to Sandy Hook. He also asked them to wear the bracelets as a visual memorial of solidarity throughout the school. And he encouraged them to engage in 26 acts of kindness toward others in an attempt to change the way they perceive and interact with one another. Newtown Connecticut community members were also motivated to form a grassroots organization called the Sandy Hook Promise (SHP), which they announced in public speeches at the Edmund Town Hall on January 13, 2013. The mission of SHP is to bring people together all over the world to do everything we can to "encourage and support common sense solutions to make [our] communit[ies] and our country safer from similar acts of violence".[27] Similarly, Jeremy Anthony, a high school junior in Iowa City, wanted to shift focus from the negative things that happen in school to the positive. So he started a Twitter feed (@westhighbros) as a place to post uplifting messages and compliments to encourage others.

1-4b Speaker

The **speaker** is the source or originator of the speech. As the speaker, what you discuss, and how you express those ideas, will depend on your interests, beliefs, background, and public speaking skills. You will choose topics that you care about, know something about, and want to inform or persuade others about. Dominic, for example, will be training his coworkers to use the new purchase order requisition and tracking program based on personal knowledge he gained earlier. Diana will share stories about her grandmother, someone she knew well and loved dearly, in ways that will likely lead her audience to feel warmly about her grandmother, too.

1-4c Audience

The **audience** is the specific group of people to whom your speech is directed. **Audience analysis** is the process of learning about the diverse characteristics of audience members and **audience adaptation** is the process of tailoring your message to address exigence in terms of their unique interests, needs, and expectations. For example, organizers of benefit concerts today recognize that many audience members are tech savvy, so they appeal for donations online and via text messages in addition to staffing toll-free phone lines (Photo 1.4).

1-4d Occasion

The **occasion** encompasses the expected purpose for the speech and the **setting** (a.k.a. location) where it will be given. When the congregation assembles at a church, synagogue, or mosque, they expect to hear a message about religious texts or principles. When physicians attend professional meetings, they expect to hear scientific presentations about new treatments. Imagine what would happen if the local rabbi were to present his sermon to the physicians and the physician were to present her findings at the synagogue service! The setting is also an important aspect of the occasion. The speech you prepare to give in a large auditorium for an audience of more than 1,000 is likely to be

SPEECH SNIPPET

Exigence

For Chen Chen, exigence stemmed from the fact that she was one of the best servers at the restaurant and her manager believed in her. By sharing what she does so well in the form of a pep talk, other servers could improve their skills too. As a result, customers would benefit also.

speaker: the source or originator of the speech

audience: the specific group of people to whom the speech is directed

audience analysis: a study made to learn about the diverse characteristics of audience members and then, based on these characteristics, to predict how audience members are apt to listen to, understand, and be motivated to act on your speech

Rick Davis/Splash News/Newscom

Photo 1.4 Celebrity performers often make pleas during benefits to aid those experiencing crises.

audience adaptation: the process of tailoring your speech's information to the needs, interests, and expectations of your listeners

occasion: the expected purpose and setting for the speech

setting: the location where the speech will be given

different than the speech you would prepare to give in a restaurant to an audience of 20 (Photo 1.5). Dominic's approach will be different, for example, when he addresses all 60 of his coworkers during the overview session than when he meets with smaller groups of 10 to 15 in breakout sessions throughout the day. In addition, because the overview speech would be recorded and posted on the company website, he would also need to address that *virtual audience* while he spoke. One way he could do so is to address the camera as if it is another "person" in the group.

© iStockphoto.com/Andresr

Photo 1.5 Speakers tailor their speech to adapt to the size of the audience.

So while effective speeches are tailored to address audience exigence, they do so in ways that adhere to the overlapping elements and constraints of the entire rhetorical situation. Now let's consider how effective public speakers do so via the primary principles of effective speeches: content, structure, and delivery.

1-5 EFFECTIVE SPEECH COMPONENTS

When we give a speech, our goal is to create and achieve shared meaning with our audience members. We do so through the rhetorical appeals of ethos, pathos, and logos.[28] **Ethos** includes everything we say and do to convey competence and good character. Dressing appropriately, being poised as we speak, citing credible sources, and speaking within the time parameters allotted, for instance, convey ethos. **Pathos** consists of everything we say and do to appeal to emotions, which can range from negative emotions such as fear or dread to positive emotions such as adventure or joy. **Logos** includes everything we say and do to appeal to logic and sound reasoning. Essentially, effective speeches use ethos, pathos, and logos in content, structure, and delivery.

ethos: everything you say and do to convey competence and good character

pathos: everything you say and do to appeal to emotions

logos: everything you say and do to appeal to logic and sound reasoning

content: the information and ideas you present

1-5a Content

Content is the information and ideas you present. It includes the speech purpose and main points as well as the evidence, supporting material, and reasoning used to develop each main idea. Evidence consists of all the facts, examples, and so forth, which help clarify or explain, your main ideas. Evidence can come from your own experiences as well as from research materials you collect. Effective evidence has sufficient breadth and depth. *Breadth* refers to the amount and types of evidence you use. *Depth* is the level of detail you provide from each piece of evidence. Evidence is effective when it is logically linked to the main idea it supports. The ideas you choose to present depend on what is appropriate for your audience and the occasion, and you adapt your content so that it includes **listener-relevance links**, which are statements informing listeners of how and why they should be interested in or care about an idea. Doing so makes the exigence of your ideas transparent. Diana's purpose was to praise her grandmother's attributes. She decided to focus on two main values her grandmother both preached and practiced: a positive attitude and perseverance. She planned to begin each main point with a listener relevance statement about the universal nature of her grandmother's values. She would then develop each main point with several brief examples to provide breadth and one more detailed story to add depth.

listener-relevance links: statements of how and why the ideas you offer are relevant to your listeners

1-5b Structure

Structure is the framework that organizes the speech content. Clear structure helps listeners follow your ideas as they listen.[29] Effective structure consists of both macrostructure and microstructure elements. **Macrostructure** is the overall organizational framework used to present your speech content. Effective macrostructure is comprised of four elements: the introduction, body, conclusion, and transitions. You may not realize it, but you have already studied macrostructure—you use it when you write formal papers for school. Now you will learn how to adapt what you have already learned to formal, oral messages.

structure: the framework you use to organize your speech content

macrostructure: the overall organizational framework you use to present your speech content

Careful attention to macrostructure is even more important when you craft a speech than when you write an essay. A reader can easily reread a poorly written essay to try to understand the author's intent, but an audience does not usually have the opportunity to listen to a speech again, unless it is being recorded and posted to an accessible website. So the introduction should be structured to build audience interest in your topic and preview your main points (tell them what you are going to tell them). The speech body contains the main ideas and supporting material used to develop each one (tell them). The conclusion reminds the audience of your main ideas and motivates them to remember what you have said (tell them what you told them). Speech macrostructure also includes **transitions**—statements that verbally summarize one main point and introduce the next one.

transition: a sentence or two that summarizes one main point and introduces the next one

Whereas macrostructure is the overall framework for your speech, **microstructure** is the specific language and style you use within your sentences. Effective speeches are understandable and memorable when speakers use appropriate, accurate, clear, and vivid language, and when they use rhetorical style devices such as alliteration, onomatopoeia, personification, similes, metaphors, and analogies.

microstructure: the specific language and style choices you use as you frame your ideas and verbalize them to your audience

1-5c Delivery

Delivery, how you use your voice and body to convey your message, can dramatically affect the audience's ability to understand, remember, and possibly act on your message.[30] Effective speakers are conversational, intelligible, poised, and expressive in their delivery. Being conversational means sounding as though you are having a spontaneous conversation with your audience, rather than simply reading to them or performing in front of them. Intelligible speakers use a rate, volume, and pitch that is easily understood. If you are speaking in a second language, have a pronounced accent, or a speech impediment, you might find that speaking somewhat slower improves your intelligibility. (See *Public Speaking in the Real World* to learn how Oscar-winning actress Julia Roberts learned to manage her tendency to stutter.) Poised speakers stand confidently without fidgeting, swaying, or using any other potentially distracting bodily action. Being poised also means making eye contact

delivery: how you use your voice and body to convey your message

Julia Roberts and Intelligibility

Today, Oscar-winning actress Julia Roberts is among the most sought after in Hollywood. Few realize, however, that she was born with a genetic predisposition to stutter. In fact, both Julia and her brother, best supporting actor nominee Eric, appear on the Stuttering Foundation of America's (SFA) "Famous People Who Stutter List." According to the Stuttering Foundation of America, over three million Americans stutter.[31] However, stuttering can be managed effectively with the help of speech therapy and does not need to limit your intelligibility or success when speaking in public. Certainly, Julia and brother, Eric, serve as evidence of that, and they are not alone. Other stutterers who went on to lead successful lives in fields where public speaking skills are paramount include actors James Earl Jones, Bruce Willis, Marilyn Monroe, and Emily Blunt; singer-songwriter Carly Simon; and sports icons Tiger Woods and Bill Walton. What do they suggest doing to reduce stuttering and increase intelligibility? (1) Slow down your thoughts and think about what you are saying now rather than three or four sentences ahead. (2) Read out loud and even in front of a mirror where you can watch yourself as others will see you. (3) When you stumble, remember that everyone makes mistakes. Stop and then simply start again. As Walton says, "It's what you do after those mistakes that will determine your ultimate success."[32]

Kevin Mazur/WireImage/Getty Images

with your audience members in face-to-face settings, or with the camera when delivering ideas via media, rather than focusing solely on your notes. Being expressive means changing your pitch, volume, rate, and so forth to emphasize emotional intent of your ideas. Generally, you want to sound a bit more dramatic than you would in casual conversation. For example, you might speak more quickly or loudly to underscore your emotional convictions or to stress key words or phrases, or you might pause strategically to call attention to important ideas. Being expressive also means using appropriate facial expressions to reflect your conviction about the topic and gestures to reinforce important points.

" speech assignment "

Speech of Self-Introduction

Prepare a two- to three-minute speech about a "hero" in your life. Offer two or three main points about the values they hold that you admire and why. Offer specific personal examples and stories to support each of your main points. Use Diana's speech outline as a guide to help you prepare, as well as the Speech Evaluation Checklist that follows as you practice to make sure your speech includes all the elements of an effective speech.

❝ speech evaluation checklist ❞

General Criteria

You can use this checklist to critique a speech you hear in class. (You can also use it to critique your own speech.)

Content

_____ 1. Were all main points addressed per the assignment?

_____ 2. Were two to three pieces of evidence provided for each main point (breadth)?

_____ 3. Was one extended piece of evidence provided for each main point (depth)?

_____ 4. Were listener-relevance links provided for each main point?

_____ 5. Did the speech fall within the time constraints of the assignment?

Structure

1. Did the speech provide all the basic elements of an effective speech: introduction, body, conclusion, and transitions? (*macrostructure*)

2. Did the introduction catch the audience's interest? _____ identify the speech topic/goal? _____ preview the main points? _____

3. Were transitions provided between each main point? _____

4. Did the conclusion remind the audience of the main points? _____ motivate the audience to remember the main ideas of the speech? _____

5. Did the speaker use words that were appropriate and inclusive? _____ accurate and clear? _____ vivid and expressive? (*microstructure*)

Delivery

1. Was the speaker intelligible in terms of volume? _____ rate? _____ pronunciation? _____ enunciation? _____

2. Was the speaker conversational? _____

3. Did the speaker look up from his or her notes most of the time and make eye contact with the audience? _____

4. Did the speaker appear professional, poised, and confident? _____

5. Was the speaker expressive in term of changes in rate and volume? _____ Strategic pauses? _____ Appropriate facial expressions? _____ Appropriate gestures?

 MindTap™

Access this checklist on your MindTap for *Challenge*.

What follows is an outline of Diana's speech of tribute to her grandmother with commentary. As you read, consider how you might address the rhetorical situation effectively as you develop the content and structure, as well as practice the delivery of your speeches. Then, answer these questions about content and structure.

1. Content: What are Diana's main points? What kinds of evidence does she use to support her main points? Where are examples of breadth, depth, and listener relevance in the body of her speech?

2. Structure: What does Diana do to get the attention of her listeners? What does she say to lead listeners from one main point to the next? How does she provide a sense of closure and motivate listeners to remember the speech? What wording seems to demonstrate inclusion, provide clarity, and evoke vivid images?

Grandma Frances: My Hero

INTRODUCTION

Attention getter

I. [Diana shows a visual aid image of several well-known superheroes from popular culture.] What makes someone a hero? Do you have any? Who are they and why do you consider them heroes?

Listener relevance and credibility

II. A simple definition of a hero is someone who is admired for noble qualities. So a hero doesn't have to be someone famous.

Based on this definition, I bet most of us in this room can identify at least one hero, one person we admire and look up to. When I think of my heroes, one important person always comes to mind: my Grandma Frances. [show visual aid photograph of Grandma Frances]

Thesis statement with main point preview

III. In the next few minutes, let's talk about my grandma Frances as a hero who taught me by her example of how to maintain a positive attitude and to persevere through good times and bad.

BODY

First main point

I. I consider Grandma Frances a hero because she modeled a positive attitude in all situations.

Subpoints (Listener Relevance)

A. We all want to be happy and healthy. Did you know that study after study shows a direct link between a positive attitude and improved mental and physical health? Who wouldn't want that?

Subpoints

B. When it came to having a positive attitude, Grandma Frances was a "rock star." You couldn't get to her.

1. One story that really shows how grandma would "turn lemons into lemonade" with a smile on her face the whole time occurred one summer when I was about 9 years old and my parents and two brothers joined grandma and grandpa on a week-long fishing expedition in Canada. [show visual of our family just before leaving for the trip]

Notice how Diana uses a series of questions to pique curiosity and then motivates listeners more by addressing listener relevance before previewing the main points she will focus on in the body of the speech.

2. As we packed for the trip, grandpa announced that we wouldn't need to pack food because we were going to eat what we caught and really live off the land (or in this case off the water, I suppose). I don't know whether grandpa knew it at the time, but grandma packed a few things just to be safe. With that, we headed out on our family fishing adventure from our comfortable homes in central Minnesota to the rugged countryside of Saskatchewan, Canada.

Diana provides listener relevance by pointing out how a positive attitude can actually make us healthier.

3. As luck would have it, we couldn't catch a fish to save our souls. We tried fishing early in the morning, throughout the day, and into the evening. We hired guides who took us to "secret spots" where they claimed we would be sure to catch fish. We had pretty much exhausted the food supplies Grandma Frances had packed, having just finished the last package of hot dogs. We wondered what we would eat for the next four days as grandma was saving the water we had used to boil the franks. My mom asked Grandma Frances what she was doing with the water, grandma responded, "Well, we might need to make weiner water soup." So you see when I talk about grandma as an eternal optimist, I don't necessarily think about making lemonade from lemons, but I surely do think about making soup out of leftover weiner water.

4. After doing the dishes, Grandma Frances said she was going to try her luck fishing right off the dock. No one from our group had tried fishing from the dock because we were told that nobody catches anything that way. Well, all I can say is they didn't know my Grandma Frances! When the fish started biting for grandma, the whole family joined her catching our limit right off the dock. In fact, we caught so many fish for the next three days that we ate fish for every meal and still came home from our adventure with coolers full. [show picture of our family holding a stringer of fish standing on the dock]

Not only do I consider grandma a hero for teaching me to have a positive attitude but also for teaching me to persevere.

II. Grandma Frances was always doing things that demonstrated her will to persevere and encouraging me to do so, as well.

A. Throughout our lives, most of us have been inundated with messages about the importance of believing in ourselves and persevering whether from children's stories like The Little Engine that Could, or songs like "I will Survive," or movies like Rocky, or even symbols like Nike's "Just Do It" brand [show a visual of the Nike symbol]. In fact, perseverance could even be considered a cultural norm about how we ought to live.

B. One way Grandma Frances taught me the value of perseverance was through modeling when people could have discouraged her. When people made fun of her for using unusual words as way to improve her vocabulary, she didn't let it get to her. She kept on doing so. For example, she would do the crossword puzzle in the newspaper every day and then use at least two words she learned doing it in conversation that day. I remember one time she used an unfamiliar word and her friends responded by teasing her with a made up word: "polly-go." Grandma Frances just smiled and kept on doing puzzles and using new words every day.

C. Another way Grandma Frances taught the value of perseverance was by encouraging me when others discouraged me. One example that stands out happened when I was in grade school. As many of you know, I come from a family of singers, and one time my brothers and I were singing. I guess I didn't hit all the right notes, and I recall a family member saying my brothers were really good singers, but I didn't seem to have the "gene." Grandma responded with "she just has a smaller range right now. It will get larger as she gets older." I never forgot what Grandma Frances said. I kept singing and practicing and luckily for my music professors in college and the kids I work with in the choirs I direct now, my range did expand. I sometimes wonder about what I would be doing today if I would have listened to the discouragers rather than Grandma Frances.

CONCLUSION

I. We all have heroes we admire for their noble qualities. Grandma Frances, who taught me the value of a positive attitude and perseverance, was my hero.

II. [Diane shows visual aid again of superheroes from popular culture] Grandma Frances may not be able to fly through the air like Superman, scale buildings like Spider-Man, or even wield a Lasso of Truth like Wonder Woman, but she will always be a superhero to me.

Here Diana provides a detailed story to provide breadth in terms of content.

Transition

A good transition statement can be as simple as Diana's is here. It works because it reminds listeners of the main point she just finished talking about—a positive attitude—and introduces the next one—perseverance.

Second main point

Supporting material (listener relevance)

Supporting material

Supporting Material

Thesis restatement and main point review

Notice how quickly Diana reviews her thesis and main points in one short sentence.

Main point review and clincher

Diana does a nice job of clinching by tying her closing back to her attention getter in a meaningful way.

MindTap™

Reflection and Assessment

Public speaking is important to achieving success in nearly every walk of life. Effective public speaking makes it possible to enact our civic engagement responsibility actively and ethically. To assess how well you've learned what we addressed in these pages, answer the following questions. If you have trouble answering any of them, go back and review that material. Once you can answer each question accurately, you are ready to move ahead to read the next chapter.

1. What is the nature and purpose of public speaking as a liberal art?
2. What are five ethical responsibilities of public speakers?
3. What is communication and public speaking as a form of it?
4. What is the rhetorical situation and how can it help you determine an appropriate speech goal?
5. What are the components of an effective audience-centered public speech?

 MindTap™

Challenge Resource and Assessment Center

Now that you have read Chapter 1, go to your MindTap for *The Challenge of Effective Speaking in a Digital Age* for quick access to the electronic resources that accompany this text. These resources include:

- **Study tools** that will help you assess your learning and prepare for exams (*digital glossary, key term flash cards, review quizzes*).

- **Activities and assignments** that will help you hone your knowledge and build your public speaking skills throughout the course (Practice, Do). Many of these activities allow you to compare your answers with those provided by the author, and, if requested, submit your answers to your instructor.

- **Media resources**—all of which are available on your MindTap for *Challenge*—will help you explore communication concepts online (Practice), develop your speech outlines (Do), watch and critique videos of sample speeches (Do), and upload your speech videos for instructor feedback and critique other students' speeches. (Do)

- **Web Links that provide you with additional information or resources related to the topics discussed in this chapter.**
  - **1.1** The Basics of Ethics (p. 6)
  - **1.2** Ethics Connection (p. 6)

- **Video resources allow you to see other students giving speeches and record your own speech.** Go to the Practice and Present section of MindTap to upload a video of your own speech of self-introduction for feedback from your instructor and classmates. Or search for other students' first speeches—do their speeches make your speech more effective?

Applying What You've Learned

1. **Impromptu Speech Activity:** Identify one of your "heroes." Your hero may or may not be famous. Identify one of the five ethical principles this hero's life adheres to and why. In your two- to three-minute impromptu speech, provide at least two incidents that serve as evidence regarding how this person demonstrates/demonstrated the principle.

2. **Assessment Activity A:** Visit the home page on Facebook. If you don't have an account, you might make one to observe while completing this course. Read through the postings on the "news feed" and identify which of them adhere to and do not adhere to the ethical communication principles proposed in this chapter.

3. **Assessment Activity B:** Visit a local retail store in a nearby mall. Spend time observing what you see. Describe what you observe according to the elements of the rhetorical situation (occasion, speaker, and audience). Do you think the sales clerk you observed was effective? Again, based on what you observed regarding the rhetorical situation, why or why not?

2 "your first speech"

WHEN YOU'VE FINISHED THIS CHAPTER, YOU WILL BE ABLE TO:

2-1 Describe the nature of public speaking apprehension

2-2 Practice several public speaking apprehension management methods and techniques

2-3 Identify the six steps in an effective speech action plan

2-4 Employ the steps to prepare and present a speech of self-introduction

MindTap™

Review the chapter **Learning Objectives** and **Start** with quick warm up activity.

ⓔ Ethical communicators behave responsibly by thoroughly preparing and practicing their speeches.

Kira had been staring at the computer screen for over an hour. Every time she started to type some ideas for her self-introduction speech assignment, her heart would start to race and she would freeze with thoughts of fear. "What if my classmates think my speech is boring? What if I make a mistake and they laugh at me or think I'm stupid? I'm too shy to give a speech. I'm just not good at it. I'm sure my voice will crack. If I do get up the nerve to do this, I hope I don't faint." She thought about dropping the class, but it is a required course that she'd registered for and dropped twice already. She knew she would eventually have to complete this class, but in her mind it had no real value. "I'm certainly not planning to be a public speaker in real life." She couldn't ask any of her family members for advice. None of them went to college, so they had no experience with public speaking classes. She didn't want to admit to her friends that she was so terrified. She sighed, shut down her computer, and picked up a textbook for another class.

You might be thinking, "Poor, Kira. If she's that nervous, her school should really let her opt out of the course." Or you might relate to Kira. You might even be thinking that people like you and Kira who suffer from severe public speaking apprehension—or stage fright—should not be put through such turmoil.

What you might not know, however, is that as many as 76 percent of experienced public speakers claim to feel fearful before presenting a speech.[1] For example, did you know that award-winning actors Meryl Streep, Kim Basinger, and Harrison Ford, singer Barbara Streisand, singer/actor Donny Osmond, former professional football player Ricky Williams, and evangelist Billy Graham all experience fear about speaking in front of others? In spite of their fear, all are effective public speakers today because they employ strategies for managing their nervousness—strategies we will discuss in this chapter.

We begin by explaining what scholars call public speaking apprehension. Then we discuss the causes and benefits–yes, we said *benefits*—of it. Finally, we'll propose several strategies for managing anxiety successfully. Perhaps most important is the role careful preparation plays in helping you develop and display confidence, which we'll describe by walking you through Kira's step-by-step process of preparing and practicing her speech of self-introduction.

2-1 UNDERSTANDING THE NATURE OF PUBLIC SPEAKING APPREHENSION

Public speaking apprehension is the level of fear a person experiences when anticipating or actually speaking to an audience. Almost all of us have some level of public speaking apprehension, and about 15 percent of the U.S. population experiences high levels of apprehension.[2] Even people with high levels of apprehension can be effective and confident public speakers. In fact, having some public speaking apprehension makes one a better public speaker than having none at all. Why? Because those feelings we label as fear are really a sign of the adrenaline boost that will help us perform at our best. Just as an adrenaline boost helps us perform better as athletes, musicians, and actors, it also helps us deliver better public speeches when we manage it effectively.[3] So, if you are lackadaisical about giving a speech, you probably will not do a good job.[4] Because at least some tension is constructive, the goal is not to eliminate nervousness but to learn how to manage it.[5]

"What if my classmates think my speech is boring? What if I make a mistake and they laugh at me or think I'm stupid?"

public speaking apprehension: the level of fear a person experiences when anticipating or actually speaking to an audience

Now that we understand that some public speaking apprehension is normal and can actually help you do a better job, let's identify some symptoms you may experience and the causes for speaking apprehension. Then we'll describe several techniques you can use to manage public speaking apprehension in ways that will make you a more effective public speaker.

2-1a Symptoms

The symptoms of public speaking apprehension vary from individual to individual and range from mild to debilitating. Symptoms can be cognitive, physical, or emotional. Cognitive symptoms include negative self-talk, which is also the most common cause of public speaking apprehension.[6] For example, a highly apprehensive person might do what Kira did in the opening vignette and dwell on thoughts such as "I'm going to make a fool of myself," or "I just know that I'll blow it." Physical symptoms may be stomach upset (or butterflies), flushed skin, sweating, shaking, lightheadedness, rapid or pounding heartbeats, stuttering, and vocalized pauses ("like," "you know," "ah," "um"). Emotional symptoms include feeling anxious, worried, or upset.

Luckily, public speaking apprehension gradually decreases for most of us as we speak. Researchers have identified three phases we proceed through: anticipation, confrontation, and adaptation.[7] Exhibit 2.1 depicts this cycle visually.

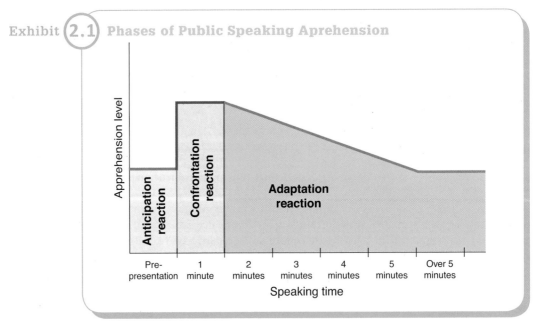

Exhibit **2.1** **Phases of Public Speaking Aprehension**

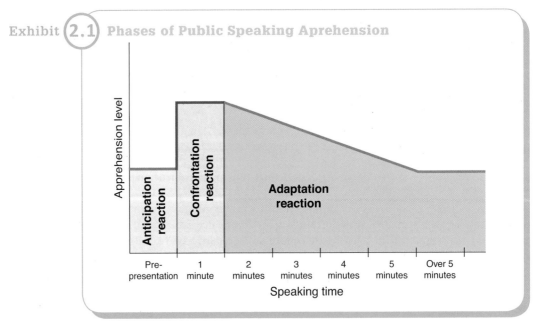

Copyright © Cengage Learning

anticipation phase: the anxiety you experience prior to giving the speech

confrontation phase: the surge of anxiety you feel as you begin delivering your speech

adaptation phase: the period during which your anxiety level gradually decreases

The **anticipation phase** is the anxiety we experience before giving the speech, both while preparing it and waiting to speak. The **confrontation phase** is the surge of anxiety we feel as we begin delivering the speech. This begins to fall about a minute or so into the speech. The **adaptation phase** is the period during which our anxiety level gradually decreases. It typically begins about one minute into the presentation and tends to level off after about five minutes.[8] So, it's normal to be nervous before you speak and, when managed effectively, can result in a better speech than having no nervousness at all.

There are many ways to measure your level of public speaking apprehension. Exhibit 2.2 presents a short self-assessment survey you can complete to gauge your level of apprehension.

xhibit

2.2 **Personal Report of Public Speaking Apprehension***

These statements give you a chance to express how you feel about speaking in public. Please indicate in the space provided the degree to which each statement applies to you by marking whether you:

1 = strongly agree; 2 = agree; 3 = are undecided; 4 = disagree; 5 = strongly disagree

_____ **1.** I have no fear of giving a speech.
_____ **2.** Certain parts of my body feel very tense and rigid while giving a speech.
_____ **3.** I feel relaxed while giving a speech.
_____ **4.** My thoughts become confused and jumbled when I am giving a speech.
_____ **5.** I face the prospect of giving a speech with confidence.
_____ **6.** While giving a speech, I get so nervous I forget the facts I really know.
_____ **TOTAL**

SCORING: Begin by reversing the numbers you assigned to statements 2, 4, and 6 (1 = 5, 2 = 4, 3 = 3, 4 = 2, 5 = 1). Then, add all six numbers.

INTERPRETING: If your total is more than 24, you may experience a high level of public speaking apprehension. People who are highly apprehensive will benefit most from applying the techniques designed to reduce anxiety.

*Taken from the PRCA-24, subscale Public Speaking. See Rich, V. P., & McCroskey, J. C. (1997). *Communication apprehension, avoidance, and effectiveness.* Scottsdale, AZ: Gorsuch Scarisbrick.

2-1b Causes

Public speaking apprehension is most commonly caused by negative self-talk.[9] **Self-talk** is defined as intrapersonal communication regarding perceived success or failure in a particular situation. Negative self-talk increases anxiety. Negative self-talk generally focuses on a fear of being stared at, a fear of the unknown, a fear of failure, or a fear of becoming fearful. Where do these negative thoughts come from? Research suggests three common roots: biologically based temperament, previous experience, and level of skills.

self-talk: intrapersonal communication regarding success or failure in a particular situation

Biologically Based Temperament

For a few of us, public speaking apprehension stems from our biologically based temperament. According to this theory, people who are extroverted tend to experience lower levels of public speaking apprehension than people who are introverted. Similarly, people who are generally anxious or shy tend to experience higher anxiety than people who are not.[10] Does this mean that naturally introverted, anxious, and shy people are doomed to be ineffective public speakers? Of course not. Remember the successful celebrities we mentioned earlier? Many of them are introverted, generally anxious, or shy, yet all of them enjoy a great deal of public speaking success. Believe it or not, even though one of your textbook authors is introverted, she has won multiple national titles in competitive collegiate speech tournaments.

Previous Experience

Our level of apprehension may also result from our experiences with public speaking while growing up. In other words, some of us actually learned to fear public speaking! Research tells us that most public speaking apprehension stems from such socialization.[11] We are socialized in two main ways: through modeling and reinforcement. **Modeling** is learning by observing and then imitating those you admire or are close to.[12] **Reinforcement** is learning from personal experiences so that past responses to our behavior shape expectations about how our future behavior will be received.[13]

Consider your past. How did modeling affect your current communication behavior? What was oral communication like growing up in your home and in your community? Did family or community members talk openly with each other a great deal, or were they

modeling: learning by observing and then imitating those you admire or are close to

reinforcement: learning from personal experiences and past responses to our behavior

Photo 2.1 Tina Fey modeled the public speaking behaviors she observed from family members when growing up.

© lev radin/Shutterstock.com

quiet and reserved? What was it like around the dinner table or at community events? Did any of your family members do much public speaking? What were their experiences? Did they avoid public speaking if they could? If your family tended to be quiet and reserved and avoided speaking in public or showed fear about it, your own preferences and fears may stem from modeling. Emmy-winning actress, writer, and comedian, Tina Fey, was once asked what it was like around her dinner table growing up. She remarked that "the whole family played to each other," her "mom's a dry wit," and her dad "has a good sense of silliness." Their modeling not only rubbed off on her as a comedian, but also helped her eventually overcome being a "shy, nerdy" teenager (Photo 2.1).[14]

How others have reinforced our public speaking efforts also influences how apprehensive we feel about it. We have all had many "public speaking" experiences, from reading aloud in elementary school, to giving an oral report in science class, to accepting a sports award at a banquet. If the responses to your speaking in the past were generally positive, you probably learned to feel confident about your ability. If, on the other hand, the responses were negative, you probably learned to feel fearful of public speaking. If your elementary school teacher humiliated you when you read aloud, if you flubbed that science report, or if friends laughed at your acceptance speech, you will probably be more apprehensive about speaking in public than if you had been praised for your efforts. Kira, for example, kept thinking about the time she gave a short speech in her eighth grade social studies class. The entire class chuckled when she mispronounced "synonym" as "cinnamon." The teacher reprimanded the class and asked Kira to continue, but she couldn't do it. The instructor allowed her to return to her seat without finishing the speech. Embarrassed and shaking, Kira learned to believe she was not a good public speaker and vowed never to do another speech. If you, like Kira, experience public speaking apprehension because of negative past experiences, you can learn strategies to manage apprehension and become an effective public speaker (Photo 2.2). We will discuss some of these strategies in the next section.

Level of Skills

An important source of public speaking apprehension comes from having underdeveloped speaking skills. This "skill deficit" theory suggests that most of us become apprehensive because we don't know how to (or choose not to) plan or prepare effectively for our public presentations. As you become skilled at using the six-step speech-planning and preparation process we introduce in this chapter, you will gain confidence and become a more effective public speaker.

2-2 MANAGING PUBLIC SPEAKING APPREHENSION

Because public speaking apprehension has multiple causes, we describe a few general methods, several specific techniques, and a six-step speech-planning and preparation process that will help manage anxiety and boost your confidence about public speaking.

2-2a General Methods

1. **Communication orientation motivation (COM) methods** is designed to reduce anxiety by adopting a "communication" rather than a "performance" orientation.[15] According to communication researcher Michael Motley, speakers with a **performance orientation** view public speaking as demanding special delivery techniques that will impress audiences "aesthetically"[16] and audience members as hypercritical judges who will not overlook even minor mistakes. When we approach public speaking with a performance orientation, our self-talk tends to

communication orientation motivation (COM) methods: designed to reduce anxiety by helping the speaker adopt a "communication" rather than a "performance" orientation toward the speech

performance orientation: viewing public speaking as a situation demanding special delivery techniques to impress an audience focus on our fear of failing, which increases our anxiety. On the other hand, speakers with a **communication orientation** view public speaking as an opportunity to engage in conversation with a number of people about an important topic. When we have a communication orientation, we focus on getting our message across rather than on how the people in our audience are judging us as a performer.

2. **Visualization** is a general method for reducing apprehension that involves picturing ourselves giving a masterful speech. Like COM techniques, visualization helps us overcome cognitive and emotional symptoms of apprehension arising from a fear of failure. Joe Ayres and Theodore S. Hopf, two scholars who have conducted extensive research on visualization, found that if people can visualize themselves going through an entire speech-preparation and speech-making process effectively, they will have a much better chance of succeeding when they actually give their speeches.[17]

Chuck Savage/Flirt/CORBIS

Photo 2.2 Effective speakers demonstrate integrity not by eliminating nervousness but by managing it effectively.

Visualization has been used extensively to improve athletic performances. In a study of basketball players trying to improve their foul-shooting percentages, for example, players were divided into three groups. One group never practiced, another group practiced making foul shots, and a third group "practiced" by visualizing themselves making foul shots. As we would expect, those who physically practiced improved far more than those who didn't practice at all. But those who simply *visualized* practicing improved almost as much as those who actually practiced.[18] Imagine what happens when you both visualize *and* practice (Photo 2.3)!

So, you can use visualization activities to manage apprehension as you prepare your speeches. Go to **Web Link 2.1, Visualizing Your Success,** in MindTap for *Challenge*. This audio activity will guide you through a visualization in which you will imagine that you successfully accomplish the complete speech preparation and presentation process.

3. **Relaxation exercises** include breathing techniques and progressive muscle relaxation exercises. For these exercises to be effective, you must learn how to do them and practice them regularly so they eventually become habitual. Then you will be able to use them to calm yourself in the moments before you speak.

Let's take a closer look at breathing techniques. We were all born breathing correctly—using the muscles in our abdomen to draw air into and push air out of our lungs. But when we become anxious, the muscles in our abdomens become tense and so we take shallower breaths, often raising our shoulders to get air into our lungs and dropping them to expel the air. Shallow breathing contributes to anxiety, depression, and fatigue.[19] Think of your lungs as balloons that fill up with air. Have you ever seen someone making balloon animals? If so, you probably noticed that, when the artist wanted part of the balloon to remain uninflated, he or she squeezed that area off with the hand. Shallow breathing is like filling only the top half of the balloon because, when your abdominal muscles tighten, you stop air from filling the bottom half of your lungs. Fortunately, we can retrain ourselves to breath from the abdomen and thereby reduce our anxiety. Exhibit 2.3 offers some suggestions.

Similarly, we can train our bodies to relax by practicing progressive muscle relaxation exercises. Essentially, you systematically tense certain muscle groups

communication orientation: viewing a speech as just an opportunity to talk with a number of people about an important topic

visualization: a method that reduces apprehension by helping speakers develop a mental picture of themselves giving a masterful speech

relaxation exercises: breathing techniques and progressive muscle relaxation exercises that help reduce anxiety for about ten seconds and then relax them for another ten seconds while focusing on what the relaxed state feels like.[20] Once you teach your body to relax on command, you can call it to do so before beginning to give your speech, again allowing the adrenaline rush to work for you.

Exhibit 2.3 **Breathing and Relaxation Exercises**

1. **Abdominal breathing:** Lie on the floor and place your hand on your abdomen. Consciously focus on filling your abdomen with air when you inhale by watching your hand rise. Then, as you release the air, watch your hand lower again.

2. **Sighing:** By sighing right before it is your turn to speak, you can release tension and lower your anxiety level, allowing the inevitable rush of adrenaline to work for you, not against you.[21]

3. **Progressive muscle relaxation exercises:** Consciously tense and relax each of these muscle groups twice and then move on to the next group: hands, arms, shoulders, neck, lips, tongue, mouth, eyes and forehead, abdomen, back, midsection, thighs, stomach, calves, feet, and toes.

Copyright © Cengage Learning

---

4. **Systematic desensitization** is a method that reduces apprehension by gradually visualizing yourself in and then performing increasingly more frightening events while remaining in a relaxed state.[22] Research tells us that more than 80 percent of those who try this method reduce their level of anxiety.[23] Essentially, once you are in a relaxed state, you imagine yourself in successively more stressful speech-planning and speech-making situations—for example, researching a speech topic in the library, practicing the speech out loud in front of a roommate, and delivering the final speech to your audience. Once you can maintain a relaxed state while visualizing yourself in each event, you try performing each event while maintaining the learned state of calmness. The ultimate goal of systematic desensitization is to transfer the calm feelings we attain while visualizing to the actual speaking event. Calmness on command—and it works.

5. **Cognitive restructuring** is a process designed to help you change your intrapersonal communication about public speaking. The goal is to replace anxiety-arousing negative self-talk with anxiety-reducing positive self-talk. The process consists of four steps.

- Identify your fears. Write down all the fears that come to mind when you know you must give a speech.

- Analyze how rational these fears are. Most fears about public speaking are, in fact, irrational because public speaking is not life threatening.

- Develop positive coping statements to replace each negative self-talk statement. Exhibit 2.4 is an example of how Kira used this process to help manage her anxiety. There is no one list of coping statements that will work for everyone, but you can develop your own list of positive coping statements to replace negative self-talk. Psychologist Richard Heimberg of the State University of New York at Albany asks his clients to consider just how many listeners in an audience of 100 would even notice or care if the clients did what they're afraid of doing when giving a speech. Ultimately, he concludes with the question, "Can you cope with the one or two people who [notice or criticize or] get upset?"[24]

Photo by John McDonnell/The Washington/Getty Images

Photo 2.3 If people can visualize themselves going through an entire process, they will have a much better chance of succeeding when they are in the actual situation.

- Incorporate your positive coping statements into your life so that they're second nature. You can do this by writing your statements down and reading them aloud to yourself each day, as well as before you give a speech. The more you repeat your coping statements to yourself, silently and aloud, the more natural they will become and the more unnatural your negative thoughts will seem.

Exhibit (2.4) **Negative Self-talk Versus Positive Coping Statements**

Kira decided to try cognitive restructuring to reduce her anxiety about giving speeches in front of her classmates. Here is how she worked through the process:

Negative self-talk
1. I'm afraid I'll stumble over my words and look foolish.
2. I'm afraid everyone will be able to tell that I'm nervous.
3. I'm afraid my voice will crack.
4. I'm afraid I'll sound boring.

Positive coping statements
1. Even if I stumble, I will have succeeded as long as I get my message across.
2. They probably won't be able to tell I'm nervous, but as long as I focus on getting my message across, that's what matters.
3. Even if my voice cracks, as long as I keep going and focus on getting my message across, I'll succeed at what matters most.
4. I won't sound bored if I focus on how important this message is to me and to my audience. I don't have to do somersaults to keep their attention because my topic is relevant to them.

systematic desensitization: a method that reduces apprehension by gradually having people visualize and perform increasingly more frightening events while remaining in a relaxed state

cognitive restructuring: a process designed to help you systematically change your intrapersonal communication (self-talk) about public speaking

All of these methods for reducing public speaking apprehension have successfully helped people reduce their anxiety. If you think you'll experience public speaking apprehension in this course, which of these techniques do you think might help you? Have you already tried some of them in other situations? If they helped, do you think you could apply them to reduce your anxiety about giving a speech? For most people, using several of them yields the best results.[25] For an activity that will help you develop positive coping statements to replace negative self-talk, go to **Web Link 2.2, Restructure Your Expectations,** in your MindTap for *Challenge*.

 MindTap™

PUBLIC SPEAKING IN THE REAL WORLD

Harrison Ford and Public Speaking Anxiety

Although Harrison Ford is one of the highest grossing movie stars of all time, he struggles with public speaking anxiety. In his own words, public speaking is "a mixed bag of terror and anxiety."[26] Not only that, he even feels fear when a character he is playing must give a speech.[27] The former philosophy major and Sigma Nu fraternity member at Ripon College in Wisconsin manages his anxiety using a modified version of Motley's communication orientation motivation (COM) method. As Ford says, "I don't want to be a movie star. I want to be in movies that are stars. For me, it's not about performance. It's about storytelling."[28]

Pascal Le Segretain/Getty Images

2-2b Specific Techniques

In addition to these five general methods, we recommend several specific techniques to employ in the days before you deliver your speech and on the day you actually give it.

1. **Allow sufficient time to prepare.** As soon as you know the day you are to give your speech and the expectations for it, identify the topic and begin to prepare. Ideally, you should spend at least a week or ten days researching, organizing, and practicing your speech.

2. **Use presentational aids.** Recall that one of the major fears that increase public speaking anxiety is the fear of being stared at. Although it is human nature to enjoy being recognized for things we've done well, it is not human nature to be the constant center of attention for a prolonged amount of time.[29] When giving a public speech, all eyes are focused constantly on us, and we can feel conspicuous. Using presentational aids allows us to direct the audience's attention toward something else at carefully placed points during the speech, which can diminish the sense of being constantly stared at and the anxiety that can accompany it.

3. **Practice your speech aloud.** When you practice your speech aloud, you get comfortable hearing yourself talk about your topic. You identify sections of the speech where your ideas may not flow and where you need to do additional preparation. By the third or fourth time you have practiced aloud, you will notice your delivery becoming easier, and you will gain confidence in your ability to present your ideas to others.

Many successful speakers not only practice aloud alone but also practice in front of trusted friends who serve as a "practice" audience and give the speaker feedback (Photo 2.4). If possible, practice your speech in the room where you'll ultimately deliver it. Hearing your voice in the room where you'll speak reduces anxiety that can arise as a result of the fear of the unknown because you now know what it will feel like to present your speech in that room. Finally, on the night before your speech, review your speech plan immediately before you go to sleep. That way, as you sleep, your mind will continue to prepare.[30]

4. **Dress up.** We tend to feel more confident when we know we look good. By dressing up a bit for our speech, we reduce anxiety about being stared at because we feel good about how we look. Not only that, dressing up enhances credibility (ethos) because doing so sends a message that we care about the audience, the occasion, and the message we want to get across to our listeners.

5. **Choose an appropriate time to speak.** If you have a choice about whether you will give your speech first, last, or somewhere in between, pick the time that works best for you. Some speakers become more nervous when they sit and listen to others, so they are better off speaking early in the class period. Others find that listening to their peers calms them, so they are better off speaking later in the class period. If given a chance, choose to speak at the time that is optimal for you.

6. **Use positive self-talk.** Immediately prior to getting up to speak, coach yourself with a short "pregame pep talk." Remind yourself about the importance of what you have to say. Remember all the hard work you have done to be prepared and recall how good you are when you are at your best. Remind yourself that nervousness is normal and useful. Tell yourself that you are confident and ready.

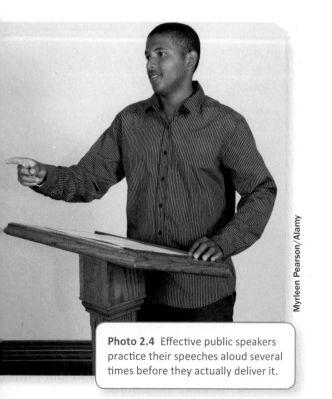

Myrleen Pearson/Alamy

Photo 2.4 Effective public speakers practice their speeches aloud several times before they actually deliver it.

7. **Face the audience.** Face the audience with confidence. When it is time, walk purposefully to the front. Plant yourself firmly yet comfortably, and take a second or two to look at the audience. Take a deep breath (you might even silently count to five while reviewing the first lines of your speech in your head) and begin your well-rehearsed introduction.

8. **Focus on sharing your message.** Although you may feel nervous, your audience rarely "sees" it. Continue to focus on sharing your ideas with the audience rather than focusing on your nerves.

2-3 DEVELOPING AN EFFECTIVE SPEECH PLAN

Whether you are a marketing account manager presenting an advertising campaign idea to clients, a coach trying to motivate your team for its game with your arch rival, or a student giving a speech in class, you can manage anxiety, demonstrate confidence, and be more effective when you develop and follow an effective **speech plan**—a strategy for achieving your goal.

> **speech plan:** a strategy for achieving your goal

In this section and throughout the chapters that follow, we will work through a six-step process for planning and preparing speeches grounded in the works of major speech scholars across the ages. Ancient Roman philosophers actually clarified the five general rules for effective public speeches more than 2,000 years ago. These rules, known as the **canons of rhetoric** still hold true today.[31] These five canons are invention (an effective speech has convincing content), arrangement (an effective speech is clearly organized), style (an effective speech uses appropriate language), delivery (an effective speaker delivers the oration with confidence, fluency, and strategic retention aids), and memory (an effective speaker integrates creative content, language, presentational aids, and delivery). While classical approaches to speech planning were speaker-focused, scholars now recognize that effective speeches are audience centered and address the rhetorical situation.[32] So, the speech making skills we propose are both rooted in ancient wisdom and informed by contemporary research. The six speech action plan steps are:

> **canons of rhetoric:** five general rules for effective public speeches

1. Select a specific speech goal that is appropriate to the rhetorical situation.

2. Understand your audience and adapt to it.

3. Gather and evaluate information.

4. Organize ideas into a well-structured outline.

5. Choose, prepare, and use appropriate presentational aids.

6. Practice oral language and delivery style.

These are also illustrated in Exhibit 2.5. Let's briefly preview what you will learn in each step and how Kira worked through each one to prepare her speech of self-introduction.

2-3a Step 1: Select a Specific Speech Goal That Is Appropriate to the Rhetorical Situation

Your **speech goal** is a specific statement of what you want your audience to know, believe, or do. To arrive at an appropriate speech goal, you need to consider yourself as the speaker, the audience, and the occasion. Doing so will encourage your audience to pay attention because they will perceive your speech as relevant to them.

> **speech goal:** a specific statement of what you want your listeners to know, believe, or do

Begin by selecting a topic that you know something about, that interests you, and is important to you. Although you might occasionally speak on a topic that is unfamiliar to you, you will usually speak on topics that meet these tests. Kira's speech topic was to be about herself.

Goal

1. Select a specific speech goal that is appropriate to the rhetorical situation.

Audience

2. Understand your audience and adapt to it.

Research

3. Gather and evaluate information.

Organization

4. Organize ideas into a well-structured outline.

Presentational Aids

5. Choose, prepare, and use appropriate presentational aids.

Delivery

6. Practice oral language and delivery style.

Audience icon, © Sielan/Shutterstock; all other icons, © CoraMax/Shutterstock

Next you need to think about your audience so you can address the topic in ways that will be relevant to their needs, interests, and desires. Who are they? What do they need to know about your topic? What do they already know? To answer these questions, you need to make a preliminary audience analysis based on their gender, culture, average age, education level, occupation, income level, and group affiliation. Then, you can assess the kinds of material and information they are likely to be motivated to listen to. Kira's audience includes her classmates and her instructor. Because she didn't know any of them before enrolling in the course, pretty much everything about her will be new to them. She counted 14 females and 11 males. Almost everyone appeared to be 18 to 24 years old except for one female who had mentioned having a 13-year-old daughter. She was probably in her 30s. She didn't know about religion or ethnicity. Although most of her classmates appeared to be Caucasian, she wasn't really sure if that was true. She figured a couple students—Xialing and Min—were of Asian descent, but she didn't know if they were international students or Asian Americans. She did know, however, that everyone was pursuing an undergraduate degree at the same school in the same state. She decided to talk about why she decided to go to college, to attend this university, and to pursue her major. She figured everyone could relate to that in some way.

You also need to consider the occasion. What is the size of the audience? When will the speech be given? Where will the speech be given? Are there any peculiarities of the room? What is the time limit for the speech? What are the particular expectations for the speech? The room Kira will be speaking in is pretty typical for a speech class. Kira is expected to introduce herself in a two- to three-minute speech using the lectern and including at least two presentational aids. Her instructor will be recording all the speeches, so students can critique and assess their performance later.

Once you determine a topic based on your interest and expertise, the audience, and the occasion, you are ready to phrase your speech goal. Every speech has a general and a specific goal. For most classroom speeches, the general goal is usually either to inform, where your goal is shared understanding; or to persuade, where your goal is to convince your audience to believe something or persuade them to take action. We will discuss several other general goals, which Aristotle called ceremonial speeches (e.g., to introduce, to entertain, and to celebrate), in later chapters.[33]

Your specific speech goal articulates exactly what you want your audience to understand, believe, or do. For instance, Gina, who is majoring in health and nutrition, might phrase her informative speech goal as, "I want the audience to understand three methods for ridding our bodies of harmful toxins." And Glen, a bioengineering major, might phrase his persuasive speech goal as, "I want to convince my audience of the value of genetic engineering." Kira was glad the instructor told everyone to focus on the same three main points for this speech. She phrased her specific speech goal as, "I want my audience to understand a bit about my personal background, what I am majoring in, and what I plan to do when I graduate."

2-3b Step 2: Understand Your Audience and Adapt to It

Once you have a clear and specific speech goal based on the speaker, audience, and occasion, you begin the task of understanding your audience more fully and how to adapt your speech to it. **Audience adaptation** is the process of tailoring your speech's information to the needs, interests, and expectations of your listeners (Photo 2.5). You will want to do so continually throughout the speech-planning and speech-practicing process.

For any speech, it is important to consider the audience's initial level of interest in your goal, their ability to understand the content of the speech, and their attitude toward you and your topic. If you believe your audience has very little interest in your topic, you will need to adapt by explaining how and why the topic is important or relevant to them. Not only will you need to adapt your speech by piquing audience interest, but if you believe that your audience doesn't know much about your topic, you will want to provide the basic information they need to understand your speech. For instance, in his speech about genetic engineering, Glen may need to begin by talking about how genetic engineering differs from organically grown foods. Kira decided that not everyone would know what a "first-generation student" is. So she would define it for them as an undergraduate student whose parents never attended college.

audience adaptation: the process of tailoring your speech's information to the needs, interests, and expectations of your listeners

SPEECH SNIPPET

Capture Audience Interest

To pique audience interest in his speech on genetic engineering, Glen decided to talk about foods commonly eaten that have been genetically modified.

Bill Aron/PhotoEdit

Photo 2.5 Suppose you were giving a speech on genetic engineering. Your adaptation challenges would differ between the audience pictured here and an audience composed of young college students.

Finally, you will need to adapt to your audience's initial attitude toward your topic. Glen should do some research to learn where his audience stands on this topic before he begins. If the majority of his audience is against genetic engineering, he will adapt by selecting arguments and evidence that can be accepted by the audience. Kira's post-graduation goal is to return to Eastern Kentucky to help develop college readiness skills in kids whose parents never attended college. She figured none of her classmates would be opposed to this idea. But they also might not really care one way or another about her background or goals. So, she decided to work hard on ways to overcome apathy by identifying common values of college students in her listener-relevance links.

2-3c Step 3: Gather and Evaluate Information

In addition to drawing on material from your own knowledge and experiences, you can draw on the expertise of others by reading printed materials, conducting interviews and surveys, and searching online. You should gather and evaluate verbal, visual, and audio-visual material that you might draw on to develop your speech outline or your presentational aids. Kira, for example, gathered photographs of her hometown and her cohort of first-generation students at college, as well as college preparation and readiness checklists for grades 9, 10, 11, and 12 she found online. You will need to evaluate the information and sources and select only the items you deem to be truthful and credible. For instance, as a student of bioengineering, Glen is able to explain the process of genetic engineering because he studied it in his classes. His personal knowledge also helps him evaluate and select additional information and sources he locates doing research on his topic. And Kira, who is a first-generation student herself, can speak from experience about the additional challenges such students must overcome in order to succeed.

2-3d Step 4: Organize Ideas into a Well-Structured Outline

Begin organizing your speech by identifying the two to four major ideas you want your audience to remember. Then turn each major idea into a complete sentence. These sentences will become the main points for the body of your speech. Next you combine your speech goal with each major idea into a succinct thesis statement with a main point preview that describes specifically what you want your audience to understand, believe, or do when you have finished speaking. This process provides the overarching framework, or macrostructure, of your speech. Kira's first draft of a thesis statement with main point preview looked like this:

Today, I'm going to tell you a bit about who I am by focusing on my personal background, what I am majoring in, and what I plan to do after I graduate.

Main points must be arranged in an organizational framework that helps the audience understand and remember them. Two of the most basic organizational frameworks are chronological and topical. **Chronological** means following an order that moves from first to last. You can see by looking at Kira's thesis statement with main point preview that her speech will be organized chronologically. **Topical** means following an order of interest. For instance, Gina, who decides to inform her audience about the three proven methods for removing harmful toxins from the body, may begin with the simplest one—keeping hydrated—and ending with the most difficult one—eating more natural whole foods.

chronological: following an order that moves from first to last

topical: following an order of interest

Having identified and ordered the main points, you are ready to outline the speech body. You do so by adding information as subpoints to support each of your two to four main points. At least one subpoint used to elaborate on each main point should provide listener relevance by articulating why or how the information relates to the audience's needs, interests, or desires. After you have outlined the speech body, you will outline your introduction and conclusion. Your introduction should get attention, establish listener relevance and speaker credibility, and lead into the body of the speech. Your conclusion should provide closure by reminding the audience of your main points and speech goal in a positively memorable way.

2-3e Step 5: Choose, Prepare, and Use Appropriate Presentational Aids

We live in what many have dubbed the "digital age." As a result of the plethora of technological sources available to us—computers, laptops, iPads, iPods, smart phones, etc.— today we need to present public speeches via multimodal messages (visual, oral, written) and channels (face-to-face, print, technology enhanced). Whereas presentational aids were once considered optional embellishments, today most audiences expect them. So, even for a very short speech, you may decide to use a presentational aid to clarify, emphasize, or dramatize your goal and main points. You might convey various ideas through models, charts, graphs, pictures, audios, videos, or audiovisuals—usually using computer technology to assist you. Note in your outline precisely where you will use them and practice using them when you rehearse your speech.

> **SPEECH SNIPPET**
>
> **Organizing Your Speech**
>
> Nora is giving a speech on how to perform CPR. She decides to organize it chronologically according to the first, second, and third steps to follow.

2-3f Step 6: Practice Oral Language and Delivery Style

In your practice sessions, you need to choose the wording of main points and supporting materials carefully. If you have not practiced various ways of phrasing your key ideas, you run the risk of missing a major opportunity for communicating your ideas effectively. In practice sessions, work on the appropriateness, accuracy, clarity, and vividness of your wording. Recall that these language choices make up the microstructure of your speech.

Although a speech is composed of words, how effective you will be is also largely a matter of how well you use your voice and body to deliver your speech. You will want to present the speech in a way that others will understand it (intelligibly), conversationally, and expressively. You will also want to use good posture and eye contact (look at members of the audience while you are speaking) to appear confident and comfortable, as well as use facial expressions and gestures that emphasize emotional intentions and clarify structure.

> **SPEECH SNIPPET**
>
> **Establish Listener Relevance**
>
> Kira established listener relevance for her personal background main point by relating to a value she knew her audience shared with her—growing up as a UK Wildcat fan.

Very few people can present speeches effectively without considerable practice. Practicing out loud gives you confidence that you can talk conversationally and expressively to accomplish your speech goal within the time limit. Don't try to memorize the speech, which is likely to increase anxiety because you may fear forgetting what you planned to say. Instead, practice delivering your speech extemporaneously based on speaking notes comprised of key words and phrases that remind you of structure, main points, and delivery cues.

Reflect on Ethics

FOOTBALL COACH FORCED TO RESIGN OVER INACCURATE RESUME

After taking the Georgia Tech football team to five straight bowl games and earning a 52–33 win-loss record there, George O'Leary was delighted to be selected as the new football coach at the University of Notre Dame in 2001. However, after admitting he lied on his resume, he resigned five days later.[34] O'Leary's resume claimed he had earned a master's degree in education from New York University in 1972 and that he was a three-time letter winner in football at the University of New Hampshire. In fact, O'Leary was a student at NYU but never earned a degree from there. In addition, he was on the football team at UNH, but he never played in a game.

He justified his lies by saying that "many years ago, as a young married father," he was pursuing his dream to become a college football coach and that these inaccuracies were never removed from his resume or biographical statement "in later years." Some said he did the right thing by resigning, because Notre Dame needs a coach they can trust—his actions must demonstrate honesty and loyalty. Others, like UNH football coach

Sean McDonnell, were "surprised and shocked that he had to resign because of something like this," claiming he "was a guy with great integrity."

1. What, if any, ethical principles did O'Leary violate and how?

2. Some people justify exaggerating, or even lying, on their resumes by saying that everybody does it. And if they don't also do it, they will hurt their chances of getting a good job. In fact, according to CareerBuilder.com, 38 percent of those surveyed admitted to embellishing their job responsibilities on their resumes, and 18 percent admitted to lying about their skill sets. Given these numbers, are the justifications reasonable? Why or why not?

3. If you believe stretching the truth is acceptable in certain circumstances, how far can you go before you cross the line into unacceptable behavior?

4. Do you think O'Leary should have resigned over this issue? Why or why not?

speech assignment

Speech of Self-Introduction

Prepare a two- to three-minute speech of self-introduction. Use the following as your main points:

1. Your personal background.

2. Your academic major.

3. What you hope to do after you graduate.

Remember that an effective speech is based on audience-centered content (breadth, depth, listener relevance), structure (macro- and micro-), and delivery (use of voice, body, and presentational aids). As you prepare, use the Speech Evaluation Checklist that follows and Kira's sample speech to make sure your speech includes all the elements of an effective speech.

speech evaluation checklist

General Criteria

You can use this checklist to critique a speech of self-introduction that you hear in class. (You can also use it to critique your own speech.) As you listen to the speaker, consider what makes a speech effective. Then, answer the following questions.

Content

1. Were all main points addressed per the assignment?_____

2. Were two or three pieces of evidence used to develop each main point (breadth)? _____

3. Was one extended piece of evidence used to add depth? _____

4. Were listener-relevance links provided for each main point? _____

5. Did presentational aids enhance clarity, embellish key ideas, or dramatize an important point?

6. Did the speech fall within the time constraints of the assignment? _____

Structure

1. Did the speech provide all the basic elements of an effective speech: introduction, body, conclusion, and transitions? *(macrostructure)* _____

2. Did the introduction catch the audience's interest? _____ identify the speech topic/goal? _____ preview the main points? _____

3. Were transitions provided between each main point? _____

4. Did the conclusion remind the audience of the main points? _____ motivate the -audience to remember the main ideas of the speech? _____

5. Did the speaker use words that were appropriate and inclusive? accurate and clear? _____ vivid and expressive? *(microstructure)* _____

6. Were the presentational aids constructed and displayed Effectively?

Delivery

1. Was the speaker intelligible in terms of volume? _____ Rate? _____ Pronunciation? _____ Enunciation? _____

2. Was the speaker conversational? _____

3. Did the speaker look up from his or her notes most of the time and make eye contact with the audience?

_____

4. Did the speaker appear professional, poised, and confident? _____

5. Was the speaker expressive in terms of changes in rate and volume? _____ Strategic pauses? _____ Appropriate faical expressions? _____ gestures?_____

6. Did the speaker integrate presentational aids gracefully? _____

MindTap™

Access this checklist on your MindTap for *Challenge.*

What follows is an outline of Kira's speech of self-introduction. As you read, consider how you might address the rhetorical situation effectively as you develop a speech of self-introduction for your audience. How will you organize your ideas, practice you delivery, and what presentation aids will you include? Then, answer these questions about Kira's content and structure.

1. Content: What are Kira's main points? What kinds of evidence does she use to support them? What are some examples of breadth, depth, and listener relevance in the body of her speech?

2. Structure: What does Kira do to get the attention of her audience? What does she say to lead her audience with her from one point to the next? How does she wrap up the speech to help her audience remember her ideas? What wording seems to demonstrate inclusion, provide clarity, and evoke vivid images?

On Being First

INTRODUCTION

Attention Getter

I. What comes to mind when someone shouts "We're number one! We're number one!"? If you're like most people I know, that chant probably conjures up images about winning a sporting event.

Notice how Kira piques interest by asking a question about a chant most of her audience is likely to be familiar with and then leads them to her topic gradually by offering another meaning.

Listener Relevance and Speaker Credibility

II. Like you, I too think about winning games. But that's not the only thought that comes to mind for me. I also think about the fact that I'm "number one" because I am the first person in my family to attend college. As a first-generation college student, I can't help but think about what a tremendous opportunity all of us have to pursue our dreams because we here in college today.

Thesis Statement and Main Point Review

III. Today, I'd like to introduce myself to you by talking about my unique personal background as a first-generation college student, my choice of majors, and my goals after graduation.

Kira very simply states her thesis with main point preview so her audience can get her main points firmly in mind.

BODY

First Main Point

I. To begin, let's talk about my personal background and how it shaped my decision to apply to the University of Kentucky.

Subpoint (Listener Relevance)

A. [show presentational aid/photo of fans cheering at a UK sporting event] Like most of you, I grew up in Kentucky cheering for the Wildcats and daydreaming about what it would be like to attend college here someday.

Subpoint

Kira knows most of her classmates are Wildcat fans so she decides to play on that to keep them listening.

B. Unlike most of you, though, I am also a first-generation college student, which means I am the first person in my family to attend college.

Kira defines what a first-generation college student is in case some of her listeners are unfamiliar with the phrase

1. [photo of my family] I was raised in Harlan County where my dad works as a miner, my mom works as a server at a local café, and my brother attends high school.

2. Although my parents supported my dream to go to college, they couldn't afford to pay for it, to give me advice about what college would be like, to help me prepare for it, including how to study for the ACT, or to help me fill out my college application.

3. [presentational aid of collage of books/websites/teachers] Instead, I had to seek out information and advice from books, Internet websites, and school teachers and counsellors.

4. I learned that I would need to develop a strong resume. So I put extra effort into doing so by studying hard to earn good grades, volunteering as a Sunday School teacher, singing in the school choir, and participating on the swim team.

Use your MindTap for *Challenge* to watch a video clip of Kira presenting her speech in class. Also use the speech evaluation checklist that precedes this outline to evaluate Kira's content (breadth, depth, listener relevance, choice of presentational aids), structure (macrostructure, microstructure, construction of presentational aids), and delivery (voice, body, integration of presentational aids).

5. Knowing I would have to pay for school myself, I also worked part-time throughout high school and applied for every scholarship, grant, and low interest loan I was eligible for. [conceal presentational aid]

Listing several examples is a way to add breadth.

Now that you know a little bit about my personal background as a first-generation college student, you probably also understand why I never take for granted the fact that I am a student here at UK. What you probably don't know, however is what I am majoring in and why.

Transition

II. I am actually pursuing a major in teacher education.

Second Main Point

Kira offers a complete transition statement that both restates the main point she finished discussing and introduces the upcoming main point.

A. If you're like me, you are pursuing a college degree for reasons beyond the fact that we'll probably make more money as a result.
   1. Many of us want to learn knowledge and skills in a particular field of study.
   2. Many of us want to gain self-confidence about our abilities.
   3. Many of us want to develop strong leadership skills.
   4. These reasons help each of us pick a major.

Subpoint (Listener Relevance)

Kira's use of "us" rather than "I" is an example of inclusive language.

B. I am pursuing my degree in social studies education because the teacher education program here has a great reputation for preparing students to be effective teachers.
   1. Coursework in the Teacher Education program will help me develop leadership skills to work effectively with middle school and high school students in an educational setting.
   2. Becoming certified as a K–12 teacher will provide the credentials needed to obtain employment in a K–12 educational system.
   3. The experiences I will gain by working in the innovative P-20 initiative in the College of Education here at UK will set me apart from other job seekers when I graduate. [show graph of the P-20 program offerings and explain how it works, then conceal it]
   4. The Teacher Education Program's job placement rate statistics are remarkable.

Subpoint

Kira points to the fact about the programs placement statistics for supporting material. She could have also used a visual aid showing the actual job placement statistics to add depth.

So I chose to earn my degree in teacher education to gain the confidence and skills I will need to make a difference in the world. Let's look more specifically at how I hope to make a difference after I graduate.

Transition

III. I have several goals for my life after graduation.

Main Point

A. Because we can all expect to spend more time at work than anywhere else once we graduate, we all aspire to being in a career that we love. For me, and I assume for many of you too, that means being in a career where I can make a difference. I know I want to pay it forward by helping other potential first-generation college students achieve their college preparation and placement goals and dreams.

Subpoint (Listener Relevance)

Again Kira uses inclusive "we" language and the phrase "and I assume for many of you too" to help her listeners feel included in the public speaking conversation with her.

Subpoint

B. When I graduate, I want to return to Eastern Kentucky, maybe even to Harlan County, to teach social studies to middle school students, high school students, or both.

1. I plan to embed activities focused on career planning that will encourage students to discover and then have the courage to pursue their dreams.

2. I also plan to develop after-school programming for students who would be first-generation college students like me to provide them the information and skills they need to succeed.

3. I hope to ultimately turn the program into a nonprofit organization where I train others to create similar programs across the state.

Kira adds depth to this point by showing the first of her step-by-step long term goals.

Subpoint

C. My long-term goal is return to UK to pursue a Masters degree in Counselling Psychology.

1. In doing so, I can learn more about how to make a difference in the lives of students who may face a variety of potential barriers to success.

2. I can then use that knowledge and those skills to broaden my goals from helping potential first-year college students to also helping other students with special needs remove barriers for success.

CONCLUSION

Thesis Restatement with Main Point Review

I. So now you know a little bit about me as a first-generation college student, why I chose to major in Teacher Education, and how I hope to pay it forward when I graduate from UK.

Clincher

II. [show UK fans cheering "We're Number 1"] And even more than that, whenever you find yourself chanting "We're number 1" you'll think about my speech today, not just in terms of what it means to be a first-generation college student, but also in terms of how each of us can achieve our career *goals* by landing a good job AND our career *dreams* by making a difference.

Kira offers a visually reinforced clincher that ties back to the emotion-arousing attention catcher to motivate listeners to remember her speech.

🌐 MindTap™

Reflection and Assessment

This chapter focused on public speaking apprehension and how to manage it in ways that will help you become a confident and effective public speaker. To assess how well you've learned what we addressed in these pages, answer the following questions. If you have trouble answering any of them, go back and review that material. Once you can answer each question accurately, you are ready to move ahead to read the next chapter.

1. What is public speaking apprehension, its symptoms, and its causes?
2. Why is the goal of effective public speakers to manage apprehension rather than eliminate it?
3. What are some methods and techniques you can use to manage public speaking apprehension effectively?
4. What are the six steps in an effective speech plan?

Challenge Resource and Assessment Center

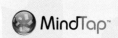

Now that you have read Chapter 2, go to MindTap for *The Challenge of Public Speaking in a Digital Age* for quick access to the electronic resources that accompany this text. These resources include:

- **Study tools** that will help you access your learning and prepare for exams (*digital glossary, key term flash cards, review quizzes*).

- **Activities and assignments** that will help you hone your knowledge and build your public speaking skills throughout the course (Practice, Do). Many of these activities allow you to compare your answers with those provided by the authors, and, if requested, submit your answers to your instructor.

- **Media resources**—all of which are available on your MindTap for *Challenge*—will help you explore communication concepts online (Practice), develop your speech outlines (Do), watch and critique videos of sample speeches (Do), and upload your speech videos for instructor feedback and critique other students' speeches. (Do)

- **Web Links that provide you with additional information or resources related to the topics discussed in this chapter.**
  2.1 Visualizing Your Success (p. 25)
  2.2 Restructure Your Expectations (p. 27)

- **Video resource allow you to see other students giving speeches and record your own speech.** Go to the Practice and Present section of MindTap to upload a video of your own narrative/personal experience speech for feedback from your instructor and classmates. Or search for other students' narrative speeches—do their speeches give you ideas for how you could make your speech more effective?

Applying What You've Learned

1. **Impromptu Speech Activity:** Identify a character from a favorite comic strip or cartoon where you believe a character communicates either ethically or unethically. Prepare a two- to three-minute speech explaining why. Be sure to tell your story with details about the setting, the characters, and the event(s) that support the life lesson or moral of your story.

2. **Assessment Activity A:** Practice a calming sigh to reduce anxiety right before you get up to give your speech. (1) Inhale deeply but gently through your nose. (2) Slowly let the air out while saying "Ahhhh." (3) Let your body go limp for a couple of moments. (4) Repeat. Do you feel more relaxed as you get up to speak?

3. **Assessment Activity B:** Prepare and practice your personal cognitive restructuring by following this five-step process. (1) Create your own negative self-talk list by writing down four or five fears that come to mind when you know you must give a speech. (2) Identify why that fear is irrational, that is, how you're blowing it out of proportion. (3) Create a positive self-talk statement to replace each negative one. (4) Place these statements on a small notecard you can keep in your pocket or wallet. (5) Practice your positive self-talk statements daily until they become second nature.

3 "listening"

○ **WHAT'S THE POINT?
WHEN YOU'VE FINISHED THIS
CHAPTER YOU'LL BE ABLE TO:**

3-1 Explain what listening is and why it's important to study in a public speaking course.

3-2 Describe why effective listening is so challenging.

3-3 Employ specific strategies to improve your listening skills.

3-4 Practice providing constructive speech critiques.

Review the chapter **Learning Objectives** and **Start** with quick warm up activity.

© iStockphoto.com/Wendy Carter

ⓔ Ethical listeners hear speakers out even when they present an opposing point of view.

As Beth pours another cup of coffee, Bart storms into the kitchen and bursts out, "Beth, do you have my car keys? I can't find them and I have to take the car or I'll be late for class."

No," Beth replies, "but it doesn't matter because . . ."

Before Beth can finish, Bart interrupts, "I can't believe it. I was sure I left them here on the counter last night. It figures. Just because I'm in a hurry, I can't find them." *Bart starts shuffling through the papers on the counter and digging through the drawers.*

"Bart, I . . ."

"I swear I put them here on the counter," *Bart continues, growing noticeably more agitated* "Are you sure you didn't stuff them in a drawer when you were cleaning the kitchen or something?"

"Bart, chill out."

"Chill out?! If I'm late, I won't be able to do my presentation and it's worth 50 percent of the course grade! I won't pass the class and I need at least a B to declare my major. Beth, this is a very big deal."

"Beth, this is a very big deal."

"Bart, I've been trying to tell you . . ."

"Oh, sure—I'll just go into the Professor Harrington's office and say, 'By the way, the reason I wasn't in class was that I couldn't find my car keys. Can I please do my presentation tomorrow?' I'll sound like a slacker who wasn't ready. There's no way he'll buy that argument even if it is true."

Beth takes Bart's hands in hers, looks him in the eye, and says calmly but firmly, "Bart, listen. I've been trying to tell you—I went out to get milk this morning and knew you would be leaving soon, so I left the keys in the car for you."

"Gee whiz, Beth, why didn't you tell me?"

> *"Chill out?! If I'm late, I won't be able to do my presentation and it's worth 50 percent of the course grade! I won't pass the class and I need at least a B to declare my major."*

Does this conversation sound familiar? Do you ever find yourself jumping to conclusions like Bart, especially when you're under pressure? We shouldn't underestimate the importance of listening; it can provide clarification, help us understand and remember material, improve our personal and professional relationships, and increase our ability to evaluate information effectively.[1] In fact, survey after survey reports that listening is one of the most important skills employers seek in job candidates. So the skills you learn and apply from this chapter will set you apart in ways that will benefit you both personally and professionally.

We begin with a discussion of what listening is and some challenges we must overcome to listen effectively. Then we offer several specific strategies to improve listening skills related to each of the steps in the active listening process. Finally, we provide guidelines to follow as you prepare effective and ethical constructive speech critiques.

3-1 WHAT IS LISTENING?

Recall that communication is the process of creating shared meaning. So to be effective, *speakers* must present messages clearly and compellingly and *listeners* must accurately interpret what is said.

hearing: the biological process that occurs when the brain detects sound waves

listening: the process of receiving, attending to, constructing meaning from, and responding to spoken or nonverbal messages

People sometimes make the mistake of thinking that hearing and listening are the same thing, but they're not. **Hearing** is a physiological process and listening is a cognitive one. According to the International Listening Association, "**Listening** is the process of receiving, attending to, constructing meaning from, and responding to spoken or nonverbal messages."[2] Listening is important because, of our time spent communicating, 50 percent or more is spent listening.[3] Yet, even when we try to listen carefully, most people remember only about 50 percent of what we hear shortly after hearing it and only about 25 percent two days later.[4]

As we've already mentioned, effective listening is a key to success in most occupations. One survey of top-level North American executives revealed that 80 percent believe listening is one of the most important skills needed in the corporate environment.[5] Listening skills (or lack thereof) are often at the root of company success or failure. When employees fail to listen effectively to instructions, they usually make mistakes. Mistakes cost the organization time and money. And when supervisors don't listen effectively to employees when they share concerns about potential problems or their creative ideas and solutions, again, the result may be lost time and money. Results of one large study of more than 6,000 organizational crisis events revealed that, in nearly every instance, employees and others had warned management repeatedly about potential problems. Had management listened effectively, the crises may have been avoided.[6] Of course, when the employees of a company do not listen and respond to customers, they are bound to fail. So it simply makes sense to improve listening skills.

Photo 3.1 Listening to music for enjoyment is a form of appreciative listening

Bubbles Photolibrary/Alamy

We choose to listen for various reasons depending on the situation. For example, when we listen to music for enjoyment and to speakers because we like their style, we engage in *appreciative listening* (Photo 3.1). When we listen to infer what more a speaker might mean beyond the actual words being spoken, we engage in *discriminative listening*. For instance, when a doctor is explaining test results, we might also try to discern whether the results are troubling or routine. When our goal is to understand, remember, and recall information—for example, material a professor shares during a classroom lecture—we engage in *comprehensive listening*. When we listen to provide emotional support, we engage in *empathic listening*. Finally, when we want to really understand and critically evaluate the worth of a message, we engage in *critical listening*. Because we need to hear, understand, evaluate, and assign worth to the message, as well as remember and recall it, critical listening requires more psychological processing than the others.

3-2 LISTENING CHALLENGES

To become effective listeners in any situation, we need to first overcome three key challenges. These challenges are rooted in our listening apprehension, our preferred listening style, and our approach to processing what we hear.

3-2a Apprehension

listening apprehension: the anxiety we feel about listening

Listening apprehension is the anxiety we feel about listening. Listening apprehension may increase when we are worry about misinterpreting the message, or when we are concerned about how the message may affect us psychologically.[7] For example, if you're in an important meeting or job training session, you may worry about trying to absorb all the important technical information needed to do your job well. Or you might feel anxiety when the material you need to absorb is difficult or confusing. Likewise, your anxiety may increase when you feel ill, tired, or stressed about something else going on in your life at the time. Listening apprehension makes it difficult to focus on the message (Photo 3.2).

Photo 3.2 Listening apprehension that arises in stressful situations can make it difficult to focus on the message.

3-2b Style

Listening style is our favored and usually unconscious approach to listening.[8] Each of us favors one of four listening styles and only a few people can switch effectively between styles based on the situation.[9]

Content-oriented listeners focus on and evaluate the facts and evidence. Content-oriented listeners appreciate details and enjoy processing complex messages that may include a good deal of technical information. Content-oriented listeners are likely to ask questions to get even more information.

People-oriented listeners focus on the feelings their conversational partners may have about what they are saying. For example, people-oriented listeners tend to notice whether their partners are pleased or upset and will encourage them to continue based on nonverbal cues like head nods, eye contact, and smiles.

Action-oriented listeners focus on the ultimate point the speaker is trying to make. Action-oriented listeners tend to get frustrated when ideas are disorganized and when people ramble. Action-oriented listeners also often anticipate what the speaker is going to say and may even finish the speaker's sentence for them.

Finally, **time-oriented listeners** prefer brief and hurried conversations and often use nonverbal and verbal cues to signal that their partner needs to be more concise. Time-oriented listeners may tell others exactly how much time they have to listen, interrupt when feeling time pressures, regularly check the time on smart phones, watches, or clocks, and may even nod their heads rapidly to encourage others to pick up the pace.

Each of these styles has advantages and disadvantages. Content-oriented listeners are likely to understand and remember details, but miss the overall point of the message and be unaware of the speaker's feelings. People-oriented listeners are likely to understand how the speaker feels, empathize, and offer comfort and support. However, they might become so focused on the speaker's feelings that they miss important details or fail to evaluate the facts offered as evidence. Action-oriented listeners may notice inconsistencies but, because they tend to anticipate what will be said rather than hearing the speaker out, may miss important details. Finally, time-oriented listeners are prone to only partially listen to messages while also thinking about their time constraints; thus, they might miss important details and be insensitive to their partner's emotional needs. In our opening scenario, Bart fell victim to the consequences of being too action-oriented and time-oriented when listening to Beth. With these challenges in mind, let's turn now to some specific techniques we can employ to improve our active listening skills in both face-to-face and virtual settings.

3-2c Processing Approach

Research suggests that people tend to listen in two ways—passively or actively—based on the rhetorical situation. In other words, we listen more carefully when the topic

listening style: the favored and usually unconscious approach to listening

content-oriented listeners: listeners who focus on and evaluate the facts and evidence

people-oriented listeners: listeners who focus on the feelings their conversational partners may have about what they are saying

action-oriented listeners: listeners who focus on the ultimate point the speaker is trying to make

time-oriented listeners: listeners who prefer brief and hurried conversations

passive listening: the habitual and unconscious process of receiving messages

active listening: the deliberate and conscious process of attending to, understanding, remembering, evaluating, and responding to messages

seems important (exigence) to us (audience), we trust and respect the sender, and during times when we are not constrained by other distractions or obligations (occasion). **Passive listening** is the habitual and unconscious process of receiving messages. When we listen passively, we are on automatic pilot. We may attend only to certain parts of a message and assume the rest. We tend to listen passively when we aren't really interested or when we are trying to multitask. By contrast, **active listening** is the deliberate and conscious process of attending to, understanding, remembering, evaluating, and responding to messages. Active listening requires practice. The rest of this chapter focuses on helping you become a better active listener.

3-3 ACTIVE LISTENING IMPROVEMENT STRATEGIES

Effective active listening is a complex psychological process made up of five steps. In this section, we offer techniques to improve listening related to each step (see Exhibit 3.1).

Exhibit **3.1** **Effective and Ineffective Listening Behaviors**

	Effective listening behavior	Ineffective listening behavior
Attending to the speech	Physically and mentally focusing on what is being said, even when information doesn't seem relevant	Seeming to listen but looking out the window and letting your mind wander
	Adjusting listening behavior to the specific requirements of the situation	Listening the same way regardless of type of material
Understanding/ remembering speech information	Determining organization by identifying goals, main points, and supporting information	Listening to individual bits of information without regard for structure
	Asking yourself questions to help identify key aspects of the speech	Seldom or never reconsidering what was said
	Silently paraphrasing to solidify understanding	Seldom or never paraphrasing
	Seeking out subtle meanings based on nonverbal cues	Ignoring nonverbal cues
	Taking good notes	Relying on memory alone
Evaluating and responding	Assessing quality of content, structure, and delivery	Relying on gut reactions

Copyright © Cengage Learning

3-3a Attending

attend: paying attention to what the speaker is saying regardless of extraneous interference

Effective active listening begins with attending. **Attending** is the process of intentionally perceiving and focusing on a message.[10] Poor listeners have difficulty exercising control over what they attend to, often letting their mind drift to thoughts totally unrelated to the topic. One reason for this stems from the fact that people typically speak at a rate of about 120 to 150 words per minute, but our brains can process between 400 and 800 words per minute.[11] This means we usually assume we know what a speaker is going to say before he or she finishes saying it. So our minds have lots of time to wander from the message. In our opening vignette, Bart seemed to have trouble attending to Beth, in part, because he thought he knew what she was going to say before she said it.

Not only does the gap between speaking rate and processing create opportunities for inattention, but research suggests that the average attention span for adults today is twenty minutes or less.[12] Some reports even claim that, thanks to the Internet, satellite TV, DVR, and smart phone technology, our attention spans have become considerably shorter.[13] Consider your own experiences listening to speeches, class lectures, and other extended presentations. Do you ever find yourself daydreaming, reading a text message, or checking email or Facebook? Do you find yourself multitasking in similar ways when participating in a teleconference, webinar, or other online presentation? If you want to find out how long your attention span is, go to **Web Link 3.1, Attention Span Self-Test,** in MindTap for *Challenge.*

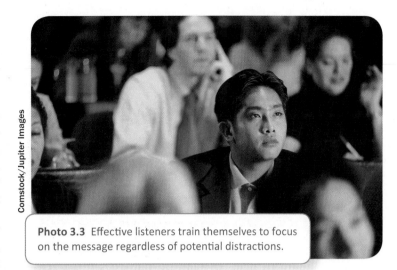

Comstock/Jupiter Images

Photo 3.3 Effective listeners train themselves to focus on the message regardless of potential distractions.

The first step to becoming an effective active listener, then, is to train ourselves to focus on or *attend* to what people are saying regardless of potential distractions (Photo 3.3). Let's consider four techniques for doing so.

1. **Get physically ready to listen.** Good listeners create a physical environment that reduces potential distractions and adopt a listening posture. For example, you might turn off background music, your cell phone, and your computer so you won't be tempted to turn your attention to them when you are trying to listen. You can also adopt a listening posture by sitting upright in your chair, leaning slightly forward, and looking directly at the speaker or screen.[14]

2. **Resist mental distractions.** Work consciously to block out wandering thoughts while listening to a speech or webcast that might come from a visual distraction (e.g., someone entering the room), an auditory distraction (e.g., people chatting), or a physical distraction (e.g., headache, growling stomach).

3. **Hear the speaker out.** Far too often, we stop listening because we disagree with something a speaker says, we assume we know what the speaker is going to say, or we become offended by an example or word used. We must train ourselves not to interrupt or even mentally argue with a speaker and stay focused throughout the message. When Beth realized Bart was not hearing her out, she helped him regain focus by taking his hands in hers and looking him in the eye.

4. **Find personal relevance.** Sometimes speakers articulate relevance for us like when a professor says, "Pay attention because this will be on the test." But we can also discover relevance for ourselves by consciously considering how we might benefit from learning the information to improve some aspect of our life.

3-3b Understanding

Understanding is accurately interpreting a message. Sometimes we may not fully understand a speaker's message because the speaker uses words that are not in our vocabulary or discusses complex technical concepts that are new to us. As a result, we might miss the emotional intent of the message. Let's discuss four strategies that can improve listening to understand.

> **SPEECH SNIPPET**
>
> Jill really wanted to learn the material in the webinar that was about to begin. So she put her phone on *silent* and even put it in her purse so she wouldn't be tempted to check messages during the session.

understand: assigning accurate meaning to what is said

Reflect on Ethics

KANYE WEST STEALS TAYLOR SWIFT'S MOMENT

The video of Kanye West jumping on stage and interrupting Taylor Swift's acceptance speech at the 2009 MTV Video Music Awards (VMA), saying, "Yo, Taylor. I'm happy for ya. I'm gonna let you finish. But Beyonce had one of the best videos of all time. One of the best videos of all time" quickly went viral.[15] In fact, we can still find it easily online today. Many have offered their opinions about how West was an unethical communicator at that moment because he violated the ethical principle of demonstrating respect for others. Similarly, many have commented about how Swift and Beyonce reacted to the situation ethically because they adhered to that same principle. West has retorted that his actions were okay because he was adhering to the ethical principle of honesty—he believed he was telling the truth. Three years after the incident, stories like the one published in *Hollywood Life.com* entitled "Kanye West Will Not Apologize to Taylor Swift at VMAs" continue referring to it. In that article, a source for West said "Kanye don't make no apologies . . . even when he's in the wrong."[16] One commenter, "Down n TX," posted a comment on Alison Bonaguro's CMT blog that he or she wished Swift had hit West over the head with the award. Another commenter, "Bree," said "As for Pink, and all the other celebs bad-mouthing Kanye, more power to you!! What he did was cold, and he deserves everything he's gonna get."

1. How would you respond to West's contention about ethics and honesty?

2. How might your answer change (if at all) after reading what the source speaking for Kanye was quoted as saying in the 2012 *Hollywood Life* article and why?

3. Do you support Down n TX's and Bree's reactions? Why or why not?

4. What advice would you give to someone who disagreed as vehemently as West did to a public message?

5. Do you think reporters that write stories about episodes that occurred years ago demonstrate ethical communication behavior? Why or why not?

---

1. **Identify the goal and main points.** Sometimes people's thoughts are well organized and easy to follow. Other times, however, we must work hard to decode the speaker's goal, main points, and some of the key details.

   For instance, during a PTA meeting, a teacher gives a short presentation on the problem of bullying. Her goal is to explain what can be done in school to deter this behavior. In her speech, she presents two main ideas: what teachers can do and what students who are harassed can do. She gives examples, statistics, and specific recommendations to develop each of the points she makes. When she is finished, audience members who have listened carefully can remember her goal and state steps that both teachers and harassed students can take even though they may not remember the specific examples and statistics that she used to develop each point. To be an effective listener, ask yourself, "What does the speaker want me to know or do?" (goal); then ask, "What are each of the main points?"; and finally ask, "What details explain or support each of the main points?"

question: a statement designed to clarify information or get additional details

2. **Ask questions.** A **question** is a statement designed to clarify information or get additional details. Although ethical listeners demonstrate respect by waiting until the speaker is finished to ask questions, you can make notes of any questions you have as you listen. Some of these questions may eventually be answered as the speaker moves through the presentation. However, others may not. Then, you can pose these remaining questions during the question-and-answer period following the presentation, privately approach the speaker after the presentation, or use the questions to do additional research about the topic yourself later.

paraphrase: putting into your own words the meaning you have assigned to a message

3. **Paraphrase silently. Paraphrasing** is putting a message into your own words. It is not simply repeating what is said. After listening, try to summarize your

understanding. So, after the speaker explains the criteria for selecting the best cell phone plan, you might say to yourself, "In other words, the key to deciding whether an unlimited plan is cost effective depends on how many minutes I'm likely to spend talking and texting on the phone each month."

4. **Observe nonverbal cues.** We interpret messages more accurately when we observe the nonverbal behaviors that accompany the words. Good speakers use their tone of voice, facial expressions, and gestures to emphasize important points and clarify structure. You can improve your listening skills by noticing where and how the speaker is attempting to emphasize or clarify points and then keying in on those comments. Had Bart observed Beth's nonverbal cues, he could have saved himself unnecessary emotional frustration about finding his keys and getting to school in time for class.

3-3c Remembering

Remembering is being able to retain and recall information later. In other words, it is the process of moving information from short-term to long-term memory. We may find remembering difficult, for instance, because we filter out information that doesn't fit our listening style, our listening anxiety prevents us from recalling what we have heard, we engage in passive listening, we practice selective listening and remember only what supports our position, and we fall victim to the primacy-recency effect of remembering only what is said at the beginning and end of a message. Let's consider three techniques to improve memory.

1. **Repeat the information. Repetition**—saying something mentally two, three, or four times—helps store information in long-term memory.[17] So if a speaker makes an important point or offers a key statistic, repeat it in your head two or three times to help make it "stick."

2. **Construct mnemonics.** A **mnemonic device** associates a special word or very short statement with new and longer information. One of the most common mnemonic techniques is to form a word with the first letters of a list of items you are trying to remember (Photo 3.4). For example, most beginning music students learn the mnemonic "*every good boy deserves fudge*" for the notes on the lines of the treble clef (E, G, B, D, F) and the word *face* (F, A, C, E) for the notes on the spaces of the treble. So you might try to construct a mnemonic to help remember the two to four main points in a speech.

3. **Take notes.** Note taking is a powerful method for improving your memory of what you have heard in a speech. Not only does note taking provide a written record that you can go back to, but also by taking notes, you take a more active role in the listening process.[18, 19]

   What constitutes good notes varies by situation. For a short speech, good notes may consist of a statement of the goal, a brief list of main points, and a few of the most significant details. Or they might be a short summary of the entire concept (a type of paraphrase). For lengthy presentations, good notes will also include more detailed statements of supporting material,

repetition: restating words, phrases, or sentences for emphasis

mnemonic device: associates a special word or very short statement with new and longer information

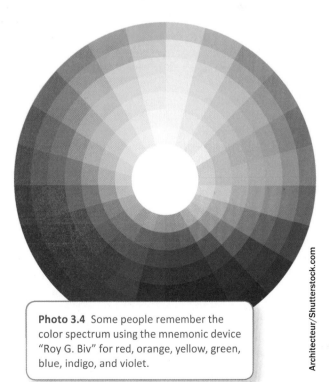

Photo 3.4 Some people remember the color spectrum using the mnemonic device "Roy G. Biv" for red, orange, yellow, green, blue, indigo, and violet.

Architecteur/Shutterstock.com

as well as questions that arise while listening. Review the basics of effective listening and note taking by going to **Web Link 3.2, Effective Listening and Note Taking,** in MindTap for *Challenge*.

3-3d Evaluating

evaluating: critically analyzing what is said to determine its truthfulness, utility, and trustworthiness

Evaluating is critically analyzing a message to determine its truthfulness, utility, and trustworthiness. Critical analysis is especially important when being persuaded to believe, support, or act on what was said. If you don't critically analyze messages, you risk going along with ideas that violate your values.

facts: statements whose accuracy can be verified as true

To evaluate messages effectively as you listen, try to separate facts from inferences. **Facts** are statements whose accuracy can be verified as true. If a statement is offered as a fact, analyze it thoughtfully to determine if it is true. **Inferences** are assertions based on the facts presented. When a speaker makes an inference, you need to determine whether the inference is valid. You can ask: (1) What are the facts that support this inference? (2) Is this information really central to the inference? (3) Is there other information that would contradict this inference? Separating facts from inferences helps us realize the difference between a verifiable observation and an opinion related to that observation. Separating facts from inferences is important because inferences may be false, even if they are based on verifiable facts.

inferences: assertions based on the facts presented

3-3e Responding

responding: providing feedback to the speaker about what is being said; usually occurs in the form of nonverbal behaviors

Responding is providing feedback. When Beth wasn't getting through to Bart, she added nonverbal cues to help him focus on what she was saying. Responding during a speech also usually occurs through nonverbal behaviors (e.g., smiling, head nodding, brow furrowing). Sometimes, however, you need to prepare a formal written evaluation, or critique, of a presentation by a classmate, colleague, or employee. Typically, a critique is based on your critical analysis of how well the speech and speaker performed on specific key criteria. In the next section, we focus on techniques for responding effectively and ethically in constructive speech critiques.

3-4 CONSTRUCTIVE CRITIQUES

A **constructive critique** is an evaluative response that identifies what was effective and what could be improved in a message. Constructive critiques are comprised of statements that evaluate all elements of a speech.

3-4a Constructive Critique Statements

constructive critique: an analysis of a speech or presentation that evaluates how well a speaker meets a specific speaking goal while following the norms for good speaking and that recommends how the presentation could be improved

Constructive critique statements follow four guidelines.

1. **Constructive critique statements are specific.** Comments like "great job" or "slow down" are too vague to truly help a speaker improve. Instead, describe specific things the speaker did to make you conclude that the speech was great. For example, did she use transitions in a way that helped you follow her train of thought? Or point out specific places where you would have liked the speaker to present the material at a slower pace.

2. **Constructive critique statements begin with observations about what was effective or done well.** Begin with positive observations so that you reinforce what the speaker did well. When we are reinforced for what we have done, we are more likely to continue doing it. By the same token, there is room for improvement in any speech. Because the goal of a critique is to help the speaker improve, describe the specific problems you observe in the speech and then offer suggestions for overcoming them.

PUBLIC SPEAKING IN THE REAL WORLD

Dale Carnegie's Tips for Talking and Listening

Everett Collection Inc./Alamy

Dale Carnegie's best selling book, *How to Win Friends and Influence People*,[20] was first published in 1936. Before you dismiss its relevance for success in the 21st century, read on. The advice Carnegie offered in that book more than 75 years ago has stood the test of time. Having sold over 15 million copies, his book remains one of the most influential self-help communication guides available today. Not only that, Dale Carnegie Training, a communication leadership program he founded in 1912, continues to flourish worldwide with offices in over 80 countries. His advice on public speaking, leadership, teambuilding, interpersonal communication, and human relations has trained more than 8 million people worldwide and includes over 400 Fortune 500 companies on its client list. In fact, Warren Buffet, whom many consider to be the most successful business investor and philanthropist of the 20th century, credits much of his success to what he learned from taking the Dale Carnegie Training course (BBC Presents Warren Buffett on Dale Carnegie—Dale Carnegie Training).[21]

Carnegie's advice for winning friends and influencing people can be summarized in the form of six key principles:

1. *Become genuinely interested in other people.*

2. *Smile.*

3. *Remember that a person's name is to that person the sweetest and most important sound in any language.*

4. ***Be a good listener. Encourage others to talk about themselves.***

5. *Talk in terms of the other person's interests.*

6. *Make the other person feel important – and do it sincerely. (Carnegie, 1936, pp. 110–111)*

He elaborates on principle number 4—be a good listener—in this way:

If you want to know how to make people shun you and laugh at you behind your back and even despise you, here is the recipe: Never listen to anyone for long. Talk incessantly about yourself. If you have an idea while the other person is talking, don't wait for him or her to finish: bust right in and interrupt in the middle of a sentence.

If you aspire to be a good conversationalist, be an attentive listener. Ask questions that other persons will enjoy answering. Encourage them to talk about themselves and their accomplishments.

Remember that the people you are talking to are a hundred times more interested in themselves and their wants and problems than they are in you and your problems. A person's toothache means more to that person than a famine in China which kills a million people. A boil on one's neck interests one more than forty earthquakes in Africa. Think of that the next time you start a conversation. (pp. 95–96)

Dale Carnegie realized long ago that being an attentive listener is critical to success. His books and training programs have taught many successful public speakers and business leaders this, too.

3. **Constructive critique statements explain how and why the observed behavior affected the speech.** For example, if you suggest that the speaker slow down while previewing the speech's main points, your statement will be more helpful if you also explain that the speaker's rate did not allow the audience time to remember the points.

4. **Constructive critique statements are phrased as personal perceptions.** You can ensure this by using "I" rather than "you" language. For example, instead of using "you" language to say, "You need to slow down," use "I" language. For example, "During the preview of main points, I had trouble listening because they were presented faster than I could understand and remember them." In our opening vignette, Beth did a good job of using "I" statements when trying to get Bart to comprehend her critique. Think about how much more critical the tone of her message would have been if she had said:

"Bart you're not listening to me. If you would ever listen to me you would understand that your keys are in your car. I left them there because I know you're in a hurry to get to class" rather than what she did say:

> **SPEECH SNIPPET**
>
> Max phrased his constructive critique statement about content this way: I appreciate the use of statistics to support your first main point. It would have helped me understand and remember them if they had also been reinforced visually on a bar graph presentational aid.

"Bart, listen. I've been trying to tell you—I went out to get milk this morning and knew you would be leaving soon, so I left the keys in the car for you."

3-4b Constructive Critique Elements

Constructive critiques are comprised of statements about a speech's content, structure, and delivery.

1. **Content critique statements focus on the goal, main points, and supporting material used to develop them.** For example, you might comment on how effectively the speaker used reasoning to tie a piece of evidence to the main point it supports. Or you might comment on the breadth and depth of the information used to develop each main idea. You might observe how relevant, recent, or credible the speaker's evidence seemed to be. Or you might talk about how effective content offered in a presentational aid was or could have been. Exhibit 3.2 illustrates ineffective and effective constructive critique statements regarding content.

Exhibit 3.2   Ineffective and Effective Comments about Speech Content

Ineffective	Effective
• Interesting stories.	• I liked the story about your trip to the carnival. The many details you provided made it sound really fun!
• Too short.	• I would have liked to hear another example for each main point. This would have helped me better understand why the carnival was so significant to you.

Copyright © Cengage Learning

2. **Structure critique statements focus on macrostructure (overall framework) and microstructure (language and style).** You might provide feedback on elements of the introduction (e.g., attention grabber, listener relevance, speaker credibility, thesis statement with main point preview), body (e.g., organizational pattern, transitions), or conclusion (e.g., thesis restatement with main point review, clincher, call to action). You might also offer statements about the speaker's language and style choices (e.g., appropriate, inclusive, accurate, clear, vivid, expressive). And you might offer statements about the construction of presentational aids (e.g., size, color, labels, layout, design). Exhibit 3.3 offers some examples of ineffective and effective constructive critique statements regarding structure.

3. **Delivery critique statements focus on use of voice and body.** In commenting on voice, you might consider intelligibility (e.g., understandable rate, volume, pronunciation, enunciation), conversational style (e.g., fluent, spontaneous), and emotional expression (e.g., changes in rate, pitch, or volume; strategic pauses; stresses on key words). In commenting on body, you might consider attire, poise, posture, eye contact, facial expressions, gestures, and movement. You can consider if the speaker's mannerisms distracted you from the message or enhanced it. You can comment on how well the speaker used voice and body

Ineffective and Effective Comments about Speech Structure

Ineffective	Effective
• Nice transitions.	• Your transitions reminded me of the main point.
• Boring introduction.	• Because you finished one main point and introduced the upcoming main point in your transition. I found it easy to follow your ideas.
	• I would have tuned in to the speech more quickly if you had begun with a great story about the carnival to capture my attention before stating your thesis.

to integrate presentational aids (e.g., conceal, reveal, reference). Exhibit 3.4 provides a couple of examples of ineffective and effective constructive critique comments regarding delivery.

Certainly, you can help other speakers improve by offering constructive critiques. You can also help yourself by completing a self-critique after each speech you give using the same approach you use to critique others. This self-critique approach is actually a form of cognitive restructuring that can help reduce your anxiety because it forces you to temper negative self-talk with positive self-talk immediately after your speech. Exhibit 3.5 presents a list of general criteria for preparing a constructive critique.

Ineffective and Effective Comments about Speech Delivery

Ineffective	Effective
• Great gestures!	• I really liked how you gestured while you stated your transitions. It made it even clearer to me that we were moving to the next main point.
• Slow down.	• It would have been helpful for me if you slowed down while previewing your main points. I had a hard time catching them. Slowing down would have helped me follow the structure throughout the body of your speech.

1. **Content**
   - Does the speaker establish common ground and adapt the content to the audience's interests, knowledge, and attitudes?
   - Does the speaker seem to have expertise in the subject areas?
   - Does the speaker have high-quality sources for the information given in the speech?
   - Does the speaker reveal the sources of the information?
   - Are the sources relevant? recent? varied? distributed throughout the speech?
   - Does the information presented explain or support each of the main points?
   - Are presentational aids appropriate and well used?
   - Is each main point supported with breadth? depth? listener relevance?

2. **Structure**
   - Does the introduction of the speech get attention, establish listener relevance and credibility, and lead into the topic?
   - Has the speaker stated a clear goal for the speech?
   - Are the main points of the speech clearly stated, parallel, and meaningful?
   - Do transitions lead smoothly from one point to another?
   - Does the information presented explain or support each of the main points?
   - Does the speaker use language that is appropriate, accurate, clear and vivid?
   - Does the speaker use a compelling style?
   - Does the conclusion summarize the main points and end with a clincher?

3. **Delivery**
   - Does the speaker sound intelligible? conversational? expressive?
   - Is the presentation fluent?
   - Does the speaker look at the audience?
   - Does the speaker use appropriate facial expressions?
   - Were the pronunciation and articulation acceptable?
   - Does the speaker have good posture?
   - Does the speaker have sufficient poise?

Copyright © Cengage Learning

IMPROMPTU SPEECH CHALLENGE

Constructive Critique Statements

Draw a card from a pile supplied by your instructor. Each card will have a different speech evaluation observation statement on it (e.g., the statistics were difficult (or easy) to understand, the organization was easy (or hard) to follow, the speaker talked fast). Prepare an effective constructive critique statement for the comment listed on your card. Then share it for the class in the form of a one- to two-minute impromptu speech. Be sure to explain why your critique statement is effective in your speech.

" speech assignment "

Preparing a Constructive Critique

 MindTap™

Go to your MindTap for *Challenge* to access and watch the speech, **"Meat Free and Me."** Prepare a constructive critique of this speech, using the general criteria offered in this chapter.

" speech evaluation checklist "

General Criteria

You can use this checklist to critique a speech you hear in class. (You can also use it to critique your own speech.)

Content

_____ **1.** Did you offer specific statements?

_____ **2.** Did you begin with statements about what the speaker did well?

_____ **3.** Did you offer statements for improvement?

_____ **4.** Did you provide an explanation (why) for each statement?

_____ **5.** Did you use "I" language to phrase each statement as a personal perception?

_____ **6.** Did you offer statements about content?

_____ **7.** Did you offer statements about structure?

_____ **8.** Did you offer statements about delivery?

_____ **9.** Did you offer statements about presentational aids?

Reflection and Assessment

Effective active listening takes conscious effort. Being an effective listener is crucial to the communication process or creating shared meaning. To assess how well you've learned what we've discussed in this chapter, answer the following questions. If you have trouble answering any of them, go back and review that material. Once you can answer each question accurately, you are ready to move ahead to read the next chapter.

1. What is listening and why study it in a public speaking course?
2. Why is effective listening challenging and what makes it most challenging for you?
3. What are some specific strategies you will employ to improve your listening skills?
4. What makes an effective and ethical constructive critique statement?
5. What elements should be addressed in an effective constructive speech critique?

Challenge Resource and Assessment Center

Now that you have read Chapter 3, go to your MindTap for *The Challenge of Effective Speaking in a Digital Age* for quick access to the electronic resources that accompany this text. These resources include:

- **Study tools** that will help you assess your learning and prepare for exams (*digital glossary, key term flash cards, review quizzes*).
- **Activities and assignments** that will help you hone your knowledge and build your public speaking skills throughout the course (Practice, Do). Many of these activities allow you to compare your answers with those provided by the authors, and, if requested, submit your answers to your instructor.
- **Media resources**—all of which are available on your MindTap for *Challenge*— will help you explore communication concepts online (Practice), develop your speech outlines (Do), watch and critique videos of sample speeches (Do), and upload your speech videos for instructor feedback and critique other students' speeches (Do).
- **Web Links that provide you with additional information or resources related to the topics discussed in this chapter.**
  3.1 Attention Span Self-Text (p. 45)
  3.2 Effective Listening and Note Taking (p. 48)

Applying What You've Learned

1. **Impromptu Speech Activity:** Consider the last time you listened to music. Prepare and present a two- to three-minute impromptu speech describing the situation, the type of listening you engaged in, and what you remember about the song(s) you heard.
2. **Assessment Activity A:** Dale Carnegie once said "You can make more friends in two months by becoming interested in other people than you can in two years by trying to get other people interested in you."[22] Try this experiment at your workplace: Ask a coworker his or her opinion about something and really listen to the response. Follow up with a "why" or "how" question, and really listen again. Write a short one- to two-page reflection paper about how you are received.
3. **Assessment Activity B:** Keep a log of three conversations you have with a friend, family member, or coworker. Try to limit how much talking you do. Keep the other person talking by asking "how" and "why" questions. Assess

the experience in written form by answering the following questions: (a) How much of the conversations can you describe here? (b) Was it difficult to keep quiet? Why or why not? (c) Were you able to stay focused? If so, how? If not, why? (d) Do you think the other person noticed your efforts to listen rather than speak? Explain.

4 "determining an appropriate speech goal"

WHAT'S THE POINT? WHEN YOU'VE FINISHED THIS CHAPTER, YOU WILL BE ABLE TO:

4-1 Identify potential speech topics

4-2 Analyze audience demographic and subject-related data

4-3 Use audience data ethically

4-4 Analyze the occasion for your speech

4-5 Select a speech topic appropriate to the rhetorical situation

4-6 Write a specific speech goal statement tailored to the rhetorical situation

 MindTap™

Review the chapter **Learning Objectives** and **Start** with quick warm up activity.

Mirjam van der Hoek/Hollandse Hoogte/Redux

1 Determine a speech goal that is appropriate to the rhetorical situation.

A. Brainstorm and concept map for topics.
B. Analyze the rhetorical situation.
C. Develop a speech goal statement that is adapted to the rhetorical situation.

© CoraMax/Shutterstock

e Ethical communicators demonstrate respect by selecting a speech goal that is appropriate for the rhetorical situation

The bell rang, and Kameron and Kayla headed out of the classroom together.

"What is your speech going to be about?" Kayla asked.

"I have no idea," Kameron said. The two looked down at the floor as they walked down the hall together.

After a few moments of silence Kameron said, "Hey, I do have an idea, but no, it's probably not such a good idea. Remember, we're supposed to think about our audience."

"I know, but what's your idea?" Kayla asked.

Kameron looked around him. The hallway was loud and busy. No one was paying any attention to them, but Kameron lowered his voice anyway. "Well, I know President Obama talked about supporting gay marriage. I agree with him—that two people who are the same sex should be allowed to get married. I thought maybe my speech could be about that. But I'm not sure our class is the right audience for it. What do you think?"

"Hmm. . . it's a great idea, but I don't know what others in our class would think," Kayla said. "Maybe you should think about some other topics that more of the people in our class can relate to."

Whenever we are invited to give a speech, whether in the classroom or some other setting, the first thing we have to do is decide upon a speech topic and goal. For many of us, this can feel pretty daunting. But it doesn't have to be. In this chapter, we'll walk you through an efficient process for determining a specific speech goal that is appropriate to the rhetorical situation.

Recall from Chapter 1, and as is reiterated in Exhibit 4.1, the elements of the rhetorical situation include you (and your knowledge and intentions), the audience (and

"After a few moments of silence Kameron said, 'Hey, I do have an idea, but no, it's probably not such a good idea. Remember, we're supposed to think about our audience.'"

Exhibit 4.1 **The Rhetorical Situation**

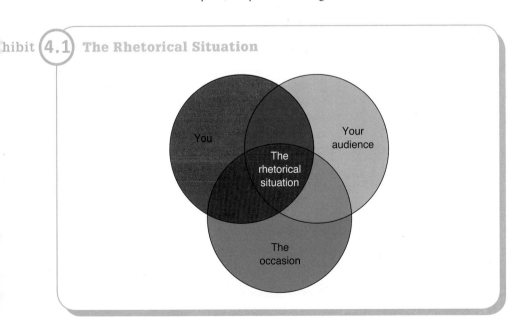

You

Your audience

The rhetorical situation

The occasion

PUBLIC SPEAKING IN THE REAL WORLD

Aaron Sorkin's Attention to the Rhetorical Situation

Even speeches by characters on TV and film are most compelling when they address the rhetorical situation. Oscar and Emmy award-winning screenwriter, Aaron Sorkin, is responsible for monumental films and TV programs such as *A Few Good Men*, *The American President*, *Charlie Wilson's War*, *The Social Network*, *The West Wing*, and *The Newsroom*. He intentionally writes character monologues that address exigence because they focus on real events. When asked about what he was thinking when creating *The Newsroom*, he said, "I like writing about heroes [who] don't wear capes or disguises. You feel like, 'Gee, this looks like the real world and feels like the real world—why can't that be the real world?'"

He goes on to discuss how he deliberately focuses on events that really occurred in the recent past because "writing fictional news . . . would take us too far from reality." Thus, as Sorkin's mouthpiece, Will McAvoy (played by Jeff Daniels) vows to cover stories because they're important and not for the ratings. Whether or not you like *The Newsroom* or Sorkin's other works, he certainly seems to understand how to identify a specific goal tailored to the rhetorical situation.[1]

---

audience analysis: the study of the intended audience for your speech

audience adaptation: the process of tailoring your speech's information to the needs, interests, and expectations of your listeners

their knowledge and expectations), and the occasion (the setting, purpose, and constraints). Because the audience is a crucial component of the rhetorical situation, effective speech goals are based on **audience analysis**, the process of learning about the diverse characteristics of audience members, and **audience adaptation**, the process of tailoring your message to address their unique needs, interests, and expectations. This step in the speechmaking process is rooted in what communication scholars refer to as uncertainty reduction theory.[2] Although effective speakers adapt to their audience throughout the speechmaking process, they begin at the point of determining a specific speech goal.

To determine a specific speech goal adapted to the rhetorical situation, begin by identifying lots of subjects and topics that interest you. Then based on your analysis of both the audience and the occasion, narrow your topic list down to include only those that (a) interest you and you know something about, (b) can be adapted to address the needs, interests, and expectations of the audience, and (c) are appropriate for the occasion.

4-1 IDENTIFY POTENTIAL SPEECH TOPICS

subject: a broad area of expertise, such as movies, renewable energy, computer technology, or the Middle East

topic: some specific aspect of a subject

Good speech topics come from subjects we have some knowledge about and interest in. What is the difference between a subject and a topic? A **subject** is a broad area of knowledge, such as contemporary cinema, renewable energy, computer technology, or the Middle East. A **topic** is a narrower aspect of a subject. So, if your broad area of expertise is contemporary cinema, you might feel qualified to speak on a variety of narrower topics such as how the Academy Awards nomination process works; the relationships among movie producers, directors, and distributors; or how technology is changing movie production. Let's look more closely at how you can identify subjects that interest you and then potential topics you might explore for an upcoming speech.

4-1a Subjects

You can identify subjects by listing those that (1) are important to you and (2) you know something about. Subjects may be related to careers that interest you, your major area of study, special skills or competencies you have or admire, your hobbies, as well as social, economic, or political issues that interest you. So, if your major is marketing, your hobbies are skateboarding and snowboarding, and issues that concern you include illiteracy, substance abuse, and obesity, then these are *subjects* from which you can identify potential speech topics.

Exhibit 4.2 Kameron's Subject Lists

Career Interests	Hobbies	Issues of Concerns
Web site Designer	Bouldering	Climate change
Teacher	Bird watching	Human Rights
Computer programmer	Disc golf	Civil Rights
Event planner	Video games	Fracking

At this point, you might be thinking, "What if my audience isn't interested in the subjects and topics that interest me?" In reality, topics in any subject area can be made interesting when they are adapted to address the needs and expectations of the audience.

Exhibit 4.2 contains subject lists that Kayla helped Kameron come up with for the speech contest. They chose to organize the subjects by using three broad headings: (1) career interests, (2) hobbies, and (3) issues of concern.

4-1b Brainstorming and Concept Mapping

A topic is a specific aspect of a subject, so from one subject you can identify many topics related to that subject. Two methods for doing so are brainstorming and concept mapping. **Brainstorming** is an uncritical, nonevaluative process of generating associated ideas. When you brainstorm, you list as many ideas as you can without evaluating them. If the subject for Kameron's speech was civil rights, he could brainstorm to come up with a list of potential topics, such as: the role of women suffragists in gaining the right to vote; the rise and fall of Jim Crowe in the American South; the pro-life/pro-choice debate; gun control; and same-sex marriage. For practice with brainstorming, access **Web Link 4.1, Brainstorming,** in your MindTap for *Challenge.*

Concept mapping is a visual means of exploring connections between a subject and related ideas.[3] To generate connections, you might ask yourself questions about your subject, focusing on who, what, where, when, and how. In Exhibit 4.3, you can see an example of what Kameron's concept map looked like for the gun control topic. Notice how concept mapping allowed him to think more deeply about a general topic idea.

Speech-Planning Action Step 1, Activity 1A will help you develop a list of topic ideas to use for your speeches in this course. See the Student Response box immediately following the activity for a sample of how one student completed this exercise.

4-2 ANALYZE THE AUDIENCE

Because addressing the specific needs and expectations of your intended audience is integral to the rhetorical situation, you need to examine who they are by collecting both demographic and subject-related data. This information will help you select and tailor your topic and goal to meet the needs, interests, and expectations of your audience. Let's consider what types of demographic and subject-related audience data you might collect, data-gathering methods you might use to do so, and specific things to consider for using audience data ethically in your speeches (Photo 4.1). To read an interesting article on the importance of careful audience analysis, go to **Web Link 4.2, Defining Your Audience,** in your MindTap for *Challenge.*

4-2a Demographic Audience Data

Helpful demographic information includes, for example, each person's approximate age, education level, sex, occupation, socioeconomic status, race, ethnicity, religion,

brainstorming: an uncritical, nonevaluative process of generating associated ideas

concept mapping: a visual means of exploring connections between a subject and related ideas

Exhibit **4.3** Kameron's Concept Map

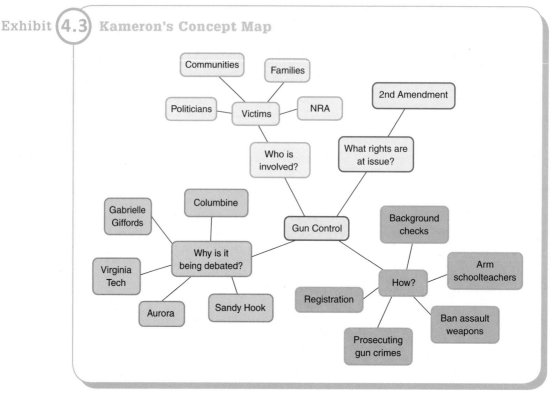

geographic uniqueness, and first language. Exhibit 4.4 presents a list of questions that may help you uncover important demographic information.

4-2b Subject-Related Audience Data

In addition to demographic data, you will also want to collect subject-related audience disposition data. More specifically, you ought to consider their level of knowledge, initial level of interest in, and attitude toward your potential topics. You might also ponder how credible they might perceive you to be about each of your potential topics. Once you know this information, you can use a process of elimination to choose a topic and goal that will offer some new information, insight, or perspective on a topic for that particular audience. Let's take a closer look at each of these aspects of subject-related audience disposition data.

Photo 4.1 Ethical speakers select a topic that is appropriate to the rhetorical situation.

allesfoto/ImageBroker/Glow Images

1. **Audience knowledge.** What can you expect your average audience member to already know about your subject? What topics are likely to provide new information for most of them? How can you adjust the perspective you take on the topic to go beyond what most of them probably already know? Because we live in a digital age where most people have instant access to general information on nearly any topic by doing a quick *Google* search on our laptops, *iPads,* and smart phones, determining this piece of subject-related audience data is crucial when selecting a speech topic. When you choose a topic that most audience members already know about or can learn about quickly on their own via an Internet search, you will bore them if you are not really creative. On the other hand, if you choose a topic

(continued page 63)

Exhibit 4.4 **Demographic Audience Analysis Questions**

Age. What is the age range of your audience, and what is the average age?

Education. What percentage of your audience has a high school, college, or postgraduate education?

Sex. What percentage of your audience is male? female?

Socioeconomic background. What percentage of your audience comes from high-, middle-, or low-income families?

Occupation. Is a majority of your audience from a single occupational group or industry, or do audience members come from diverse occupational groups?

Race. Are most members of your audience of the same race, or is there a mixture of races?

Ethnicity. What ethnic groups are in the audience? Are most audience members from the same cultural background?

Religion. What religious traditions are followed by audience members?

Geographic uniqueness. Are audience members from the same state, city, or neighborhood?

Language. What languages do a significant number of members of the audience speak as a first language? What language (if any) is common to all audience members?

Knowledge of subject. What can I expect the audience already knows about my subject? How varied is the knowledge level of audience members?

Attitude toward subject. What can I expect my audience's feelings to be about my subject?

1A SPEECH PLANNING

Identify Potential Speech Topics

The goal of this activity is to help you identify potential speech topics.

Step 1: Develop a subject list.

    a. Divide a sheet of paper into three columns. Label column 1 "major and career interests," label column 2 "hobbies and activities," and label column 3 "issues of concern."

    b. Working on one column at a time, identify subjects of interest to you. Try to identify at least three subjects in each column.

    c. Place a check mark next to the one subject in each list that you would most enjoy speaking about.

    d. Keep the lists for future use in choosing a topic for an assigned speech.

Step 2: For each subject you have checked, brainstorm a list of topics that relate to that subject. Look at the topics you have brainstormed. In which do you have the most interest and expertise? Place a check mark beside one or two of these.

Step 3: Then, for each item on the brainstorm list that you have checked, develop a concept map to identify smaller topic areas and related ideas that might be developed into future speeches.

Access **Action Step 1, Activity 1A** on your MindTap for *Challenge*.

(1A) STUDENT RESPONSE

Identify Potential Speech Topics

Step 1: Develop a subject list

Major and career interests	Hobbies and activities	Issues of concern
Teaching	Singing	School violence
✔ Early childhood education	✔ Volunteering	Breast cancer research
Chef	Rock climbing	Cyberbullying
Coaching	Swimming	✔ Childhood obesity

Step 2: Brainstorm List for "Childcare"

parental care	in-home group care
family care	parent cooperatives
nannies	day care

Step 3: Concept Map for "Day Care"

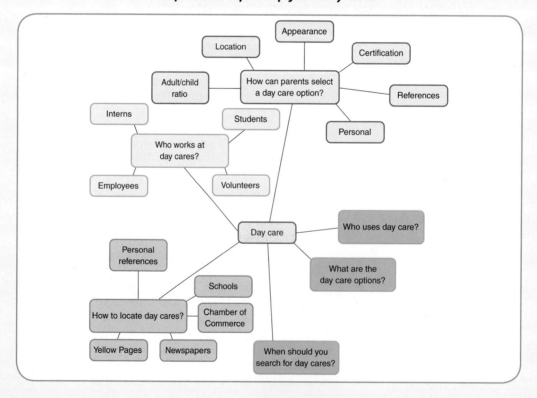

Activity

for which your audience has insufficient background knowledge, you will have to provide the background or risk confusing them. For instance, if your subject is music, you can expect that an audience of traditional-age college students will know the general history of rock 'n' roll, including the major performers. So the topic "A Brief History of Rock 'n' Roll" might bore them because you aren't offering new information or insight or perspective. However, a speech on the contributions of girl bands to the development of rock 'n' roll might draw on the audience's background knowledge but offer new information to most audience members.

2. **Audience interest.** How likely are audience members to be interested in your topic? You can actually make educated guesses about this piece of subject-related data based on the demographic data you collect. For instance, suppose you would like to speak on the subject of cancer drugs. If your audience is made up of health-care professionals, they might well be interested in the topic, but also might already know a good deal about it. You would need to make sure to delve deeper into the topic to ensure interest. On the other hand, if your audience is a beginning public speaking class made up mostly of 18- and 19-year-old students, then unless they have had personal experience with cancer, they may not naturally be interested in the topic. So you can either choose another topic or make an extra effort to determine why 18- and 19-year-olds ought to know about cancer drugs and articulate this relevance throughout the speech.

3. **Audience attitude.** What might your audience's initial disposition be toward your topic? This is especially important when trying to influence their beliefs or move them to take action. You can determine your audience's attitudes toward your topic directly by surveying them, which we will discuss in the next section. If you cannot survey the audience directly, you might try to see if published opinion polls related to your subject are available. Then you can estimate your audience members' attitudes by studying these opinion polls and extrapolating their results to your audience. Go to **Web Link 4.3, Public Opinion Polls,** in your MindTap for *Challenge* to access links to respected polling organizations.

Once you have an idea about your audience's initial attitude toward the topic, you can tailor your specific goal in ways that will allow you to influence rather than alienate them (Photo 4.2). For example, one reason the gun control debate tends to be so heated stems from different attitudes based on personal experiences. Friends and family members of those killed at places such as Columbine, Virginia Tech, Aurora, and Sandy Hook Elementary School would likely come to the speaking occasion with a different initial attitude than others who may be avid hunters living in

SPEECH SNIPPET

Audience Interest
Laura wanted to give a speech on the prevalence of unnecessary hysterectomies. Because her audience included males and females, she took care to make her speech relevant for everyone by talking about how we are all affected by the increases in insurance rates that result from unnecessary operations, and how a patient's emotional trauma caused by an unnecessary hysterectomy can have a profound effect on family and friends.

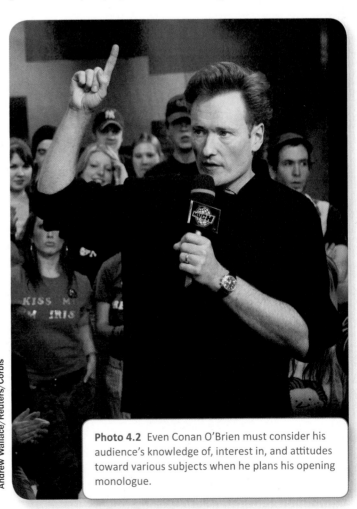

Photo 4.2 Even Conan O'Brien must consider his audience's knowledge of, interest in, and attitudes toward various subjects when he plans his opening monologue.

rural areas where they appreciate the sense of protection owning a firearm provides them.

4. **Audience perception.** Will your audience recognize you as a subject-matter expert? Will you need to establish your credibility as you speak? **Credibility** is the audience's perception of you as knowledgeable about the topic, trustworthy (honest, dependable, and ethical), and personable (friendly; sincere; genuinely committed to the topic, occasion, and audience). Consider, for example, transnational celebrity activism. Although superstars from George Clooney to Angelina Jolie to Madonna to Bono might be easily perceived as credible when speaking about their careers as actors or singers, they might need to take additional measures to ensure that audiences perceive them as credible when speaking about issues related to global politics.

Tailoring your speech to your audience based on both demographic and subject-related data is crucial not only to determine an appropriate topic and goal but throughout the speech preparation and delivery process. Thus, we devote the next chapter to a deeper discussion about how to do so when gathering information, developing and organizing your ideas, making language choices, and delivering the speech. In this chapter, we turn now to some methods you can use to gather audience data.

4-2c Data-Gathering Methods

You can employ a number of different methods to gather audience data. We focus on four of them here.

1. **Conduct a survey.** Although it is not always possible, the most direct way to collect audience data is to survey the audience. A **survey** is a direct examination of people to gather information about their ideas and opinions. Some surveys are done as interviews; others as written questionnaires. Four common items used in surveys are two-sided, multiple response, scaled, and open ended.

   • **Two-sided items** force respondents to choose between two answers, such as yes/no, for/against, or pro/con. Suppose you wanted to understand your audience members' attitudes on violence in adult video games. You might phrase several questions with two-sided answers, such as:

   Do you believe adult video games contain too much violence?

   _____ Yes _____ No

   Do you play adult video games (e.g., Bioshock, Grand Theft Auto)?

   _____ Yes _____ No

   Respondents can answer two-sided items quickly and they are easy to sort during analysis.

   • **Multiple-response items** give respondents several alternatives from which to choose and are especially useful for gathering demographic data. For example:

   What is the highest level of education you have completed?

   ___ some high school   ___ high school diploma   ___ some college
   ___ Associate's degree   ___ Bachelor's degree   ___ Master's degree
   ___ Doctorate degree   ___ Post-doctorate   ___ Other

   Multiple-response items can also be used to assess the extent of knowledge audience members have about a topic. For example:

credibility: the perception that you are knowledgeable, trustworthy, and personable

IMPROMPTU SPEECH CHALLENGE

Consider a time when you questioned the credibility of a speaker as knowledgeable about the topic. Prepare and present a two- to three-minute impromptu speech explaining why.

survey: a canvassing of people to get information about their ideas and opinions

two-sided items: survey items that force the respondent to choose between two answers, such as yes/no, for/against, or pro/con

multiple-response items: survey items that give the respondent several alternative answers from which to choose

Indicate what you know about diamonds by placing an X next to each topic you already know about.

_____How to value a diamond

_____How diamonds are made

_____How to tell the difference between a real diamond and a fake

_____What are Blood diamonds

- **Scaled items** measure the direction or intensity of respondents' feelings or attitudes toward something (on a scale from 1 to 5 with 5 being "very likely,". . .). For example:

Indicate the extent to which you agree or disagree with the following statement:

Adult video games contain too much violence.

_____ Strongly agree _____ Agree _____ Neutral _____ Disagree
_____ Strongly disagree

Scaled items can also be used to assess audience interest. For example:

Please place a check next to the response that best describes your interest in learning about each of the following.

How to value diamonds:
_____Very interested _____ Somewhat interested _____ Uninterested

How diamonds are cut:
_____ Very interested _____ Somewhat interested _____ Uninterested

What are Blood diamonds:
_____ Very interested _____ Somewhat interested _____ Uninterested

> **scaled items:** survey items that measure the direction and/or intensity of an audience member's feeling or attitude toward something

- **Open-ended items** encourage respondents to elaborate on their opinions without forcing them to answer in a predetermined way. These items yield rich information, but the wide variety of responses can be difficult to analyze. For example, to determine what you would need to do to establish your credibility on the subject of video game violence, you might ask:

How can you tell if someone is an expert on video game violence?

> **open-ended items:** survey items that encourage respondents to elaborate on their opinions without forcing them to answer in a predetermined way

2. **Observe informally.** If you are familiar with members of your audience (as you are with members of your classroom audience), you can learn a lot through informal observation. For instance, after being in class for even a couple of sessions, you should be able to estimate the approximate age or age range and the ratio of men to women. Because you are all in college, you know the educational level. As you listen to your classmates talk, you will learn more about their interest in, knowledge of, and attitudes about many issues.

3. **Question a representative.** When you are invited to speak to a group you are unfamiliar with, ask your contact person for demographic and subject-related audience data (Photo 4.3). You should specifically ask for data that will help you narrow the focus of your topic and goal, as well as tailor the speech itself to address their needs, interests, and expectations.

Photo 4.3 Sometimes you can find out about an audience by questioning a representative.

marginalizing: ignoring the values, needs, and interests of certain audience members, leaving them feeling excluded from the speaking situation

stereotyping: assuming all members of a group have similar behaviors or beliefs simply because they belong to the group

audience diversity: the range of demographic and subject-related differences represented in an audience

occasion: the setting, which includes the purpose, audience expectations, and location

4. **Make educated guesses.** If you can't get information any other way, you can make educated guesses based on indirect data such as the general makeup of the people who live in a specific community, belong to a certain or similar organization, or are likely to attend an event of this nature. Suppose, for example, a nonprofit group you support asks you to give a speech on volunteer opportunities they offer. You are to give the speech to high school guidance counselors who oversee community service projects for students. You can infer a number of things about audience members. First, all will be college-educated high school counselors in your community. There will be both women and men. They will be interested in your topic, but their knowledge about specific opportunities at the nonprofit you will discuss will vary.

4-3 ETHICAL USE OF AUDIENCE DATA

Once you have collected audience data, you can use it to tailor your speech to their interests, needs, and expectations. To demonstrate respect for everyone, you will want to avoid making inappropriate or inaccurate assumptions based on demographic or subject-related information you have collected. Two potential pitfalls you'll want to avoid are marginalizing and stereotyping.

Marginalizing is the practice of ignoring the values, needs, and interests of some audience members, leaving them to feel excluded. For example, if you discover that most of your audience members have played adult video games, you will want to avoid marginalizing the few members who have never done so. So you might quickly describe the goal and show a brief demonstration of a popular adult video game in the introduction of your speech on violence in adult video games.

Stereotyping is assuming all members of a group have similar knowledge, behaviors, or beliefs simply because they belong to that group. If, for example, you find out that the average age of your audience is 65, you might stereotype by assuming that most of them know nothing about video games when, in fact, many have either played them or observed family members doing so. To avoid stereotyping based on demographic data, you need to collect subject-related data from them as well.

You can also reduce your chances of marginalizing or stereotyping by recognizing and acknowledging the diversity represented in your audience. **Audience diversity** is the range of demographic and subject-related differences represented in an audience. So while the average age of your audience may be 65, there may also be some in the audience who are much younger. Similarly, although most audience members may be familiar with adult video games, a few may know very little about them.

Exhibit 4.5 is a form you can use to summarize the demographic and subject-related audience data you collect. Now that you understand audience analysis, you can complete Speech-Planning Action Step 1, Activity 1B. See the Student Response box immediately following the activity for a sample of how one student completed this exercise.

4-4 ANALYZE THE OCCASION

The **occasion** is made up of the expected purpose of and setting (location) for the speech. Answers to several key questions about the occasion should guide you when selecting your topic and throughout the speech-making process.

1. **What is the intended purpose (exigence) of the speech?** In other words, why does the audience think this speech is being given? At a religious service, for example, the congregation expects the sermon to have a religious theme. At a national sales meeting, the field representatives expect to hear about new products. For your classroom speeches, a major expectation is that your speech will meet the assignment criteria.

(continued on page 70)

Exhibit (4.5) **Audience Analysis Summary Form**

My subject is _____

Data were collected:
_____ by survey
_____ by direct observation
_____ by questioning the person who invited me
_____ by educated guessing

Demographic Data

1. The average audience member's education level is _____ high school _____ college _____ postgraduate.

2. The ages range from _____ to _____. The average age is about _____.

3. The audience is approximately _____ percent male and _____ percent female.

4. My estimate of the average income level of the audience is _____ upper _____ middle _____ lower.

5. Most audience members are of _____ the same occupation/major (which is _____) _____ different occupations/majors.

6. Most audience members are of _____ the same race (which is _____) _____ a mixture of races.

7. Most audience members are of _____ the same religion (which is _____) _____ a mixture of religions.

8. Most audience members are of _____ the same nationality (which is _____) _____ a mixture of nationalities.

9. Most audience members are from _____ the same state _____ the same city _____ the same neighborhood _____ different areas.

10. Most audience members _____ speak English as their first language _____ English as a second language (ESL).

Subject-Specific Data

1. The average audience member's knowledge of the subject is likely to be _____ extensive _____ moderate _____ limited because _____

2. The average audience member's interest in this subject is likely to be _____ high _____ moderate _____ low because _____ _____.

3. The average audience member's attitude toward my subject is likely to be _____ positive _____ neutral _____ negative because _____.

4. My initial credibility with the audience is likely to be _____ high _____ medium _____ low because _____ _____ _____.

Conclusion

Based on these data _____
_____
_____,
which relate to my speech topic in the following ways: _____
_____,
_____,
I will tailor my speech in the following ways: _____
_____,
_____,

SPEECH SNIPPET

Audience Diversity

Ian's classmates ranged from first-year 18-year-old students to 30-somethings, some of them married. To be audience-centered, Ian realized he needed to adapt to audience diversity regarding fire safety. So he decided to talk about fire safety measures that would be appropriate not only for students living in residence halls but also for people who own their own homes.

(1B) SPEECH PLANNING

Analyzing Your Audience

Step 1: Decide on a method for gathering audience data and collect it.

Step 2: Use the information gathered to complete the Audience Analysis Summary Form (Exhibit 4.5).

Step 3: Write two short paragraphs to describe what these audience demographics and subject-related data might suggest about their knowledge, interests, attitudes, and expectations toward your topic.

 MindTap™

Go to your MindTap for *Challenge* to download a copy of the **Audience Analysis Summary Form**.

(1B) STUDENT RESPONSE

Analyzing Your Audience

Step 1: Decide on a method

1. I gathered audience data through informal observation.

Step 2: Complete the Audience Analysis Summary Form

1. The average audience member's education level is ____ high school __X__ college ____ postgraduate.

2. The ages range from __19__ to __24__ The average age is about __20__ .

3. The audience is approximately __65__ percent male and __35__ percent female.

4. My estimate of the average income level of the audience is ____ upper __X__ middle ____ lower.

5. Most audience members are of ____ similar occupations/majors __X__ different occupations/majors.

6. Most audience members are of ____ the same race __X__ a mixture of races.

7. Most audience members are of ____ the same religion __X__ a mixture of religions (because I can't really tell).

(continued)

1B STUDENT RESPONSE *(continued)*

8. Most audience members are of __X__ the same nationality (*which is* <u>American</u>) ____ a mixture of nationalities.

9. Most audience members are from __X__ the same state ____ the same city ____ the same neighborhood ____ different areas.

10. Most audience members speak __X__ English as their first language ____ English as a second language (ESL).

Subject-Specific Data

1. The average audience member's knowledge of the subject is likely to be ____ extensive ____ moderate __X__ limited because <u>*my audience members are mostly*</u> <u>*communication students, not geology or mineralogy students*</u>

2. The average audience member's interest in this subject is likely to be ____ high __X__ moderate ____ low because <u>*without encouragement, they have no need to know*</u> <u>*about this subject. Mineralogy is hardly a trendy subject.*</u>

3. The average audience member's attitude toward my subject is likely to be ____ positive __X__ neutral ____ negative because <u>*the audience doesn't really have any informa-*</u> <u>*tion about the topic.*</u>

4. My initial credibility with the audience is likely to be ____ high ____ medium __X__ low because <u>*this is our first speech and they don't know I am a Geology major or that*</u> <u>*my family owns a jewelry store.*</u>

Step 3: Write summary paragraphs

From these data, I conclude that most audience members are similar to one another and to me. We are all students at U.K. Most of us are around 20 years old, which suggests that we have a common generational view. There are more men than women in the class, and we are mixture of different races. I can't really tell if we are similar or different in terms of religious affiliation. I would have to probe more specifically for that information if it seems pertinent for my ultimate topic and speech goal. Although most audience members speak English as their first language, there are also two international students who do not speak English as their first language. I will want to avoid marginalizing them by using visual aids to help them comprehend important information throughout the speech.

Most audience members don't know a lot about diamonds and probably have only a moderate interest in the subject. I will need to make sure to explain how and why this information may be important to them throughout the speech. Since they don't know about my expertise regarding diamonds, I will need to establish my credibility during the introduction and periodically throughout the speech.

Photo 4.4 Even musicians ought to demonstrate respect for their audiences by adhering to time limit expectations.

2. **What is the expected length?** Time limits for classroom speeches are usually quite short, so you will want to choose a topic that is narrow enough to be accomplished in the time allotted. "Three Major Causes of the Declining Honey bee Population" could probably be presented in five minutes, but "A History of Human Impact on the Environment" could not. Time limit expectations are not unique to classroom speeches (Photo 4.4). Adhering to audience time limit expectations demonstrates respect. For example, consider when you paid a hefty ticket price to attend a live concert or other public event. If the main event was shorter than you expected it to be, you probably felt cheated. Or consider when a teacher kept you in class longer than the allotted time. You may have become frustrated because it seemed the instructor failed to respect the other commitments (e.g., other classes, jobs) you juggled along with that particular course. Speakers who speak for more or less time than has been allotted can seriously interfere with event programming and lose the respect of both their hosts and their audiences.

3. **Where will the speech be given?** Rooms vary in size, lighting, and seating arrangements. Some are single level, some have stages or platforms, and some have tiered seating. The space affects the speech. For example, in a long, narrow room, you may need to speak loudly to be heard in the back row. If you are speaking in an auditorium to a large group of people, you will need to speak loudly and perhaps use a microphone. You will also need to use large gestures and presentational aids that can be seen and heard easily in all parts of the room. The brightness of the room and the availability of room darkening shades may impact what kinds of visual aids you can use. So you will want to know and consider the layout of the room as you plan your speech. If possible, visit the room in advance either physically or virtually via online photo galleries or virtual tours posted on the venue's website. The more you know about the location where you will be giving your speech, the better you will be able to tailor it to be most effective in that setting.

4. **When will the speech be given?** A speech given early in the morning requires a different approach from one given right after lunch or in the evening. If a speech is scheduled after a meal, for instance, the audience may be lethargic, mellow, or even on the verge of sleep. So you may want to plan to insert more material designed to gain and regain audience interest throughout. Similarly, where you are placed on the schedule of events should influence your speech planning. For example, if you are first, you may need to "warm up" the audience and be prepared to deal with the distraction of latecomers entering the room while you are speaking. If you speak later in the program, you may need to integrate attention-catching material to keep the interest of a weary audience.

5. **What equipment is necessary and available?** Would you like to use a microphone, lectern, flip chart, smartboard, or computer and LCD projector to display visuals or audiovisuals? If so, does the room have an adequate means for displaying visuals and projecting audio? Do you plan to use Internet and, if so, is the room wired for Internet or wi-fi? It is your responsibility to check with your host to make sure the equipment can be made available or to make alternative arrangements. Regardless of the arrangements made, however, experienced speakers expect that something may go wrong and always prepare a backup plan. So if you plan to show a computerized slide show, you might also prepare handouts of key slides in case the equipment fails.

Speech-Planning Action Step 1, Activity 1C will help you understand the occasion so that you take into consideration your purpose, audience expectations, and location as you choose your topic and develop your speech. See the Student Response box immediately following the activity for a sample of how one student completed this exercise.

Activity

(1C) SPEECH PLANNING

Analyzing the Occasion

The goal of this activity is to help you understand your speech occasion. Fill in answers to the following questions:

1. What is the intended purpose (exigence) for the speech? _____

2. What is the expected length? _____

3. Where will the speech be given? _____

4. When will the speech be given? _____

5. What equipment is necessary and available? _____

Write a short paragraph mentioning which aspects of the occasion are most important to consider as you prepare your speech and why.

_____

_____

Access Action Step 1, Activity 1C on your MindTap for *Challenge*.

Activity

(1C) STUDENT RESPONSE

Analyzing the Occasion

1. What is the intended purpose (exigence) for the speech? *A persuasive speech*

2. What is the expected length? *4–6 minutes*

3. Where will the speech be given? *Memorial Auditorium to about 100 people (including students, teachers, administrators, communication experts, and community members)*

4. When will the speech be given? *I am the first of eight speakers to compete at 9:30 a.m. on Monday morning.*

5. What equipment is necessary and available? *LCD projector, computer, and screen Time is certainly important: Four to six minutes is not very long. I plan to time my speech when I practice to make sure I stay within the expected time limits.*

4-5 SELECT A TOPIC

As you review your topic list, compare each to your audience profile. Are any topics too simple or too difficult for this audience's knowledge base? If so, eliminate those topics. Are some topics likely to bore the audience and you can't think of any way to pique their interest with new insight or a new perspective on them? Eliminate those, as well. How might the audience's age range, ethnicity, and other demographic features mesh with

Reflect on Ethics

JIM CRAMER AND CNBC'S MAD MONEY

Jim Cramer hosts CNBC's *Mad Money*, a program devoted to providing financial advice to its viewers. In an interview on Comedy Central's *The Daily Show*, Jon Stewart claimed both Stewart and Cramer are "snake oil salesmen" but that *The Daily Show* is labeled as such. Stewart was essentially arguing that his program on Comedy Central admits to being satire whereas CNBC's *Mad Money* is duping viewers by claiming to offer sound financial advice, when actually it is not. For example, Stewart showed footage of Cramer recommending that his viewers buy Bear Stearns stock just before it collapsed. If you are personally unfamiliar with the show, watch at least one episode before answering the following questions. Then, with regard to *Mad Money*, consider the elements of the rhetorical situation we've discussed in this chapter (purpose, audience expectations, and location).

1 How would you respond to Stewart's claim that *Mad Money's* host is being unethical?

2 How might Cramer be demonstrating or violating the ethical principle of honesty in terms of the program's purpose?

3 How might Cramer be demonstrating or violating the ethical principle of integrity with regard to audience expectations?

4 Why might the fact that *Mad Money* is shown on CNBC (and not Comedy Central) influence your decision about its host as an ethical communicator?

5 Given that many people now rely on *The Daily Show* to get their news, was Jon Stewart behaving ethically when he made his charge? How does the fact that he made the claim on *The Daily Show* influence your decision?

each topic? By asking these and similar questions, you will be able to identify topics that are appropriate for the audience.

Next, consider the occasion. Are some topics inappropriate for the intended purpose? Are some too broad to cover adequately in the time allotted? Would any require equipment that cannot be made available where you will be speaking? Answers to these kinds of questions will help you identify topics appropriate to the occasion.

4-6 WRITE A SPEECH GOAL STATEMENT

Once you have chosen your topic, you are ready to identify and write the general goal of your speech and then to write your specific goal statement tailored to the audience and occasion.

4-6a Understanding General and Specific Speech Goals

general goal: the overall intent of the speech

The **general goal** is the overall intent of the speech. Most speeches intend to entertain, to inform, or to persuade, even though each type of speech may include elements of other types. Consider the following examples. Jimmy Kimmel's opening monologue on *Jimmy Kimmel Live* is generally intended to entertain, even though it may include persuasion. Likewise, presidential campaign speeches are generally intended to persuade, even though they also include informative material. The general goal is usually dictated by the occasion. (In classroom speeches, the instructor usually specifies it.)

Speech-Planning Action Step 1, Activity 1D will help you select your topic. See the Student Response box immediately following the activity for a sample of how one student completed this exercise.

specific goal: a single statement that identifies the exact response the speaker wants from the audience

Whereas the general goal is typically determined by the occasion, the **specific goal** (or specific purpose) is a single statement that identifies the exact response a speaker wants from the audience. For a speech about "Vanishing Honeybees," you might state the specific goal as, "I would like the audience to understand the four reasons honeybees are vanishing" if your general goal is to inform. If your general goal is to persuade, you might state instead, "I intend to convince the audience to donate money to *Honeybee Advocacy International*." In the first example, the goal is informative: The speaker wants the audience to understand the reasons. In the second example, the goal is persuasive: The speaker wants to persuade the audience to donate money.

4-6b Phrasing a Specific Speech Goal

A specific speech goal statement must be carefully crafted because it lays the foundation for organizing your speech. The following guidelines can help you do so.

1. **Write a first draft of your speech goal in one complete sentence.** Remember Kameron from our opening vignette? He ultimately decided on the topic of same-sex marriage for his speech. He wrote his first speech goal draft this way:

   I want my audience to agree that same-sex marriage should be allowed.

   Kameron's draft is a complete sentence, and it specifies the response he wants from the audience: *to agree* that same-sex couples should be allowed to marry. Thus, he is planning to give a persuasive speech.

1D SPEECH PLANNING

Activity

Selecting a Topic

Use your responses to Action Step Activities 1A, 1B, and 1C to complete this activity.

1. Look over the concept map you prepared in Activity 1A. List each of the specific topics that you generated:

   _____   _____   _____

   _____   _____   _____

   _____   _____   _____

2. Using the information you compiled in Activity 1B (audience analysis), compare each topic to your audience profile. Eliminate topics that seem less appropriate for this specific audience. List the remaining topics:

   _____   _____   _____

   _____   _____   _____

3. Compare each of the remaining topics to the information you compiled in Activity 1C (analysis of the occasion). Eliminate topics that seem less appropriate. List each of the remaining topics:

   _____   _____   _____

4. The remaining topics are appropriate to the rhetorical situation (you, the audience, and the occasion). So, select the topic from this list that you are most excited about sharing with others. My topic will be: _____

 MindTap™

Access this activity on your MindTap for *Challenge*.

Selecting a Topic

1. Look over the concept map you prepared in Activity 1A. List each of the specific topics that you generated:

   Low-cost ways to travel   *Study abroad programs*
   Youth hostels   *Working on cruise ships*
   Organizing alternative   *Elderhostel*
   spring break group trips

2. Using the information you compiled in Activity 1B (audience analysis), compare each topic to your audience profile. Eliminate topics that seem less appropriate. List the remaining topics:

   Low-cost ways to travel   *Study abroad programs*
   Youth hostels   *Organizing alternative spring*
                                      break group trips

3. Compare each of the remaining topics to the information you compiled in Activity 1C (analysis of the occasion). Eliminate topics that seem less appropriate for this specific audience. List each of the remaining topics:

   Study abroad programs   *Youth hostels*
   Organizing alternative spring
   break group trips

4. The remaining topics are appropriate to the rhetorical situation (you, the audience, and the occasion). So, select the topic from this list that you are most excited about sharing with others. My topic will be *organizing alternative spring break group trips.*

2. **Make sure the goal statement contains only one idea.** Suppose Kameron had first written:

   I would like the audience to agree that same-sex marriage should be allowed and that parents and teachers should talk to children about these issues without shame.

   This statement would need to be revised because it includes two distinct ideas: allowing same-sex marriage and talking to children about it without shame. Either one could be a worthy goal—but not both in one short speech. Kameron needs to choose one of these ideas. If your goal statement includes the word *and*, you probably have more than one idea and need to narrow your focus.

3. **Revise the statement until it clearly articulates the general goal.** If your general goal is to inform, you might use phrases such as "to understand," "to recognize," "to distinguish," or "to identify." If the general goal is to persuade, you might use phrases such as "to believe," "to accept," "to change," or "to do." If Kameron wanted to inform his audience, his specific goal might be worded:

I want my audience to understand the issues surrounding same-sex marriage.

This general goal, *to understand*, suggests that Kameron would lay out the various perspectives about same-sex marriage and stop short of advocating one position over the others.

4. **Revise your statement until it articulates the precise focus of your speech tailored to the audience.** Kameron's draft "I want my audience to agree that same-sex marriage should be allowed" is still fairly vague. Exactly what is it about same-sex marriage that Kameron wants his audience to believe? Here is where you need to consider your audience analysis and adapt your specific goal in ways that address their needs, interests, and expectations. What is it about the topic that your particular audience should know and why?

Kameron reasons that his audience members are citizens in a nation that values and respects human rights for all, so he revises his specific speech goal this way:

> *I want my audience to agree that anyone in a committed relationship based on mutual love and respect should have the right to marry.*

Before we close this chapter, we want to tell you a bit more about Kameron from the opening vignette and his speech. Although Kayla is not a real person, Kameron is based on a real student named Kameron Slade from Queens, New York. Kameron actually won a speech competition in 2012 for a speech in which he advocated for same-sex marriage. His performance earned him the right to compete in a much larger speech contest. When he was told he would not be allowed to compete unless he changed his topic, a public outcry went viral (Photo 4.5). He did ultimately get to deliver his speech and even went on to give it to the New York City Council.[4] But why did the contest organizers want to censor the topic? They did not believe Kameron had the needed subject-related credibility for such a speech because Kameron was only 10 years-old. You can watch his speech to the New York City Council on **Web Link 4.4, Kameron Slade,** in your MindTap for *Challenge*.

A good specific speech goal statement will guide you as you research your speech. Once you have completed your research, you will revise your specific speech goal into a thesis statement, which will be the foundation on which you will organize the speech. Exhibit 4.6 gives several additional examples of general and specific informative and persuasive goals.

Exhibit 4.6 is a form you can use to summarize the demographic and subject-related audience data you collect. Now that you understand audience analysis, you can complete Speech-Planning Action Step 1, Activity 1B. See the Student Response box immediately following the activity for a sample of how one student completed this exercise.

Speech-Planning Action Step 1, Activity 1E will help you develop a well-written specific goal statement for your speech. See the Student Response box immediately following the activity for a sample of how one student completed that exercise.

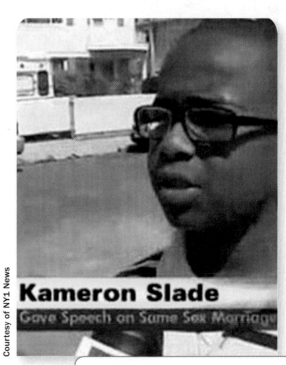

Courtesy of NY1 News

Kameron Slade
Gave Speech on Same Sex Marriage

Photo 4.5 Kameron Slade's winning speech on same sex marriage went viral and earned him an opportunity to give it for the New York City Council.

Exhibit (4.6) **General and Specific Speech Goals**

Informative Goals

General goal: To inform the audience about e-books

Specific goal: I want the audience to understand the differences between the Kindle and the Sony/iPad approaches to electronic books.

General goal: To inform the audience about forms of mystery stories

Specific goal: I want the audience to be able to identify the three basic forms of mystery stories.

Persuasive Goals

General goal: To persuade the audience that saving for retirement is important

Specific goal: I want the audience to begin a personal ROTH IRA funded this year with at least 2 percent of their income.

General goal: To persuade the audience to get involved with the food bank

Specific goal: I want to persuade the audience to volunteer to work on the campus food drive for our local food bank.

1E SPEECH PLANNING

Activity

Writing a Specific Goal

Type of speech: _____

1. Write a first draft of your specific speech goal using a complete sentence that specifies the type of response you want from the audience.

2. If the statement contains more than one idea, select one and rewrite the statement.

3. Revise the statement until it clearly articulates the general goal.

4. Revise the statement until it articulates the precise focus of your speech tailored to your intended audience.

Write the final draft of the specific speech goal:

_____

_____

_____

 MindTap™

Do this activity with Speech Builder Express. Access this activity on your MindTap for *Challenge.*

1E STUDENT RESPONSE

Activity

Writing a Specific Goal

Type of speech: _informative_

1. Write a first draft of your specific speech goal using a complete sentence that specifies the type of response you want from the audience.

    I want the audience to understand how a fire is lit without a match.

2. If the statement contains more than one idea, select one and rewrite the statement.

    I want my audience to recognize the basic steps necessary in lighting a fire without a match.

3. Revise the statement until it clearly articulates the general goal.

    I want to teach the audience how to light a fire without a match.

4. Revise the statement until it articulates the precise focus of your speech tailored to your intended audience. Write the final draft of the specific goal:

    I want to teach my audience to recognize the three basic steps involved in lighting a fire without a match.

Reflection and Assessment

The first step in preparing an effective speech is to identify a topic and goal. An appropriate topic is one that addresses the rhetorical situation (you, your audience, and the occasion). To assess how well you've learned what we've discussed in this chapter answer the following questions. If you have trouble answering any of them, go back and review the material. Once you can answer each question accurately, you are ready to move ahead to read the next chapter.

1. How do you go about brainstorming for potential speech topics?
2. What are some kinds of demographic and subject-related audience data you should collect?
3. What methods might you employ to collect audience data?
4. What do we mean by using audience data ethically?
5. What are the characteristics of an effective specific speech goal statement?

Challenge Resource and Assessment Center

Now that you have read Chapter 4, go to your MindTap for *The Challenge of Effective Speaking in a Digital Age* for quick access to the electronic resources that accompany this text. These resources include:

- **Study tools** that will help you assess your learning and prepare for exams (*digital glossary, key term flash cards, review quizzes*).
- **Activities and assignments** that will help you hone your knowledge and build your public speaking skills throughout the course (*Applying What You've Learned,* the *Student Workbook,* and *Action Step Activities*). Many of these activities allow you to compare your answers with those provided by the authors, and, if requested, submit your answers to your instructor.
- **Media resources**—all of which are available on your MindTap for *Challenge*—will help you explore communication concepts online (Practice), develop your speech outlines (Do), watch and critique videos of sample speeches (Do), and upload your speech videos for instructor feedback and critique other students' speeches (Do).
- **Speech-Planning Action Steps identified earlier in the chapter.**
  - **1A:** Use Brainstorming and Concept Mapping to Identify Speech Topics (p. 61)
  - **1B:** Analyzing Your Audience (p. 68)
  - **1C:** Analyzing the Occasion (p. 71)
  - **1D:** Selecting a Topic (p. 73)
  - **1E:** Writing a Specific Goal (p. 76)
- **Web Links that provide you with additional information or resources related to the topics discussed in this chapter.**
  - **4.1** Brainstorming (p. 59)
  - **4.2** Defining Your Audience (p. 59)
  - **4.3** Public Opinion Polls (p. 63)
  - **4.4** Kameron Slade (p. 75)
- **Video resources allow you to see other students giving speeches and record your own speech.**
  1. Go to MindTap (Do) and browse the speeches posted there. Do any of the topics of the speeches you see give you ideas for your own classroom speeches? Do some of the topics inspire you to brainstorm for more topics?

2. Go to the Practice and Present section of MindTap and upload a video of a speech you're working on. Ask your instructor and classmates for feedback on the statement of your specific goal. Or look through other students' speeches to see how effectively they state their specific goals—do their statements give you ideas for how you could make your statement more effective?

Applying What You've Learned

1. **Impromptu Speech Activity:** Identify a pet peeve and prepare a two- to three-minute impromptu speech describing the pet peeve and why it bothers you. Include in your reasons which ethical communication principle(s) it violates in your opinion and why.

2. **Assessment Activity A:** Complete Action Steps 1A through 1E for one of the speeches you may give this semester.

3. **Assessment Activity B:** Suppose you were asked to give a speech about some aspect of your work to a group of your coworkers and managers. Explain what demographic and subject-specific information you would need, how you would collect it, and how you might use it in your speech planning. How would your approach differ if your audience were your speech classmates?

5 "adapting to audiences"

WHAT'S THE POINT?
WHEN YOU'VE FINISHED THIS CHAPTER, YOU WILL BE ABLE TO:

5-1 Address initial audience disposition toward your topic.

5-2 Highlight common ground with your audience.

5-3 Articulate the relevance of your speech to your audience

5-4 Establish your credibility as knowledgeable, trustworthy, and personable.

5-5 Employ strategies to enhance comprehension and retention

5-6 Overcome potential language and cultural differences

5-7 Create your own audience adaptation plan

 MindTap™

Review the chapter **Learning Objectives** and **Start** with quick warm up activity.

2 Understand your audience and adapt to it.

A. Understand audience diversity.
B. Tailor your speech to address their needs, interests, and expectations.

e Ethical communicators demonstrate respect by adapting their message to the audience at all points in the speech-making process.

Read, highlight, and take notes online.

Megan decided to do her speech on the causes and effects of hurricanes. Hurricane Katrina had destroyed her family's home several years ago. They still hadn't fully recovered from it. When she watched news reports of Super Storm Sandy, the awful memories came flooding back. Her heart ached for the victims. She really wanted her classmates to better understand the physical and emotional havoc raised by hurricanes. But how would she gain and maintain the interest of classmates who live in a landlocked state nowhere near a coastline? Her instructor said nearly any topic can be tailored to address the needs, interests, and expectations of the audience. Still, Megan couldn't help but think this was going to pose quite a challenge.

J.J. chose to do his speech on cell phone distracted driving. Audience analysis had confirmed his assumption that most of his classmates realized they shouldn't talk or text while driving. Yet, their survey responses revealed that 90 percent of them did so anyway. Many of them indicated they were very careful. They did not believe they were likely to get in an accident while texting and most certainly not while merely talking on the phone. He knew better. But he also knew that convincing them to agree with him and to stop engaging in this dangerous behavior would be a real challenge.

> "Her instructor said nearly any topic can be tailored to address the needs, interests, and expectations of the audience. Still, Megan couldn't help but think this was going to pose quite a challenge."

In the previous chapter, we talked about how to conduct an audience analysis and then use it to narrow your topic and determine your speech goal. Recall, however, that effective speakers don't stop there. Effective speakers use *audience adaptation*—the process of tailoring the speech to the needs, interests, and expectations of the audience—to inform everything from researching the topic to organizing the main points to developing them with supporting material to making language choices and practicing delivery. In this chapter, we offer guidelines for adapting to your audience by acknowledging initial audience disposition, establishing common ground, demonstrating relevance, gaining credibility, enhancing information comprehension and retention, and overcoming potential language and cultural differences.

5-1 INITIAL AUDIENCE DISPOSITION

Initial audience disposition is the knowledge and opinions your audience has about your topic before they hear you speak. Recall that this information helped you narrow the topic and determine your speech goal. You also want to consider initial audience disposition when determining your main points, selecting supporting material, and making language choices. For example, if you were giving a speech on refinishing wood furniture, you may face an audience whose initial attitude is that refinishing furniture is complicated and boring. On the other hand, you may face an audience of young homeowners who love HGTV and are really looking forward to your talk. Although the process you describe in both situations will be the same, your approach to explaining the steps will differ somewhat. If your audience thinks refinishing furniture is boring and complicated, you will need to pique their interest and convince them that the process is really simpler than they initially thought. And if you know your audience enjoys watching HGTV, you can play upon these interests by making reference to some popular HGTV shows (Photo 5.1).

initial audience disposition: the knowledge of and opinions about your topic that your listeners have before they hear you speak

common ground: the background, knowledge, attitudes, experiences, and philosophies audience members and the speaker share

personal pronouns: "we," "us," and "our"— pronouns that directly link the speaker to members of the audience

rhetorical questions: questions phrased to stimulate a mental response rather than an actual spoken response from the audience

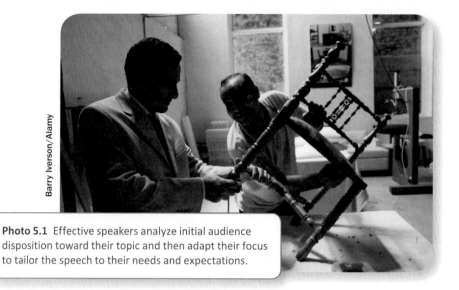

Barry Iverson/Alamy

Photo 5.1 Effective speakers analyze initial audience disposition toward their topic and then adapt their focus to tailor the speech to their needs and expectations.

5-2 COMMON GROUND

People are unique, with different knowledge, attitudes, philosophies, experiences, and ways of perceiving the world. So it is easy for audience members to assume they have nothing in common with you or with the other audience members. As a speaker, your goal is to identify and highlight **common ground**, a sense of shared background, knowledge, attitudes, experiences, and philosophies. You can do so by using personal pronouns, asking rhetorical questions, and drawing on common experiences.

5-2a Use Personal Pronouns

One way to establish common ground is to use the **personal pronouns**—"we," "us," and "our." For example, in her speech about hurricanes, Megan used personal pronouns to establish common ground in this way:

> *Let's discuss how hurricanes form and the varying degrees of intensity of them.*

By using "let's discuss" rather than "I'll explain," Megan created a sense of common ground that she and her audience would work together to form a common understanding about hurricanes.

5-2b Ask Rhetorical Questions

A second way to establish common ground is to pose **rhetorical questions**—questions phrased to stimulate a mental response on the part of the audience. Rhetorical questions are often used in speech introductions but can also be used effectively in transitions and other parts of the speech. For instance, notice how this transition, phrased as a rhetorical question, creates common ground:

> *When watching a particularly violent TV program, have you ever asked yourself, "Did they really need to be this graphic to make the point?"*

Used in this way, rhetorical questions highlight similar attitudes among the speaker and audience members and pique interest about the content that is to come.

5-2c Draw from Common Experiences

Another way to establish common ground is by sharing personal stories and examples illustrating things you and your audience have in common. In her speech about hurricanes, Megan tried to establish common ground in her introduction in this way:

> *Close your eyes and think about a time when you were absolutely terrified. Maybe it was when you were a child and afraid of a bully on the playground. Or maybe it was a time when you were scared about getting in an accident while driving during a terrible snow, sleet, or hail storm. Or maybe you were terrified as a child when you got lost in a crowd at the shopping center or county fair. In any case, all you wanted to do was get home where you would be safely surrounded by family and friends. Now imagine feeling that petrified AND having no idea if your home would even be there when you arrived. Well, that's exactly how I felt when Hurricane Katrina hit the Louisiana coastline a few years ago.*

Although Megan realized that very few, if any, of her classmates had probably ever experienced a hurricane, she drew upon a common experience she knew they could all relate to: that of being afraid.

5-3 RELEVANCE

Another important way to tailor your speech to your audience is by demonstrating **relevance**—adapting information in ways that help audience members realize its importance to them. Listeners pay attention to and are interested in ideas that affect them personally in some way ("What does this have to do with me?") and lose interest when they don't see how a speech relates to them. You can demonstrate relevance by emphasizing timeliness, proximity, and personal impact of the ideas you share throughout your speech (Photo 5.2).

relevance: adapting the information in a speech so that audience members view it as important to them

5-3a Emphasize Timeliness

Information has **timeliness** when it is useful now or in the near future. For example, in a speech about the hazards of cell phone distracted driving, J.J. demonstrated relevance via timeliness with this introduction:

timeliness: showing how information is useful now or in the near future

> *Most of us in this room, as many as 90 percent of us in fact, are a danger to society. Why? It's because we talk or text on our cell phones while driving. Recent reports released in 2012 from the National Safety Council reveal that cell phone distracted driving is the most common cause of accidents today—even more common than driving under the influence (DUI). Did you know that when you talk on the phone when you're driving—even if you do so on a hands-free set—you're four times more likely to get into a serious crash than if you're not doing so? This issue is far from harmless and is certainly one each of us should take seriously.*

By referencing recent statistics not only about texting but also about talking on the phone while driving, J.J. demonstrates relevance that the topic of his speech is timely. Megan did so by talking not only about her own experiences with Hurricane Katrina, which may not seem timely to her listeners, but also more-recent stories from those attempting to recover from Super Storm Sandy.

To see an example of how timeliness can affect a message—President Ronald Reagan's 1986 speech on the *Challenger* space shuttle disaster—go to **Web Link 5.1, Demonstrating Timeliness,** in your MindTap for *Challenge.*

Matthew Rambo/Photodisc/Getty Images

Photo 5.2 How might you establish relevance in a speech about driving while phoning or texting?

5-3b Emphasize Proximity

Listeners are more likely to be interested in information that has **proximity**, a relationship to their personal "space." Psychologically, we pay more attention to information related to our "territory"—to us, our family, our neighborhood, or our city, state, or country. You have probably heard speakers say, "Let me bring this close to home for you . . ." and then make their point by using a local example. As you do research, look for statistics and examples that emphasize proximity for your audience. For example, J.J. used the latest cell phone distracted driving accident statistics in his state and a story reported in the local paper of a young mother who was killed as a result of cell phone distracted driving.

5-3c Emphasize Personal Impact

When you emphasize a serious physical, economic, or psychological impact of your topic, audience members are interested in what you have to say. Consider, for example, how you perk up when your instructor says, "you might want to jot this down because it will be on the test." That's an example of emphasizing personal impact because remembering it will help you earn a better grade. Megan emphasized personal impact by highlighting ripple effects of hurricanes such as skyrocketing gasoline prices and energy costs. J.J. emphasized personal impact by showing how much higher everyone's auto insurance is today as a result of cell phone distracted traffic accidents.

5-4 SPEAKER CREDIBILITY

Credibility is the audience's perception of a speaker as trustworthy and knowledgeable about the topic. The impact of credibility on speaker success has been a fundamental concept in public speaking since Aristotle described it as *ethos* more than 2,000 years ago. Having been understood as a key concept for so long, it is no wonder that several theories exist about how speakers develop credibility. You can read a summary of these theories by going to **Web Link 5.2, Holistic Theory of Speaker Credibility,** in your MindTap for *Challenge.*

Some people are widely known as experts on a particular topic (Photo 5.3). When these people give a speech, they don't have to do much to establish their credibility. For example, in November 2008 Nancy Nielsen, president of the American Medical Association, spoke to fellow physicians on the subject of standing up for patients when health plans don't—no one listening would have questioned her credibility.

However, most of us need to adapt our remarks to help establish credibility with our audience. We can do so by articulating our knowledge and expertise, conveying trustworthiness, and displaying personableness.

Photo 5.3 Sometimes speakers, such as Warren Buffet, a well-known and successful business investor and philanthropist, come to the occasion with established credibility as an expert on a topic.

Gyi Nsea/EdStock/IStockphoto.com

5-4a Articulate Knowledge and Expertise

Audience members' assessment of your **knowledge and expertise** depends on how well you convince them that you are qualified to speak on this topic. You can do so directly and indirectly.

You can articulate your expertise directly by disclosing your personal experiences with the topic, including formal education, special study, demonstrated skill, and your "track record." For example, in his cell phone distracted driving speech, J.J. explained:

I became interested in the issue of cell phone distracted driving after being involved personally in an accident caused by a driver who was talking on the phone. Since then, I've done a great deal of research on the subject and am involved in a grassroots organization devoted to passing legislation to ban driving while phoning or texting in our state.

Megan articulated knowledge and expertise by sharing her personal stories about experiencing Hurricane Katrina and the things she and her family did and continue to do to live according to what she described as a "new normal." When you can articulate personal experience with your topic, your audience will perceive you as knowledgeable about the material.

Similarly, when ideas are developed through specific statistics and high-quality examples, audience members are more likely to view a speaker as knowledgeable. J.J. did so by citing the most recent statistics release by the National Safety Council and Megan did so by citing reports she found in *The Washington Post* and statistics published by the *National Weather Service.*

Audience members also assess knowledge and expertise through indirect means. Audiences have an almost instinctive sense of when a speaker is "winging it." Most audiences will perceive speakers who do not appear to have command of the material as less knowledgeable and speakers who are confident, fluent, and easy to follow as more knowledgeable.

5-4b Convey Trustworthiness

Trustworthiness is the extent to which the audience believes what you say is accurate, true, and in their best interests. People assess trustworthiness by judging the speaker's character and motives.

As you prepare, consider how you will demonstrate good character—that you are honest, industrious, dependable, and ethical (Photo 5.4). For example, when you credit the source of your information as you speak, you demonstrate good character. You are confirming you did not make up the information (honesty), and you are not plagiarizing (ethics).

How trustworthy you seem also depends on how the audience views your motives. If people believe that what you are saying is self-serving rather than in their best interests, they will be suspicious and view you as less trustworthy. Early in your speech, show how audience members will benefit from what you are saying. For example, in his speech on toxic waste, Brandon described how one community's ignorance of toxic waste disposal allowed a toxic waste dump to be located in their community, which led to serious health issues. He then shared his motive by saying, "My hope is that this speech will give you the information you need to thoughtfully participate in decisions like these that may face your community."

5-4c Display Personableness

Personableness is the extent to which one projects a pleasing personality. Quite simply, we have more confidence in people we like. We quickly decide how much we like a new person based on our first impressions. This fact is actually based on a communication concept known as impression formation and management, which is rooted in the theory of symbolic interactionism.[1] These first impressions are based on what we infer about people from what we see, such as how they dress, how physically attractive

knowledge and expertise: how well you convince your audience that you are qualified to speak on the topic

trustworthiness: the extent to which the audience can believe that what you say is accurate, true, and in their best interests

personableness: the extent to which you project an agreeable or pleasing personality

AP Photo/Jason DeCrow

Photo 5.4 Ethical speakers are fair in that they present all sides of an issue, not just the one they favor. Would you describe Stephen Colbert as ethical in this regard?

Reflect on Ethics

In his *Sports Illustrated* interview in 2012, University of Notre Dame football player, Manti Te'o, was clearly devastated. Why? Both his grandmother and his girlfriend, Lennay Kekua, had died ten days earlier. During the interview, Te'o described his girlfriend as having graduated from Stanford and living in Carson, California. He explained that she discovered she had leukemia while recovering from injuries incurred from being hit by a drunk driver on April 28, 2012. At the time, Te'o was described as a hero: the "physical and emotional center" of the team who somehow found inspiration in the memories of his grandmother and girlfriend and persevered. The public later learned that Lennay Kekua never existed. She was fake. Some said she was a hoax created to help Te'o's chances to win the Heisman trophy. (He ultimately came in second place.) Some said Te'o was "in on it" all along and others said he had been duped. In an interview with Katie Couric in January 2013, Te'o said he wasn't lying. He was in love with a girl he met online and had never met in person. As he himself said, "What I went through was real. You know, the feelings, the pain, the sorrow—that was all real, and that's something that I can't fake".[2] While we may never know the truth, some speculate that Te'o's teammates were inspired to play harder because of his resilience in the face of what appeared to be the tragic deaths of two loved ones.

1. Is it ethical to adapt in a way that resonates with your audience even if it is not entirely true?

2. Do Te'o's claims that Kakua was "real" to him make a difference regarding the ethics of his statements and behaviors?

3. How (if at all) did Te'o's perceived credibility change among various audiences (e.g., teammates, fans) after learning that Kakua didn't exist?

4. What would you do if you were Te'o in this situation and why?

we find them, how well they speak, whether they smile and appear friendly, and even how they carry themselves. Although first impressions are not always correct, we still use them. That's why a successful business professional might wear an oversize graphic T-shirt, baggy shorts, and a backward ball cap when hanging out with friends; put on khakis and a polo shirt to go to the office; and dress in a formal blue suit to make a major presentation at a professional conference. He or she adjusts appearance to convey appropriate personableness in different settings.

Besides dressing appropriately, you can increase the chances that the audience will like you by smiling at individual audience members before beginning your remarks and by looking at individuals as you speak, acknowledging them with a quick nod. You can

PUBLIC SPEAKING IN THE REAL WORLD

Oprah Winfrey on Knowing Your Audience

Frederick M. Brown/Getty Images

Billionaire Oprah Winfrey is one of the richest women in America according to *Forbes* magazine.[3] Although new episodes are no longer being produced, her award-winning "Oprah Winfrey Show" remains one of the most highly rated talk shows in TV history. But how did she do it? Oprah herself has credited her success from knowing what her audience wants and then, not only giving it to them, but giving them even more.[4] It seems Oprah understands the value of analyzing and adapting to her audience. In fact, her new kind of TV talk show replaced the common practice of reporting celebrity gossip with engaging in conversations designed to build rapport, empathy, as well as self-awareness and esteem. Deborah Tannen described Oprah's unique ability to adapt to her audience in a *Time* magazine article as linking strangers "over public airwaves . . . in the privacy of our homes [and making] people care because she cares. That is Winfrey's genius, and will be her legacy, as the changes she has wrought in the talk show continue to permeate our culture and shape our lives."[5]

also demonstrate personableness by using appropriate humor. By appropriate humor, we mean humor that demonstrates respect for diverse listeners by not potentially offending a particular group (e.g., sexist, ageist, racist) or the values held by them.

5-5 INFORMATION COMPREHENSION AND RETENTION

You also need to adapt your speech to ensure comprehension and retention throughout it. Five ways to do so are (1) appealing to diverse learning styles, (2) using transitions, (3) choosing specific and familiar language, (4) using vivid language and examples, and (5) comparing unfamiliar ideas with familiar ones.

5-5a Appeal to Diverse Learning Styles

A **learning style** is a person's preferred way of receiving information. Because we differ in our preferred learning styles, you should present your ideas in ways that make it easy for all audience members to understand and remember what you are saying. Models for understanding learning styles have been developed by many scholars.[6] One prominent model, called Kolb's cycle of learning, conceptualizes learning preferences along four dimensions: feeling, thinking, watching, and doing.[7] Kolb's model is actually rooted in John Dewey's experiential learning theory.[8] Exhibit 5.1 illustrates the watching, doing, feeling, and thinking dimensions of the learning cycle.

learning style: a person's preferred way of receiving information

Exhibit (5.1) Kolb's Cycle of Learning

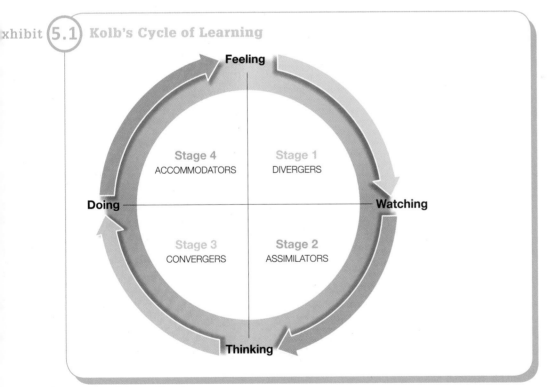

Copyright © Cengage Learning

Some people prefer to learn by "watching" and easily understand and remember things they see and relate to well-designed visual aids and vivid examples they can picture in their minds. Others prefer to learn by doing. For these people, hands-on activities aid their comprehension and memory. People who prefer to learn by doing relate well when speakers provide real-life applications and clearly state how the speech topic is relevant to their personal or professional lives.

Some people learn best when their feelings are engaged. These people learn well from stories and other supporting material that appeal to their emotions or senses. Other people learn well by thinking about factual material and connect well when ideas are supported with detailed definitions, explanations, facts, and statistics.

Although each of us has a preferred learning style, research also reveals that all people learn most effectively when ideas are presented in ways that "round" the entire cycle of learning.[9] So as you develop your speech, adapt to diverse learning styles by presenting information in ways that appeal to each of the four dimensions (watching, feeling, doing, and thinking).

For example, suppose you are trying to make the point that understanding simple directions can be a problem for functionally illiterate people. You could do so by saying:

For instance, a person who is functionally illiterate might not be able to read or understand a label that says, "Take three times a day after eating."

Now look at how much richer this explanation becomes when it is developed in ways that appeal to different learning styles:

Many Americans are functionally illiterate. In fact, about 35 million people, or 20 percent of the adult population, have serious difficulties with common reading tasks (thinking). *That means that one of every five people cannot read well enough to understand how to bake a frozen pizza, how to assemble a child's bicycle from printed instructions, or which bus to catch from the signs at the stop* (feeling). *Many functionally illiterate people don't read well enough to follow the directions on this bottle [show an enlarged image of the label on a medicine bottle that reads, "Take three times a day after eating"]* (watching). *Not only that, they wouldn't know they need to "press down while turning" to remove this cap [demonstrate removing the cap from the pill bottle]* (doing). *So the directions on a prescription bottle like this [show visual aid of enlarged prescription bottle with directions written in garbled nonsense words] are basically meaningless.*

5-5b Use Transitions

When listeners have trouble following a speaker's organization, we have difficulty understanding the message. So you should use transitions to help your audience follow along. Recall from chapter 1 that a transition is a sentence or two that summarizes one main point and introduces the next one. Suppose your goal is to explain the three phases of a clinical trial a cancer drug must pass through to earn FDA approval. After explaining the goals of the first phase, you might use a transition like this: "So the goal of the first phase is to see whether a drug that is safe in animals is also safe in humans. Phase I trials are not designed to determine whether or not the drug works; that is actually the goal in Phase II trials."

To see an excellent example of orienting listeners—former President Bill Clinton's speech outlining the reasons for NATO involvement in Kosovo—go to **Web Link 5.3, Orienting Listeners,** in your MindTap for *Challenge.*

5-5c Choose Specific and Familiar Language

Words have many meanings, so you want to make sure your listeners understand the meaning you intend. You can do so by using specific language and choosing familiar terms. Specific words clear up the confusion caused by general words by narrowing the focus in some way. For example, saying "a feisty little year-old Yorkshire terrier" is more specific than "a dog." Narrowing the meaning encourages your listeners to picture the same thing you are.

You also want to use familiar words. Avoid jargon and slang terms unless (1) you define them clearly the first time you use them, and (2) they are central to your

transition: a sentence or two that summarizes one main point and introduces the next one speech goal. For instance, in a speech on the four major problems faced by functionally illiterate people in the workplace, your audience will need to understand what you mean by "functionally illiterate." You should offer your definition early in the speech: "By 'functionally illiterate,' I mean people who have trouble accomplishing simple reading and writing tasks."

5-5d Use Vivid Language and Examples

Vivid examples help audience members understand and remember abstract, complex, and novel material. One vivid example can help us understand a complicated concept. As you prepare, find or create real or hypothetical examples and illustrations to help your audience understand new and complex information. For example, in the functionally illiterate definition, the description "people who have trouble accomplishing simple reading and writing tasks" can be made more vivid by adding: "For instance, a functionally illiterate person could not read and understand the directions on a prescription label that states, 'Take three times a day with a glass of water. Do not take on an empty stomach.'"

5-5e Compare Unfamiliar Ideas with Familiar Ones

An easy way to adapt material to your audience is to compare new ideas with ones the audience already understands (Photo 5.5). As you prepare, identify places where you can use comparisons. In the speech on functional illiteracy, if you want the audience of literates to sense what functionally illiterate people experience, you might compare it to the experience of surviving in a country where one is not fluent in the language:

Many of us have taken a foreign language in school. So we figure we can visit a place where that language is spoken and "get along," right? But when we get to the country, we are often appalled to discover that even the road signs are written in this "foreign" language. And we can't quite make the signs out, at least not at 60 kilometers an hour. I was in France last summer, equipped with my three years of high school French, and I saw a sign that indicated that the train station I was looking for was "à droit"—"to the right," or is it "to the left"? I knew it was one or

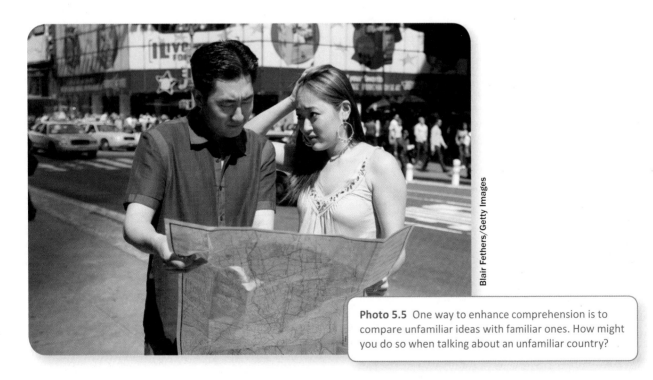

Blair Fethers/Getty Images

Photo 5.5 One way to enhance comprehension is to compare unfamiliar ideas with familiar ones. How might you do so when talking about an unfamiliar country?

In his speech about skydiving, Kyron related the sensation of falling out of a plane to something most listeners could probably relate to in this way: "The first thing you feel when you finally jump is that stomach-in-the-mouth sensation that is similar to something we've all experienced when we have lurched because we've missed a step going down a staircase or when we have momentarily gone airborne in a car from approaching the crest of a hill too fast."

IMPROMPTU SPEECH CHALLENGE

Draw a slip of paper from a stack provided by your instructor. The paper has the name of a common object on it. Prepare a one- to two-minute speech describing the object without saying what it is. Then ask your classmates to guess what you described. Discuss why they did or did not get it right.

the other. Unfortunately, I couldn't remember and took a shot that it was to the left. Bad move. By the time I figured it out, I was 10 miles in the wrong direction and ended up missing my train. At that moment, I could imagine how tough life must be for functionally illiterate people. So many "little details" of life require the ability to comprehend written messages.

Devon, a student at the University of California, used comparisons in his speech on how the Japanese economy affects U.S. markets. To help his audience understand geographic data about Japan, he could just quote the following statistics:[10]

Japan is small and densely populated. The nation's 128 million people live in a land area of 146,000 square miles, giving them a population density of 877 persons per square mile.

Instead, he used a comparison to enhance understanding:

Japan is a small, densely populated nation. Its population of 128 million is nearly half that of the United States. Yet the Japanese are crowded into a land area of only 146,000 square miles—roughly the same size as California. Just think of the implications of having half the population of the United States living here in California, where 30 million people—about one-fifth of that total—now live. In fact, Japan packs 877 persons into every square mile of land, whereas in the United States we average about 74 persons per square mile. Overall, then, Japan is about 12 times as crowded as the United States.

Even though most of his listeners probably don't know the total land area of the United States, they do know that the United States covers a great deal of territory. Likewise, his California audience would have a sense of the size of their home state compared with the rest of the nation. Devon researched statistics on the United States and California in order to make these comparisons. If Devon was speaking to an audience in another state, he could tailor his ideas by using information about that state instead of California.

5-6 LANGUAGE AND CULTURAL DIFFERENCES

Western European speaking traditions inform the approach to public speaking we discuss in this book. However, public speaking is a social act that varies across cultures. So when you address an audience comprised of people from ethnic and language groups different from your own, you should make two adaptations: try to be understandable when speaking in a second language, and show respect by choosing culturally appropriate supporting material.

5-6a Work to Be Understood When Speaking in Your Second Language

When speaking to an audience in a language that is not your native language, audience members may have difficulty understanding you because you may speak with an accent, mispronounce words, choose inappropriate words, or misuse idioms. You can help your audience understand you by speaking more slowly and articulating as clearly as you can. By slowing your speaking rate, you give yourself additional time to pronounce difficult sounds and choose words whose meanings you know. You can also use visual aids to reinforce key terms and concepts as you move through your speech. Doing so assures listeners that they've understood you correctly.

One of the best ways to improve is to practice in front of friends who are native speakers. Ask them to take note of words and phrases that you mispronounce or misuse. Then they can work with you to correct your pronunciation or to help you choose better words to express your ideas. Also, keep in mind that the more you practice speaking the language, the more comfortable you will become with it.

5-6b Choose Culturally Appropriate Supporting Material

When speaking to audiences who are vastly different from you, it will take work to find out about their culture and experiences, so you can adapt your ideas and information to them. This may mean conducting additional research to find relevant supporting material. Or it may require you to elaborate on ideas that might be self-explanatory in your own culture. For example, suppose that Maria, a Mexican-American exchange student, was giving a narrative/personal experience speech for her speech class at Yeshiva University in Israel on the *quinceañera* party she had when she turned fifteen. Because students in Israel probably don't have any experience with the Mexican coming-of-age tradition of *quinceañera* parties, they may have trouble understanding the significance of this event unless Maria uses her knowledge of the bar mitzvah and bat mitzvah coming-of-age ritual Jewish celebrations as comparisons.

5-7 FORMING A SPECIFIC AUDIENCE ADAPTATION PLAN

You now understand the challenges speakers face in developing and maintaining audience interest and understanding, and you have read about the adaptation techniques that can help you overcome these challenges. At this point, you can develop your own adaptation plan by answering the following questions:

1. **What is my audience's initial disposition toward my topic?** What can I do to enhance audience interest?

2. **What common ground do audience members share with one another and with me?** How and where can I use personal pronouns, rhetorical questions, and common experiences to enhance the perception of common ground?

3. **How relevant will the audience find this material?** How can I demonstrate that the material is timely, proximate, and has personal impact for audience members?

4. **What can I do to enhance my credibility?** How did I develop my expertise on this topic, and how can I share that with the audience? How can I demonstrate my trustworthiness as I speak? What will I do to help the audience perceive me as personable?

5. **How can I make it easier for audience members to comprehend and remember the information?** What types of material can I use to appeal to different learning style preferences? What key terms will I need to define? What new concepts might I develop with vivid language and examples? What new ideas might I want to compare to ones the audience is already familiar with?

6. **What language or cultural differences do audience members have with one another and with me?** If I will be speaking in a second language, how will I increase the likelihood that the audience will understand me? What cultural differences do I need to be sensitive to, and what culturally appropriate material might I search for and use?

Speech-Planning Action Step 2, Activity 2 will help you identify opportunities for audience adaptation as you develop your speeches. See the Student Response box immediately following the activity for a sample of how one student completed this exercise.

② SPEECH PLANNING

Recognizing Opportunities for Audience Adaptation

To identify opportunities for audience adaptation, state your potential topic and then answer the following questions.

Potential topic: _____

1. What is my audience's initial disposition toward my topic?

2. What common ground do audience members share with one another and with me?

3. How relevant will the audience find this material? How can I demonstrate that the material is timely, proximate, and has personal impact for this audience?

4. What can I do to enhance my credibility?

5. How can I make it easier for audience members to comprehend and remember the information?

6. What language or cultural differences do audience members have with one another and with me?

 MindTap™

Access this activity on your MindTap for *Challenge*.

Activity

(2) STUDENT RESPONSE

Recognizing Opportunities for Audience Adaptation

Potential topic: *The overall effects of hurricanes*

1. What is my audience's initial disposition toward my topic?

   Most audience members will be only mildly interested in and not well informed about hurricanes when I begin. I hope to pique and maintain their interest by using vivid language and examples, as well as graphic photos.

2. What common ground do audience members share with one another and with me?

   Because most audience members are my age and are from the same national culture, we share areas of common ground I can draw on. First, hurricanes occur every year and affect weather patterns throughout the country when they do. I should also be able to use personal pronouns and rhetorical questions to create common ground. We are different in that I have actually lived through the devastation of a hurricane in my hometown, so I'll have to keep in mind that most of my listeners have not. That means I'll have to be careful not to assume they know more than general facts about hurricanes.

3. How relevant will the audience find this material?

   Initially, since they don't live on a coast, they are not likely to see it as relevant.

   How can I demonstrate that the material is timely, proximate, and has personal impact on the members of this audience?

   I can make the information timely by talking about Super Storm Sandy, a fairly recent hurricane that most people are aware of, which affected many people, and that even affected the weather in other states.

4. What can I do to enhance my credibility?

   I will build credibility through solid research and oral citations of sources. Early in my introduction, I'll mention where I live on the Gulf Coast and the fact that I've lived through several hurricanes.

5. How can I make it easier for audience members to comprehend and remember the information?

   I will round the cycle of learning by talking about my personal experiences (feeling), showing photographs (watching), offering facts and statistics about the effects of hurricanes (thinking), and providing clear instructions about how to categorize hurricanes and act appropriately to ensure safety (doing). I'll also describe the effects using vivid language and examples, and I'll compare them to other natural disasters my audience members may have experienced such as thunderstorms, tornados, and floods.

6. What language or cultural differences do audience members have with one another and with me?

   I will not be speaking in a second language, but I will need to be careful not to use too many technical terms that may be "jargon" to my audience, and, when I do, I need to be sure to define them clearly. Although most audience members are U.S. nationals, there are three international students in class. I will do some research to see if any of them live in a country that experiences hurricanes, and, if so, I'll include some examples from their countries, as well.

MindTap™

Reflection and Assessment

Audience adaptation is the process of tailoring your speech to the needs, interests, and expectations of your specific audience. To assess how well you've learned what we've discussed in this chapter, answer the following questions. If you have trouble answering any of them, go back and review that material. Once you can answer each question accurately, you are ready to move ahead to read the next chapter.

1. How can you find out about and then address initial audience disposition toward your topic?
2. What techniques can you use to emphasize aspects of common ground you share with your audience?
3. What are some ways you can point out the relevance of your speech to your audience?
4. How can you establish yourself as a credible speaker?
5. In what ways might you promote audience comprehension and retention?
6. What might you do to overcome potential language and cultural differences?

MindTap™

Challenge Resource and Assessment Center

Now that you have read Chapter 5, go to your MindTap for *The Challenge of Effective Speaking in a Digital Age* for quick access to the electronic resources that accompany this text. These resources include the following:

- **Study tools** that will help you assess your learning and prepare for exams (*digital glossary, key term flash cards, review quizzes*).

- **Activities and assignments** that will help you hone your knowledge and build your public speaking skills throughout the course (Practice, Do). Many of these activities allow you to compare your answers with those provided by the authors, and, if requested, submit your answers to your instructor.

- **Media resources**—all of which are available on your MindTap for *Challenge*—will help you explore communication concepts online (Practice), develop your speech outlines (Do), watch and critique videos of sample speeches (Do), and upload your speech videos for instructor feedback and critique other students' speeches (Do).

- **Speech-Planning Action Step identified earlier in the chapter.**

  Activity 2: Recognizing Opportunities for Audience Adaptation (p. 92)

- **Web Links that provide you with additional information or resources related to the topics discussed in this chapter.**

  5.1: Demonstrating Timeliness (p. 83)

  5.2: Holistic Theory of Speaker Credibility (p. 84)

  5.3: Orienting Listeners (p. 88)

- **Video resources allow you to see other students giving speeches and record your own speech.**

  1. Use your Interactive Video Activities (Do) to watch, analyze, and see the transcripts and outlines for the speech, "We Must Save NASA."

  2. View how other speakers adapted to their audiences. What did they do to demonstrate relevance, establish common ground, enhance their credibility, and adapt to cultural or language differences? Or go to the Practice and Present section of MindTap and record a speech you're working on, upload it, and ask your peers for their feedback. What feedback could you use to fine-tune your audience adaptation before you give your speech in class?

Applying What You've Learned

1. **Impromptu Speech Activity:** Identify a common practice that is taken for granted in your family or your community that may be an unusual or unique practice for other families or in other communities. (For example, one family celebrated Hanukkah-like birthdays where a present was received each day of the birthday week.) Prepare and present a two- to three-minute impromptu speech describing the practice in ways that employ the audience adaptation guidelines proposed in this chapter.

2. **Assessment Activity A:** Identify a cultural group in your community with which you have limited experience. Learn more about this group by (1) observing an event or other gathering, (2) participating in a cultural practice, (3) interviewing a member of the culture, as well as (4) doing some secondary source research. Then write a two- to three-page paper in which you begin by comparing and contrasting what you have learned about this culture. Then, in the second part of the paper, imagine that you were going to give a speech to an audience composed of members of this cultural group. Your assigned topic for the speech is "Reality TV." Based on what you have learned about this culture, which three of the six issues of adaptation that would be the most important for you to address, and describe how might you do that.

3. **Assessment Activity B:** Volunteer at a local service organization regularly (at least twice per week) for four weeks. Before doing so, consider some specific things you will do to seek common ground and gain credibility. Keep a journal throughout the experience, noting what worked and did not work. After four weeks, prepare a two- to three-page reflection paper regarding your adaptation experience. Focus on what you expected the experience to be like, what it was like (rewards and challenges), and what you learned about others and yourself as a result.

4. **Assessment Activity C:** Complete Action Step 2 for one of the speeches you may give this semester.

6

topic development

WHAT'S THE POINT?
WHEN YOU'VE FINISHED THIS
CHAPTER, YOU WILL BE ABLE TO:

6-1   Locate and evaluate information sources about your topic

6-2   Select relevant information about your topic

6-3   Record information accurately

6-4   Cite sources appropriately

 MindTap™

Review the chapter **Learning Objectives** and **Start** with quick warm up activity.

---

3 Gather and evaluate information

A. Examine areas where you need additional information.
B. Locate, evaluate, and select a variety of information types and sources.
C. Record information.
D. Cite sources.

Ⓔ Ethical speakers ensure that what they say is truthful by carefully researching their topic and evaluating information and source credibility.

Justin was concerned. He was scheduled to give his speech in a week, but he hadn't even begun to conduct any research. A couple of months ago, he had read a magazine article about the vanishing honey bees while in the doctor's office waiting room and decided that would be an interesting topic for his informative speech. Although he couldn't remember the name of the magazine, he pulled out his laptop and Googled "vanishing honey bees." To his surprise, he got 14,600,000 hits. He wondered how in the world he would go about sorting through all this information and all these sources to determine which ones would be best for his speech.

Justin's experience is not unusual. Most of us have formed opinions about a variety of subjects based on our personal experiences, interactions with others, and things we've read or watched online or on television. But when it comes to presenting our ideas in a public forum, we need to do research to find evidence to support them. **Evidence** is essentially any information that clarifies, explains, or otherwise adds depth or breadth to a topic. What is particularly challenging in the digital age we live in today is not an inability to find the information we're looking for, but sorting through the array of information at our fingertips to evaluate and select the best information for our speeches. In this chapter, we explain how to locate and evaluate a variety of information types and sources, identify and select the best information, and then cite the sources of that information appropriately in your speech.

6-1 LOCATE AND EVALUATE INFORMATION SOURCES

How can you quickly find the best information related to your specific speech goal? You can start by assessing your own knowledge and experience. Then you can move to **secondary research**, which is the process of locating information discovered by other people. This includes doing Internet and library searches for relevant books, articles, general references, and websites. Information (a.k.a. evidence) can come in written, visual, audio, and audiovisual forms. Justin, for example, discovered an interview with actress Ellen Page done by Bill Maher and posted on YouTube, an informative video posted on the USDA's website, and a chart showing the progression of this crisis over the past decade posted by the National Agriculture Statistics Service. If the information you find from secondary sources doesn't answer all your questions, you may need to conduct **primary research**, which is the process of collecting data about your topic directly from the real world.

6-1a Personal Knowledge and Experience

One form of evidence can be personal knowledge and experiences. For instance, saxophone players know how to select and care for a reed, entrepreneurs know the key features of a good business plan, and dieticians know a good deal about healthy diets. So Diane, a skilled long-distance runner, can draw from her own knowledge and experience to develop her speech on "How to Train for a Marathon." If you have personal knowledge and experience about the topic, however, you should also share your **credentials**—your experience or education that qualifies you to speak with authority on a specific subject. For Diane, establishing her credentials means briefly mentioning her training and expertise as a long-distance runner before she launches into her speech about training for a marathon (Photo 6.1).

"A couple of months ago, he had read a magazine article about the vanishing honey bees while in the doctor's office waiting room and decided that would be an interesting topic for an informative speech."

evidence: any information that clarifies, explains, or otherwise adds depth or breadth to a topic

secondary research: the process of locating information that has been discovered by other people

primary research: the process of conducting your own study to acquire the information you need

credentials: your experiences or education that qualifies you to speak with authority on a specific subject

Photo 6.1 Someone who runs marathons would have credibility when speaking about running injuries. Can you think of topics where you would have similar credibility?

6-1b Secondary Research

Most of us usually begin to develop a topic by searching online for sources and information. For example, we can search websites, blogs, YouTube, and discussion boards, as well as online libraries and databases. Some sources are available digitally either free or for a fee. Some might require a visit to a library to pick up hard copies or through interlibrary loan. We can also ask librarians for help online via "ask the librarian" links or in person at a library. Because most of us do research online these days, we begin this section with a discussion of some guidelines for doing so effectively, efficiently, and ethically. We focus specifically on using search engines, encyclopedias such as Wikipedia, commercial and nonprofit organization websites, personal and corporate blogs, and online social networks. Then we talk about different types of sources you can find both online and in local libraries and how to evaluate them.

Internet Sources

Thanks to the major advances in computer technology that have occurred in recent years—including laptops, tablets, and smart phones, as well as wireless and personal hot spot Internet accessibility—we literally have instant access to a plethora of information about any topic. The challenge for us comes in the form of sifting through all this information and evaluating it in order to select the best information to use as evidence to support our claims. We typically begin online searches by typing key words into a general search engine such as Google or Bing, metasearch engines such as Dogpile or Metacrawler, or online library databases such as EBSCOhost, GoogleScholar, or LexisNexis. Links to many different library databases can be found on any library's website. These searches reveal hits, which are links to all sorts of web pages, images, videos, articles, and other sources that include material about the key words. In our opening vignette, recall that Justin typed the words "vanishing honey bees" into Google and got 14,600,000 hits.

Many times one of the hits will be to an online encyclopedia entry in *Wikipedia*. These entries can be a good starting point for learning general information and for locating additional references about a given topic. Justin read the *Wikipedia* entry that came up from his "vanishing honey bees" search and learned that the official name for the phenomenon is colony collapse disorder. He also perused the Reference List and Further Reading list where he found articles published by the *New York Times, Science News,* and the *Proceedings of the National Academies of Science* among others. And he discovered several helpful websites listed under External Links from organizations such as the United States Department of Agriculture (USDA) and the National Honey Board. There is nothing wrong with starting the research process by reading a *Wikipedia* entry. In fact, doing so can be quite helpful.

Other hits may include commercial websites, which are created and maintained by for-profit organizations. Commercial website URLs typically end in .com. Commercial websites can be helpful for locating information about a company such as the National Honey Bee Board, for finding current or popular culture material, and for finding presentational aids. Justin found a short audiovisual clip to use in his speech about the vanishing honey bee phenomenon.

Nonprofit organization websites can be distinguished from commercial ones because their URLs will usually end in .org. These organizations are dedicated to issues or causes and can often provide emotional appeals examples. Justin found some startling statistics about $15 billion in crops the United States would lose without the bees needed to pollinate the plants.

Blogs are websites that provide personal viewpoints of their author. They can be created and maintained by an individual or an organization. They might be focused on a particular subject and include images, audios, and audiovisuals. Because they are often biased toward the opinion of the blogger, information on them may have to be verified with other sources. However, they can be a good source for finding public opinion examples and to humanize the topic. The most efficient way to find blogs is to use a blog search engine such as Google Blog Search or Blogarama. Justin found some interesting opinions on Dady Cherie's *News Junkie Post* blog. Because blogs can be written by anyone, you will need to determine whether the author is a credible source by locating his or her credentials. If you cannot determine their credentials—and, thus, their credibility as was the case for Justin—you should not use the information in your speech.

blogs: websites that provide personal viewpoints of their author

Online social networks are websites where communities of people interact with one another over the Internet. Some popular examples include Facebook, LinkedIn, Twitter, and Instagram. Like blogs, postings on these sites can be used to find supporting material to humanize a topic, appeal to emotions, and serve as presentational aids. For links to some of the websites referred to in this section, go to **Web Link 6.1, Online Source Examples,** in your MindTap for *Challenge*.

online social networks: websites where communities of people interact with one another over the Internet

Other Types of Sources

You can also find pertinent information in sources that can be found online or in a local library. These include, for example, encyclopedias, books, articles in academic journals and magazines, news media, statistical sources, biographies, quotation books, websites, and government documents.

1. **Encyclopedias.** Encyclopedia entries (including Wikipedia which we discussed earlier) can serve as a good starting point by providing an overview about your topic. But because encyclopedias provide only overviews, they should never be the only source you rely on. General encyclopedias contain short articles about a wide variety of subjects. In addition, specialized encyclopedias focus on areas such as art, history, religion, philosophy, and science (e.g., *African American Encyclopedia, Latino Encyclopedia, Asian American Encyclopedia, Encyclopedia of Computer Science, Encyclopedia of Women, Encyclopedia of Women in American Politics*). As we have already mentioned, Wikipedia is a popular research tool that is also controversial because there is no way to confirm the credibility of the people posting information in its entries. Nevertheless, reference lists and notes sections can point you in the direction of good sources you can use to develop your speech.

2. **Books.** If your topic has been around for awhile, there are likely to be books written about it. Although books are excellent sources of in-depth information about a topic, keep in mind that most of the information in a book is likely to be at least two years old by the time it is published. So books are not a good resource if your topic is very recent or if you're looking for the latest information on a topic. You can also use the call number for one book to physically locate other books on the same subject. For example, when Diane went to the shelves to locate a book called *Improving Sports Performance in Middle and Long-Distance Running*, she discovered a number of related books located in the same area including one she would also use in her speech titled *Advanced Sports Nutrition* by Dr. Dan Benardot.

3. **Articles.** Articles, which may contain more current or highly specialized information on your topic than a book would, are published in **periodicals**—magazines and journals published at regular intervals. The information in periodical articles is often

periodicals: magazines and journals that appear at fixed periods

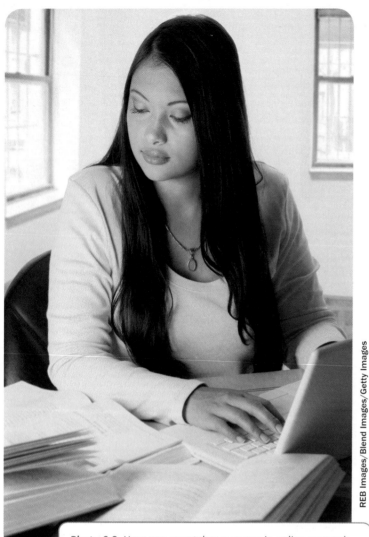

Photo 6.2 Have you ever taken a course in online research at your school's library? If not, consider doing so. You will save yourself a lot of time and will locate great sources of useful information.

REB Images/Blend Images/Getty Images

more current than that published in books because many periodicals are published weekly, biweekly, or monthly. So a periodical article is likely to be a better source if a topic is one that's currently "in the news." Most libraries subscribe to electronic databases that index periodicals and many can be found via a general online search (Photo 6.2). Justin's general search using Google, for example, revealed articles in online periodicals by *Time*, *Newsweek*, and *Science News*.

4. **News Media.** News media articles can provide facts about and interpretations of both contemporary and historical issues. They can also provide information about local issues and perspectives. Keep in mind, however, that most authors of news media articles are journalists who are not experts themselves on the topics they write about. So it is best not to rely solely on news media articles for your speech. Today, most traditional news media publications are available online (e.g., *New York Times*, *Wall Street Journal*), which makes them very accessible. Two electronic newspaper indexes that are most useful if they are available to you are the *National Newspaper Index*, which indexes five major newspapers—the *New York Times*, *Wall Street Journal*, *Christian Science Monitor*, *Washington Post*, and *Los Angeles Times*—and *Newsbank*, which provides not only the indexes but also the text of articles from more than 450 U.S. and Canadian newspapers. You might also find good information in new media online only sources such as the *Huffington Post* and the *Drudge Report*.

5. **Statistical sources.** Statistical sources present numerical information on a wide variety of subjects. When you need facts about demography, continents, heads of state, weather, or similar subjects, access one of the many single-volume sources such as *The Statistical Abstract of the United States*, that report such data. Justin, for example, consulted the *National Agriculture Statistics Service* to gather statistics about the declining honey bee population in the United States. For links to other web-based statistical sources, and an interesting essay on the improper use of statistics, go to **Web Link 6.2, Online Statistics,** in your MindTap for *Challenge*.

6. **Biographies.** When you need an account of a person's life, from thumbnail sketches to reasonably complete essays, you can consult a biographical reference source. Some examples include *Who's Who in America* and *International Who's Who*, *Contemporary Black Biography*, *Dictionary of Hispanic Biography*, *Native American Women*, *Who's Who of American Women*, and *Who's Who among Asian Americans*. You can find them easily

PUBLIC SPEAKING IN THE REAL WORLD

Daniel Day Lewis and Sally Field on Doing Research

David James/TM/20th Century Fox Film Corp/ Everett Collection

Most of us realize good research is required to develop effective research papers and public speeches. Did you know, however, that the best actors and actresses also do good research to play their roles well? Award-winning actors Daniel Day Lewis and Sally Field, for example, did their homework in order to play Abraham and Mary Todd Lincoln in the 2012 award-winning film, *Lincoln*. Day-Lewis secretly toured the Old State Capitol in Springfield, Illinois where Lincoln famously said "A house divided against itself cannot stand" to feel Lincoln's presence. He called the time he spent doing research "really important."[1] Sally

Field said, "I did every bit of research I could do" to play the role of Mary Todd Lincoln. "I read five books. I went to her childhood home [and] I visited the best collections of Lincoln and Mary memorabilia."[2] Doing good research pays off in the end—for writers, for public speakers, and even for actors.

at a local library or bookstore, as well as online at outlets such as Amazon.com. Many famous people also have some of their biographical information posted on websites. For her speech about running, Diane found biographical information about Paula Radcliff by reading several websites about the famous female marathoner. For Web Links to collections of biographical references access **Web Link 6.3, Online Biographical References,** in your MindTap for *Challenge*.

7. **Quotation books and websites.** A good quotation can be especially provocative as well as informative, and there are times you want to use a quotation from a respected person. *Bartlett's Familiar Quotations* is a popular source of quotes from both historical and contemporary figures. Some others include *The International Thesaurus of Quotations, Harper Book of American Quotations, My Soul Looks Back, 'Less I Forget: A Collection of Quotations by People of Color, The New Quotable Woman,* and *The Oxford Dictionary of Quotations.* Some popular quotation websites include *The Quotations Page* and *Quoteland.com.* You might also find good quotations on social networking sites such as Twitter and Facebook. For Web Links to quotation websites access **Web Link 6.4, Online Quotations,** in your MindTap for *Challenge*.

8. **Government documents.** If your topic is related to public policy, government documents may provide useful information. The *Federal Register* publishes daily regulations and legal notices issued by the U.S. executive branch and all federal agencies. It is divided into sections, such as rules and regulations and Sunshine Act meetings. Of special interest are announcements of hearings and investigations, committee meetings, and agency decisions and rulings. The *Monthly Catalog of United States Government Publications* covers publications of all branches of the federal government. For Web Links to several frequently used U.S. federal government documents access **Web Link 6.5, Online Government Publications,** in your MindTap for *Challenge*.

Skim Sources

Because your search of sources is likely to uncover far more information than you can use, you will want to skim sources to determine whether or not to read them in full. **Skimming** is a method of rapidly going through a work to determine what is covered and how.

skimming: a method of rapidly going through a work to determine what is covered and how

As you skim an article, think about whether the source really presents information on the area of the topic you are exploring and whether it contains any documented statistics, examples, meaningful visuals, or quotable opinions. You can start by reading the **abstract**—a short paragraph summarizing the research findings. As you a skim a book, read the table of contents carefully, look at the index, and review the headings and visuals in pertinent chapters, asking the same questions as you would for a magazine article. A few minutes spent skimming will save hours of time.

Evaluate Sources

The validity, accuracy, and reliability of sources vary. **Valid sources** report factual information that can be counted on to be true. Tabloid and gossip magazines and newspapers are generally considered less valid sources than mainline news publications that use "fact-checkers" before publishing articles. **Accurate sources** attempt to present unbiased information and often include a balanced discussion of controversial topics. For example, the *Congressional Record* presents an accurate account of what each member of U.S. Congress said on the House or Senate floor. A newspaper account of a member's speech, however, may only report part of what was said and may even distort the remark by taking it out of context. **Reliable sources** are those that have a history of presenting valid and accurate information. Four criteria can help you evaluate the validity, accuracy, and reliability of sources.

1. **Authority.** The first test of a source is the expertise of its author and/or the reputation of the publishing or sponsoring organization. When an author is listed, you can check the author's credentials through biographical references or by seeing if the author has a home page listing professional qualifications. You can use the electronic periodical indexes or check the Library of Congress to see what else the author has published in the field.

   On the Internet, you will find information that is anonymous or credited to someone whose background is not clear. In these cases, your ability to trust the information depends on evaluating the qualifications of the sponsoring organization. URLs ending in ".gov" (governmental), ".edu" (educational), and ".org" (organizational) are noncommercial sites with institutional publishers. The URL ".com" indicates that the sponsor is a for-profit organization. If you do not know whether you can trust the sources, then do not use the information.

2. **Objectivity.** Although all authors have a **stance**—an attitude, perspective, or viewpoint on a topic—be wary of information that seems excessively slanted. Documents that have been published by business, government, or public interest groups should be carefully scrutinized for obvious biases or good public relations fronts. To evaluate stance in articles and books, read the preface or identify the thesis statement. These often reveal the author's point of view. When evaluating a website, look for its purpose. Most home pages contain a purpose or mission statement (sometimes in a link called "About"). Armed with this information, you are in a better position to evaluate stance and recognize excessive source bias regarding the topic.

3. **Currency.** In general, more recent information is preferred (unless, for example, you are documenting a historical event). So be sure to consult the latest information you can find. One of the reasons for using Web-based sources is that they often provide more up-to-date information than printed sources,[3] but that isn't always the case. To determine how current the information is, you need to find out when the book was published, the article was written, the study was conducted, or the article was placed on the Web or revised. Web page dates are usually listed at the end of the article. If no dates are listed, you have no way of judging how current the information is.

4. **Relevance.** During your research, you will likely come across a great deal of interesting information. Whether that information is appropriate for your speech

abstract: a short paragraph summarizing the research findings

valid sources: report factual information that can be counted on to be true

accurate sources: attempt to present unbiased information and often include a balanced discussion of controversial topics

reliable sources: are those that have a history of presenting valid and accurate information

stance: An author's attitude, perspective or viewpoint on a topic is another matter. Relevant information is directly related to your topic and supports your main points, making your speech easier to follow and understand. Irrelevant information will only confuse listeners, so you should avoid using it no matter how interesting it is.

Go to **Web Link 6.6, Analyzing Information Sources,** in your MindTap for *Challenge* for additional criteria you can use to evaluate your sources. For more information on evaluating websites as sources of information, go to **Web Link 6.7, Evaluating Internet Sources,** in your MindTap for *Challenge.*

6-1c Primary Research

When there is little secondary research available on your topic or on a main idea you want to develop in your speech, or when you wonder whether what you are reading about is true in a particular setting, consider doing *primary research*, which is conducting your own study in the real world. But keep in mind that primary research is much more labor intensive and time consuming than secondary research, and in the professional world, much more costly. You can conduct fieldwork observations, surveys, interviews, original artifact or document examinations, or experiments.

Fieldwork Observations

You might choose to learn about a group of people and their practices by conducting *fieldwork observations,* which is a method also known as **ethnography**. Essentially, you carefully observe people or groups of people while immersed in their community. You can conduct fieldwork as a *participant observer* by engaging in interactions and activities with the people you are studying or as a *nonparticipant observer* by observing but not engaging with them. If, for instance, you are planning to talk about how social service agencies help homeless people find shelter and job training, or the process involved in adopting a pet, you can learn more by visiting or even volunteering for a period of time at a homeless shelter or humane society. By focusing on specific behaviors and taking notes on your observations and interpretations of them, you will have a record of specific information to use in your speech.

ethnography: a form of primary research based on fieldwork observations

Surveys

Recall that a *survey* is a canvassing of people to get information about their ideas and opinions. Surveys may be conducted in person, over the phone, via the Internet, or in paper-and-pencil documents. At times, your secondary research will reveal publications that summarize findings from surveys, which have been conducted by other people or organizations. At other times, you may want to conduct your own survey. For example, you might prepare a brief survey using SurveyMonkey or Qualtrix and post a link to it on Facebook or Twitter. If you decide to conduct your own survey, **Web Link 6.8, Conducting Surveys,** in MindTap for *Challenge* will provide you with important tips for collecting good information.

> **SPEECH SNIPPET**
>
> Lauren wanted to know what addicts experience as they go through recovery, so she arranged to volunteer at a local treatment center to observe while she helped out.

Interviews

Like media reporters, you may get some of your best information from an **interview**—a highly structured conversation where one person asks questions and another answers them. You might conduct your interview in person, over the telephone, or online using software such as Skype or Adobe Connect. To be effective, you'll want to select the best person to interview, prepare a solid **interview protocol** (the list of questions you plan to ask), and adhere to several ethical guidelines when conducting and then processing the actual interview.

1. **Selecting the best person.** Somewhere on campus or in the larger community are people who have expertise in the topic area of your speech. Usually a bit of research and a few emails or telephone calls will lead you to a good person to talk with about your topic. For instance, for a speech on "how to get a music recording

interview: a planned, structured conversation where one person asks questions and another answers them

interview protocol: the list of questions you plan to ask

rapport-building questions: nonthreatening questions designed to put the interviewee at ease and demonstrate your respect for them

primary questions: introductory questions about each major interview topic

secondary questions: questions designed to probe the answers given to primary questions

open questions: broadbased questions that ask the interviewee to provide perspective, ideas, information, or opinions

SPEECH SNIPPET

Scheduling an Interview

For his speech on vanishing honey bees, Justin looked at the Biology Department website and discovered a faculty member who had published two papers on vanishing honey bees. He read the papers and learned the phenomenon is referred to as Colony Collapse Disorder (CCD). He decided to try to set up an interview with the professor to learn more. Justin first called the professor and left a voicemail message, which he followed up with the following email message:

My name is Justin Martin, and I am a student here at the university. I am preparing a classroom speech on CCD, and I know you are an expert on this subject. I'd like to make an appointment to talk with you about your research findings. Would you be available to talk with me for fifteen or twenty minutes sometime this week?

contract," you might begin by asking a professor in the music department for the name of a music production agency in your community or nearby. Or you could find one by searching online. Once you find a website, you can usually find an "About Us" or "Contact Us" link on it, which will offer names, titles, email addresses, and phone numbers. You should be able to find someone appropriate to your purpose from this list. Once you have identified a potential interviewee, you should contact the person to make an appointment. You can do so either by email or telephone. Be forthright in your reasons for scheduling the interview. Whether your interview is for a class speech or for a different audience, say so. You should also tell the person how long you expect the interview to take and suggest several dates and time ranges so the person can select the date and time that works best for him or her. If you make the appointment more than a few days in advance, you should contact them again the day before the interview to confirm the date, time, and location (in person or Internet address information) of the interview.

Before your interview, make sure you have researched the topic, especially anything the interviewee has written about it. Likewise, do your research to understand the expert's credentials. Interviewees are more likely to talk with you if you appear informed, and being informed will ensure that you ask better questions. You don't want to waste the interviewee's time by asking questions you could find the answers to elsewhere.

2. **Preparing the interview protocol.** The heart of an effective interview is the **interview protocol,** which is a list of good questions you plan to ask. How many questions you ask depends on how much time you will have for the interview. Begin by listing the topics you want to cover. Exhibit 6.1 presents a list of topics for an interview with a music producer when the goal is to learning about how to find and sign new talent. Then prepare a couple of **rapport-building questions**, which are nonthreatening questions designed to put the interviewee at ease and demonstrate your respect for them. For his speech on vanishing honey bees and colony collapse disorder (CCD), Justin began his interview with "How did you get interested in doing research on CCD?"

Just as the topics in a well-developed speech are structured in an outline with main points, subpoints, and supporting material, a good interview protocol is structured into primary and secondary questions. **Primary questions** are introductory questions about each major interview topic. **Secondary questions** are follow-up questions designed to probe the answers given to primary questions. Some follow-up questions probe by simply encouraging the interviewee to continue ("And then?" "Is there more?"). Others probe into a specific detail the interviewee mentioned or failed to mention. For the music producer interview, for example, you might probe with: "You didn't mention genre. What role might that play in your decision to offer a contract?" And finally, some probe into feelings: "How did it feel when her first album went platinum?"

Open questions are broad-based queries that allow freedom regarding what specific information or opinions to talk about ("Why do you think the vanishing

Exhibit **6.1** **Music Producer Interview Topics**

- Finding artists
- Decision processes
- Criteria
- Stories of success and failure

From Verderber/Verderber/Sellnow, *Communicate!*, 14e. © 2014 Cengage Learning.

honey bee crisis is happening so quickly and dramatically today?" "What are some kinds of behaviors you have seen bees exhibit when afflicted with this disease?" "What would you recommend people like me who aren't scientists or beekeepers do to help?" "What research studies are you working on next?").[4]

Closed questions are narrowly focused and require very brief (one- or two-word) answers. Some require a simple yes or no ("Do you believe we can stop the CCD crisis?"); others need only a short response ("What do you believe to be the most significant cause of CCD?"). By asking closed questions, interviewers can control the interview and obtain specific information quickly. But the answers cannot reveal the nuances behind responses, nor are they likely to capture the complexities surrounding the topic.[5]

closed questions: narrowly focused questions that require only very brief answers

Open and closed questions may also be neutral or leading.

Neutral questions do not direct a person's answers. "What can you tell me about your work with Habitat for Humanity?" and "What criteria do you use in deciding whether or not to offer an artist a contract?" are neutral questions. By contrast, **leading questions** guide respondents toward providing certain types of information and imply that the interviewer prefers one answer over another. "What do you like about working for Habitat for Humanity?" and "Having a 'commercial sound' is an important criteria, isn't it?" are leading questions.

neutral questions: questions phrased in ways that do not direct a person's answers

leading questions: questions phrased in a way that suggests the interviewer has a preferred answer

Exhibit 6.2 lists some of the questions you might ask in an interview with a music producer.

3. **Conducting the interview.** To guide you in the process of conducting effective and ethical interviews, we offer this list of best practices.

   • **Dress professionally.** Doing so sends a message to the interviewee that you *respect* the time they are giving and take the interview seriously.

Exhibit 6.2 Sample Interview Questions

Rapport-Building Opener

How did you get interested in becoming a music producer?

Major Topic Questions

Primary Question #1: How do you find artists to consider for contract?

    Secondary Question: Is this different from the methods used by other producers?

    Secondary Question: Do artists ever come to you in other ways?

Primary Question #2: Once an artist has been brought to your attention, what course of action follows?

    Secondary Question: Do you ever just see an artist or band and immediately sign them?

    Secondary Question: What's the longest period of time you "auditioned" an artist or band before signing them?

Primary Question #3: What criteria do you use in deciding to offer a contract?

    Secondary Question: How important are the artist's age, sex, or ethnicity?

Primary Question #4: Can you tell me the story of how you came to sign one of your most successful artists?

    Secondary Question: What do you think made the artist so successful?

Primary Question #5: Can you tell me the story of an artist you signed that was not successful?

    Secondary Question: Why do you think this artist failed?

    Secondary Question: Do you think it was a mistake to sign this artist?

    Secondary Question: In retrospect, what could you or the artist have done differently that might have helped him or her succeed?

- **Be prompt.** You also demonstrate *respect* by showing up prepared to begin at the time you have agreed to. If you are conducting the interview in person, remember to allow enough time for potential traffic or parking problems.

- **Be courteous.** Begin by introducing yourself and thanking the person for taking the time to talk to you. Remember, although interviewees may enjoy talking about the subject, and be flattered, they most likely have nothing to gain from the interview. So you should let them know you are grateful for their time. Most of all, *respect* what the interviewee says regardless of what you may think of the answers.

- **Ask permission to record the interview.** If the interviewee says "no," *respect* his or her wishes and take careful notes instead.

- **Listen carefully.** At key places in the interview, repeat what the interviewee has said in your own words to be sure you really understand. This will ensure them that you will report the answers *truthfully* and *fairly* during your speech.

- **Keep the interview moving.** You do not want to rush the person, but you do want to behave *responsibly* by getting your questions answered during the allotted time.

- **Monitor your nonverbal reactions.** Demonstrate *integrity* by maintaining good eye contact. Nod to show understanding, and smile occasionally to maintain a friendly persona. How you look and act is likely to determine whether the person will warm up to you and give you an informative interview.

- **Get permission to quote.** Be sure to get permission for exact quotes. Doing so demonstrates that you *respect* the interviewee and want to report his or her ideas *honestly* and *fairly*. Doing so also communicates that you have *integrity* and strive to act *responsibly*. You might even offer to let the person see a copy of the formal outline before you give the speech. That way, he or she can double-check the accuracy of direct quotations.

- **Confirm credentials.** Before you leave, be sure to confirm your interviewee's professional title and the company or organization he or she represents. Doing so is acting *responsibly* because you'll need these details when explaining why you chose to interview this person.

- **End on time.** As with arriving promptly, ending the interview when you said you would demonstrates *respect* for the interviewee and his or her valuable time and that you act *responsibly* and with *integrity* (Photo 6.3).

transcribe: translating responses word for word into written form

- **Thank the interviewee.** Always close the interview by thanking the interviewee. This closure leads to positive rapport should you need to follow up with them later. It also demonstrates that you *respect* his or her valuable time. You may even follow up with a short thank you note after you leave.

Rob Loud/Getty Images

Photo 6.3 Ethical interviewers demonstrate honesty, respect, integrity, fairness, and responsibility by following several "best practices" for conducting interviews.

4. **Processing the interview.** Because your interview notes were probably taken in an outline or bullet-point form, the longer you wait to translate them the more difficult doing so will be. Sit down with your notes as soon as possible after the interview to make more extensive notes of the information you may want to use in your speech. If you recorded the interview, take some time to **transcribe** the responses by translating them word for word into written form. If at

any point you are not sure whether you have accurately transcribed what the person said, take a minute to telephone or email them to double-check.

Although it is typically a best practice to conduct your interviews in person, that is not always possible. When time or distance make a face-to-face interview impossible, people will instead conduct an interview over the telephone, via email, or using videoconferencing software such as Skype or Googlechat.

Original Artifact or Document Examinations

Sometimes the information you need has not been published. Rather, it may exist in an original unpublished source, such as an ancient manuscript, a diary, personal correspondence, or company files. Or you may need to view an object to get the information you need, such as a geographic feature, a building, a monument, or an artifact in a museum (Photo 6.4). Today many original artifacts and documents or illustrations of them can be found online, as well.

Experiments

You can design a study to test a **hypothesis**, which is an educated guess about a cause-and-effect relationship between two or more things. Then you can report the results of your experiment in your speech. Keep in mind that conducting experiments well can take time, and you must understand the principles

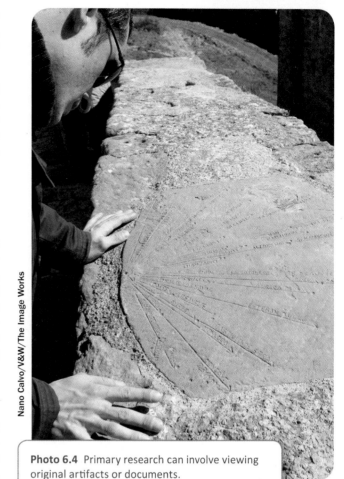

Nano Calvo/V&W/The Image Works

Photo 6.4 Primary research can involve viewing original artifacts or documents.

of the scientific process to be able to trust results of a formal experiment (Photo 6.5). However, sometimes you can do an informal experiment to test the results of a study you learn about elsewhere.

hypothesis: an educated guess about a cause-and-effect relationship between two or more things

6-2 SELECT RELEVANT INFORMATION

Once you have collected a variety of sources, you need to identify different types of information to use as evidence in your speech. You might select factual statements, expert opinions, and elaborations conveyed in written, oral, and/or visual forms.

6-2a Factual Statements

Factual statements are those that can be verified. "A recent study confirmed that preschoolers watch an average of twenty-eight hours of television a week" and "The microprocessor, which was invented by Ted Hoff at Intel in 1971, made the creation of personal computers possible" are both statements of fact that can be verified. The chart Justin found illustrating decreasing honey bee population in the U.S. over time and the recorded excerpt Marney played from Taylor Swift's platinum album are also examples of factual evidence that can be verified.

factual statements: information that can be verified

One way to verify factual information is to check it against other sources on the same subject. Never use any information that is not carefully documented unless you have corroborating sources. Factual statements may come in the form of statistics, examples, and definitions.

Photo 6.5 Each episode of the television program *MythBusters* is actually made up of a series of simple experiments.

statistics: numerical facts

Speech-Planning Action Step 3, Activity 3A will help you evaluate and compile a list of potential sources for your speeches in this course. See the Student Response box immediately following the activity for a sample of how one student completed this exercise.

Statistics

Statistics are numerical facts. Statistical statements, such as, "Only five of every ten local citizens voted in the last election" or "The national unemployment rate for January 2013 was 7.9 percent" can provide impressive support for a point, but when statistics are poorly used in a speech, they may be boring and, in some instances, downright deceiving. Here are some ethical guidelines for using statistics.

1. **Use only statistics you can verify to be reliable and valid.** Taking statistics from only the most reliable sources and double-checking any startling statistics with another source will guard against the use of faulty statistics (Photo 6.6).

2. **Use only recent statistics so your audience will not be misled.**

3. **Use statistics comparatively.** You can show growth, decline, gain, or loss by comparing two numbers. For example, according to the Bureau of Labor Statistics, the national unemployment rate for January 2013 was 7.9 percent. This statistic is more meaningful when you also mention that this figure has held about steady for three months or when you compare it with 8.3 percent in January 2012 or 5.1 percent in March 2008.

4. **Use statistics sparingly.** A few pertinent numbers are far more effective than a battery of statistics.

Photo 6.6 Ethical speakers use statistics only from the most reliable sources and double-check any startling statistics with another source.

3A SPEECH PLANNING

Gathering and Evaluating Information Sources

The goal of this activity is to help you compile a list of potential sources for your speech.

1. Brainstorm a list of keywords related to your speech goal.

2. Identify gaps in your current knowledge about the topic.

3. Use a search engine like Google or Bing to identify potential information sources.

4. Use a library database (either at the library or online) to identify additional potential information sources.

5. Skim the sources to decide which are likely to be the most useful.

6. Evaluate each source for validity, accuracy, and reliability.

7. Determine what (if any) primary research you might conduct to fill remaining gaps.

 MindTap™

Complete this activity on your MindTap for *Challenge*.

3A STUDENT RESPONSE

Gathering and Evaluating Information Sources

Speech goal: *I would like the audience to understand why honey bees are vanishing.*

1. Brainstorm a list of keywords related to your speech goal. *honey bees, bumblebees, beekeepers, colony collapse disorder*

2. Identify gaps in your current knowledge about the topic. *Because I'm a biology major and have done an eight-week internship in the field, I am familiar with the kinds of work I'll need to seek out in order to fill any gaps in my knowledge.*

3. Use a search engine like Google or Bing to identify potential information sources. *I searched using Google and found a Wikipedia entry I used as a starting point to locate other websites, a YouTube video by the USDA, an interview with a beekeeper, and an interview by Bill Maher with Ellen Page I could use in my speech.*

4. Use a library database (either at the library or online) to identify additional potential information sources. *Journal of Bee Biology, Science, Biology Quarterly, Entomol,*

5. Skim the sources to decide which are likely to be the most useful.

6. Evaluate each source for validity, accuracy, and reliability.

7. Determine what (if any) primary research you might conduct to fill remaining gaps. *I will interview my adviser, who has been studying the vanishing bees since 2006.*

5. **Display statistics visually.** Your audience is more likely to understand statistics when you illustrate them on a chart, graph, or some other visual aid.

6. **Remember that statistics are biased.** Mark Twain once said there are three kinds of lies: "lies, damned lies, and statistics."[6] Not all statistics are lies, of course, but consider the source of the statistics you'd like to use, what that source may have been trying to prove with these data, and how that situation might have influenced the way the data were collected and interpreted. In other words, evaluate the source thoughtfully for validity, accuracy, and reliability.[7]

Examples

examples: specific instances that illustrate or explain a general factual statement

Examples are specific instances that illustrate or explain a general factual statement. One or two short examples such as the following ones provide concrete details that help make a generalization meaningful.

One way a company increases its power is to acquire another company. When Delta bought out Northwest Airlines it became the world's largest airline company.

Professional figure skaters practice many long hours every day. 2010 Olympic Gold medalist Adam Rippon practices twenty to twenty-five hours per week.

hypothetical examples: specific instances based on reflections about future events

Examples can be real like these, or hypothetical. **Hypothetical examples** are specific illustrations based on reflections about future events. They develop the idea "What if . . . ?" In the following excerpt, John A. Ahladas presents some hypothetical examples of what it will be like in the year 2039 if global warming continues.

In New York, workers are building levees to hold back the rising tidal waters of the Hudson River, now lined with palm trees. In Louisiana, 100,000 acres of wetland are steadily being claimed by the sea. In Kansas, farmers learn to live with drought as a way of life and struggle to eke out an existence in the increasingly dry and dusty heartland. . . . And reports arrive from Siberia of bumper crops of corn and wheat from a longer and warmer growing season.[8]

Because hypothetical examples are not themselves factual, you must be very careful to check that the facts on which they are based are accurate. Three principles should guide your use of examples. First, use at least one example to support every generalization. A generalization without an example (or other piece of evidence to support it) can be judged by the audience as nothing more than your opinion. Second, the examples should be clear and specific enough to create a picture the audience can understand. Consider the following generalization and supporting example.

Generalization: Electronics is one of the few areas in which products are significantly cheaper today than they were in the 1980s.

Supporting example: In the mid-1980s, Motorola sold cell phones for $5,000 each; now a person can buy a cell phone for under $50.

With this single example, the listener has a vivid picture of the tremendous difference in about a thirty-year period. You can often achieve this first guideline best by sharing it in the form of a presentational aid. For example, you could show an enlarged advertisement for a Motorola cell phone in the 1980s along with a recent one.

Third, the examples you use should be representative. If cell phones were the *only* electronics product whose prices had dropped so much over that same period, this vivid example would be misleading and unethical. Any misuse of data is unethical, especially if the user knows better. To extend our thinking about illustrating examples, you might show several advertisements for different electronic devices from the 1980s and today.

Definitions

A **definition** is a statement that clarifies the meaning of a word or phrase. Definitions serve to clarify in three ways. First, definitions clarify the meaning of terminology that is specialized, technical, or otherwise likely to be unfamiliar to your audience. For example, when Dan talked about bioluminescence, he clarified the meaning of the word *bioluminescence* with the following definition: "According to *Encyclopaedia Britannica Online*, bioluminescence is the emission of visible light by living organisms like fireflies." Although dictionaries and encyclopedias contain definitions, your speech topic might be such that you have to find definitions through prominent researchers or professional practitioners. For example, in a speech about eating disorders, you might go to the website of the American Dietetic Association for your definition of the term *eating disorders*.

Second, definitions clarify words and terms that have more than one meaning. For example, because *child abuse* is a term that encompasses a broad range of behaviors, you might choose to define it in a way that acknowledges which behaviors you intend to focus on in your speech.

Third, particularly with controversial subjects, definitions clarify your stance on the subject. For example, in a speech about domestic violence against women, former U.S. Secretary of Health and Human Services Donna Shalala defined such violence as "terrorism in the home."[9]

6-2b Expert Opinions

Expert opinions are interpretations and judgments made by an authority in a particular subject area. They can help explain what facts mean or put them in perspective. "Watching twenty-eight hours of television a week is far too much for young children" and "Having a firewire port on your computer is absolutely necessary" are opinions. Whether they are expert opinions or not depends on who made the statements. An **expert** is a person recognized as having mastered a specific subject, usually through long-term study. When you use expert opinions in your speech, remember to cite their credentials.

6-2c Elaborations

Both factual statements and expert opinions can be elaborated on through anecdotes and narratives, comparisons and contrasts, or quotations.

Anecdotes and Narratives

Anecdotes are brief, often amusing stories; **narratives** are accounts, personal experiences, tales, or lengthier stories. Because holding audience interest is important and because audience attention is likely to be captured by a story, anecdotes and narratives are worth looking for or creating (Photo 6.7). The key to using them is to be sure the point of the story directly addresses the point you are making in your speech. Good stories may be humorous, sentimental, suspenseful, or dramatic. Speakers often find anecdotes and brief narratives on social media sites such as YouTube.

In the following speech excerpt, John Howard makes a point about failure to follow guidelines.

The knight was returning to the castle after a long, hard day. His face was bruised and badly swollen. His armor was dented. The plume on his helmet was broken, and his steed was limping. He was a sad sight.

The lord of the castle ran out and asked, "What hath befallen you, Sir Timothy?"

definition: a statement that clarifies the meaning of a word or phrase

expert opinions: interpretations and judgments made by authorities in a particular subject area

expert: a person recognized as having mastered a specific subject, usually through long-term study

anecdotes: brief, often amusing stories

narratives: accounts, personal experiences, tales, or lengthier stories

Photo 6.7 Much of the success of actor and stand-up comedian, Jamie Foxx, can be attributed to his ability to tell great stories.

"Oh, Sire," he said, "I have been laboring all day in your service, bloodying and pillaging your enemies to the West."

"You've been doing what?" gasped the astonished nobleman. "I haven't any enemies to the West!"

"Oh!" said Timothy. "Well, I think you do now."

There is a moral to this little story. Enthusiasm is not enough. You need to have a sense of direction.[10]

Comparisons and Contrasts

One of the best ways to give meaning to new ideas is through comparison and contrast. **Comparisons** illuminate a point by showing similarities, whereas **contrasts** highlight differences. Although comparisons and contrasts may be literal, like comparing and contrasting the murder rates in different countries or during different eras, they may also be figurative.

Figurative Comparison:

In short, living without health insurances is as much of a risk as having uncontrolled diabetes or driving without a safety belt.[11]

Figurative Contrast:

If this morning you had bacon and eggs for breakfast, I think it illustrates the difference. The eggs represented "participation" on the part of the chicken. The bacon represented "total commitment" on the part of the pig![12]

comparison: illuminating a point by showing similarities

contrast: illuminating a point by highlighting differences

QUOTATIONS

At times, information you find will be so well stated that you want to quote it directly in your speech. Because audiences want to listen to your ideas and arguments, they do not want to hear a string of long quotations. Nevertheless, a well-selected quotation may be perfect in one or two key places.

Quotations can both explain and enliven. Look for quotations that make a point in a particularly clear or vivid way. For example, in his speech "Enduring Values for a Secular Age," Hans Becherer, executive officer at Deere & Company, used this Henry Ford quote to show the importance of enthusiasm to progress:

Enthusiasm is at the heart of all progress. With it, there is accomplishment. Without it, there are only alibis.[13]

Frequently, historical or literary quotations can reinforce a point vividly. Cynthia Opheim, chair of the Department of Political Science at Southwest Texas State University, in her speech "Making Democracy Work," used this quote from Mark Twain on the frustration of witnessing legislative decision making:

There are two things you should never watch being made: sausage and legislation.[14]

plagiarism: the unethical act of representing another person's work as your own

When you use a direct quotation, you need to verbally acknowledge the person it came from. Using any quotation or close paraphrase without crediting its source is **plagiarism**, the unethical act of representing another person's work as your own.

Handout/Getty Images

Reflect on Ethics

COLDPLAY ADMITS TO PLAGIARISM

In 2005 the popular British rock band Coldplay admitted to *Rolling Stone* magazine that they plagiarized from various musical sources on their 2005 album *X & Y*. After admitting it, they also admitted that the album should have included a bibliography, discography, or references for the "borrowed" material. Despite their admission, they suffered no repercussions. Then, according to a report published in the December 5, 2008, issue of *Rolling Stone,* songwriter and guitarist Joe Satriani sued the band for "ripping off his 2004 track 'If I Could Fly'" for their own Grammy-nominated hit "Viva La Vida." The case was dismissed on September 14, 2009. Although Satriani's lawyer would not say whether a financial settlement was involved, one thing was clear: "Under terms of the dismissal, Coldplay won't have to admit to any wrongdoing."[15]

1. Which ethical principles did Coldplay demonstrate or violate in 2005?

2. Which ethical principles did the band demonstrate or violate in 2008?

3. Do you think Coldplay will plagiarize from other artists again? Why or why not? Be sure to point to ethical principles in your answer.

4. Would you consider that Satriani's actions, his lawyer's actions, and the court's actions demonstrated ethical behavior? Why or why not?

5. What would you do if you were in Coldplay's position? Satriani's position?

6-2d Diverse Cultural Perspectives

When identifying factual statements, expert opinions, and elaborations to develop your speech be sure to include a variety of cultural perspectives. For example, when Carrie was preparing her speech on proficiency testing in grade schools, she purpose-fully searched for articles written by noted Hispanic, Asian, and African American, as well as European American, authors. In addition, she interviewed two local school superintendents—one from an urban district and another from a suburban district. Doing so boosted Carrie's confidence that her speech would accurately reflect diverse perspectives on the issue of proficiency testing.

6-3 RECORD INFORMATION

As you find information to use as evidence in your speech, you need to record it accurately and keep a careful account of your sources so you can city them appropriately during your speech. How should you keep track of these sources and information? One way to do so is to compile an annotated bibliography of the sources you believe are relevant and prepare a hand-written or electronic research card for each piece of information you might use in the speech.

6-3a Annotated Bibliography

An **annotated bibliography** is a preliminary record of the relevant sources you find pertaining to your topic. It includes a short summary of the information in that source and how it might be used to support your speech. Your annotated bibliography can be used to create your research cards as well as your speech reference list later. A good annotated bibliography includes:

annotated bibliography: a preliminary record of the relevant sources you find pertaining to your topic

- A complete bibliographic citation for each source using an appropriate style guide such as APA or MLA;

- Two or three sentences summarizing the information in the source;

research cards: are individual index cards or electronic facsimiles that identify (a) one piece of information relevant to your speech, (b) a key word or theme the information represents, and (c) the bibliographic data identifying where you found it

- Two or three sentences explaining how the information might support your speech; and

- Any direct quotations you might want to include verbatim in your speech.

6-3b Research Cards

Although not necessary, some speakers find research cards useful for arranging the information they might cite during the speech. **Research cards** are individual 3 × 5 or 4 × 6-inch index cards or electronic facsimiles that identify (a) one piece of information relevant to your speech, (b) a key word or theme the information represents, and (c) the bibliographic data identifying where you found it. Then you can easily find, arrange, and rearrange individual pieces of information according to key word or theme while you prepare your speech. Exhibit 6.3 shows a sample research card.

Exhibit **6.3** **A Sample Research Card**

Topic: Fracking

Key Term/Main Idea: Health issues

Theo Colborn, president of The Endocrine Disruption Exchange in Paonia, Colorado, believes that some drilling and fracking additives that can end up in produced water are neurotoxic; among these are 2-butoxyethanol. "If you compare [such chemicals] with the health problems the people have," Colborn says, "they match up."

From Verderber/Verderber/Sellnow, *Communicate!* 14e. © 2014 Cengage Learning.

The number of sources and pieces of information you will need depends in part on the type of speech you are giving and your own expertise. A five-minute speech on the causes and effects of Ebola would probably require three or more research cards from different sources under each heading. Selecting and using a variety of information types from several different sources helps you develop an original approach to your topic, a broader research base, and multiple perspectives on it.

Activity 3B, will help you prepare research cards for the sources you compiled in Activity 3A. See the Student Response box after the activity for a sample of how one student completed this exercise.

(3B) SPEECH PLANNING

Record Relevant Information

The goal of this activity is to review the source material that you identified in Action Step Activity 3A and to record specific information you might use on research cards.

1. Carefully read all sources and information you have identified and evaluated as appropriate for your speech.

2. As you review an information item you think might be useful in your speech, record it on a research card or on the appropriate electronic research card form available in MindTap for *Challenge*.

 MindTap™

Complete this activity on your MindTap for *Challenge*.

(3B) STUDENT RESPONSE

Record Relevant Information

Speech goal: *I would like the audience to agree that domestic violence is a problem, realize some of its underlying causes, and be convinced of strategies to reduce domestic violence in the United States today.*

Card 1

Topic: *The problem*

Heading: *Scope*

Three million women per year are physically abused by their husbands or boyfriends. And about 31 percent of American women report being sexually or physically abused by a male partner during her lifetime. (In other words, of the twenty women in my speech class, about six will be assaulted by a male partner during her lifetime!)

Futures without Violence website (2009). "The Facts on Domestic, Dating and Sexual Violence." http://www.futureswithoutviolence.org. Accessed February 26, 2013.

Card 2

Topic: *The problem*

Heading: *Severity*

There were 248,300 rapes/sexual assaults in 2007, more than 500 per day, up from 190,600 in 2005.

Goodman, A. (2010, March 2). Domestic Violence: A pre-existing condition? TruthDig.com. Retrieved on February 26, 2013 at http://www.truthdig.com/report/item/domestic_ violence_a_pre-existing_condition_20100302/

Card 3

Topic: *Causes*

Heading: *Power and control*

Men often resort to violence to gain power over women when they feel threatened and subordinate and want to maintain a sense of control.

Johnson, Michael P., and Ferraro, Kathleen J. (2000). "Research on domestic violence in the 1990s: Making distinctions." Journal of Marriage and Family, 62(4), pp. 948–963.

Card 4

Topic: *Causes*

Heading: *Power and control*

Most abused women would leave if human capital such as housing and employment were more readily available to them.

Christy-McMullin, K., and Shobe, M. A. (2007). "The role of economic resources and human capital with woman abuse." Journal of Policy Practice, 6(1), pp. 3–26.

oral footnote: reference to an original source, made at the point in the speech where information from that source is presented

6-4 CITE SOURCES

In your speeches, as in any communication in which you use information beyond your own personal knowledge and experience, you need to acknowledge the sources. Specifically mentioning your sources not only helps the audience evaluate the content but also adds to your credibility. Frankly, failure to cite sources constitutes plagiarism. Just as you would provide internal references or footnotes in a written document, so must you provide oral footnotes during your speech. **Oral footnotes** are references to an original source, made at the point in the speech where information from that source is presented. The key to preparing oral footnotes is to include enough information for listeners to access the sources themselves and to offer enough credentials to enhance the credibility of the information you are citing. You need to cite oral footnotes for any information including, for example, visuals, audiovisuals, and interviews. Justin provided this oral footnote for his interview with the honey bee expert: "I had the privilege of interviewing one of the nation's leading colony collapse disorder scholars, Dr. Susan Stromme. She explained that the radiation emitted from cell phones is one cause of death for the bees." Exhibit 6.4 gives several examples of appropriate speech source citations.

Speech-Planning Action Step 3, Activity 3C, will help you prepare oral citations for the sources you recorded in Activity 3B. See the Student Response box after the activity for a sample of how one student completed this exercise.

IMPROMPTU SPEECH CHALLENGE

Citing oral footnotes

Select a newspaper article, magazine article, book, or Internet source from a stack of materials provided by your instructor. Select a piece of information and prepare a short impromptu speech articulating how you would cite the source effectively in a speech and why.

3C SPEECH PLANNING

Citing Sources

On the back of each research card, write a short phrase you can use as an oral footnote during your speech.

3C STUDENT RESPONSE

Citing Sources

According to J. S. Gordon in his book Helping Survivors of Domestic Violence: The Effects of Medial, Mental Health, and Community Services, *domestic violence is the number-one reason for emergency room visits by women.*

xhibit **6.4** **Appropriate Speech Source Citations**

Books

Cite the title of the book and the name of its author. You may cite the book's publication date or the author's credentials if doing so boosts credibility.

"Thomas Friedman, noted international editor for the *New York Times*, stated in his book *Hot, Flat, and Crowded. . .*"

"But to get a complete picture we have to look at the statistics. According to the 2007 *Statistical Abstract*, the level of production for the European Economic Community rose from . . ."

Journal or magazine articles

Cite the name and date of the publication in which you found the article. You may cite the article's author and title if doing so adds credibility.

"According to an article about the Federal Reserve in last week's *Newsweek* magazine . . ."

"In the latest Gallup poll cited in the February 10 issue of *Newsweek* . . ."

"Timothy Sellnow, professor of communication at The University of Kentucky, wrote in an article published in 2009 in the *Journal of Applied Communication* that . . ."

Newspapers

Cite the name of the newspaper and date of the article. You may cite the article's author and his or her credentials if it adds credibility.

"According to a May 2010 article in the *Washington Post*. . ."

Interviews

Cite the name and credentials of the person interviewed and the date the interview took place. If you cite the interview more than once, you need only cite the interviewee's name in subsequent oral footnotes.

"In an interview with *The Wall Street Journal* in February 22, 2010, Treasury Secretary Timothy Geithner stated . . ."

"In my telephone interview on September 29 with Dr. Susan Nissen, physician for physical medicine in Kansas City, Kansas, I learned that . . ."

Internet sources

Cite the website's author, his or her credentials, and the date of the site's most recent revision. If there is no author, cite the credentials of the website's sponsoring organization. Do not cite the URL as part of your oral footnote.

"According to a January 2010 posting on the official website of the American Heart Association . . ."

Television programs

Cite the name of the program and the date of the original broadcast. You may also cite the name of the reporter for news programs if it boosts credibility.

"According to an October 2009 CNN special broadcast called 'Latino in America'. . ."

Public speeches

Cite the name and credentials of the speaker, as well as the occasion and date of the speech.

"In a speech on the need for fi nancial education during times of financial crises delivered to the Kansas City Federal Reserve Interagency Consumer Complaint Conference in April of 2009, Susan C. Keating, president of the National Foundation of Credit Counseling, stated . . ."

Reflection and Assessment

Effective speeches are developed by doing good research. To do good research, you need to know where to locate different types of information and sources, as well as how to evaluate them. You also need to know how to integrate the information into your speech effectively and ethically. To assess how well you've learned what we've discussed in this chapter, answer the following questions. If you have trouble answering any of them, go back and review that material. Once you can answer each question accurately, you are ready to move ahead to read the next chapter.

1. How do you locate and evaluate information sources to develop your topic?
2. What information types might you use as relevant evidence to support your topic?
3. How can you go about recording information accurately?
4. How do you cite sources appropriately?

 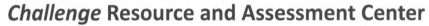

Challenge Resource and Assessment Center

Now that you have read Chapter 6, go to your MindTap for *The Challenge of Effective Speaking in a Digital Age* for quick access to the electronic resources that accompany this text. These resources include the following:

- **Study tools** that will help you assess your learning and prepare for exams (*digital glossary, key term flash cards, review quizzes*).
- **Activities and assignments** that will help you hone your knowledge and build your public speaking skills throughout the course (Practice, Do). Many of these activities allow you to compare your answers with those provided by the authors and, if requested, submit your answers to your instructor.
- **Media resources**—all of which are available on your MindTap for *Challenge*— will help you explore communication concepts online (Practice), develop your speech outlines (Do), watch and critique videos of sample speeches (Do), and upload your speech videos for instructor feedback and critique other students' speeches (Do).
- **Speech-Planning Action Steps, identified earlier in the chapter.**
  - **3A:** Gathering and Evaluating Information Sources (p. 109)
  - **3B:** Record Relevant Information (p. 114)
  - **3C:** Citing Sources (p. 116)
- **Web Links that provide you with additional information or resources related to the topics discussed in this chapter.**
  - **6.1** Online Source Examples (p. 99)
  - **6.2** Online Statistics (p. 100)
  - **6.3** Online Bibliographical References (p. 101)
  - **6.4** Online Quotations (p. 101)
  - **6.5** Online Government Publications (p. 101)
  - **6.6** Analyzing Information Sources (p. 103)
  - **6.7** Evaluating Internet Sources (p. 103)
  - **6.8** Conducting Surveys (p. 103)

- **Video resources allow you to see other students giving speeches and record your own speech.**

    1. Use your interactive Video Activities on your MindTap for *Challenge* to watch, analyze, see the transcript and outlines for the student speech, "Teaching Critical Media Studies in Elementary Schools."
    2. View how other students cite their sources in their speeches. Or go to the Practice and Present section of your MindTap to record a speech you're working on, upload it, and ask your peers for their feedback. What feedback could you use to fine-tune your oral source citations before you give your speech in class?

Applying What You've Learned

1. **Impromptu Speech Activity:** Draw an information source from a box in the front of the room. It might be a book; magazine or academic journal article; printout from a discussion board, blog, or website; and so forth. Read or skim the source. Then prepare a proper APA reference citation. Go to the front of the room and write the citation on the board. Then present a two- to three-minute informative speech on how well the source meets each of the four evaluation criteria for a speech on a related topic. Provide evidence for your assessments. Be sure to quote something from the information source using a proper oral footnote during the speech.

2. **Assessment Activity A:** Go to the VS Video Productions website and click on Corporate Videos. What kinds of information and information sources are used to compel viewers to use this company's services? Which are most compelling to you and why?

3. **Assessment Activity B:** Watch an opening story on a local or national news broadcast. Identify what information types and sources are used to support the story. Do they meet the criteria for good sources? Why or why not?

7 "organizing the speech body"

WHAT'S THE POINT?
WHEN YOU'VE FINISHED THIS
CHAPTER, YOU'LL BE ABLE TO:

7-1 Organize your speech body into two to four main points using an appropriate main point pattern

7-2 Construct a clear thesis statement

7-3 Develop each main point with subpoints and supporting material

7-4 Create effective transitions

7-5 Outline the speech body

 MindTap™

Review the chapter **Learning Objectives** and **Start** with quick warm up activity.

4 **Organize ideas into a well-structured outline (the body).**

A. Identify two to four main points.
B. Write a thesis statement with main point preview.
C. Develop your main points with subpoints and supporting material.
D. Outline the speech body (with transitions).

Ethical communicators behave responsibly by taking the time to organize the material they plan to share in their speeches.

Alberto Pomares/Getty Images

©CoraMax/Shutterstock

Katie and Alyssa are taking a public speaking course online over the summer. That way they can still make progress toward graduation while living at home where they both have great summer jobs. Most of the class is conducted asynchronously; but every Monday afternoon from 1:00–3:00 p.m., all students are required to "attend class virtually" using Adobe Connect. That's when students deliver their formal speeches. Matt just finished delivering his speech when Alyssa got a text from Katie:

> *"Matt's speech was awesome! So many powerful stories!"*
>
> *Alyssa replied: "Great stories but hard to follow. What were his main points?"*
>
> *Katie responded, "Hmmm . . . Not sure. I hope mine will be easier to follow."*
>
> *"Mine too," Alyssa exclaimed. "Uh oh. Late for work. CU."*

Read, highlight, and take notes online.

"A well-organized speech has three identifiable parts: an introduction, a body, and a conclusion."

Katie and Alyssa's experience is not that unusual. Even well-known speakers sometimes give speeches that are hard to follow. Yet when your speech is well organized, you are far more likely to achieve your goal. In this chapter and the next, we explain the fourth speech plan action step: Organize your ideas into a well-structured outline. A well-organized speech has three identifiable parts: an introduction, a body, and a conclusion. This chapter focuses on the speech body and the next one will examine introductions and conclusions. Here we describe how to: (1) identify **main points** and arrange them using an appropriate main point pattern; (2) use them to construct a clear thesis statement; (3) develop each main point with appropriate supporting material (evidence and reasoning); (4) create transitions that move the speech smoothly from one main point to the next; and (5) outline the speech body.

7-1 ORGANIZE MAIN POINTS

Organizing, the process of arranging your speech material, is guided by what you learned from your audience analysis. Begin by identifying two to four main points that will help you achieve your speech goal. In fact, the difference between an effective five-minute speech and an effective twenty-five-minute speech with the same speech goal is not the number of main points, but the extent to which each one is developed with supporting material.

7-1a Identify Main Point Ideas

For some goals, identifying main point ideas is easy. For example, if your goal is to demonstrate how to create a website, your main ideas will likely be the steps involved in developing a very basic one. Most times, however, determining main point ideas is more complex. How can you identify the main ideas when they aren't so obvious? First, begin by listing the ideas you believe relate to your specific goal. You will probably find it easy to list as many as nine or more. Second, eliminate ideas that you believe this audience already understands. Third, eliminate any ideas that might be too complicated or too broad for this audience to comprehend in the time allotted. Fourth, check to see if some of the ideas can be grouped together under a broader theme. Finally, from the ideas that remain, choose two to four that will help you accomplish your specific speech goal.

Let's look at how Katie used these steps to identify the main point ideas for her speech to inform about "the growing problem of Adderall® use among college students." To begin, Katie listed ideas she discovered while doing her research.

what is a prescription drug

what is Adderall

what are the ingredients in Adderall

main points: complete sentence statements of the two to four central ideas the audience needs to understand for your speech goal to be realized

organizing: the process of arranging your speech material, guided by what you learned from your audience analysis

how is Adderall made

what is the history of Adderall

who takes Adderall

why is Adderall prescribed

what are its benefits

what are its risks

how many college students take Adderall without a prescription

what are the demographics of college students who take Adderall without a prescription

why do college students who don't have a prescription take it (perceived benefits)

what are the benefit myths

what are the actual results and/or consequences of taking Adderall without a prescription

Second, Katie eliminated the idea "what is a prescription drug" because she knew her audience already understood this. Third, Katie decided the ingredients, history, and how Adderall is made were too broad to cover adequately in the time allotted for the speech and were not directly related to her goal. Fourth, Katie noticed that several ideas seemed to be related. What is Adderall, why is it prescribed, who takes it, as well as its risks and benefits seemed to go together. How many take it, demographics, and perceived benefits of college students who take Adderall without a prescription also seemed to be related. And benefit myths and actual results/consequences could be grouped together. Finally, Katie decided that her main point ideas would be (1) understanding the nature and purpose of Adderall as a prescription drug, (2) its growing popularity as a study aid among college students, and (3) problems involved with using Adderall without a prescription. This process left Katie with three broad main point ideas she could focus on to develop her speech. The figure below illustrates what Katie's list looked like after she finished her analysis and synthesis.

Speech-Planning Action Step 4, Activity 4A, will help you identify main point ideas to use for your speeches in this course. See the Student Response box after the activity for a sample of how one student completed this exercise.

4A SPEECH PLANNING

Identify Main Point Ideas

1. List all the ideas you found that relate to your speech topic.

2. Next, limit the number by:

   a. Drawing a line through each idea you believe the audience already understands or that seems too broad or too complicated to cover in the time allotted.

   b. Combining ideas that can be grouped together under a common theme.

3. From the remaining ideas, choose the two to four that will best accomplish your speech goal.

Do this activity with Speech Builder Express. Access this activity on your MindTap for *Challenge*.

Remember the number of main point ideas does not determine speech length, but rather, how thoroughly you develop each of them. The same two to four main point ideas can be developed into a speech that will last for three to five minutes, five to seven minutes, eight to ten minutes, or even into a fifty-minute major presentation.

7-1b Word Main Points

Once you have identified your two to four main point ideas, you can begin to shape each one into a clear main point. Write out a complete sentence for each main area. Let's look at how Katie did this.

Recall that Katie's main point ideas are understanding the nature and purpose of Adderall as a prescription drug, its growing popularity as a study aid among college students, and the risks involved in doing so. Suppose she wrote her first draft of main points as follows:

    I. What exactly is Adderall, and why is it prescribed?

   II. College student use

  III. Risks

Some people refer to this first version of wording main points as a **preparation outline**. It provides a draft of main points but doesn't specify clearly how each main point is related to the speech goal. To begin clarifying these relationships, Katie next needs to create complete sentences for each. So she might clarify her main points like this:

    I. What exactly is Adderall?

   II. An increasing number of American college students are using Adderall.

  III. Abusing Adderall is risky.

Study these statements. Do they seem a bit vague? Sometimes, the first draft of a main point doesn't quite capture what we want to say. So we need to rework our points to make them clearer. Let's consider Katie's draft statements more carefully. Her three main points are complete sentences. To assure herself that she has achieved the best wording for her main points, Katie next applies two test questions to them.

preparation outline: provides a starting point of main points but doesn't specify clearly how each main point is related to the goal

Identify Main Point Ideas

General goal: *I want to inform my audience.*

Specific goal: *I want my audience to understand the basics of seasonal affective disorder (SAD).*

1. List all the ideas you found that relate to your speech.

    what is SAD
    symptoms
    causes of SAD
    historical background
    discoverer
    types of depression
    vitamin deficiencies
    locations and prevalence
    diagnoses
    medical treatments
    organic treatments
    therapeutic treatments
    the role of sunshine
    light therapy
    myths
    realities

2. Next limit the number by:

    a. Drawing a line through each idea you believe the audience already understands or that seems too broad or too complicated to cover in the time allotted.

    b. Combining ideas that can be grouped together under a common theme.

3. From the remaining ideas, choose the two to four that will best accomplish your speech goal.

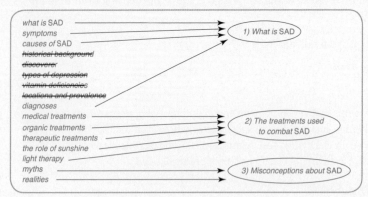

Main point Ideas:

Causes
Symptoms
Misconceptions
Treatments

1. **Is the relationship between each main point statement and the goal statement clearly specified?** Katie's first main point statement doesn't indicate what purposes Adderall serves as a prescription medicine. So she improved this statement by saying:

What exactly is Adderall actually prescribed for?

Similarly, she improved the second main point statement by saying:

Adderall abuse is becoming increasingly popular among American college students.

And she revised the third main point to state:

Abusing Adderall as a study aid is dangerous.

2. **Are the main points parallel in structure? Parallel structure** means the main points follow the same structural pattern, often using the same introductory words. Parallel structure is not a requirement, but it can help the audience recognize main points when you deliver your speech. So Katie made one more small adjustment:

> I. *First, what exactly is Adderall, and why is it prescribed?*
>
> II. *Second, a growing number of American college students are using Adderall.*
>
> III. *Third, abusing Adderall as a study aid is dangerous.*

Parallel structure can be achieved in many ways. Katie used numbering: "first . . . second . . . third." Another way is to start each sentence with an active verb. Suppose Adam wants his audience to understand the steps involved in writing an effective job application cover letter. Adam's first draft of main points was:

> I. *Format the heading elements correctly.*
>
> II. *The body of the letter should be three paragraphs long.*
>
> III. *When concluding, use "sincerely" or "regards."*
>
> IV. *Then you need to proofread the letter carefully.*

Adam revised his main points to make them parallel by using active verbs (italicized):

> I. *Format* the heading elements correctly.
>
> II. *Organize* the body into three paragraphs.
>
> III. *Conclude* the letter with "sincerely" or "regards."
>
> IV. *Proofread* the letter carefully.

parallel structure: when the main points follow the same structural pattern, often using the same introductory words

7-1c Select a Main Point Pattern

A speech can be organized in many different ways. Remember your objective is to help the audience make sense of the material. Although speeches may follow many different organizational patterns, four fundamental types are time (a.k.a. sequential or chronological) order, narrative order, topical order, and logical reasons order.

1. **Time order**, sometimes called *sequential order or chronological order*, arranges main points in sequence or by steps in a process. When you explain how to do something, how to make something, how something works, or how something happened, you use time order (Photo 7.1). Adam's speech on the *steps* in writing a job application and cover letter is an example of time order. Here is another example.

   General goal: *I want to inform my audience.*

time order: organizing the main points in sequence or by steps in a process

narrative order: organizing the main points as a story or series of stories

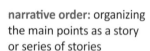
Specific goal: I want the audience to understand the four steps involved in developing a personal network.

Main Points:

> I. First, analyze your current networking potential.
>
> II. Second, position yourself in places for opportunity.
>
> III. Third, advertise yourself.
>
> IV. Fourth, follow up on contacts.

2. **Narrative order** conveys ideas through a story or series of stories. Narrative order is rooted in narrative theory, which suggests that one important way people communicate is through storytelling. We use stories to teach and to learn, to entertain, and to make sense of the world around us.[3] Although a narrative may be presented in chronological order, it may also use a series of flashbacks or flash forwards to increase dramatic effect. Each main point may be an event in a single story or each main point may be a different story that illustrates the thesis. Lana shared her story about having anorexia using three stories as main points.

General goal: I want to inform my audience.

Specific goal: I want my audience to understand how anorexia nervosa affects the lives of its victims and their loved ones.

Main points:

> I. First, let's talk about the story of a typical day as a recovering anorexic.
>
> II. Next, let's focus on a historical account about how I became anorexic.
>
> III. Finally, let's discuss an inspirational story about two people who basically saved my life.

3. **Topical order** arranges the main points using some logical relationship among them. Main points might progress from general to specific, least important to most important, most to least familiar, and so forth. Katie used topical order from least to most important for achieving her speech goal. Here is another example:

General goal: I want to inform my audience.

Specific goal: I want the audience to understand three proven methods for ridding our bodies of harmful toxins.

Main Points:

> *I. One proven method for ridding our bodies of harmful toxins is keeping well hydrated.*
>
> *II. A second proven method for ridding our bodies of harmful toxins is reducing our intake of animal products.*
>
> *III. A third proven method for ridding our bodies of harmful toxins is eating more natural whole foods.*

4. **Logical reasons order** organizes the main points according to reasons for accepting the thesis as desirable or true. Logical reasons order is often used when your general goal is to persuade (Photo 7.2).

General goal: I want to persuade my audience.

Specific goal: I want the audience to donate money to the United Way.

Main points:

> *I. When you donate to the United Way, your one donation covers many charities.*
>
> *II. When you donate to the United Way, you can stipulate which charities you wish to support.*
>
> *III. When you donate to the United Way, you know that a high percentage of your donation will go directly to the charities you've selected.*

These four organizational patterns are the most basic ones. We will introduce you to several additional patterns in later chapters.

Speech-Planning Action Step 4, Activity 4B, will help you organize your main points. See the Student Response box immediately following the activity for a sample of how one student completed this exercise.

Jeff Greenberg/Alamy

Photo 7.1 Time order is appropriate when you are showing others how to do or make something or how something works.

topical order: organizing the main points of the speech by categories or divisions of a subject

logical reasons order: organizing the main points of a persuasive speech by the reasons that support the speech goal

Kevork Djansezian/Getty Images

Photo 7.2 Logical reasons order is often used when trying to persuade others to agree with you or to take action.

4B) SPEECH PLANNING

Organize Main Points

The goal of this activity is to help you organize your main points.

1. Write your general and specific speech goal statements.

2. Write down the two to four main point ideas you identified in Activity 4A.

3. Write one sentence that summarizes what you want your audience to know about each idea.

4. Review the main points as a group.

   a. Is the relationship between each main point statement and the goal statement clearly specified? If not, revise.

   b. Are the main points parallel in structure? If not, consider why and revise.

5. Identify the organizational pattern you used.

 MindTap™

Do this activity with Speech Builder Express. Access this activity on your MindTap for *Challenge*.

7-2 CONSTRUCT A CLEAR THESIS STATEMENT

thesis statement: a one or two-sentence summary of the speech that incorporates the general and specific goals and previews the main points

Once you have identified and worded your main points using an appropriate organizational pattern, you are ready to construct your thesis statement. A **thesis statement** is a one- or two-sentence summary of your speech that incorporates your general and specific goals and previews the main points of the speech. A thesis statement provides a blueprint of the speech body organization. Exhibit 7.1 provides several examples of specific speech goals and thesis statements.

7-3 DEVELOP MAIN POINTS

subpoints: statements that elaborate on a main point

supporting material: developmental material, including personal experiences, examples, illustrations, anecdotes, statistics, and quotations

listener relevance link: a statement alerting listeners about how a main point or subpoint relates to them or why they should care about it

Once you have identified the main points and used them to form your thesis statement, you need to develop each one with subpoints and supporting material. **Subpoints** are statements that elaborate on a main point. A main point may have two, three, or more subpoints depending on the complexity of it. Each subpoint is developed further with **supporting material**—evidence you gathered through secondary and primary research along with the logical reasoning you use to link it to the main point it supports. You can identify subpoints by sorting through the research you compiled in your annotated bibliography and/or on research cards to find evidence (e.g., definitions, examples, facts, statistics, stories) that supports each of your main points. Once you have listed the items of information that make the point, look for relationships between and among ideas. As you analyze, you can draw lines connecting items of information that fit together logically and cross out information that seems irrelevant. Finally, one subpoint under each main point should be a **listener relevance link**, a statement alerting listeners to why the main point is important to them.

Subpoints should also be written in full sentences. It also helps to include internal references for information you found in secondary sources. Doing so will remind you to cite it during the speech, which will enhance listeners' perception of you as credible

(4B) STUDENT RESPONSE

Activity

Organize Main Points

1. Write your general and specific goal statements.

   General Goal: *I want to inform my audience.*

   Specific Goal: *I want my audience to understand the three tests to determine whether a diamond is real.*

2. Write down the two to four main point ideas identified in Activity 4A.

   Acid test

   Streak test

   Hardness test

3. Write one sentence that summarizes what you want your audience to know about each idea.

   I. *One way to identify a diamond is by using the acid test.*

   II. *The streak test can also be used to identify a diamond.*

   III. *You can also identify a diamond by using the hardness test.*

4. Review the main points as a group.

   a. Is the relationship between each main point statement and the goal-statement clearly specified? If not, revise.

   No. The purpose of each test is to identify whether the diamond is real. The following revision puts emphasis in the right place.

   Revision:

   I. *One way to identify whether a diamond is real is by using the acid test.*

   II. *The streak test can also be used to identify whether a diamond is real.*

   III. *You can also identify whether a diamond is real by using the hardness test.*

   b. Are the main points parallel in structure? If not, consider why and revise.

   Revision:

   I. *One way to determine whether a diamond is real is to use the acid test.*

   II. *A second way to determine whether a diamond is real is to use the streak test.*

   III. *A third way to determine whether a diamond is real is to use the hardness test.*

5. Identify the organizational pattern you used.

   Topical

and help you avoid plagiarism. As with main points, subpoints should be revised until they are clearly stated.

7-4 CREATE TRANSITIONS

Transitions are words, phrases, or sentences that show the relationship between two ideas. Transitions act like tour guides leading the audience from point to point throughout the speech. Good transitions are certainly important in writing; however, they are crucial for formal public speeches. If listeners get lost or think they've missed something, they can't go back and check as they can when reading. Transitions come in the form of section transitions and signposts.

transitions: words, phrases, or sentences that show a relationship between, or bridge, two ideas

Exhibit 7.1 Sample Speech Goals and Thesis Statements

General goal: I want to inform my audience.

Specific goal: I want my audience to understand how to improve their grades in college.

Thesis statement: Three proven techniques for improving test scores in college are to attend classes regularly, develop a positive attitude, and study efficiently.

General goal: I want to inform my audience.

Specific goal: I want the audience to understand the benefits of volunteering.

Thesis statement: Some important benefits of volunteering include helping underprivileged populations, supporting nonprofit organizations, and improving your own self-esteem.

General goal: I want to persuade my audience.

Specific goal: I want my audience to believe that parents should limit the time their children spend viewing television.

Thesis statement: Parents should limit the time their children spend viewing television because heavy television viewing increases violent tendencies in children.

General goal: I want to persuade my audience.

Specific goal: I want my audience to believe that they should learn to speak Spanish.

Thesis statement: You should learn to speak Spanish because it will benefit you personally, economically, and practically.

4C SPEECH PLANNING

Construct a Thesis Statement

The goal of this activity is to develop a well-worded thesis statement for your speech.

1. Write the general and specific goals you identified in Activity 4A.

2. List the main point ideas you identified in Activity 4A.

3. Now write one or two complete sentences that combine your goals with your main point ideas.

Do this activity with Speech Builder Express. Access this activity on your MindTap for *Challenge*.

---

section transitions: complete sentences that show the relationship between, or bridge, major parts of a speech

Section transitions are complete sentences that show the relationship between and bridge major parts of the speech. They typically summarize what has just been said in one main point and preview the one coming up next. Essentially, section transitions are the glue that holds the macrostructure of your speech together.

For example, suppose Adam has just finished the introduction of his speech on creating a cover letter and is now ready to launch into his main points. Before stating his first main point, he might say, "Creating a good cover letter is a four-step process. Now let's consider the first one." When his listeners hear this transition, they are signaled to

4C STUDENT RESPONSE

Activity

Construct a Thesis Statement

1. Write the general and specific goals you identified in Activity 4A.
   General goal: I want to inform my audience.
   Specific goal: I want my audience to understand the nature of seasonal affective disorder.

2. List the main point ideas you identified in Activity 4A.
   Causes
   Symptoms
   Misconceptions
   Treatments

3. Now write one or two complete sentences that combine your general and specific goals with your main point ideas.
   Seasonal affective disorder, also known as SAD, is a fairly common mood disorder people experience regularly in winter, summer, spring, or autumn. To better understand the nature of this form of depression, let's look at its causes and symptoms, some misconceptions, and several treatment methods.

mentally prepare to listen to and remember the first main point. When he finishes his first main point, he may say: "Now that we understand what is involved in creating the heading elements, we can move on to discuss what to include in the body of the letter."

Section transitions are important for two reasons. First, they help the audience follow the organization of ideas in the speech. Second, they help audience members remember information.

Signposts are words or phrases that connect pieces of supporting material to the main point or subpoint they address. Whereas section transitions are complete sentences, signposts are usually one-word references. Sometimes, signposts highlight numerical order: "first," "second," "third," or "fourth." Sometimes, they help the audience focus on a key idea (Photo 7.3): "foremost," "most important," or "above all." They can also be used to signify an explanation: "to illustrate," "for example," "in other words," "essentially," or "to clarify." Signposts can also signal that an important idea, or even the speech itself, is coming to an end: "in short," "finally," "in conclusion," or "to summarize." Just as section transitions serve as the glue that holds your macrostructure together, signposts serve as the glue that holds your subpoints and supporting material together within each main point.

signposts: words or phrases that connect pieces of supporting material to the main point or subpoint they address

formal speech outline: a sentence representation of the hierarchical and sequential relationships among the ideas presented in the speech

7-5 OUTLINE THE SPEECH BODY

Once you have developed each main point with supporting material and formed transition statements to link them together, you are ready to begin putting a formal speech outline together. A **formal speech outline** is a sentence representation of the hierarchical and sequential relationships among ideas in the speech. In other words, it is a diagram of your speech material. For most speeches, you will use main points (Roman

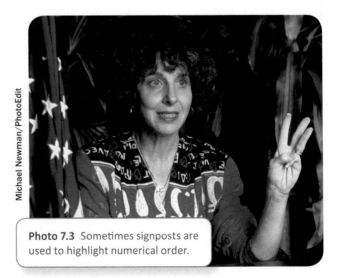

Michael Newman/PhotoEdit

Photo 7.3 Sometimes signposts are used to highlight numerical order.

I. **Main point one**
    A. Subpoint A for main point one
        1. Sub-subpoint one
           a. Elaboration material (if needed)
           b. Elaboration material (if needed)
        2. Sub-subpoint two
           a. Elaboration material (if needed)
           b. Elaboration material (if needed)
    B. Subpoint B for main point one
        1. Sub-subpoint one
           a. Elaboration material (if needed)
           b. Elaboration material (if needed)
        2. Sub-subpoint two
           a. Elaboration material (if needed)
           b. Elaboration material (if needed)

II. **Main point two**
    A. Subpoint A for main point two
        1. Sub-subpoint one
           a. Elaboration material (if needed)
           b. Elaboration material (if needed)
        2. Sub-subpoint two
           a. Elaboration material (if needed)
           b. Elaboration material (if needed)
    B. Subpoint B for main point two
        1. Sub-subpoint one
           a. Elaboration material (if needed)
           b. Elaboration material (if needed)
        2. Sub-subpoint two
           a. Elaboration material (if needed)
           b. Elaboration material (if needed)
        3. Sub-subpoint three
           a. Elaboration material (if needed)
           b. Elaboration material (if needed)
    C. Subpoint C for main point two
        1. Sub-subpoint one
           a. Elaboration material (if needed)
           b. Elaboration material (if needed)
        2. Sub-subpoint two
           a. Elaboration material (if needed)
           b. Elaboration material (if needed)
        3. Sub-subpoint three
           a. Elaboration material (if needed)
           b. Elaboration material (if needed)
        . . . etc.

SPEECH SNIPPET

Section Transitions

In her speech about methods of disciplining children, Darla used this section transition between her first and second main point: "Certainly, the behavioral modification approach based on B. F. Skinner's work can be an effective method for disciplining children. It is not the only method, however, which leads us to a second method, based on Sigmund Freud's work."

IMPROMPTU SPEECH CHALLENGE

Select a favorite YouTube video you've seen. Prepare a two- to three-minute speech explaining why it is your favorite. Your speech should consist of a thesis statement as the introduction, the two to four main points linked with section transitions for the body, and a thesis restatement for the conclusion. Be sure to consider the wording of your thesis statement and the best organizational pattern for your main points. Finally, support each main point with one or two subpoints.

---

numerals: I, II, III, etc.), subpoints (capital letters: A, B, C, etc.), and sometimes sub-subpoints (Arabic numerals: 1, 2, 3, etc.). Exhibit 7.2 shows a diagram of this general form for formal speech outlines.

Speech-Planning Action Step 4, Activity 4D, will help you complete the outline for the body of your speech. See the Student Response box immediately following the activity for a sample of how one student completed this exercise.

(4D) SPEECH PLANNING

Activity

Outline the Speech Body

The goal of this exercise is to help you get started on the formal speech outline for the body of your speech. Using complete sentences, write the following:

1. The general and specific speech goals you identified in Activity 4A.

2. The thesis statement you developed in Activity 4C.

3. A transition to the first main point.

4. The first main point you developed in Activity 4B.

5. The subpoints and supporting material for your first main point.

6. A transition from your first to second main point.

7. The other main points, subpoints, support, section transitions, and signposts. Use the format shown in the Student Response to Activity 4D.

 MindTap™

Do this activity with Speech Builder Express. Access this activity on your MindTap for *Challenge*.

(4D) STUDENT RESPONSE

Activity

Outline the Speech Body

Here is Katie's speech body outline.

General goal: *I want to inform my audience.*
Specific speech goal: *I would like the audience to understand the uses and abuses of Adderall.*
Thesis statement: *Off-label Adderall usage by college students is a growing problem across the U.S. To clarify, let's discuss the nature and legal uses of Adderall, its growing popularity as a study aid for college students, and the problems associated with using Adderall without a prescription.*

Body

I. *Adderall is a psychostimulant prescribed to treat three conditions.*

   A. *Listener relevance link: Understanding the intended medical uses of the drug Adderall may help you understand why the drug is so widely abused by collegians.*

   B. *Adderall, the brand name for amphetamikne-dextroamphetamine, is a psychostimulant, one of a class of drugs intended to promote concentration, suppress hyperactivity, and promote healthy social experiences for patients (Willis, 2001).*

(continued)

1. *Adderall stimulates the central nervous system by increasing the amount of dopamine and norepinephrine in the brain. These chemicals are neurotransmitters that help the brain send signals between nerve cells (Daley, 2004, April 20).*

2. *Mentally, Adderall brings about a temporary improvement in alertness, wakefulness, endurance, and motivation.*

3. *Physically, it can increase heart rate and blood pressure and decrease perceived need for food or sleep.*

C. *Adderall is prescribed for the medical treatment of attention deficit hyperactivity disorder (ADHD) in children and adults as well as for narcolepsy and clinical depression.*

1. *ADHD is a neurobehavioral developmental disorder characterized by problems of attention coupled with hyperactivity.*

a. *Since the mid-1990s, there has been a documented increase in the number of American children diagnosed with and treated for ADHD (McCabe, Teter, & Boyd, 2004).*

b. *According to the Diagnostic and Statistical Manual of Mental Disorders (2000), symptoms must be present for at least six months for diagnosis, and symptoms must be excessive for medicinal treatment.*

c. *The drugs Ritalin and Dexedrine are also used to treat ADHD. Adderall, however, remains the most widely prescribed of these drugs (Willis, 2001).*

d. *According to the Centers for Disease Control and Prevention, approximately 4.4 million American children have been diagnosed with ADHD, and more than 2.5 million of those patients have been prescribed medicine to treat the condition (2005).*

2. *Adderall is also prescribed to treat narcolepsy, which occurs when the brain can't normally regulate cycles of sleep and waking.*

a. *Sufferers of narcolepsy experience excessive daytime sleepiness that results in episodes of suddenly falling asleep.*

b. *A chronic sleep disorder, narcolepsy affects 1 in every 2,000 Americans (American Academy of Sleep Medicine, 2005).*

3. *Adderall can also be used to treat clinical depression.*

a. *Clinical depression is a disorder characterized by low mood, a loss of interest in normal activities, and low self-esteem.*

b. *According to the National Institute of Mental Health, 9.5 percent of the adult population—that is, nearly 1.8 million American adults—suffer from clinical depression.*

Transition: Now that we understand the basic properties and medical uses of the drug Adderall, let's assess the increasing level of abuse of the drug by college students.

II. *Unfortunately, Adderall has become popular among college students who use it "off label" as a study aid and for recreational purposes.*

A. *Listener relevance link: As college students, we need to be aware of what students believe about Adderall and why they are abusing it.*

(continued)

(4D) STUDENT RESPONSE

B. College students who don't suffer from ADHD, narcolepsy, or depression will take it with no prescription because they believe that it will improve their focus and concentration, allowing them to perform better on academic tasks (Teter, McCabe, Crandford, Boyd, & Gunthrie, 2005).

   1. Adderall abuse among college students occurs especially at stressful times of the semester when students get little sleep.

      a. DeSantis, Webb, and Noar (2007) found that 72 percent of the students they surveyed reported using the drug to stay awake so that they could study longer when they had many assignments due.

      b. Katherine Stump, a Georgetown University student, reported in the school newspaper: "During finals week here at Georgetown, campus turns into an Adderall drug den. Everyone from a cappella singers to newspaper writers become addicts, while anyone with a prescription and an understanding of the free market becomes an instant pusherman" (Jaffe, 2006, January 1).

      c. Collegians report using the drug frequently during stressful times of the semester. One student said, "I use it every time I have a major paper due" (Daley, 2004, April 20).

   2. Students also use Adderall for purposes other than academic ones.

      a. A survey of undergraduate and graduate students revealed that students engage in Adderall abuse for partying at a frequency just slightly less than taking the drug for academic purposes (Prudhomme White, Becker-Blease, & Grace-Bishop, 2006).

      b. DeSantis, Webb, and Noar (2007) report that students take the drug for its energizing effects. Other students report taking the drug to make them more social and outgoing at parties.

      c. Some college students, especially women, report using the drug for its use as an appetite suppressant for dieting purposes (Daley, 2004, April 20).

C. Adderall abuse is pervasive at the University of Kentucky.

   1. I lived on campus my freshman year of college, and I currently still live in the dorms. By living in close proximity with other students, I learned a great deal about the individuals on my floor. I personally knew several students who used Adderall without a prescription. One student obtained the medication from a younger sibling diagnosed with ADHD, and another student purchased the pills from a friend on campus. The students would take the medicine to focus more intently when they had a short amount of time to complete a task. Both told me that they had used the drug as a study aid whenever they had several assignments to complete around the same time.

   2. Adderall is easily obtained at the University of Kentucky. A male friend of mine told me that he had no problem finding someone to sell him the medication once he approached his first exam week as a college freshman. He told me that he merely had to ask around, and within no time, he was able to find a fellow student who agreed

(continued)

Activity

to sell him Adderall. As with any major university, the University of Kentucky is not impervious to the widespread abuse of Adderall by its students.

D. *Adderall is easily obtained on college campuses because students with prescriptions for medical stimulants are distributing or diverting their medications to nonprescribed users.*

1. *Nearly one-third of college students with a prescription for Adderall have either sold or given away their medication at least once while being treated for ADHD (Garnier et al., 2010).*

2. *Sepúlveda et al. (2011) found that 36 percent of their sample of prescribed users have diverted their medical stimulants to nonprescribed users.*

Transition: Now that we understand that Adderall abuse is prevalent on university campuses among students, it is important to understand the detrimental effects that can accompany the illegal use of Adderall.

III. *Whether students acknowledge the dangers or not, there are great risks involved in illegally using Adderall.*

A. *Listener relevance link: As we have now discussed the pervasiveness of Adderall abuse, statistically, it is likely that several of you have used this substance without a prescription to either enhance your academic performance or your social outings. Thus, it is important that we all recognize the adverse effects that result from taking Adderall without a prescription.*

B. *Adderall abuse can cause negative health effects for individuals not diagnosed with ADHD (Daley, 2004, April 20).*

1. *Adderall is reported to cause a heightened risk for heart problems when used inappropriately. Problems include sudden heart attack or stroke, sudden death in individuals with heart conditions, and increased blood pressure and heart rate (FDA, 2010).*

2. *Adderall abuse also can result in a myriad of mental problems including manifestation of bipolar disorder, an increase of aggressive thoughts, and a heightened risk for psychosis similar to schizophrenia (FDA, 2010).*

C. *Adderall is highly addictive.*

1. *Adderall is an amphetamine, and while amphetamines were once used to treat a variety of ailments including weight loss in the 1950s and '60s, the drugs began to be much more closely regulated once their addictive nature was realized (Daley, 2004, April 20).*

2. *Adderall has similar properties to cocaine, and, as a result, abuse of the drug can lead to substance dependence (FDA, 2010).*

D. *Though clear risks are associated with the illegal use of Adderall, unlike other drugs, collegians do not view the inappropriate use of Adderall as harmful or illegal.*

1. *College students typically view stimulant abuse as morally acceptable and physically harmless. In a 2010 study, DeSantis and Hane found that students were quick to justify their stimulant abuse by claiming its use was fine in moderation.*

(continued)

(4D) STUDENT RESPONSE

2. *The Kentucky Kernel, the student newspaper at the University of Kentucky, published an editorial of a student who flippantly described the use of Adderall among college students. He states, "If you want to abuse ice cream, amphetamines or alcohol, then there are going to be serious problems; however, let's not pretend a person using Adderall twice a semester to help them study is in any way likely to die a horrible death or suffer terrible side effects" (Riley, 2010, May 3).*

3. *In a study assessing the attitudes of college students toward the inappropriate use of stimulants, the authors found that "the majority of students who reported misuse or abuse were not concerned about the misuse and abuse of prescription stimulants, and a number of students thought that they should be more readily available" (Prudhomme White, Becker-Blease, & Grace-Bishop, 2006, p. 265).*

4. *Those students who distribute their medical stimulants to nonprescribed users do not perceive their actions to be harmful or dangerous (Jardin, Looby, & Earlywine 2011).*

Transition: Now that we understand the risks involved in illegally using Adderall, hopefully you have a better understanding of why using the drug without a prescription is so dangerous.

Reflect on Ethics

WHAT WOULD *YOU* DO?

A SNAKE IN THE GRASS

Harriet Ziefert's children's book, *A Snake Is Totally Tail*, was to be published in early 2006 when a New York public librarian, John Peters, noticed that more than half of the text exactly matched a book by Judi Barrett. First published in 1983, Barrett's book was by then out of print. Peters posted his observation to a listserv, and Ziefert responded with, "I have no recollection of ever seeing Ms. Barrett's book—though it would be foolish of me not to consider the possibility that I might have seen it decades ago and that its structure and some of its language imprinted somewhere on my subconscious."[4] Although no formal suit was ever filed against Ziefert, the publisher decided not to publish the book after Peters's listserv posting was made public.[5]

1. Do you believe Ziefert's explanation? Why or why not?

2. Suppose that Ziefert's book did not match the earlier book word for word but instead just followed a very similar plotline that was organized the same way and used the same narrative voice. Would your opinion of Ziefert change?

3. Do you believe John Peters acted ethically? Why or why not?

Reflection and Assessment

Effective public speeches are well organized. The body of the speech includes main points and subpoints that should be written in complete sentences and checked to make sure that they are clear, parallel in structure, meaningful, and limited in number to four or fewer. To assess how well you've learned what we've discussed in this chapter, answer the following questions. If you have trouble answering any of them, go back and review that material. Once you can answer each question accurately, you are ready to move ahead to read the next chapter.

1. Why organize your speech body into two to four main points using an appropriate main point pattern?
2. How do you construct a clear thesis statement?
3. How do you go about developing main points?
4. How are effective section transitions constructed and why are they important in public speeches?
5. What is a formal speech outline?

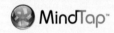

Challenge Resource and Assessment Center

Now that you have read Chapter 7, go to your MindTap for *The Challenge of Effective Speaking in a Digital Age* for quick access to the electronic resources that accompany this text. These resources include the following:

- **Study tools** that will help you assess your learning and prepare for exams (*digital glossary, key term flash cards, review quizzes*).
- **Activities and assignments** that will help you hone your knowledge and build your public speaking skills throughout the course (Practice, Do). Many of these activities allow you to compare your answers with those provided by the authors and, if requested, submit your answers to your instructor.
- **Media resources**—all of which are available on your MindTap for *Challenge*— will help you explore communication concepts online (Practice), develop your speech outlines (Do), watch and critique videos of sample speeches (Do), and upload your speech videos for instructor feedback and critique other students' speeches (Do)."
- **Speech-Planning Action Steps identified earlier in the chapter.**
    4A: Identify Main Points (p. 123)
    4B: Construct a Thesis Statement (p. 128)
    4C: Organize Main Points (p. 130)
    4D: Outline the Speech body (p. 133)
- **Web Link that provides you with additional information or resources related to the topics discussed in this chapter.**
    7.1 Steve Jobs' Speech (p. 126)
- **Video resources allow you to see other students giving speeches and record your own speech.**
    1. Use your Interactive Video Activities on your MindTap for Challenge to watch, analyze, see the transcript and outlines for the student videos, "Flag Etiquette," "Making Ethanol," and Don't Chat and Drive."
    2. Go to MindTap (Do) to see how other students worded their thesis statements. Or go the the Practice and Present section of your MindTap to record a speech you're working on, upload it to Speech Studio, and ask your peers for their feedback. What feedback could you use to fine-tune your thesis statement before you give your speech in class?

Applying What You've Learned

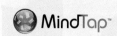

1. **Impromptu Speech Activity:** Identify a favorite toy or game you enjoyed as a child. Come up with a goal statement and two to four main points you could talk about concerning that toy or game. Present a short speech consisting of a thesis statement as the introduction, the two to four main points linked with section transitions for the body, and a thesis restatement for the conclusion. Be sure to consider the wording of your thesis statement and the best organizational pattern for your main points. Be prepared to defend your choices if asked to do so.

2. **Assessment Activity A:** Complete Action Steps 4A, 4B, 4C, and 4D for a speech you may give this semester.

3. **Assessment Activity B:** Watch a speaker in person or on television who demonstrates how to make or do something. Try to identify the thesis statement and main points. Does the speaker use parallel phrasing, section transitions, and/or signposts? How does using or not using them influence your ability to follow along?

8 "the introduction and conclusion"

WHAT'S THE POINT?
WHEN YOU'VE FINISHED THIS CHAPTER, YOU'LL BE ABLE TO:

8-1 Explain why solid introductions and conclusions are so important to effective public speaking

8-2 Create an effective speech introduction

8-3 Create an effective speech conclusion

8-4 Complete your outline and reference list

 MindTap™

Review the chapter **Learning Objectives** and **Start** with quick warm up activity.

4 Organize and develop ideas into a well-structured outline.

E. Create the speech introduction.
F. Create the speech conclusion.
G. Compile the reference list.
H. Complete the formal speech outline.

e Ethical communicators demonstrate integrity when they begin and end each of their speeches with an introduction and conclusion that meets all the goals intended in them.

WaveBreak Media Ltd./Alloy/Corbis

© CoraMax/Shutterstock

Katie asked Alyssa to listen to her rehearse her speech. As she stood in front of the room where she was practicing, she began, "Adderall—a psychostimulant prescription drug—is becoming more and more popular as a study aid among college students today and this is a real problem. In the next few minutes, I'll explain why."

"Whoa, Katie," Alyssa said. "That's your introduction?"

"Yes," Katie replied. "I've got a lot of information to share and don't have a lot of time to say it. So, I don't want to waste any more time than necessary on my introduction."

Katie's response might sound reasonable at first. But what she is failing to realize is that not everyone in the audience may be ready to listen to her speech about Adderall abuse. People might think the topic is boring, irrelevant to them, or for some other reason not worth their time. They might also wonder what makes Katie a credible speaker on the subject. How well you start the speech may determine whether people even listen, and how well you finish your speech can play a major role in determining whether they will remember what you've said.

One reason the introduction and conclusion are so important is based on what psychologists call the **primacy-recency effect**: We are more likely to remember the first and last items conveyed orally in a series than the items in between.[1] This means listeners are more likely to remember the beginning and ending of your speech than what you say in the body. Another reason stems from the need for listeners to quickly grasp your goal and main points in order to follow along, as well as remember them after you've finished.

In the previous chapter, we described the tasks involved in organizing the speech body. In this chapter, we focus on creating an introduction that both gets attention and leads into the body of the speech; creating a conclusion that both summarizes main points and motivates listeners to remember; writing a title; and completing a reference list.

8-1 THE INTRODUCTION

Once you have developed the speech body, you need to decide how to introduce it. Because the introduction is so important to success, you will want to develop two or three different introductions and then select the one that seems best for the audience you will be addressing. An introduction is generally about 10 percent of the length of the entire speech, so for a five-minute speech (approximately 750 words), an introduction of about thirty seconds (approximately 60 to 85 words) is appropriate.

An effective introduction achieves four primary goals: to get attention, convey listener relevance, establish speaker credibility, and identify the thesis statement (speech goal and main point preview). In our opening scenario, Katie didn't really achieve any of these goals. Rather, she simply identified and defined the topic and then moved right into her first main point.

8-1a Get Attention

An audience's physical presence does not guarantee that people will actually listen to your speech. Your first goal, then, is to create an opening that will arouse curiosity and motivate your audience to want to know more about your topic. Some rhetorical strategies for doing so include startling statements, questions, stories, jokes, personal references, quotations, action, and suspense. You can determine which attention-getting device to use by considering what emotional tone is appropriate for your topic. A humorous attention getter will signal a lighthearted tone; a serious one signals a more thoughtful or somber tone. For instance, a speaker who starts with a funny story will

"I've got a lot of information to share and don't have a lot time to say it. So, I don't want to waste any more time than necessary on my introduction."

primacy-recency effect: the tendency to remember the first and last items conveyed orally in a series put the audience in a lighthearted mood. If that speaker then says, "Now let's turn to the subject of abortion" (or nuclear war or drug abuse), the audience will be confused by the speaker's initial words, which signaled a far different type of subject.

startling statement: a sentence or two that grabs your listeners' attention by shocking them in some way

1. A **startling statement** is a shocking expression or example. Chris used this startling statement to get his listeners' attention for his speech about how automobile emissions contribute to global warming:

   Look around. Each one of you is sitting next to a killer. That's right. You are sitting next to a cold-blooded killer. Before you think about jumping up and running out of this room, let me explain. Everyone who drives an automobile is a killer of the environment. Every time you turn the key to your ignition, you are helping to destroy our precious surroundings.

questions: requests for additional information

rhetorical question: a question that seeks a mental rather than an overt response

2. **Questions** are requests for information that encourage your audience to think about something related to your topic. Questions can be *rhetorical* or *direct*. A **rhetorical question** doesn't require an overt response. Notice how this student began his speech on counterfeiting with these three short rhetorical questions:

   What would you do with this $20 bill if I gave it to you? Take your friend to a movie? Treat yourself to a pizza and drinks? Well, if you did either of these things, you could get in big trouble—this bill is counterfeit!

direct question: a question that seeks an overt response from the audience, usually by a show of hands

   Unlike a rhetorical question, a **direct question** seeks an overt response from the audience. It might be a "yea" or "nay" or a show of hands (Photo 8.1). For example, here's how author and motivational speaker Harvey Mackay started his commencement address at the University of Southern California:

   Let me start by asking all of you in the audience this question: How many people talk to themselves? Please raise your hands. I count approximately 50 percent.

   To the other 50 percent who didn't raise your hands, I can just hear you now, saying to yourself: "Who me? I don't talk to myself!"

   Well I think all of you will be talking to yourself about the day's events on your way home this evening. This is an unforgettable moment among many fine hours you will have in your career and life.[2]

   Direct questions can be helpful in getting audience attention because they require a physical response. However, getting listeners to actually comply with your request can also pose a challenge.

story: an account of something that has happened (actual) or could happen (hypothetical)

3. A **story** is an account of something that has happened (actual) or could happen (hypothetical). Most people enjoy a well-told story, so it makes a good attention getter. One drawback of stories is that they are often lengthy and can take more time to tell than is appropriate for the length of your speech. Use a story only if it is short or if you can abbreviate it so that it is just right for your speech length. Yash Gupta, dean of the Carey Business School at Johns Hopkins University, used a story to get attention about assumptions, prejudices, and policies about older people:

   Imagine this.

   You are boarding a routine business flight. As you get on the plane you notice the pilot looks perhaps a bit . . . grandfatherly. In fact, he is only two years away from his FAA-mandated retirement age.

   You sit and open a magazine. You know, in advertisements flight attendants always

Photo 8.1 Speakers typically ask for a show of hands when getting attention with a direct question.

AP photo/Hani Mohammed

look like the champagne they are pouring: fresh and bubbly. But looking around the cabin at the flight crew the words that instead come to mind are mature and no-nonsense. All three flight attendants are in their 50s.

You are belted comfortably, your seat is in the upright position, and you have just felt the wheels lift off the runway from LaGuardia Airport.

Only a couple minutes into your flight there is a loud bang, followed by another loud bang. Flames shoot out from the plane's two jet engines, and then they both go silent. Less than three minutes later, the pilot makes one terse announcement: prepare for impact.

The next thing you know you're floating on the Hudson River and the flight crew is quickly and efficiently moving you onto the wings of the aircraft. They know their jobs.

Flight attendant Doreen Welsh is 58. She's been flying since 1970—almost 40 years' experience. Sheila Daily is 57. She's been flying since 1980, and the other flight attendant, 51-year-old Donna Dent, has been flying since 1982.

As you watch the rescue boats approach, one thought goes through your mind: At moments like this, who needs fresh and bubbly?

The story of Flight 1549 suggests that in our society perhaps we have been too quick to praise youth, too ready to underestimate the value of age, wisdom and experience. One thing is certain: as we look forward to the middle years of the 21st century, we are going to have ample opportunity to discover if our assumptions, our prejudices, and our policies about older people are valid—or if perhaps we have some serious reconsidering to do.[3]

> **SPEECH SNIPPET**
>
> **Rhetorical Questions and Startling Statements**
>
> Lana used a combination of rhetorical questions and a startling statement to get her listeners' attention for her speech on eating disorders: "Who are five of the most important women in your life? Your mother? Your sister? Your daughter? Your wife? Your best friend? Now which one of them has an eating disorder? Before you disregard my question, listen to what research tells us. One in every five women in the United States has an eating disorder."

4. A **joke** is an anecdote or a piece of wordplay designed to make people laugh (Photo 8.2). A joke can be used to get audience attention when it meets the three R's test: It must be realistic, relevant, and repeatable.[4] In other words, it can't be too far-fetched, unrelated to the speech purpose, or potentially offensive to some listeners. In his speech about being a person of integrity, for example, Joel Osteen offered this joke to get attention:

   A kindergarten teacher asked one of her students what she was drawing a picture of. The little girl said, "I'm drawing a picture of God." The teacher replied, "Oh honey, nobody knows what God looks like." Without missing a beat, the little girl replied, "They will in a minute . . .".[5]

   When jokes work, they adhere to the three R's test, but if you decide to use one, be sure to consider how you will handle the situation if nobody laughs.

joke: an anecdote or a piece of wordplay designed to make people laugh

personal reference: a brief account about something that happened to you or a hypothetical situation that listeners can imagine themselves in

5. A **personal reference** is a brief account about something that happened to you or a hypothetical situation that listeners can imagine themselves in. In addition to getting attention, a personal reference can be especially effective at engaging listeners as active participants. A personal reference like this one on exercise is suitable for a speech of any length:

   Were you panting when you got to the top of those four flights of stairs this morning? I'll bet there were a few of you who vowed you'd never take a class on the top floor of this building again. But did you ever stop to think that maybe the problem isn't that this class is on the top floor? It just might be that you are not getting enough exercise.

Kevin Winter/Getty Images

Photo 8.2 A joke can make a good attention getter as long as it is realistic, relevant, and repeatable.

quotation: a comment made by and attributed to someone other than the speaker

6. A **quotation** is a comment made by and attributed to someone other than the speaker. A particularly vivid or thought-provoking quotation can make an excellent attention getter as long as it relates to your topic. Although it is common to quote famous people, a good quotation from *any* source can create interest in your topic. For instance, notice how Sally Mason, provost at Purdue University, used the following quotation to get the attention of her audience, the Lafayette, Indiana, YWCA:

There is an ancient saying, "May you live in interesting times." It is actually an ancient curse. It might sound great to live in interesting times. But interesting times are times of change and even turmoil. They are times of struggle. They are exciting. But, at the same time, they are difficult. People of my generation have certainly lived through interesting times and they continue today.[6]

Thanks to the Internet and search engines like Google and Bing, finding compelling and relevant quotations is easier today than it was in the past. Some ideas can be found at **Web Link 8.1, Quotations Websites,** on your MindTap for *Challenge.*

7. An **action** is an attention-getting act designed to highlight and arouse interest in your topic. You can perform an action yourself, just as Juan did when he split a stack of boards with his hand to get attention for his speech on karate. Or you can ask volunteers from the audience to perform the action. For example, Cindria used three audience members to participate in breaking a piñata to create interest in her speech on the history of the piñata. If you choose to use audience members, consider soliciting participants ahead of time to avoid the possibility of having no volunteers when you ask during your speech. Finally, you can ask your entire audience to perform some action related to your speech topic. If you'd like to ask your whole audience to perform an action, realistically assess whether what you are asking is something your audience is likely to comply with.

8. To **create suspense,** you word your attention getter so that what is described generates uncertainty or mystery and excites the audience. When you get the audience to ask, "What is she leading up to?" you have created suspense. A suspenseful opening is especially valuable when your audience is not particularly interested in hearing about your topic. Consider this suspenseful statement:

It costs the United States more than $116 billion per year. It has cost the loss of more jobs than a recession. It accounts for nearly 100,000 deaths a year. I'm not talking about cocaine abuse—the problem is alcoholism. Today I want to show you how we can avoid this inhumane killer by abstaining from it.

Notice that by introducing the problem, alcoholism, at the end of the statement, the speaker encourages the audience to try to anticipate the answer. And because the audience may well be thinking that the problem is narcotics, the revelation that it is alcoholism is likely to be that much more effective.

For more tips about how to use these and other types of attention getters, go to MindTap for *Challenge* to access **Web Link 8.2: Strategies for Introducing Speeches.**

8-1b Establish Relevance

Even if you successfully get the attention of your listeners, to *keep* their attention you will need to motivate them to listen to your speech. You can do this by creating a clear listener relevance link, a statement of how and why your speech relates to or might affect your audience. Doing this in the introduction and again for each main point helps your audience realize its exigence.[7] Sometimes your attention-getting statement will serve this function, but if it doesn't, you will need to provide a personal connection between your topic and your audience (Photo 8.3). When creating a listener relevance link, answer these questions: Why should my listeners care about what I'm saying? In what way(s) might

Reflect on Ethics

Award show hosts actually provide the introduction for the ceremony in the form of an opening monologue. On February 24, 2013, Seth McFarlane—actor, animator, screenwriter, comedian, producer, director, and singer; as well as creator of the popular animated TV program *Family Guy*—served as host of the 85th annual Academy Awards. Producers selected MacFarlane in hopes of raising ratings, particularly among younger viewers. In that sense, the strategy worked. In fact, 40.3 million viewers tuned in to watch, up 3 percent from 2012. Not only that, the number of 18 to 34 year old viewers grew a whopping 20 percent from the year before.[8] Like many hosts, MacFarlane used humor to get attention, set the tone, and preview what was to come. However, many later criticized his jokes as, at best, in poor taste and, at worst, downright offensive. In his opening song (performed with the Los Angeles Gay Men's Chorus), "We Saw Your Boobs," he poked fun at specific actresses who bared their breasts in films. Jokes were dubbed as bordering on anti-Semitism, racism,

and sexism. He even quipped that *Django Unchained*, a film about a woman "subjected to unthinkable violence" was what Chris Brown and Rihanna would call "a date movie".[9] Not long after the media published an array of criticism, MacFarlane responded to a tweet asking if he'd ever host the show again with "No way" and "Lotta fun to have done it, though".[10]

1. Do you think MacFarlane's use of humor was ethical? Why or why not?

2. If people laugh, does that make potentially offensive humor ok? Why or why not?

3. Given that ratings went up overall and among the 18 to 34 year old demographic, do you think MacFarlane should consider hosting the program again? Why or why not?

4. What advice would you give to MacFarlane or others who might host the awards show in the future with regard to use of humor and ethics?

---

they benefit from hearing about it? How might my speech relate to my listeners' needs or desires for health, wealth, well-being, self-esteem, success, and so forth?

8-1c Establish Credibility

If someone hasn't formally introduced you, audience members are going to wonder who you are and why they should pay attention to what you say. So, another goal of the introduction is to begin to build your credibility. The theoretical grounding for this goal actually dates back to ancient Greek philosophy of Aristotle in his treatise

action: an attention-getting act designed to arouse interest in your topic

creating suspense: wording an attention getter so that what is described generates initial uncertainty or mystery and excites the audience

Bill Aron/PhotoEdit

Photo 8.3 Telling a story is a time-honored way to get attention for a speech.

The Rhetoric.[11] In it, he asserted that listeners would be motivated to both listen to and believe a speaker based on their perception of his or her *ethos* (competence, good character, and goodwill), *pathos* (appeals to emotions), and *logos* (perception of truthfulness through evidence and reasoning). To be successful, you need to begin to establish ethos during your introductory remarks. This initial ethos responds to the questions listeners may be thinking, such as: Why should I trust you? What makes you an authority on the subject? Why should I believe you? Do you seem sincere? Do you seem like a likeable person? Do your words and actions demonstrate respect for me and this occasion? Remember, though, that your goal is to highlight how you are a credible speaker on this topic, one who respects the audience and occasion, not that you are *the* or even *a* final authority on the subject. Carmen Mariano, principal of Archbishop Williams High School, established credibility and goodwill in a "welcome back, students" speech this way:

> *Ladies and gentlemen, you will hear one word many times this morning. That word is welcome. Please know how much we mean that word. Please know how much I mean that word.*
>
> *Why will we mean that word so much?*
>
> *Because without you, this is just a building on 80 Independence Avenue. And with you, this is Archbishop Williams High School. That's right. When you walked through those doors this morning, you made this building a school again.*
>
> *So welcome back.*
>
> *And welcome to your school.*[12]

8-1d State the Thesis

Because audiences want to know what your speech is going to be about, it's important to state your thesis. After Miguel gained the audience's attention and established relevance and credibility he said, "In the next five minutes, I'd like to explain to you that romantic love is composed of three elements: passion, intimacy, and commitment."

Stating your main points in the introduction is necessary unless you have some special reason for not revealing the details of the thesis. For instance, after getting the attention of his audience, Miguel might say, "In the next five minutes, I'd like to explain the three aspects of romantic love," a statement that specifies the number of main points but leaves the details for a preview statement that immediately precedes the main points. Steve Jobs, in his commencement address at Stanford, did so this way: "Today I want to tell you three stories from my life. That's it. No big deal. Just three stories."[13]

8-2 SELECTING THE BEST INTRODUCTION

Because the introduction is critical in establishing a relationship with your audience and identifying your topic and goal, it's worth investing the time to compare different openings. Try working on two or three different introductions; then, pick the one you believe will work best for your specific audience and speech goal.

For instance, Jamie created two introductions for her speech on obesity. The first used a personal reference for an attention getter. Notice how she established listener relevance and credibility by citing the U.S. Department of Health and Human Services statistic before offering her thesis statement:

> *Imagine a table full of all the food you eat in one week. That's a lot of food, right? Now, imagine eating all that food in one day! Believe it or not, there are people who do this. This condition, called binge eating, is contributing to a national epidemic: obesity. According to the U.S. Department of Health and Human Services, obesity*

may soon overtake tobacco as the leading cause of preventable death. In order to reduce obesity, let's examine the scope of the problem and its causes followed by some practical solutions. (ninety-two words)

Her second introduction used a startling statement and rhetorical question to get attention:

Tom is a 135-pound male who enjoys playing computer games and loves pizza. Sounds like an average person, right? Well, what would you think if I told you that Tom is only six years old? According to the U.S. Department of Health and Human Services, obesity may soon overtake tobacco as the leading cause of preventable death. Obesity is a serious problem in our society and warrants our attention. To prove my point, let's examine the scope of the problem and its causes followed by some practical solutions. (eighty-nine words)

Which of Jamie's introductions do you prefer? Why?

Your speech introduction should meet all four goals and be long enough to encourage listeners to hear you out, but not so long that it leaves too little time to develop the substance of your speech. Of course, the shorter the speech, the shorter the introduction.

Speech-Planning Action Step 4, Activity 4E, will help you develop three choices for your speech introduction. See the Student Response box after the activity for a sample of how one student completed this exercise.

8-3 THE CONCLUSION

Shakespeare once said, "All's well that ends well." Effective conclusions heighten the impact of a good speech by summarizing the main ideas and leaving the audience with a vivid impression (Photo 8.4). Even though the conclusion is a relatively short part of the speech—seldom more than 5 percent (thirty-five to forty-five words for a five-minute speech)—your conclusion should be carefully planned.

 SPEECH PLANNING

Activity

Creating Speech Introductions

The goal of this activity is to create several speech introductions from which to choose.

1. For the speech body you outlined earlier, write three different introductions—using different rhetorical devices (startling statement, a question, a story, a personal reference, a joke, a quotation, action, or suspense) to get attention—that you believe meet the primary goals of effective introductions and would be appropriate for your speech goal and audience.

2. Of the three introductions you drafted, which do you believe is the best? Why?

3. Write that introduction in outline form, indicating in parentheses where you are meeting each goal.

Do this activity with Speech Builder Express. Go to your MindTap for *Challenge*.

4E STUDENT RESPONSE

Activity

Creating Speech Introductions

1. For the speech body you outlined earlier, write three different introductions—using different rhetorical devices (startling statement, a question, a story, a personal reference, a joke, a quotation, action, or suspense) to get attention—that you believe meet the goals of effective introductions and would be appropriate for your speech goal and audience.

   Specific goal: I would like the audience to understand the three ways to tell if a diamond is real.

   (1) We are at an age where buying diamonds might be on our minds. I would like to tell you how you can know for sure if your diamond is real.

   (2) Have you ever wondered if you would know if the diamond the jeweler is trying to sell you is real? Nobody wants to be duped into spending a lot of money on a fake. As a geology major, I have actually studied how to determine whether a diamond is real and would like to share three things you can look for to do so.

   (3) Calcite, quartz, cubic zirconia, diamond. How can you tell these minerals apart? They are all colorless and can sometimes look alike. But let me tell you three ways that you can tell if you are holding a diamond.

2. Of the three introductions you drafted, which do you believe is the best? Why?

   I believe the second one is the best because the rhetorical question and listener relevance link are likely to motivate the audience to listen, I share why they can believe me, and lead into the body in my thesis statement with main point preview.

3. Write that introduction in outline form, indicating in parentheses where you are meeting each goal.

   I. *Have you ever wondered if you would know if the diamond that the jeweler is trying to sell you is real? (attention getter)*

   II. *Nobody wants to be duped into spending a lot of money on a fake. (listener relevance)*

   III. *I have actually studied how to determine whether a diamond is real and would like to share three things you can look for do to so. (speaker credibility and thesis statement with main point preview).*

The conclusion of a speech has two major goals. The first is to summarize the goal and main points. The second is to provide a sense of closure by driving home the importance of your message in a memorable way. As with your speech introduction, you should prepare two or three conclusions and then choose the one you believe will be most effective for the audience and occasion.

8-3a Summarize Goal and Main Points

An effective speech conclusion includes an abbreviated restatement of your goal and main points. A summary for an informative speech on how to improve your grades might be, "So I hope you now understand *[informative goal]* that three techniques to improve your grades are to attend classes regularly, to develop a positive attitude toward the course, and to study systematically *[main points]*." A short summary for a persuasive speech on why you should exercise might be "So you should exercise for at least 30 minutes each day *[persuasive goal]* to improve your appearance, as well as your physical and mental health *[main points]*."

> **SPEECH SNIPPET**
>
> **Summarizing Main Points**
>
> Courtney offered this summary for her speech on the benefits of eating organic food:
>
> *So I hope you now understand how eating organically produced food contributes to physical health, a cleaner environment, and animal welfare.*

8-3b Clinch

Although a good summary helps the audience remember your main points, a good clincher leaves the audience with a vivid impression. A **clincher** is a short statement that provides a sense of closure by driving home the importance of your speech in a memorable way. If you can, try to devise a clincher that refers back to the introductory comments in some way. Two effective strategies for clinching are using vivid imagery and appealing to action.

Vivid Imagery

To develop vivid imagery, you can use any of the devices we discussed for getting attention (startling statement, question, story, joke, personal reference, quotation, action, or suspense). For example, in Tiffany's speech about being a vegetarian, she referred back to the personal reference she had made in her introduction about a vegetarian Thanksgiving meal:

Photo 8.4 The conclusion offers one final chance to leave a lasting impression.

Purestockh/Jupiter Images

> *So now you know why I made the choice to become a vegetarian and how this choice affects my life today. As a vegetarian, I've discovered a world of food I never knew existed. Believe me, I am salivating just thinking about the meal I have planned for this Thanksgiving: fennel and blood orange salad; followed by baked polenta layered with tomato, fontina, and Gorgonzola cheeses; an acorn squash tart, marinated tofu; and with what else but pumpkin pie for dessert!*

clincher: a one- or two-sentence statement that provides a sense of closure by driving home the importance of your speech in a memorable way

Sounds good doesn't it? Clinchers that foster vivid imagery are appropriate for both informative and persuasive speeches because they leave listeners with a vibrant picture imprinted in their minds.

Appeal to Action

The appeal to action is a common clincher for persuasive speeches. The **appeal to action** describes the behavior you want your listeners to follow after they have heard your arguments. Notice how Matthew Cossolott, president and founder of Study Abroad Alumni International, concludes his speech on global awareness and responsibility with a strong appeal to action:

appeal to action: a statement that describes the behavior you want your listeners to follow after they have heard your arguments

> *So, yes, you should have this re-entry program. Yes, you should network and explore international career opportunities. That's all good.*
>
> *But I also encourage you to Globalize Your Locality. I urge you to Think Global . . . Act Global . . . Be Global.*
>
> *This is an urgent call to action . . . for you and other study abroad alumni . . . to help us reduce the global awareness deficit.*
>
> *You can do so by becoming involved with SAAI . . . and other organizations such as the National Council for International Visitors, Sister Cities, or Rotary International.*
>
> *You can speak to local schools and community organizations about your study abroad experience and the need for more global awareness.*
>
> *When you studied abroad, I'm sure you were told many times that you would be serving as unofficial ambassadors of the United States . . . your campus . . . and even your community back home.*

Now that you're home again, I hope you'll become ambassadors for the value of the study abroad experience and for the need for greater international awareness.

In wrapping up . . . I'd like to leave you with this image . . . just picture in your mind's eye that iconic photograph of planet earth. I'm sure you've seen it. Taken over four decades ago . . . in December 1968 . . . on the Apollo 8 mission to the moon.

The photograph—dubbed Earthrise—shows our small, blue planet rising above a desolate lunar landscape. This photo was a true watershed in human history . . . marking the first time earthlings . . . fellow global citizens had traveled outside earth's orbit and looked back on our lonely planet.

The widespread publication of Earthrise had a lot to do with launching the world-wide environmental movement. It's no accident that the first Earth Day—on April 22, 1970—took place so soon after the publication of this remarkable photograph.

We're all privileged to inhabit this same planet—truly an island in space. And voices to the contrary notwithstanding . . . whether we want to admit it or not . . . we are all, undeniably and by definition, citizens of the world.

The only question is: will we accept the responsibilities of global citizenship?

Your future . . . and perhaps the survival of the planet . . . just may depend on how many of us answer yes to that question.[14]

8-4 SELECTING THE BEST CONCLUSION

As with the introduction, create two or three conclusions and then choose the best one for the audience and occasion. For her short speech on Adderall, Katie created the following three variations of summaries for consideration. Which do you like best?

Adderall is a prescription stimulant that is being used more and more among college students especially as a study aid, and there are serious risks associated with using the drug illegally. The next time you or a friend considers taking Adderall as a study aid, think again. The potential harm the drug could cause to your body is not worth even a perfect grade point average.

Adderall is a prescription drug that is being abused by college students across the country. The stimulant is meant to treat medical conditions but is now being used illegally as a study aid. The harms in doing so are alarming. So if you've considered taking Adderall as a study aid, I hope you consider what we've talked about today before you do. Not taking it is not only better for you in the long run, just like wearing your seatbelt and not drinking and driving, but it's also obeying the law.

So, Adderall is a stimulant that is prescribed to treat real problems but is now being abused by more and more college students as a study aid, which is, quite frankly, breaking the law. I won't ask for a show of hands this time, but I will ask the question once more. If you've used Adderall illegally as a study aid, will you think twice before you do it again? If you know someone who uses it illegally as a study aid, will you share what you've learned today with that person? I sincerely hope so. It really is a matter of life and health.

For speeches that are no longer than five minutes, a one- to three-sentence conclusion is often appropriate.

Speech-Planning Action Step 4, Activity 4F, will help you develop choices for your speech conclusion. See the Student Response box after the activity for a sample of how one student completed this exercise.

IMPROMPTU SPEECH CHALLENGE

Identify a favorite game or toy you enjoyed as a child. Come up with an introduction and conclusion for a speech about that game or toy. At your instructor's request, come to the front of the room to share the introduction and conclusion you prepared. Be prepared to hear critiques from your classmates and to offer suggestions on theirs, as well.

4F · SPEECH PLANNING

Creating Speech Conclusions

The goal of this activity is to help you create several speech conclusions from which to choose.

1. For the speech body you outlined earlier, write three different conclusions that review important points you want the audience to remember, and include a clincher that provides closure by leaving the audience with a vivid impression.

2. Which do you believe is the best? Why?

3. Write that conclusion in outline form.

 MindTap™

Do this activity with Speech Builder Express. Go to your MindTap for *Challenge*.

4F · STUDENT RESPONSE

Creating Speech Conclusions

1. For the speech body you outlined earlier, write three different conclusions that review important points you want the audience to remember, and include a clincher that provides closure by leaving the audience with a vivid impression.

   Specific goal: I would like the audience to understand the three ways to tell if a diamond is real.

   (1) So, the next time you buy or receive a diamond, you will know how to do the acid, streak, and hardness tests to make sure the diamond is real.

   (2) Before making your final diamond selection, make sure it can pass the acid test, streak test, and hardness test. Remember, you want to make sure you're buying a real diamond and not a fake!

   (3) Now we all know how to tell if a diamond is real. So, folks, if you discover that the gem you're considering effervesces in acid, has a streak that is not clear, or can be scratched, you will know that it is a fake. As a result, none of us will fall victim to being duped by a crook!

2. Which do you believe is the best? Why?

   The third one because it restates the characteristics and leaves a vivid impression.

3. Write that conclusion in outline form.

   I. *Now we all know how to tell if a diamond is real. (Goal restatement)*

   II. *If it effervesces, streaks, or scratches, it is a fake. (main point review)*

   III. *As a result, none of us will be duped by a crook! (clincher)*

PUBLIC SPEAKING IN THE REAL WORLD

Public Speaking Lessons Learned from Lady Gaga

PETER FOLEY/EPA/Newscom

Ryan Avery is an international professional public speaker that also teaches others to become better communicators. The 2012 World Champion of Public Speaking does keynote speeches and conducts workshops regularly designed to help improve communication among the younger generation. He says he learned a lot about the importance of a strong introduction and conclusion from singer and performer, Lady Gaga. Here's what he posted on his blog, AVERYTODAY, after attending one of her concerts:

"Life Lesson: Keep your eyes open for learning new lessons from others. I learned how to be a better speaker from one of the most famous musicians of our time.

- Strong opening. She opened with a bang! She got the crowed excited and on their feet, and within the first 30 seconds you already want more. What are you doing to grab your audience's attention and have them saying "wow, I want more of what this person is giving me?"

- Strong closing. Cute girls are crying, boys are hugging, hands are in the air, and she sings her last note! You walk out and people are on cloud nine. After two hours of dancing, singing, and burning more than 2,000 calories, people are not tired. They are energized. They were left on a high note and reminded to go for their dreams. How well are you ending your speech or presentation?

Being a better communicator will help you become a person of influence. Gaga is a great communicator with tremendous influence. Take these lessons and implement them when you give your next speech or presentation."[15] As Avery points out, a strong introduction and conclusion can make any presentation better, whether that presentation comes in the form of a public speech, professional workshop, or even a musical performance.

8-5 THE COMPLETE FORMAL OUTLINE WITH REFERENCE LIST

formal outline: A full sentence outline of your speech that includes internal references and a reference list

After drafting your introduction and conclusion, you have essentially drafted an outline of your speech. To complete the **formal outline**, you need to compile a list of the sources you draw from in the speech, create a title (if required), and then review your outline to make sure that it conforms to a logical structure.

8-5a Listing Sources

Regardless of the type or length of the speech, you need to prepare a list of the sources you use in it. This list will enable you to direct audience members to the specific source of any information you used and will allow you to quickly find the information at a later date. You also want to use internal references throughout the formal speech outline to help you remember what to cite and where during your speech. Doing so will ultimately enhance your credibility and help you avoid unintentional plagiarism.

Many formal bibliographical styles can be used to compile your source list (for example, MLA, APA, Chicago, CBE). Exhibit 8.1 gives examples of citations according to the Modern Language Association (MLA) and American Psychological Association (APA) style guides. The "correct" form differs by professional or academic discipline. Check to see if your instructor has a preference about which style you use in class.

Speech-Planning Action Step 4, Activity 4G will help you compile a list of sources used in your speech. See the Student Response box after the activity for a sample of how one student completed this exercise.

Exhibit 8.1 **Examples of the MLA and APA Citation Formats**

	MLA style	APA style
Book	Miller, Roberta B. *The Five Paths to Persuasion: The Art of Selling Your Message.* New York: Warner Business Books, 2004. Print.	Miller, R. B. (2004). *The five paths to persuasion: The art of selling your message.* New York: Warner Business Books.
Edited book	Janzen, Rod. "Five Paradigms of Ethnic Relations." *Intercultural Communication.* 10th ed. Eds. Larry Samovar and Richard Porter. Belmont, CA: Wadsworth, 2003. 36–42. Print.	Janzen, R. (2003). Five paradigms of ethnic relations. In L. Samovar & R. Porter (Eds.), *Intercultural communication* (10th ed., pp. 36–42). Belmont, CA: Wadsworth.
Academic journal	Barge, J. Kevin. "Reflexivity and Managerial Practice." *Communication Monographs* 71 (Mar. 2004): 70-96. Print.	Barge, J. K. (2004, March). Reflexivity and managerial practice. *Communication Monographs, 71,* 70–96.
Magazine	Krauthammer, Charles. "What Makes the Bush Haters So Mad?" *Time* 22 Sept. 2003: 84. Print.	Krauthammer, C. (2003, September 22). What makes the Bush haters so mad? *Time,* 84.
Newspaper	Cohen, Richard. "Wall Street Scandal: Whatever the Market Will Bear." *The Cincinnati Enquirer* 17 Sept. 2003: C6. Print.	Cohen, R. (2003, September 17). Wall Street scandal: Whatever the market will bear. *The Cincinnati Enquirer,* p. C6.
Electronic article based on print source	Friedman, Thomas L. "Connect the Dots." *The New York Times.* 25 Sept. 2003. Web. 20 Aug. 2004.	Friedman, T. L. (2003, September 25). Connect the dots. *The New York Times.* Retrieved from http://www.nytimes.com/2003/09/25/opinion/25FRIED.html
Electronic article from Internet-only publication	Osterweil, Neil, and Michelle Smith. "Does Stress Cause Breast Cancer?" *Web M.D. Health.* WebMD Inc. 24 Sept. 2003. Web. 20 Aug. 2004.	Osterweil, N., & Smith, M. (2003, September 24). Does stress cause breast cancer? *Web M.D. Health.* Retrieved from http://my.webmd.com/contents/article/74/89170.htm?z3734_00000_1000_ts_01
Electronic article retrieved from database	Grabe, Mark. "Voluntary Use of Online Lecture Notes: Correlates of Note Use and Note Use as an Alternative to Class Attendance." *Computers and Education* 44 (2005): 409-21. *ScienceDirect.* Web. 28 May 2006.	Grabe, M. (2005). Voluntary use of online lecture notes: Correlates of note use and note use as an alternative to class attendance. *Computers and Education, 44,* 409–421. Retrieved from *ScienceDirect.*
Movie	*Pirates of the Caribbean: Dead Man's Chest.* Dir. Gore Verbinksi. Perf. Johnny Depp, Orlando Bloom, Keira Knightley. 2006. The Walt Disney Company, 2007. DVD.	Bruckheimer, J. (Producer), & Verbinksi, G. (Director). (2006). *Pirates of the Caribbean: Dead man's chest* [Motion picture]. United States: Walt Disney Pictures.
Television program episode	"Truth Be Told." *Dexter.* Showtime. 10 Dec. 2006. Television.	Gordon, K. (Director). (2006, December 10). Truth be told. [Television series episode]. In J. Manos Jr. (Executive producer), *Dexter.* New York, NY: Showtime Networks Inc.
Music recording	Nirvana. "Smells Like Teen Spirit." *Nevermind.* Geffen, 1991. CD.	Nirvana. (1991). Smells like teen spirit. On *Nevermind* [CD]. Santa Monica, CA: Geffen.
Personal interview	Mueller, Bruno. Personal interview. 19 March 2004.	APA style dictates that no personal interview is included in a reference list. Rather, cite this type of source orally in your speech, mentioning the name of the person you interviewed and the date of the interview.

From Verderber/Verderber/Sellnow, *Communicate!,* 14e. © 2014 Cengage Learning.

(4G) SPEECH PLANNING

Compiling a List of Sources

The goal of this activity is to record a list of sources for your speech.

1. Review your annotated bibliography and/or research cards, as well as formal speech outline. Identify each source that you drew information from for your speech.

2. Note on your outline where you'll reference the source during your speech.

3. List the sources used in your speech by copying the bibliographical information recorded on the annotated bibliography and/or research card.

4. Using the style guide required for your class, record the bibliographic citation for each source in an alphabetical list.

 MindTap™

Do this activity with **Speech Builder Express**. Go to your MindTap for *Challenge*.

(4G) STUDENT RESPONSE

Compiling a List of Sources

1. Review your annotated bibliography and/or research cards, as well as formal speech outline. Identify each source that you drew information from for your speech.

2. Note on your outline where you'll reference the source during your speech.

3. List the sources used in your speech by copying the bibliographical information recorded on the annotated bibliography and/or research card.

4. Using the style guide required for your class, record the bibliographic citation for each source in an alphabetical list.

Sources

Dixon, Dougal. The Practical Geologist. *New York: Simon & Schuster*, 1992.

Farver, John. Personal interview. 23 June 2004.

Klein, Cornelius and Barbara Dutrow. Manual of Mineral Science. *3rd ed. New York: John Wiley & Sons*, 2008.

Montgomery, Carla W. Fundamentals of Geology. *3rd ed. Dubuque, IA: Wm. C. Brown*, 1997.

8-5b Writing a Title

In most speech situations outside the classroom, it helps to have a title that lets the audience know what to expect (Photo 8.5). A title is probably necessary when you will be formally introduced, when the speech is publicized, or when the speech will be published. A good title helps to attract an audience and build interest in what you will say. Titles should be brief, descriptive of the content, and, if possible, creative. Most speakers don't settle on a title until the rest of the speech preparation is complete.

Three kinds of titles can be created: a simple statement of subject, a question, or a creative title.

1. **Simple statement of subject.** This straight-forward title captures the subject of the speech in a few words.

   Courage to Grow

   Selling Safety

   The Dignity of Work

   America's Destiny

2. **Question.** To spark greater interest, you can create a title by phrasing your speech goal as a question. A prospective listener may then be motivated to attend the speech to find out the answer.

   Do We Need a Department of Play?

   Are Farmers on the Way Out?

   What Is the Impact of Computers on Our Behavior?

   Are We Living in a Moral Stone Age?

3. **Creative title.** A more creative approach is to combine a familiar saying or metaphor with the simple statement of subject.

   Teaching Old Dogs New Tricks: The Need for Adult Computer Literacy

   Promises to Keep: Broadcasting and the Public Interest

   The Tangled Web: How Environmental Climate Has Changed

   Freeze or Freedom: On the Limits of Morals and Worth of Politics

Photo 8.5 You don't always need one, but titles are useful for professional speeches that will be publicized or published. What are some interesting speech titles you've heard or read?

The simple statement of the subject gives a clear idea of the topic but is not especially eye- or ear-catching. Questions and creative titles capture interest but may not give a clear idea of content. Creative titles often require subtitles.

8-5c Reviewing the Outline

Now that you have created all parts of the outline, it is time to put them together in complete formal outline form and review them to make sure the outline is well organized and well worded. Use this checklist to guide you.

1. **Have I used a standard set of symbols to indicate structure?** Main points are indicated by Roman numerals, major subpoints by capital letters, sub-subpoints by Arabic numerals, and further subdivisions by lowercase letters.

2. **Have I written main points and major subpoints as complete sentences?** Complete sentences help you to see (1) whether each main point actually develops your speech goal and (2) whether the wording makes your intended point.

3. **Do main points and main subpoints each contain a single idea?** This guideline ensures that the development of each part of the speech will be relevant to the point. Thus, rather than:

   Organically produced food is good for the environment and for animals.
   divide the sentence so each part is stated separately:

   I. *Organically produced food is good for the environment.*

   II. *Organically produced food is good for animals.*

4H SPEECH PLANNING

Completing the Formal Speech Outline

Write and review a complete-sentence outline of your speech using material you've developed so far with the Action Steps in Chapters 4 through 8.

MindTap

Do this activity with **Speech Builder Express**. Go to your MindTap for *Challenge*.

4. **Does each major subpoint relate to or support its major point?** This principle, called subordination, ensures that you don't wander off point and confuse your audience. For example:

   I. Proper equipment is necessary for successful play.

   A. Good gym shoes are needed for maneuverability.

   B. Padded gloves help protect your hands.

   C. A lively ball provides sufficient bounce.

   D. And a good attitude doesn't hurt either.

   Notice that the main point deals with equipment. A, B, and C (shoes, gloves, and ball) all relate to the main point. But D, attitude, is not equipment and should appear somewhere else, if at all.

5. **Are all subpoint elaborations indicated?** Recall that subpoint elaborations help develop the speech. Because you don't know how long it might take to discuss these elaborations, you should include more than you are likely to use. During rehearsals, you may discuss each in a different way.

Now that we have considered the various parts of an outline, let us put them together for a final look. The outline in Exhibit 8.2 illustrates the principles in practice.

Speech-Planning Action Step 4, Activity 4H, will help you write and review a complete-sentence outline of your speech. For this activity, refer to Katie's complete outline (Exhibit 8.2) as the student response.

Exhibit 8.2 Sample Complete Formal Outline

Using and Abusing Adderall: What's the Big Deal?
by Katie Anthony
University of Kentucky

General goal: I want to inform my audience.

Specific goal: I would like the audience to understand the uses and abuses of Adderall by college students.

Thesis statement: I want to inform you about the growing problem of off-label Adderall usage by college students, explaining the nature and legal uses of Adderall, its growing popularity as a study aid for college students, and the problems associated with abusing Adderall.

Introduction

   I. *Attention getter:* Raise your hand if anyone you know has taken the drug Adderall. Keep your hand raised if the person is doing so without a prescription for the drug.

   II. *Listener relevance:* The illegal use of stimulants like Adderall among college students has increased dramatically over the past decade. The latest National Study on Drug Use and Health found that nearly 7 percent of full-time college students reported using Adderall without a prescription. So if you know ten people who are in college, it is likely that you know someone who is abusing Adderall.

III. *Speaker credibility:* I became interested in this topic my freshman year when my roommate received a call from her mother telling her that her best friend, who was a sophomore at a different college, had died suddenly from an Adderall-induced heart attack. Because I had several friends who were also using Adderall without a prescription but who thought it was safe to do so, I began to read all I could about the drug, its use, and its risks. Not only have I become versed in the written information on Adderall, but I have also interviewed several faculty here who are studying the problem, and I have become an undergraduate research assistant helping one faculty member to collect data on this problem. Today, I want to share with you some of what I have learned.

IV. *Thesis statement:* Specifically, I want to inform you about the growing problem of off-label Adderall usage by college students, explaining the nature and legal uses of Adderall, its growing popularity as a study aid for college students, and the problems associated with abusing Adderall.

Body

I. Adderall is a psychostimulant prescribed to treat three conditions.

Listener relevance link: Understanding the intended medical uses of the drug Adderall may help you understand why the drug is so widely abused by collegians.

   A. Adderall, the brand name for amphetamikne-dextroamphetamine, is a psychostimulant, one of a class of drugs intended to promote concentration, suppress hyperactivity, and promote healthy social experiences for patients (Willis, 2001).

     1. Adderall stimulates the central nervous system by increasing the amount of dopamine and norepinephrine in the brain. These chemicals are neurotransmitters that help the brain send signals between nerve cells (Daley, 2004, April 20).

     2. Mentally, Adderall brings about a temporary improvement in alertness, wakefulness, endurance, and motivation.

     3. Physically, it can increase heart rate and blood pressure and decrease perceived need for food or sleep.

   B. Adderall is prescribed for the medical treatment of attention deficit hyperactivity disorder (ADHD) in children and adults as well as for narcolepsy and clinical depression.

     1. ADHD is a neurobehavioral developmental disorder characterized by problems of attention coupled with hyperactivity.

       a. Since the mid-1990s, there has been a documented increase in the number of American children diagnosed and treated for ADHD (McCabe, Teter, & Boyd, 2004).

       b. According to the *Diagnostic and Statistical Manual of Mental Disorders* (2000), symptoms must be present for at least six months for diagnosis and symptoms must be excessive for medicinal treatment.

       c. The drugs Ritalin and Dexedrine are also used to treat ADHD. Adderall, however, remains the most widely prescribed of these drugs (Willis, 2001).

       d. According to the Centers for Disease Control, approximately 4.4 million American children have been diagnosed with ADHD, and over 2.5 million of those patients have been prescribed medicine to treat the condition (2005).

     2. Adderall is also prescribed to treat narcolepsy, which occurs when the brain can't normally regulate cycles of sleep and waking.

       a. Sufferers of narcolepsy experience excessive daytime sleepiness that results in episodes of suddenly falling asleep.

       b. A chronic sleep disorder, narcolepsy affects between 50,000 and 2.4 million Americans. (National Heart, Lung, and Blood Institute, 2008).

     3. Adderall can also be used to treat clinical depression.

       a. Clinical depression is a disorder characterized by low mood, a loss of interest in normal activities, and low self-esteem.

       b. According to the National Institute of Mental Health, 9.5% of the adult population—that is nearly 1.8 million American adults—suffer from clinical depression.

Transition: Now that we understand the basic properties and medical uses of the drug Adderall, let's assess the increasing level of abuse of the drug by college students.

(continued)

Exhibit (8.2) **Sample Complete Formal Outline** *(continued)*

II. Unfortunately, Adderall has become popular among college students who use it as a study aid and for recreational purposes.

> *Listener relevance link:* As college students, we need to be aware of what students believe about Adderall and why they are abusing it.

A. College students who don't suffer ADHD, narcolepsy, or depression will take it with no prescription because they believe that it will improve their focus and concentration, allowing them to perform better on academic tasks (Teter, McCabe, Crandford, Boyd, & Gunthrie, 2005).

1. Adderall abuse among college students occurs especially at stressful times of the semester when students get little sleep.
    a. DeSantis, Webb, and Noar (2008) found that 72 percent of the students they surveyed reported using the drug to stay awake so that they could study longer when they had many assignments due.
    b. Katherine Stump, a Georgetown University student, reported in the school newspaper: "During finals week here at Georgetown, campus turns into an Adderall drug den. Everyone from a cappella singers to newspaper writers become addicts, while anyone with a prescription and an understanding of the free market becomes an instant pusherman" (Jaffe, 2006, January 1).
    c. Collegians report using the drug frequently during stressful times of the semester. One student said, "I use it every time I have a major paper due" (Daley, 2004, April 20).

B. Students also use Adderall for purposes other than academic ones.

1. A survey of undergraduate and graduate students revealed that students engage in Adderall abuse for partying at a frequency just slightly less than taking the drug for academic purposes (Prudhomme White, Becker-Blease, & Grace-Bishop, 2006).
2. DeSantis, Webb, and Noar (2007) report that students take the drug for its energizing effects. Other students report taking the drug to make them more social and outgoing at parties.
3. Some college students, especially women, report using the drug for its use as an appetite suppressant for dieting purposes (Daley, 2004, April 20).

Transition: Now that we understand that Adderall abuse is prevalent on university campuses among students, let's focus on the detrimental effects that can accompany the illegal use of Adderall.

III. Whether students acknowledge the dangers or not, there are great risks involved in illegally using Adderall.

> *Listener relevance link:* As we have now discussed the pervasiveness of Adderall abuse, statistically, it is likely that several of you have used this substance without a prescription to either enhance your academic performance or your social outings. Thus, it is important that we all recognize the adverse effects that result from taking Adderall without a prescription.

A. Adderall abuse can cause negative health effects for individuals not diagnosed with ADHD (Daley, 2004, April 20).

1. Adderall is reported to cause a heightened risk for heart problems when used inappropriately. Problems include sudden heart attack or stroke, sudden death in individuals with heart conditions, and increased blood pressure and heart rate (FDA, 2010).
2. Adderall abuse also can result in a myriad of mental problems, including manifestation of bipolar disorder, an increase of aggressive thoughts, and a heightened risk for psychosis similar to schizophrenia (FDA, 2010).

B. Adderall is highly addictive.

1. Adderall is an amphetamine, and while amphetamines were once used to treat a variety of ailments including weight loss in the 1950s and '60s, the drugs began to be much more closely regulated once their addictive nature was realized (Daley, 2004, April 20).
2. Adderall has similar properties to cocaine, and, as a result, abuse of the drug can lead to substance dependence (FDA, 2010).

C. Though clear risks are associated with the illegal use of Adderall, unlike other drugs, collegians do not view the inappropriate use of Adderall as harmful or illegal.

1. College students typically view stimulant abuse as morally acceptable and physically harmless. In a 2010 study, DeSantis and Hane found that students were quick to justify their stimulant abuse by claiming its use was fine in moderation.

2. The *Kentucky Kernel*, the student newspaper at the University of Kentucky, published an editorial of a student who flippantly described the use of Adderall among college students. He states, "If you want to abuse ice cream, amphetamines or alcohol, then there are going to be serious problems; however, let's not pretend a person using Adderall twice a semester to help them study is in any way likely to die a horrible death or suffer terrible side effects" (Riley, 2010, May 3).

3. In a study assessing the atitudes of college students toward the inappropriate use of stimulants, the authors found that "the majority of students who reported misuse or abuse were not concerned about the misuse and abuse of prescription stimulants, and a number of students thought that they should be more readily available (Prudhomme White, Becker-Blease, & Grace-Bishop, 2006, p. 265).

Transition: Now that we understand the risks involved in illegally using Adderall, hopefully you have a better understanding of why using the drug without a prescription is so dangerous.

Conclusion

I. *Restatement of thesis:* Adderall is a prescription stimulant that is increasingly being abused by college students primarily as a study aid.

II. *Main point review:* We have examined today what the drug Adderall is, its growing popularity among college students especially as a study aid, and the risks associated with using the drug illegally.

III. *Clincher:* The next time you or a friend considers taking Adderall as a study aid, think again. The potential harm that the drug could cause to your body is not worth even a perfect grade point average.

References

American Psychiatric Association. *(2000). Diagnostic and statistical manual of mental disorders.* Arlington, VA: Author.

Centers for Disease Control and Prevention. (2005, September 2). *Morbidity and Mortality Weekly Report (MMWR).* Retrieved from http://www.cdc.gov

Daley, B. (2004, April 20). Perspective: Miracle drug? Adderall is prescribed for individuals with ADD and ADHD; for nonprescribed users there can be some serious risks. *Daily Pennsylvanian.* Retrieved from http://www.vpul.upenn.edu

DeSantis, A. D., & Hane, A. C. (2010). "Adderall is definitely not a drug": Justifications for the illegal use of ADHD stimulants. *Substance Use & Misuse, 45,* 31–46.

DeSantis, A. D., Webb, E. M., & Noar, S. M. (2008). Illicit use of prescription ADHD medications on a college campus: A multimethodological approach. *Journal of American College Health, 57,* 315–324.

Food and Drug Administration. (2010). *Drugs @ FDS: FDA approved drug products.* Retrieved from http://www.accessdata.fda.gov.

National Heart, Blood, and Lung Insitute (2008). "What is narcolepsy?" *National Heart, Blood, and Lung Institute Diseases and Conditions Index.* Retrieved from http://www.nhlbi.nih.gov/health/dci/Diseases/nar/nar_what.html

Jaffe, H. (2006, January 1). ADD and abusing Adderall. *The Washingtonian.* Retrieved from http://www.washingtonian.com

McCabe, S. E., Teter, C. J., & Boyd, C. J. (2004). The use, misuse and diversion of prescription stimulants among middle and high school students. *Substance Use and Misuse, 39,* 1095–1116.

Prudhomme White, B., Becker-Blease, K. A., & Grace-Bishop, K. (2006). Stimulant medication use, misuse, and abuse in an undergraduate and graduate student sample. *Journal of American College Health, 54,* 261–268.

Riley, T. (2010, May 3). Prescription drug abuse is a personal choice. *Kentucky Kernel.* Retrieved from http://kykernel.com

Substance Abuse and Mental Health Services Administration, Office of Applied Studies. (April 7, 2009). *The NSDUH Report: Nonmedical Use of Adderall among Full-Time College Students.* Rockville, MD.

Teter, J. C., McCabe, S. E., Crandford, J. A., Boyd, C. J., & Gunthrie, S. K. (2005). Prevalence and motives for illicit use of prescription stimulants in an undergraduate student sample. *Journal of American College Health, 53,* 253–262.

Willis, F. (2001). Attention deficit disorder. *Modern Drug Discovery, 4,* 84–86.

Reflection and Assessment

You finish organizing you speech by preparing an introduction and a conclusion, as well as listing the sources used, writing a title (if required), and reviewing the formal outline. To assess how well you've learned what we've discussed in this chapter, answer the following questions. If you have trouble answering any of them, go back and review that material. Once you can answer each question accurately, you are ready to move ahead to read the next chapter.

1. What are the goals of an effective speech introduction?
2. What are the goals an effective speech conclusion?
3. How do you go about completing the outline and reference list?

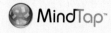

Challenge Resource and Assessment Center

Now that you have read Chapter 8, go to your MindTap for *The Challenge of Effective Speaking in a Digital Age* for quick access to the electronic resources that accompany this text. These resources include the following:

- **Study tools** that will help you assess your learning and prepare for exams (*digital glossary, key term flash cards, review quizzes*).

- **Activities and assignments** that will help you hone your knowledge and build your public speaking skills throughout the course (Practice, Do). Many of these activities allow you to compare your answers with those provided by the authors and, if requested, submit your answers to your instructor.

- **Media resources**—all of which are available on your MindTap for *Challenge*—will help you explore communication concepts online (Practice), develop your speech outlines (Do), watch and critique videos of sample speeches (Do), and upload your speech videos for instructor feedback and critique other students' speeches (Do).

- **Speech-Planning Action Steps identified earlier in the chapter.**
  4E: Creating Speech Introductions (p. 147)
  4F: Creating Speech Conclusions (p. 151)
  4G: Compiling a List of Sources (p. 154)
  4H: Completing the Speech Outline (p. 156)

- **Web Links that provide you with additional information or resources related to the topics discussed in this chapter.**
  8.1 Quotations Websites (p. 144)
  8.2 Strategies for Introducing Speeches (p. 144)

- **Video resources allow you to see other students giving speeches and record your own speech.**
  1. To see an example of a speech introduction and conclusion view "Chinese Fortune Telling" on your MindTap for *Challenge*. Each video features a sample student speech, including a speech transcript, complete and speaking outlines, and speaking notes.
  2. Viet introductions and conclusions other students created for their speeches. Or go to the Practice and Present section of MindTap and record a speech you're working on, upload it to Speech Studio, and ask your peers for their feedback. What feedback could you use to fine-tune your introduction and conclusion before you give your speech in class?

Applying What You've Learned

1. **Impromptu Speech Activity:** From a basket of thesis statements provided by your instructor, create two introductions and conclusions following the guidelines offered in this chapter. (Be sure to address all the goals of an introduction and conclusion.) Deliver both versions to the class as though you were giving an actual speech on the topic. Ask for feedback regarding which version the class liked better and why.

2. **Assessment Activity A:** Attend a public presentation on campus or in your community or watch and listen to one of the speeches you'll find on your MindTap for *Challenge*. Listen carefully to the speaker's introduction and conclusion. Did he or she address all the goals we identified in this chapter for introductions and conclusions? In your opinion, what could he or she have done differently to improve and why?

3. **Assessment Activity B:** Complete Action Step 4 for one of the speeches you may give this semester.

9 "presentational aids"

Oso Media/Alamy

○ **WHAT'S THE POINT?**
WHEN YOU'VE FINISHED THIS
CHAPTER, YOU'LL BE ABLE TO:

9-1 Identify the benefits of using presentational aids in your speech

9-2 Describe different types of presentational aids

9-3 Choose appropriate presentational aids for your speech

9-4 Prepare effective presentational aids

9-5 Display presentational aids effectively for your speech

9-6 Plan when and how to use presentational aids during your speech

 MindTap™

Review the chapter **Learning Objectives** and **Start** with quick warm up activity.

---

5 **Choose, prepare, and use appropriate presentational aids**

A. Identify presentational aids that will clarify, emphasize, or dramatize your message.

B. Use a symbol system other (or in addition to) words in your aids.

C. Make sure your visual aids are large enough to be seen and audio aids are loud enough to be heard.

D. Prepare and display your presentational aids professionally.

E. Plan when to use aids and integrate them during your speech.

© CoraMax/Shutterstock

ⓔ Ethical communicators demonstrate respect for their audiences by using presentational aids that enhance the verbal message in ways that are not likely to offend.

Read, highlight, and take notes online.

It's April 29, 2009. Scott and Carrie are driving home from an Ignite® Seattle 6 event in which industrial designer Dominic Muren just gave a five-minute PowerPoint-aided presentation called "Humblefacturing a Sustainable Electronic Future."[1] Ignite is a worldwide speaking movement in which speakers give five-minute presentations, often on technical topics, aided by twenty self-projecting PowerPoint slides. "Wow! Dominic's speech was really great," says Carrie. I learned so much about what we could do to develop more sustainable electronics."

"Yeah, I know what you mean," replies Scott. "I've even got some ideas for reducing the e-waste he talked about."

"You know, what's really amazing to me is how much I learned from such a short talk," says Carrie.

"I know what you mean. When I heard these were going to be PowerPoint presentations, all I could think was 'Oh no! Here we go again! It's going to be Death by PowerPoint: a darkened room and a faceless speaker talking to an oversized screen.' Thank goodness I was wrong," says Scott. "Dominic's visuals really helped me, but he and his message was still the focus. And the slides helped me visualize and reinforced the important points he was making. My manager could benefit from watching someone like Dominic."

"I know. I can't believe we learned so much in five minutes! Tomorrow when I get into the office, I'm going to check out Dominic's blog."

Unlike the "death by PowerPoint" speeches Scott alluded to and we've all had to suffer through, the speeches given at these events are adapted to people today—people for whom interacting on several different social networking sites, talking or texting on mobile phones, watching TV, and eating dinner are simultaneous activities. We live in an era when the written, oral, visual, and digital modes of communicating are merging. Whether it is a TV news program, your professor's lecture, or a motivational speech, audiences have come to expect messages to be enhanced with presentational aids. This means that as you prepare your speech, you will need to decide what presentational aids will enhance your verbal message and motivate your audience to both pay attention and remember it. In fact, as we mentioned in Chapter 6, presentational aids have become so important that they are essentially a form of supporting material you should be looking for as you conduct research to develop your topic. Ultimately, you might use them to get attention in the introduction, to support a main point in the body, as well as to clinch in the conclusion.

A **presentational aid** is any visual, audio, audiovisual, or other sensory material used to enhance a message. **Visual aids** enhance a speech by allowing audience members to see what the speaker is describing or explaining. Examples of visual aids include actual objects, models, photographs, drawings and diagrams, maps, charts, and graphs. **Audio aids** enhance the speaker's verbal message with sound. Examples include musical clips from CDs and iTunes, and recorded clips from conversations, interviews, and famous speeches, as well as recordings of nature sounds like bird calls and whale sounds. **Audiovisual aids** enhance the speech using a combination of sight and sound. Examples of audiovisual aids include clips from movies and television, YouTube videos, and podcasts, as well as other events or observations captured on video. **Other sensory aids** include materials that enhance verbal

> "I know what you mean. When I heard these were going to be PowerPoint presentations, all I could think was 'Oh no! Here we go again! It's going to be Death by PowerPoint: a darkened room and a faceless speaker talking to an oversized screen.' Thank goodness I was wrong."

presentational aid: any visual, audio, audiovisual, or other sensory material used in a speech

visual aid: a presentational aid that allows the audience to see what the speaker is describing or explaining

audio aid: a presentational aid that enhances the speaker's verbal message with additional sound

audiovisual aid: a presentational aid that enhances the speech using a combination of sight and sound

other sensory aid: a presentational aid that enhances the speech by appealing to smell, taste, or touch

messages by appealing to smell, touch, or taste. For example, a verbal description of a perfume's fragrance can be clarified by allowing audience members to smell it, and the flavor of a particular entrée can be clarified by allowing audience members to taste it.

9-1 BENEFITS OF PRESENTATIONAL AIDS

Research documents several benefits of using presentational aids. First, they clarify and dramatize your verbal message. Second, they help audiences remember your message.[2] Third, they allow you to address the diverse learning style preferences of your audience.[3] Fourth, they increase persuasive appeal. In fact, some research suggests that speakers who use presentational aids are almost twice as likely to persuade listeners than those who do not.[4] Finally, using presentational aids may help you to feel more competent and confident.[5]

Today, presentational aids are usually developed into computerized slide shows using presentation software such as PowerPoint®, MediaPro®, Adobe®, Acrobat®, Prezzi, or Photodex® and are projected onto a large screen via a computer and LCD projector. These programs allow you to embed audio and audiovisual links from local files and the Internet, which makes it fairly simple to create effective multimedia presentations. Whether creating multimedia presentations or developing simpler presentational aids, your purpose for using them is the same: to enhance your message without overpowering it. Speakers who violate this principle end up with what Scott called "death by PowerPoint" in the chapter opener. In this chapter, we describe various types of presentational aids, criteria to consider when choosing and preparing them, and how to display and use them during your speech.

9-2 TYPES OF PRESENTATIONAL AIDS

Presentational aids range from those that are readily available from existing sources you found while conducting your research to those that are custom produced for your specific speech. As we mentioned earlier, types can come in the form of visual, audio, audiovisual, or other sensory aids.

9-2a Visual Aids

Visual aids enhance the verbal message by allowing audiences to see what it is you are describing or explaining. They include actual objects and models, photographs, drawings and diagrams, maps, charts, and graphs.

Actual Objects

actual object: an inanimate or animate sample of the idea you are communicating

Actual objects are inanimate or animate physical samples of the idea you are communicating. Inanimate objects make good visual aids if they are (1) large enough to be seen by all audience members, (2) small enough to transport to the site of the speech, (3) simple enough to understand visually, and (4) safe. A set of golf clubs or a Muslim prayer rug would be appropriate in size for audiences of twenty to thirty. An iPhone or Blackberry might be okay if the speech goal is simply to show what a smartphone looks like, but it might be too small if you want to demonstrate how to use any of its specialized functions.

On occasion, *you* can be an effective visual aid. For instance, you can demonstrate the motions involved in swinging a golf club or use your attire to illustrate the native dress of a particular country. Sometimes it can be appropriate to use another person as a visual aid, such as when Jenny used a friend to demonstrate the Heimlich maneuver. Animals can also be effective visual aids. For example, Josh used his AKC Obedience Champion dog to demonstrate the basics of dog training. But keep in mind that animals placed in unfamiliar settings can become difficult to control and then distract from your message.

Models

When an actual object is too large or too small for the room where you'll be speaking, too complex to understand visually, or potentially unsafe or uncontrollable, a model of it can be an effective visual aid. A **model** is a three-dimensional scaled-down or scaled-up version of an actual object that may be simplified to aid understanding (Photo 9.1). In a speech on the physics of bridge construction, a scale model of a suspension bridge would be an effective visual aid.

Photographs

If an exact reproduction of material is needed, photographs can be excellent visual aids. In a speech on smart weapons, for example, before and after photos of target sites would be effective in helping the audience understand the pinpoint accuracy of these weapons. When choosing photographs, be sure that the image is large enough for the audience to see, that the object of interest in the photo is clearly identified, and ideally, that the object of interest is in the foreground. For example, if you are giving a speech about your grandmother, and you show a photo of her with her college graduating class, you might circle her image so she's easily seen.

Simple Drawings and Diagrams

Simple drawings and **diagrams** (a type of drawing that shows how the whole relates to its parts) can be effective because you can choose how much detail to include. To make sure they look professional, you can prepare them using a basic computer software drawing program or find them already prepared in a book, an article, or on the Internet. If you do this, however, be sure to credit the source during your speech to enhance your credibility and avoid plagiarism. Andria's diagram of the human body and its pressure points, for example, visually clarified her message (see Exhibit 9.1).

Maps

Maps allow you to orient audiences to landmarks (mountains, rivers, and lakes), states, cities, land routes, weather systems, and so on. As with drawings and diagrams, include only the details that are relevant to your purpose. Exhibit 9.2 shows a map that focuses on weather systems.

Charts

A **chart** is a graphic representation that distills a lot of information into an easily interpreted visual format. Flowcharts, organizational charts, and pie charts are the most common types. A **flowchart** uses symbols and connecting lines to diagram a sequence of steps through a complicated process. Tim used a flowchart to help listeners move through the sequence of steps to assess their weight (see Exhibit 9.3). An **organizational chart** shows the structure of an organization in terms of rank and chain of command. The chart in Exhibit 9.4 illustrates the organization of a student union board. A **pie chart** shows the relationships among parts of a single unit. Ideally, pie charts have two to five "slices," or wedges—more than eight wedges clutter a pie chart. If your chart includes too many wedges, use another kind of chart unless you can consolidate several of the

model: a three-dimensional scaled-down or scaled-up version of an actual object

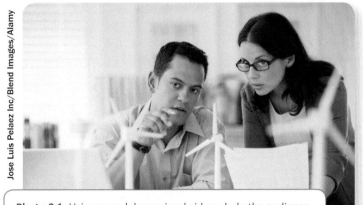

Jose Luis Pelaez Inc/Blend Images/Alamy

Photo 9.1 Using a model as a visual aid can help the audience understand your topic. This model of a wind turbine helps the speaker clarify his explanation of how it works to harness the wind and convert it into power.

Exhibit (9.1) Diagram

diagram: a type of drawing that shows the whole and its parts

chart: a graphic representation that distills a lot of information and presents it in an easily interpreted visual format

flowchart: diagrams a sequence of steps through a complicated process

organizational chart: shows the structure of an organization in terms of rank and chain of command

Copyright © Cengage Learning

Exhibit (9.2) Map

pie chart: shows the relationships among parts of a single unit

graph: presents numerical comparisons in visual form

bar graph: uses vertical or horizontal bars to show relationships between or among two or more variables

line graph: indicates changes in one or more variables over time

Copyright © Cengage Learning

SPEECH SNIPPET

A Map as a Visual Aid

For his speech about "places to visit in Tuscany," Paolo showed a map to orient his listeners where Italy is located in relation to Europe and the Tuscany region in relation to the rest of Italy.

less important wedges into the category of "other," as Tim did to show the percentage of total calories that should come from the various components of food (see Exhibit 9.5).

Graphs

A **graph** presents numerical information in visual form. A **bar graph** uses vertical or horizontal bars to show relationships between or among two or more variables. For instance, Jacqueline used a bar graph to compare the amounts of caffeine found in one serving each of chocolate, coffee, tea, and cola (see Exhibit 9.6). A **line graph** indicates changes in one or more variables over time. In a speech about the U.S. population, for example, the line graph in Exhibit 9.7 illustrates how it has increased, in millions, from 1810 to 2010.

Exhibit 9.3 Flowchart

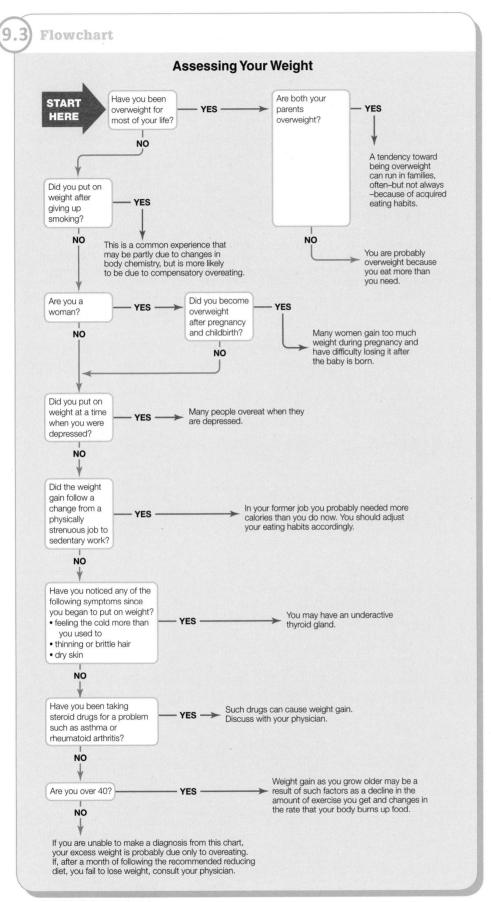

Assessing Your Weight

START HERE → Have you been overweight for most of your life?

— YES → Are both your parents overweight?

— YES → A tendency toward being overweight can run in families, often—but not always—because of acquired eating habits.

(Are both your parents overweight?) NO → You are probably overweight because you eat more than you need.

(Have you been overweight for most of your life?) NO → Did you put on weight after giving up smoking?

— YES → This is a common experience that may be partly due to changes in body chemistry, but is more likely to be due to compensatory overeating.

(Did you put on weight after giving up smoking?) NO → Are you a woman?

— YES → Did you become overweight after pregnancy and childbirth?

— YES → Many women gain too much weight during pregnancy and have difficulty losing it after the baby is born.

(Did you become overweight after pregnancy and childbirth?) NO →

(Are you a woman?) NO → Did you put on weight at a time when you were depressed?

— YES → Many people overeat when they are depressed.

(Did you put on weight at a time when you were depressed?) NO → Did the weight gain follow a change from a physically strenuous job to sedentary work?

— YES → In your former job you probably needed more calories than you do now. You should adjust your eating habits accordingly.

(Did the weight gain follow a change from a physically strenuous job to sedentary work?) NO → Have you noticed any of the following symptoms since you began to put on weight?
• feeling the cold more than you used to
• thinning or brittle hair
• dry skin

— YES → You may have an underactive thyroid gland.

NO → Have you been taking steroid drugs for a problem such as asthma or rheumatoid arthritis?

— YES → Such drugs can cause weight gain. Discuss with your physician.

NO → Are you over 40?

— YES → Weight gain as you grow older may be a result of such factors as a decline in the amount of exercise you get and changes in the rate that your body burns up food.

NO → If you are unable to make a diagnosis from this chart, your excess weight is probably due only to overeating. If, after a month of following the recommended reducing diet, you fail to lose weight, consult your physician.

Exhibit **9.4** **Organizational Chart**

Student Union Board

Exhibit **9.5** **Pie Chart**

Calorie Counts

Exhibit **9.6** **Bar Graph**

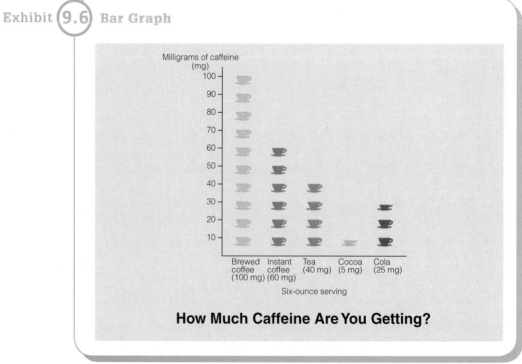

How Much Caffeine Are You Getting?

Exhibit 9.7 Line Graph

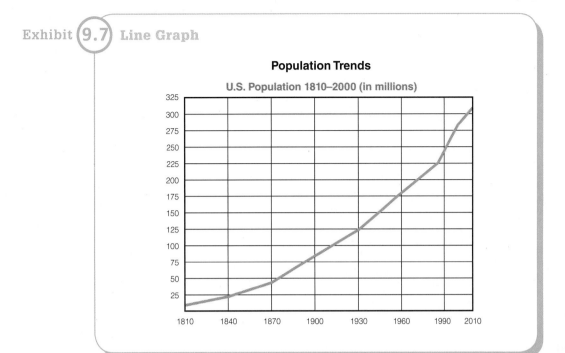

Population Trends

U.S. Population 1810–2000 (in millions)

From Verderber/Verderber/Sellnow, *Communicate!*, 14e, © 2014 Cengage Learning.

9-2b Audio Aids

Audio aids enhance a verbal message through sound. They are especially useful when it is difficult, if not impossible, to describe a sound in words. For example, in David's speech about the three types of trumpet mutes and how they alter the trumpet's sound, he played his trumpet so listeners could hear what he meant. If you can't or don't want to make your own sounds, you can use recorded excerpts from sources such as famous speeches, radio programs, interviews, and recordings of music or environmental sounds. For example, Susan chose to begin her speech on the future of the NASA space program with a recording of Neil Armstrong's first words as he stepped on the surface of the moon: "That's one small step for a man, one giant leap for mankind." Before using audio material, make sure you have enough time to present it (no more than about 5 percent of your speaking time) and that you have access to a quality sound system.

9-2c Audiovisual Aids

Audiovisual aids enhance a verbal message using a combination of sight and sound. For example, you can use short clips from films and videos that are relatively easy to access on Internet sites such as YouTube. They are also easy to import as hyperlinks into computerized slide shows. During his speech about the use of robots in automobile production, Chad, who worked as a technician at the local Ford plant, showed a twenty-second video clip of a car being painted in a robotic paint booth. Audiovisual aids should take no more than 5 percent of your speaking time.

9-2d Other Sensory Aids

Depending on your topic, other sensory aids that appeal to smell, touch, or taste may effectively enhance your speech. For example, a speech about making perfume might benefit from allowing your audience to smell scented swatches as you describe the ingredients used to make the scents. In a speech about Braille, Javier handed out copies of his outline written in Braille for audience members to touch. And in his speech about name brand and generic foods, Greg actually had his audience members do a taste test of two products.

SPEECH SNIPPET

Music as an Audio Aid

Chas played a recorded excerpt from a song he wrote for the attention catcher and clincher on his speech about following your dreams.

SPEECH SNIPPET

YouTube Clip as Audiovisual Aid

For his speech on what happens to race horses after they retire, Paul began by playing a short clip he found on YouTube showing Secretariat's famous Kentucky Derby win.

9-3 CHOOSING PRESENTATIONAL AIDS

With so many different types of presentational aids, you have to decide which ones will best illustrate the content you want to highlight (Photo 9.2). In our opening scenario, Carrie and Scott were motivated to pay attention and remember Dominic's Ignite speech in part because he took the time to carefully choose presentational aids that would best illustrate his points. Some simple guidelines can help you make good choices. Choose aids that:

Gilbert Carrasguillo/Getty Images

Photo 9.2 Celebrity chefs often ask observers to sample their product to confirm that it really tastes good.

- Illustrate the most important ideas to understand and remember.

- Clarify complex ideas that are difficult to explain verbally.

- Are appropriate for the size of the audience.

- Make dull information and details more interesting.

- You feel comfortable using and transporting to the speech site.

- Enhance rather than overwhelm the verbal message.

- You have the time and money to prepare.

- Demonstrate cultural sensitivity that will not offend members of your audience.

Reflect on Ethics

WHAT WOULD YOU DO?

ETHICS AND VISUAL IMAGES IN ADVERTISEMENTS

The International Charter is an organization dedicated to promoting best practices for businesses across the world.[6] Regarding ethical standards in advertising, the organization advocates that:

- Advertisements should not contain statements or visual presentations which offend prevailing standards of decency; and

- Advertisements should not condone any form of discrimination, including that based upon race, national origin, religion, sex or age, nor should they in any way undermine human dignity.

That said, the ultimate goal of all advertisements is to sell products or services and we all know that sex and humor and shock appeal sell. This paradox gives rise to an ongoing debate about where to draw the line. Consider the controversial Go Daddy commercial where sexy supermodel, Bar Rafaeli, engages in a sloppy kiss with some smart nerd named Walter; the Volkswagon commercial that came under fire as racist because a white man spoke with a thick Jamaican accent; the Lynx ad's relentless play on the double entendre "balls"; or the Reebok commercial that told viewers to "cheat on your girlfriend, not on your workout." For decades, the ethics line has often been drawn in the court of public opinion. In other words, if an advertisement causes outrage among enough people, the advertisement gets pulled and a public apology is offered. Today, however, even when such advertisements are removed, they remain easily accessible online via a simple Google search.

1. Because the U.S. Constitution guarantees the right to free speech, advertisers have every right to publish potentially controversial ads. How do you reconcile what is ethical with what is legal?

2. Who should determine whether an advertisement is ethical and in what ways, if any, should advertisers who cross the line be held accountable?

3. Many outraged Super Bowl viewers claim such ads should not be aired on programs intended to be "family friendly." Does where the ad appears make a difference in terms of the ethical advertising line? Explain.

4. Does the fact that ads pulled from publication can still be accessed on social media sites such a YouTube make a difference in where the ethical advertising line should be drawn? Explain.

9-4 PREPARING PRESENTATIONAL AIDS

IMPROMPTU SPEECH CHALLENGE

Locate an advertisement (e.g., billboard magazine, TV, YouTube) that seems to do a good job following the guidelines of effective and ethical aids or one that does not. Prepare a short two- to three- minute speech articulating why you believe it is or is not effective and ethical according to what you've learned in this chapter.

However simple your presentational aids, you still need to produce them carefully. You may need to find or create charts, graphs, diagrams, maps, or drawings. You may need to search for and prepare photographs. You may choose to look for audio, video, or audiovisual clips and then convert them to a format that you can use at your speech site. The goal is to prepare professional-looking and sounding presentational aids that will enhance your ethos (perceived competence, credibility, and character) in addition to clarifying your message and making it more memorable. To do so, follow these guidelines.

1. **Limit the reading required of the audience.** The audience should be listening to you not reading the presentational aid. So use key words and short phrases rather than complete sentences.

2. **Customize presentational aids from other sources.** As you conducted research, you probably found potential supporting material already represented in visual, audio, or audiovisual form. In these cases, simplify your aid to include only the information that is relevant to your speech. For example, Jia Li was preparing a speech on alcohol abuse by young adults. During her research, she found a graph called "Current, Binge, and Heavy Alcohol Use among Persons Aged 12 or Older by Age." The graph presented information pertaining to drinkers from the ages 12 to 65+, which was much more information than Jia Li needed. So she simplified it about her presentation and used only the information about young adults.

3. **Use a photo, print, or type size that can be seen easily and a volume and sound quality that can be heard easily by your entire audience.** Check photo, chart, and lettering size by moving as far away from the presentational aid as the farthest person in your audience will be sitting. If you can see the image, lettering, and pertinent details from that distance, your aid is large enough. If not, create another and check it again. Check audio materials for volume and sound quality in a similar way.

4. **Use a consistent print style that is easy to read.** Avoid fancy print styles and stick to one print style on the aid and throughout the computerized slide show. In addition, use uppercase and lowercase letters rather than ALL CAPS as doing so is actually easier to read.

5. **Make sure information is laid out in a way that is aesthetically pleasing.** Leave sufficient white space around the whole visual making it easy to identify each component. Also, use typefaces and indenting to visually represent relationships between ideas.

6. **Use graphic illustrations in visuals.** To truly enhance a verbal message, a presentational aid should consist of symbols other than or more than just words.[7] Visual symbols can increase retention by appealing to diverse learning styles.[8] Even something as simple as a relevant piece of clip art can make the verbal message more memorable. Of course, clip art can be overdone so be careful not to let your message be overpowered by unnecessary pictures or animations.

7. **Use color strategically.** Although black and white can work well for your visual aids, consider using color strategically to emphasize points. Here are some suggestions for doing so:

   - Use the same background color for all your presentational aids and theme for all of the slides on your computerized slide show.

   - Use the same color to show similarities, and use opposite colors (on a color wheel) to show differences between ideas.

   - Use bright colors, such as red, to highlight important information. Be sure to avoid using red and green together, however, because audience members who are color-blind may not be able to distinguish between them.

I WANT YOU TO REMEMBER THE THREE R'S OF RECYCLING

Reduce the amount of waste people produce, like overpacking or using material that won't recycle.

Reuse by relying on cloth towels rather than paper towels, earthenware dishes rather than paper or plastic plates, and glass bottles rather than aluminum cans.

Recycle by collecting recyclable products, sorting them correctly, and getting them to the appropriate recycling agency.

- Use dark colors for lettering on a white background and light colors for lettering on black or deep blue backgrounds.

- Use no more than two or three colors on any presentational aid that is not a photograph or video clip.

- Pretend you are your audience. Sit as far away as they will be sitting, and evaluate the colors you have chosen for their readability and appeal.

Let's see if we can put all of these principles to work. Exhibit 9.8 contains a lot of important information, but notice how unpleasant it is to the eye. As you can see, this visual aid ignores all the principles we've discussed. However, with some thoughtful simplification, this speaker could produce the visual aid shown in Exhibit 9.9, which sharpens the focus by emphasizing the key words (reduce, reuse, recycle), highlighting the major details, and adding clip art for a professional touch.

Exhibit A Simple but Effective Visual Aid

Remember the Three R's of Recycling

Reduce waste

Reuse
cloth towels
dishes
glass bottles

Recycle
collect
sort
deliver

9-5 DISPLAYING PRESENTATIONAL AIDS

Once you have decided on the specific presentational aids for your speech, you need to choose a method for displaying them. As with choosing and preparing aids, your goal is to display them using a method that is professional looking and sounding to enhance your ethos, as well as your verbal message. Speakers can choose from the following methods for displaying presentational aids.

9-5a Posters

The easiest method for displaying simple drawings, charts, maps, photos, and graphs is on a poster. Because poster boards tend to be fairly small, use them only with smaller audiences (thirty people or fewer). Many professional conference presentations use poster boards to explain complex research projects (Photo 9.3).

9-5b Whiteboards or Chalkboards

Because a whiteboard or chalkboard is a staple in every college classroom, many novice (and ill-prepared) speakers rely on this method for displaying their visual aids. Unfortunately, a whiteboard or chalkboard is easy to misuse and overuse. Moreover, they are not suitable for depicting complex material. Writing on a whiteboard or chalkboard is appropriate only for very short items of information that can be written in a few seconds. Nevertheless, being able to use a whiteboard or chalkboard effectively should be a part of any speaker's repertoire.

Whiteboards or chalkboards should be written on prior to speaking or during a break in speaking. Otherwise, the visual is likely to be either illegible or partly obscured by your body as you write. Or you may end up talking to the board rather than the audience. Should you need to draw or write on the board while you are talking, you should practice doing so in advance. If you are right-handed, stand to the right of what

Jeff Greenberg/Alamy

Photo 9.3 Posterboards are often used by professionals to help explain research projects.

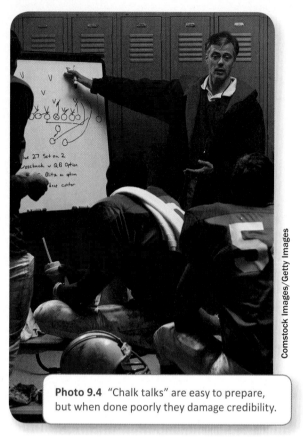

Photo 9.4 "Chalk talks" are easy to prepare, but when done poorly they damage credibility.

Comstock Images/Getty Images

you are drawing. Try to face at least part of the audience while you work (Photo 9.4). Although it may seem awkward at first, doing so will allow you to maintain eye contact with your audience and will allow the audience to see what you are doing while you are doing it.

9-5c Flipcharts

A **flipchart**, a large pad of paper mounted on an easel, can be an effective method for presenting visual aids. Flipcharts (and easels) are available in many sizes. For a presentation to four or five people, a small tabletop version works well; for a larger audience, use a larger pad (thirty-by-forty inches).

As with whiteboards and chalkboards, you should prepare them prior to giving the speech. In some situations, you may write down some information before the speech begins and add information while speaking. Also, be sure to leave a blank page between each visual on the pad to serve as both a transition page and a cover sheet. Because you want your audience to focus on visual material only when it is being discussed, you can flip to the empty page while you are talking about material not covered by visuals on the flip chart. Flipcharts can be comfortably used with smaller audiences (fewer than 100 people) but are not appropriate for larger settings.

flipchart: a pad of paper mounted on an easel

handout: material printed on sheets of paper

9-5d Handouts

At times, it may be useful for each member of the audience to have a personal copy of the visual aid. In these situations, you can prepare a **handout** (material printed on sheets of paper). The benefit is that all people in the audience can have a copy to refer to and take with them after the speech. The drawback is that distributing handouts during a speech can distract listeners' attention from you and your message.

Before you decide to use handouts, carefully consider why they would be better than some other method. Handouts are effective for information you want listeners to refer to after the speech, such as a set of steps to follow later, useful telephone numbers and addresses, or mathematical formulas.

If you do decide on handouts, distribute them at the end of the speech. If you want to refer to information on the handout during the speech, create another visual aid that you can reveal only when discussing it for use during your speech.

9-5e Document Cameras

Another simple way to display drawings, charts, photos, and graphs is with a document camera, such as an Elmo®. If you choose this method, be sure to transfer drawings, charts, photos, and graphs from original sources onto sheets of eight-by-eleven-inch paper so you can display them smoothly and professionally.

9-5f Computers, CD/DVD Players, and LCD Projectors

Most people today prefer to present audio and audiovisual recordings, as well as computerized slideshows using a computer and an LCD projector. However, you should always prepare back-up aids to use if equipment fails. Also, to ensure that audience

PUBLIC SPEAKING IN THE REAL WORLD

The Power of Presentational Aids and Ignite Speeches

The first Ignite event was conceived in 2006 as a way for the tech community in the Seattle, Washington area to share their personal and professional passions. An Ignite event typically consists of 15–20 speeches by people who submitted ideas in advance and were selected to present by event organizers. The rules for presenters are to use 20 self-propelling slides to help tell their story in a formal presentation limited to five minutes or less. Since then, Ignite has literally gone global with events taking place in over 100 cities around the world. Today, however, Ignite events are no longer limited to tech topics and are open to anyone who submits a good idea. These speeches are also posted online, which means speakers have the potential to reach millions of viewers with their ideas.[9, 10]

Drew Peneton, for instance, is a U.S. Army veteran, business entrepreneur, and finance professional at a Fortune 50 corporation. He speaks regularly at Ignite events across the country to promote Boots To Suits, a nonprofit organization he founded in 2009 to help military veterans reintegrate into the workforce when they return to civilian life. Peneton realizes the value of Ignite public speaking events as a forum for getting the word out about the plight of military veterans when they return from active duty, and as a platform for persuading people to help the cause. Speaking at Ignite events has helped him grow the Boots to Suits nonprofit organization from an online resource for veterans to a nationwide network of volunteers who have helped hundreds of thousands of veterans become gainfully employed.[11] You can watch

Peneton's 2012 Ignite speech and another sample Ignite speech by going to **Web Link 9.1, Ignite Speeches,** in your MindTap for *Challenge*.

There are at least four reasons why Ignite speeches resonate with so many people, and why they are such an effective public speech format:

1. Good Ignite speakers leave audiences both satisfied AND motivated to learn more.

2. Good Ignite speakers are less likely to bore audiences because they must be concise. They don't have time to ramble.

3. Good Ignite speakers must practice in advance or they won't be able to integrate their verbal message with the self-propelling slides. Practicing results in better speeches.

4. Good Ignite speakers choose, create, and use presentational aids effectively to enhance the telling of their story.

As Ignite co-creator, Brady Forrest explains: "It's not about slides, it's not even about your words, it's about a performance that marries the two together and lets people walk away with at least one new idea."[12]

Devon Christopher Adams

---

members focus their attention on you when you're not talking about one of your slides or clips, insert blank screens between slides, press the "B" key on your computer, or use the "mute" key on your projector remote to display blank screens. As Scott and Carrie realized after watching Dominic's Ignite speech in the opening vignette, computerized slideshows do not have to result in a "death by PowerPoint" experience when prepared, displayed, and used effectively.

 MindTap

9-6 USING PRESENTATIONAL AIDS

Many speakers think that once they have chosen and prepared good presentational aids, they will have no trouble using them during the speech. However, effective speakers also practice using them in advance. Although we will spend more time explaining how to do so in Chapter 11 (Delivery), we introduce several guidelines for using them here, as well.

1. Plan carefully when to use each presentational aid and make a note of it on your formal outline and in your speaking notes.

2. Position presentational aids and equipment so all audience members can see and/or hear them before beginning the speech.

3. Show or play presentational aids only when talking about them so they do not distract audience members from your message (Photo 9.5).

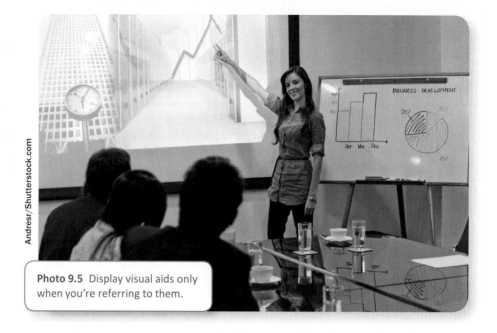

Photo 9.5 Display visual aids only when you're referring to them.

Andresr/Shutterstock.com

4. Pass objects and handouts around AFTER rather than during the speech so they do not distract audience members from your message.

5. Talk about the visual aid while showing it, and the audio or audiovisual aid just before and just after playing it.

6. Make eye contact with the audience while talking about the presentational aid.

 Go to **Web Link 9.2, Enhancing Written and Spoken Presentations**, in MindTap for *Challenge* to find out more about how and when to use visual aids in a speech.

 SPEECH PLANNING

Choosing, Preparing, and Using Presentational Aids

The goal of this activity is to identify where a presentational aid would increase audience interest, understanding, and retention and what type of presentational aid to prepare to do so.

1. Identify the key ideas in your speech for which you believe a presentational aid would increase audience interest, facilitate understanding, or increase retention.

2. For each idea you identified, list the type of presentational aid you think would be most appropriate and effective.

3. For each aid you identified, decide how you will find and/or design it.

4. For each aid you identified, decide on the method you will use to display it and how you will reference it during the speech.

Do this activity with Speech Builder Express. Access this activity on your MindTap for *Challenge*.

(5A) STUDENT RESPONSE

Activity

Choosing, Preparing, and Using Presentational Aids

Speech goal: *I would like my audience to learn to identify common poisonous plants that grow in our area.*

1. Identify the key ideas in your speech where a presentational aid would increase audience interest, facilitate understanding, or increase retention.

   Leaf shape, size, and color; habitat; signs of contact

2. For each idea you identified, list the type of presentational aid you think would be most appropriate and effective.

   I will use two color photographs of each type of plant. The first will show the entire plant; the second will be a close-up of the leaves. I will also use photos to show the habitat in which each plant is usually found. Finally, I will use photographs to show the reactions that occur as a result of contact with the plants. I will have actual plant samples available for closer inspection after my speech.

3. For each aid you identified, decide how you will find and/or design it.

   I will use my digital camera to take photographs of each plant and the habitats in which I found them. These will be transferred to my computer, and then I will create a computerized slide show using PowerPoint. I will locate images of reactions to each plant online, download them, and add them to the computerized slide show. I will also collect samples of each type of plant and bring them with me to the speech.

4. For each aid you identified, decide on the method you will use to display it and how you will reference it during the speech.

   I will bring a memory stick with the PowerPoint presentation on it with me and use the computer and LCD projector that is available at the speaking site. I will also have backup overheads of all my photos and slides. I will reference it using a pointer because I will be speaking to an audience of at least fifty people.

Reflection and Assessment

Presentational aids are useful when they help audience members understand and remember important information. To assess how well you've learned what we've discussed in this chapter, answer the following questions. If you have trouble answering any of them, go back and review that material. Once you can answer each question accurately, you are ready to move ahead to read the next chapter.

1. What are the benefits of using presentational aids in your speech?
2. Identify the different types of presentational aids.
3. What are some criteria for choosing appropriate presentational aids?
4. What are some guidelines you can follow when preparing presentational aids?
5. How might you display presentational aids in a speech?
6. What should you consider when using presentational aids during your speech?

 MindTap™

Challenge Resource and Assessment Center

Now that you have read Chapter 9, go to your MindTap for *The Challenge of Effective Speaking in a Digital Age* for quick access to the electronic resources that accompany this text. These resources include the following:

- **Study tools** that will help you assess your learning and prepare for exams (*digital glossary, key term flash cards, review quizzes*).

- **Activities and assignments** that will help you hone your knowledge and build your public speaking skills throughout the course (Practice, Do). Many of these activities allow you to compare your answers with those provided by the authors and, if requested, submit your answers to your instructor.

- **Media resources**—all of which are available on your MindTap for *Challenge*—will help you explore communication concepts online (Practice), develop your speech outlines (Do), watch and critique videos of sample speeches (Do), and upload your speech videos for instructor feedback and critique other students' speeches (Do).

- **Speech-Planning Action Step identified earlier in the chapter.**

  5A: Choosing, Preparing, and Using Presentational Aids (p. 176)

- **Web Links that provide you with additional information or resources related to the topics discussed in this chapter.**

  9.1: Ignite Speeches (p. 175)

  9.2: Enhancing Written and Spoken Presentations (p. 176)

- **Video resources allow you to see other students giving speeches and record your own speech.**

  1. Use your Interactive Video Activities to watch, analyze, and see the transcript and outline for the student speech "What Is Down Syndrome"?

  2. View how other students use presentational aids in their speeches. Do any of the speeches you see give you good ideas for how to use presentational aids in your own speeches? Or go to the Practice and Present section of MindTap to record a speech you're working on, upload it and ask your peers for their feedback. What feedback could you use to fine-tune your presentational aids before you give your speech in class?

Applying What You've Learned

1. **Impromptu Speech Activity:** Battle of the Visual Aids. Form groups of four or five people. Your instructor will provide you with three sample visual aids that might be used in a speech. Based on the criteria and guidelines you learned in this chapter, evaluate each visual aid and select the best one. At your instructor's request, one member of each team should go to the front of the room and give a two- to three-minute speech that makes a case for why the visual aid you selected is the best of the three. After all groups have made their presentations, vote as a class on the best one and discuss why.

2. **Assessment Activity A:** Complete Action Plan Step 5 for a speech you give this semester.

3. **Assessment Activity B:** Locate a visual, audio, and audiovisual aid example that you believe represents an effective and ineffective presentational aid based on the information and guidelines offered in this chapter. Prepare a two- to three-page paper explaining why you assessed them as you did.

10 "language and oral style"

WHAT'S THE POINT?
WHEN YOU'VE FINISHED THIS
CHAPTER, YOU'LL BE ABLE TO:

10-1 Explain how oral style differs from written style

10-2 Use appropriate words for the audience and occasion

10-3 Choose the most accurate words to convey your ideas

10-4 Use clear language

10-5 Select vivid words that appeal to the senses and draw on rhetorical devices

MindTap

Review the chapter **Learning Objectives** and **Start** with quick warm up activity.

6 Practice oral language and delivery style.

A. Practice to develop an oral style using language that is appropriate, accurate, clear, and vivid.

Ethical communicators make language choices that demonstrate respect for other individuals and groups.

Inna Felker/iStockphoto.com

© CoraMax/Shutterstock

Nathan asked his friend Josh to read through his formal speech outline and provide suggestions for improvement. After reading the outline for Nathan's informative speech about the congenital condition known as a Meckel's Diverticulum, Josh asked, "What class are you giving this speech for? Isn't it your public speaking class?"

"Yeah, why?" Nathan responded.

"Well" Josh replied, "Don't take this the wrong way, ok? I actually think it would be great for classmates in your Human Anatomy and Physiology class. But it seems awfully technical for classmates who come from all sorts of majors. I'm afraid it might go over their heads."

Nathan sounded bummed as he responded, "Oh, good point. Darn it! I guess I'll have to go back to the drawing board and pick a different topic."

"Actually," said Josh, "I don't think you have to start over. You just need to adjust some of your language to be appropriate and clear for a more general audience. Here let me show you . . ."

"I don't think you'll have to start over. You just need to adjust some of your language . . ."

With your outline in hand and presentational aids prepared, you are ready to move to the next step in the preparation process. In other words, you turn your focus from the macrostructure (the overall framework for organizing your speech content) to the microstructure (the specific language and style choices used to verbalize your ideas to a particular audience). In the chapter opening, Josh realizes that Nathan's speech can be adapted to his public speech class audience by choosing appropriate, accurate, clear, and vivid language.

In written communication, effective style evolves through a repetitious process of reading and revising. In a speech, effective style develops through a repetitious process of practicing aloud and revising. In this chapter, you will learn to develop language and style that is instantly intelligible to the *ear* so listeners interpret your messages as you intend.

Let's begin by clarifying how oral style differs from written style, as well as how the formal oral style used in public speeches differs from the informal oral style we use in casual conversations with family and friends. Then we'll offer some specific strategies you can employ to ensure that your language is appropriate, accurate, clear, and vivid.

10-1 ORAL STYLE

Oral style refers to how we convey messages through the spoken word. An effective oral style differs quite a bit from written style, though when giving a speech your oral style is still more formal than everyday talk. In fact, the degree of formality required to be an effective public speaker is based on the rhetorical situation. In other words, your goal is to adapt your language to the purpose, the audience, and the occasion. For example, although your language when speaking to a small audience of colleagues at a business meeting will be more formal than when conversing with a friend at dinner, it will not be as formal as when speaking to an audience of 100 or more at a professional conference or workshop. Still, even in a formal public speaking situation, you must *establish a relationship* with your listeners. Although your oral style is slightly more formal than in everyday conversation, it should still reflect a personal tone that encourages

PUBLIC SPEAKING IN THE REAL WORLD

The President's Way With Words

In the NPR news story, "The Art Of Language, Obama-Style," correspondent Linton Weeks explains that President Barack Obama understands that carefully selected language and oral style are powerful means for reaching the hearts and minds of listeners. How does he do it? He does it by following the guidelines for effective oral style.

First, he relies on simple language. He begins sentences with "look" or "listen" and uses everyday expressions such as "screwed up" and "folks." In other words, "he doesn't use $5 words when nickel ones will suffice".[1] In fact, according to a study that tracked language patterns of presidential candidates from 1948 to 2012 conducted by communication professors Roderick Hart and Kathleen Hall Jamieson,[2] Obama scored lower than anyone else on both "complexity" (average word size) and "embellishment" (number of words used to make a point). As a result, Obama comes across as a "plain spoken Midwesterner."

Second, according to political science professor John Geer, is the President's unique ability to "reach rhetorical heights" by finding the most descriptive words to express his worldview and make his point. In his article published in *The Guardian*, Sam Leith compared the President's brilliant use of rhetorical figures and structures of speech as equivalent to "a greatest hits album knocked out in time for Christmas. All his favourite oratorical devices were on display."[3]

© Ryan Rodrick Beiler/Shutterstock.com

And, he draws upon his "rare gift" and "real strength" for sounding conversational and appearing "comfortable whether scripted or extemporaneous" (Geer as cited in Weeks, 2009). He does so by using personal pronouns like "we" and "our" as he claims, for example, that "we're going to win this struggle" by working together and "our journey is not complete until."[4]

Whether or not one agrees with his politics, President Obama capitalizes on his own unique language and oral style to appeal effectively to the "folks" in his audience.

---

oral style: how one conveys messages through the spoken word

listeners to perceive you to be *having a conversation with them*. Four primary characteristics distinguish an effective oral style from an effective written style.

1. **An effective oral style tends toward short sentences and familiar language.** Because listeners expect to grasp the main ideas in your speech while they listen, work to ensure your words are ones that your audience is likely to understand without having to look up definitions. Likewise, opt for short, simple sentences rather than complex ones that would require additional time for audience members to decipher. We certainly live in a digital age where live public speeches can be recorded and even posted online to be heard multiple times. Even when watching a recorded public speech, however, listeners should not be required to press "pause" to look up word meanings or "reverse" to replay complex sentences. So adapting oral style to your audience means using short sentences and familiar language.

2. **An effective oral style features plural personal pronouns.** Using personal pronouns such as "we," "us," and "our" creates a sense of relationship with the audience; it demonstrates respect for the audience as participants in the rhetorical situation. Remember your goal is to create a perception of conversing *with* your audience rather than presenting *to* or *in front of* them. Personal pronouns encourage that perception.

3. **An effective oral style features descriptive words and phrases that appeal to the ear in ways that sustain listener interest and promote retention.** By using colorful adjectives and adverbs that appeal to the senses, and rhetorical figures of speech (discussed later in this chapter), you will capture the interest of your audience and motivate them to stay focused throughout the speech.

4. **An effective oral style incorporates clear macrostructural elements** (e.g., main point preview, section transitions, and signposts as discussed in Chapters 7 and 8). Unless your speech is being recorded and posted for additional viewing, listeners will be afforded the opportunity to hear it only once. Consequently, you need to intentionally articulate a preview of your main ideas, so listeners can place them firmly in their minds at the outset. Similarly, you need to provide clear section transitions that verbally signal when you are moving from one major idea to the next, and signposts such as "first," "second," "third," and "fourth" to help listeners follow your train of thought as the speech progresses.

Now that you have a sense of the nature of oral style as it differs from written style, let's turn our attention to some specific language choices you might make as you practice and revise your speech.

10-2 SPEAKING APPROPRIATELY

Speaking appropriately means using language that adapts to the needs, interests, knowledge, and attitudes of your listeners and avoiding language that might alienate anyone (Photo 10.1). In the communication field, we use the term **verbal immediacy** to describe language used to reduce the psychological distance between you and your audience.[5] In other words, speaking appropriately means making language choices that enhance a sense of connection between you and your audience members. In this section, we discuss specific strategies for making appropriate language choices.

10-2a Relevance

Your first challenge is to help the audience see the relevance of your topic to them. Listeners pay attention to and are motivated to listen to ideas that have a personal impact (when they can answer the question, "What does this have to do with me?"). Recall from Chapter 5 that you can help the audience perceive your topic and purpose as relevant by highlighting its timeliness, proximity, and personal impact for them. Listeners are more likely to be interested in information they perceive as timely. So whenever possible, use present tense as you explain your ideas. They see your topic as relevant when they understand how they can use it *now* or in the near future; when they see that it occurs where they live (not just in some far away place); and when they realize its potential physical, economic, or psychological impact on them personally. Josh, from the opening vignette, suggested that Nathan pique listener interest in this way by pointing out that major league pitcher, Chan Ho Park, was diagnosed with the defect in 2006. Doing so added relevance, since Park pitches for the team located right here where they are attending school.

10-2b Plural Personal Pronouns

As we've already mentioned, using plural personal pronouns like "we," "our," and "us" rather than "you" or "they," also conveys a sense of connection with your listeners. When used appropriately, "we" language fosters a sense of having a conversation *with* your audience rather than speaking or presenting *in front of* them. As a result, your audience will be more open to listening to you, believing what you say, and remembering your ideas.[6] You can easily replace "I" and "you" language

speaking appropriately: using language that adapts to the needs, interests, knowledge, and attitudes of the listener and avoiding language that alienates audience members

verbal immediacy: language that reduces the psychological distance between you and your audience

Photo 10.1 Speaking appropriately means avoiding language that might offend or alienate audience members. Doing so demonstrates respect and bolsters credibility.

© Featureflash/Shutterstock.com

Using "We" Language

Pete used "we" language to introduce his speech in this way: "Today, we'll see why Tok Pisin of Papua New Guinea should be considered a legitimate language. We'll do this by looking at what kind of language Tok Pisin is, some of the features of the Tok Pisin language, and why this language is necessary in New Guinea."

generic language:
language that uses words that apply only to one sex, race, or other group as though they represent everyone

with "we" language in the macrostructural elements of your speech. In your thesis statement, you can say, for example, "let's discuss . . ." rather than "I will inform you . . .," and in your section transitions, you can say "Now that we all have a clearer understanding of . . ." rather than "Now that I've explained . . ." and so on. For his Meckel's Diverticulum speech, Josh suggested Nathan introduce his thesis and preview using "we" language this way: "In the next few minutes, let's explore the symptoms, diagnosis, and treatment of a fairly unknown defect in the small intestine known as a Meckel's Diverticulum."

10-2c Linguistic Sensitivity

To demonstrate linguistic sensitivity, choose words that are respectful of others and avoid potentially offensive language. You can enhance verbal immediacy in this way by avoiding generic language, nonparallelism, potentially offensive humor, as well as profanity and vulgarity.[7]

1. **Generic language** uses words that apply only to one sex, race, or other group as though they represent everyone. In the past, English speakers used the masculine pronoun *he* to stand for all humans regardless of sex. This example of generic language excludes 50 percent of most audiences. The best way to avoid generic language is to use plurals: "When we shop, we should have a clear idea of what we want to buy."[8]

   A second problem of generic language results from the traditional use of *man*.[9] Consider the term *manmade*. What this really means is "made by human beings," but its underlying tone is that a *male* human being made the item. Bias-free alternatives do exist—for instance, *police officer* instead of *policeman*, *synthetic* instead of *manmade*, *humankind* instead of *mankind*, *flight attendant* instead of *stewardess*, and *server* instead of *waitress*. Bias-free language is not only more appropriate but, quite frankly, also more accurate (Photo 10.2).

2. **Nonparallelism** denotes when terms are changed because of the sex, race, or other group characteristics of the individual. Two common forms of nonparallelism are marking and irrelevant association.

   Marking is the *addition* of sex, race, age, or other group designations to a description. For instance, a doctor is a person with a medical degree who is licensed to practice medicine. Notice the difference between the following two sentences:

   > Jones is a good doctor.

   > Jones is a good black doctor.

   In the second sentence, use of the marker "black" has nothing to do with doctoring. Marking is inappropriate because it trivializes the person's role by introducing an irrelevant characteristic.[10] The speaker may be intending to praise Jones, but listeners may interpret the sentence as saying that Jones is a good doctor for a black person (or a woman or an old person) but not that Jones is as good as a good white doctor (or a male doctor or a young doctor).

   A second form of nonparallelism is **irrelevant association**, which is when we emphasize one person's relationship to another when that

Photo 10.2 Why does referring to these people as policemen fail to demonstrate linguistic sensitivity?

Tom Carter/Photolibrary/Getty Images

relationship is irrelevant to our point. For example, introducing a speaker as "Gladys Thompson, whose husband is CEO of Acme Inc., is the chairperson for this year's United Way campaign" is inappropriate. Mentioning her husband's status implies that Gladys Thompson is chairperson because of her *husband's* accomplishments, not her own.

3. **Offensive Humor**—such as dirty jokes and racist, sexist, or other "-ist" remarks—may not be intended to be offensive, but if some listeners are offended, you will have lost verbal immediacy. To be most effective with your formal public speeches, avoid humorous comments or jokes that may be offensive to some listeners. As a general rule, when in doubt, leave it out.

4. **Profanity and Vulgar** expressions are not considered appropriate language. Fifty years ago, a child was punished for saying "hell" or "damn," and adults used profanity and vulgarity only in rare situations to express strong emotions. Today, "casual swearing"—profanity injected into regular conversation—is commonplace in some language communities, including college campuses.[11] As a result, some of us have become desensitized to them as shocking or offensive (Photo 10.3). However, when giving a public speech, we need to remember that some people in our audience may still be offended by swearing. People who casually pepper their speech with profanity and vulgar expressions are often perceived as abrasive and lacking in character, maturity, intelligence, manners, and emotional control.[12]

Unfortunately, profanity and vulgarity are habits that are easily acquired and hard to extinguish. Tips for how to "tame your tongue" can be found can be found at **Web Link 10.1, Cuss Control Academy**, on MindTap for *Challenge*.

nonparallelism: when terms are changed because of the sex, race, or other group characteristics of the individual

marking: the addition of sex, race, age, or other group designations to a description

irrelevant association: emphasizing one person's relationship to another when that relationship is irrelevant to the point

10-2d Cultural Diversity

Language rules and expectations vary from culture to culture. One major theory used to explain such similarities and differences is individualism versus collectivism.[13] In general, individualistic cultures tend to use low-context communication, in which information is (1) embedded mainly in the messages transmitted and (2) presented directly. Collectivistic cultures tend to use high-context communication, in which people (1) expect others to know how they're thinking and feeling and (2) present some messages indirectly to avoid embarrassing the other person. Thus, speakers from low-context cultures tend to operate on the principle of saying what they mean and getting to the point. Their approach may be characterized by such expressions as "Say what you mean" and "Don't beat around the bush."[14] In contrast, speakers from high-context cultures are likely to use language that is intentionally indirect and listeners are expected to understand the message not only based on the words but also from the context in which they are uttered.

What does this mean for public speakers? When you address an audience comprised of people from ethnic and language groups different from your own, make extra effort to ensure that you are being understood. When the first language spoken by audience members is different from yours, they may

©iStockphoto.com/EdStock

Photo 10.3 Some comedians rely on profanity for humor; however, in doing so, they often offend some listeners.

Reflect on Ethics

On April 21, 2010, National Security Advisor James L. Jones opened his speech at the Washington Institute for Near East Policy—a pro-Israel think tank—with a joke. Many in the largely Jewish crowd laughed, while others claimed that it demonstrated a lack of sensitivity. Here's the joke:

A member of the Taliban who gets separated from his fighting party stumbles upon a shack, which it turns out is a little store owned by a Jewish merchant.

"I need water," the Taliban fighter says to the merchant. "Get me some water."

"I'm sorry I don't have any water, but would you like to buy a tie?" the merchant says. "We have a nice sale on ties today."

The Taliban warrior goes on a tirade against the merchant, against Jews, about Israel. "I need water; you try to sell me ties. You people don't get it."

"Well, I'm sorry, I don't have water for you," the merchant says. "I forgive you for all of the insults you've levied against me, my family, my country. But I will help you out."

The merchant steers the Taliban toward a restaurant two miles away.

"They have all the water you'll need," the merchant says.

The Taliban fighter walks toward the restaurant, then returns about an hour later.

"Your brother tells me I need a tie to get in the restaurant," he says.

Ba-dum-bum.

Jake Tapper, who was ABC Senior White House Correspondent at the time, called it the worst kind of joke Jones could have told in trying to reach out to the Jewish community. A Jewish member of Congress responded by saying ABC News should "lighten up." General Jones later offered this statement regarding his comments: "I wish that I had not made this off the cuff joke at the top of my remarks, and I apologize to anyone who was offended by it. It also distracted from the larger message I carried that day: that the United States' commitment to Israel's security is sacrosanct."[15]

1. What ethical communication principles do you believe Jones adhered to and violated in telling this joke?

2. Would your answer change if he had been speaking to an audience not made up primarily of Jewish individuals? Why or why not?

3. How would you evaluate Jones's apology in terms of ethical communication and why?

4. What will you do regarding cultural sensitivity and humor in your speeches and why?

---

not be able to understand what you are saying because you may speak with an accent, mispronounce words, choose inappropriate words, and misuse idioms.

Speaking in a second language can sometimes make us feel self-conscious. But most audience members are more tolerant of mistakes made by a second language speaker than they are of those made by a native speaker. Nevertheless, when you are speaking in a second language, you can help your audience by speaking more slowly and articulating as clearly as you can. By slowing your speaking rate, you give yourself additional time to pronounce difficult sounds and choose words whose meanings you know. You also give your audience members additional time to adjust their ears to more easily process what your are saying. You can also use visual aids to reinforce key terms and concepts as you move through the speech. Doing so assures listeners that they've understood you correctly.

One of the best ways to improve when you are giving a speech in a second language is to practice in front of friends who are native speakers. Ask them to take note of words and phrases that you mispronounce or misuse. Then they can work with you to correct the pronunciation or to choose other words that better express your idea. Also, keep in mind that the more you practice speaking the language, the more comfortable you will become with it.

 You can read more about how to adapt your language to be appropriate with audiences from diverse cultures at **Web Link 10.2, Speaking to International Audiences,** on your MindTap for *Challenge*.

10-3 SPEAKING ACCURATELY

Using **accurate language** means using words that convey your meaning precisely. On the surface, speaking accurately seems simple enough. In fact, however, speaking accurately is not that simple. Here are three reasons why.

accurate language: words that convey your meaning precisely

words: arbitrary symbols used to represent things

1. **Language is arbitrary.** The **words** we use to represent things are arbitrary symbols. In other words, there is not necessarily any literal connection between a word and the thing it represents. For a word to have meaning, it must be recognized by both or all parties as standing for a particular object, idea, or feeling.[16] In communication studies, we often simply say the *word* is not the *thing*. In their

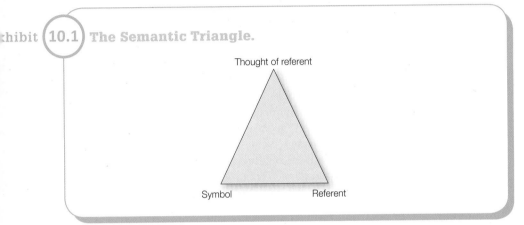

Exhibit 10.1 The Semantic Triangle.

Thought of referent

Symbol   Referent

Copyright © Cengage Learning

influential book, *The Meaning of Meaning: A Study of the Influence of Language upon Thought and the Science of Symbolism*, I. A. Richards and C. K. Ogden clarify this idea using the semantic triangle.[17] As depicted in Exhibit 10.1, a "referent" is the *thing* (object or idea) we refer to with a word, which is the "symbol" we use to refer to it. Our audience then attaches meaning to that symbol, which is what Richards and Ogden label the "thought of referent." The word D-O-G is nothing more than three letters used together unless all parties agree that it stands for a certain four-legged animal. To clarify, think about the fact that different groups use different word symbols for the same phenomenon. In Spanish, for instance, *el perro* stands for the same thing as *dog* in English. And the storage compartment of an automobile is called a "trunk" in the United States and a "boot" in England.

2. **Language is abstract.** Not only is language arbitrary, but it is also abstract. In the United States, for example, the word "pet" is commonly understood to be an animal kept for companionship. Still, if Rema refers simply to her "pet," Margi may think of a dog, cat, snake, bird, or hamster. Even if Rema specifically mentions her dog, Margi still might think of dogs of various breeds, sizes, colors, and temperaments.

Because language is abstract, two people might interpret the same word quite differently (Photo 10.4). For example, when James tells Chrissie that he liked going to the movie with her, Chrissie might interpret "liked" as enjoying the movie or spending time with her.

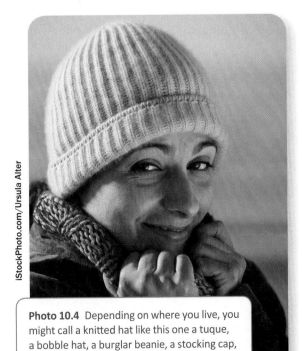

iStockPhoto.com/Ursula Alter

Photo 10.4 Depending on where you live, you might call a knitted hat like this one a tuque, a bobble hat, a burglar beanie, a stocking cap, or a toboggan. What would you call it?

3. **Language changes over time.** New words are constantly being invented and existing words abandoned or assigned new meanings. Just think, for example, of the words that have been invented to represent new technologies, such as *texting, Googling, cyberbullying, tweeting, retweeting, webinar, app, emoticon,* and *emoji.* Some of the new words most recently added to English dictionaries include *vanity sizing* (the deliberate undersizing of clothes), *twirt* (flirt on Twitter), *mankle* (the male ankle), and *cougar* (an older woman in a romantic relationship with a younger man). Did you know that the *Oxford English Dictionary* now also includes *OMG, LOL,* and *<3* as actual words?

Some words become obsolete because the thing they represent becomes obsolete. For example, today we use *photocopiers* and *computers* to make multiple copies of print documents rather than *mimeographs* (low-cost printing presses) and *stencils.* We record audio and video data using *smart phones* rather than using *tape recorders, cassette tapes,* and *videotapes.* And we take notes on *iPads* and *laptops* rather than on paper that we organize in a *Trapper Keeper* (a loose-leaf 3-ring binder used by school children in the U.S. during the 1980s).

Sometimes meanings of existing words change. For example, in the United States, the word *gay* once meant *happy* and only that. Today its more common usage references one's sexual orientation. In some communities, *bad* might mean *not good,* in others it might mean *naughty,* and in others it might mean *really great* (e.g., "That movie was really bad."). Language can also change as a result of melding aspects of multiple languages. *Tex-Mex* and *Spanglish,* for instance, both blend English and Spanish, and we don't think twice about the fact that children go to *kindergarten,* a word absorbed by the United States from German immigrants.

Using accurate language is crucial to effective speaking because it helps you be **intelligible**, or clearly understood. If listeners don't understand you or what you mean, your attempt to communicate is doomed. To help ensure that the language you use in speeches is accurate, let's take a look at three concepts that affect how words are interpreted: denotation, connotation, and dialect.

10-3a Denotation

A word's **denotation** is its explicit dictionary definition. So, denotatively, when Melissa said her dog died, she meant that her domesticated canine no longer demonstrates physical life. Nathan from the opening vignette offered the dictionary definition of a Meckel's Diverticulum as a congenital defect in the small intestine. Keep in mind that in some situations the denotative meaning of a word may not be clear. Why? One reason is that dictionary definitions reflect current and past practices in the language community. Another reason is that dictionaries often offer more than one definition for a given word. And dictionaries use words (which are abstract) to define words. The end result is that words are defined differently in various dictionaries and may include multiple meanings that also may change over time.

Moreover, meaning may vary depending on the **context** —the position of a word in a sentence and its relationship to the words around it. For example, the dictionary definition of *right* includes both (1) correct (adjective) and (2) a moral or ethical principle (noun). The situation in which a word is spoken may also clarify its denotative meaning. For example, if you're at the beach and you say you are "surfing," you probably mean you're riding the waves. But if you're sitting at your desk in front of your computer, you probably mean you're searching the Internet for information.

10-3b Connotation

A word's **connotation** is the positive, neutral, or negative feelings or evaluations we associate with it. For example, consider how your impression of Dave would differ if

---

intelligible: capable of being understood

denotation: the explicit dictionary definition of a word

context: the position of a word in a sentence and its relationship to the words around it

connotation: the positive, neutral, or negative feelings or evaluations we associate with a word someone said he was "cheap" versus "frugal." The denotative meaning of both words indicates someone who doesn't like to spend a lot of money, but for most of us "frugal" has a more positive connotation than "cheap" does. Thus, our perception of a word's connotation may be even more important than its denotation in how we interpret the meaning of the word. Connotations can be neutral, positive, or negative and can be quite different for different people. For example, the word "cop" can conjure up very different connotations for different people based on previous experiences.

Ogden and Richards were among the first scholars to consider the misunderstandings that result from the failure of communicators to realize that their subjective reactions to words are a product of their life experiences.[18] For instance, when Melissa told Trish that her dog died, Trish's understanding of the message depends on the extent to which her feelings about pets and death—her connotations of the words—correspond to the feelings Melissa has about pets and death. Whereas Melissa (who sees dogs as truly indispensable friends) may be intending to communicate her overwhelming grief, Trish (who doesn't particularly care for pets in general or dogs in particular) may miss the emotional meaning of Melissa's statement.

Connotations give emotional power to words, so much so that people will even fight and die for them. Consider the connotative meanings people assign to words like *freedom* and *honor* and *justice*. For this reason, connotations can increase the emotional appeal of your message. As you consider language options, be sure to consider audience disposition toward them and steer clear of words that might arouse unintended connotations.

10-3c Dialect

Dialect is a unique form of a more general language spoken by a specific cultural or co-cultural group.[19] These smaller groups that speak a common dialect are called **speech communities**. Dialects evolve over time, and the manner in which they differ from the "standard" of the language may be influenced by other languages spoken in the region or by the ethnic group. For instance, in her book *Chicano English in Context*, Carmen Fought explains how the English spoken by some Hispanic people in the Los Angeles area differs from Standard English.[20] Regional differences are also reflected in the words used to represent common things. For example, in some places a car's turn signal is called a "blinker," a seesaw is a "teeter-totter," and a soft drink is a "pop" or a "coke." Some dialects also incorporate what is considered non-standard grammar, such as "he don't," "I says," "this here book," and "beings as how he was sick." If your audience doesn't share the dialect you normally speak, using it during your speeches can interfere with intelligibility. Not only that, it can also affect your ethos (the audience's perception of your competence and credibility). Because most audiences are diverse, the best way to ensure being understood by all and conveying positive ethos is to use **Standard English** (which is taught in American schools and detailed in grammar handbooks like *Hodges Harbrace Handbook*, 18th ed.[21]).

dialect: a regional variety of a language

speech communities: a group of people who speak a common dialect

Standard English: form of English described in an English grammar handbook

10-4 SPEAKING CLEARLY

Speaking clearly results from explaining potentially ambiguous language. Compare the clarity of the following two descriptions of the same incident:

> *Some nut almost ran into me last week.*

> *Last Saturday afternoon, an older man in a banged-up Honda Civic ran through the red light at Calhoun and Clifton and came within inches of hitting my car while I was waiting to turn left.*

Let's look at four strategies for improving clarity: use specific language, choose familiar terms, provide details and examples, and limit vocalized pauses.

SPEECH SNIPPET

Adjusting for Dialect

As Maren, who is from Minnesota, prepared to practice her speech on the effect drinking sugared sodas has on childhood obesity, she thought about how her roommate would tease her when she referred to "soda" as "pop." As she practiced, she made notes to always say "soda" during her speech.

10-4a Use Specific Language

specific language: words that clarify meaning by narrowing what is understood from a general category to a particular item or group within that category

Specific language clarifies meaning by using precise words that narrow what is understood from a general category to a particular item or group within that category. For instance, if in her speech Nevah refers to a "blue-collar worker," you might picture any number of occupations that fall within this broad category. If, instead, she says "construction worker," the number of possible images you can picture is reduced. Now you select your image from the subcategory of construction worker, and your meaning is likely to be closer to the one she intended. If she is even more specific, she may say "bulldozer operator." Now you are even clearer on the specific occupation. To see a video clip of a student speaker using specific language, go to your MindTap for *Challenge* to access the Interactive Video Activities for Chapter 10. Select the clip called "Shakespeare."

Choosing specific language is easier when you have a large working vocabulary. As a speaker, the larger your vocabulary, the more choices you have from which to select the word you want. As a listener, the larger your vocabulary, the more likely you are to understand the words used by others.

One way to increase your vocabulary is to study one of the many vocabulary-building books, such as *Word Smart: How to Build a More Educated Vocabulary*, 5th ed.[22] To take a vocabulary test online, go to **Web Link 10.3, Vocabulary-Building Challenge,** on your MindTap for *Challenge.*

A second way to increase your vocabulary is to take note of unfamiliar words you read or that people use in conversations and look them up. For instance, suppose you read or hear, "I was inundated with phone calls today!" If you wrote down *inundated* and looked it up in a dictionary later, you would find its it means "overwhelmed" or "flooded." If you then say to yourself, "She was inundated—overwhelmed or flooded—with phone calls today," you are likely to remember its meaning.

A third way to increase your vocabulary is to use a thesaurus to identify synonyms that may be more specific options. Most computer programs like Microsoft Word offer a thesaurus under the "Tools" option, or there are various options online. But be careful—avoid unfamiliar words that may make you sound intelligent but could reduce your intelligibility. For example, *somnolent* is an interesting word, but most people don't know that it is a synonym for *sleepy*. You can access **Web Link 10.4, Merriam-Webster Online,** on your MindTap for *Challenge.*

Having a larger vocabulary won't help your speaking unless you use it as you practice. Suppose you were practicing a speech on registering for classes and said, "Preregistration is awful." If this word isn't quite right, you can quickly brainstorm better words, such as *frustrating, demeaning, cumbersome,* and *annoying.* Then, as you continue to practice, you might say, "Preregistration is a cumbersome process."

Some speakers think that to be effective they must impress their audience with their extensive vocabulary. As a result, instead of looking for specific and precise words, they use words that appear pompous, affected, or stilted to the listener. Speaking precisely and specifically does not mean speaking obscurely. The following story illustrates the problem with pretentious words:

> A plumber wrote to a government agency, saying that he found that hydrochloric acid quickly opened drainpipes but that he wasn't sure whether it was a good thing to use. A scientist at the agency replied, "The efficacy of hydrochloric acid is indisputable, but the corrosive residue is incompatible with metallic permanence."

> The plumber wrote back thanking him for the assurance that hydrochloric acid was all right. Disturbed by this turn of affairs, the scientist showed the letter to his boss, another scientist, who then wrote to the plumber: "We cannot assume responsibility

for the production of toxic and noxious residue with hydrochloric acid and suggest you use an alternative procedure."

The plumber wrote back that he agreed. Hydrochloric acid worked fine. Greatly disturbed by this misunderstanding, the scientists took their problem to the top boss. She wrote to the plumber: "Don't use hydrochloric acid. It eats the hell out of pipes."

So, use a more difficult word *only* when you believe that it is the very best word for a specific context. Let's suppose you wanted to use a more precise or specific word for *building*. Using the guideline of familiarity, you might select *house, apartment, high-rise,* or *skyscraper*, but you would avoid *edifice*. Each of the other choices is more precise or more specific, but *edifice* is neither more precise nor more specific, and in addition to being less well understood, it will be perceived as affected or stilted.

10-4b Choose Familiar Terms

Using familiar terms is just as important as using specific words. Avoid jargon, slang, abbreviations, and acronyms unless (1) you define them clearly the first time they are used and (2) using them is central to your speech goal.

Jargon is the unique technical terminology of a trade or profession that is not generally understood by outsiders. We might forget that people who are not in our same line of work or who do not have the same hobbies may not understand the jargon that seems such a part of our daily communication. For instance, when Jenny starts talking with her computer-illiterate friend Sarah about "social MUDs based on fictional universes," Sarah is likely to be totally lost. If, however, Jenny recognizes Sarah's lack of familiarity with cyberlanguage, she can make her message clear by discussing the concepts in words her friend understands. In short, limit your use of jargon in speeches to general audiences and always define jargon in simple terms the first time you use it. Josh suggested that Nathan not only say that a technetium-99m scan is the test used to diagnose a Meckel's Diverticulum, but also what it is. So, Nathan added a sentence to say that technetium-99m is a radioactive material that is injected into a vein in your arm. Then a special camera positioned outside your body can help detect the deformity.

jargon: the unique technical terminology of a trade or profession

Slang refers to informal, nonstandard vocabulary and definitions assigned to words by a social group or co-culture (Photo 10.5). For example, today the word *wicked*, which has a standard definition denoting something wrong or immoral, can mean quite the opposite in some social groups and co-cultures.[23] You should generally avoid slang in your public speeches not only because you risk being misunderstood but also because slang doesn't sound professional and can hurt your credibility (ethos). Slang is so pervasive that there are special dictionaries devoted to the specialized vocabulary of different communities. To access one created by a former student of the University of California, Berkeley, go to **Web Link 10.5, Slang Dictionary,** on your MindTap for *Challenge*.

slang: informal, nonstandard vocabulary and definitions assigned to words by a social group or co-culture

Photo 10.5 Slang that is generally understood within a co-culture may not be clear to all audience members for a public speech.

Overusing and misusing abbreviations and acronyms can also hinder clarity. Even if you think the abbreviation or acronym is a common one, to ensure intelligibility, always define it the first time you use it in the speech. For example, in a speech about NASCAR, refer to it initially by the organization's full name and then provide the acronym: "National Association for Stock Car Auto Racing, or NASCAR." Providing the full and abbreviated forms of the name will ensure clarity for all listeners. If you are assuming right now that everyone knows what NASCAR is, it might benefit you to know one of your authors had to look it up to include it in this book!

10-4c Provide Details and Examples

Sometimes the word we use may not have a precise synonym. In these situations, clarity can be achieved by adding details or examples. Saying "He lives in a really big house" can be clarified by adding details: "He lives in a fourteen-room Tudor mansion on a six-acre estate."

10-4d Limit Vocalized Pauses

Vocalized pauses are unnecessary words interjected into sentences to fill moments of silence. Words commonly used for this purpose are "like," "you know," "really," and "basically," as well as "um" and "uh." We sometimes refer to vocalized pauses as "verbal garbage" because they do not serve a meaningful purpose and when used excessively actually distract listeners from the message. Although a few vocalized pauses typically don't hinder clarity, practicing your speech aloud will help you eliminate them.

10-5 SPEAKING VIVIDLY

Speaking vividly is one effective way to gain and maintain audience interest and help them remember what you say. **Vivid language** is full of life—vigorous, bright, and intense. For example, a mediocre baseball announcer might say, "Jackson made a great catch," but a better commentator's vivid account might be, "Jackson leaped and made a spectacular one-handed catch just as he crashed into the center field wall." The words *leaped, spectacular, one-handed catch*, and *crashed* paint an intense verbal picture of the action. You can make your ideas come to life by using sensory language and by using rhetorical figures and structures of speech.

vocalized pauses: unnecessary words interjected into sentences to fill moments of silence

vivid language: language that is full of life—vigorous, bright, and intense

10-5a Use Sensory Language

Sensory language appeals to the senses of seeing, hearing, tasting, smelling, and feeling. Vivid sensory language begins with vivid thought. You are much more likely to express yourself vividly if you can physically or psychologically sense the meanings you are trying to convey. If you feel the "bite of the wind" or "the sting of freezing rain," if you hear and smell "the thick, juicy sirloin steaks sizzling on the grill," you will be able to describe these sensations. Does the cake merely "taste good" or do your taste buds "quiver with the sweet double-chocolate icing and velvety feel of the rich, moist cake"?

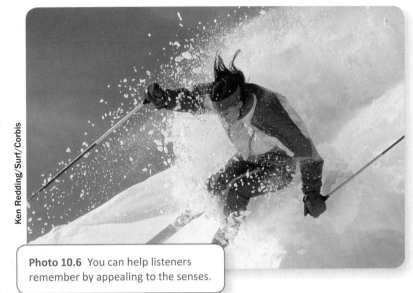

Ken Redding/Surf/Corbis

Photo 10.6 You can help listeners remember by appealing to the senses.

To develop vivid sensory language, begin by considering how you can re-create what something, someone, or some place *looks like*. Consider, too, how you can help listeners imagine how something *sounds*. How can you use language to convey the way something *feels* (textures, shapes, temperatures)? How can language re-create a sense of how something *tastes* or *smells*? To achieve this in your speech, use colorful descriptors. They make your ideas more concrete and can arouse emotions. They invite listeners to imagine details. Here's an example about downhill skiing:

> *Sight:* As you climb the hill, the bright winter sunshine glistening on the snow is blinding.
>
> *Touch and feel:* Just before you take off, you gently slip your goggles over your eyes. They are bitterly cold and sting your nose for a moment.
>
> *Taste:* You start the descent and, as you gradually pick up speed, the taste of air and ice and snow in your mouth invigorates you (Photo 10.6).
>
> *Sound:* An odd silence fills the air. You hear nothing but the swish of your skis against the snow beneath your feet. At last, you arrive at the bottom of the slope. Reality hits as you hear the hustle and bustle of other skiers and instructors directing them to their next session.
>
> *Smell and feel:* You enter the warming house. As your fingers thaw in the warm air, the aroma from the wood stove in the corner comforts you as you drift off into sleep.

By using colorful descriptors that appeal to the senses, you arouse and maintain listener interest and make your ideas more memorable.

10-5b Use Rhetorical Figures and Structures of Speech

Rhetorical figures of speech make striking comparisons between things that are not obviously alike to help listeners visualize or internalize what you are saying. **Rhetorical structures of speech** combine ideas in a particular way. Any of these devices can serve to make your speech more memorable as long as they aren't overused. Let's look at some examples.

A **simile** is a direct comparison of dissimilar things using the word *like* or *as*. Clichés such as "He walks like a duck" and "She's as busy as a bee" are similes. If you've

sensory language: appeals to the senses of seeing, hearing, tasting, smelling, and feeling

IMPROMPTU SPEECH CHALLENGE

Draw a card from a stack provided by your instructor. Each card names an event or activity such as *mowing the lawn, eating tacos, riding a bicycle,* or *being stuck in traffic.* Prepare a short one- to two-minute speech about it by appealing to each of the five senses (sight, touch/feel, taste, sound, smell)

rhetorical figures of speech: phrases that make striking comparisons between things that are not obviously alike

rhetorical structures of speech: phrases that combine ideas in a particular way

simile: a direct comparison of dissimilar things using *like* or *as*

Dan decided to use a metaphor to help explain the complex concept of bioluminescence to his listeners. He said that "bioluminescence is a miniature flashlight that fireflies turn on and off at will."

metaphor: an implied comparison between two unlike things without using *like* or *as*

analogy: an extended metaphor

alliteration: repetition of consonant sounds at the beginning of words that are near one another

assonance: repetition of vowel sounds in a phrase or phrases

onomatopoeia: words that sound like the things they stand for

personification: attributing human qualities to a concept or an inanimate object

repetition: restating words, phrases, or sentences for emphasis

seen the movie *Forrest Gump*, you might recall Forrest's use of similes: "Life is like a box of chocolates. You never know what you're going to get" and "Stupid is as stupid does." An elementary school teacher used a simile by saying that being back at school after a long absence "was like trying to hold 35 corks under water at the same time."[24] Similes can be effective because they make ideas more vivid in listeners' minds. But they should be used sparingly or they lose their appeal. Clichés should be avoided because their predictability reduces their effectiveness.

A **metaphor** is an implied comparison between two unlike things, expressed without using *like* or *as*. Instead of saying that one thing is *like* another, a metaphor says that one thing *is* another. Thus, a problem car is a "lemon" and a leaky roof is a "sieve." Metaphors can be effective because they make an abstract concept more concrete, strengthen an important point, or heighten emotions. Notice how one speaker used a metaphor effectively to conclude a speech: "It is imperative that we weave our fabric of the future with durable thread."[25]

An **analogy** is an extended metaphor. Sometimes, you can develop a story from a metaphor that makes a concept more vivid. If you were to describe a family member as the "black sheep in the barnyard," that's a metaphor. If you went on to talk about the other members of the family as different animals on the farm and the roles ascribed to them, you would be extending the metaphor into an analogy. Analogies can be effective for holding your speech together in a creative and vivid way. Analogies are particularly useful to highlight the similarities between a complex or unfamiliar concept and a familiar one.

Alliteration is the repetition of consonant sounds at the beginning of words that are near one another. Tongue twisters such as "She sells seashells by the seashore" use alliteration. In her speech about the history of jelly beans, Sharla used alliteration when she said, "And today there are more than fifty fabulous fruity flavors from which to choose." Used sparingly, alliteration can catch listeners' attention and make the speech memorable. But overuse can hurt the message because listeners might focus on the technique rather than the speech content.

Assonance is the repetition of vowel sounds in a phrase or phrases. "How now brown cow" is a common example. Sometimes, the words rhyme, but they don't have to. As with alliteration, assonance can make your speech more memorable as long as it's not overused.

Onomatopoeia is the use of words that sound like the things they stand for, such as "buzz," "hiss," "crack," and "plop." In the speech about skiing, the "swish" of the skis is an example of onomatopoeia.

Personification is attributing human qualities to a concept or an inanimate object. When Madison talked about her truck, "Big Red," as her trusted friend and companion, she used personification. Likewise, when Rick talked about flowers dancing on the front lawn, he used personification.

Repetition is restating words, phrases, or sentences for emphasis. Martin Luther King Jr.'s "I Have a Dream" speech is a classic example:

I say to you today, my friends, so even though we face the difficulties of today and tomorrow, I still have a dream. It is a dream deeply rooted in the American dream.

I have a dream that one day this nation will rise up and live out the true meaning of its creed: "We hold these truths to be self-evident: that all men are created equal."

I have a dream that one day on the red hills of Georgia the sons of former slaves and the sons of former slave owners will be able to sit down together at the table of brotherhood.

I have a dream that one day even the state of Mississippi, a state sweltering with the heat of injustice, sweltering with the heat of oppression, will be transformed into the oasis of freedom and justice.

I have a dream that my four little children will one day live in a nation where they will not be judged by the color of their skin but by the content of their character. I have a dream today.

© 1963 Dr. Martin Luther King Jr. © 1991 Copyright renewed by Coretta Scott King.

Antithesis is combining contrasting ideas in the same sentence, as when John F. Kennedy said, "Ask not what your country can do for you. Ask what you can do for your country." Likewise, astronaut Neil Armstrong used antithesis when he first stepped on the moon: "One small step for man, one giant leap for mankind." Speeches that offer antithesis in the concluding remarks are often very memorable.

antithesis: combining contrasting ideas in the same sentence

Reflection and Assessment

Your overall goal with regard to language and oral style is to be appropriate, accurate, clear, and vivid. To assess how well you've learned what we've discussed in this chapter, answer the following questions. If you have trouble answering any of them, go back and review that material. Once you can answer each question accurately, you are ready to move ahead to read the next chapter.

1. In what ways does oral style differ from written style?
2. What are some guidelines to determine appropriate words for the audience and occasion?
3. How do you choose the most accurate words to convey your ideas?
4. What does it mean to use clear language?
5. What are some examples of vivid words that appeal to the senses or draw on rhetorical devices?

Challenge Resource and Assessment Center

Now that you have read Chapter 10, go to your MindTap for *The Challenge of Effective Speaking in a Digital Age* for quick access to the electronic resources that accompany this text. These resources include the following:

- **Study tools** that will help you assess your learning and prepare for exams (*digital glossary, key term flash cards, review quizzes*).

- **Activities and assignments** that will help you hone your knowledge and build your public speaking skills throughout the course (Practice, Do). Many of these activities allow you to compare your answers with those provided by the authors and, if requested, submit your answers to your instructor.

- **Media resources**—all of which are available on your MindTap for *Challenge*—will help you explore communication concepts online (Practice), develop your speech outlines (Do), watch and critique videos of sample speeches (Do), and upload your speech videos for instructor feedback and critique other students' speeches (Do).

- **Web Links that provide you with additional information or resources related to the topics discussed in this chapter.**
  - **10.1:** Cuss Control Academy (p. 185)
  - **10.2:** Speaking to International Audiences (p. 186)
  - **10.3:** Vocabulary-Building Challenge (p. 190)
  - **10.4:** Merriam-Webster Online (p. 190)
  - **10.5:** Slang Dictionary (p. 191)

- **Video resources allow you to see other students giving speeches and record your own speech.**
  1. Use your Interactive Video Activities (Do) to watch, analyze, and see the transcript and outlines for Hillary Carter-Liget's informative speech "Shakespeare."
  2. View how other students use language in their speeches. Or go to the Practice and Present section of MindTap to record a speech you're working on, upload it, and ask your peers for their feedback. What feedback could you use to fine-tune your language and oral style before you give your speech in class?

Applying What You've Learned

1. **Impromptu Speech Activity:** Draw a nonsensical word from a stack of cards created by your instructor (e.g., photomaniac, alienitus, caninicopia, aquatiphobia). Develop your own definition for this word. Then, prepare and deliver a two- to three-minute impromptu speech explaining the meaning of the word using specific language, familiar terms, details, and examples.

2. **Assessment Activity A:** Go online to the *American Rhetoric: Top 100 Speeches* website. Select and listen to one of the speeches posted there. As you listen, take notes regarding the speaker's vivid language choices (sensory language and rhetorical figures and structures of speech). To what degree does the use of them pique your interest and add to the memorability of the message? Explain.

3. **Assessment Activity B:** Select one of these popular television sitcoms: *Modern Family, How I Met Your Mother, Parks and Recreation, Girls, Big Bang Theory,* or *Family Guy.* Watch an episode and record the following for each of the main characters use of (a) "we" language, (b) profanity and vulgarity, (c) offensive humor, and (d) linguistic insensitivity. To what degree is each main character portrayed as a role model for viewers? Based on the kinds and number of appropriate and inappropriate language behaviors exhibited and the nature of the character as an intended role model, what message is being sent to viewers about what "appropriate" language usage is?

11 "delivery"

WHAT'S THE POINT?
WHEN YOU'VE FINISHED THIS
CHAPTER, YOU'LL BE ABLE TO:

11-1 Describe the characteristics of effective delivery

11-2 Use your voice effectively to deliver your speech

11-3 Use your body effectively to deliver your speech

11-4 Understand different speech delivery methods

11-5 Engage in effective speech rehearsals

11-6 Adapt delivery appropriately while presenting your speech

11-7 Adapt your speech and delivery for virtual audiences

 MindTap™

Review the chapter **Learning Objectives** and **Start** with quick warm up activity.

---

6 **Practice oral language and delivery style.**

B. Practice until the delivery is conversational, intelligible, and expressive.

C. Practice integrating presentational aids until you can do so smoothly and confidently.

D. Practice until you can deliver your speech extemporaneously within the time limit.

Mode Ian O'Leary/Mode Images/Alamy

© CoraMax/Shutterstock

e Ethical communicators demonstrate respect for their listeners by practicing delivery in advance.

When Alyssa and Katie finished watching a recording of Alyssa's first speech practice, Alyssa said:

"Ugh! That was horrible. I bored myself. I just don't get it. I have all this great information. Why is it so hard to stay focused? My speech is only 5 1/2 minutes long."

Katie responded, "Don't be so hard on yourself Alyssa. Your speech is good. The topic is interesting and relevant, you cite great evidence, it's well organized, and you use compelling language. You just need to work a bit more on your delivery to make it sound conversational and dynamic. Let's add some delivery cues to your speaking notes to help you remember to emphasize key points with your voice and gestures and to clarify structure with gestures and movement. Then you can practice a few more times until you sound and look spontaneous."

"Ok," Alyssa replied. "After watching that rehearsal, I'll try anything . . ."

> "You just need to work a bit on your delivery to make it sound more conversational and dynamic."

What both Alyssa and Katie recognize is that the difference between a good speech and a great speech is often how well it is delivered. In fact, research suggests that listeners are influenced more by delivery than by the content of speeches.[1] A speaker's delivery alone cannot compensate for a poorly researched, organized, or developed speech, but a well-delivered speech can rise above the ordinary and really capture an audience.

In this chapter, we begin by talking about the characteristics of effective delivery. We then describe the elements of effective delivery: use of voice and use of body. Next, we discuss three speech delivery methods and the settings in which each is most appropriate. Finally, we suggest a process for rehearsing your speech and ways to adapt to your audience while giving it in face-to-face settings and for virtual audiences.

11-1 CHARACTERISTICS OF EFFECTIVE DELIVERY

Think about the best speaker you have ever heard. What made this person stand out in your mind? In all likelihood, how the speaker delivered the speech had a lot to do with it. **Delivery** is how a message is communicated nonverbally through your voice and body. **Nonverbal communication** includes all speech elements other than the actual words themselves.[2] These elements include your use of voice (e.g., pitch, volume, rate, quality, articulation, pronunciation, and pauses) and use of body (e.g., facial expressions, eye contact, gestures, body language, and even appearance). Effective delivery is both conversational and animated.

11-1a Conversational

You have probably heard ineffective speakers whose delivery was overly dramatic and affected or stiff and mechanical. In contrast, effective delivery is **conversational**, meaning your audience perceives you as *talking with* them and not *performing in front of* or *reading to* them. The hallmark of a conversational style is spontaneity. **Spontaneity** is the ability to sound natural—as though you are really thinking about the ideas *and* getting them across to the audience—no matter how many times you've practiced.

The secret to developing a conversational style is to learn the *ideas* of your speech rather than trying to memorize every *word*. As you study your outline, you absorb these ideas, and as you rehearse out loud, you can focus on conveying them in a conversational way.

11-1b Animated

Have you ever been bored by a professor reading a well-structured lecture while mostly looking at the lecture notes rather than at the students and making few gestures other than turning the pages of those notes? Even a well-written speech given by an expert can bore an audience unless its delivery is **animated**, that is, lively and dynamic (Photo 11.1).

How can we be conversational and animated at the same time? The secret is to focus on conveying the passion we feel about the topic through our voice and body. When we are passionate about sharing something with someone, almost all of us become more animated in our delivery. The goal is to duplicate this level of liveliness when delivering our speeches. The next two sections focus on how to use the voice and body to achieve effective conversational and animated delivery. To see a video clip of a student speaker with an animated delivery, go to MindTap for *Challenge* to access the speech "Why Pi?" in the Chapter 11 resources.

Photo 11.1 Animated delivery motivates audience members to listen to you.

© Iofoto/Shutterstock.com

🌑 MindTap™

delivery: how a message is communicated through the use of voice and body

nonverbal communication: all speech elements other than the words themselves

conversational: delivery that seems spontaneous, as though one is talking with an audience

spontaneity: sounding natural no matter how many times one has practiced

animated: delivery that is lively, and dynamic

voice: the sound you produce using your vocal organs

pitch: the highness or lowness of the sounds produced in your larynx

volume: how loudly or softly you speak

11-2 USE OF VOICE

Your **voice** is the sound you produce using your vocal organs (including your larynx, tongue, teeth, lips, etc.). How your voice sounds depends on its pitch, volume, rate, and quality. **Pitch** is the highness or lowness of the sounds you produce. **Volume** is how loudly or softly you speak. **Rate** is the speed at which you talk. **Quality** is the timbre that distinguishes your voice from others. Your goal in public speaking is to vary your pitch, volume, rate, and quality to achieve a conversational and animated style that is both intelligible and expressive.

11-2a Intelligibility

To be intelligible means to be understandable. All of us have experienced situations when we couldn't understand what was being said because the speaker was talking too softly or too quickly. If you practice your speech using appropriate vocal pitch, volume, rate, and vocal quality, you can improve the likelihood that you will be intelligible to your audience.

Most of us speak at a pitch that is appropriate for us and intelligible to listeners. However, some people naturally have voices that are higher or lower in register or become accustomed to talking in tones that are above or below their natural pitch. Speaking at an appropriate pitch is particularly important if your audience includes people who have hearing loss because they may find it difficult to hear a pitch that is too high or too low. Intelligibility is also affected by how much a speaker fluctuates his or her pitch. In normal conversation, pitch fluctuates frequently, and perhaps even a bit more during a speech. Pitch that doesn't fluctuate may hinder intelligibility. For example, in English, a sentence that is meant to be a question is vocalized with rising pitch. If pitch doesn't rise at the end of a question, listeners may interpret the sentence as a statement instead.

Appropriate volume is the key to intelligibility. You must speak loudly enough, with or without a microphone, to be heard easily by audience members seated in the back of the room but not so loudly as to bring discomfort to listeners seated near the front. Similarly, when recording a speech to post online, you want to be heard easily but not sound as though you are shouting.

The rate at which you speak can also influence intelligibility. Speaking too slowly gives your listeners time to let their minds wander after they've processed an idea. Speaking too quickly, especially when sharing complex ideas and arguments, may not give your listeners enough time to process the information completely. Because nervousness may cause you to speak more quickly than normal, you will want to monitor your speaking rate and intentionally slow down if necessary. To complete a simple test to see if your typical rate of speech is within the range that is intelligible to most people, go to **Web Link 11.1, Your Speech Rate,** on your MindTap for *Challenge*.

In addition to vocal characteristics, articulation, pronunciation, and accent problems can affect how intelligible you are. **Articulation** is using the tongue, palate, teeth, jaw movement, and lips to shape vocalized sounds that combine to produce a word. Many of us suffer from minor articulation and **pronunciation** problems such as adding a sound where none appears ("athalete" for *athlete*), leaving out a sound where one occurs ("libary" for *library*), transposing sounds ("revalent" for *relevant*), and distorting sounds ("truf" for *truth*). Exhibit 11.1 lists many common words that people are likely to mispronounce or misarticulate.

rate: the speed at which you talk

quality: the tone, timbre, or sound of your voice

 MindTap™

articulation: using the tongue, palate, teeth, jaw movement, and lips to shape vocalized sounds that combine to produce a word

pronunciation: the form and accent of various syllables of a word

hibit 11.1 Words Commonly Mispronounced

Word	Incorrect	Correct
arctic	ar'-tic	arc'-tic
athlete	ath'-a-lete	ath'-lete
family	fam'-ly	fam'-a-ly
February	Feb'-yu-ary	Feb'-ru-ary
get	git	get
hundred	hun'-derd	hun'-dred
larynx	lar'-nix	ler'-inks
library	ly'-ber-y	ly'-brer-y
nuclear	nu'-kyu-ler	nu'-klee-er
particular	par-tik'-ler	par-tik'-yu-ler
picture	pitch'-er	pic'-ture
recognize	rek'-a-nize	rek'-ig-nize
relevant	rev'-e-lant	rel'-e-vant
theater	thee-ay'-ter	thee'-a-ter
truth	truf	truth
with	wit or wid	with

Copyright © Cengage Learning

Accent is the inflection, tone, and speech habits typical of native speakers of a language. When you misarticulate or speak with a heavy accent during a conversation, your listeners can ask you to repeat yourself until they understand you. But in a speech setting, audience members are unlikely to interrupt to ask you to repeat something.

Accent can be a major concern for second language speakers or speakers from various regions of a country (Photo 11.2). Everyone speaks with some kind of accent, because "accent" means any tone or inflection that differs from the way others speak. To clarify, natives of a particular city or region in the United States will speak with inflections and tones that they believe are "normal" spoken English—for instance, people from the Northeast who drop the *r* sound (saying "cah" for *car*) or people from the South who elongate their vowels and "drawl," or people from the upper Midwest who elongate certain vowels (e.g., "Min-ne-SOOO-ta"). But when they visit a different city or region, they are perceived as having an accent. If your accent is "thick" or very different

accent: the inflection, tone, and speech habits typical of native speakers of a language

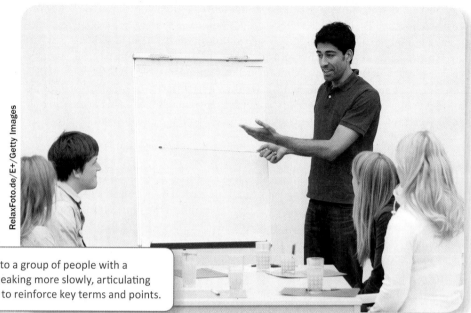

RelaxFoto.de/ E+/ Getty Images

Photo 11.2 When speaking to a group of people with a different accent adjust by speaking more slowly, articulating clearly, and using visual aids to reinforce key terms and points.

vocal expression: variety you create in your voice through changing pitch, volume, and rate, as well as stressing certain words and using pauses

monotone: a voice in which the pitch, volume, and rate remain constant, with no word, idea, or sentence differing significantly from any other

from that of most of your audience, practice pronouncing key words so that you are easily understood; speak slowly to allow your audience members more time to process your message; and consider using visual aids to reinforce key terms, concepts, and important points. Alyssa from our opening scenario grew up in Arkansas before moving to Lexington to attend college at the University of Kentucky. Although her accent was similar to most of her classmates, she decided to ask Katie to listen to her speech and point out any words she might want to articulate differently or reinforce on visual aids.

11-2b Vocal Expression

Vocal expression is achieved by changing your pitch, volume, and rate, stressing certain words; and using pauses strategically. Doing so clarifies the emotional intent of your message and helps animate your delivery. Generally, speeding up your rate, raising your pitch, or increasing your volume reinforces emotions such as joy, enthusiasm, excitement, anticipation, and a sense of urgency or fear. Slowing down your rate, lowering your pitch, or decreasing your volume can communicate resolution, peacefulness, remorse, disgust, or sadness.

A total lack of vocal expressiveness produces a **monotone**—a voice in which the pitch, volume, and rate remain constant, with no word, idea, or sentence differing significantly in sound from any other. Although few people speak in a true monotone, many severely limit themselves by using only two or three pitch levels and relatively unchanging volume and rate. An actual or near monotone not only lulls an audience to sleep but, more important, diminishes the chances of audience understanding. For instance, if the sentence "Congress should pass laws limiting the sale of pornography" is presented in a monotone, listeners will be uncertain whether the speaker is concerned with *who* should take action, *what* Congress *should do*, or *what* the laws should be.

Creating vocally expressive messages is a complex process. For example, Nick introduced his speech on legalizing marijuana as a painkiller this way:

Millions of Americans suffer needlessly each year. These people endure unbearable pain needlessly because, although our government is capable of helping them, it chooses to ignore their pain. Our government has no compassion, no empathy, no regard for human feeling. I'm here today to convince you to support my efforts toward legalizing marijuana as a painkiller for terminally ill patients.

To reinforce the emotional elements of anger, disgust, and seriousness, Nick gradually slowed his rate, decreased his volume, and lowered his pitch as he emphasized, "Our government has no compassion, no empathy, no regard for human feeling."

He also used **stress**, an emphasis placed on certain words by speaking them more loudly than the rest of the sentence, to shape his meaning. Read the following sentence from Nick's speech:

Millions of Americans suffer needlessly each year.

What did Nick intend the focus of that sentence to be? Without hearing it spoken, it is difficult to say because its focus would change depending on which word Nick chose to stress. Read the sentence aloud several times. Each time, stress a different word, and listen to how your stress changes the meaning. If you stress *millions*, the emphasis is on the number of people affected. When you stress *Americans*, the fact that the problem is on a national scale is emphasized. When you stress *suffer*, notice how much more you feel the pain. When you stress *needlessly*, you can sense Nick's frustration with how unnecessary the suffering is. And when you stress *each year*, the ongoing nature of the unnecessary suffering becomes the focus. Thus, the words you stress in a sentence affect meaning.

Pauses, moments of silence strategically placed to enhance meaning, can also mark important ideas. If you use one or more sentences in your speech to express an important idea, pause before each sentence to signal that something important is coming up, or pause afterward to allow the ideas to sink in. Pausing one or more times within a sentence can add further impact. Nick included several short pauses within and a long pause after his line, "Our government has no compassion (*pause*), no empathy (*pause*), no regard for human feeling" (*longer pause*).

> **stress:** emphasis placed on certain words by speaking them more loudly than the rest of the sentence

> **pauses:** moments of silence strategically placed to enhance meaning

11-3 USE OF BODY

Because your audience can see as well as hear you, how you use your body also contributes to how conversational and animated your audience perceives you to be. Body language elements that affect delivery are appearance, posture, poise, eye contact, facial expressions, gestures, and movement.

11-3a Appearance

Some speakers think that what they wear doesn't or shouldn't influence the success of their speech. But your **appearance**, the way you look to others, does matter. Studies show that a neatly groomed and professional appearance sends important messages about a speaker's commitment to the topic and occasion, as well as the speaker's credibility (ethos).[3] Your appearance should complement your message, not detract from it. Three guidelines can help you decide how to dress for your speech.

> **appearance:** the way you look to others

1. **Consider the audience and occasion.** Dress a bit more formally than you expect members of your audience to dress. If you dress too formally, your audience is likely to perceive you as untrustworthy and insincere,[4] and if you dress too casually, the audience may view you as uncommitted to your topic or disrespectful of them or the occasion.[5]

2. **Consider your topic and purpose.** In general, the more serious your topic, the more formally you should dress. For example, if your topic is AIDS and you are trying to persuade your audience to be tested for HIV, you will want to look like someone who is an authority by dressing the part. But if your topic is spinning and you are trying to convince your audience they would enjoy taking a class at the new campus recreation center, you might dress more casually or even in sportswear.

3. **Avoid extremes.** Your attire shouldn't detract from your speech. Avoid gaudy jewelry, over- or undersized clothing, or sexually suggestive attire. Remember, you want your audience to focus on your message, so your appearance should be neutral, not distracting.

Alyssa would be delivering her speech to an audience of about 15 students who would be present in the classroom and another 10–15 students who would watch online. Because most would probably be wearing anything from pajamas or sweatpants to jeans and t-shirts, she decided to dress a bit more formally in khaki pants and a navy blouse.

11-3b Posture

posture: the position or bearing of the body

Posture is how you hold your body. When giving a speech, an upright stance and squared shoulders communicate a sense of confidence. Speakers who slouch may be perceived as lacking self-confidence and not caring about the topic, audience, and occasion. To read a thought-provoking discussion of how use of body may affect audience attention during a speech, go to **Web Link 11.2, Body Motions and Audience Attention,** on your MindTap for *Challenge*.

11-3c Poise

poise: the graceful and controlled use of the body that gives the impression

Poise is a graceful and controlled use of the body that gives the impression that you are self-assured, calm, and dignified. Mannerisms that convey nervousness, (swaying from side to side, drumming fingers on the lectern, taking off or putting on glasses, jiggling pocket change, smacking the tongue, or scratching the nose, hand, or arm) should be noted during practice sessions and avoided during the speech.

11-3d Eye Contact

eye contact: looking at the people to whom you are speaking

When giving a speech, effective **eye contact** involves looking at people in all parts of the room throughout the speech. As long as you are looking at someone (those in front of you, in the left rear of the room, in the right center of the room, etc.) and not at your notes or the ceiling, floor, or window, everyone in the audience will perceive you as having good eye contact with them. Generally, you should look at your audience at least 90 percent of the time, glancing at your notes only when you need a quick reference point. Maintaining eye contact is important for several reasons.

1. **Maintaining eye contact helps audiences concentrate on the speech.** If you do not look at audience members while you talk, they are unlikely to maintain eye contact with you. This break in mutual eye contact often decreases concentration on the message.

2. **Maintaining eye contact bolsters ethos.** Just as you are likely to be skeptical of people who do not look you in the eye as they converse, audiences also will be skeptical of speakers who do not look at them. In the United States, eye contact is perceived as a sign of sincerity. Speakers who fail to maintain eye contact with audiences are perceived almost always as ill at ease and often as insincere or dishonest.[6] In some cultures across the world and co-cultures within the United States, however, direct eye contact may be perceived as disrespectful. Many Native American nations, such as the Hopi, Cherokee, Navajo, and Sioux, believe indirect eye contact demonstrates humility and respect.[7] Knowing your audience becomes extremely important as you determine what kind of eye contact is most appropriate.

3. **Maintaining eye contact helps you gauge audience reaction to your ideas.** Because communication is two-way, audience members communicate with you while you are speaking to them. In conversation, the audience's response is likely to be both verbal and nonverbal. In public speaking, the audience's response

is likely to only be through nonverbal cues. Bored audience members may yawn, look out the window, slouch in their chairs, and even sleep. Confused audience members may look puzzled by furrowing their brows or shaking their heads. Audience members who understand or agree with something may smile or nod their heads. By monitoring your audience's behavior, you can adjust by becoming more animated, offering additional examples, or moving more quickly through a point (Photo 11.3).

Photo 11.3 Maintaining eye contact helps keep your audience engaged as you speak.

When speaking to large audiences of 100 or more people, you must create a *sense* of looking listeners in the eye even though you actually cannot. This process is called **audience contact**. You can create audience contact by mentally dividing your audience into small groups scattered around the room. Then, at random, talk for four to six seconds with each group. Perhaps start with a Z pattern. Talk with the group in the back left for a few seconds, then glance at people in the far right for a few seconds, and then move to a group in the middle, a group in the front left, and then a group in the front right, and so forth. Then perhaps reverse the order, starting in the back right. Eventually, you will find yourself using a random pattern to look at all groups over a period of a few minutes. Such a pattern also helps you avoid spending a disproportionate amount of time talking with those in one part of the room.

audience contact: creating a sense of looking listeners in the eye when speaking to large audiences

11-3e Facial Expressions

Facial expressions are the eye and mouth movements that convey emotions. When you talk with friends, your facial expressions are naturally animated. Audiences expect your expressions to be similarly animated when giving a speech. Effective facial expressions convey **nonverbal immediacy** by communicating that you are personable and likeable. Speakers who do not vary their facial expressions during their speech and instead wear deadpan expressions, perpetual grins, or permanent scowls tend to be perceived as boring, insincere, or stern. Audiences respond positively to natural facial expressions that appear to spontaneously reflect what you're saying and how you feel about it. To assess whether you are using effective facial expressions, practice delivering your speech to yourself in front of a mirror or record your rehearsal and evaluate your facial expressions as you watch it (Photo 11.4).

facial expressions: eye and mouth movements that convey emotions

11-3f Gestures

Gestures are the movements of your hands, arms, and fingers. Effective gestures emphasize important points and ideas, refer to presentational aids, or clarify structure. For example, as Aaron began to speak about the advantages of smart phone apps, he said, "on one hand" and lifted his right hand face up. When he got to the disadvantages, he lifted his left hand face up as he said, "on the other hand." Some of the most common gestures used by speakers are shown in Exhibit 11.2.

Some people who are nervous when giving a speech clasp their hands behind their backs, bury them in their pockets, or grip

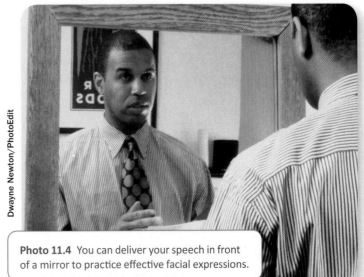
Photo 11.4 You can deliver your speech in front of a mirror to practice effective facial expressions.

Exhibit (11.2) **Common Hand Gestures Used by Speakers.**

- The supine hand with palm upward to express good humor, frankness, and generalization.

nonverbal immediacy: a perception of being personable and likeable

gestures: movements of hands, arms, and fingers

- The vertical hand with palm outward to indicate warding off, pushing from, or a disagreeable thought.

Using Appropriate Facial Expressions

Nancy furrowed her brows and pursed her lips when she told the story of two young children who were abandoned in a parking lot—her facial expression conveyed seriousness and disgust. Thad, on the other hand, raised his eyebrows and smiled slightly as he talked about the many new forms of entertainment a domed stadium would bring to the city.

- The clenched hand to reinforce anger or defiance or to emphasize an important point.

- The prone hand with palm downward to show superposition or the resting of one thing upon another.

Using Appropriate Gestures

For emphasis, Marcella repeatedly slammed her right fist into her left palm to emphasize her frustration as she said, "Over and over and over again, we have tried to stop child pornography, but to no avail."

- The index finger to specialize or reinforce the first in a sequence of events.

the lectern. Unable to pry their hands free gracefully, they wiggle their elbows or appear stiff, which can distract audience members from the message. As with facial expressions, effective gestures must appear spontaneous and natural even though they are carefully planned and practiced (Photo 11.5). When you practice and then deliver your speech, leave your hands free so that they will be available to gesture as you normally do.

11-3g Movement

Movement refers to changing your body position. During your speech, engage only in **motivated movement**, movement with a specific purpose such as emphasizing an important idea, referencing a presentational aid, or clarifying macrostructure. For example, you might take a few steps to one side of the stage or the other each time you begin a new main point. Or, to emphasize a particular point, you might move closer to the audience. To create a feeling of intimacy before you tell a personal story, you might walk out from behind a lectern and sit down on a chair placed at the edge of the stage. To use motivated movement effectively, you need to practice when and how you will move until you can do so in a way that appears spontaneous and natural while remaining "open" to the audience (not turning your back to them).

Avoid unmotivated movement such as bobbing, weaving, shifting from foot to foot, or pacing from one side of the room to the other because unplanned movements distract the audience from your message. Because many unplanned movements result from nervousness, you can minimize them by paying mindful attention to your body as you speak. At the beginning of your speech, consciously stand up straight on both feet. Whenever you find yourself fidgeting, readjust and position your body with your weight equally distributed on both feet.

During speech practice sessions, try various methods to monitor or alter your bodily action. Video recording provides an excellent means of monitoring your use of body to determine whether it is enhancing the message or distracting from it. You may also want to practice in front of a mirror to see how you look to others when you speak. Another good method is to get a willing listener to critique your use of body and help you improve. Once you have identified the behavior you want to change, tell your helper what to look for. For instance, you might say, "Raise your hand every time I begin to rock back and forth." By getting specific feedback when the behavior occurs, you can make immediate adjustments.

To see a video clip of a student speaker using effective bodily action, go to MindTap for *Challenge* to access the speech "No More Sugar" in the Chapter 11 resources.

11-4 DELIVERY METHODS

Speeches vary in the amount of content preparation and the amount of practice you do ahead of time. The three most common delivery methods are impromptu, scripted, and extemporaneous.

Bill Aron/PhotoEdit

Photo 11.5 When a person speaks, we expect appropriate facial expressions, gestures, and movement.

IMPROMPTU SPEECH CHALLENGE

Draw an index card from a stack provided by your instructor. The index card will identify an emotion (e.g., fear, excitement, anger, sorrow). Prepare a short one- to three-minute impromptu speech describing how you would convey that emotion in a speech. Be sure to focus on the use of voice and use of body strategies provided in this chapter.

movement: changing the position or location of the entire body

motivated movement: movement with a specific purpose

impromptu speech: delivered with only seconds or minutes of advance notice for preparation and is usually presented without referring to notes of any kind

scripted speech: prepared by creating a complete written manuscript and delivered by reading from or memorizing a printed copy

extemporaneous speech: researched and planned ahead of time, but the exact wording is not scripted and will vary from presentation to presentation

11-4a Impromptu Speeches

An **impromptu speech** is one that is delivered with only seconds or minutes of advance notice for preparation and is usually presented without referring to notes of any kind. You may have already given an impromptu speech in class, so you know the kind of pressures and problems this type of speaking creates.

Because impromptu speakers must quickly gather their thoughts just before and while they speak, carefully organizing and developing ideas can be challenging. As a result, they may leave out important information or confuse audience members. Delivery can suffer as speakers use "ah," "um," "like," and "you know" to buy time as they scramble to collect their thoughts. That's why the more opportunities you have to use the impromptu method, the better you'll become at doing so.

Some of the most common situations that require using the impromptu method are during employment and performance review interviews, at business meetings, in class, at social ceremonies, and to the media. In each situation, having practiced organizing ideas quickly and conveying them intelligibly and expressively will bolster your ethos and help you succeed.

You can improve your impromptu performances by practicing "mock" impromptu speeches. For example, if you are taking a class where the professor often calls on students to answer questions, you can prepare by anticipating the questions that might be asked and by practicing giving your answers out loud. Over time, you will become more adept at quickly organizing your ideas and "thinking on your feet."

11-4b Scripted Speeches

At the other extreme, a **scripted speech** is one that is prepared by creating a complete written manuscript and delivered by reading from or memorizing a written copy. Obviously, effective scripted speeches take a great deal of time because both an outline and a word-for-word transcript must be prepared, practiced, and then delivered in a way that sounds both conversational and animated. When you memorize a scripted speech, you face the increased anxiety of forgetting your lines. When you read a scripted speech from a manuscript or teleprompter, you must become adept at looking at the script with your peripheral vision so that you don't appear to be reading and you must still sound conversational and animated. While politicians, talk show hosts, and television news anchors are usually good at achieving conversational style while reading from printed manuscripts and teleprompters, most speakers sound like they are reading and find it difficult to sound spontaneous and conversational (Photo 11.6).

Because of the time and skill required to effectively prepare and deliver a scripted speech, they are usually reserved for important occasions that have important consequences. Political speeches, keynote addresses, commencement addresses, and CEO remarks at annual stockholder meetings are examples of occasions when a scripted speech might be appropriate and worth the extra effort.

11-4c Extemporaneous Speeches

Most speeches, whether in the workplace, in the community, or in class, are delivered extemporaneously. An **extemporaneous speech** is researched and planned ahead of time, but the exact wording is not scripted and will vary somewhat from presentation to presentation. When speaking extemporaneously, you refer to speaking notes reminding you of key ideas, structure, and delivery cues as you speak. Some speakers today use their computerized slideshows as speaking notes. If you choose to do so, however, be careful not to include too many words on any given slide, which will ultimately distract listeners from focusing on you as you speak.

Extemporaneous speeches are the easiest to give effectively. Unlike impromptu speeches, when speaking extemporaneously, you are able to prepare your thoughts ahead of time and to have notes to prompt you. Unlike scripted speeches, extemporaneous speeches do not require as lengthy a preparation and practice process to be effective. In the next section, we describe how to rehearse successfully for an extemporaneous speech.

11-5 REHEARSAL

Rehearsing is the iterative process of practicing your speech aloud. Inexperienced speakers often wrongly believe they are ready to present the speech once they have finished their outline. A speech that is not practiced out loud is likely to be far less effective than it would have been had you given yourself sufficient time to revise, evaluate, and mull over all aspects of the speech.[10] Exhibit 11.3 provides a useful timetable for preparing and practicing your speech for an introductory communication course. In the sections that follow, we describe how to rehearse effectively by preparing speaking notes; handling presentational aids; and recording, analyzing, and refining delivery.

Photo 11.6 News anchors read from scripted speeches from a teleprompter but still sound spontaneous and conversational.

AP Photo/NBC,Dana Edelson

rehearsing: the iterative process of practicing your speech aloud

11-5a Speaking Notes

Prior to your first rehearsal session, prepare a draft of your speaking notes. **Speaking notes** are a key-word outline of your speech including hard-to-remember information and delivery cues. The best notes contain the fewest words possible written in lettering large enough to be seen instantly at a distance.

To develop your notes, begin by reducing your speech outline to an abbreviated outline of key words and phrases. Then, if there are details you must cite exactly—such as a specific example, quotation, or set of statistics—add these in the appropriate places. You might also use separate "Quotation Cards" for direct quotations, which is what Alyssa did (see Exhibit 11.4). Next, indicate exactly where you plan

speaking notes: a keyword outline of your speech, plus hard-to-remember information and delivery cues

---

xhibit **11.3** Timetable for Preparing a Speech

7 days before	Select topic; begin research
6 days before	Continue research
5 days before	Outline body of speech
4 days before	Work on introduction and conclusion
3 days before	Finish outline; find additional material if needed; have all presentational aids completed
2 days before	First rehearsal session
1 day before	Second rehearsal session
Due date	Give speech

Exhibit (11.4) Alyssa's Speaking Outline on Four Note Cards

a. NOTE CARD 1: Introduction

PLANT FEET....DIRECT EYE CONTACT....POISE/ETHOS! ☺

I. Famous Indian peace activist Mahatma Gandhi: "We must become the change we seek in the world."
Tall order....We can make a difference right here in Lexington, KY

II. Think for a moment....child/homework, neighbor/leaves, stranger/groceries....It's easy for college students like us to get involved.

III. I volunteer at LRM and reaped benefits (Slide 1)

IV. Benefits volunteering....
a. get acquainted
b. responsibility & privilege
c. resumé-building skills

BLANK SLIDE, WALK RIGHT, EYE C.: Let's begin by explaining the ways volunteering can help us connect to our local community.

b. NOTE CARD 2: Body

I. GREAT WAY to become acquainted ☺ ☺
LR: Comforts of home....unfamiliar city....volunteering....easy and quick way....
Natalie Cunningham—May 2nd (Q. CARD #1)
Social issues and conditions
Acc. to a 1991 article published in the *J. of Prevention and Intervention in the Community* by Cohen, Mowbray, Gillette, and Thompson raise awareness....
My experience at LRM (SLIDES 2 & 3)
BLANK SLIDE, WALK LEFT, EYE C.: Not only is volunteering important....familiar and social issues....FRANKLY....dem society....

II. Civic responsibility AND privilege....LR: We benefit college....give back.
I agree with Wilson and Musick who said in their 1997 article in *Social Forces* **active participation or deprived**. (SLIDES 4 &5)
Also a privilege....make a difference....feel good....self-actualization (SLIDE #6)

c. NOTE CARD 3: Body & Conclusion

BLANK SLIDE, WALK RIGHT, EYE C: privilege & responsibility....resume-building....
III. Life skills
Article "Employability Credentials: A Key to Successful Youth Transition to Work" by I. Charner—1988 issue of the *Journal of Career Development*....(Q. CARD #2)
Laura Hatfield....leadership, teamwork, and listening skills
Andrea Stockelman, volunteer (SLIDE #7) (Q. CARD #3)
MY RESUMÉ (SLIDE #8)
BLANK SLIDE, WALK TO CENTER, EYE C: Today, we've discussed....get acquainted, responsibility & privilege, resumé-building life skills help after grad.
CL: So, I'm hoping the next time you recall....not distant past. Instead, I hope you'll be thinking bout how you **ARE** being the change you seek in the world by **volunteering right here //in Lexington///right now!**
PAUSE, EYE CONTACT, POISE, NOD ☺

d. Quotation Card

#1: "My first group of students needed rides to all the various volunteer sites b/c they had no idea where things were in the city. It was really easy for the students who lived on campus to remain ignorant of their city, but while volunteering they become acquainted with Lexington and the important issues going on here."

#2: "Employers rely on credentials to certify that a young person will become a valuable employee. Credentials that document the experiences and employability skills, knowledge, and attitude."

#3: "I learned that there was a lot more that went into preparing food for the homeless than I ever thought possible. It was neat to be a part of that process."

PUBLIC SPEAKING IN THE REAL WORLD

Anne Hathaway on the Importance of Practicing Your Speech

© Sydney Alford/Alamy

You might know that, on February 24, 2013, Anne Hathaway won an Oscar for her best-supporting actress role in "Les Miserables." What you might not know, however, is that the acclaimed star actually rehearsed her acceptance speech *a lot*. Why? To begin, her feelings had been hurt by the waves of criticism she got from many for doing such a poor job delivering her Golden Globe acceptance speech a few weeks earlier. More important, however, is that she learned from her mistake and worked hard practicing her Oscar acceptance speech "many, many times."[8] In addition to thanking the academy in her "It Came True!" speech, her goal was to be perceived as "more likeable."[9] Because appearing personable through delivery is one characteristic of effective public speakers, it appears that Hathaway understands the truth in the old adage: Practice makes perfect!

to share presentational aids. Finally, incorporate delivery cues indicating where you want to make use of your voice and body to enhance intelligibility or expressiveness. For example, indicate where you want to pause, gesture, or make a motivated movement. Capitalize or underline words you want to stress. Use slash marks (//) to remind yourself to pause. Use an upward-pointing arrow to remind yourself to increase rate or volume.

For a three- to five-minute speech, you will need no more than three 3- by 5-inch note cards to record your speaking notes. For longer speeches, you might need one card for the introduction, one for each main point, and one for the conclusion. If your speech contains a particularly important and long quotation or a complicated set of statistics, you can record this information in detail on a separate card. Exhibit 11.4 shows Alyssa's speaking notes for her speech outline, which you can find at the end of this chapter. When you use a computerized slideshow, you can also use the "notes" feature for your speaking notes.

Use your notes during practice sessions just as you will when you actually give the speech. If you will use a lectern, set the notes on the speaker's stand or, alternatively, hold them in one hand and refer to them only when needed. How important is it to construct good speaking notes? Speakers often find that the act of making a note card is so effective in helping cement ideas in the mind that during practice, or later during the speech itself, they rarely use the notes at all.

11-5b Presentational Aids

Some speakers think that once they have prepared good presentational aids, they will have no trouble using them in the speech. However, many speeches with good aids have become a shambles because the aids were not well handled. You can avoid problems by following these guidelines.

1. **Carefully plan when to use the presentational aids.** Indicate in your speaking notes/outline exactly when you will reveal and conceal each presentational aid. Practice introducing and using your aids until you can do so comfortably and smoothly.

Reflect on Ethics

During her speech at the First National Tea Party Convention in February 2010, former Alaska Governor Sarah Palin exclaimed that the Tea Party movement is "bigger than any charismatic guy with a teleprompter." She was referring to President Barack Obama, who often uses a teleprompter to deliver scripted speeches. Later, it was revealed in visual recordings of her speech and the question-and-answer session she participated in that she had relied on a "cheat sheet" of notes written on her hand. CNN political editor Mark Preston (among others) criticized Palin as a hypocrite:

Look, the fact that she wrote on her hand isn't really that big of a deal. We all work off of notes, certainly in television. But the fact that she was critical of President

Obama and called him "that charismatic guy with the teleprompter"—and as you just saw, I looked down at my notes to give that direct quote. It's very hard to be critical of one person when you yourself are using the same kind of aids when you're speaking.[11]

1. Do you agree with Preston's assessment of Palin's use of notes? Explain.

2. What, if any, ethical principles did Palin violate?

3. What, if any, ethical principles did the political media analysts violate in the way they covered this story?

4. Can you think of situations where the delivery method chosen for a speech might raise ethical questions or violate ethical principles? Explain.

2. **Consider audience needs carefully.** As you practice, eliminate any presentational aid that does not contribute directly to the audience's attention to, understanding of, or retention of the key ideas in your speech.

3. **Position presentational aids and equipment before beginning your speech.** Make sure your aids and equipment are where you want them and that everything is ready and in working order. Test electronic equipment to make sure everything from visual displays to sound to hyperlinks work and are cued correctly.

4. **Share a presentational aid only when talking about it.** Because presentational aids will draw audience attention, practice sharing them only when you are talking about them and then concealing them when they are no longer the focus of attention. Because a single presentational aid may contain several bits of information, practice only exposing the portion you are currently discussing. On computerized slideshows, you can do so by using the "custom animation" feature to allow only one item to appear at a time, by striking the "B" key for a black screen when you aren't directly referencing the aid, and by inserting blank slides where your ideas are not being supplemented by something on the slideshow.

5. **Display presentational aids so that everyone in the audience can see and hear them.** It's frustrating not to be able to see or hear an aid. If possible, practice in the space where you will give your speech so you can adjust equipment accordingly. If you cannot practice in the space ahead of time, then arrive early enough on the day of the presentation to practice quickly with the equipment you will use.

6. **Reference the presentational aid during the speech.** Because you already know what you want your audience to see in a visual aid, tell your audience what to look for, explain the various elements in it, and interpret figures, symbols, and percentages. For an audio or audiovisual aid, point out what you want your audience to listen for before playing the excerpt. When showing a visual or audiovisual aid, use the "turn-touch-talk" technique.

   - When you display the visual, walk to the screen—that's where everyone will look anyway. Slightly turn to the visual and touch it—that is, point to it with an arm gesture or a pointer. Then, with your back to the screen and your body still facing the audience at a slight 45-degree angle, talk to your audience about it.

- When you finish making your comments about the visual, return to the lectern or your speaking position and conceal the aid.

7. **Talk to your audience, not to the presentational aid.** Although you will want to acknowledge the presentational aid by looking at it occasionally, it is important to maintain eye contact with your audience as much as possible. As you practice, resist the urge to stare at or read from your presentational aid.

8. **Resist the temptation to pass objects through the audience.** People look at, read, handle, and think about whatever they hold in their hands. While they are so occupied, they are not likely to be listening to you. If you have handouts or objects, distribute them after the speech rather than during it.

11-5c Practice Rounds

As with any other activity, effective speech delivery requires practice. Each practice round should consist of (a) practicing aloud, (b) analyzing and making adjustments, and (c) practicing aloud again. The more you practice, the better your speech will be. During each practice round, evaluate your language choices, as well as your use of voice, body, and presentational aids. You should do as many practice rounds as needed to deliver a speech that is conversational and animated. For most speakers, we suggest a minimum of four practice rounds.

First Practice

1. Record (audio and video) your practice session so you can analyze it and make improvements. You may also want to have a friend sit in on your practice and offer suggestions afterward.

2. Read through your complete sentence outline once or twice to refresh your memory. Then, put the outline out of sight and practice using your speaking notes.

3. Make the practice as similar to the speech situation as possible, including using the presentational aids you've prepared. Stand up and face your imaginary audience. Pretend the chairs, lamps, books, and other objects in the room are people.

4. Write down the time that you begin or set a digital timer on your smart phone or computer.

5. Begin speaking. Regardless of what happens, keep going until you have presented your entire speech. If you goof, make a repair and keep going as if you were actually delivering the speech to an audience.

6. Write down the time you finish or stop the timer. Compute the length.

Analysis

Watch and listen to your recorded performance while reviewing your complete outline. How did it go? Did you leave out any key ideas? Did you talk too long on any one point and not long enough on another? Did you clarify each of your points? Did you adapt to your anticipated audience? Were your notes effective? How well did you do with your presentational aids? If a friend sat in, ask him or her for input, as well. Make any necessary changes before your second practice.

Second Practice

Repeat the six steps listed for the first practice. By practicing a second time right after your analysis, you are more likely to make the kind of adjustments that begin to improve the speech.

(6) SPEECH PLANNING

Rehearsing Your Speech

The goal of this activity is to rehearse your speech by practicing it, analyzing and refining it, and then practicing it again.

1. After you have prepared your speaking notes, find a place where you can be alone (or with a friend) to practice your speech. Follow the six points of the first practice

2. Watch and listen to the recording. Review your outline as you do so and then complete a speech evaluation checklist to see how well you delivered your speech. (You can find the Speech Evaluation Checklist: General Criteria on page 14 in Chapter 1, a more detailed checklist in this chapter, and checklists for informative and persuasive speeches in later chapters.)

   List three specific changes you will make in your next practice.

   One: _____

   Two: _____

   Three: _____

3. Go through the six practice steps again. Then assess: Did you achieve the goals you set for the second practice?

Reevaluate the speech using the checklist and do additional practice rounds until you are satisfied with your presentation.

Do this activity with **Speech Builder Express**. Go to your MindTap for *Challenge*.

Additional Practice Rounds

After you have completed one full practice round, put the speech away for a while. Although you should practice the speech at least a couple more times, you will not benefit from cramming all the practices into one long rehearsal time. You may find that a final practice right before you go to bed will be very helpful; while you are sleeping, your subconscious will continue to work on the speech. As a result, you are likely to find significant improvement in delivery when you practice again the next day.

11-6 ADAPTING WHILE DELIVERING THE SPEECH

Even when you've practiced your speech to the point that you know it inside and out, you must be prepared to adapt to your audience and possibly change course a bit as you give your speech. Remember that your primary goal is to generate shared understanding, so pay attention to the audience's feedback as you speak and adjust accordingly. Here are six tips to guide you.

1. **Be aware of and respond to audience feedback.** As you make eye contact with members of your audience, notice how they react to what you say. For instance, if you see quizzical looks on the faces of several listeners, you may need to explain a particular point in a different way. On the other hand, if you

see listeners nodding impatiently, you don't need to belabor your point and can move on. If many audience members look bored, try to rekindle their interest by conveying more enthusiasm in your voice and body.

2. **Be prepared to use alternative developmental material.** Your ability to adjust to your audience's needs depends on how much additional alternative information you have to share. If you have prepared only one example, you wouldn't be ready if your audience is confused and needs another. If you have prepared only one definition for a term, you may be unable to rephrase it if needed. As you prepare, try to anticipate where your audience may be confused or already knowledgeable and practice adding or dropping examples and other details.

3. **Correct yourself when you misspeak.** Every speaker makes mistakes. They stumble over words, mispronounce terms, forget information, and mishandle presentational aids. So expect that you will make a few mistakes. It's normal. If you stumble over a phrase or mispronounce a word, correct yourself and move on. Don't make a big deal of it by laughing, rolling your eyes, or in other ways drawing unnecessary attention to it. If you suddenly remember that you forgot to provide some information, consider how important it is for your audience to have that information. If what you forgot to say will make it difficult for your audience to understand an upcoming point, figure out how and when to provide the information later in your speech. Usually, however, information we forgot to share is not critical to the audience's understanding and its better to leave it out and move on.

4. **Adapt to unexpected events.** Maintain your composure if something unexpected happens, such as a cell phone ringing or someone entering the room while you're speaking. Simply pause until the disruption ceases and then move on. If the disruption causes you to lose your train of thought or has distracted the audience, take a deep breath, look at your speaking notes, and continue your speech at a point slightly before the interruption occurred. This will allow both you and your audience to refocus on your speech. You might acknowledge that you are backtracking by saying something like, "Let's back up a bit and remember where we were—."

5. **Adapt to unexpected audience reactions.** Sometimes, you'll encounter listeners who disagree strongly with your message. They might show their disagreement by being inattentive, heckling you, or rolling their eyes when you try to make eye contact with them. If these behaviors are limited to one or two members of your audience, ignore them and focus on the rest of your listeners. If the majority of your audience is hostile to what you are saying, try to anticipate and address their concerns. You might begin by acknowledging their feedback and then try to persuade your audience to suspend their judgment while they listen. For example, you could say something like, "I can see that many of you don't agree with my first point. But let me ask you to put aside your initial reaction and think along with me on this next point. Even if we end up disagreeing, at least you will understand my position."

6. **Handle questions respectfully.** It is rare for audience members to interrupt speakers with questions during a speech. But if you are interrupted, be prepared to respond respectfully. If the question is directly related to understanding the point you are making, answer it immediately. If not, acknowledge the question, indicate that you will answer it later, and then remember to do so. In most professional settings, you will be expected to answer questions when you've finished your speech. Some people will ask you to clarify information. Some will ask you for an opinion or to draw conclusions beyond what you have said.

Whenever you answer a question, be honest about what you know and don't know. If an audience member asks a question you don't know the answer to, admit it by saying something like, "That's an excellent question. I'm not sure of the answer, but I would be happy to follow up on it later if you're interested." Then move on to the next question. If someone asks you to state an opinion about a matter you haven't thought much about, it's okay to say, "You know, I don't think I have given that enough thought to have a valid opinion."

Be sure to monitor how much time you have to answer questions. When the time is nearly up, mention that you'll entertain one more question so as to warn listeners that the question-and-answer period is almost over. You might also suggest that you'll be happy to talk more with individuals one on one later—this provides your more reserved listeners an opportunity to follow up with you.

11-7 ADAPTING YOUR SPEECH FOR VIRTUAL AUDIENCES

When Plato, Aristotle, and Cicero engaged in public speaking thousands of years ago, the communication event occurred in real time with both the speaker and the audience physically present. Thanks to technology, however, public speeches today may be delivered in both face-to-face and virtual environments. In the opening scenario, for example, Alyssa and Katie would be delivering their speeches in a classroom with some audience members present while simultaneously streaming to several classmates who would be watching online via their computers. Their speeches would also be uploaded to the class website so they could watch, critique, and prepare reflective written assessments of themselves later.

Technology makes it possible to speak publicly to multiple audiences across the country and around the world. For example, Alyssa planned to post her speech to YouTube and link to it from her Facebook and Twitter accounts for extra credit. In doing so, she hoped to reach many more college students with her volunteerism and civic engagement speech than just those sitting in the classroom. The bottom line is this. Although public speaking certainly still occurs in traditional face-to-face settings, it is no longer limited by place and time—far from it!

President Franklin Delano Roosevelt (FDR) is credited as one of the first public figures to capitalize on the benefits of electronic media to break through the *place* limitation to reach a wider audience. Throughout his presidency in the 1930s and 1940s, FDR delivered *fireside chats*, weekly radio addresses about issues facing the country.[12] These speeches could be heard by anyone who chose to tune in. U.S. presidents have been offering weekly addresses ever since! In fact, today President Obama even posts weekly addresses on YouTube and the White House website.[13]

Perhaps one of the most significant examples of technology overcoming the limitation of *time* comes from Martin Luther King, Jr. Over 200,000 people were at the political rally in Washington, D.C., on August 28, 1963, to hear his famous "I Have a Dream" speech live and in person. More than 50 years later, we can join the 200,000 who made up that first audience to hear him delivery his powerful oration by clicking on any number of websites where it is archived. In fact, a quick *Google* search of it yields more than 37,400,000 hits.

To reach multiple audiences successfully, we must consider not just those who are informed about the topic, but also those who may not be informed, may be apathetic, and may even be hostile toward it. Those who have analyzed Dr. King's speech, for instance, claim he was successful in part because he used a black preacher style while also transcending it to reach broader audiences. To clarify, he began by addressing the grievances of black Americans and then transitioned to focus more broadly on the bedrock of American values. Linking civil rights to the American Dream appealed not only to the audience present on the Washington Mall, but also to the millions of uncommitted American who watched the speech on TV.[14] In doing so, it has transcended time. Today, his speech continues to resonate as representing core American values and the American dream.

With the proliferation of Internet accessibility comes both additional opportunities and challenges. For example, because speeches today may be easily uploaded to websites like YouTube with or without our permission and then quickly go viral, we also must always be cognizant of possible audiences we never intended to target. Failing to do so could result in devastating consequences. In 2001, for instance, Texas governor and then GOP presidential hopeful Rick Perry discovered this when a speech he delivered to a group of supporters in New Hampshire went viral. Blog posts and newspaper editorials blamed his giggling and rambling remarks on being "drunk" or "drugged".[15]

Obviously, we ought to consider how to adapt our delivery for virtual audiences. Although we are only beginning to discover the ways in which we should do so, here are a few guidelines to consider when adapting your speeches for virtual audiences.

1. **Adapt your speech to address multiple audiences.** Assume that any speech you give may be recorded and made available to those who are not in your immediate audience. Always consider how you might adapt not only your delivery, but also your content and structure, to accurately and respectfully address uninformed, apathetic, and oppositional audiences who may view your speech virtually.

2. **Adapt your speech to account for unintended audiences.** Similarly, don't say anything to one specific audience that you would not want broadcasted to a wider audience. With just a few clicks of a smart phone or iPad, an audience member can record a video and post it online. So make sure your speech content, humorous anecdotes, use of voice, and use of body are accurate and respectful.

3. **Choose presentational aids carefully.** Make sure the visuals and audiovisuals you use can be easily viewed and heard in an online format. Also, be sure to explain them so that those who only have audio access or who view them on a small smart phone screen can understand the information on them.

4. **Become proficient with technology.** Technological proficiency is no longer considered a value-added skill; it is expected of professionals today. Make it a regular practice to consult with communication technology experts at your university or place of business to learn initially how to use and subsequently how to stay up-to-date on how to use available technologies effectively. Because technology continues to expand at astonishing rates, you can expect to need regular ongoing training to keep pace with it.

5. **Employ the fundamentals of effective public speaking.** Although it might seem to go without saying, be sure to adhere to the strategies of effective public speaking even when delivering your speech online. The steps we have discussed regarding topic selection and development, organization, language, and delivery remain fundamental to effective speechmaking for face-to-face and virtual audiences. Treat the camera as a person. As you do so, use your voice and body in ways that are intelligible, conversational, animated, and poised just as you would if the camera were someone in the room with you.

speech assignment

Presenting an Informative Speech with Presentational Aids

Based on the specific assignment of your instructor, prepare a three- to five-minute speech by completing the Speech-Planning Action Step activities. Go to your MindTap for *Challenge* to help you prepare you speech and your outline. You can see an example of Alyssa's outline and speech in the sample speech at the end of this chapter.

Do this activity with Speech Builder Express.

speech evaluation checklist

Speech Evaluation Checklist

Check items that were accomplished effectively.

Content

_____ 1. Was the goal of the speech clear?

_____ 2. Did the speaker offer breadth and depth to support each main point?

_____ 3. Did the speaker use high-quality information and sources?

_____ 4. Did the speaker use a variety of kinds of developmental material?

_____ 5. Were presentational aids appropriate?

_____ 6. Did the speaker establish common ground and adapt the content to the audience with listener relevance links?

Macrostructure

_____ 1. Did the introduction gain attention, establish credibility and listener relevance, as well as state the goal of the speech and preview the main points?

_____ 2. Were the main points clear, parallel, and meaningful complete sentences?

_____ 3. Did section transitions lead smoothly from one point to another?

_____ 4. Did the conclusion tie the speech together by summarizing the main goal and points and offering a clincher?

Microstructure

_____ 1. Was the language appropriate?

_____ 2. Was the language accurate?

_____ 3. Was the language clear?

_____ 4. Was the language vivid?

Delivery

_____1. Did the speaker appear and sound conversational?

_____2. Did the speaker appear and sound animated?

_____3. Was the speaker intelligible?

_____4. Was the speaker vocally expressive?

_____5. Was the speaker's appearance and attire appropriate?

_____6. Did the speaker use effective eye/audience contact throughout the speech?

_____7. Did the speaker use appropriate facial expressions?

_____8. Did the speaker have good posture that communicated poise and confidence?

_____9. Were the speaker's gestures and movement appropriate?

_____10. Did the speaker conceal and reveal the presentational aids effectively?

_____11. Did the speaker reference the presentational aids effectively while discussing them?

Based on these criteria, evaluate the speech as (check one):

_____ excellent _____ good _____ satisfactory _____ fair _____ poor

MindTap™

Access this checklist on your MindTap for _Challenge._

Sample Informative Speech with Presentational Aids

This section presents a sample informative speech with presentational aids, given by a student and including an adaptation plan, an outline, and a transcript.

College Student Volunteering and Civic Engagement

By Alyssa Grace Millner, University of Kentucky[16]

ADAPTATION PLAN

1. **Key aspects of audience.** The majority of listeners know what volunteering is in a general sense, but they probably don't know the ways it can benefit them as college students.

2. **Establishing and maintaining common ground.** I'll use personal pronouns throughout the speech, as well as specific examples about volunteering from volunteers right here in Lexington.

3. **Building and maintaining interest.** I'll insert listener relevance links in the introduction and for each main point that point out how volunteering is directly related to improving the lives of college students in some way.

4. **Building credibility.** I will point out right away that I volunteer and that I've done a good deal of research on it. I'll insert examples of my own experiences throughout the speech, as well as cite credible research to support my claims.

5. **Audience attitudes.** Some may be indifferent, but according the research I've found, most will probably be open to the idea of volunteering. They might not know how easy it can be to get started though.

6. **Adapting to audiences from different cultures and language communities.** Although most of my classmates are U.S. citizens, there are a couple of international students in the class. So, when I talk about volunteering being a civic responsibility, I'll make sure to talk about how all of us are reaping benefits of a U.S. education; that's why we are all responsible for giving back in some way. I'll talk about it as an ethical responsibility.

7. **Use presentational aids.** I will show photographs of people engaged in volunteer work throughout the speech. I think this will make my ideas very concrete for the audience and will enhance pathos (emotional appeal). I'll also show some graphs about homelessness in Lexington and the percentage of college students who believe in volunteering. I think these will bolster my ethos as the audience will see I've done research. Finally, I'll show my résumé with elements highlighted that I've been able to include because I've volunteered. I think this will drive home my point about the future benefits for college students who volunteer while still in school.

Formal Speech Outline

General goal: To inform my audience.

Specific goal: I want my audience to realize the benefits of volunteering in Lexington while we are still students at the University of Kentucky.

INTRODUCTION

I. The famous Indian Peace activist and spiritual leader Mahatma Gandhi is known for saying "We must become the change we seek in the world." That sounds at first like an awfully tall order, but today I'd like to show you how each of us can do just that and make a difference right here in Lexington, Kentucky.

II. Think for a moment of a time in your life when you did something kind for someone else. Maybe you helped a child do homework, or a neighbor rake leaves, or even a stranger get groceries from the store to the car. Do you remember how that made you feel? Well, that feeling can be a normal part of your week when you choose to be a volunteer. And for college students like us, it's easy to get involved as volunteers in our local community.

III. Personally, I volunteer at the Lexington Rescue Mission and have reaped many benefits by doing so. *(Show Slide 1: picture of me volunteering at the Mission.)* I've also done extensive research on volunteering and civic engagement.

IV. So, let's spend the next few minutes discussing the benefits volunteering can have for us as college students by focusing on how volunteering helps us get acquainted with the local community, why civic engagement is the responsibility of every one of us, and what volunteering can do to teach us new skills and build our résumés.

Let's begin by explaining the ways volunteering can connect each of us to our local community.

Attention getter

Listener relevance

Speaker credibility

Thesis statement with main point preview

Transition

BODY

I. Volunteering is a great way to become acquainted with a community beyond the university campus.

Most college students move away from the comforts of home to a new and unfamiliar city. Not knowing what there is to do or even how to get around can be overwhelming and isolating. Volunteering is an easy way to quickly become familiar with and begin to feel a part of this new city in addition to the campus community.

Listener relevance

A. Volunteering allows you to learn your way around town.
   1. In an interview I had with Natalie Cunningham, the volunteer coordinator of the Lexington Rescue Mission, she said, "I've been working with students for several years now. While every group is different, one lingering trend is each group's unawareness of their city. It is easy for the students who live on campus to stay in their 'on-campus bubble.' Volunteering allows students to become acquainted with Lexington and the important issues facing their new home." (personal communication, January 2, 2013).
   2. It seems like a silly thing, but knowing your way around town starts to make any city feel like home. Volunteering gets you out into the local area and helps you begin to get acquainted with new people and places.

B. Volunteering can also open your eyes to local social issues and conditions.
   1. Many nonprofit organizations and volunteer-centered groups strive to raise awareness of important social issues by getting willing volunteers involved in the local community and issues impacting the area, things like hunger and homelessness (Norris Center, 2013).

2. The second time I showed up to volunteer at the Lexington Rescue Mission, I served food to the homeless. *(Show Slide 2: group of volunteers in the kitchen.)*

    a. I served soup and hung out with other volunteers and local homeless people. One of the "veteran" volunteers explained to me that Lexington has approximately 3,000 homeless people. *(Show Slide 3: homelessness statistics in Lexington.)*

    b. I was shocked to learn that we had such a large number of men, women, and children without a regular place to sleep. I wouldn't have known about this problem or the organizations working to end homelessness if I hadn't been a volunteer.

Transition   *Not only is volunteering important because it helps us become familiar with a town and its social issues; frankly, as members of a democratic society, volunteering is our civic responsibility.*

II. Giving back to the community through volunteer work is our civic responsibility and a privilege.

Listener relevance   Each of us in this room—whether as U.S. citizens or international students— are reaping the benefits of earning college degrees in this democratic society. With that benefit comes the responsibility and privilege of giving back.

    A. Volunteering is our civic responsibility.

        1. Wilson and Musick (1997) explain that, without active participation in the local community, civil society becomes deprived.

        2. Many Americans take this responsibility seriously. In fact, the US Bureau of Labor Statistics (2012) reports "About 64.3 million people volunteered through or for an organization at least once between September 2010 and September 2011." I agree that it's important to volunteer. Giving back by volunteering helps a community in so many ways. *(Show Slides 4 and 5: volunteers sorting clothes at the mission and then volunteers playing cards with people served at the shelter.)*

    B. Volunteering is also a privilege. Making a difference by volunteering ends up making us feel better about ourselves and our role in the world around us.

        1. In fact, college students aged sixteen to twenty-four represent the largest growth in percentages of volunteers across the country (Corporation for National and Community Service, 2006). *(Show Slide 6: bar graph of growth.)*

        2. A study of first-year college students done by the Higher Education Research Institute published in January 2009 revealed that 69.7 percent of students believe it is *essential or very important* to volunteer in order to help people in need (Pryor et al., 2009).

Transition   *Certainly, the privilege of giving back as volunteers is our civic responsibility and helps our local community, but we can also reap valuable résumé-building life skills by volunteering.*

III. Volunteering helps teach us new skills.

Listener relevance   These new skills and talents can actually make us more marketable for better jobs once we graduate.

    A. Being a consistent volunteer at a nonprofit organization while attending college can strengthen your résumé.

        1. "Employers rely on credentials to certify that a young person will become a valuable employee. Credentials that document the experiences and employability skills, knowledge, and attitude" (Charner, 1988, p. 30).

2. Laura Hatfield, director of the Center for Community Outreach at the University of Kentucky, points out that volunteers can include leadership, teamwork, and listening skills on their résumés because they can document the experiences where they had to use them effectively in the real world.

3. Andrea Stockelman, another volunteer at the Lexington Rescue Mission, explained some of the new skills she picked up with volunteering. She said, "I learned that there was a lot more that went into preparing food for the homeless than I ever thought possible. It was neat to be a part of that process" (personal communication, April 28, 2010). *(Show Slide 7: photo of Andrea preparing food.)*

B. Volunteering at the Lexington Rescue Mission taught me new skills that bolstered my résumé. *(Show Slide 8: résumé with skills highlighted.)*

1. I learned to coordinate the schedules of other volunteers.

2. I also practiced important people skills such as teamwork, empathy, conflict management, and listening.

CONCLUSION

I. Today we've discussed why volunteering is beneficial to college students by focusing on how volunteering can connect us quickly and easily to our local community, why it's both our responsibility and a privilege to do so, and how volunteering will benefit us after we graduate.

> **Thesis restatement with main point summary**

II. So, I'm hoping the next time you recall a time you really enjoyed making a difference by helping someone, that memory won't come from the distant past. Instead, I hope you'll be thinking about how you are being the change you seek in the world by volunteering right here in Lexington right now.

> **Clincher**

REFERENCES

Charner, I. (1988). Employability credentials: A key to successful youth transition to work. *Journal of Career Development, 15*(1), 30–40.

Corporation for National and Community Service. (2006). *College students helping America.* Washington, DC: Author.

Norris Center. (2013, January 2). *Center for student involvement: Volunteer opportunities.* Northwestern University. Retrieved from http://www.norris.northwestern.edu/csi/community/volunteer-opportunities/

Pryor, J. H., Hurtado, S., DeAngelo, L., Sharkness, J., Romero, L., Korn, W. S., & Tran, S. (2009). *The American freshman: National norms for fall 2008.* Los Angeles, CA: Higher Education Research Institute.

United States Bureau of Labor Statistics. (2012, February 22). *Economic news release: Volunteering in the United States, 2011.* Retrieved from http://www.bls.gov/news.release/volun.nr0.htm

Wilson, J., & Musick, M. A. (1997). Work and volunteering: The long arm of the job. *Social Forces, 76*(1), 251–272.

speech and analysis

Speech

The famous Indian peace activist and spiritual leader Mahatma Gandhi is known for saying "We must become the change we seek in the world." That sounds at first like an awfully tall order, but today I'd like to show you how each of us can do just that and make a difference right here in Lexington, Kentucky. Think for a moment of a time in your life when you did something kind for someone else. Maybe you helped a child do homework, or a neighbor rake leaves, or even a stranger get groceries from the store to the car. Do you remember how that made you feel? Well, that feeling can be a normal part of your week when you choose to be a volunteer. And for college students like us, it's easy to get involved as volunteers in our local community. Personally, I volunteer at the Lexington Rescue Mission and have reaped many benefits by doing so. *(Show Slide 1: picture of me volunteering at the Mission.)* I've also done extensive research on volunteering and civic engagement. So, let's spend the next few minutes discussing the benefits volunteering can have for us as college students by focusing on how volunteering helps us get acquainted with the local community, why civic engagement is the responsibility of every citizen, and what volunteering can do to teach us new skills and build our résumés. Let's begin by explaining the ways volunteering can connect each of us to our local community.

Volunteering is a great way to become acquainted with a community beyond the university campus. Most college students move away from the comforts of home to a new and unfamiliar city. Not knowing what there is to do or even how to get around can be overwhelming and isolating. Volunteering is an easy way to quickly become familiar with and begin to feel a part of this new city in addition to the campus community.

Volunteering allows you to learn your way around town. In an interview I had with Natalie Cunningham, the volunteer coordinator of the Lexington Rescue Mission, she said, "I've been working with students for several years now. While every group is different, one lingering trend is each group's unawareness of their city. It is easy for the students who live on campus to stay in their 'on-campus bubble.' Volunteering allows students to become acquainted with Lexington and the important issues facing their new home." It seems like a silly thing, but knowing your way around town starts to make any city feel like home. Volunteering gets you out into the local area and helps you begin to get acquainted with new people and places.

Volunteering can also open your eyes to local social issues and conditions. According to the Norris Center many nonprofit organizations and volunteer-centered groups strive to raise awareness of important social issues by getting willing volunteers involved in the local community and issues impacting the area, things like hunger and homelessness. The second time I showed up to volunteer at the Lexington Rescue Mission, I served food to the homeless. *(Show Slide 2: group of volunteers in the kitchen.)* I served soup and hung out with other volunteers and local homeless people. One of the "veteran" volunteers explained to me that Lexington has approximately 3,000 homeless people. *(Show Slide 3: homelessness statistics in Lexington.)* I was shocked to learn that we had such a large number of men, women, and children without a regular place to sleep. I wouldn't have known about this problem or the organizations working to end homelessness if I hadn't been a volunteer. Not only is volunteering important because it helps us become familiar with a town and its social issues; frankly, as members of a democratic society, volunteering is our civic responsibility.

Giving back to the community through volunteer work is our civic responsibility and a privilege. Each of us in this room—whether as U.S. citizens or international students—are reaping the benefits of earning college degrees in this democratic society. With that benefit comes the responsibility and privilege of giving back. Volunteering is our civic responsibility. Wilson and Musick explain that, without active participation in the local community, civil society becomes deprived. Many Americans

Analysis

Notice how Alyssa uses a famous quotation to get the attention of her audience in a way that also piques interest about the topic.

Here, Alyssa establishes listener relevance by pointing out that helping others makes us feel good and volunteering can be easy. Alyssa mentions that she volunteers, which bolsters ethos and establishes her credibility to speak on the topic.

Notice how Alyssa's thesis with main point preview gives us a sense of the organizational framework for her ideas.

Again, as Alyssa introduces the first main point, she gets us to tune in because we all know how overwhelming and isolating we can feel when we move to a new place.

Quoting the volunteer coordinator is a great piece of developmental material that encourages us to trust that Alyssa's message is trustworthy. (Note that interviews are not included in the reference section but are cited in the text of the outline.)

Alyssa intersperses actual photos of her and others volunteering throughout the speech. Doing so enhances her verbal message but doesn't replace it. The photos also provide pathos, making her ideas more emotionally compelling.

Here and throughout the speech, notice how Alyssa uses effective section transitions to verbally tie the point she is wrapping up with an introduction of the point to come. This makes her speech flow smoothly so listeners can follow her

take this responsibility seriously. In fact, the US Bureau of Labor Statistics reports "About 64.3 million people volunteered through or for an organization at least once between September 2010 and September 2011." I agree that it's important to volunteer. Giving back by volunteering helps the community in so many ways. *(Show Slides 4 and 5: volunteers sorting clothes at the mission and then volunteers playing cards with people served at the shelter.)*

Volunteering is also a privilege. Making a difference by volunteering ends up making us feel better about ourselves and our role in the world around us. In fact, research conducted by the Corporation for National and Community Service from 2002 to 2005 shows that college students age sixteen to twenty-four represent the fastest growing demographic of volunteers in this country. *(Show Slide 6: bar graph showing growth.)* Not only that, a study done by the Higher Education Research Institute published in January of 2009 shows that a whopping 69.7 percent of first-year college students believe it is essential or very important to volunteer to help people in need. Certainly, the privilege of giving back as volunteers is our civic responsibility and helps our local community, but we can also reap valuable résumé-building life skills by volunteering.

Volunteering helps teach us new skills. These new skills and talents can actually make us more marketable for better jobs once we graduate. Being a consistent volunteer at a nonprofit organization while attending college can strengthen your résumé. According to Charmer, in the *Journal of Career Development*, "Employers rely on credentials to certify that a young person will become a valuable employee. Credentials that document the experiences and employability skills, knowledge, and attitude." Laura Hatfield, director of the Center for Community Outreach at the University of Kentucky, points out that volunteers can include leadership, teamwork, and listening skills on their résumés because they can document the experiences where they had to use them effectively in the real world. Andrea Stockelman, another volunteer at the Lexington Rescue Mission, explained some of the new skills she picked up with volunteering. She said, "I learned that there was a lot more that went into preparing food for the homeless than I ever thought possible. It was neat to be a part of that process." *(Show Slide 7: photo of Andrea preparing food.)*

Volunteering at the Lexington Rescue Mission taught me new skills that bolstered my résumé. *(Show Slide 8: résumé with skills highlighted.)* I learned to coordinate the schedules of other volunteers. I also practiced important people skills such as teamwork, empathy, conflict management, and listening.

Today we've discussed why volunteering is beneficial to college students by focusing on how volunteering can connect us quickly and easily to our local community, why it's both our responsibility and a privilege to do so, and how volunteering will benefit us after we graduate. So, I'm hoping the next time you recall a time you really enjoyed making a difference by helping someone, that memory won't come from the distant past. Instead, I hope you'll be thinking about how you are being the change you seek in the world by volunteering right here in Lexington right now.

---

train of thought and bolsters her ethos because she sounds prepared. Alyssa's careful audience analysis reveals itself here as she reminds her audience that even those who are not American citizens are benefiting as students in our educational system and, thus, have a responsibility to give back in some way.

Alyssa's choice to include national statistics of college student volunteers bolsters her credibility and provides listener relevance by reinforcing that college students are doing this, want to do this, and feel good about doing this kind of work.

Students want to know how to market themselves to get good jobs. So this main point will help maintain listener interest at a point when minds might tend to wander.

By including a quotation from another volunteer, we don't have to take Alyssa's word alone.

This very clear thesis restatement with main point summary signals a sense of closure.

Notice how Alyssa ties back to her opening quotation in her clincher. This provides a sense of wrapping up without saying thank you that helps listeners feel like the speech is complete in a memorable way.

Reflection and Assessment

Delivery refers to the use of voice and body in presenting speeches. Effective delivery is conversational and animated. To assess how well you've learned what we've discussed in this chapter, answer the following questions. If you have trouble answering any of them, go back and review that material. Once you can answer each question accurately, you are ready to move ahead to read the next chapter.

1. What are the characteristics of effective delivery?
2. How do you use your voice effectively to deliver a speech?
3. How do you use your body effectively to deliver a speech?
4. What are the different speech delivery methods?
5. How do you go about rehearsing your speech?
6. What can you do to adapt delivery while giving your speech?
7. What special adaptation guidelines should you consider when delivering your speech to virtual audiences?

Challenge Resource and Assessment Center

Now that you have read Chapter 11, go to your MindTap for *The Challenge of Effective Speaking in a Digital Age* for quick access to the electronic resources that accompany this text. These resources include the following:

- **Study tools** that will help you assess your learning and prepare for exams (*digital glossary, key term flash cards, review quizzes*).
- **Activities and assignments** that will help you hone your knowledge and build your public speaking skills throughout the course (Practice, Do). Many of these activities allow you to compare your answers with those provided by the authors and, if requested, submit your answers to your instructor.
- **Media resources**—all of which are available on your MindTap for *Challenge*—will help you explore communication concepts online (Practice), develop your speech outlines (Do), watch and critique videos of sample speeches (Do), and upload your speech videos for instructor feedback and critique other students' speeches (Do)."
- **Speech-Planning Action Step identified earlier in the chapter.**
  6: Rehearsing Your Speech (p. 214)
- **Web Links that provide you with additional information or resources related to the topics discussed in this chapter.**
  11.1: Your Speech Rate (p. 201)
  11.2: Body Motions and Audience Attention (p. 204)
- **Video resources allow you to see other students giving speeches and record your own speech.**
  1. Use your Interactive Video Activities (Do) to watch, analyze, and see the transcript and outlines for the student speeches "Why Pi?," "No More Sugar," and "College Student Volunteering and Civic Engagement."
  2. View how other students deliver their speeches. Or go to the Practice and Present section of MindTap and record a speech you're working on, upload it, and ask your peers for their feedback. What feedback could you use to fine-tune your delivery before you give your speech in class?

Applying What You've Learned

 MindTap™

1. **Impromptu Speech Activity:** Draw a slip of paper from a container provided by your instructor. The slip of paper will identify an element we've discussed about effective speech preparation (identifying a topic and writing a speech goal, audience analysis and adaptation, locating and evaluating secondary research sources, types of developmental material, conducting primary research, elements of an effective macrostructure, elements of effective microstructure, constructing presentational aids, effective delivery, use of voice, use of body, delivery methods, rehearsal sessions, and so on). Prepare and present a two- to three-minute impromptu speech explaining the element with specific examples.

2. **Assessment Activity A:** Complete Action Step 6 (Rehearsing Your Speech) for a speech you will deliver this term.

3. **Assessment Activity B:** Go to your Interactive Activities for *Challenge* through your CourseMate and select a sample speech recorded there. Using the Speech Evaluation Checklist provided in this chapter, assess the speech. After doing so, provide a brief narrative critique of the speaker's delivery (use of voice and body). Be sure to answer these questions in your assessment: (1) What did the speaker do particularly well and why? (2) What could the speaker do to improve delivery, why, and how? (3) What will you do during your own rehearsal sessions based on your critique of this speaker's delivery?

12 "informative speaking"

WHAT'S THE POINT?
WHEN YOU'VE FINISHED THIS CHAPTER, YOU'LL BE ABLE TO:

12-1 Explain the characteristics of informative speeches

12-2 Describe the major methods of informing

12-3 Prepare an informative process speech

12-4 Prepare an informative expository speech

MindTap™

Review the chapter **Learning Objectives** and **Start** with quick warm up activity.

Ⓔ Ethical communicators demonstrate honesty and responsibility by providing listeners with the facts.

As Logan finished his informative speech, the class burst into spontaneous applause. Anna turned to her friend Ryan and whispered, "Wow, when Logan said his speech was going to be on online social networks I thought it would be boring. We all use Facebook and YouTube all the time. What could he possibly teach us? Was I ever wrong."

"I know what you mean," Ryan responded. "I guess Professor Gaffney was right. You really can make a familiar topic interesting if you can share new and relevant insight about it."

"Yeah," Anna continued. "Now I'm really glad I don't speak today. I'm going to take another look at my speech tonight to make sure I'm sharing new and relevant insight about online identity theft."

After listening to Logan, Anna and Ryan discovered first-hand what makes informative speeches effective. Effective information speeches don't just share information. They share information that is both new and relevant for a particular audience. Not only that, Ryan and Anna also learned that even familiar topics can be intellectually stimulating when speakers share new and relevant insight about them. In this chapter, we'll share some guidelines to help you develop effective informative speeches.

An **informative speech** is one whose goal is to explain or describe facts, truths, and principles in a way that stimulates interest, facilitates understanding, and increases the likelihood of remembering. In short, informative speeches are designed to educate audiences. Thus, most classroom lectures are basically informative speeches (although they may range from excellent to poor in quality). Informative speeches answer questions about a topic, such as those beginning with who, when, what, where, why, how to, and how does. For example, your informative speech might describe who popular singer-songwriter Adele is, define Scientology, compare and contrast the similarities and differences between Twitter and Facebook, narrate the story of golf professional Rory McIllroy's rise to fame, or demonstrate how to create and post a video on a website like YouTube. Informative speaking differs from other speech forms (such as speaking to persuade, to entertain, or to celebrate) in that your goal is simply to achieve mutual understanding about an object, person, place, process, event, idea, concept, or issue.

In this chapter, we first discuss five distinguishing characteristics of informing. Next, we describe five methods of informing. And, finally, we discuss two common types of informative speeches and provide examples of each.

12-1 CHARACTERISTICS OF EFFECTIVE INFORMATIVE SPEAKING

We face some unique challenges to gain and sustain listener attention when giving informative speeches. We can address them successfully by attending to five key characteristics of effective informative speeches.

1. **Intellectually Stimulating**

   Your audience will perceive information to be **intellectually stimulating** when it is new to them and when it is explained in a way that piques their curiosity and interest (Photo 12.1). By *new*, we mean new information that most of your audience is unfamiliar with or new insights into a topic with which they are already familiar.

   If your audience is unfamiliar with your topic, you should consider how you might tap their natural curiosity. Imagine you are an anthropology major who

> *"You really can make a familiar topic interesting if you can share new and relevant insight about it."*

informative speech: a speech whose goal is to explain or describe facts, truths, and principles in a way that stimulates interest, facilitates understanding, and increases the likelihood of remembering

intellectually stimulating: information that is new to audience members and is explained in a way that piques their curiosity

Photo 12.1 You can make familiar topics intellectually stimulating with new and relevant insight.

is interested in prehistoric humans, not an interest shared by most members of your audience. You know that in 1991, a 5,300-year-old man, Otzi, as he has become known, was found surprisingly well preserved in an ice field in the mountains between Austria and Italy. Even though the discovery was big news at the time, it is unlikely that your audience knows much about it. You can draw on their natural curiosity, however, as you present "Unraveling the Mystery of the Iceman," where you describe scientists' efforts to understand who Otzi was and what happened to him.[1]

If your audience is familiar with your topic, you will need to identify new insight about it. Begin by asking yourself: What things about my topic do listeners probably not know? Then, consider depth and breadth as you answer the question. *Depth* has to do with going into more detail than people's general knowledge of the topic. Logan did so by sharing details about the history of online social networks; something his audience of young users probably never thought about before. If you've ever watched programs on the *Food Channel*, that's what they do. Most people know basic recipes, but these programs show new ways to cook the same foods. *Breadth* has to do with looking at how your topic relates to associated topics. Trace considered breadth when he informed listeners about Type 1 diabetes. He discussed not only the physical and emotional effects on a person with diabetes but also the emotional and relational effects on the person's family and friends, as well as the financial implications of it society.

2. **Relevant**

A general rule to remember when preparing informative speeches is this: Don't assume your listeners will recognize how the information you share is relevant to them. Remember to incorporate *listener relevance links* throughout the speech. As you prepare each main point, ask and answer the question: How would knowing this information make my listeners happier, healthier, wealthier, wiser, and so forth? In other words, answer the question: Why should they care?

3. **Creative**

Your audience will perceive your information to be **creative** when it yields innovative ideas. You may not ordinarily consider yourself to be creative, but that may be because you have never recognized or fully developed your own innovative ideas. Contrary to what you may think, creativity is not a gift that some have and some don't; rather, it is the result of hard work. Creativity comes from doing good research, taking time, and practicing productive thinking.

Creative informative speeches begin with good research. The more you learn about a topic, the more you will have to work with to develop it creatively. Speakers who present information creatively do so because they have given themselves lots of supporting material to work with.

For the creative process to work, you have to give yourself time to think. Rarely do creative ideas come when we are in a time crunch. Instead, they are likely to come when we least expect it—when we're driving our car, preparing for bed, or daydreaming. We need time to mull over ideas. If you complete a draft of your outline several days before you speak, you will have time to consider how to present your ideas creatively.

For the creative process to work, you also have to think productively. **Productive thinking** occurs when we contemplate something from a variety of

---

creative: the ability to produce original, innovative ideas

productive thinking: to contemplate something from a variety of perspectives

---

SPEECH SNIPPET

Making Your Informative Speech Relevant

In her speech about date rape, Jenny offered a **listener relevance link** regarding the statistic that one in four women will be raped at some point in her lifetime. She said, "We can reason, then, that two or three of the eleven women in our classroom may be raped during her lifetime. Not only that, if you have a mother, an aunt, a sister or two, or a daughter, one of them could conceivably be raped in her lifetime."

perspectives. Then, with numerous ideas to choose from, we can select the ones that are best suited to our particular audience. In the article "Thinking Like a Genius," author Michael Michalko describes several strategies you can use to become a productive thinker. They include:

SPEECH SNIPPET

Doing Good Research to Stimulate Creative Thinking

To nurture creative thinking about transnational celebrity activism, Anne Marie not only conducted an extensive library search on several databases, but she also researched the topic by reading celebrity gossip magazines and visiting the websites of celebrities known for practicing it (e.g., Angelina Jolie, Matt Damon, George Clooney, Madonna).

- **Rethink a topic, issue, or problem from many perspectives.** Albert Einstein actually came up with the theory of relativity this way. As you brainstorm, try to think about a possible topic as it might be perceived by many different cultural and co-cultural groups. Then, as you conduct research, try to find sources that represent a variety of perspectives, as well.

- **Make your thoughts visible by sketching drawings, diagrams, and graphs.** Galileo revolutionized science by doing this. Try concept mapping as you generate topics and approaches to them.

- **Set regular goals to actually *produce something*.** The great NHL hockey player, Wayne Gretzky, put it this way: "You miss every shot you don't take." So take some shots (Photo 12.2)! Thomas Edison actually set a goal to produce an invention every ten days. J. S. Bach produced one cantata per week. And T. S. Eliot's many drafts of *The Waste Land* eventually became a masterpiece. Don't let writer's block keep you from drafting an initial outline. You need to start somewhere. Getting ideas out of your head and onto paper or a computer screen gives you something to work with and revise. After all, you can't edit air.

- **Combine and recombine ideas, images and thoughts in different ways.** The Austrian monk, Gregor Mendel, combined mathematics and biology to come up with the laws of heredity, which still ground the modern science of genetics today. Jennifer's list of possible speech topics included gardening (something she loved to do) and rising college tuition costs. She put the two ideas together and came up with the idea of doing an informative speech about how to use gardening (services, produce, and products) to raise money to help pay for college.

4. **Memorable**

If your speech is really informative, your audience will hear a lot of new information but will need help remembering what is most important. Emphasizing your specific goal, main points, and key facts are good starting points. Exhibit 12.1 illustrates several memory-enhancing techniques you might also use.

5. **Diverse Learning Styles**

Because audience members differ in how they prefer to learn, you will be most effective when you address diverse learning styles. You can appeal to people who prefer to learn through the feeling dimension by providing concrete, vivid images, examples, stories, and testimonials. You can address the watching dimension by using visual aids and by using appropriate facial expressions and gestures. You can address the thinking dimension through clear macrostructure as well as definitions, explanations, and statistics. Finally, you can address the doing dimension by providing your listeners with an opportunity to do something during the speech or afterward. Rounding the cycle ensures that you address the diverse learning styles of your audience and make the speech understandable, meaningful, and memorable for all. Logan rounded the learning cycle with personal stories to address feeling, PowerPoint slides to address watching, clear definitions and statistics

AP Images/Chris O'Meara

Photo 12.2 If you take a shot and write something down, even if it's not very good, you have something to revise. If you don't take a shot, you most assuredly have nothing to work with.

Exhibit (12.1) **Techniques for Making Informative Speech Material Memorable**

Technique	Use	Example
Presentational aids	To provide the opportunity for the audience to retain a visual as well as an audio memory of important or difficult material	A diagram of the process of making ethanol.
Repetition	To give the audience a second or third chance to retain important information by repeating or paraphrasing it	"The first dimension of romantic love is passion; that is, it can't really be romantic love if there is no sexual attraction."
Transitions	To increase the likelihood that the audience will retain the relationships among the information being presented, including which information is primary and which is supporting	"So the three characteristics of romantic love are passion, intimacy, and commitment. Now let's look at each of the five ways you can keep love alive. The first is through small talk."
Humor and other emotional anecdotes	To create an emotional memory link to important ideas	"True love is like a pair of socks: you've got to have two, and they've got to match. So you and your partner need to be mutually committed and compatible."
Mnemonics and acronyms	To provide an easily remembered memory prompt or shortcut to increase the likelihood that a list is retained	"You can remember the four criteria for evaluating a diamond as the four C's: carat, clarity, cut, and color." or "As you can see, useful goals are SMART: S—Specific, M—Measurable, A—Action oriented, R—Reasonable, and T—Time bound. That's SMART."

Addressing Diverse Learning Styles

In his speech about what it is like to do a tour of duty as a soldier in Iraq, Ray rounded the cycle of learning by sharing stories of his own experiences (feeling), showing visual aids of the places he has been and the equipment he has used (watching), explaining why the days were structured as they were (thinking), and asking his audience to respond silently to four questions every soldier must answer "yes" to (doing).

to address thinking, and by asking audience members to write down their own examples of social media sites they participate on to address doing.

12-2 METHODS OF INFORMING

Several methods exist for developing informative speech content. We can inform by describing, defining, comparing and contrasting, narrating, and demonstrating. Let's look at each of these methods more closely.

12-2a Description

Description is a method used to create an accurate, vivid, verbal picture of an object, geographic feature, setting, event, person, or image. This method usually answers an overarching "who," "what," or "where" question. If the thing to be described is simple and familiar (like a light bulb or a river), the description may not need to be detailed. But if the thing to be described is complex and unfamiliar (like a sextant or holograph), the description will be more exhaustive. Descriptions are of course easier if you have a presentational aid, but vivid verbal descriptions can also create informative mental pictures. To describe something effectively, you can explain its size, shape, weight, color, composition, age, condition, and spatial organization.

You can describe size subjectively as large or small and objectively by noting specific numerical measurements. For example, you can describe New York City subjectively as the largest in the United States or more objectively as home to more than 8 million people with more than 26,000 people per square mile.

You can describe shape by reference to common geometric forms such as round, triangular, oblong, spherical, conical, cylindrical, or rectangular, or by reference to common objects such as a book or a milk carton. For example, the lower peninsula of Michigan is often described as a left-handed mitten (Photo 12.3). Shape is made more vivid by using adjectives such as smooth or jagged.

You can describe weight subjectively as heavy or light and objectively by pounds and ounces or kilograms, grams, and milligrams. As with size, you can clarify weight with comparisons. So you can describe a Humvee (Hummer) objectively as weighing about 7,600 pounds, or subjectively as about the same as three Honda Civics.

You can describe color by coupling a basic color (such as black, white, red, or yellow) with a familiar object. For instance, instead of describing something as puce or ocher, you might describe the object as "eggplant purple" or "lime green."

You can describe the composition of something by indicating what it is made of. So you can describe a building as being made of brick, concrete, wood, or aluminum siding. At times, you might describe something as what it looks like rather than what it is. For example, you might say something looks metallic even though it is actually made of plastic rather than metal.

You can also describe something by age and by condition. Together, descriptions of age and condition can give the audience cues about the worth of what is being described. For example, describing a coin as old but in mint condition indicates that it may be worth far more than its face value. Similarly, describing a city as ancient and well-kept produces different mental pictures than does describing a city as old and war torn.

Finally, you can describe spatial organization going from top to bottom, left to right, outer to inner, and so forth. A description of the Sistine Chapel might go from the floor to the ceiling; a description of a painting might proceed from foreground to background; and a description of a NASCAR automobile might go from the body to the engine to the interior (Photo 12.4).

©iStockphoto.com/Classix

Photo 12.3 The shape of the Lower Peninsula of Michigan can be described as looking like the left hand of a mitten.

description: the informative method used to create an accurate, vivid, verbal picture of an object, geographic feature, selling, or image

12-2b Definition

Definition is a method that explains the meaning of something. There are four ways to define something.

First, you can define a word or idea by classifying it and differentiating it from similar words or ideas. For example, in a speech on vegetarianism, you might use information from the Vegan Society's website (http://www.vegansociety.com) to define a vegan: "A vegan is a vegetarian who is seeking a lifestyle free from animal products for the benefit of people, animals, and the environment. Vegans eat a plant-based diet free from all animal products, including milk, eggs, and honey. Vegans also don't wear leather, wool, or silk and avoid other animal-based products."

definition: a method of informing that explains its meaning

Second, you can define a word by explaining its derivation or history. For instance, the word *vegan* is made from the beginning and end of the word VEGetariAN and was coined in the United Kingdom in 1944 when the Vegan Society was founded.[2] Offering this etymology will help your audience remember the meaning of vegan.

Third, you can define a word by explaining its use or function. For example, in vegan recipes, you can use tofu or tempeh to replace meat and almond or soy milk to replace cow's milk.

The fourth and perhaps the quickest way to define something is by using a familiar synonym or antonym. A **synonym** is a word that has the same or a similar meaning; an **antonym** is a word that is directly opposite in meaning. So, you could define a *vegan* by comparing it to the word *vegetarian*, which is a synonym with a similar although not identical meaning, or to the word *carnivore*, which is an antonym.

12-2c Comparison and Contrast

Comparison and contrast is a method of informing that focuses on how something is similar to and different from other things. For example, in a speech on veganism, you might tell your audience how vegans are similar to and different from other types of vegetarians. You can point out that like vegetarians, vegans don't eat meat. In contrast, semi-vegetarians eat fish or poultry. Like lacto-vegetarians, vegans don't eat eggs, but unlike this group and lacto-ovo-vegetarians, vegans don't use dairy products. So of all vegetarians, vegans have the most restrictive diet. Because comparisons and contrasts can be figurative or literal, you can use metaphors and analogies as well as making direct comparisons.

12-2d Narration

Narration is a method that recounts an autobiographical or biographical event, myth, or other story. Narratives usually have four parts. First, the narration orients the listener by describing when and where the event took place and by introducing important characters. Second, the narration explains the sequence of events that led to a complication or problem, including details that enhance the development. Third, the narration discusses how the complication or problem affected key characters. Finally, the narration recounts how the complication or problem was solved. The characteristics of a good narration include a strong story line; use of descriptive language and details that enhance the plot, people, setting, and events; effective use of dialogue; pacing that builds suspense; and a strong voice.[3]

Narrations can be presented in a first-, second-, or third-person voice. When you use first person, you report what you have personally experienced or observed, using the pronouns "I," "me," and "my" as you recount the events (Photo 12.5). Your narration will be effective if your audience can identify and empathize with you and the events you describe. "Let me tell you about the first time I tried to water ski" might be the opening for a narrative story told in first person. When you use second person, you place your audience "at the scene" by using the pronouns "you" and "your." Second-person narration can be effective because it asks the audience to

Jason Smith/Getty Images for NASCAR

Photo 12.4 You can describe a NASCAR automobile spatially proceeding from the engine to the interior.

synonym: a word that has the same or a similar meaning

antonym: a word that is directly opposite in meaning

comparison and contrast: a method of informing that explains something by focusing on how it is similar to and different from other things recall an event as though they are an "actor" in the story. You might say, for example, "Imagine that you have just gotten off the plane in Hong Kong. You look at the signs but can't read a thing. Which way is the terminal?" When you use third person, you describe what has happened, is happening, or will happen to other people by using pronouns like "he," "her," and "they." For example, you might say "When the students arrived in Venice for their study-abroad experience, the first thing they saw was. . . ." Third-person narration is effective when your audience can identify with key characters and their experiences.

12-2e Demonstration

Demonstration is a method that shows how something is done, displays the stages of a process, or depicts how something works. Demonstrations range from very simple with a few easy-to-follow steps (such as how to iron a shirt) to very complex

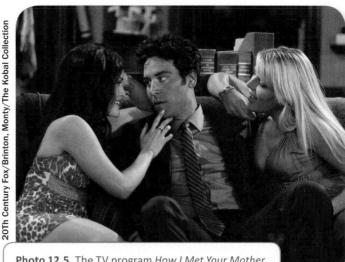

Photo 12.5 The TV program *How I Met Your Mother* is an example of informing using the first-person narrative method. How does it capture and maintain audience interest?

20Th Century Fox/Brinton, Monty/The Kobal Collection

(such as demonstrating how a nuclear reactor works). Regardless of whether the topic is simple or complex, effective demonstrations require expertise, a hierarchy of steps, and vivid language and presentational aids.

In a demonstration, your experience with what you are demonstrating is critical. Expertise gives you the necessary background to supplement bare-bones instructions with personally lived experience. During a demonstration, you speak from that experience as you guide your audience through the steps. Why are TV cooking shows so popular? Because the chef doesn't just read the recipe and do what it says. Rather, while performing each step, the chef shares tips that aren't mentioned in any cookbook. It is the chef's experience that allows him or her to say that one egg will work or how to tell if the cake is really done.

In a demonstration, you organize the steps from first to last to help your audience remember the sequence accurately. If there are many steps, grouping them will also help audiences remember. For example, suppose you want to demonstrate the steps in using a touch-screen voting machine. If, rather than presenting fourteen separate points, you group them under four headings—(1) get ready to vote; (2) vote; (3) review your choices; (4) cast your ballot—chances are much higher that the audience will be able to remember most if not all the items in each of the four groups.

Most demonstrations involve actually showing the audience the process or parts of the process. That's in part why TV shows like *What Not to Wear* and *Flip This House* are so popular. If what you are explaining is relatively simple, you can demonstrate the entire process from start to finish. However, if the process is lengthy or complex, you may choose to pre-prepare material for some of the steps. Although you will show all stages in the process, you will not have to take the time for every single step as the audience watches. For example, many of the ingredients used by TV chefs are already cut up and measured into little bowls.

Effective demonstrations require practice. Remember that, under the pressure of speaking to an audience, even the simplest task can become difficult (Have you ever tried to thread a needle with twenty-five people watching you?). As you practice, you will want to consider the size of your audience and the configuration of the room. Be sure that everyone in your audience will be able to see what you are doing.

narration: a method of informing that explains something by recounting events

demonstration: a method of informing that shows how something is done, displays the stages of a process, or depicts how something works

To see a video clip of an effective demonstration from a student informative speech, go to your MindTap for *Challenge* to access the video clip "Flag Etiquette."

12-3 INFORMATIVE PROCESS SPEECHES

Two of the most common patterns for organizing the macrostructure of informative speeches are process patterns and expository patterns. In this section, we focus specifically on process speeches. In the section that follows, we'll talk about expository speeches.

process speech: a speech that explains and shows how something is done, is made, or works

The goal of a **process speech** is to explain and show how something is done, is made, or works. Effective process speeches require you to carefully delineate the steps and the order in which they occur. The steps typically become the main points and explanations of each step become the subpoints. Most process speeches rely heavily on the demonstration method of informing.

For example, Allie is a floral designer and has been asked by her former art teacher to speak on the basics of floral arrangement to a high school art class. The teacher allotted five minutes for her presentation. Allie recognized that she could not demonstrate an entire floral display of any size in just five minutes. So she opted to physically demonstrate only parts of the process and bring additional arrangements in various stages of completion. For example, the first step is to choose the right vase and frog (flower holder). So she brought in vases and frogs of various sizes and shapes to show as she explained how to choose one based on the types of flowers used and the desired visual effect. The second step is to prepare the basic triangle of blooms. Allie began to demonstrate how to place the flowers she had brought to form one triangle. Rather than trying to get everything perfect in the few seconds she had, however, she also brought out several other partially finished arrangements that were behind a draped

How to do it	How to make it	How it works
Select running shoes	compost bin	3-D movies
Apply for a loan	rope knots	stem cell reproduction
Install a toilet water saving device	lefse	solar energy
Bouldering	fishing flies	digital synchronization

IMPROMPTU SPEECH CHALLENGE

Identify a food item that is fairly simple to make (e.g., peanut butter and jelly sandwich, bowl of cereal, cheese and crackers, meal in a can or box such as soup or macaroni and cheese, Kool-Aid). Prepare and present a short two- to three-minute process speech explaining how to make it.

table. These showed other carefully completed triangles that used other types of flowers. The third step is placing additional flowers and greenery to complete an arrangement and achieve various artistic effects. Again, Allie actually demonstrated how to place several blooms, and then, as she described them, she brought out several completed arrangements that illustrated various artistic effects. Even though Allie did not physically perform every part of each step, her visual presentation was an excellent demonstration of floral arranging.

Although some process speeches require you to demonstrate, others are not suited to demonstrations. For these, you can use visual or audiovisual aids to help the audience "see" the steps in the process. In a speech on remodeling a kitchen, it would not be practical to demonstrate the process; however, you could greatly enhance the verbal description by showing pictures before, during, and after the remodeling. Exhibit 12.2 provides some topic examples for process speeches.

" speech assignment "

Process Speech

Prepare a three- to six-minute process speech explaining how something is made, how something is done, or how something works. An adaptation plan and a complete outline are required. To help you prepare your speech and your outline, go to your MindTap for *Challenge* and complete the Speech-Planning Action Step Activities.

Notice that the sample Process Speech Evaluation Form includes both specific criteria related to process speeches and general criteria items that are common to all speeches.

 MindTap™

Do this activity with **Speech Builder Express**.

speech evaluation checklist

Process Speech Evaluation Checklist

You can use this form to critique a process speech.

General Criteria

_____ 1. Was the specific goal clear?

_____ 2. Was the introduction effective in creating interest, as well as introducing the thesis and main points?

_____ 3. Was the macrostructure easy to follow?

_____ 4. Was the language appropriate, accurate, clear, and vivid?

_____ 5. Were the main points developed with appropriate breadth, depth, and supporting material?

_____ 6. Was the conclusion effective in summarizing the thesis and main points, as well as clinching?

_____ 7. Was the speaker's use of voice conversational, intelligible, and expressive?

_____ 8. Did the speaker's use of body (e.g., appearance, posture, poise, eye contact, facial expressions, gestures, and movement) appear poised, spontaneous, appropriate, and effective?

Specific Criteria

_____ 1. Was the specific goal appropriate for a process speech (how to do it, how to make it, how it works)?

_____ 2. Did the speaker show personal expertise with the process?

_____ 3. Did the speaker emphasize the process steps?

_____ 4. If the speaker demonstrated a process or parts of a process, was the demonstration fluid and skillful?

_____ 5. Were presentational aids constructed effectively to help explain the process?

_____ 6. Were presentational aids used effectively to help explain the process and easily seen by all audience members?

Based on these criteria, evaluate the speech as (check one):

_____ excellent _____ good _____ satisfactory _____ fair _____ poor

Explain:

🌐 MindTap™

Access this checklist online on MindTap for *Challenge*.

SAMPLE SPEECH

Sample Process Speech

This section presents a sample informative speech given by a student, including an adaptation plan, an outline, and a transcript.

Internet Identity Theft: Self-Protection Steps

By Anna Rankin

ADAPTATION PLAN

1. **Key aspects of audience**. Most people in my audience are probably aware of identity theft but probably don't know all the steps they can take to protect themselves from becoming victims of it.

2. **Establishing and maintaining common ground.** I will begin my speech by using a hypothetical example placing them as victims of Internet identity theft. Throughout the speech, I will refer to the audience's previous knowledge and experience.

3. **Building and maintaining interest.** I will try to gain interest in the introduction by relating the problem of internet identity theft to college students. Throughout the speech, I will use common analogies and metaphors to explain the self-protection steps. Finally, I will use a well-designed PowerPoint presentation to capture and maintain attention.

4. **Audience knowledge and sophistication.** Because most of the class is probably not familiar with the actual self-protection steps regarding Internet identity theft, I will focus specifically on them throughout my speech.

5. **Building credibility.** Early in the speech, I will tell the audience how I got interested in Internet identity theft and the research I did to learn about it as a pre-law student.

6. **Audience attitudes.** I will try to address audience apathy by using interesting examples and compelling stories they can easily relate to.

7. **Adapting to audiences from different cultures and language-communities.** I will use visual and audiovisual aids in my PowerPoint presentation to help those listeners from different cultures understand what I'm talking about even though English is not their native language.

8. **Using presentational aids to enhance understanding and memory.** Throughout the speech, I will use color-coded PowerPoint slides with headers to reinforce the steps being discussed.

Outline

General goal: To inform

Specific goal: I want my audience to understand the steps to protect themselves from online identity theft.

INTRODUCTION

I. Imagine this: you are filing your income tax return after starting your first real job after college. After completing the tedious online forms, you hit the "calculate" button. You are ecstatic when the online filing system says you are due a return of a whopping $2,800! Then, imagine hitting "file" to submit your

Read the speech adaptation plan, outline, and transcript of a speech by Anna Rankin. You can access a video clip of Anna's speech through the Chapter 12 resources of your MindTap for *Challenge*. You can also use your MindTap to identify some of the strengths of Anna's speech by completing an evaluation checklist and preparing a one- to two-page critique identifying what she did well and what she could improve on regarding content, structure, delivery, and presentational aids.

Attention getter

tax return and you get the error message "*Your tax return has already been processed.*" Someone has stolen your identity and pocketed your return.

Listener relevance
II. If you think this cannot happen to you, think again! According to the U.S. Government Accountability Office (White, 2012), approximately 642,000 cases of tax-related identity theft were reported in the first nine months of 2012 alone.

Speaker credibility and Listener relevance
III. Through my research, I discovered that 8.3 million Americans were victims of identity theft in 2005 (FTC, 2007). Identity theft can happen when someone simply digs through your trash for bank statements and most of us now shred such items before discarding them. Recently, however, Internet identity theft is becoming far more prevalent (U.S. Department of Justice, n.d.). An identity thief who accesses your information online can apply for jobs, loans, and credit cards, can receive medical care or prescription drugs, and can make large purchases all under your name (FTC, 2012).

Thesis statement with main point preview
IV. Today, let's discuss several simple steps we can all take to prevent Internet identity theft (*Show Slide 1: Three Steps to Prevent Identity Theft*). These three steps are designed to help prevent phishing, hacking, and pharming.

BODY

I. The first step in preventing online identity theft is to protect yourself from phishing (*Show Slide 2: Email Phishing [Photo]*).

   A. Most likely, everyone in this room receives hundreds of email messages every week. Whether it is an update from our college professor or coupons from our favorite retail stores, we are bombarded with emails that we do not hesitate to open or reply to.

   B. Phishing is a process through which identity thieves persuade Internet users to provide personal information by posing as legitimate organizations (NCPC, 2013).

      1. Identity thieves might send you an email that appears to be from a legitimate organization.

      2. In it, they will ask you to provide personal information such as your bank account numbers, Social Security number, or personal passwords.

   C. One way to prevent phishing is by never providing personal information online without verifying the legitimacy of the sender.

      1. Always contact the organization's customer service number provided to verify the legitimacy of the email.

      2. And make it a standard practices to always provide such information over the phone rather than via email (FTC, 2012).

   D. Another way to avoid becoming a victim of identity theft through phishing is never to click on links in emails from unknown sources (NCPC, 2013).

      1. Clicking on these links can automatically install software on your computer that re-routes your personal information to the identity thief's personal data collection website.

      2. Once the thief or thieves have this information, they can basically "become you" all over the Internet.

Transition
Now that we all know what we can do to keep our identity safe through good email practices, let's consider how we can prevent identity theft by surfing the Internet wisely.

II. The second step we can take to protect ourselves from identity theft is to prevent hacking (*Show Slide 3: Computer Hacking [Photo]*).

A. Take a moment to think about all the personal and financial information you have stored on your electronic devices. If someone were to gain open access to your computer, or even to your smart phone for that matter, he or she would be able to steal your identity in a few swipes of the keys.

Listener relevance

B. Hacking refers to a process through which an identity thief gains access to your personal computer to view documents, files, and personal information (NCPC, 2013).

C. Here are a few simple steps you can take to protect yourself from becoming a victim of hacking.

    1. The first step is to password-protect all of your accounts and devices, and to get creative with your passwords (FTC, 2012).

        a. Avoid using personal information such as your name, date of birth, address, or other personal information that is easily discovered by others (NCPC, 2013).

        b. Never use words that are found in the dictionary—some hacking programs can quickly attempt every word found in the dictionary to access your information.

        c. Try creating acronyms that you will always remember. For example, the phrase "I graduate from college in 2016" could turn into the password IgFcI2k16—a strong and unique password that you can easily remember (*Show Slide 4: Unique Password Examples*)!

        d. Finally, avoid sharing too much information on social networking sites. If an identity thief finds out enough about your personal life, they can easily answer those "challenge" questions you use to keep your accounts and devices protected.

    2. The second step to protect identity theft from hacking is to be sure you wipe clean any of your electronic devices before selling them or disposing of them (FTC, 2012).

        a. Before you dispose of your laptop or smart phone, eliminate any personal information including saved passwords, photos, web search histories, and contact information.

        b. There are several programs you can use to wipe your hard drive clean. However, the National Crime Protection Council (2005) suggests removing and destroying your computer's hard drive altogether before selling or disposing of your laptop.

So now that we know how to protect our email accounts from phishing and our computers from hacking, let's focus on what we need to do to protect ourselves from the most advanced method of online identity theft.

Transition

III. The third step in protecting ourselves from identity theft is to prevent pharming (*Show Slide 5: Pharming Website Dangers [Photo]*).

A. Virtually every day, we engage in online transactions. We may log on to our online banking to make sure we have enough money for dinner with friends, we may purchase a gift for someone using Amazon.com, or we may pay tuition using the online payment system.

B. Pharming, one of the toughest methods of online identity theft to detect, is a process through which criminals hack established websites, such as Amazon.com, and re-route the website to a "poser" website that looks very similar and allows them to gather our personal information during a transaction (NCPC, 2005).

    C. Although pharming is the most difficult method of identity theft to detect, there are a few steps we can take to protect ourselves when making online transactions.

       1. First, look for the "lock" icon on your Internet browser's status bar. This lock indicates that the website you are on is safe (*Show Slide 6: Internet Browser Safety Features*).

       2. Next, verify that the website is secure by inspecting the URL. A safe website URL will begin with https:// instead of http://

       3. Finally, you can purchase encryption software that makes sure any information you send over the Internet is jumbled and unreadable to others.

CONCLUSION

Thesis restatement

    I. As you can see, the Internet is literally a gold mine for identity thieves when our personal information is not protected.

Main point summary

    II. Fortunately, we can take steps to protect ourselves from phishing, hacking, and pharming (*Show Slide 7 [same as slide 1]*).

    III. According to a 2011 article in the *New York Times* (Perlroth, 2011), it is extremely difficult to prosecute online identity thieves even though they deserve it. One thing we can do, however, is to put a padlock on our goldmines so these criminals can't access them in the first place!

Clincher

REFERENCES

Federal Trade Commission. (2007). FTC releases survey of identity theft in the U.S. study shows 8.3 million victims in 2005. Retrieved from http://www.ftc.gov/opa/2007/11/idtheft.shtm

Federal Trade Commission. (2012). Identity theft. Retrieved from http://www.consumer.ftc.gov/features/feature-0014-identity-theft

Koster, C. (n.d.) Identity theft. Retrieved from the Missouri Attorney General website: http://ago.mo.gov/publications/idtheft.htm#header3

National Crime Prevention Council. (2013). Evolving with technology: A comprehensive introduction to cybercrime with links to resources. Retrieved from: http://www.ncpc.org/topics/fraud-and-identity-theft/evolving-with-technology

Perlroth, N. (2011, December 19). A unit to fight cybercrimes. *The New York Times*. Retrieved from http://query.nytimes.com/

U.S. Department of Justice. (n.d.). Identity theft and fraud. Retrieved from http://www.justice.gov/criminal/fraud/websites/idtheft.html

White, J. R. (2012). *Identity theft: Total extent of refund fraud using stolen identities is unknown* (GAO Publication No. GAO-13-132T). Washington, DC: U.S. Government Accountability Office. Retrieved from http://www.gao.gov/assets/660/650365.pdf

speech and analysis

Speech

Imagine this: you are filing your income tax return after starting your first real job after college. After completing the tedious online forms, you hit the "calculate" button. You are ecstatic when the online filing system says you are due a return of a whopping $2,800! Then, imagine hitting "file" to submit your tax return and you get the error message *"Your tax return has already been processed."* Someone has stolen your identity and pocketed your return.

If you think this cannot happen to you, think again! According to a U.S. Government Accountability Office report published in 2012, approximately 642,000 cases of tax-related identity theft were reported in the first nine months of 2012 alone. Through my research, I discovered that 8.3 million Americans were victims of identity theft in 2005. Of course, identity theft can happen when someone simply digs through your trash for bank statements and most of us now shred such items before discarding them. Recently, however, according the U.S. Department of Justice, Internet identity theft is becoming far more prevalent. According to the Federal Trade Commission, an identity thief who accesses your information online can apply for jobs, loans, and credit cards, can receive medical care or prescription drugs, and can make large purchases all under your name.

Today, let's discuss several simple steps we can all take to prevent Internet identity theft (*Show Slide 1: Three Steps to Prevent Identity Theft*). These three steps are designed to help prevent phishing, hacking, and pharming.

The first step in preventing online identity theft is to protect ourselves from phishing (*Show Slide 2: Email Phishing [Photo]*). Most likely, everyone in this room receives hundreds of email messages every week. Whether it is an update from our college professor or coupons from our favorite retail stores, we are bombarded with emails that we do not hesitate to open or reply to.

According to the National Crime Protection Council, phishing is a process through which identity thieves persuade Internet users to provide personal information by posing as legitimate organizations. Identity thieves might send you an email that appears to be from a legitimate organization. In it, they will ask you to provide personal information such as your bank account numbers, social security number, or personal passwords.

One way to prevent phishing is by never providing personal information online without verifying the legitimacy of the sender. Always contact the organization's customer service number provided to verify the legitimacy of the email. And make it a standard practice to always provide your information over the phone rather than via email.

Another way to avoid becoming a victim of identity theft through phishing is never to click on links in emails from unknown sources. Clicking on these links can automatically install software on your computer that re-routes your personal information to the identity thief's personal data collection website. Once the thief or thieves have this information, they can basically "become you" all over the Internet.

Now that we all know what we can do to keep our identity safe through good email practices, let's consider how we can prevent identity theft by surfing the Internet wisely.

The second step we can take to protect ourselves from identity theft is to prevent hacking (*Show Slide 3: Computer Hacking [Photo]*).

Take a moment to think about all the personal and financial information you have stored on your electronic devices. If someone were to gain open access to

Analysis

Notice how Anna uses a hypothetical example to draw her audience into her speech with this attention getter. Not only that, she also offers listener relevance by using a dollar amount that most college students would find enticing.

This paragraph is chock full of listener relevant statements supported with evidence from reputable sources, which serve to establish Anna's credibility very well.

Anna very succinctly offers her thesis and main point preview using personal pronouns and "we" language that foster a sense of immediacy with her audience.

As Anna presents her first main point, she also incorporates a listener relevance link that piques audience member interest.

Anna appeals to the thinking dimension of the learning cycle here with a clear definition and explanation of what phishing is.

Here Anna appeals to the doing dimension of the learning cycle by offering specific things listeners can do to protect themselves from online identity theft.

Although this is another great action step, Anna could have improved by offering a narrative from someone who experienced this or referencing a feature film focused on this topic.

Anna does a great job here of tying the two points together using "we" language that fosters immediacy.

your computer, or even to your smart phone for that matter, he or she would be able to steal your identity in a few swipes of the keys.

Hacking refers to a process through which an identity thief gains access to our personal computers to view documents, files, and personal information. Fortunately, the Federal Trade Commission and the National Crime Protection Council outline several things we can do to protect ourselves from becoming a victim of hacking. The first step is to password-protect all of our accounts and devices, and to get creative with our passwords. We can avoid using personal information such as name, date of birth, address, or other personal information that is easily discovered by others. We can also avoid using words that are found in the dictionary—some hacking programs can quickly attempt every word found in the dictionary to access our information. And we can create acronyms that we will always remember. For example, the phrase "I graduate from college in 2016" could turn into the password IgFcI2k16—a strong and unique password that you can easily remember if you are graduating in 2016 (*Show Slide 4: Unique Password Examples*)! Finally, we can avoid sharing too much information on social networking sites. If an identity thief finds out enough about our personal life, they can easily answer those "challenge" questions we use to keep our accounts and devices protected.

Another way to protect identity theft from hacking is to be sure you wipe clean any of your electronic devices before selling them or disposing of them. Before you dispose of your laptop or smart phone, eliminate any personal information including saved passwords, photos, web search histories, and contact information. There are several programs you can use to wipe your hard drive clean. However, the National Crime Protection Council suggests removing and destroying your computer's hard drive altogether before selling or disposing of your laptop.

So now that we know how to protect our email accounts from phishing and our computers from hacking, let's focus on what we need to do to protect ourselves from the most advanced method of online identity theft.

The third step in protecting ourselves from identity theft is to prevent pharming (*Show Slide 5: Pharming Website Dangers [Photo]*).

Virtually every day, we engage in online transactions. We may log on to our online banking to make sure we have enough money for dinner with friends, we may purchase a gift for someone using Amazon.com, or we may pay our tuition using the online payment system.

Pharming, according to the National Crime Protection Council, is one of the toughest methods of online identity theft to detect. It is essentially a process through which criminals hack established websites, such as Amazon.com, and re-route the website to a "poser" website that looks very similar and allows them to gather our personal information during a transaction. Although pharming is the most difficult method of identity theft to detect, there are a few steps we can take to protect ourselves when making online transactions. First, we can look for the "lock" icon on the Internet browser's status bar. This lock indicates that the website we are on is safe (*Show Slide 6: Internet Browser Safety Features*). And we can verify that the website is secure by inspecting the URL. A safe website URL will begin with https:// instead of http:// Finally, we can purchase encryption software that makes sure any information we send over the Internet is jumbled and unreadable to others.

As you can see, the Internet is literally a gold mine for identity thieves when our personal information is not protected. Fortunately, we can take steps to protect ourselves from phishing, hacking, and pharming (*Show Slide 7 [same as slide 1]*). According to a 2011 article in the *New York Times*, it is extremely difficult to prosecute online identity thieves even though they deserve it. One thing we can do, however, is to put a padlock on our goldmines so these criminals can't access them in the first place!

Here again Anna does a great job establishing personal relevance for her second main point.

Although this is great information, it might be clearly for the listener if Anna would break it into two points: (1) password protection and (2) creative passwords.

Again, this is interesting and helpful information that could be more compelling with oral footnotes to reputable sources and a narrative account from someone who experienced it.

Notice how Anna again provides a transition that verbally ties the two main points together creating a fluent sense of forward motion into her next main point.

Here Anna provides great examples that should help her classmates see the relevance of what she is discussing and, thus, motivate them to stay tuned in.

Here and throughout the speech Anna provides excellent information. What is missing, however, are personal quotations, stories, and testimonials that would appeal to the feeling dimension of the learning cycle.

Anna makes her conclusion more memorable by using the analogy of a "goldmine" to refer to our identities and identity thieves as "criminals."

12-4 INFORMATIVE EXPOSITORY SPEECHES

The goal of an **expository speech** is to provide carefully researched in-depth knowledge about a complex topic (Photo 12.6). For example, "understanding the gun control debate," "the origins and classifications of nursery rhymes," "the sociobiological theory of child abuse," and "viewing hip-hop music as poetry" are all topics on which you could give an interesting expository speech. Lengthy expository speeches are known as lectures.

All expository speeches require speakers to draw from an extensive research base, choose an organizational pattern best suited to the topic and goal, and use a variety of informative methods (e.g., descriptions, definitions, comparisons and contrasts, narrations, short demonstrations) to sustain the audience's attention and help them understand the material presented.

Expository speeches include those that explain a political, economic, social, religious, or ethical issue; events or forces of history; a theory, principle, or law; and a creative work.

Photo 12.6 An expository speech, like a classroom lecture, is an informative presentation that provides in-depth knowledge of a subject.

© Andresr/Shutterstock.com

12-4a Exposition of Political, Economic, Social, Religious, or Ethical Issues

In an expository speech, you have the opportunity to help the audience understand the background or context of an issue, including the forces that gave rise to the issue and continue to affect it. You may also present the various positions held about the issue and the reasoning behind these positions. Finally, you may discuss various ways that have been presented for resolving the issue.

The general goal of your speech is to inform, not to persuade. So you will want to present all sides of controversial issues without advocating which side is better. You will also want to make sure the sources you are drawing from are respected experts and are objective in what they report. Finally, you will want to present complex issues in a straightforward manner that helps your audience to understand while not oversimplifying knotty issues. For example, while research a speech on fracking—the controversial method for extracting nature gas deposits—you need to be careful to consult articles and experts on all sides of the issue and fairly represent and incorporate these views in your speech. If time is limited you might discuss all sides of just one or two of these issues, but you should also at least mention the others, as well. Exhibit 12.3 provides examples of topic ideas for an expository speech about a political, economic, social, religious, or ethical issues.

expository speech: an informative presentation that provides carefully researched in-depth knowledge about a complex topic

Exhibit 12.3 Topic Ideas for Expository Speeches About Political, Economic, Social, Religious, or Ethical Issues.

gay marriage	stem cell research
affirmative action	health care reform
climate change	school vouchers
media bias	digital remixing
gun control	home schooling
immigration	fracking
genetic engineering	celebrity culture

Reflect on Ethics

WHAT WOULD *YOU* DO?

ETHICS OF ONLINE NEWS: "GIZMODOGATE" AS A HISTORICAL EVENT

Today more and more people are getting their news online, not only from online newspapers, but also from blogs and social networking sites, like Twitter and Facebook. In March 2010, one of these news sources, tech blog Gizmodo, became news itself.

Allegedly, Gizmodo paid to obtain a prototype of Apple's iPhone 4G, which an Apple employee left at a local bar and that was then picked up by someone else.[4] Nick Denton, CEO of Gizmodo's parent company, Gawker Media, admitted he paid $5,000 for the prototype, knowing the person he was paying was not the owner.[5] Gizmodo then posted photos of the prototype, without knowing whether the prototype was even real and scooping Apple, who hadn't yet made any announcements about the phone.

Gizmodo's blog posts spurred a criminal investigation, as well as a debate about the rights and responsibilities of online journalists. As part of the investigation, county prosecutors searched the home of Gizmodo's editor, Jason Chen, and seized his computers. In response, Gizmodo claimed that this seizure violated laws that limit newsroom investigations. No employees of Gizmodo or Gawker Media were ever charged. However, the two people who found the iPhone and sold it to Gizmodo were.[6]

1. What, if any, ethical principles did Gizmodo violate by posting the photos and stories about the prototype iPhone?

2. Should online journalists who host blogs be held to the same ethical codes of fact checking and credential verification as traditional journalists? If so, how?

3. Should the laws that limit newsroom investigations also protect online journalists who work on computers in their homes? Why or why not?

12-4b Exposition of Historical Events and Forces

It has been said that those who don't understand history may be destined to repeat it. So an expositional speech about an historical event or force can be fascinating for its own sake, but it can also be relevant for what is happening today. Unfortunately, some people think history is boring. So, you have a special obligation to seek out stories and narratives that can enliven your expository speech. And you will want to analyze the event you describe and the impact it had at the time it occurred, as well as the meaning it has for us today. For example, although many of us are familiar with the historical fact that the United States developed the atomic bomb during World War II, an expository speech on the Manhattan Project (as it was known) that dramatized the race to produce the bomb and told the stories of the main players would add to our understanding of the inner workings of "secret" government-funded research projects. It might also place modern arms races and the fear of nuclear proliferation into historical context. Exhibit 12.4 offers some topic idea examples for an expository speech about historical events and forces.

Exhibit (12.4) Topic Ideas for Expository Speeches About Historical Events and Forces

genocide	Gandhi and his movement
the Papacy	the colonization of Africa
Irish immigration	building the Great Pyramids
women's suffrage	the Industrial Revolution
the Spanish flu epidemic	the Ming Dynasty
conquering Mt. Everest	the Vietnam War
assassination of MLK Jr.	the Crusades
the Balfour Declaration	Space Shuttle *Challenger* explosion

Copyright © Cengage Learning

12-4c Exposition of a Theory, Principle, or Law

The way we live is affected by natural and human laws and principles and explained by various theories. Yet there are many theories, principles, and laws that we do not completely understand—or, at least, we don't understand how they affect us. An expository speech can inform us by explaining these important phenomena. The main challenge is to find material that explains the theory, law, or principle in language that is understandable to the audience. You will want to search for or create examples and illustrations that demystify complicated concepts and terminology. Effective examples and comparing unfamiliar ideas with those that the audience already knows are techniques that can help you with this kind of speech. For example, in a speech on the psychological principles of operant conditioning, a speaker could help the audience understand the difference between continuous reinforcement and intermittent reinforcement with the following explanation:

When a behavior is reinforced continuously, each time people perform the behavior they get the reward, but when the behavior is reinforced intermittently, the reward is not always given when the behavior is displayed. Behavior that is learned by continuous reinforcement disappears quickly when the reward is no longer provided, but behavior that is learned by intermittent reinforcement continues for long periods of time, even when not reinforced. You can see examples of how behavior was conditioned in everyday encounters. For example, take the behavior of putting a coin in the slot of a machine. If the machine is a vending machine, you expect to be rewarded every time you "play." And if the machine doesn't eject the item, you might wonder if the machine is out of order and "play" just one more coin, or you might bang on the machine. In any case, you are unlikely to put in more than one more coin. But suppose the machine is a slot machine or a machine that dispenses instant winner lottery tickets. Now how many coins will you "play" before you stop and conclude that the machine is "out of order"? Why the difference? Because you have been conditioned to a vending machine on a continuous schedule, but a slot machine or automatic lottery ticket dispenser "teaches" you on an intermittent schedule.

Exhibit 12. 5 provides some examples of topic ideas for an expository speech about a theory, principle, or law.

Exhibit 12.5 **Topic Ideas for Expository Speeches About a Theory, Principle, or Law**

natural selection	diminishing returns
gravity	Boyle's law
number theory	psychoanalytic theory
Murphy's Law	intelligent design
feminist theory	Maslow's hierarchy of needs
social cognitive theory	color theory: complements and contrasts
the Peter principle	

12-4d Exposition of a Creative Work

Courses in art, theater, music, literature, and film appreciation give students tools by which to recognize the style, historical period, and quality of a particular piece or group of pieces. Yet most of us know very little about how to understand a creative work, so

Exhibit **12.6** **Topic Ideas for Expository Speeches About Creative Works**

hip-hop music	the films of Alfred Hitchcock
Impressionist painting	Lady Gaga's "Paparazzi"
salsa dancing	Kabuki theater
inaugural addresses	Iconography
MLK Jr. National Memorial	*Catcher in the Rye*: a coming-of-age novel
The Hunger Games trilogy	Spike Lee's *Mo' Better Blues*
Van Gogh's *Starry Night*	

presentations designed to explain creative works such as poems, novels, songs, or even famous speeches can be very instructive for audience members.

When developing a speech that explains a creative work, you will want to find information on the work and the artist who created it. You will also want to find sources that help you understand the period in which this work was created and learn about the criteria that critics use to evaluate works of this type. So, for example, if you wanted to give an expository speech on Frederick Douglass's Fourth of July oration of 1852 in Rochester, New York, you might need to orient your audience by first reminding them of who Douglass was. Then, you would want to explain the traditional expectation that was set for Fourth of July speakers at this point in history. After this, you might want to summarize the speech and perhaps share a few memorable quotations. Finally, you would want to discuss how speech critics view the speech and why the speech is considered "great" still today. Exhibit 12.6 provides some examples of topics for an expository speech about a creative work.

speech assignment

Expository Speech

Prepare a five- to eight-minute expository speech. To help you prepare your speech and your outline, go to your MindTap for *Challenge* and complete the Speech-Planning Action Step Activities.

Notice that the sample Expository Speech Evaluation Checklist that follows includes both specific criteria related to expository speeches and general criteria that are common to all speeches.

Do this activity with Speech Builder Express.

" speech evaluation checklist "

Expository Speech Evaluation Checklist

You can use this form to critique an expository speech that you hear in class. As you listen, outline the speech and identify which expository speech type it is. Then, answer the following questions.

Type of expository speech

_____Exposition of political, economic, social, religious, or ethical issues

_____Exposition of historical events or forces

_____Exposition of a theory, principle, or law

_____Exposition of a creative work

General Criteria

_____1. Was the specific goal clear?

_____2. Was the introduction effective in creating interest, as well as introducing the thesis and main points?

_____3. Was the macrostructure easy to follow?

_____4. Was the language appropriate, accurate, clear, and vivid?

_____5. Were the main points developed with appropriate breadth, depth, and supporting material?

_____6. Was the conclusion effective in summarizing the thesis and main points, as well as clinching?

_____7. Was the speaker's use of voice conversational, intelligible, and expressive?

_____8. Did the speaker's use of body (e.g., appearance, posture, poise, eye contact, facial expressions, gestures, and movement) appear poised, spontaneous, appropriate, and effective?

Specific Criteria

_____1. Was the specific speech goal to provide well-researched information on a complex topic?

_____2. Did the speaker effectively use a variety of informative methods?

_____3. Did the speaker emphasize the main ideas and important supporting material?

_____4. Did the speaker use a variety of supporting material?

_____5. Did the speaker present in-depth, high-quality, appropriately cited information?

Based on these criteria, evaluate the speech as (check one):

_____ excellent _____ good _____ satisfactory _____ fair _____ poor

Explain:

Access this checklist online on your MindTap for Challenge.

SAMPLE SPEECH

Sample Expository Speech

This section presents a sample expository speech adaptation plan, outline, and transcript by Logan Hurley.

Social Media and Society

By Logan Hurley, University of Kentucky[7]

Read the speech adaptation plan, outline, and transcript of a speech by Logan Hurley. You can access a video clip of Logan's speech through the Chapter 12 resources of your MindTap for *Challenge*. You can also use your MindTap to identify some of the strengths of Logan's speech by completing an evaluation checklist and preparing a one- to two-page critique identifying what he did well and what he could improve on regarding content, structure, delivery, and presentational aids.

ADAPTATION PLAN

1. **Key aspects of audience.** Because most of my classmates are not only aware of social media but also active users, I will focus instead on it as a social force impacting both politics and news reporting.

2. **Establishing and maintaining common ground.** I will use inclusive pronouns and relate all aspects of social media I discuss as they impact me and my audience.

3. **Building and maintaining interest.** I will build interest by pointing out that social media is getting more and more popular not only as a way to stay connected with friends but also altering the way we engage in politics and in news reporting too.

4. **Audience knowledge and sophistication.** The audience is made up of my classmates and all are 18 to 20 years old. Because they grew up using social media, I don't need to explain how the sites function. However, I will need to clarify what exactly I'm talking about when I say social media, because of assumptions and foreknowledge that the class will carry in with them.

5. **Building credibility.** I will cite credible sources and portray a thorough understanding of my sources in the speech.

6. **Audience attitudes.** I expect my audience to have some reservations in accepting that they do not fully understand the consequences of the social network world they are so accustomed to, but they should also be willing to accept the power of social media to affect change because they have grown up seeing its impact in their own lives.

7. **Adapt to audiences from different cultures and language communities.** The class consists of entirely English speakers. To adjust to those from different backgrounds, I will cite examples as large in scope as possible to encompass the impact of social media upon events that different culture-background students have likely heard of.

8. **Use presentational aids to enhance audience understanding and memory.** I will use PowerPoint slides of familiar images that are easily associated with the content I discuss.

Formal Speech Outline

General purpose: To inform

Speech goal: In this speech, I am going to explain the impact of social media on our world by describing its rapid historical growth as a social force and its impact on both political processes and news reporting.

INTRODUCTION

I. A man dies—cheery way to start out, right?—and ends up sitting there in front of heaven's Pearly Gates. St Peter asks, "What have you done with your life?" The man responds indignantly with, "You mean you haven't been reading my tweets!?"

Attention getter

II. All joking aside, I imagine most of us in this room use social media, whether it be Facebook, Twitter, Linked In, or even—dare I say it—Myspace—remember that one—for nostalgia. *(Show Slide 1: Scattered logos of significant or previously significant social media websites. Facebook, Twitter, Myspace, Friendster, etc.)* To illustrate my point, go ahead and take out your smart phone, notebook, or laptop and log on to any one of them. This is a race: when you're "on," raise your hand *(time them)*. Every hand went up in less than five seconds! But how many of us really understand the significant impact this modern online social network phenomenon is having our society? If we're being honest, I sincerely doubt that many of us have thought about it. We know not to post raunchy stuff on Facebook or Twitter before going to an important job interview and not to "friend" professional supervisors if we don't want them to see what we talk about online, but how much more?

Listener relevance

III. After realizing I knew next to nothing about these complex social networks I use everyday, I decided to explore what the experts have to say about the nature of online social networks and how they are shaping communication practices and society today.

Speaker credibility

IV. So today, I'd like to share what I've discovered about the history and rapid growth of our modern online social networks and how they are impacting both politics and news reporting.

Thesis statement with main point preview

BODY

I. To really understand how online social networks, that is, websites that allow users to easily create content and interact with one another about that content, affect our lives and the world we live in today, we first need to understand a bit about their convoluted, but significant history (Curtis, 2013).

First main point and Listener relevance

A. Historically speaking, online social media is rather young dating back only about twenty years to 1994 when Beverly Hills Internet created a web-hosting service called Geocities.com.

1. For the first time, users could create customizable web pages organized by interests with feedback sections and other features unavailable to noncorporate website creators at the time (Curtis, 2013).

2. According to a 2009 *LA Times* article, it wasn't in the sleek and attractive style we expect today (Milian, 2009). *(Show Slide 2: example Geocities site with its unorganized content)*

3. Although it was rather unattractive, it was still the first of its kind in being a way for users to create their own content and respond to that of others (Curtis, 2013).

B. Three short years later, blogging took off. People began creating personas for themselves and engaging in regular, frequent dialog through blog posts, responses to posts, and of course, responses to the responses of blog posts (Curtis, 2013).

1. AOL Instant Messenger changed what users wanted from the Internet as a communication tool *(Show Slide 3: AIM, MSN Messenger icons)*.

2. We all remember our grade school days of being mystified at the thought of instantly sending and receiving messages from our friends, right? Well, this was the start of that. And what's more, this was the start of a demand for instant gratification when it came to online social interaction with friends according to Oliver Gray in a *20 Something Magazine* article posted in March 2013 (Gray, 2013).

C. In 2002 and 2003, two sites that would become outrageously popular began. Although neither is a most-frequented site today, Friendster and Myspace, took the Internet by storm.

1. Users of Friendster, which was invented in 2002, catapulted to 3 million in just three short months, which was a fantastic feat.

2. By 2004, however, just one year after it was created in 2003, Myspace overtook Friendster in terms of the number of accounts created.

3. That same year, 2004, marks the point when a similar site was created by a group of students at Harvard. Dubbed the college version of Friendster, it didn't receive much attention at the time, but you may have heard of it: *(Show Slide 4: cartoon of Facebook icon on top of Myspace and Friendster icons)* Facebook (Curtis, 2013).

4. It's pretty incredible to think that Facebook is not even a decade old and, according to an article in the *Wall Street Journal,* boasts of having more than a billion members worldwide (Fowler, 2012).

D. Another dramatic shift occurred in 2005 when YouTube was founded.

1. Aspiring musicians found an outlet to post musical recordings

2. Parents began posting home videos of their kids.

3. Corporations began posting recordings to promote their products.

4. People began posting hilarious creative videos that previously could only be seen on programs such as *America's Funniest Home Videos* (Curtis, 2013).

E. Today, online social networks such as Facebook, YouTube, and Twitter are taken-for-granted communication outlets for most Americans, especially digital natives like those of us here in the room today.

If you are like I was before I did my research, you might be thinking, "so what's the big deal? Online social networks are here to stay." But, let me tell you now how they have changed and will continue to change our cultural norms; norms ranging from how we make friends, find romantic partners, and pay our taxes to how we choose our president.

II. Online social networks have changed the way a generation examines politics. *(Show Slide 6: Arrangement of President Obama, Mitt Romney, Rick Santorum, other noteworthy politicians)*

A. Social media is used for political fundraising.

1. In 2008, then-candidate Obama used social media to raise over $400 million, nearly twice as much as his opponent, John McCain, who did not use social media for such purposes.

2. In 2012, according to MGD Advertising, Obama used social media to garner the numbers by appealing to a source of money other politicians never had, those able to make small donations. By expanding past traditional targets of fundraising, he was able to access a substantial volume of smaller donations, pushing him past prior fundraising levels (O'Neill, 2012).

B. Social media is used for positive and negative campaigning.

1. In 2008 and 2012, the Obama campaign used online social media networks like Facebook and Twitter to reach a demographic that

had largely lost interest in politics and thus reinvigorating civic engagement in the United States.

    2. In the 2012 election cycle, however, social media was also being used for negative campaigning. For example, ABC News reported that Republican primary candidate Rick Santorum was ousted from the race, in part, because of his name's association with a very unsavory definition. What is crucial to point out, however, is that a savvy Internet user used his blogging influence to create an artificial definition, aided by other bloggers linking to the site with the definition, thus making it the first hit on all major search engines.

  C. Social media is used for governing.

    1. According to the American Political Journalism organization, Politico, reporters who usually interview and report on the president's doings are extremely unsatisfied with their access to President Obama.

    2. However, the President claims to have an extremely transparent administration because his staff uses social media to disseminate information in a politically savvy way.

    3. Whether it's FDR-esque videos posted to YouTube, or Facebook links to the latest EPA policy, a lot of information has been spread out by social networking channels, a trend that Politico argues will set a trend for the presidency in the future (Vandehei & Allen, 2013).

So we really can't deny the fact that online social networks have impacted and will continue to impact political process today and in years to come. Let's take a few minutes now to examine some of the ways social networks are influencing news reporting today.

Transition

III. Thanks to online social networking, news reporting is forever changed in terms of access and immediacy.

  A. Because technology now makes it possible for anyone to post news to social networking sites anywhere and anytime, viewers can see events occurring around the world as they happen. Consequently, the traditional news media can no longer set the agenda for what viewers do and do not have access to. *(Show Slide 7: Images of Iranian Protest tweets and images of the protests shared via Twitter)*

    1. Take the Iranian protests as a prominent example. Time Magazine reported in 2009 that Twitter was the primary way protestors reported on repressive activity by Iran's government.

    2. Take the 2013 Sandy Hook massacre as another example. Users knew about the massacre well before news broadcasters shared formal stories about it.

    3. And consider how news broadcasters used footage posted on Facebook and Twitter in their stories about the Boston Marathon Bombing in 2013.

  B. Social media is also more immediate than traditional news, even with the current format of a 24-hour news cycle, meaning that major news channels are always broadcasting and can respond to events as they unfold. *(Show Slide 8: Picture of plane in the Hudson River)*

    1. For example, Twitter actually broke the news story that a plane had crashed in the Hudson River. A twitterer on the scene commented about it and that comment got retweeted many times before any news organization had wind of the story (Curtis, 2013).

2. Because of the immediacy and reach that social networks offer users, traditional news is feeling the pressure to keep up as an information supplier. The Pew Research Center notes that news organizations like CNN, ABC News, and Fox News are losing audience share, and are trying to adapt to control the pressure from social media. While we've not seen how this will play out in the long term, this emphasizes our main point: that social media is forcing news reporting to change.

CONCLUSION

Thesis statement

I. Whether for better or for worse, social media is a driving force of change in our culture.

Main point summary

II. In a matter of two decades, online social networks have dramatically impacted our political and news reporting processes.

Clincher

III. I hope you now realize like I do that online social networks like Facebook and Twitter and YouTube are not just fun ways to interact with our friends. They are powerful communication phenomenon impacting our cultural norms, our communication practices, and our society. I hope you think about that the next time you read or post a comment or tweet

REFERENCES

Curtis, A. (2013). A brief history of social media. Retrieved April 5, 2013 at http://www.uncp.edu/home/acurtis/NewMedia/SocialMedia/SocialMediaHistory.html

Dwyer, D. (2011, May 10). Rick Santorum's "Google problem" resurfaces with Jon Stewart plug. ABC News. Retrieved April 10, 2013 at http://abcnews.go.com/blogs/politics/2011/05/rick-santorums-google-problem-resurfaces-with-jon-stewart-plug/

Fletcher, D. (2009, November 9). Internet atrocity! Geocities' demise erases web history. *Time.* Retrieved April 8, 2013 at http://www.time.com/time/business/article/0,8599,1936645,00.html

Fowler, G. A. (2012, October 4). Facebook: One billion and counting. *The Wall Street Journal,* Retrieved April 20, 2013 at http://online.wsj.com/article/SB10000872396390443635404578036164027386112.html

Gray, O. (2013, March 8). A valediction: AOL Messenger. *20 Something Magazine.* Retrieved April 5, 2013 at http://20somethingmagazine.com/2013/03/08/a-valediction-aol-instant-messenger/

Grossman, L. (2009, June 17). Iran protests: twitter, the medium of the movement. *Time.* Retrieved April 7 at http://www.time.com/time/world/article/0,8599,1905125,00.html

O'Neill, M. (2012, March 7). How has social media impacted political fundraising? [infographic]. Retrieved April 5, 2013 at http://socialtimes.com/political-fundraising-infographic_b91001

Sasseen, J., Olmstead, K., & Mitchell A. (2013). Digital: as mobile grows rapidly, the pressures on news intensify. Pew Research Center. Retrieved April 7, 2013 at http://stateofthemedia.org/2013/digital-as-mobile-grows-rapidly-the-pressures-on-news-intensify/

Vandehei, J. & Allen, M. (2013, February 18). Obama, the puppet master. Politico. Retrieved April 9, 2013 at http://www.politico.com/story/2013/02/obama-the-puppet-master-87764.html

speech and analysis

Speech

A man dies—cheery way to start out, right?—and ends up sitting there in front of heaven's Pearly Gates. St Peter asks, "What have you done with your life?" The man responds indignantly with, "You mean you haven't been reading my tweets!?"

All joking aside, I imagine most of us in this room use social media, whether it be Facebook, Twitter, Linked In, or even—dare I say it—Myspace—remember that one—for nostalgia. *(Show Slide 1: Scattered logos of significant or previously significant social media websites. Facebook, Twitter, Myspace, Friendster, etc.)* To illustrate my point, go ahead and take out your smart phone, notebook, or laptop and log on to any one of them. This is a race: when you're "on," raise your hand *(time them)*. Every hand went up in less than five seconds! But how many of us really understand the significant impact this modern online social network phenomenon is having our society? If we're being honest, I sincerely doubt that many of us have thought about it. We know not to post raunchy stuff on Facebook or Twitter before going to an important job interview and not to "friend" professional supervisors if we don't want them to see what we talk about online, but how much more?

After realizing I knew next to nothing about these complex social networks I use everyday, I decided to explore what the experts have to say about the nature of online social networks and how they are shaping communication practices and society today.

So today, I'd like to share what I've discovered about the history and rapid growth of our modern online social networks and how they are impacting both politics and news reporting.

To really understand how online social networks, that is, websites that allow users to easily create content and interact with one another about that content, affect our lives and the world we live in today, we first need to understand a bit about their convoluted, but significant history.

Historically speaking, online social media is rather young dating back only about twenty years to 1994 when a Beverly Hills Internet created a web-hosting service called Geocities.com. According to Dr. Anthony Curtis, professor of Mass Communication at the University of North Carolina at Pembroke, this marks the first time users could create customizable web pages organized by interests with feedback sections and other features unavailable to noncorporate website creators at the time. According to a 2009 *LA Times* article, it wasn't in the sleek and attractive style we expect today. *(Show Slide 2: Example Geocities site with its unorganized content)* Although it was rather unattractive, it was still the first of its kind in being a way for users to create their own content and respond to that of others.

Three short years later, blogging took off. People began creating personas for themselves and engaging in regular, frequent dialog through blog posts, responses to posts, and of course, responses to the responses of blog posts. For example, AOL Instant Messenger changed what users wanted from the Internet as a communication tool *(Show Slide 3: AIM, MSN Messenger icons)*. We all remember our grade school days of being mystified at the thought of instantly sending and receiving messages from our friends, right? Well, this was the start of that. And what's more, this was the start of a demand for instant gratification when it came to online social interaction with friends according to Oliver Gray in a *20 Something Magazine* article posted in March 2013.

Analysis

Notice how Logan uses a humorous anecdote to get the attention of his listeners.

Here Logan does a great job of establishing relevance with his audience of young adults and appealing to the doing dimension of the learning cycle by asking them to check their social network sites.

Logan admits not knowing much about the nature of online social networks, which make him seem trustworthy before also establishing credibility by stating that he did some homework to prepare this speech.

Here Logan shares his goal in the form of a thesis statement with main point preview. Listeners have a macrostructural framework by which to listen to the body of the speech.

Notice how Logan states his first main point in a way that also provides listener relevance, piquing curiosity to keep the audience paying attention.

Here Logan offers listener relevance that addresses the feeling dimension of the learning cycle, as well. Listeners are encouraged to reflect on their own personal memories of using AOL Instant Messenger.

In 2002 and 2003, two sites that would become outrageously popular began. Although neither is a most-frequented site today, Friendster and Myspace, took the Internet by storm. Users of Friendster, which was invented in 2002, catapulted to 3 million in just three short months, which was a fantastic feat. By 2004, however, just one year after it was created in 2003, Myspace overtook Friendster in terms of the number of accounts created. That same year, 2004, marks the point when a similar site was created by a group of students at Harvard. Dubbed the college version of Friendster, it didn't receive much attention at the time, but you may have heard of it: *(Show Slide 4: cartoon of Facebook icon on top of Myspace and Friendster icons)* Facebook. It's pretty incredible to think that Facebook is not even a decade old, and according to an article in the *Wall Street Journal,* boasts of having more than a billion members worldwide.

Another dramatic shift occurred in 2005 when YouTube was founded. Thanks to YouTube, aspiring musicians had an outlet to post musical recordings without getting a recording studio to do so. Parents also began posting home videos of their kids. Corporations began posting recordings to promote their products and people began posting hilarious creative videos that previously could only be seen on programs such as *America's Funniest Home Videos.* Today, online social networks such as Facebook, YouTube, and Twitter are taken-for-granted communication outlets for most Americans, especially digital natives like those of us here in the room today.

If you are like I was before I did my research, you might be thinking, "so what's the big deal? Online social networks are here to stay." But, let me tell you now how they have changed and will continue to change our cultural norms; norms ranging from how we make friends, find romantic partners, and pay our taxes to how we choose our president.

Online social networks have changed the way a generation examines politics. *(Show Slide 6: Arrangement of President Obama, Mitt Romney, Rick Santorum, other noteworthy politicians)*

Consider for example how social media is used today for political fundraising. In 2008, then-candidate Obama used social media to raise over $400 million, nearly twice as much as his opponent, John McCain, who did not use social media for such purposes. And, according to MGD Advertising, Obama used social media in his 2012 campaign to garner the numbers by appealing to a source of money other politicians never had, those able to make small donations. By expanding past traditional targets of fundraising, he was able to access a substantial volume of smaller donations, pushing him past prior fundraising levels.

Social media is also used for both positive and negative campaigning. In 2008 and 2012, the Obama campaign used online social media networks like Facebook and Twitter to reach a demographic that had largely lost interest in politics and thus reinvigorating civic engagement in the United States. In the 2012 election cycle, however, social media was also being used for negative campaigning. For example, ABC News reported that Republican primary candidate Rick Santorum was ousted from the race, in part, because of his name's association with a very unsavory definition. What is crucial to point out, however, is that a savvy internet user used his blogging influence to create an artificial definition, aided by other bloggers linking to the site with the definition, thus making it the first hit on all major search engines.

And, social media is also used today for governing. According to the American Political Journalism organization, *Politico,* reporters who usually interview and report on the president's doings are extremely unsatisfied with their access to President Obama. However, the president claims to have an extremely transparent administration because his staff uses social media to disseminate information in a politically savvy way. Whether it's FDR-esque videos posted to YouTube, or Facebook links to the latest EPA policy, a lot of information has been spread out by social networking

Although Logan provides a good deal of interesting supporting material here, he only cites a source for one of the facts he presents. He could have improved the speech by citing the sources for more of the information shared in this paragraph.

Logan could have made this paragraph more compelling by offering some specific examples for each of the ways in which YouTube has broken through traditional gatekeeper barriers for the general public.

Again, Logan does a great job with this transition statement that reminds his audience about the point he is done talking about and introducing the next one in a way that also highlights listener relevance for it.

This information is quite compelling, however, Logan should also have cited a source for his $400 million statistic to enhance credibility and avoid plagiarism.

Logan could have strengthened this portion of his speech with some direct quotations and stories about the facts he states.

Again, although these facts are interesting, Logan could have made them more compelling by inserting a direct quotation or by showing a sample of a Tweet or YouTube posting from the Obama presidency.

channels, a trend that Politico argues will set a trend for the presidency in the future.

So we really can't deny the fact that online social networks have impacted and will continue to impact political process today and in years to come. Let's take a few minutes now to examine some of the ways social networks are influencing news reporting today.

Thanks to online social networking, news reporting is forever changed in terms of access and immediacy. Because technology now makes it possible for anyone to post news to social networking sites anywhere and anytime, viewers can see events occurring around the world as they happen. Consequently, the traditional news media can no longer set the agenda for what viewers do and do not have access to. *(Show Slide 7: Images of Iranian Protest tweets and images of the protests shared via Twitter)* Take the Iranian protests as a prominent example. *Time Magazine* reported in 2009 that Twitter was the primary way protestors reported on repressive activity by Iran's government. Take the 2013 Sandy Hook massacre as another example. Users knew about the massacre well before news broadcasters shared formal stories about it. And consider how news broadcasters used footage posted on Facebook and Twitter in their stories about the Boston Marathon Bombing in 2013.

Notice here how Logan uses personal pronouns and "we" language to create nonverbal immediacy and a sense of talking with rather than speaking to his audience.

Although Logan's presentational aids of the Iran protest tweets and images are very effective, it would have been effective to also include visual examples from the Sandy Hook example and the Boston Marathon example,

Social media is also more immediate than traditional news, even with the current format of a 24-hour news cycle, meaning that major news channels are always broadcasting and can respond to events as they unfold. *(Show Slide 8: Picture of plane in the Hudson River)* For example, Twitter actually broke the news story that a plane had crashed in the Hudson River. A twitterer on the scene commented about it and that comment got retweeted many times before any news organization had wind of the story. Because of the immediacy and reach that social networks offer users, traditional news is feeling the pressure to keep up as an information supplier. The Pew Research Center notes that news organizations like CNN, ABC News, and Fox News are losing audience share, and are trying to adapt to control the pressure from social media. While we've not seen how this will play out in the long term, this emphasizes our main point: that social media is forcing news reporting to change.

Here it would have been nice to include the actual tweet from the Hudson River example Logan describes.

Whether for better or for worse, social media is a driving force of change in our culture. In a matter of two decades, online social networks have dramatically impacted our political and news reporting processes. I hope you now realize like I do that online social networks like Facebook and Twitter and YouTube are not just fun ways to interact with our friends. They are powerful communication phenomenon impacting our cultural norms, our communication practices, and our society. I hope you think about that the next time you read or post a comment or tweet.

Notice how nicely Logan concludes the speech with a thesis restatement and main point summary, as well a clincher encouraging his audience to think twice from this point on every time they interact with an online social network. If he is successful, his speech will have lasting impact on his audience.

Reflection and Assessment

An informative speech is one whose goal is to explain or describe facts, truths, and principles in a way that stimulates interest, facilitates understanding, and increases the likelihood that audiences will remember. In short, informative speeches are designed to educate an audience. To assess how well you've learned what we've discussed in this chapter, answer the following questions. If you have trouble answering any of them, go back and review that material. Once you can answer each question accurately, you are ready to move ahead to read the next chapter.

1. What are the characteristics of informative speeches?
2. What are the major methods of informing?
3. How do you prepare an informative process speech?
4. How do you prepare an informative expository speech?

 ## *Challenge* Resource and Assessment Center

Now that you have read Chapter 12, go to your MindTap for *The Challenge of Effective Speaking in a Digital Age* for quick access to the electronic resources that accompany this text. These resources include the following:

- **Study tools** that will help you assess your learning and prepare for exams (*digital glossary, key term flash cards, review quizzes*).

- **Activities and assignments** that will help you hone your knowledge and build your public speaking skills throughout the course (Practice, Do). Many of these activities allow you to compare your answers with those provided by the authors and, if requested, submit your answers to your instructor.

- **Media resources**—all of which are available on your MindTap for *Challenge*—will help you explore communication concepts online (Practice), develop your speech outlines (Do), watch and critique videos of sample speeches (Do), and upload your speech videos for instructor feedback and critique other students' speeches (Do).

- **Video resources**
  1. Use your Interactive Video Activities (Do) to watch, analyze, and see the transcript and outlines for the informative speeches "Flag Etiquette," "Making Ethanol," and "Understanding Hurricanes."
  2. Go to the Practice and Present section of MindTap to upload a video of your own informative speech for feedback from your instructor and classmates. Or search for other students' informative speeches—do their speeches give you ideas for how you could make your speech more effective?

Applying What You've Learned

1. **Impromptu Speech Activity:** You will draw three slips of paper from a container offered by your instructor. Each slip will identify a historical event or historical figure on it. Select one event you'd like to experience or figure you'd like to meet if you could travel back in time. Do a two- to three-minute impromptu speech about why you'd like to experience that historical event or meet that historical figure if you could travel back in time and why.

2. **Assessment Activity A:** Select a current event that's "in the news" today. Learn more about it from three different sources (e.g., a local newspaper, a national news broadcast, and an online blog or social networking site). Compare what you learn from each source and evaluate the ways in which the source cited

research, acknowledged fact checking, and established the credentials for sources. Which source seems to be most credible as a result and why? Prepare a two- to three-page reflection paper explaining your conclusion. Be sure to attach copies or transcripts of the three sources.

3. **Assessment Activity B:** Identify a celebrity (e.g., television or movie actor, sports star, singer, etc.). Learn more about the person you've identified by visiting his or her personal website or blog, a social networking site devoted to this person, and a celebrity gossip magazine. How does the information shared about this person on each source differ, and how does that shape your understanding of who he or she is? Which one seems most ethical based on the ethical communication principles we discuss in this book and why? Prepare a two- to three-page paper comparing the similarities and differences and your conclusions.

13 "persuasive messages"

**WHAT'S THE POINT?
WHEN YOU'VE FINISHED THIS
CHAPTER, YOU'LL BE ABLE TO:**

13-1 Describe the nature of persuasion

13-2 Explain how people process persuasive messages

13-3 Identify and apply logos in persuasive messages

13-4 Identify and apply ethos in persuasive messages

13-5 Identify and apply pathos in persuasive messages

MindTap™

Review the chapter **Learning Objectives** and **Start** with quick warm up activity.

B Christopher/Alamy

ⓔ **Ethical communicators use logos, ethos, and pathos in ways that demonstrate honesty, fairness, and responsibility.**

Rick loves his golden retriever, Trini. He lives in an apartment right downtown and enjoys taking Trini for walks twice a day, but he wishes there was a place nearby where he could let Trini off her leash to run. He decides to try to persuade the city council to fence off an area of a large inner-city park to turn it into a dog park where owners can let their dogs run free. He needs to circulate a petition about the idea, get at least 500 others to sign it, and collect $1,000 in donations to help pay for the fence. Within a few weeks of knocking on doors, Rick easily gathers more than enough signatures. However, he manages to raise less than half of the $1,000 he needs. He wonders what he can do to persuade more people to actually donate money for the cause.

This scenario is not unusual. As was the case with Rick and the downtown dog park, whenever we attempt to convince others to agree with our position or behave a certain way, we actually construct and present persuasive messages. How successful we are, however, depends on how effectively we employ persuasive strategies in doing so. **Persuasion** is the process of influencing people's attitudes, beliefs, values, or behaviors. **Persuasive speaking** is the process of doing so in a public speech.

Persuasive messages are pervasive. Whether we are attempting to convince others or others are attempting to influence us, we are constantly involved in influencing or being influenced. Friends persuade us to go to a particular movie or to eat at a certain restaurant, salespeople persuade us to buy a certain sweater or pair of shoes, and advertisements bombard us whenever we turn on the radio or television, or surf the Internet. It is critical to understand persuasion so you can critically examine and evaluate the persuasive messages you receive and you can create effective and ethical persuasive messages of your own.

We begin our two-chapter discussion of persuasive speaking by first describing the nature of persuasive messages and the rhetorical strategies used in them. Next, using the Elaboration Likelihood Model (ELM), we explain how people process persuasive messages. Then, we focus specifically on how to use the rhetorical strategies of logos, ethos, and pathos to develop your persuasive messages and offer guidelines for you to consider when evaluating and constructing them.

13-1 THE NATURE OF PERSUASION

Persuasive messages are fundamentally different from informative ones. Whereas the goal of an informative message is to teach, the goal of a persuasive message is to lead. So persuasive speakers are only successful when their audience members are convinced to agree, change their behavior, or take action. In the opening scenario, Rick was successful in convincing others to agree with him, but unsuccessful in getting them to take action.

As a speaker, you can develop informative and persuasive speeches on the same topic depending on your ultimate goal. For example, Susan is a petrochemical engineering student taking a speech course. Last semester, she completed a term project on the Deep Water Horizon oil spill. So she decided to use her expertise on this topic for her three required speeches. For her informative speech, her goal was to explain the errors that led to the explosion and subsequent oil spill. The goal of her first persuasive speech was to convince her audience to agree with her position. So she focused on persuading them to agree that the sequence of events leading to the Deep Water Horizon spill could not happen again and that drilling for oil offshore in deep water is safe. In her second persuasive speech, her goal was to motivate her classmates to take action. So she focused on persuading them to reduce their oil dependence by recycling the plastic they use and limiting or avoiding drinks packaged in plastic bottles.

"Within a few weeks of knocking on doors, Rick easily gathers more than enough signatures. However, he manages to raise less than half of the $1,000 he needs. He wonders what he can do to persuade more people to actually donate money for the cause."

persuasion: the process of influencing people's attitudes, beliefs, values, or behaviors

persuasive speaking: the process of influencing people's attitudes, beliefs, values, or behaviors in a public speech

In her April 25, 2010, article in the *Washington Post*, Cecilia Kang reported that "employees of companies with interests in Washington are chattering online to shape opinions in hard-to-detect ways."[1] For example, P. J. Rodriguez tweets about a variety of topics, including his opinion about Federal Communications Commission (FCC) technology policy issues. Rodriguez's Twitter profile simply says he is a "pop culture maven and cable blogger." What his profile does not say, however, is that he works for the National Cable and Telecommunications Association (NCTA) and is a public relations specialist for Comcast, Cox, and Time Warner Cable. In other words, he's a lobbyist for the telecommunications industry.

Kang goes on to report that AT&T spent 15 percent more on its lobbying budget in the first quarter of 2010 than it did in all of 2009, and Google's lobbying budget rose by 57 percent. Lobbyists once visited congressional representatives personally to make their arguments. Now they are trying to influence lawmakers in record numbers as "anyone on the Web," with no rules or regulations compelling them to disclose who they really are or whose interests they represent.

1. What, if any, ethical communication principles are lobbyists like Rodriguez violating?
2. What, if any, harm is being done by individuals who attempt to persuade others online without disclosing whose interests they represent?
3. What, if anything, should the FCC do with regard to privacy and disclosure of lobbyist interests on the Internet?
4. Where would you draw the line regarding open or restricted access to Internet users and why?

To further explain the nature of persuasion, we draw on the work of the ancient Greeks and Romans who described *persuasion* as logical and well-supported arguments developed through rhetorical appeals to logos, ethos, and pathos. Argument, in this context, is not synonymous with "quarrel" as we sometimes define it today. Rather, **argument** means articulating a position with the support of logos, ethos, and pathos.[2] **Logos** is a persuasive strategy of constructing logical arguments that support your point of view. **Ethos** is a persuasive strategy of highlighting your competence, credibility, and good character as means by which to convince others to accept your point of view. **Pathos** is a persuasive strategy of appealing to emotions in order to convince others to support your position.[3]

While all speakers are expected to behave ethically, persuasive speakers have an extra burden to demonstrate that what they are advocating is in the best interest of the audience. So persuasive speakers must evaluate their message strategies and eliminate those that violate the ethical principles of truthfulness, integrity, fairness, respect, and responsibility.

Now that we have a basic understanding of the nature of persuasion, let's look more closely at how people think about the persuasive messages they receive.

13-2 PROCESSING PERSUASIVE MESSAGES

Do you remember times when you listened thoughtfully about something someone was trying to convince you to agree with before making a deliberate decision? Do you remember other times when you only half listened and made up your mind quickly based on your "gut" feeling? What determines how closely we listen to and how carefully we evaluate the hundreds of persuasive messages we hear each day? Richard Petty and John Cacioppo developed the Elaboration Likelihood Model (ELM) to explain how likely people are to spend more or less time evaluating information (such as the arguments that they hear in a speech) before making their decisions.

The model suggests that people process information in one of two ways. Sometimes we use the "central route" and listen carefully, reflect thoughtfully, and may even mentally elaborate on the message before making a decision. In doing so, we based our decision primarily on appeals to logic and reasoning (logos). The second way, called the

argument: articulating a position with the support of logos, ethos, and pathos

logos: arguments that support your point of view

ethos: arguments based on competence, credibility, and good character

pathos: arguments that appeal to the emotions

"peripheral route," is a shortcut that relies on simple cues such as a quick evaluation of the speaker's competence, credibility, and character (ethos) or a gut check about what we feel (pathos) about the message.

We choose a route based on how important we perceive the issue to be for us. When we believe the issue is important, we will expend the energy necessary to process it using the central route. When we don't, we take the peripheral route. For example, if you have a serious chronic illness that is expensive to treat, you are more likely to pay attention to and evaluate carefully any proposals to change health care benefits. If you are healthy, you are more likely to quickly agree with suggestions from someone you perceive to be credible or with a proposal that seems compassionate. The ELM also suggests that when we form attitudes as a result of central processing, we are less likely to change our minds than when we base our decisions on peripheral cues. If you'd like to learn more about ELM, and persuasion in general, go to **Web Link 13.1, Elaboration Likelihood Model,** on your MindTap for *Challenge.*

When you prepare a persuasive speech, you will want to use strategies that address both the central and peripheral routes. To do so, be sure to integrate logos strategies that will be most influential for audience members who use the central processing route. And integrate ethos and pathos strategies to appeal to those in your audience who make their decision based on the peripheral route. Ultimately, the most compelling persuasive messages offer appeals to all three: logos, ethos, and pathos.

13-3 THE RHETORICAL STRATEGY OF LOGOS

Logos strategies are arguments built on logic and reasoning (Photo 13.1). Stephen Toulmin developed a model to explain the form of everyday arguments that has stood the test of time. His model has three major elements: The claim, the support, and the warrant.[4]

The **claim (C)** is the conclusion the persuader wants others to agree with. For example, you might *claim*: "Jim's car needs a tune-up." The **support (S)** is the evidence offered as grounds for accepting/agreeing with the claim. You can support a claim with various types of evidence such as facts, opinions, experiences, and observations. In the car example, we might note as evidence that "the car is missing at slow speeds" and "stalling at stoplights." The **warrant (W)** is the reasoning process that connects the support to the claim. Sometimes the warrant is verbalized and sometimes it is implied. In the car example, you might offer a warrant such as "missing at slow speeds and stalling at stoplights are *common indications* that a car needs a tune-up." Or you might assume that others realize these are signs that a car needs a tune-up. Not knowing whether their audience members will make these connections, the most effective public speakers verbalize their reasoning warrants.

You can connect your supporting evidence to the claim using one of two different types of reasoning warrants. You can do so inductively or deductively. **Inductive reasoning** is arriving at a general conclusion based on several pieces of specific evidence. When we reason inductively, how much our audience agrees with our conclusion depends on the number, quality, and typicality of each piece of evidence we offer. For Jim's car, an inductive reasoning argument might look like this:

claim (C): the proposition or conclusion to be proven

support (S): the evidence the speaker offers as the grounds for accepting the conclusion

warrant (W): the reasoning process that connects the support to the claim

inductive reasoning: arriving at a conclusion based on a series of pieces of evidence

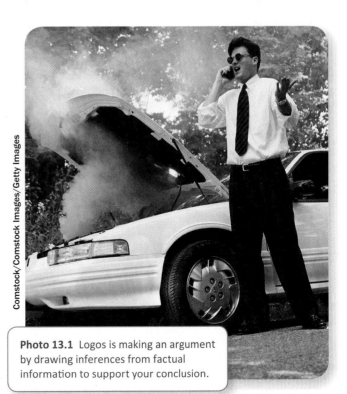

Comstock/Comstock Images/Getty Images

Photo 13.1 Logos is making an argument by drawing inferences from factual information to support your conclusion.

deductive reasoning:
arriving at a conclusion
based on a major premise
and minor premise

major premise: a general
principle that most
people agree upon

minor premise: a specific
point that fits within the
major premise

syllogism: the three-
part form of deductive
reasoning

argue from sign: to
support a claim by citing
events, characteristics, or
situations that signal the
claim information that
signals the claim

S: Jim's car is missing at slow speeds.

S: Jim's car is stalling at stoplights.

W: These are common indicators that a car needs a tune-up.

C: Jim's car needs a tune-up.

Deductive reasoning is arguing that if something is true for everything that belongs to a certain class (**major premise**) and a specific instance is part of that class (**minor premise**), then we must conclude that what is true for all members of the class must be true in the specific instance (logical conclusion/claim). This three-part form of deductive reasoning is called a **syllogism**. For Jim's car, a syllogism might look like this:

Major premise: Cars need a tune-up when the engine misses consistently at slow speeds.

Minor premise: Jim's car is missing at slow speeds.

Logical Conclusion/Claim: Jim's car needs a tune-up.

With this introduction in mind, let's look at some different types of logical arguments.

13-3a Types of Logical Arguments

Although an argument *always* includes a claim and support, different types of warrants can be used to illustrate the relationship between the claim and the support on which it is based. Four common types of logical arguments are sign, example, analogy, and causation.

Arguing from Sign

If certain events, characteristics, or situations usually or always accompany something, those events, characteristics, or situations are signs. You **argue from sign** when you support a claim by providing evidence that the events that signal the claim have occurred (Photo 13.2). The general warrant for reasoning from sign can be stated as follows: When phenomena that usually or always accompany a specific situation occur, then we can expect that specific situation is occurring (or will occur).

SPEECH SNIPPET

**Making the Right
Argument**

One reason Rick didn't
succeed in collecting
$1,000 in donations
may have been due to
the fact that his primary
argument had been
focused on convincing
people to agree that a
dog park was needed
and to sign the petition.
He decided to revise
his argument to focus
specifically on persuading
people to contribute to
the fund and try again.

© iStockphoto.com/EdStock

Photo 13.2 Political campaigners design multiple persuasive messages attempting to convince voters not only that their candidate is the best but also to actually get out and vote for them.

For example: "Hives and a slight fever are indicators (signs) of an allergic reaction. Since you have hives and a fever (sign), you must be having an allergic reaction (claim)." Signs should not be confused with causes; signs accompany a phenomenon but do not bring about, lead to, or create the claim. In fact, signs may actually be the effects of the phenomenon. A rash and fever don't cause an allergic reaction; they are indications, or effects, of a reaction.

Let's look at another example. Suppose you are supporting Juanita Martinez for president of the local neighborhood council. You believe that Juanita is electable (claim). If you notice that she has more campaign workers than all the other candidates combined (sign) and more community members are wearing "Juanita for President" than any others (sign), you might reason that "Juanita's campaign has the key signs of a presidential victory" (warrant).

When arguing from sign, you can make sure that your argument is valid by answering the following questions.

1. **Do the signs cited usually or always indicate the conclusion drawn?** If the signs cited do not usually indicate the conclusion, then the argument might not be valid because the reasoning is flawed.

2. **Are a sufficient number of signs present?** Several signs often indicate events or situations. If enough signs are not present, then the conclusion may not follow. If there are insufficient signs, then the argument may not be valid because the reasoning is flawed.

3. **Are contradictory signs in evidence?** If many signs exist that indicate different conclusions, then the argument may not be valid because the reasoning is flawed.

Arguing from Example

You **argue from example** when the evidence you use as support are examples of the claim you are making. For almost any topic, it is easy to find examples. So you are likely to use arguing from example quite frequently. The warrant for an argument from example—its underlying logic—is, "What is true in the examples provided is (or will be) true in general or in other instances."

argue from example: to support your claim by providing one or more individual examples

Let's revisit the claim that "Juanita is electable" for neighborhood council president. In examining her résumé, you find several examples of previous victories. She was elected president of her high school senior class, treasurer of her church council, and president of her college Phi Beta Kappa honor society chapter. Each of these examples supports your claim. Thus, the reasoning warrant would be, "What was true in several instances (Juanita was elected in three previous races) is true or will be true in general or in other instances (she will be electable in this situation)."

When arguing from example, you can make sure your argument is valid by answering the following questions.

1. **Are enough examples cited?** Are three elections enough examples to convince others to agree with your claim? You must cite enough examples to satisfy others that the instances are not isolated or handpicked. Otherwise the argument may not be valid because the reasoning is flawed.

2. **Are the examples typical?** Are the three offices Juanita previously held similar to the one she is now running for? Typical means that the examples cited must be similar to or representative of most or all within the category (Photo 13.3). Otherwise the argument may not be valid because the reasoning is flawed.

3. **Are negative examples accounted for?** There may be one or more examples that contradict the argument. If the exceptions are minor or infrequent, then

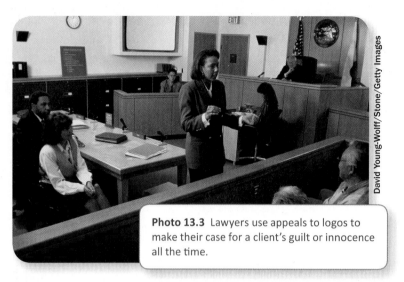

Photo 13.3 Lawyers use appeals to logos to make their case for a client's guilt or innocence all the time.

they won't invalidate the argument. For instance, perhaps Juanita ran for president of the Sociology Club in college and lost. That one failure does not necessarily invalidate the argument. If, however, Juanita had run for office twelve times and was successful on only the three occasions cited, then the argument may not be valid because the reasoning is flawed.

Arguing from Analogy

argue from analogy: to support a claim with a single comparable example that is significantly similar to the subject of the claim

You **argue from analogy** when you support a claim with a single comparable example that is so significantly similar to the subject of the claim as to be strong proof. The general statement of a warrant for an argument from analogy is, "What is true for situation A will also be true in situation B, which is similar to situation A" or "What is true for situation A will be true in all similar situations."

Suppose you wanted to argue that the Cherry Fork volunteer fire department should conduct a raffle to raise money for three portable defibrillator units (claim). You could support the claim by analogy with a single example: Jefferson City Fire Department, which is very similar to that of Cherry Fork (warrant), conducted a raffle and raised enough money to purchase four units (support).

Let us return to the claim that Juanita is electable (claim). If you discover that Juanita has essentially the same characteristics as Paula Jefferson, who was elected president two years ago (both are very bright and have a great deal of drive), then you can use the single example of Paula to form a reasoning warrant: "Juanita has the same characteristics of being bright and driven that got Paula Jefferson elected two years ago."

When arguing from analogy, you can make sure that your argument is valid by answering the following questions.

1. **Are the subjects being compared similar in every important way?** Are intelligence and drive the most important characteristics for determining electability? If the characteristics are not the most important ones, then the argument may not be valid because the reasoning is flawed.

2. **Are any of the ways in which the subjects are dissimilar important to the claim?** If Paula is a native of the community, whereas Juanita has only been in the area for a year, is this dissimilarity important? When the dissimilarities outweigh the subjects' similarities, then the argument may be invalid because the reasoning is flawed.

Arguing from Causation

argue from causation: to support a claim by citing events that have occurred that result in the claim

You **argue from causation** when you support a claim by citing events that have occurred that result in the claim. Reasoning from causation says that one or more of the events cited always (or almost always) brings about, leads to, creates, or prevents a predictable effect or set of effects.

The general warrant for arguments from causation can be stated as follows: If an event comes before another event and is associated with that event, then we can say that it is the cause of the event. "If A, which is known to bring about B, has been observed, then we can expect B to occur." For instance, you could develop a causal argument based on the relationship between mortgage interest rates and home sales: "Home sales are bound to increase during the next three months (claim) because mortgage interest rates have recently dropped markedly (causal event as support). In the past, each time interest rates were dropped, home sales increased (warrant)."

Let's return to Juanita's election campaign one more time. In researching Juanita's election campaign, you might discover that (1) she has campaigned intelligently (support), and (2) she has won the endorsement of key community leaders (support). In the past, these two events have usually been associated with victory (warrant), thus Juanita is electable (claim).

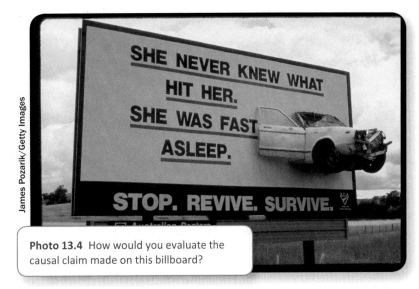

Photo 13.4 How would you evaluate the causal claim made on this billboard?

When arguing from causation, you can make sure your argument is valid by answering the following questions (Photo 13.4).

1. **Are the events alone sufficient to cause the stated effect?** Are intelligent campaigning and key endorsements alone important enough to result in winning elections? If the events are truly causes, then the effect would not occur if the event were eliminated. If the effect can occur without these two events occurring, then the argument may not be valid because the reasoning is flawed.

2. **Do other events accompanying the cited events actually cause the effect?** Are other factors (such as luck, drive, friends) more important in determining whether a person wins an election? If these other events are more important in causing the effect, then the argument may not be valid because the reasoning is flawed.

3. **Is the relationship between the causal events and the effect consistent?** Do intelligent campaigning and key endorsements always (or usually) yield electoral victories? If there are times when the effect has not followed the cause, then the argument may not be valid because the reasoning is flawed.

Combining Arguments in a Persuasive Speech

An effective persuasive speech usually uses several types of logical arguments. To convince voters that Juanita is electable, for instance, Juanita's campaign speakers might organize their speeches this way:

I. *Juanita has run successful campaigns in the past. (argument by example)*

   A. *Juanita was successful in her campaign for president of her high school class.*

   B. *Juanita was successful in her campaign for treasurer of her church council.*

   C. *Juanita was successful in her campaign for president of her college honor society.*

II. *Juanita has engaged in actions that result in campaign victory. (argued by cause)*

   A. *Juanita has campaigned intelligently.*

   B. *Juanita has secured key endorsements.*

Charlize Theron: Award Winning Actress *and* Powerful Persuasive Speaker

Many people may know Charlize Theron as an Academy award-winning actress who takes on difficult roles, such as a serial killer in *Monster*, a sexual harassment activist in *North Country*, and an evil stepmother in *Snow White and the Huntsman*. What is less well known, however, is that Theron has a genuine fear of public speaking. In fact, she nearly passed out on the first day of filming *North Country* because she had to give a public speech. She is quoted as saying "I get this really strange sensation (when public speaking) where everything goes black, and I see white spots, and I break out in hives. It's probably the most frightening thing you can make me do."[5] Nevertheless, Theron is an outspoken activist designated by the United Nations as a "Messenger of Peace" who travels across the globe giving persuasive speeches focused on eliminating violence against women, creating a better life for impoverished families in South Africa, promoting HIV prevention, and endorsing same-sex marriage.[6, 7] In spite of her fear, Theron is an effective persuasive speaker determined to get her message across to all who will listen.

---

reasoning fallacies: errors in reasoning

hasty generalization: a fallacy that presents a generalization that is either not supported with evidence or is supported with only one weak example

false cause: a fallacy that occurs when the alleged cause fails to be related to, or to produce, the effect

Avoiding Hasty Generalizations

Josh knew several classmates who abused drugs like marijuana, anabolic steroids, and prescription painkillers. To make sure he didn't make a hasty generalization that a growing percentage of young adults are doing so throughout the United States, he did an online search for statistics from credible sources such as the National Institute on Drug Abuse (NIDA), National Institute of Health (NIH), and the U.S. Department of Health and Human Services.

III. *Juanita is a strong leader. (argued by sign)*

    A. *Juanita has more volunteer campaign workers than all other candidates combined.*

    B. *Most community members are wearing Juanita's campaign buttons.*

13-3b Reasoning Fallacies

As you test the validity of your arguments from sign, example, analogy, and causation, you should check to make sure that your reasoning is sound. We refer to errors in reasoning as **reasoning fallacies**. Five common reasoning fallacies to avoid are hasty generalization, false cause, either-or, straw man, and ad hominem arguments.

1. A **hasty generalization** occurs when a claim is either not supported with evidence or is supported with only one weak example. Because the supporting material that is cited should be representative of all the supporting material that could be cited, enough supporting material must be presented to satisfy the audience that the instances are not isolated or handpicked. For example, someone who argued, "All Akitas are vicious dogs," whose sole piece of evidence was, "My neighbor had an Akita and it bit my best friend's sister," would be guilty of a hasty generalization. It is hasty to generalize about the temperament of a whole breed of dogs based on a single action of one dog.

2. A **false cause** occurs when the alleged cause fails to be related to, or to produce, the effect. The Latin term for this fallacy is *post hoc, ergo propter hoc*, meaning "after this, therefore because of this." Just because two things happen one after the other does not mean that the first necessarily caused the second. Unlike people who blame monetary setbacks and illness on black cats or broken mirrors, don't present a coincidental event as a cause unless you can prove the causal relationship. An example of a false cause fallacy is when people claim that school violence is caused by television violence, the Internet, a certain song or musical group, or lack of parental involvement. When one event follows another, there may be no connection between them at all. Or the first event might be just one of many that contribute to the second.

3. An **either/or** fallacy occurs by suggesting there are only two alternatives when, in fact, others exist. Many such cases are an oversimplification of a complex

issue. For example, when Robert claimed "we'll either have to raise taxes or close the library," he committed an either/or fallacy. He reduced a complex issue to one oversimplified solution when many other possible solutions existed.

4. A **straw man** fallacy occurs when a speaker weakens the opposing position by misrepresenting it in some way and then attacks that weaker (straw man) position. For example, in her speech advocating a seven-day waiting period to purchase handguns, Colleen favored regulation, not prohibition, of gun ownership. Bob argued against that by claiming "it is our constitutional right to bear arms." However, Colleen did not propose abolishing the right to bear arms. Hence, Bob distorted Colleen's position, making it easier for him to refute.

5. An **ad hominem** fallacy attacks or praises the person making the argument rather than addressing the argument itself. *Ad hominem* literally means "to the man." For example, if Jamal's support for his claim that his audience should buy an Apple computer is that its founder, Steve Jobs, was a genius, he is making an ad hominem argument. Jobs's intelligence isn't really a reason to buy a particular brand of computer. Unfortunately, politicians sometimes resort to ad hominem arguments when they attack their opponent's character rather than their platforms while campaigning for office. Bullying in person, over the Internet, and via text messaging is another example of ad hominem attacks that can have dire consequences. TV commercials or advertisements that feature celebrities using a particular product are often guilty of ad hominem reasoning (Photo 13.5). For example, Robert De Niro and Jerry Seinfeld have both appeared in American Express commercials, and Gwyneth Paltrow has done ads for Estée Lauder. What makes any of these celebrities experts about the products they are endorsing?

13-3c Evaluating Evidence and Sources

As you research a topic, you are likely to find far more evidence than you will be able to use in the time allotted for your speech. So you will want to evaluate your evidence and the sources you found them in and select the best ones to use in your speech. You can use answers to the following questions to guide your decision.

1. **Does the evidence come from a well-respected source?** This question involves both the people who offered the opinions or compiled the facts and the book, journal, or Internet source where they were reported. Just as some people's opinions are more reliable than others (Photo 13.6), so are some printed and Internet sources more reliable than others. Eliminate evidence that comes from a questionable, unreliable, or overly biased source.

2. **Is the evidence recent, and if not, is it still valid?** Things change, so information that was accurate for a particular time period may or may not be valid today. Consider when the evidence was gathered. Something that was believed to be true five years ago may not be true today. A trend that was forecast a year ago may have been revised since then. And a statistic that was reported last week may be based on data that were collected three years ago.

For example, the evidence "The total cost of caring for individuals with Alzheimer's is at least $100 billion, according to the Alzheimer's Association and the National Institute on Aging"[8] was cited in a 2003 National Institutes of Health publication. Although the source is credible, the date of the

Photo 13.5 Ad hominem arguments praise or attack a person rather than focus on the argument.

Splash News/Newscom

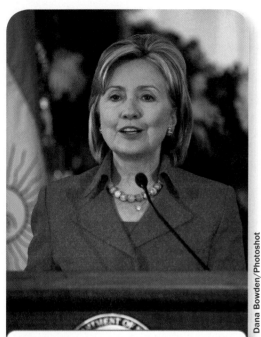

Photo 13.6 Use evidence from a well-respected expert. Who might be considered "well-respected" today?

publication suggests that the cost may no longer be accurate and, in fact, may be much higher today. Moreover, the report was actually based on information from a study conducted using 1991 data. In cases like this, you would want to find the most recent figures reported by a credible source.

3. **Does the evidence really support the claim?** Some of the evidence you find may be only indirectly related to the claim and should be eliminated in favor of evidence that provides more direct support.

4. **Will this evidence be persuasive for this audience?** Finally, you will want to choose evidence that your particular audience is likely to find persuasive. If, for example, you have two quotations from experts, you will want to use the one from the person your audience is likely to find more compelling.

13-4 THE RHETORICAL STRATEGY OF ETHOS

Not everyone will choose the central processing route to make a decision regarding a persuasive message. One important cue people use when they process information by the peripheral route is ethos. So, you will want to demonstrate good character, as well as say and do things to convey competence and credibility.

13-4a Conveying Good Character

We turn again to the ancient Greek philosopher Aristotle (384–322 B.C.E.) who first observed that a speaker's credibility is dependent on the audience's perception of the speaker's goodwill. Today, we define **goodwill** as a perception the audience forms of a speaker who they believe (1) understands them, (2) empathizes with them, and (3) is responsive to them.[9] When audience members believe in the speaker's goodwill, they are willing to believe what the speaker says. In our opening scenario, Rick was able to convey good character with other dog owners living downtown because he lived there too. So he could talk about sharing their concerns and empathizing with their frustrations.

One way to demonstrate that you understand your audience is by personalizing your information. For example, in his speech at the annual conference of the Property Casualty Insurers Association of America (PCI), Julian James, director of Worldwide Markets for Lloyds, demonstrated understanding by referencing membership facts over the past year.

> I would certainly contend that, following two consecutive record hurricane seasons, we have passed a key financial test. Debate after Katrina was largely about the detail of how we can do things better, and not about whether the industry could survive—as it was after 9/11. Not bad progress for an industry that faced almost double the value of claims from catastrophes in 2005 as it did for 9/11. . . . If we come out of this year intact, U.S. insurance industry profits in 2006 are forecast to be the best in a generation at $55 to $60 billion.[10]

Not only do you demonstrate goodwill by understanding your audience, but also by empathizing with them. **Empathy** is the ability to see the world through the eyes of someone else. Empathizing goes beyond understanding to also identify emotionally with your audience members' views. Empathizing with the views of the audience doesn't necessarily mean that you accept their views as your own. It does mean, however,

SPEECH SNIPPET

Using Well-Respected Sources

In his speech about infant and toddler automobile safety standards, Phil decided not to use the Ford, General Motors, and Chrysler companies as sources because they might be perceived as biased. Instead, he cited experts from the National Highway Traffic Safety Administration as well as academic experts from reputable transportation programs.

goodwill: a perception the audience forms of a speaker who they believe understands them, empathizes with them, and is responsive to them

empathy: the ability to see the world through the eyes of someone else that you acknowledge them as valid. Although your speech may be designed to change audience members' views, the sensitivity you show to audience members' feelings will demonstrate your goodwill. Julian James demonstrated empathy about the reputation of business and industry this way:

> So far the industry's finances have rarely looked better. But not everyone is celebrating. With success in business comes greater scrutiny—just ask the oil industry.
>
> In recent weeks we have seen a growing vilification of insurers that is unprecedented and, I believe, wholly unwarranted. Take these recent headlines I came across:
>
> From USA Today: "Insurance rates pummel Florida homeowners."
>
> From Dow Jones Market Watch: "Sweet are the uses of adversity: Are insurers reeling from disaster or reeling in the profits?" (No prizes for guessing which side the authors came down on in that one.)
>
> And from the Niagara Falls Reporter: "Insurance companies real villains in Hurricane Katrina's aftermath."
>
> If that is the kind of press the industry is getting in Niagara Falls, in upstate New York, you might wonder how we are being portrayed in the Gulf States.[11]

Finally, you can demonstrate goodwill by being responsive. Speakers who are **responsive** show that they care about the audience by acknowledging feedback, especially subtle negative cues. This feedback may occur during the presentation, but it also may have occurred prior to the speech. Let's turn again to Julian James's speech as an example:

> When I spoke to you at this conference, I posed a challenge and asked, "Do you want to take control of the insurance cycle . . . or do you want to stay a passenger?" The reaction was very interesting. One group said, "That's so obvious, why hasn't anyone said that before?" Others said, "Ah, but you're very young, you don't understand, insurance cycles are a fact of life, and you can't do anything about them." . . . Ladies and gentlemen, four years ago, it may have felt like we were standing at the cliff edge, looking into the abyss.
>
> The good news is that, in the intervening period, we have made important progress. . . . But we put our future in grave danger if we stop here. . . . The challenges we face today may be different, but the message from 2002 remains the same: "Our thinking and behaviour must change if the insurance industry is to be a stable, secure industry for our policy holders and shareholders of the future." Let's not mess it up again.[12]

responsive: when speakers show that they care about the audience by acknowledging feedback, especially subtle negative cues

13-4b Conveying Competence and Credibility

Not surprisingly, we are more likely to be persuaded when we perceive a speaker to be competent and credible, that is, when we perceive them to be well informed about the topic. We propose the following strategies so that your **terminal credibility**, the audience's perception of your expertise at the end of your speech, is greater than your **initial credibility**, their perception of your expertise at the beginning of your speech.

1. **Explain your competence.** Unless someone has formally introduced you and your qualifications to your audience, your initial credibility will be low, and as you speak, you will need to tell your audience about your expertise. Sending these types of messages during the speech results in your achieving a level of **derived credibility** with your audience. You can interweave comments about your expertise into introductory comments and at appropriate places within the body of the speech.[13] If you've done a good deal of research on the topic, say so. If you have personal experience, say so. It's important for the audience to know why they can trust what you are saying.

terminal credibility: perception of a speaker's expertise at the end of the speech

initial credibility: perception of a speaker's expertise at the beginning of the speech

derived credibility: strategies employed throughout the speech that signal a speaker's expertise

2. **Use evidence from respected sources.** You can also increase your derived credibility by using supporting material from well-recognized and respected sources. So, if you have a choice between using a statistic from a known partisan organization or from a dispassionate professional association, choose the professional association. Likewise, if you can quote a local expert who is well known and respected by your audience or an international scholar your audience may never have heard of, use the local expert's opinion.

3. **Use nonverbal delivery to enhance your credibility.** Your audience assesses your credibility not only from what it hears about you before you begin speaking but also from what it observes by looking at you. Although professional attire enhances credibility in any speaking situation, it is particularly important for persuasive speeches. Research shows that persuasive speakers dressed more formally are perceived as more credible than those dressed casually or sloppily.[14]

   The audience will also notice how confident you appear as you prepare to address them. From the moment you rise to speak, you will want to convey through your nonverbal behavior that you are competent. Plant your feet firmly, glance at your notes, and then make eye contact or audience contact with one person or group before taking a breath and beginning to speak. Likewise, pause and establish eye contact upon finishing the speech. Just as pausing and establishing eye contact or audience contact before the speech enhance credibility, doing so upon delivering the closing lines of the speech has the same result.

4. **Use vocal expression to enhance your credibility.** Research shows that credibility is strongly influenced by how you sound. Speaking fluently, using a moderately fast rate, and expressing yourself with conviction makes you appear more intelligent and competent.[15]

13-5 THE RHETORICAL STRATEGY OF PATHOS

emotions: the buildup of action-specific energy

We are more likely to be involved with a topic when we have an emotional stake in it. **Emotions** are the buildup of action-specific energy.[16] When we experience the tension associated with any emotion, we look for a way to release the energy. For example, consider how people's facial expressions change when they receive good or bad news. Smiling is one way to release built-up feelings of happiness. Crying is a way to release built-up feelings of sadness. You can increase audience involvement, then, by stimulating both negative and positive emotions in your speeches.[17]

13-5a Evoking Negative Emotions

negative emotions: disquieting feelings people experience

Negative emotions are disquieting, so when people experience them, they look for ways to eliminate them. During your speech, if you can help your audience experience negative emotions, they will be more involved with what you are saying (Photo 13.7). As a result, they will be motivated to use their energy to listen carefully to you to see if you give them a way to reduce their feelings of discomfort. Although you can tap numerous negative emotions we describe five of the most common and how you can use them in a persuasive speech.

Fear

fear: perceiving no control over a situation that threatens us

We experience **fear** when we perceive that we have no control over a situation that threatens us. We may fear physical harm or psychological harm. Fear is reduced when the threat is eliminated or when we escape. If you use examples, stories, and statistics that create fear in your audience, they will be more motivated to hear how your proposal can eliminate the source of their fear or allow them to escape. For example, in a speech whose goal was to convince the audience that they were at risk of developing high blood pressure, the speaker might use a fear appeal in this way:

One of every three Americans aged eighteen and older has high blood pressure. It is a primary cause of stroke, heart disease, heart failure, kidney disease, and blindness. It triples a person's chance of developing heart disease, boosts the chance of stroke seven times, and the chance of congestive heart failure six times. Look at the person on your right; look at the person on your left. If they don't get it, chances are, you will. Today, I'd like to convince you that you are at risk for developing high blood pressure.

Frederic J. Brown/AFP/Getty Images

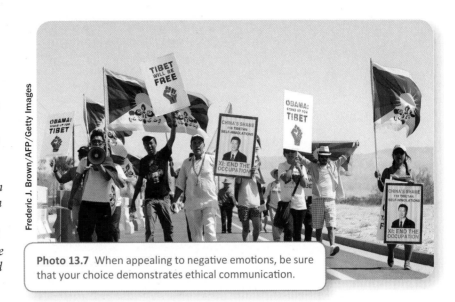

Photo 13.7 When appealing to negative emotions, be sure that your choice demonstrates ethical communication.

Guilt

We feel **guilt** when we personally violate a moral, ethical, or religious code that we hold dear. We experience guilt as a gnawing sensation that we have done something wrong. When we feel guilty, we are motivated to "make things right" or to atone for our transgression. For example, in a speech designed to motivate the audience to take their turn as designated drivers, a speaker might evoke guilt like this:

> *Have you ever promised your mom that you wouldn't ride in a car driven by someone who had been drinking? And then turned around and got in the car with your buddy even though you both had had a few? You know that wasn't right. Lying to your mother, putting yourself and your buddy at risk. . . (pause) but what can you do? Well, today I'm going to show you how you can avoid all that guilt, live up to your promises to mom, and keep both you and your buddy safe.*

guilt: feeling when we personally violate a moral, ethical, or religious code that we hold dear

Shame

We feel **shame** when a moral code we have violated is revealed to someone we think highly of. The more egregious our behavior or the more we admire the person who finds out, the more shame we experience. When we feel shame, we are motivated to "redeem" ourselves in the eyes of that person. Likewise, we can be convinced to refrain from doing something to avoid feelings of shame. If in your speech you can evoke feelings of shame and then demonstrate how your proposal can either redeem someone after a violation has occurred or prevent feelings of shame, then you can motivate the audience to carefully consider your arguments. For example, in a speech advocating thankfulness, the speaker might use a shame-based approach by quoting the old saying, "I cried because I had no shoes until I met a man who had no feet."

shame: feeling when we have violated a moral code and it is revealed to someone we think highly of

Anger

When faced with an obstacle that stands in the way of something we want, we experience **anger**. We may also experience anger when someone demeans us or someone we love. As with all emotions, the intensity of what we feel may vary from mild annoyance to blind rage. Speakers who choose to evoke anger in their audience members must be careful that they don't incite so much anger that reasoning processes are short-circuited.

In your speeches, if you can rouse your audience's anger and then show how your proposal will enable them to achieve their goals or stop the demeaning that has been occurring, you can motivate them to carefully consider your arguments. For example, suppose

anger: feeling when we are faced with an obstacle in the way of something we want you want to convince the audience to support a law requiring community notification when a convicted sex offender moves into the neighborhood. You might arouse the audience's anger to get their attention by personalizing the story of Megan Kanka.

> She was your little girl, just seven years old, and the light of your world. She had a smile that could bring you to your knees. And she loved puppies. So when that nice man who had moved in down the street invited her in to see his new puppy, she didn't hesitate. But she didn't get to see the puppy, and you didn't ever see her alive again. He beat her, he raped her, and then he strangled her. He packaged her body in an old toy chest and dumped it in a park. Your seven-year-old princess would never dig in a toy chest again or slip down the slide in that park. And that hurts. But what makes you really angry is she wasn't his first. But you didn't know that. Because no one bothered to tell you that the guy down the street was likely to kill little girls. The cops knew it. But they couldn't tell you. You, the one who was supposed to keep her safe, didn't know. Angry? You bet. Yeah, he's behind bars again, but you still don't know who's living down the street from you. But you can. There is a law pending before Congress that will require active notification of the community when a known sex offender takes up residence, and today I'm going to tell how you can help to get this passed.[18]

Sadness

When we fail to achieve a goal or experience a loss or separation, we experience **sadness**. Unlike other negative emotions whose energy is projected outward, we tend to withdraw and become isolated when we feel sad. Because sadness is an unpleasant feeling, we look for ways to end it. When we are sad, we are already "looking for answers." So speeches that help us understand and find answers for what has happened can comfort us and help relieve this unpleasant feeling. For example, after 9/11, many Americans were sad. Yes, they were also afraid and angry, but overlaying it all was profound sadness for those who had been lost and what had been lost. The questions, "Why? Why did they do this? Why do they hate us so?" capture the national melancholy. So, when politicians suggested that they understood the answers to these questions, Americans tended to perk up and listen to what they had to say.

13-5b Evoking Positive Emotions

Just as evoking negative emotions can cause audience members to internalize your arguments, so too can you tap **positive emotions**, which are feelings that people enjoy experiencing. With negative emotions, our goal is to show how our proposal will reduce or eliminate the feeling. With positive emotions, our goal is to help the audience maintain or enhance the feeling. We discuss five positive emotions here.

Happiness and Joy

Happiness or joy is the buildup of positive energy we experience when we accomplish something, when we have a satisfying interaction or relationship, or when we see or possess objects that appeal to us. Think about how you felt when you won that ribbon in grade school or when you found out that you got an "A" on that volcano project in fourth grade. Think of how you felt when you heard that special someone say, "I love you" for the very first time. Or think about the birthday when you received that toy you had been dreaming about. In each of these cases, you were happy, maybe even so happy that you were joyous. As a speaker, if you can show how your proposal will lead your audience members to be happy or joyful, then they are likely to listen and to think carefully about your proposal. For example, suppose you want to motivate your audience to attend a couples encounter weekend where they will learn how to "rekindle" their relationship with a partner. If you can remind them about how they felt early in their relationship and then suggest how the weekend can reignite those feelings, they may be more motivated to listen.

Pride

When we experience satisfaction about something we or someone we care about accomplishes, we feel **pride**. "We're number one! We're number one!" is the chant of the crowd feeling pride in the accomplishment of "their" team. Whereas happiness is related to feelings of pleasure, pride is related to feelings of self-worth. So, if you can demonstrate how your proposal will help audience members feel good about themselves, they will be more motivated to consider your arguments. For example, suppose you want to persuade your audience to volunteer to work on the newest Habitat for Humanity house being constructed in your community. You might allude to the pride they will feel when they see people moving into the house they helped to build. As Rick revised his persuasive speech campaign to raise money for a dog park, he decided to appeal to his listeners' sense of pride about helping to build a park that would provide beautiful green space in the heart of the city and, at the same time, provide a welcome place for our family friends to run and play.

pride: feeling of self-satisfaction as the result of an accomplishment

Relief

When a threatening situation has been alleviated, we feel the positive emotion of **relief**. We relax and put down our guard. As a speaker, you use relief to motivate audience members by combining it with the negative emotion of fear. For example, suppose your goal is to convince the audience that they are not at risk for high blood pressure. You might use the same personalization of statistics that was described in the example of fear appeals, but instead of stopping at convincing them that they are at risk, you could also promise relief if they hear you out and do what you advocate.

relief: feeling when a threatening situation has been alleviated

Hope

The emotional energy that stems from believing something desirable is likely to happen is called **hope**. Like relief, hope is a positive emotion that has its roots in a difficult situation. Whereas relief causes us to relax and let down our guard, hope energizes us to take action to overcome the situation. Hope empowers. As with relief, hope appeals are usually accompanied by fear appeals. So you can motivate audience members to listen by showing them how your proposal provides a plan for overcoming a difficult situation. For example, if you propose adopting a low-fat diet to reduce the risk of high blood pressure, you can use the same personalization of statistics that were cited in the example of fear but change the ending to state: "Today, I'm going to convince you to beat the odds by adopting a low-fat diet."

hope: emotional energy that stems from believing something desirable is likely to happen

compassion: feeling of selfless concern for the suffering of another

Compassion

When we feel selfless concern for the suffering of another person and that concern energizes us to try to relieve that suffering, we feel **compassion**. Speakers can evoke audience members' feelings of compassion by vividly describing the suffering endured by someone (Photo 13.8). The audience will then be motivated to listen to see how the speaker's proposal plans to end that suffering. For example, when a speaker whose goal is to have you donate to Project Peanut Butter displays a slide of an emaciated child, claims that 13 percent of all Malawi children die of malnutrition, and states that for $10 you can save a child, he or she is appealing to your compassion.

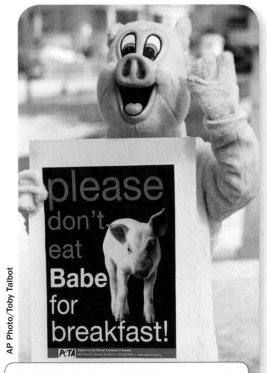

AP Photo/Toby Talbot

Photo 13.8 Speakers appeal to compassion by showing how someone is suffering and how we can help.

13-5c Guidelines for Appealing to Emotions

You can evoke negative emotions, positive emotions, or both as a way to encourage listeners to internalize your message. In this section, we offer several guidelines for doing so effectively in your speech content, language, and delivery.

1. **Tell vivid stories.** Dramatize your arguments by using stories and testimonials that personalize the issue for listeners by appealing to specific emotions. In his speech on bone marrow donation, David Slater simply could have said, "By donating bone marrow—a simple procedure—you can save lives." Instead, he dramatized both the simplicity of the bone marrow donation procedure and the lifesaving impact with a short story designed to heighten audience members' feelings of compassion.

   > When Tricia Matthews decided to undergo a simple medical procedure, she had no idea what impact it could have on her life. But more than a year later, when she saw five-year-old Tommy and his younger brother Daniel walk across the stage of the Oprah Winfrey Show, she realized that the short amount of time it took her to donate her bone marrow was well worth it. Tricia is not related to the boys who suffered from a rare immune deficiency disorder treated by a transplant of her marrow. Tricia and the boys found each other through the National Marrow Donor Program, or NMDP, a national network which strives to bring willing donors and needy patients together. Though the efforts Tricia made were minimal, few Americans made the strides she did. Few of us would deny anyone the gift of life, but sadly, few know how easily we can help.[19]

   Notice how David used a compelling example to appeal to his listeners' emotions and personalize the information for them.

   Similarly, Ryan Labor began his speech on shaken baby syndrome with the following vivid story designed to raise feelings of fear, anger, and sadness:

   > Last winter, two-year-old Cody Dannar refused to eat or play. He had a headache. Doctors said he just had the flu. After a couple weeks home with his mother, Cody felt better. Days later. . . Cody's headaches returned. Coming home from work the next afternoon, his parents found the babysitter frantically calling 911 and Cody lying rigid and unconscious on the floor. He didn't have the flu; in fact, he wasn't sick at all. The babysitter had caused his headaches. To quiet Cody down, she had shaken him, damaging the base of Cody's brain that now risked his life as he lay on the ground.[20]

2. **Use startling statistics.** Statistics don't have to be boring; instead, when used strategically, they can evoke strong emotions. To provoke emotions, statistics need to be startling. A statistic may surprise because of its sheer magnitude. For example, in a speech urging the audience to attend a local protest march organized by the Mobilization for Global Justice, Cory used the following statistic to shame and anger his audience about the global problem of wealth distribution: "Did you know that the USA has 25.4 percent of the world's wealth? And of that, the top 10 percent of Americans control 71 percent?" Sometimes, by comparing two statistics, you can increase the emotional impact. For example, during his second main point, Cory used the following comparative statistic to highlight wealth disparity. "In the U.S., not only does the top 10 percent control 71 percent of the wealth, but the bottom 40 percent of Americans control less than 1 percent!" In Ryan's speech on shaken baby syndrome, he strengthened his emotional appeal by following his vivid story with these startling statistics:

   > Unfortunately, Cody isn't alone. Over one million infants and young children suffer from shaken baby syndrome annually while thousands die. . . . Only 15 percent survive without damage. The remaining children suffer from blindness, learning disabilities, deafness, cerebral palsy, or paralysis.

3. **Incorporate listener relevance links.** You can also appeal to emotions by integrating listener relevance links because emotions are stronger when listeners feel personally involved. At a later point in Ryan's shaken baby syndrome speech, he

appealed to emotions through listener relevance. Notice how he brings the problem close to each listener by suggesting the universality of the problem.

> *Jacy Showers, director of the first National Conference on shaken baby syndrome, says "shaking occurs in families of all races, incomes, and education levels" and "81 percent of SBS offenders had no previous history of child abuse." The reason? The offenders were so young, either babysitters or new parents.*

4. **Choose striking presentational aids.** Because "a picture is worth a thousand words," consider how you can reinforce your verbal message with dramatic presentational aids. Still pictures and short video clips can at times create an emotional jolt that is difficult to achieve with words. Jonna used several before-and-after pictures of female celebrities Nicole Richie, LeeAnn Rimes, and Mary Kate Olsen to reinforce her point that emaciated celebrities were contributing to the eating disorder epidemic in teenage girls. Likewise, Anton used a fifteen-second video clip from the DVD *Zoned for Slavery: The Child Behind the Label* [21] to dramatize the problem of child labor in the global textile industry. His goal was to shame his audience members into sending one postcard to the manufacturer of their favorite brand of clothing asking about the working conditions of the workers who manufacture their clothing. Rick solicited help from a graphic designer to provide an artist rendering of what the empty space would look like once the dog park was finished.

5. **Use descriptive and provocative language.** When developing your speech, include persuasive punch words—words that evoke emotion—where you can. Here's how Ryan used persuasive punch words to strengthen his emotional appeal:

> *The worst of all epidemics is a silent one. With the majority of all victims either infants or young children, shaken baby syndrome can be classified as a stealthy plague .... When shaken, the brain is literally ricocheted inside the skull, bruising the brain and tearing blood vessels coming from the neck ... cutting off oxygen and causing the eyes to bulge.*

6. **Use nonverbal delivery to reinforce your emotional appeal.** Even the most eloquently phrased emotional appeal will lose its impact unless the nonverbal parts of delivery heighten and highlight the emotional content of the message. Practice using your voice to emphasize what you are saying with the use of pauses, volume, and pitch to heighten and highlight the emotional content of your message. A dramatic pause before a startling statistic can magnify its emotional effect. Similarly, lowering or raising the volume or pitch of your voice at strategic places can create an emotional response. If you experiment as you practice out loud, you will find a combination of vocal elements that can enhance emotional appeal when delivering your speech.

7. **Use gestures and facial expressions that highlight the emotions you are conveying.** Your message will lose its emotional impact if you deliver it with a deadpan expression or if your demeanor contradicts the emotional content of your message. So, if you want your audience to feel angry, you should model this feeling by looking annoyed or livid or furious. You might clench your fists, furrow your brows, and frown. When you want to foster feelings of joy in your audience, you can smile, nod, and use other nonverbal gestures that are natural for you when you experience joy. Remember, as an ethical speaker, you are appealing to emotions that you yourself feel about the situation, so allow yourself to experience these emotions as you practice. Then, when you give your speech, you will be more comfortable displaying your feelings for your audience.

To explore one speaker's use of emotional appeals, go to **Web Link 13.2, Terrorism and Islam: Maintaining the Faith,** on your MindTap for *Challenge*.

IMPROMPTU SPEECH CHALLENGE

Select a product advertisement online in the form of a YouTube video, or from a magazine, or on a billboard. Create a short one- to two-minute speech evaluating its use of appeals to logos, ethos, and pathos.

Reflection and Assessment

Persuasion is the process of influencing people's attitudes, beliefs, values, or behaviors, and persuasive speaking is doing so in a public speech. Persuasive messages differ from informative messages in that the primary goal is to seek agreement and sometimes to incite action. To assess how well you've learned what we've discussed in this chapter, answer the following questions. If you have trouble answering any of them, go back and review that material. Once you can answer each question accurately, you are ready to move ahead to read the next chapter.

1. What is nature of persuasive messages compared to informative ones?
2. How do people process persuasive messages?
3. What is the role of logos in persuasive messages?
4. What is the role of ethos in persuasive messages?
5. What is the role of pathos in persuasive messages?

 MindTap

Challenge Resource and Assessment Center

Now that you have read Chapter 13, go to your MindTap for *The Challenge of Effective Speaking in a Digital Age* for quick access to the electronic resources that accompany this text. These resources include the following:

- **Study tools** that will help you assess your learning and prepare for exams (*digital glossary, key term flash cards, review quizzes*).

- **Activities and assignments** that will help you hone your knowledge and build your public speaking skills throughout the course (Practice, Do). Many of these activities allow you to compare your answers with those provided by the authors and, if requested, submit your answers to your instructor.

- **Media resources**—all of which are available on your MindTap for *Challenge*—will help you explore communication concepts online (Practice), develop your speech outlines (Do), watch and critique videos of sample speeches (Do), and upload your speech videos for instructor feedback and critique other students' speeches (Do).

- **Web Links that provide you with additional information or resources related to the topics discussed in this chapter.**

  13.1: Elaboration Likelihood Model (p. 263)

  13.2: Terrorism and Islam: Maintaining the Faith (p. 277)

- **Video resource allows you to see other students giving speeches and record your own speech.**

  1. View how other students approach logos, ethos, and pathos in their persuasive speeches. Do any of them use logical fallacies in their speeches? Or record a speech you're working on, upload it to MindTap, and ask your peers for their feedback. What feedback could you use to fine-tune your persuasive speech before you give it in class?

Applying What You've Learned

1. **Impromptu Speech Activity:** Draw a common household product from a box of products your instructor provides. Some products in the box might be non-perishable foods (soup, cereal, snacks, etc.), cleaning supplies (window wash, hand soap, dishwashing liquid), and paper products (toilet paper, paper towels, napkins). Prepare a two- to three-minute speech identifying how the product you selected appeals to logos, ethos, and pathos.

2. **Assessment Activity A:** Watch a television commercial for a similar product that airs on a cable news network, sports network, and family channel. Identify similar and different rhetorical appeals used in them. Offer possible reasons based on the ELM for using similar and different appeals. Prepare a one- to two-page reflection paper describing what you discovered and the assessment you drew from it.

3. **Assessment Activity B:** Consider an interaction you had in the last week with a friend or family member who convinced you (a) *to do something* you hadn't planned on doing (e.g., go to a movie, attend an event) or (b) *not to do something* you had intended to do (e.g., a household chore, homework). What rhetorical strategies can you identify that influenced your decision? Prepare a one- to two-page paper documenting examples of logos, ethos, and pathos that persuaded you.

14 "persuasive speaking"

AP Photo/UCLA Daily Bruin, Tiffany Michalka

WHAT'S THE POINT?
WHEN YOU'VE FINISHED THIS CHAPTER, YOU'LL BE ABLE TO:

14-1 Identify the initial attitude of your target audience

14-2 Phrase your persuasive speech goal as a proposition

14-3 Identify some dispositional and actuation persuasive speech patterns

14-4 Follow ethical communication guidelines when preparing persuasive speeches

MindTap™

Review the chapter **Learning Objectives** and **Start** with quick warm up activity.

Ethical communicators demonstrate responsibility by considering implications of their persuasive message on the audience.

As Tomeka finished her speech on "Taking Back the Neighborhood: Get Out the Vote!" the audience rose to their feet and began to chant, "No more! No more! No more! No more!..." It was clear to her that she had made an impact. Not only had she convinced her audience, but she could also see that some of them were visibly angry and ready for action. As she was leaving the platform, she heard a member of the audience shout out, "You heard her. It's time! Voting won't do any good. Let's go take what is ours. Take to the streets! Get yours!" In the riot that ensued, three neighborhood shops were ransacked, ten cars were set on fire, and twenty-three people were arrested. The next day as she toured the neighborhood and saw firsthand the wreckage her speech had led to, all she could think was, "This wasn't what I meant. This isn't what I wanted."

Read, highlight, and take notes online.

In the previous chapter, we focused on how persuasive messages employ what Aristotle called the available means of persuasion (logos, ethos, and pathos) to seek agreement or to encourage action. In this chapter, we focus on how to organize those rhetorical appeals into persuasive speeches that are both effective and ethical. In the opening vignette, Tomeka's speech not only convinced her audience to agree with her point of view, but it also left them so emotionally agitated that when one member of the audience advocated action, the rest followed. And the actions they took went well beyond what Tomeka wanted the audience to do.

So what are the steps you need to follow to create persuasive speeches that are both effective and ethical? First you need to understand where your audience stands on your topic and then phrase your goal as a proposition that is appropriate to the rhetorical situation. Next you need to organize your speech using an appropriate persuasive speech pattern. Finally, you need to evaluate, and if necessary, revise your speech based on ethical guidelines for persuasive speeches.

14-1 AUDIENCE ATTITUDE

Because it is very difficult to convince people to change their minds, what you can hope to accomplish in one speech depends on where your audience stands on your topic. So you'll want to analyze your audience members' attitudes about your topic. An **attitude** is "a general or enduring positive or negative feeling about some person, object, or issue."[1] People express their attitudes about something when they give their opinions. So someone who claims "I think physical fitness is important" is expressing an opinion that reflects a favorable attitude about physical fitness.

Audience members' attitudes can range from highly favorable to strongly opposed and can be visualized as lying on a continuum like the one pictured in Exhibit 14.1. Even though an audience will include individuals whose opinions fall at nearly every point along the continuum, generally audience members' opinions tend to cluster in one area of it. For instance, the opinions of the audience represented in Exhibit 14.1 cluster around "mildly opposed," even though a few people are more hostile and a few have favorable opinions. This cluster point represents your **target audience**, the group of people you most want to persuade. Based on your target audience, you can classify your audience's initial attitude toward your topic as "in favor" (already supportive), "no opinion" (uninformed, neutral, or apathetic), or "opposed" (holding an opposite point of view).

14-1a Opposed

It is unrealistic to believe you will be able to change your target audience's attitude from "opposed" to "in favor" in only one short speech. Instead, seek **incremental**

attitude: a general or enduring positive or negative feeling about some person, object, or issue

target audience: the group of people you most want to persuade

"As she toured the neighborhood and saw firsthand the wreckage her speech had led to, all she could think was, 'This wasn't what I meant. This isn't what I wanted.'"

Exhibit (14.1) **Sample Opinion Continuum**

Highly opposed	Opposed	Mildly opposed	Neither in favor nor opposed	Mildly in favor	In favor	Highly in favor
2	2	11	1	2	2	0

Copyright © Cengage Learning

incremental change: attempting to move your audience only a small degree in your direction

change, that is, attempt to move them only a small degree in your direction, hoping for additional movement later. For example, if your target audience is opposed to the goal "I want to convince my audience that same sex marriage should be legal," you might rephrase your goal as "I want to convince my audience that committed same sex couples should be afforded the same legal protection as committed heterosexual couples through state-recognized civil unions." Then brainstorm potential objections, questions, and criticisms that might arise and shape your speech around them.

14-1b No Opinion

uninformed: the audience doesn't know enough about a topic to have formed an opinion

neutral: the audience has some information about a topic but does not really understand why one position is preferred and so still has no opinion

If your target audience has no opinion for or against your topic, consider whether they are uninformed, neutral, or apathetic. If they are **uninformed**—that is, they do not know enough about the topic to have formed an opinion—you will need to provide the basic arguments and information needed to become informed. For example, if your target audience is uninformed about same sex marriage, you might begin by highlighting the legal benefits of marriage in general. If your target audience is **neutral**; that is, they know the basics about your topic but not enough to have formed an opinion, you will want to provide evidence and reasoning illustrating why your position is superior to others (Photo 14.1). Perhaps your target audience knows the legal benefits of marriage in general but needs to understand how committed same sex couples who do not have these benefits are disadvantaged. When target audiences have no opinion because they are **apathetic**, you will need to find ways to show how it relates to them or their needs.

PUBLIC SPEAKING IN THE REAL WORLD

"Let us be outraged, let us be loud, let us be bold."

When most of us think of Brad Pitt, we probably think of the guy who seems to have it all, for instance, the four-time Oscar nominated actor, the two-time recipient of People's sexiest men alive, or the happy family man in the Pitt-Jolie clan. What we might not think of is Brad Pitt the human rights and social issues activist. Some of his more famous speech quotations are actually "heartthrobs are a dime a dozen," "you must lose everything in order to gain anything," and "success is a beast. It actually puts the emphasis on the wrong thing." Perhaps that's why for over a decade, he has devoted so much time to publicly supporting causes he believes in such as stem-cell research and same sex marriage, as well as combating AIDS and poverty in

Jeff Vespa/wire image/Getty Images

developing countries.[2] His courage for doing so in the face of critics who question his sincerity is grounded in what we talk about in this chapter: being genuinely committed to your message. In his own words:

> "Let us be the ones who say we do not accept that a child dies every three seconds simply because he does not have the drugs you and I have.
>
> Let us be the ones to say we are not satisfied that your place of birth determines your right to life.
>
> Let us be outraged, let us be loud, let us be bold."[3]

For the same sex example, you will want to address possible questions such as, "I'm not gay, so why should I care?" You can do this by including strong listener relevance links for each main point.

For more about dealing with audiences who are opposed to or have no opinion about your position, go to **Web Link 14.1: Dealing with a Hostile Audience**, and **Web Link 14.2: Dealing with a Challenging Audience** on your MindTap for *Challenge*.

14-1c In Favor

If your target audience is only mildly in favor of your proposal, your task is to reinforce and strengthen their beliefs. Audience members who favor your position may become further committed to it after hearing new reasons and more recent evidence supporting it. When your target audience strongly agrees with your position, then you can consider a goal that moves them to act on it. So, if your target audience strongly favors the idea of same sex marriage, then your goal might be "I want my audience to email or write letters to their state representatives urging them to support legislation extending the right to marry to same sex couples." In the opening vignette, Tomeka's audience was already in favor of her proposition so she focused on motivating them to act.

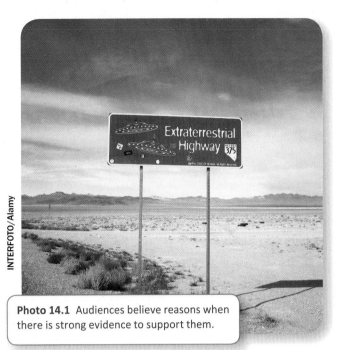

INTERFOTO/Alamy

Photo 14.1 Audiences believe reasons when there is strong evidence to support them.

14-2 IDENTIFYING YOUR PROPOSITION

Persuasive speech goals are stated as propositions. A **proposition** is a declarative sentence that clearly indicates the position you advocate. For example, "I want to convince my audience that pirating (downloading from the Internet) copyrighted media without paying for it is wrong" is a proposition. Notice how a persuasive proposition differs from an informative speech goal on the same subject: "I want to inform my audience about the practice of pirating copyrighted media." In the informative speech, you will achieve your goal if the audience understands and remembers what you talk about. In the persuasive speech, however, they must not only understand and remember, but also agree with your position and possibly even take action. The three types of propositions are fact, value, or policy.

A **proposition of fact** is a statement designed to convince your audience that something: (1) did, probably did, probably did not, or did not exist or occur; (2) is, probably is, probably is not, or is not true; or (3) will, probably will, probably will not, or will not occur. Although propositions of fact may or may not be true—both positions are arguable—they are stated as though they are, without question, true. For example, whether or not Princess Diana's death was an unfortunate car accident or an assassination is debatable. So you could argue a proposition of fact in two ways: "Princess Diana's death was nothing more than a tragic car accident" or "Princess Diana's death was, in fact, a successful assassination attempt." Examples of propositions of fact concerning the present are "God exists" or "There is no such thing as God"; and "Cell phone use causes brain cancer" or "Cell phone use does not cause brain cancer." Claims of fact concerning the future are predictions. For example, "Thanks to the Internet, paperbound books will eventually cease to exist" and "The New York Yankees will surely win the World Series next year" are both propositions of fact concerning the future.

A **proposition of value** is a statement designed to convince your audience that something is good, bad, desirable, undesirable, fair, unfair, moral, immoral, sound,

MindTap™

apathetic: the audience is uninterested in, unconcerned about, or indifferent toward your topic

SPEECH SNIPPET

When the Audience Is in Favor, Seek Action

Adam knew that most if not all of the people in his audience already agreed that bullying is bad, so he decided to focus on a speech that would get them to do their part to help stop it.

proposition: a declarative sentence that clearly indicates the position the speaker will advocate

proposition of fact: a statement designed to convince the audience that something did or did not exist or occur, is or is not true, or will or will not occur

Exhibit 14.2 Example of Persuasive Speech Propositions

Propositions of Fact	Propositions of Value	Propositions of Policy
Mahatma Gandhi was the father of passive resistance.	Mahatma Gandhi was a moral leader.	Mahatma Gandhi should be given a special award for his views on passive resistance.
Pharmaceutical advertising to consumers increases prescription drug prices.	Pharmaceutical advertising of new prescription drugs on TV is better than marketing new drugs directly to doctors.	Pharmaceutical companies should be required to refrain from advertising prescription drugs on TV.
Using paper ballots is a popular method for voting in U.S. elections.	Using paper ballots is better than using electronic voting machines.	Using paper ballots should be required for U.S. elections.

proposition of value: a statement designed to convince the audience that something is good, bad, desirable, undesirable, fair, unfair, moral, immoral, sound, unsound, beneficial, harmful, important, or unimportant

proposition of policy: a statement designed to convince the audience that they should take a specific course of action

unsound, beneficial, harmful, important, or unimportant.[4] You can attempt to convince your audience that something has more value than something else, or you can convince your audience that something meets valued standards. "Running is a better form of exercise than bicycling" is an example of the former and "The real value of a college education is that it creates an informed citizenry" is an example of the latter.

A **proposition of policy** is a statement designed to convince your audience that a particular rule, plan, or course of action should be taken. Propositions of policy will implore listeners using words such as "do it/don't do it," "should/shouldn't," or "must/must not." "All college students *should* be required to take a public speaking course," "The United States *must* stop deep sea oil drilling," "*Don't* text while driving," and "Water packaged in plastic bottles *should* be taxed to pay for the cost associated with recycling empties" are propositions of policy. Tomeka's speech focused on a proposition of policy, as well: "We must get out and vote." Exhibit 14.2 provides several examples of how propositions of fact, value, and policy can be developed from the same topic idea.

As you begin working on your persuasive speeches, you can use the Speech-Planning Action Steps and Speech Builder Express to help you organize and develop them,

 SPEECH PLANNING

Speech-Planning Action Step for Persuasive Speeches

Writing a Specific Goal as a Persuasive Proposition

1. Identify your topic and tentatively phrase your goal.

2. Check whether you believe that your target audience is opposed to, has no opinion of, or is in favor of your position. Why?

3. Rephrase your goal as a proposition of fact, value, or policy appropriately tailored to the attitude of your target audience.

Do this activity with Speech Builder Express. Access this activity on your MindTap for *Challenge.*

STUDENT RESPONSE

Student Response Action Step for Persuasive Speeches

Writing a Specific Goal as a Persuasive Proposition

1. Identify your topic and tentatively phrase your goal.

   I want to convince the audience not to download copyrighted music from the Internet without paying for it.

2. Check whether you believe that your target audience is opposed to, has no opinion of, or is in favor of your position. Why?

   Although some students may be opposed to or in favor of this proposition, I think the majority are undecided.

3. Rephrase your goal as a proposition of fact, value, or policy appropriately tailored to the attitude of your target audience.

   Because my audience is neutral, I will phrase my goal as a proposition of value: Downloading copyrighted music from the Internet without paying for it is wrong.

---

although some of the steps will be modified to provide you with guidance that is particular to persuasive speeches. You can use Activity 1Ep and the sample student response to help you develop a specific goal for a persuasive speech stated as a proposition.

14-3 PERSUASIVE SPEECH PATTERNS

Persuasive speeches are organized as speeches to convince or speeches to actuate. **Speeches to convince** focus on reinforcing or changing your audience's belief or attitude. **Speeches to actuate** focus on persuading your audience to take action.

14-3a Speeches to Convince

Most speeches to convince follow one of four organizational patterns: statement of reasons, comparative advantages, criteria satisfaction, and refutative. The following paragraphs describe each pattern and show how Tomeka's speech to convince her audience to agree with her about how they should vote on a school tax proposition might be arranged using it.

Statement of Reasons

A **statement of reasons** pattern is used to confirm propositions of fact by presenting the best-supported reasons in a meaningful order. For a speech with three reasons or more, place the strongest reason last because this is the reason you believe the audience will find most persuasive. Place the second strongest reason first because you want to start with a significant point. Place the other reasons in between.

Proposition of Fact: The proposed school tax levy is necessary.

   I. *The income is needed to restore vital programs. (second strongest)*

   II. *The income is needed to give teachers cost of living raises.*

   III. *The income is needed to maintain local control. (strongest)*

speech to convince: a speech designed to seek agreement about a belief, value, or attitude

speech to actuate: a speech designed to incite action

statement of reasons: a straightforward organization in which you present your best-supported reasons in a meaningful order

Comparative Advantages

comparative advantages: an organization that shows that a proposed change has more value than any of the alternatives.

A **comparative advantages** pattern attempts to convince others that something has more value or is better than the any of the alternatives.[5] A comparative advantages approach to the school tax proposition would look like this:

Proposition of Value: Passing the school tax levy will be better than not passing it. (compares the value of change to the status quo)

I. With new income from a tax levy, schools may reintroduce important programs that had been cut. (advantage 1)

II. New income from a tax levy may provide raises in teacher salaries, which should avert a tentative strike by them. (advantage 2)

III. New income from a tax levy will make it possible to retain local control of our schools, which will be lost to the state if additional local funding is not provided. (advantage 3)

Criteria Satisfaction

A **criteria satisfaction** pattern seeks agreement on criteria that should be considered when evaluating a particular proposition and then shows how the proposition satisfies those criteria. A criteria satisfaction pattern is especially useful when your audience is opposed to your proposition because it approaches the proposition indirectly by first focusing on criteria that the audience will probably agree with before introducing the specific proposition (Photo 14.2). A criteria satisfaction organization for the school tax proposition might look like this:

Proposition of value: Passing a school tax levy is a good way to fund our schools.

I. *We all agree that the funding method we select must meet three key criteria:*

   A. *The funding method must provide resources needed to reinstate important programs.*

   B. *The funding method must pay for teachers.*

   C. *The funding method must generate enough income to maintain local control.*

II. *Passing a local school tax levy will satisfy each of these criteria.*

   A. *A local levy will allow us to fund important programs again.*

   B. *A local levy will provide needed revenue to give teachers a raise.*

   C. *A local levy will generate enough income to maintain local control.*

Refutative

A **refutative** pattern arranges main points according to opposing arguments and then both challenges them and bolsters your own. This pattern is particularly useful when the target audience opposes your position. Begin by acknowledging the merit of opposing arguments and then showing their flaws. Once listeners understand the flaws, they will be more receptive to the arguments you present to support your proposition. A refutative pattern for the school tax proposition might look like this:

SPEECH SNIPPET

Comparative Advantages Pattern

Because Molly knew some members of her audience probably engaged in the practice of "hooking up," and others probably didn't care one way or the other, she decided to organize her persuasive speech to convince them to use a comparative advantages pattern.

criteria satisfaction: an indirect organization that seeks audience agreement on criteria that should be considered when evaluating a particular proposition and then shows how the proposition satisfies those criteria

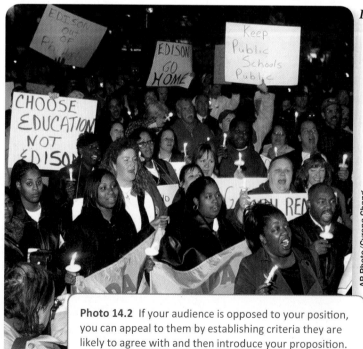

Photo 14.2 If your audience is opposed to your position, you can appeal to them by establishing criteria they are likely to agree with and then introduce your proposition.

AP Photo/Cyrena Chang

Proposition of Value: A school tax levy is the best way to fund our schools.

I. *Opponents of the tax levy argue that the tax increase will fall only on property owners.*

    A. *Landlords will recoup property taxes in the form of higher rents.*

    B. *Thus, all people will be affected.*

II. *Opponents of the tax levy argue that there are fewer students in the school district, so schools should be able to function on the same amount of revenue.*

    A. *Although there are fewer pupils, costs continue to rise.*

        1. *Salary costs are increasing.*

        2. *Energy costs are increasing.*

        3. *Maintenance costs are increasing.*

        4. *Costs from unfunded federal and state government mandates are increasing.*

    B. *Although there are fewer pupils, there are many aging school buildings that need replacing or renovating.*

III. *Opponents of the tax levy argue that parents should be responsible for the excessive cost of educating their children.*

    A. *Historically, our nation flourished under a publicly funded educational system.*

    B. *Parents today are already paying more than parents in previous generations did.*

        1. *Activity fees*

        2. *Lab fees*

        3. *Book fees*

        4. *Transportation fees*

    C. *Of school-age children today in this district, 42 percent live in families that are below the poverty line and have limited resources.*

refutative: an organization that persuades by both challenging the opposing position and bolstering one's own

" speech assignment "

Speech to Convince

1. Prepare a five- to seven-minute speech seeking agreement about a belief, value, or attitude.

2. Write a persuasive plan for adapting to your specific audience that includes:

    a. How your goal stated as a proposition adapts to whether your prevailing audience attitude is in favor, has no opinion, or is opposed.

    b. What organizational pattern you will use and why it is appropriate for the rhetorical situation.

    c. What main points you will use.

3. Write a complete speech outline.

Do this activity with your MindTap for *Challenge.*

" speech evaluation checklist "

Speech to Convince Evaluation Checklist

You can use this checklist to critique a speech to convince that you hear in class or a recording of your own. As you listen, outline the speech. Pay close attention to the reasoning process the speaker uses. Note the claims and supports used in the arguments, and identify the types of warrants used. Then, answer the following questions.

General Criteria

_____ **1.** Was the introduction effective in creating interest, involving the audience in the speech, and previewing the main points?

_____ **2.** Were section transitions used to help you follow the organization of the main points?

_____ **3.** Did the conclusion summarize the thesis and main points in a memorable way?

_____ **4.** Was the language appropriate, accurate, clear, and vivid?

_____ **5.** Was the speech delivered conversationally, intelligibly, expressively, and convincingly?

Specific Criteria

_____ **1.** Was the specific goal stated as a proposition?

_____ **2.** Was the speech organized into an appropriate pattern?

_____ Statement of reasons

_____ Comparative advantages

_____ Criteria satisfaction

_____ Refutative

_____ **3.** Did the speaker use logos effectively?

_____ Use strong evidence?

_____ Use reasoning to link evidence to claims?

_____ Avoid reasoning fallacies?

_____ **4.** Did the speaker use ethos effectively?

_____ Establish expertise?

_____ Demonstrate trustworthiness?

_____ Convey goodwill?

_____ **5.** Did the speaker use pathos effectively?

Appeal to negative emotions? If so, check all that were tapped: _____ fear _____ guilt _____ anger _____ shame _____ sadness

Appeal to positive emotions? If so, check all that were tapped: _____ happiness/joy _____ pride _____ relief _____ hope _____ compassion

Overall evaluation of the speech (check one):

_____ excellent _____ good _____ average _____ fair _____ poor

Explain:

🌐 MindTap™

Access this checklist online on your MindTap for *Challenge*.

SAMPLE SPEECH

Sample Speech to Convince

This section presents a sample speech to convince given by a student, including an adaptation plan, an outline, and a transcript.

Hooking Up, Friends-with-Benefits Relationships (FWBR), or Dating: Not Really a Tough Choice

By Molly Reynolds[6]

ADAPTATION PLAN

1. **Audience attitude**: When I asked people about their feelings concerning hookups and friends-with-benefits relationships (FWBRs), most of them regarded the practices as common and not a big deal. However, very few admitted to their own hookup or FWBRs. Instead, they talked about the involvements that "others" engaged in. Therefore, I determined that the majority of my audience is either undecided or unconcerned about the consequences.

2. **Reasons**: Dating is physically and psychologically healthier, and leads to greater relationship satisfaction, yet Bisson and Levine (2007) reported that 60% of their college sample had been involved in a FWBR.

3. **Organizational pattern**: I am going to use a comparative advantages pattern. This topic naturally lends itself to demonstrating the comparative advantages that dating has over both hooking up and friends-with-benefits relationships (FWBRs). The three primary advantages are physical health, psychological health, and relationship satisfaction.

Outline

General goal: To persuade

Specific goal: I want to convince my audience that dating relationships are better than hooking up or friends-with-benefits relationships (FWBRs).

INTRODUCTION

I. *"Well you know, they travel in threes, and she was* not *the hot one but she wasn't the fat one either. And it was late, and if I wanted to get laid the choices were getting slim, so—"*

"We were at this party, and I was dancing with this really hot guy. One thing led to another, and I thought, what the heck. He's so hot."

"Josh and I have known each other since grade school, and I've always kind of had a thing for him. Neither one of us was seeing anyone, and one night we were out with friends and dancing, and one thing led to another and we became, you know, 'friends with benefits.' But now I'm really hooked on him and he doesn't know it, and he's started to see someone who he thinks is special. But he wants to keep up our arrangement too because she won't sleep with him."

"I met this really cool girl in my biology class. She's really pretty and smart, and she seems to have a good sense of humor. So I broke the code and asked her out. We took a walk in the park, had dinner, and then went back to her place, and believe it

Attention getter

 MindTap™

Read the speech adaptation plan, outline, and transcript of a speech given by Molly Reynolds in an introductory speaking course. Access the Chapter 14 resources of your MindTap for *Challenge* to identify some of the strengths of Molly's speech by preparing an evaluation checklist and an analysis. You can then compare your answers with those of the authors.

or not, we just talked. It was so weird, but I really enjoyed it. So we've made plans to go to the movies on Saturday. So I won't be going out trolling for a bad girl this weekend. Who knows—I may be out of the action for a while. We'll see."

Listener relevance

II. We have all known someone who has engaged in the above-mentioned scenarios. Which of these scenarios appeals most to you? If you had your choice of hooking up with a stranger, having sex with a friend, or going out with someone you found interesting and attractive, what would you prefer?

Speaker credibility

III. As a member of what some call "the hookup generation," I have first-hand knowledge and some experience with the current hookup culture that is so popular on college campuses today. So I was curious about what the research says about these practices, and what I discovered might surprise you as much as it surprised me.

IV. Today, I'm here to convince you that hooking up and friends-with-benefits relationships (FWBRs) are poor substitutes for dating relationships.

Thesis statement

V. I will show why dating is the best choice by defining each relationship type and then comparing the physical risks, psychological costs, and feelings of relationship satisfaction among them.

BODY

I. Let's begin by defining each of these three types of relationships.

Listener relevance

I'm sure we have all known someone who hooked up and was disappointed when they didn't get a phone call the next day, and someone whose FWBR ended with no benefits and the loss of a friend. And I'm sure we have known friends who grieved the loss of what they thought was a solid dating relationship.

   A. Before we can examine the risks, we must define what a hookup is.
   1. "Hookups are defined as a sexual encounter which may or may not include sexual intercourse, usually occurring on only one occasion between two people who are strangers or brief acquaintances" (Paul, McManus, & Hayes, 2000, p. 76).
      a. These casual sexual encounters are essentially spontaneous sex between partners who barely had contact with each other before engaging in the sexual act (Glenn & Marquardt, 2001; Owen, Rhoades, Stanely, & Fincham, 2010; Paul et al., 2000; Winslow, Franzini, & Hwang, 1992).
      b. The nature of the sexual behavior involved is ambiguous and may vary from heavy kissing to intercourse.
   2. Not only is the behavior ambiguous, but those involved may have different goals and expectations regarding future encounters (Owen & Fincham, 2011).
   3. Even with the associated ambiguity, 50 to 75% of young adults have experienced hooking up (Owen & Fincham, 2011).
   B. Now that we understand the nature of a hookup, what exactly is a friends-with-benefits relationship (FWBR)?
   1. FWBRs are platonic friendships where partners engage in sexual behaviors ranging from kissing to sexual intercourse (Mongeau, Shaw, & Knight, 2009).
      a. FWBRs can include numerous degrees on the intimacy spectrum.
      b. These degrees range from good friends who engage in sexual activity to individuals who engage in serial hookups but have little to no interaction beyond the hookup.

2. Despite the type of FWBR, individuals usually enter into a FWBR with no intention of it evolving into a romantic relationship (Hughes, Morisson, & Asada, 2005).
   a. Sometimes one partner in a FWBR becomes interested in taking the relationship further, but these feelings aren't always mutual.
   b. Research has shown that individuals involved in FWBRs may vary in their desire to receive positive social and/or emotional consequences (e.g., Levinson, Jaccard, & Beamer, 1995; Paul, McManus, & Hayes, 2000).
   c. Justin Timberlake and Mila Kunis starred in the movie *Friends with Benefits* where their characters began as friends, moved into a FWBR, and ended up together at the end.
   d. Owen and Fincham (2011) discuss that both men and women who engage in FWBRs report more positive than negative relational consequences. Yet, not all individuals are aware of the costs and not all FWBRs have a fairy-tale ending and end up with their own version of Justin Timberlake.

C. Now that we understand the nature of hookups and FWBRs, we must define dating relationships.
   1. In dating relationships, individuals spend time getting to know each other and enter into a sexual relationship if and when both partners feel a sense of relational intimacy (Surra, Boettcher-Burke, Cottle, West, & Gray, 2007).
   2. In dating relationships, both people share more intimate thoughts and feelings as trust builds.
   3. In hookups and FWBRs there can be uncertainty and differing expectations, in dating relationships there is an emphasis on shared values and beliefs (Larson & Holmes, 1994).
   4. Relational success is more likely when partners know each other and date for an extended period before marriage and engage in positive communication (Stafford, 2008).

Now that we've established a common set of definitions, let's compare these relationships according to how they affect physical health, psychological health, and relationship satisfaction.

Transition

II. Let's begin by exploring the physical risks associated with hookups, FWBRs, and dating relationships.

Since most of us in this room are not married, we ought to understand the physical risks involved in engaging in these different types of relationships.

Listener relevance

A. Because partners often fail to practice safe sex, hookups and FWBRs increase the risk of catching a sexually transmitted disease (STD).
   1. It's true that when you have sex with someone, you also have sex with everyone they have ever had sex with.
      a. Listen to the testimony of someone suffering from pelvic inflammatory disease (PID), a bacterial infection of the uterus, fallopian tubes, and ovaries:
      "I have suffered with pelvic inflammatory disease now for fifteen years. I have in the last three years had a full hysterectomy and now suffer worse pain than ever and have severe adhesions and chronic pain. My life is ruined. My PID was silent but deadly— one day no pain; next day I was crippled. PID is a horrible disease—and you don't have to be promiscuous to get it. Just

sleeping with someone you don't know and whose sexual past is unknown can put you in jeopardy of this disease."

    b. PID is most frequently caused by gonorrhea and chlamydia, two common STDs.

  2. There are numerous risks associated specifically with hooking up (Downing-Maltibag & Geisinger, 2009).

    a. Students who did not use protection often trusted that their hookup partners were STD-free based on appearance or informal character assessments.

    b. They also tended to rationalize that because there were low rates of HIV/AIDS in the region where they lived, they did not have to protect themselves against it (p. 1204).

  3. People aren't any safer in FWBRs.

    a. People who engage in *hookups* report being more careful when engaging in sexual intercourse with unknown or lesser-known individuals than with people they already know (Morr & Mongeau, 2004).

    b. Just because you know someone as a "friend" and have a FWBR with that person does not mean you know what he or she is doing sexually.

      i. FWBRs by their very nature are not meant to be exclusive, so he or she may have other partners who, by association, you are also sleeping with.

      ii. Even if you are both monogamous during your relationship, unless you are both tested prior to having sex, you are still at risk.

    c. In hookups and in FWBRs, the emphasis is on each partner's personal needs for sex and physical satisfaction, so the partner is an "insignificant other."

B. Because partners involved in hookups and FWBRs are less likely to practice safe sex, the likelihood of an unplanned pregnancy also increases.

  1. Listen to the experience of a woman who posted her story on Yahoo! Answers:

"I was with this guy for a very short time. It pretty much ended up being a one-night stand, even though we texted a little afterwards. When I found out I was pregnant, I decided to tell him, especially since I didn't know what I was going to do yet. But whatever I was going to do was part of his responsibility (i.e., bills for an abortion, child support, or choosing of an adoptive family). When I told him, he just begged me to get an abortion over and over until I finally agreed and told him I had gotten the abortion to get him to stop texting me every five seconds and begging while I could get some quiet time to figure out what I really wanted to do."

Notice, guys, it was what she wanted to do. A man who fathers a hookup child is legally responsible for supporting that child until it is an adult. You have no say—it is her body and her decision. So, in addition to your college loans, you may have a significant financial responsibility for the next eighteen years. And every time you get a raise, your child gets part of it. It's the risk you take. And if you're morally or religiously opposed to abortion? Tough. Her body, her decision. You can try to change her mind, but if she decides on abortion, there is nothing you can do. And remember, even when condoms are used they are only 95 percent effective as a contraceptive. Think about it.

Listener relevance

2. Unintended pregnancy is a risk in any sexual relationship.
    a. But people who are dating and have built some degree of respect and intimacy are more likely to come to a mutual understanding about the woman's choice.
    b. Or they can adjust to co-parenting tasks, even if they choose to end their romantic relationship.

C. While physical risks are inherent in any sexual relationship, dating is physically healthier than either hooking up or engaging in a FWBR.

Not only do hookups and FWBRs put you at more risk physically, but they are also more likely to do psychological damage. Transition

III. Both hooking up and engaging in FWBRs create psychological distress. Listener relevance

How many of you know someone who says they feel more confident and have higher self-esteem following a hookup? After sleeping with their best friend? Not many, right? More often, we listen to our friends express feelings of guilt, shame, and embarrassment. People, it's called a "walk of shame" for a reason.

A. People who hook up have lower self-esteem, greater depression, and more feelings of guilt than those who don't (Grello, Welsh, & Harper, 2006; Sprecher, Barbee, & Schwartz, 1995).
    1. Women who engage in hooking up experience more loss of self-esteem and depression than men.
    2. It is not clear whether depression leads to casual sexual behavior or whether casual sexual behavior leads to depression.
    3. Women who engage in casual sex express feelings of good old-fashioned guilt.
    4. Men don't necessarily feel guilty for hooking up with strangers, but they do feel guilty if they get drunk and hook up with a friend.

B. While breaking up a dating relationship can also lead to depression, research has found that although the first breakup can lead to depression, subsequent breakups are unlikely to do so.
    1. The first act of breaking up seems to "inoculate" us, probably because we figure that there is life after a breakup.
    2. The opposite seems to be true in more casual sexual relationships—the more you do it, the more guilty and depressed you become.

Because of the many negative physical and psychological consequences of hooking up and FWBRs, dating tends to produce more satisfying relationships in the end. Transition

IV. Hooking up and FWBRs lead to less satisfying relationships than dating.
    A. In a hookup, ideally neither partner wants or expects anything other than sexual satisfaction (Grello et al., 2006).
        1. Half of all college students who engage in sexual intercourse during a hookup never see the other person again.
        2. But 18 percent of women view a hookup as stepping stone to a romantic relationship.
    B. In the ideal FWBR, two friends simply become "sex" buddies without damaging the friendship.
    C. According to that famous philosopher, Harry Burns in the 1989 movie When *Harry Met Sally*, "Men and women can never be friends because the sex part always gets in the way." Was Harry wrong? Yes and no.
        1. In 2010 study, Lehmiller and colleagues found yes:
           "Sex was a more common motivation for men in FWBRs, whereas emotional connection was a more common motivation for women.

> *In addition, men were more likely to hope that the relationship stays the same over time, whereas women expressed more desire for change into either a full-fledged romance or a basic friendship."*

2. This is understandable when you consider the biology of sex, according to sex therapist Dr. Ian Kerner, speaking on the *Today Show* in 2007:

   > *"During sex, women produce lots of oxytocin, a hormone that stimulates a strong emotional connection. As a result, women are more emotionally integrated when it comes to sex. That's why casual sex and hookups often backfire for lots of women. Guys produce little to no oxytocin, and can easily have sex without any sense of emotional connection. It's sex with no emotional strings attached."*

3. One of the inherent problems in FWBRs is the ambiguity partners can feel about what they can expect. Euphoria posted this to the sex forum on Women's-Health.com:

   > *"We have a very good relationship as friends; we're very close. We've been 'talking' since November, and one night I slept over his house and it just happened. The thing that bothers me is that he didn't kiss me in the morning and didn't talk to me until the next night. And on New Year's Eve I also slept over [at] his house, along with other people, and I was probably setting myself up for it cause it happened again. I had left early that morning, around eight, and my friend had told me later on that day that he came into the room she was sleeping in and practically woke her up to kiss her. We did agree to be friends with benefits, but I meant that I'm the only one he should [be] doing it with. Should I say something to him, or do I have no right since we're FWB?"*

4. During my research, I came upon an article by Marilyn Murphey on the Askmen.com website that talked about the pros and cons of FWBRs.

   a. Seventy-five percent of the 139 posts responding to the article talked about how a FWBR produced problems.

   b. These problems stemmed from one partner wanting the relationship to evolve into something more serious.

5. But *no*, Harry wasn't right in one sense—both men and women in a FWBR were ultimately more committed to the friendship than to the sexual aspect of the relationship (Lehmiller et al., 2010).

D. Although not all dating relationships lead to "happily ever after," successful dating leads to more satisfactory relationships in terms of intimacy and safe sexual fulfillment.

1. Dating is the preferred type of relationship for both men and women (Glenn & Marquardt, 2001).

   a. In a national survey of over 1,000 college women published in 2001, 83 percent agreed with the statement "Being married is very important to me."

   b. And 63 percent agreed with the statement "I would like to meet my future husband/wife in college."

   c. Yet 50 percent of the women sampled had had fewer than two dates since starting college.

   d. A 2010 study found that 87 percent of women and 64 percent of men indicated a preference for dating over hooking up, particularly when they might be interested in a long-term relationship (Bradshaw et al., 2010).

2. As "Bad Reputation" put it in his online post, "There are girls you date and girls you have sex with." So I ask you, ladies: Who do you want to be?

CONCLUSION

I. Based on analysis, I'm sure you can see that dating, while scary and angst-ridden, is still superior to hooking up or having a FWBR.

II. Both hookups and FWBRs have more physical and psychological risks than dating relationships.

III. So, before you go out this weekend get smashed and find yourself looking for love in all the wrong places, consider giving that someone you've had your eye on a call and see if you can make a date for a movie, or concert, or just a cup of coffee. While it might not lead to a romantic relationship, who knows—it just might.

Thesis statement

Main point summary

Clincher

REFERENCES

Bisson, M. A., & Levine, T. R. (2007). Negotiating a friends with benefits relationship. *Archives of Sexual Behavior, 38*, 66–73.

Carroll, J. L., Volk, K. D., & Hyde, J. S. (1985). Differences between males and females in motives for engaging in sexual intercourse. *Archives of Sexual Behavior, 14*, 131–139.

Cohen, E. (2010). "The downside of friends with benefits." *CNN.com.* Accessed at http://www.cnn.com/2010/HEALTH/04/15/friends.benefits.stds/index.html

Downing-Maltibag, T. M., & Geisinger, B. (2009). Hooking up and sexual risk taking among college students: A health belief model perspective. *Qualitative Health Research, 19*, 1196–1204.

Glenn, N., & Marquardt, E. (2001). *Hooking up, hanging out, and hoping for Mr. Right: College women on dating and mating today.* A report conducted by the Institute for American Values for the Independent Women's Forum.

Grello, C. M., Welsh, D. P., & Harper, M. S. (2006). No strings attached: The nature of casual sex in college students. *The Journal of Sex Research, 43*, 255–267.

Hughes, M., Morrison, K., & Asada, K. J. K. (2005). What's love got to do with it? Exploring the impact of maintenance rules, love attitudes, and network support on friends-with-benefits relationships. *Western Journal of Communication, 69*(1), 49–66.

Kerner, I. (2007). "The biggest sex mistakes that men and women make." *The Today Show, September 27, 2007.* Accessed at http://www.today.msnbc.msn.com/id/20955254/ns/today-today_relationships//

Larson, J. H., & Holmes, T. B. (1994). Premarital predictors of marital quality and stability. *Family Relations, 43*, 228–237. Accessed at http://www.jstor.org/stable/585327

Lehmiller, J. J., VanderDrift, L. E. & Kelly, J. R. (2010). Sex differences in approaching friends-with-benefits relationships. *Journal of Sex Research*, doi:10.1080/00224491003721694

Monroe, S. M., Rohde, P., Seeley, J. R., Lewinsohn, P. M. (Nov 1999). Life events and depression in adolescence: Relationship loss as a prospective risk factor for first onset of major depressive disorder. *Journal of Abnormal Psychology*, Vol 108(4), 606–614.

Morr, M., C., & Mongeau, P. A. (2004). First-date expectations: The impact of sex of initiator, alcohol consumption, and relationship type. *Communication Research, 31*(1), 3–35.

Murphy, M. (2009). "The pro's and con's of casual sex between friends." *Askmen.Com.* Accessed at http://www.askmen.com/includes/components/posts/postPage.php?id=910517&p=3

No name. (Nov 1, 2009). "I'm pregnant, but it was only a hookup. Should I tell him?" *Yahoo! Answers.* Accessed at http://answers.yahoo.com/questions/index?qid=20091101094838AAnz4l1

Owen, J., & Fincham, F. D. (2011). The effects of gender and psychosocial factors on "friends with benefits" relationships among young adults. *Archives of Sexual Behavior, 40*, 311–320.

Owen, J. J., Stanley, S. M., & Fincham, F. D. (2010). "Hooking up" among college students: Demographic and psychosocial correlates. *Archives of Sexual Behavior, 39*, 653–663.

Paul, E. L., McManus, B., & Hayes, A. (2000). "Hookups": Characteristics and correlates of college students' spontaneous and anonymous sexual experiences. *Journal of Sex Research, 37*, 76–88.

Paul, E. L., & Hayes, K. A. (2002). The casualties of "casual" sex: A qualitative exploration of the phenomenology of college students' hookups. *Journal of Social and Personal Relationships, 19*, 639–660.

Sprecher, S., Barbee, A., & Schwartz, P. (1995). "Was it good for you too?": Gender differences in first intercourse experiences. *The Journal of Sex Research, 32*(1), 3–15.

Stafford, L. (2008). Dating relationships. In Wolfgang Donsbach (Ed.), *The international encyclopedia of communication* (Vol. 3, pp. 1167–1171). Malden, MA: Blackwell Publishing Ltd.

_____. (2010). "Chalmydia CDC Fact Sheet." U.S. Department of Health and Human Services Center for Disease Control. Accessed at http://www.cdc.gov/std/chlamydia/stdfact-chlamydia.htm

_____. (2008). "Gonorrhea CDC Fact Sheet." U.S. Department of Health and Human Services Center for Disease Control. Accessed at: http://www.cdc.gov/std/Gonorrhea/STDFact-gonorrhea.htm

Surra, C. A., Boettcher-Burke, T. M. J., Cottle, N. R., West, A. R., & Gray, C. R. (2007). The treatment of relationship status in research on dating and mate selection. *Journal of Marriage and Family, 69*, 207–221.

Winslow, R. W., Franzini, L. R., & Hwang, J. (1992). Perceived peer norms, casual sex, and AIDS risk prevention. *Journal of Applied Social Psychology, 22* (24), 1559–1816.

" speech and analysis "

The Speech

"Well you know, they travel in threes, and she was not the hot one but she wasn't the fat one either. And it was late, and if I wanted to get laid the choices were getting slim, so—"

"We were at this party, and I was dancing with this really hot guy. One thing led to another, and I thought, what the heck. He's so hot."

"Josh and I have known each other since grade school, and I've always kind of had a thing for him. Neither one of us was seeing anyone, and one night we were out with friends and dancing, and one thing led to another and we became, you know, 'friends with benefits.' But now I'm really hooked on him and he doesn't know it, and he's started to see someone who he thinks is special. But he wants to keep up our arrangement too because she won't sleep with him."

"I met this really cool girl in my biology class. She's really pretty and smart, and she seems to have a good sense of humor. So I broke the code and asked her out. We took a walk in the park, had dinner, and then went back to her place, and believe it or not, we just talked. It was so weird, but I really enjoyed it. So we've made plans to go to the movies on Saturday. So I won't be going out trolling for a bad girl this weekend. Who knows—I may be out of the action for a while. We'll see."

We have all known someone who has engaged in the above-mentioned scenarios. Which of these scenarios appeals most to you? If you had your choice of hooking up with a stranger, having sex with a friend, or going out with someone you found interesting and attractive, what would you prefer?

Analysis

Molly uses four hypothetical scenarios to grab her audience's attention. Doing so is particularly effective because they are scenarios that most of her classmates can probably relate to.

Here Molly establishes listener relevance by asking a series of rhetorical questions, which engages her audience from the outset.

As a member of what some call "the hookup generation," I have first-hand knowledge and some experience with the current hookup culture that is so popular on college campuses today. So I was curious about what the research says about these practices, and what I discovered might surprise you as much as it surprised me.

Today I'm here to convince you that hooking up and friends-with-benefits relationships (FWBRs) are poor substitutes for dating relationships. I will show why dating is the best choice by defining each relationship type and then comparing the physical risks, psychological costs, and feelings of relationship satisfaction among them.

Let's begin by defining each of these three types of relationships. I'm sure we have all known someone who hooked up and was disappointed when they didn't get a phone call the next day, and someone whose FWBR ended with no benefits and the loss of a friend. And I'm sure we have known friends who grieved the loss of what they thought was a solid dating relationship. Therefore, before we can examine the associated risks, we must begin by defining what a hookup actually is.

According to Paul, McManus, and Hayes in their 2000 article "'Hookups': Characteristics and correlates of college students' spontaneous and anonymous sexual experiences," published in the *Journal of Sex Research*, "Hookups are defined as a sexual encounter which may or may not include sexual intercourse, usually occurring on only one occasion between two people who are strangers or brief acquaintances." Winslow, Franzini, and Hwang explain further in their article published in the *Journal of Applied Social Psychology* that these casual sexual encounters are essentially spontaneous sex between partners who barely had contact with each other before engaging in the sexual act. The exact nature of the sexual behavior involved during a hookup is somewhat ambiguous and may vary from heavy kissing to intercourse. Not only is the behavior ambiguous, but according to their article published in a 2001 issue of the *Archives of Sexual Behavior*, Owen and Fincham explain that those involved may have different goals and expectations regarding future encounters. Even so, as many as 50 to 75% of young adults today have hooked up.

Now that we understand the nature of a hookup, what exactly is a friends-with-benefits relationship (FWBR)? Lehmiller, VanderDrift, and Kelly, in their article "Sex differences in approaching friends-with-benefits relationships," published in a 2010 issue of the *Journal of Sex Research*, explored the nature of a FWBR as platonic friendships where partners engage in sexual behaviors ranging from kissing to sexual intercourse. The authors found FWBRs can include numerous degrees on the intimacy spectrum, ranging from good friends who engage in sexual activity to individuals who engage in serial hookups but have little to no interaction beyond the hookup.

Despite the type of FWBR, Hughes, Morrison, and Asada reported in their article "What's love got to do with it?" published in a 2005 issue of the *Western Journal of Communication*, individuals usually enter into a FWBR with no intention of it evolving into a romantic one. Sometimes one partner in a FWBR becomes interested in taking the relationship further. However, these feelings aren't always mutual. Some of you might have watched the movie *Friends with Benefits*. In the movie, Justin Timberlake and Mila Kunis began as friends, moved into a FWBR, and ended up together at the end. Unfortunately, according to Owen and Fincham's 2011 article in the *Archives of Sexual Behavior*, FWBRs rarely have this fairy-tale ending in real life.

Now that we understand the nature of hookups and FWBRs, we need to define dating relationships. In dating relationships, individuals spend time getting to know each other and enter into a sexual relationship if and when both partners feel a sense of relational intimacy. In dating relationships, both people share more intimate thoughts and feelings with each other as trust builds. In her 2008 reference in the *International Encyclopedia of Communication*, Stafford explains that relational success is more likely when

---

Molly establishes credibility by pointing out her personal experience with the topic as part of the "hookup generation" and that she was surprised at what she learned from the research.

We clearly understand what Molly's proposition is and how she will organize her arguments to convince us to agree with her about this issue.

Molly realizes that she can't succeed with her goal unless she knows that her listeners understand the nature of the different types of relationships she's discussing. So she makes this subject her first main point.

Molly bolsters her ethos by using an oral citation. Doing so enhances her credibility, telling the audience that she is informed as well as ethical.

Molly does a nice job of using a rhetorical question to verbally tie the point she has finished talking about to the point she is introducing.

Although Molly cites a number of reputable sources for this point, she could improve by integrating a variety of types of evidence, perhaps a testimonial or a personal story.

Molly could improve by offering some kind of warrant to support this claim.

Again, Molly offers a transition that verbally ties her main points together. She also uses inclusive language when she says "we" rather than "I".

Molly could improve by elaborating on this "dating" main point. Perhaps she assumed her listeners already know what a dating relationship is.

partners know each other and date for an extended period before marriage and engage in positive communication.

Now that we've established a common set of definitions, let's compare these relationships according to how they affect physical health, psychological health, and relationship satisfaction. Let's begin by exploring the physical risks associated with hookups, FWBRs, and dating relationships. Since most of us in this room are not married, we ought to understand the physical risks involved in engaging in these different types of relationships.

Hookups and FWBRs increase the risk of catching an STD because partners often fail to practice safe sex. The old saying that when you have sex with someone, you also have sex with everyone they have ever had sex with is true. Listen to the testimony of someone suffering from PID (pelvic inflammatory disease), a bacterial infection of the uterus, fallopian tubes, and ovaries. PID is most frequently caused by gonorrhea and chlamydia, two common STDs that can be devastating. Listen to one sufferer's story:

I have suffered with pelvic inflammatory disease now for fifteen years. I have in the last three years had a full hysterectomy and now suffer worse pain than ever and have severe adhesions and chronic pain. My life is ruined. My PID was silent but deadly—one day no pain; next day I was crippled. PID is a horrible disease—and you don't have to be promiscuous to get it. Just sleeping with someone you don't know and whose sexual past is unknown can put you in jeopardy of this disease.

Molly's decision to include a personal testimonial appeals to the feelings of listeners via a rhetorical appeal to pathos.

In their article "Hooking up and sexual risk taking among college students: A health belief model perspective," published in a 2009 issue of the *Qualitative Health Research Journal*, Downing-Maltibag and Geisinger also discovered numerous risks associated with hooking up. Specifically, students who did not use protection often trusted that their hookup partners were STD-free based on appearance or informal character assessments. They also tended to rationalize that because there were low rates of HIV/AIDS in the region where they lived, they did not have to protect themselves against it.

Ironically, people aren't any safer in FWBRs. In fact, according to an article published in *Communication Research* by Morr and Mongeau in 2004, people actually report being more careful when engaging in sexual intercourse with unknown or lesser known individuals than with people they already know. Just because you know someone as a "friend" does not mean you know what they are doing sexually. FWBRs, by their very nature, are not meant to be exclusive, so while you're sleeping with your friend, he or she may also have other partners who, by association, you are also sleeping with. And even if you are both monogamous during your relationship, unless you are both tested prior to having sex, you are still at risk. In hookups and in FWBRs, the emphasis is on each partner's personal needs for sex and physical satisfaction, so the partner is an "insignificant other."

Some of Molly's listeners might find this fact startling, which will keep their interest focused on learning more.

Because partners involved in hookups and FWBRs are less likely to practice safe sex, the likelihood of an unplanned pregnancy also increases. Listen to the experience of a woman who posted her story on Yahoo! Answers:

I was with this guy for a very short time. It pretty much ended up being a one-night stand, even though we texted a little afterwards. When I found out I was pregnant, I decided to tell him, especially since I didn't know what I was going to do yet. But whatever I was going to do was part of his responsibility (i.e., bills for an abortion, child support, or choosing of an adoptive family). When I told him, he just begged me to get an abortion over and over until I finally agreed and told him I had gotten the abortion to get him to stop texting me every five seconds and begging while I could get some quiet time to figure out what I really wanted to do.

Molly again uses personal testimony to appeal to pathos in her speech.

Notice, guys, it was what *she* wanted to do. A man who fathers a hookup child is legally responsible for supporting that child until it is an adult. You have no say—it is her body and her decision. So, in addition to your college loans, you

Offering this listener relevance link helps males in Molly's audience see how the story of one person's pregnancy relates to them as well.

may have a significant financial responsibility for the next eighteen years. And every time you get a raise, your child gets part of it. It's the risk you take. And if you're morally or religiously opposed to abortion? Tough. Her body, her decision. You can try to change her mind. But if she decides on abortion there is nothing you can do. And remember, even when condoms are used, they are only 95 percent effective as a contraceptive. Think about it.

While unintended pregnancy is a risk in any sexual relationship, it stands to reason that people who are dating—who have built some degree of respect and intimacy—are more likely to be equipped to come to a mutual understanding about the woman's choice and to adjust to co-parenting tasks, even if they choose to end their romantic relationship.

While physical risks are inherent in any sexual relationship, dating is physically healthier than either hooking up or engaging in a FWBR. Not only do hookups and FWBRs put you at more risk physically, but they are also more likely to do psychological damage. Both hooking up and FWB create psychological distress.

How many of you know someone who says they feel more confident and have higher self-esteem following a hookup? After sleeping with their best friend? Not many, right? More often, we listen to our friends express feelings guilt, shame, and embarrassment. People, it's called a "walk of shame" for a reason. People who hook up have lower self-esteem, as well as greater depression and feelings of guilt than those who don't. In their 2006 article "No strings attached: The nature of casual sex in college students," published in *The Journal of Sex Research*, Grello, Welsh, and Harper report that women who engage in hooking up experience more loss of self-esteem and depression than men—it is not clear whether depression leads to casual sexual behavior or casual sexual behavior leads to depression. Not only that, women who engage in casual sex express feelings of good old-fashioned guilt. Men, however, don't necessarily feel guilty for hooking up with strangers, but do feel guilty if they get drunk and hook up with a friend.

While breaking up a dating relationship can also lead to depression, research has found that while the first breakup of a first dating relationship can lead to depression, subsequent breakups are unlikely to do so. The first act of breaking up seems to "inoculate" us, probably because we figure that there is life after a breakup. The opposite seems to be true in more casual sexual relationships. The more you do it, the more guilty and depressed you become. Because of the many negative physical and psychological consequences of hooking up and friends-with-benefits relationships, dating tends to produce more satisfying relationships in the end.

Finally, hooking up and FWBRs lead to less satisfying relationships than dating. In a hookup, ideally neither partner wants or expects anything other than sexual satisfaction. Did you know that, according to that 2006 article by Grello, Welsh, and Harper, half of all college students who engage in sexual intercourse during a hook up never see the other person again? Not only that, 18 percent of women reported in that same study that they consider a hookup to be a stepping-stone toward developing a romantic relationship.

In the ideal FWBR, two friends simply become "sex" buddies without damaging the friendship. But, according to that famous philosopher, Harry Burns in the 1989 movie *When Harry Met Sally*, "Men and women can never be friends because the sex part always gets in the way." Was Harry wrong? Well, as it turns out, yes and no.

In their 2010 study published in the *Journal of Sex Research*, Lehmiller and his colleagues found yes, and I quote:

Sex was a more common motivation for men to FWB relationships, whereas emotional connection was a more common motivation for women. In addition, men were more likely to hope that the relationship stays the same over time, whereas women expressed more desire for change into either a full-fledged romance or a basic friendship.

One thing Molly does extremely well throughout her speech is provide transitions. With each transition, she uses inclusive "we" language, which enhances a conversational style and helps listeners easily follow along.

Again, Molly uses rhetorical questions in her listener relevance link to keep listeners focused on how this message is important to them.

Here Molly failed to offer an oral citation for the Sprecher research. She missed an opportunity here to bolster her ethos, and she violated the ethic of honesty because failing to cite a source is considered plagiarism.

Citing a quotation from popular culture—in this case the movie When Harry Met Sally— can be an effective strategy for maintaining listener attention, particularly when giving a heavy speech like this one.

Molly's speech tends to rely heavily on academic journal articles. Doing so is fine, but interjecting a few contemporary sources like this one keeps the speech from becoming too academic at the expense of intelligibility and conversationality.

This is understandable when you consider the biology of sex. According to sex therapist Dr. Ian Kerner, speaking on the Today Show in 2007:

During sex, women produce lots of oxytocin, a hormone that stimulates a strong emotional connection. As a result, women are more emotionally integrated when it comes to sex. That's why casual sex and hookups often backfire for lots of women. Guys produce little to no oxytocin, and can easily have sex without any sense of emotional connection. It's sex with no emotional strings attached.

One of the inherent problems in FWBRs is the ambiguity partners can feel about what they can expect. Euphoria posted this to the sex forum on Women's-Health.com:

We have a very good relationship as friends; we're very close. We've been 'talking' since November, and one night I slept over [at] his house and it just happened. The thing that bothers me is that he didn't kiss me in the morning and didn't talk to me until the next night. And on New Year's Eve I also slept over [at] his house, along with other people, and I was probably setting myself up for it cause it happened again. I had left early that morning, around eight, and my friend had told me later on that day that he came into the room she was sleeping in and practically woke her up to kiss her. We did agree to be friends with benefits, but I meant that I'm the only one he should [be] doing it with. Should I say something to him, or do I have no right since we're FWB?

Again, sources like this one—as long as they are only peppered throughout the speech—make it real and potentially more relevant to her audience.

As I was researching this issue, I came upon an article by Marilyn Murphey on the Askmen.com website that talked about the pros and cons of FWBRs. What I found most interesting was that this article had 139 posts reacting to it. And when I analyzed these posts, 75 percent of them talked about how a FWBR that either the poster or a friend of the poster had been in actually produced problems stemming from one partner wanting the relationship to evolve into something more serious.

But no, Harry wasn't right in one sense. Lehmiller, Venderdrift, and Kelly, in their 2010 article in the *Journal of Sex Research*, also unexpectedly found that both men and women were ultimately more committed to the friendship than to the sexual aspect of the relationship.

Molly could have easily left this statement out, because it contradicts the point she is trying to make. However, including it demonstrates the ethic of fairness.

Of course, not all dating relationships lead to "happily ever after" either. However, dating leads to more satisfactory relationships since, if successful, it leads to both intimacy and safe sexual fulfillment. It should come as no surprise that it's the preferred type of relationship of both men and women. In a national survey of over 1,000 college women by Glenn and Marquardt that was published in 2001, 83 percent of them agreed with the statement "Being married is very important to me." And 63 percent agreed with the statement "I would like to meet my future husband/wife in college." Yet 50 percent of the women sampled had had fewer than two dates since starting college. Caroline Bradshaw and her colleagues reported in her 2010 study that 87 percent of women, and even 64 percent of men, indicated a preference for dating over hooking up, particularly when they might be interested in a long-term relationship. As "Bad Reputation" put it in his online post, "There are girls you date and girls you have sex with." So I ask you, ladies, who do you want to be?

This survey of both women and men is particularly compelling because it demonstrates not only that research suggests dating is preferred over hooking up or FWBRs, but also that young people themselves prefer dating for initiating long-term relationships.

Based on analysis, I'm sure you can see that dating, while scary and angst-ridden, is still a better choice than hooking up or having a FWBR. Both hookups and FWBRs have more physical and psychological risks than dating relationships.

So, before you go out this weekend, get smashed, and find yourself looking for love in all the wrong places, consider giving that someone you've had your eye on a call and see if you can make a date for a movie, or concert, or just a cup of coffee. While it might not lead to a romantic relationship, who knows—it just might.

Molly does a nice job of restating her proposition and providing a clincher that ties back nicely to the opening scenarios.

14-3b Speeches to Actuate

Implicit in speeches to actuate is the assumption that there is a problem that audience members can help solve by taking certain actions. As a result, most actuation persuasive speeches follow one of three organizational frameworks: problem-solution, problem-cause-solution, and the motivated sequence.

Problem-Solution

A **problem-solution** pattern explains the nature of a problem and proposes a solution. This pattern is particularly effective when the audience is neutral or agrees that there is a problem but has no opinion about a particular solution. A problem-solution speech usually has three main points. The first examines the problem, the second presents the solution(s), and the third suggests what action the listener should take.

problem-solution: a persuasive organizational pattern that reveals the nature of a problem and proposes a solution to it

To convince the audience that there is a problem, you need to explore the breadth and depth of the issue, as well as provide listener relevance links. You provide breadth by showing the scope or scale of the problem, for example, giving the number of people it affects and proving upward trends over time, including forecasted trends if the problem is not solved. You might provide depth by showing the gravity of the problem. Both breadth and depth may be described through stories and startling statistics. When you describe the solution, you should be detailed enough for the audience to understand how and why it will solve the problem (Photo 14.3). The call to action should provide your audience with specific steps that they ought to take to help implement the solution(s).

A problem-solution organization for Tomeka's speech about the school tax levy proposition might look like this:

Proposition of Policy: We must solve the current fiscal crisis in the school district.

I. *The current funding is insufficient.* (statement of the problem)
   A. *The schools have had to cut programs.*
   B. *Teachers have not had a cost of living raise in five years.*
   C. *The state could take over control.*

II. *The proposed tax levy will address these problems.* (proposed solution)
   A. *The schools will be able to reinstate important programs.*
   B. *Teachers will be afforded raises.*
   C. *The district will be able to maintain control.*

III. *We must do our part to make this happen.* (call to action)
   A. *Vote "yes."*
   B. *Encourage your friends and neighbors to vote "yes."*

problem-cause-solution: a form of persuasive organization that examines a problem, its cause(s), and solutions designed to eliminate or alleviate the underlying cause(s)

Problem-Cause-Solution

A **problem-cause-solution** pattern is similar to a problem-solution pattern but differs from it by adding a main point that reveals the causes of the problem and then proposes a solution designed to alleviate those causes. This pattern is particularly useful for addressing seemingly intractable problems that have been dealt with unsuccessfully in the past as a result of treating symptoms rather than underlying causes. A problem-cause-solution pattern for the school tax levy proposition might look like this:

Photo 14.3 The same speech topic is arranged differently depending on your specific goal stated as a proposition.

Image Source/Cultura RM/Alamy

Proposition of Policy: *We must solve the current fiscal crisis in the school district.*

   I. *The current funding is insufficient.* (statement of the problem)
      A. *The schools have had to cut programs.*
      B. *Teachers have not had a cost of living raise in five years.*
      C. *The state could take over control.*

   II. *We can trace these problems to several key things.* (causes)
      A. *Dwindling government support.*
      B. *Rising costs for operating expenses.*

   III. *The proposed tax levy will address these issues.* (solutions)
      A. *The levy will supplement inadequate government support.*
      B. *The levy will fill the gap in operating expense needs.*

   IV. *We each have a responsibility to make sure the tax levy proposition passes.* (call to action)
      A. *Vote "yes."*
      B. *Encourage your friends and neighbors to vote "yes."*

Motivated Sequence

The **motivated sequence** is an organizational pattern that combines a problem-solution pattern with explicit appeals designed to motivate the audience to act. Allan Monroe articulated the motivated sequence as a distinct speech pattern in the 1930s. In the motivated sequence, the normal introduction, body, and conclusion are unified into a five-step sequence described as follows:

1. **The attention step** is essentially the introduction. It should begin by piquing the audience's curiosity referring to the knowledge and experiences you have that build your credibility. As in any introduction, you will want to clearly identify your goal stated as a proposition and preview the main points of your speech.

2. **The need step** explores the nature of the problem that gives rise to the need for change. In it, you point out the conditions that are unsatisfactory using statistics, examples, and expert opinion to bolster your argument. Then, you describe the implications or ramifications of this problem. What is happening because the condition is allowed to continue? Finally, you allude to how the audience might be instrumental in changing the situation.

3. **The satisfaction step** explains the proposed solution to the problem. In this step, you show, point by point, how what you are proposing will satisfy each of the needs that you articulated in the previous step. If there are other places where your proposal has been tried successfully, you will want to mention these. In addition, you present and refute any objections to the proposal that you can anticipate.

4. **The visualization step** asks the audience to imagine what will happen if your proposal is implemented and is successful. You might also ask the audience to visualize how things will be if your proposal is not adopted. This step draws heavily on rhetorical appeals to pathos.

5. **The action appeal step** is essentially the conclusion. In it, emphasize the specific action(s) you advocate. You also state or restate your own commitment to it and actions taken. You also offer a direct call to action indicating what your listeners are to do and how. Finally, you conclude with a quote, story, or other element that is emotionally compelling.

motivated sequence: a persuasive organization that combines a problem-solution pattern with explicit appeals designed to motivate the audience to act

the attention step: the introduction

the need step: explores the nature of the problem

the satisfaction step: explains the proposed solution to the problem

the visualization step: asks the audience to imagine what will happen if your proposal is implemented and is successful and/or not implemented

the action appeal step: the conclusion

A motivated sequence pattern for the school tax levy proposition might look like this:

Proposition of Policy: We must solve the current fiscal crisis in the school district.

I. **Attention step**
   A. *Comparisons of worldwide test scores in math and science show the United States continues to lose ground.*
   B. *I've made an extensive study of this problem, and today I'm going to tell you how you can help stop this decline.*
   C. *I'll start by describing the problem; then, I will tell you what you should do and why it will help.*

II. **Need step:** *The local schools are underfunded.*
   A. *The current funding is insufficient and has resulted in program cuts.*
   B. *Qualified teachers leave because of stagnant wages.*
   C. *A threatened state takeover of local schools would lead to more bureaucracy and less learning.*

III. **Satisfaction step:** *The proposed local tax levy is large enough to solve these problems.*
   A. *Programs will be restored.*
   B. *Qualified teachers will be compensated so they will stay.*
   C. *We will retain local control.*
   D. *You'll once again have pride in your community.*

IV. **Visualization step:** *Imagine the best, and imagine the worst.*
   A. *What it will be like if we pass the levy. How will you feel?*
   B. *What it will be like if we don't. How will you feel?*

V. **Action appeal step:** *Vote "yes" for the levy in November.*
   A. *If you want to see schools improve and the United States catch up to the rest of the world, vote for the levy.*
   B. *Come join me. I'm registered, I'm ready, I'm voting for the levy.*
   C. *It costs to be the best in the world. Where there is pain, there is gain.*
   D. *They say it takes a village, so you can make a difference.*

SPEECH SNIPPET

Monroe's Motivated Sequence

Daniel decided to arrange his speech to actuate about ending the practice of deep sea oil drilling using the motivated sequence. He did so because he wanted to spend a good deal of time visualizing a positive and negative future to help persuade his listeners to lobby legislators to create and vote for laws to stop the practice.

" speech assignment "

Actuation Persuasive Speech

1. Prepare a five- to seven-minute persuasive speech to actuate. To help you prepare your speech and your outline, go to your MindTap for *Challenge* and complete the Speech-Planning Action Step Activities.

2. As an addendum to the outline, write a persuasive speech adaptation plan in which you describe:
   a. Target audience initial attitude and background knowledge.
   b. Organizational pattern you will use and why.
   c. Arguments you will make to support your proposition (logos).
   d. How you will demonstrate competence, credibility, and good character (ethos).
   e. How you will appeal to emotions (pathos).

 MindTap™

Do this activity with **Speech Builder Express**.

" speech evaluation checklist "

Speech to Actuate Evaluation Checklist

General Criteria

_____ 1. Was the introduction effective in creating interest, involving the audience in the speech, and previewing the main points?

_____ 2. Were section transitions used to help you follow the organization of the main points?

_____ 3. Did the conclusion summarize the thesis and main points in a memorable way?

_____ 4. Was the language appropriate, accurate, clear, and vivid?

_____ 5. Was the speech delivered conversationally, intelligibly, expressively, and convincingly?

Specific Criteria

_____ 1. Was the specific goal clear and phrased as a proposition of policy?

_____ 2. Was the speech organized into an appropriate actuation persuasive speech framework?

      _____ Problem-solution

      _____ Problem-cause-solution

      _____ Motivated sequence

_____ 3. Did the speaker use logos effectively?

      _____ Use strong evidence?

      _____ Use reasoning to link evidence to claims?

      _____ Avoid fallacies?

_____ 4. Did the speaker use ethos effectively?

      _____ Establish expertise?

      _____ Demonstrate trustworthiness?

      _____ Convey goodwill?

_____ 5. Did the speaker use pathos effectively?

      Appeal to negative emotions? If so, check all that were tapped: _____ fear _____ guilt _____ anger _____ shame _____ sadness

      Appeal to positive emotions? If so, check all that were tapped: _____ happiness/joy _____ pride _____ relief _____ hope _____ compassion

_____ 6. Did the speaker offer a compelling call to action?

Based on these criteria, evaluate the speech as (check one):

      _____ excellent _____ good _____ average _____ fair _____ poor

Explain:

 MindTap™

Access this checklist on your MindTap for *Challenge*.

SAMPLE SPEECH

Sample Actuation Persuasive Speech

This section presents a sample speech to actuate given by a student, including an adaptation plan, an outline, and a transcript.

Together, We Can Stop Cyber-Bullying[7]

By Adam Parrish

ADAPTATION PLAN

1. **Target audience initial attitude and background knowledge**: My audience is composed of traditional-aged college students with varying majors and classes. Most are from middle-class backgrounds. The initial attitude about bullying for most will be to agree with me already that it's a bad thing. So I will try to get them to take action. My perception is that my audience knows about cyber-bullying but not the nuances of it.

2. **Organizational pattern**: I will organize my speech using a problem-cause-solution framework because my audience already agrees that bullying is bad but may not know what they can and should do to help stop it.

3. **Arguments (logos)**: I will demonstrate what widespread (breadth) and harmful (depth of effects) cyber-bullying is and why it persists (causes). Once I've convinced my audience, I will propose solutions that must be taken and cite specifically what we must do to help stop this horrible practice.

4. **Building competence, credibility, and good character (ethos)**: I will use credible sources to support my claims and cite them using oral footnotes. I will also offer personal stories to create goodwill.

5. **Creating and maintaining interest (pathos)**: I will involve my audience by appealing to several emotions, including guilt, sadness, relief, hope, and compassion.

Outline

General goal: To persuade

Specific goal: To convince my audience to take action to help stop cyber-bullying.

INTRODUCTION

I. "I'll miss just being around her." "I didn't want to believe it." "It's such a sad thing." These quotes are from the friends and family of 15-year-old Phoebe Prince, who, on January 14, 2010, committed suicide by hanging herself. Why did this senseless act occur? The answer is simple: Phoebe Prince was bullied to death.

II. Many of us know someone who has been bullied in school. Perhaps they were teased in the parking lot or in the locker room. In the past, bullying occurred primarily in and around schools. However, with the advent of new communication technologies such as cell phones with text messaging capability, instant messaging, e-mails, blogs, and social networking sites, bullies can now follow their victims anywhere, even into their own bedrooms. Using electronic communications to tease, harass, threaten, and intimidate another person is called cyber-bullying.

Read the speech adaptation plan, outline, and transcript of a speech given by Adam Parrish in an introductory speaking course. You can access a video clip of Adam's speech through the Chapter 14 resources on MindTap for *Challenge*. You can also use your MindTap to identify some of the strengths of Adam's speech by preparing an evaluation checklist and an analysis. You can then compare your answers with those of the authors.

Attention getter

Listener relevance

III. As a tutor and mentor to young students, I have witnessed cyber-bullying firsthand, and by examining current research, I believe I understand the problem, its causes, and how we can help end cyber-bullying.

IV. Cyber-bullying is a devastating form of abuse that must be confronted and stopped.

V. Today, we will examine the widespread and harmful nature of cyber-bullying, discover how and why it persists, and propose some simple solutions that we must engage in to thwart cyber-bullies and comfort their victims.

Let's begin by tackling the problem head on.

BODY

I. Cyber-bullying is a pervasive and dangerous behavior.

Many of us have read rude, insensitive, or nasty statements posted about us or someone we care about on social networking sites like Twitter and Facebook. Whether or not those comments were actually intended to hurt another person's feelings, they are perfect examples of cyber-bullying.

A. Cyber-bullying takes place all over the world through a wide array of electronic media.

1. According to *Statisticbrain.com*, as of 2012, 52 percent of American middle-school students had experienced instances of cyber-bullying ranging from hurtful comments to threats of physical violence (Statisticbrain.com, 2012).

2. Females are just as likely as males to engage in cyber-bullying, although women are 10 percent more likely to be victimized (Li, 2007).

3. A 2011 study reported in the journal *Pediatrics* noted that instances of bullying via text messages have risen significantly since 2006 (Ybarra, Mitchell, & Korchmaros, 2011).

4. Quing Li (2007), a researcher of computer-mediated communication, noted that Internet and cell-phone technologies have been used by bullies to harass, torment, and threaten young people in North America, Europe, and Asia.

5. A particularly disturbing incident occurred in Dallas, Texas, where an overweight student with multiple sclerosis was targeted on a school's social networking page. One message read, "I guess I'll have to wait until you kill yourself, which I hope is not long from now, or I'll have to wait until your disease kills you" (Keith & Martin, 2005, p. 226).

Clearly, cyber-bullying is a widespread problem. What is most disturbing about cyber-bullying, however, is its effects upon victims, bystanders, and perhaps even upon the bullies themselves.

B. Cyber-bullying can lead to traumatic physical psychological injuries upon its victims.

1. According to a 2007 article in the *Journal of Adolescent Health*, 36 percent of the victims of cyber-bullies are also harassed by their attackers in school (Ybarra, Diener-West, & Leaf, 2007).

2. For example, the Dallas student with MS had eggs thrown at her car and a bottle of acid thrown at her house (Keith & Martin, 2005).

3. Ybarra et al. (2007) reported that victims of cyber-bullying experience such severe emotional distress that they often exhibit behavioral problems such as poor grades, skipping school, and receiving detentions and suspensions.

4. Smith et al. (2008) suggested that even a few instances of cyber-bullying can have these long-lasting and heartbreaking results.

5. What is even more alarming is that victims of cyber-bullying are significantly more likely to carry weapons to school as a result of feeling threatened (Ybarra et al., 2007). Obviously, this could lead to violent, and perhaps even deadly, outcomes for bullies, victims, and even bystanders.

Now that we realize the devastating nature, scope, and effects of cyber-bullying, let's look at its causes.

Transition

II. Cyber-bullying is perpetuated because victims and bystanders do not report their abusers to authorities.

The cause

Think back to a time when you may have seen a friend or loved one being harassed online. Did you report the bully to the network administrator or other authorities? Did you console the victim? I know I didn't. If you are like me, we may unknowingly be enabling future instances of cyber-bullying.

Listener relevance

A. Cyber-bullies are cowards who attack their victims anonymously.
   1. Ybarra et al. (2007) discovered that 13 percent of cyber-bullying victims did not know who was tormenting them.
   2. This is an important statistic because, as Keith and Martin (2005) point out, traditional bullying takes place face to face and often ends when students leave school. However, today, students are subjected to bullying in their own homes.
   3. Perhaps the anonymous nature of cyber-attacks partially explains why Li (2007) found that nearly 76 percent of victims of cyber-bullying and 75 percent of bystanders never reported instances of bullying to adults.

B. Victims and bystanders who do not report attacks from cyber-bullies can unintentionally enable bullies.
   1. According to De Nies, Donaldson, and Netter of *ABCNews.com* (2010) several of Phoebe Prince's classmates were aware that she was being harassed but did not inform the school's administration.
   2. Li (2007) suggested that victims and bystanders often do not believe that adults will actually intervene to stop cyber-bullying.
   3. However, *ABCNews.com* (2010) reports that 41 states have laws against bullying in schools, and 23 of those states target cyber-bullying specifically.

Now that we realize that victims of cyber-bullies desperately need the help of witnesses and bystanders to report their attacks, we should arm ourselves with the information necessary to provide that assistance.

Transition

III. Cyber-bullying must be confronted on national, local, and personal levels.

The solution

Think about the next time you see a friend or loved one being tormented or harassed online. What would you be willing to do to help?

Listener relevance

A. There should be a comprehensive national law confronting cyber-bullying in schools. Certain statutes currently in state laws should be amalgamated to create the strongest protections for victims and the most effective punishments for bullies as possible.
   1. According to Limber and Small's (2003) article titled *State Laws and Policies to Address Bullying in Schools*, Georgia law requires faculty and staff to be trained on the nature of bullying and what actions to take if they see students being bullied.
   2. Furthermore, Connecticut law *requires* school employees to report bullying as part of their hiring contract (Limber & Small, 2003). Washington takes this a step further by protecting employees from

any legal action if a reported bully is proven to be innocent (Limber & Small, 2003).

3. When it comes to protecting victims, West Virginia law demands that schools must ensure that a bullied student does not receive additional abuse at the hands of his or her bully (Limber & Small, 2003).

4. Legislating punishment for bullies is difficult. As Limber and Small (2003) noted, zero-tolerance polices often perpetuate violence because at-risk youth (bullies) are removed from all of the benefits of school, which might help make them less abusive.

5. A comprehensive anti-cyber-bullying law should incorporate the best aspects of these state laws and find a way to punish bullies that is both punitive and has the ability to rehabilitate abusers.

B. Local communities must organize and mobilize to attack the problem of cyber-bullying.

1. According to Greene (2006), communities need to support bullying prevention programs by conducting a school-based bullying survey for individual school districts. We can't know how to best protect victims in our community without knowing how they are affected by the problem.

2. It is critical to know this information. As Greene noted, only 3 percent of teachers in the United States perceive bullying to be a problem in their schools (Greene, 2006).

3. Local school districts should create a Coordinating Committee made up of "administrators, teachers, students, parents, school staff, and community partners" to gather bullying data and rally support to confront the problem (Greene, 2006, p. 73).

4. Even if your local school district is unable or unwilling to mobilize behind this dire cause, there are some important actions you can take personally to safeguard those you love against cyber-bullying.

C. Take note of these warning signs that might indicate a friend or loved one is a victim of a cyber-bully.

1. Victims of cyber-bullies often use electronic communication more frequently than do people who are not being bullied.

2. Victims of cyber-bullies have mood swings and difficulty sleeping (Keith & Martin, 2005).

3. Victims of cyber-bullies seem depressed and/or become anxious (Keith & Martin, 2005).

4. Victims of cyber-bullies become withdrawn from social activities and fall behind in scholastic responsibilities (Keith & Martin, 2005).

D. If you see a friend or loved one exhibiting any of these signs, I implore you not to ignore them. Rather take action. Get involved. Do something to stop it.

1. According to Raskauskas and Stoltz (2007), witnesses of cyber-bullying should inform victims to take the attacks seriously, especially if the bullies threaten violence.

2. Tell victims to report their attacks to police or other authority figures (Raskauskas & Stoltz, 2007).

3. Tell victims to block harmful messages by blocking e-mail accounts and cell phone numbers (Raskauskas & Stoltz, 2007).

4. Tell victims to save copies of attacks and provide them to authorities (Raskauskas & Stoltz, 2007).

5. If you personally know the bully and feel safe confronting him or her, do so! As Raskauskas and Stoltz (2007) noted, bullies will often back down when confronted by peers.

6. By being a good friend and by giving good advice, you can help a victim report his or her attacks from cyber-bullies and take a major step toward eliminating this horrendous problem.

So, you see, we are not helpless to stop the cyber-bullying problem as long as we make the choice NOT to ignore it.

Transition

CONCLUSION

I. Cyber-bullying is a devastating form of abuse that must be reported to authorities.

Thesis statement

II. Cyber-bullying is a worldwide problem perpetuated by the silence of both victims and bystanders. By paying attention to certain warning signs, we can empower ourselves to console victims and report their abusers.

Main point summary

III. Today, I implore you to do your part to help stop cyber-bullying. I know that you agree that stopping cyber-bullying must be a priority. First, although other states have cyber-bullying laws in place, ours does not. So I'm asking you to sign this petition that I will forward to our district's state legislators. We need to make our voices heard that we want specific laws passed to stop this horrific practice and to punish those caught doing it. Second, I'm also asking you to be vigilant in noticing signs of cyber-bullying and then taking action. Look for signs that your friend, brother, sister, cousin, boyfriend, girlfriend, or loved one might be a victim of cyber-bullying and then get involved to help stop it! Phoebe Prince showed the warning signs, and she did not deserve to die so senselessly. None of us would ever want to say, "I'll miss just being around her," "I didn't want to believe it," "It's such a sad thing" about our own friends or family members. We must work to ensure that victims are supported and bullies are confronted nationally, locally, and personally. I know that, if we stand together and refuse to be silent, we can and will stop cyber-bullying.

Call to action and clincher

REFERENCES

Cyber-Bullying Statistics (2012). Retrieved from http://www.statisticbrain.com/cyber-bullying-statistics/

De Nies, Y., Donaldson, S., & Netter, S. (2010, January 28). Mean girls: Cyberbullying blamed for teen suicides. *ABCNews.com*. Retrieved from http://abcnews.go.com/GMA/Parenting/girls-teen-suicide-calls-attention-cyberbullying/story?id = 9685026

Greene, M. B. (2006). Bullying in schools: A plea for measure of human rights. *Journal of Social Issues, 62*(1), 63–79.

Keith, S., & Martin, M. (2005). Cyber-bullying: Creating a culture of respect in the cyber world. *Reclaiming Children and Youth, 13*(4), 224–228.

Li, Q. (2007). New bottle of old wine: A research of cyberbullying in schools. *Computers in Human Behavior, 23,* 1777–1791.

Limber, S. P., & Small, M. A. (2003). State laws and policies to address bullying in schools. *School Psychology Review, 32*(3), 445–455.

Raskauskas, J., & Stoltz, A. D. (2007). Involvement in traditional and electronic bullying among adolescents. *Developmental Psychology, 43*(3), 564–575.

Smith, P. K., Mahdavi, J., Carvalho, M., Fisher, S. Russel, S., & Tippett, N. (2008). Cyberbullying: Its nature and impact in secondary school pupils. *Journal of Child Psychology and Psychiatry, 49*(4), 374–385.

Ybarra, M. L., Diener-West, M., & Leaf, P. J. (2007). Examining the overlap in internet harassment and school bullying: Implications for school intervention. *Journal of Adolescent Health, 41,* S42–S50.

Ybarra, M. L., Mitchell, K. J., Wolak, J., & Finkelhor, D. (2006). Examining characteristics and associated distress related to Internet harassment: Findings from the second Youth Internet Safety Survey. *Pediatrics, 118,* 1169–1177.

Ybarra, M. L., Mitchell, K. M., & Korchmaros, J. D. (2011). National trends in exposure to and experiences of violence on the Internet among children. *Pediatrics,* Retrieved from http://pediatrics.aappublications.org/content/early/2011/11/16/peds.2011-0118. full.pdf+html

" speech and analysis "

The Speech

"I'll miss just being around her." "I didn't want to believe it." "It's such a sad thing." These quotes are from the friends and family of 15-year-old Phoebe Prince, who, on January 14, 2010, committed suicide by hanging herself. Why did this senseless act occur? The answer is simple . . . Phoebe Prince was bullied to death.

Many of us know someone who has been bullied in school. Perhaps they were teased in the parking lot or in the locker room. In the past, bullying occurred primarily in school. However, with the advent of new communication technologies such as cell phones, text messaging, instant messaging, blogs, and social networking sites, bullies can now follow and terrorize their victims anywhere, even into their own bedrooms. Using electronic communications to tease, harass, threaten, and intimidate another person is called cyber-bullying.

As a tutor and mentor to young students, I have witnessed cyber-bullying firsthand, and by examining current research, I believe I understand the problem, its causes, and how we can help end cyber-bullying. What I know for sure is that cyber-bullying is a devastating form of abuse that must be confronted on national, local, and personal levels.

Today, we will examine the widespread and harmful nature of cyber-bullying, uncover how and why it persists, and pinpoint some simple solutions we must begin to enact in order to thwart cyber-bullies and comfort their victims. Let's begin by tackling the problem head on.

Many of us have read rude, insensitive, or nasty statements posted about us or someone we care about on social networking sites like Twitter and Facebook. Well, whether or not those comments were actually intended to hurt another person's feelings, if they did hurt their feelings, then they are perfect examples of cyber-bullying.

Cyber-bullying is a pervasive and dangerous behavior. It takes place all over the world and through a wide array of electronic media. According to *Statisticbrain.com,* as of 2012, 52 percent of American middle-school students had experienced instances of cyber-bullying ranging from hurtful comments to threats of physical violence. Quing Li's article published in the journal *Computers in Human Behavior* noted that cyber-bullying is not gender biased. According to Li, females are just as likely as males to engage in cyber-bullying, although women are 10 percent more likely to be victimized.

A 2011 study reported in the journal *Pediatrics* noted that instances of bullying via text messages have risen significantly since 2006. The problem does not exist in the United States alone.

Li noted that Internet and cell-phone technologies have been used by bullies to harass, torment, and threaten young people in North America, Europe, and Asia. However, some of the most horrific attacks happen right here at home.

Analysis

Adam uses quotes from family and friends of cyber-bullying victim Phoebe Prince to get attention and lead into his proposition.

Here Adam further entices his listeners to pay attention by offering listener relevance that we all can relate to.

Using the vivid term "terrorize," Adam appeals to negative emotions (pathos).

Adam begins to establish ethos by mentioning why he has credibility about this topic. Mentioning that he is a tutor and mentor also conveys goodwill. Listeners are likely to think he must have good character if he volunteers as a tutor and mentor.

Adam does a nice job of previewing his problem-cause-solution organizational framework, but his thesis statement phrased as a proposition is somewhat lost and could be made more overtly here.

Again, Adam's use of a listener relevance helps keep listeners tuned in and interested in hearing more.

Here Adam bolsters his ethos (and avoids plagiarism) by citing an oral footnote for his statistics.

Notice Adam's word choices (harass, torment, threaten, horrific) to enhance pathos.

According to Keith and Martin, a particularly disturbing incident occurred in Dallas, Texas, where an overweight student with multiple sclerosis was targeted on a school's social networking page. One message read, "I guess I'll have to wait until you kill yourself which I hope is not long from now, or I'll have to wait until your disease kills you." Clearly, the cyber-bullying is a worldwide and perverse phenomenon. What is most disturbing about cyber-bullying is its effects upon victims, bystanders, and perhaps even upon bullies themselves.

Cyber-bullying can lead to physical and psychological injuries upon its victims. According to a 2007 article in the *Journal of Adolescent Health,* Ybarra and colleagues noted that 36 percent of the victims of cyber-bullies are also harassed by their attackers in school. For example, the Dallas student with MS had eggs thrown at her car and a bottle of acid thrown at her house.

Ybarra et al. reported that victims of cyber-bullying experience such severe emotional distress that they often exhibit behavioral problems such as poor grades, skipping school, and receiving detentions and suspensions. Furthermore, Smith et al. suggested that even a few instances of cyber-bullying can have these long-lasting negative effects.

What is even more alarming is that, according to Ybarra and colleagues, victims of cyber-bullying are significantly more likely to carry weapons to school as a result of feeling threatened. Obviously, this could lead to violent outcomes for bullies, victims, and even bystanders.

Now that we have heard about the nature, scope, and effects of cyber-bullying, let's see if we can discover its causes. Let's think back to a time when we may have seen a friend or loved one being harassed online. Did we report the bully to the network administrator or other authorities? Did we console the victim? I know I didn't. If you are like me, we may unknowingly be enabling future instances of cyber-bullying.

Cyber-bullying occurs because of the anonymity offered to bullies by cell phone and Internet technologies, as well as the failure of victims and bystanders to report incidents of cyber-bullying. You see, unlike schoolyard bullies, cyber-bullies can attack their victims anonymously.

Ybarra and colleagues discovered that 13 percent of cyber-bullying victims did not know who was tormenting them. This devastating statistic is important because, as Keith and Martin noted, traditional bullying takes place face to face and often ends when students leave school. However, today, students are subjected to nonstop bullying, even when they are alone in their own homes.

Perhaps the anonymous nature of cyber-attacks partially explains why Li found that nearly 76 percent of victims of cyber-bullying and 75 percent of bystanders never reported instances of bullying to adults. Victims and bystanders who do not report attacks from cyber-bullies can unintentionally enable bullies.

According to De Nies, Donaldson, and Netter of *ABCNews.com* (2010), several of Phoebe Prince's classmates were aware that she was being harassed but did not inform the school's administration. Li suggested that victims and bystanders often do not believe that adults will actually intervene to stop cyber-bullying. However, *ABCNews.com* reports that 41 states have laws against bullying in schools, and 23 of those states target cyber-bullying specifically.

Now that we know that victims of cyber-bullies desperately need the help of witnesses and bystanders to report their attacks, we should arm ourselves with the information necessary to provide that assistance. Think about the next time you see a friend or loved one being tormented or harassed online. What would you be willing to do to help?

Cyber-bullying must be confronted on national, local, and personal levels. There should be a comprehensive national law confronting cyber-bullying in schools. Certain statutes currently in state laws should be amalgamated to create the strongest protections for victims and the most effective punishments for bullies as possible.

According to Limber and Small's article titled *State Laws and Policies to Address Bullying in Schools*, Georgia law requires faculty and staff to be trained on the nature of bullying and what actions to take if they see students being bullied.

Furthermore, Connecticut law *requires* school employees to report bullying as part of their hiring contract. Washington takes this a step further by protecting employees from any legal action if a reported bully is proven to be innocent. When it comes to protecting victims, West Virginia law demands that schools must ensure that a bullied student does not receive additional abuse at the hands of his or her bully.

This example provides an emotional appeal by offering a real example of a real victim in Dallas, Texas.

This vivid example enhances pathos.

Now that Adam has established the breadth of the problem as widespread, he moves into a discussion about the depth of the effects it can have on victims.

Here Adam helps pique listener interest by pointing out how bystanders could also be hurt if we don't do something to stop this form of terrorism.

Notice how Adam's transition verbally ties the point he is finishing (problem) to the next point (causes) clearly using inclusive "we" language. This, too, bolsters a sense of goodwill and uses a conversational style that keeps listeners engaged.

Again, Adam does a nice job with his transition.

Notice how Adam gets right to the point about needing to take action on a variety of levels to stop this practice.

Adam gives credence to his policy statement by pointing to several states that have already succeeded in creating such laws.

Legislating punishment for bullies is difficult. As Limber and Small noted, zero-tolerance polices often perpetuate violence because at-risk youth, i.e., bullies, are removed from all of the benefits of school, which might help make them less abusive. A comprehensive anti-cyber-bullying law should incorporate the best aspects of these state laws and find a way to punish bullies that is both punitive and has the ability to rehabilitate abusers. However, for national laws to be effective, local communities need to be supportive.

Here Adam points to the need for consequences for bullying behavior when it is caught.

Local communities must organize and mobilize to attack the problem of cyber-bullying. According to Greene's 2006 article published in the *Journal of Social Issues*, communities need to support bullying prevention programs by conducting a school-based bullying survey for individual school districts. We can't know how to best protect victims in our community without knowing how they are affected by the problem. It is critical to know this information. As Greene noted, only 3 percent of teachers in the United States perceive bullying to be a problem in their schools.

Adam offers specific action steps that communities ought to do to help stop cyber-bullying.

Local school districts should create a Coordinating Committee made up of administrators, teachers, students, parents, school staff, and community partners to gather bullying data and rally support to confront the problem. Even if your local school district is unable or unwilling to mobilize behind this dire cause, there are some important actions you can take personally to safeguard those you love against cyber-bullying.

Here Adam gets personal when he points out that each person in the room has an ethical responsibility to help stop cyber-bullying.

There are several warning signs that might indicate a friend or loved one is a victim of a cyber-bully. If you see a friend or loved one exhibiting these signs, the decision to get involved can be the difference between life and death.

According to Keith and Martin's article *Cyber-Bullying: Creating a Culture of Respect in a Cyber World*, victims of cyber-bullies often use electronic communication more frequently than do people who are not being bullied. Victims of cyber-bullies have mood swings and difficulty sleeping. They seem depressed and/or become anxious. Victims can also become withdrawn from social activities and fall behind in scholastic responsibilities. If you witness your friends or family members exhibiting these symptoms, there are several ways you can help.

According to Raskauskas and Stoltz's 2007 article in *Developmental Psychology,* witnesses of cyber-bullying should inform victims to take the attacks seriously, especially if the bullies threaten violence. You should tell victims to report their attacks to police or other authorities, to block harmful messages by blocking e-mail accounts and cell phone numbers, and to save copies of attacks and provide them to authorities.

Adam could make this statement more compelling by offering a specific example of what one might tell the police, as well as how to install blockers on email and cell phones.

If you personally know the bully and feel safe confronting him or her, do so! As Raskauskas and Stoltz noted, bullies will often back down when confronted by peers. By being a good friend and by giving good advice, you can help a victim report his or her attacks from cyber-bullies and take a major step toward eliminating this horrendous problem. So, you see, we are not helpless to stop the cyber-bulling problem as long as we make the choice NOT to ignore it.

To conclude, cyber-bullying is a devastating form of abuse that must be reported to authorities. Cyber-bullying is a worldwide problem perpetuated by the silence of both victims and bystanders. By paying attention to certain warning signs, we can empower ourselves to console victims and report their abusers.

Here Adam restates his proposition, but it actually could be more comprehensive (beyond just our need to report bullying to authorities).

Today, I'm imploring you to do your part to help stop cyber-bullying. I know that you agree that stopping cyber-bullying must be a priority. First, although other states have cyber-bullying laws in place, ours does not. So I'm asking you to sign this petition that I will forward to our district's state legislators. We need to make our voices heard that we want specific laws passed to stop this horrific practice and to punish those caught doing it.

Adam reminds us of his specific call to action and even asks listeners to sign a petition today. His approach encourages listeners to follow through with his goal, that is, to actuate.

Second, I'm also asking you to be vigilant in noticing signs of cyber-bullying and then taking action. Look for signs that your friend, brother, sister, cousin, boyfriend, girlfriend, or loved one might be a victim of cyber-bullying, and then get involved to help stop it! Phoebe Prince showed the warning signs, and she did not deserve to die so senselessly. None of us would ever want to say, "I'll miss just being around her," "I didn't want to believe it," "It's such a sad thing" about our own friends or family members. We must work to ensure that victims are supported and bullies are confronted nationally, locally, and personally.

Adam does a nice job with his clincher in terms of tying back to the Phoebe story in his attention catcher. Doing so also appeals to emotions (pathos) in a way that should make his speech very memorable.

I know that, if we stand together and refuse to be silent, we can and will stop cyber-bullying.

14-4 ETHICAL GUIDELINES FOR PERSUASIVE SPEECHES

Throughout this book, we have discussed the fundamental behaviors of ethical communicators. At this point, we want to look at six ethical guidelines speakers should follow when their specific goal is to convince the audience to agree with a proposition or to move the audience to action.

Photo 14.4 Ethical persuasion requires speakers to admit their expertise and trustworthiness honestly, which includes acknowledging personal values that might directly influence one's position.

1. **Ethical persuasive speeches advocate the genuine beliefs of the speaker.** Sometimes people get excited about playing devil's advocate—that is, arguing for a belief or action just to stir up discussion. However, it is unethical to give a speech on a proposition that you do not genuinely endorse.

2. **Ethical persuasive speeches provide choice.** Ethical persuasive speeches let audiences evaluate what is said before making up their own minds.

3. **Ethical persuasive speeches use representative supporting information.** You can probably find a piece of "evidence" to support any claim, but ethical speakers make sure the evidence they cite is representative of all the evidence that could be used. It is unethical to misrepresent what a *body* of evidence (as opposed to a single item) would show if all of it were presented to the audience.

4. **Ethical persuasive speeches use emotional appeals conscientiously.** Emotional appeals are a legitimate strategy to get an audience involved in your persuasive speech. However, using excessive emotional appeals as the basis of persuasion, without strong evidence and reasoning, is unethical.

5. **Ethical persuasive speeches honestly present the speaker's credibility.** Ethical speakers present their expertise and trustworthiness honestly (Photo 14.4). It is unethical to act as if you know a great deal about a subject when you do not. Ethical speakers also disclose interests that may influence stance on the issue. You might say, for example, "I work for the Literacy Project as a paid intern, so my experiences there do influence my position on what must be done regarding illiteracy in this country."

Reflect on Ethics

DAVID ORTIZ'S EMOTIONAL PRE-GAME SPEECH SPARKS DEBATE

Shortly after the horrific Boston Marathon Bombings on April 15, 2013, the city of Boston went on lock down while law enforcement officials searched for the terrorists. The city, the nation, and the world followed breaking stories throughout the unprecedented manhunt and breathed a collective sigh of relief when it was finally over. One perpetrator was dead and the other arrested. Boston residents could come out of their homes and resume their lives.

Fans made their way back to Fenway Park to watch their beloved Boston Red Sox on April 20. A pre-game ceremony was held to honor the victims, the law enforcement responders, and the people of Boston and branded it *Boston Proud*. David Ortiz, designated hitter for the Red Sox, was handed the microphone, and he said when he looked out "at the faces in the crowd ... he felt what they were feeling".[8] His short speech rocked the house by precisely capturing their emotions.

He clinched his speech with conviction saying, "this is our [explicative] city, and nobody is going to dictate our freedom. Stay strong." Though emotionally compelling and clearly representative of the passionate feelings of those in his audience, Ortiz's clincher sparked controversy. Why? Because Ortiz, who is also known as Big Papi, dropped an F-bomb at a family-friendly event, which was also broadcast on national television. Later, Ortiz apologized, saying, "It just came out. If I offended anyone, I apologize".[9]

The Federal Communications Commission (FCC), which is tasked with policing such profanity, also did something unprecedented. They chose not to fine major league baseball, the Boston Red Sox, or Ortiz.[10] In fact, Julius Genachowski, Chair of the FCC, tweeted: "David Ortiz spoke from the heart at today's Red Sox game. I stand with Big Papi and the people of Boston – Julius".[11]

1. What, if any, ethical communication principles did Ortiz violate in his speech?

2. Does the fact that he apologized later make a difference? Why or why not?

3. Do you think the FCC's decision not to fine Ortiz, the Boston Red Sox, or major league baseball was ethical? Why or why not?

Rudy K. Lawidjaja/Sipa Press/march.010/ 0910122206/Newscom

Reflection and Assessment

Persuasive speeches are designed to influence the attitudes, beliefs, values, or behaviors of audience members. This chapter focused on creating effective and ethical persuasive speeches. To assess how well you've learned what we've discussed in this chapter, answer the following questions. If you have trouble answering any of them, go back and review that material. Once you can answer each question accurately, you are ready to move ahead to read the next chapter.

1. Why is it important to consider the initial audience attitude when constructing your persuasive speech goal?
2. How do you phrase a persuasive speech goal as a proposition?
3. What are some dispositional and actuation persuasive speech frameworks?
4. What ethical communication guidelines should you follow as a persuasive speaker?

Challenge Resource and Assessment Center

Now that you have read Chapter 14, go to your MindTap for *The Challenge of Effective Speaking in a Digital Age* for quick access to the electronic resources that accompany this text. These resources include the following:

- **Study tools** that will help you assess your learning and prepare for exams (*digital glossary, key term flash cards, review quizzes*).

- **Activities and assignments** that will help you hone your knowledge and build your public speaking skills throughout the course (Practice, Do). Many of these activities allow you to compare your answers with those provided by the authors and, if requested, submit your answers to your instructor.

- **Media resources**—all of which are available on your MindTap for *Challenge*—will help you explore communication concepts online (Practice), develop your speech outlines (Do), watch and critique videos of sample speeches (Do), and upload your speech videos for instructor feedback and critique other students' speeches. (Do)

- **Speech-Planning Action Steps identified earlier in the chapter.**
    1. Writing a Specific Goal as a Persuasive Proposition

- **Web Links that provide you with additional information or resources related to the topics discussed in this chapter.**

    14.1: Dealing with a Hostile Audience (p. 283)

    14.2: Dealing with a Challenging Audience (p. 283)

- **Video resources allow you to see other students giving speeches and record your own speech.**
    1. Use your Interactive Video Activities (Do) to watch, analyze, and see the transcript and outlines for Adam's speech to actuate, "Together, We Can Stop Cyber-Bullying." (p. 305)
    2. View persuasive speeches to convince and to actuate given by other students. How effective and ethical were their speeches? Or go to the Practice and Present section of MindTap and record a speech you're working on, upload it to Speech Studio, and ask your peers for their feedback. What feedback could you use to fine-tune your persuasive speech before you give it in class?

Applying What You've Learned

1. **Impromptu Speech Activity:** Select an item from a box provided by your instructor. Items could be anything from a small toy to an eating utensil to a tool to a knick-knack. Prepare a two- to three-minute impromptu speech attempting to "sell" the item to the target audience using the motivated sequence organizational framework. Alternatively, groups of three students might do so in a role-play impromptu "television advertisement" selling the product as it fulfills some "unique need" for college students. The "need" might not be what the item is typically intended for.

2. **Impromptu Speech Activity:** You and a partner will draw a slip of paper from a container provided by your instructor. The paper will identify competing topics (e.g., superman versus batman, butter versus margarine, eat eggs/don't eat eggs, fly versus drive, running versus walking for exercise). Each of you will prepare a one- to two-minute persuasive impromptu speech advocating opposing positions as a point/counterpoint activity.

3. **Assessment Activity A:** Watch a television commercial and identify the following: Who is the target audience for the product, and why do you believe so? What would you believe their initial attitude is for the product and why? Identify how the advertisement addresses each element of the motivated sequence and whether it does so effectively. If it does not address an element effectively, suggest how it could be modified to improve. Write up your assessment in the form of a one- to two-page reflection paper.

4. **Assessment Activity B:** Complete all the Action Step activities for a persuasive speech you will give in class.

15 "ceremonial speaking"

WHAT'S THE POINT?
WHEN YOU'VE FINISHED THIS CHAPTER, YOU'LL BE ABLE TO:

15-1 Determine what you should include in a speech of welcome

15-2 Identify why a speech of introduction should be brief

15-3 Declare the goal of your speech of nomination

15-4 Know when you might be expected to give a speech of recognition

15-5 Determine the key things to say in a speech of acceptance

15-6 List some common types of speeches of tribute

15-7 Identify additional types of ceremonial speeches

Review the chapter **Learning Objectives** and **Start** with quick warm up activity.

e Ethical communicators demonstrate respect for their audiences by considering the context for the ceremonial speech they'll be giving.

Because Ben didn't know his biological father, his grandfather had been like a father to him. He and his grandfather used to spend hours playing ball, fishing, or simply watching television together. Although Ben's grandfather had lived a long and fruitful life, Ben found it difficult to say goodbye. Still, he wanted to give the eulogy at the funeral. How could he find the right words to do justice to his grandfather's memory?

"How could he find the right words to do justice to his grandfather's memory?"

On special occasions, such as weddings and funerals, we may be called on to "say a few words." On these ceremonial occasions, your audience has distinct expectations for what they will hear. So, although the speech plan action steps you have learned will help you prepare your remarks, you also need to understand how expectations of these special occasions affect the way you should shape your speech.

The goal of ceremonial speaking lies somewhere between informing and persuading. In ceremonial speeches, you invite listeners to agree with you about the value of the person, object, event, or place the special occasion revolves around. Another characteristic of most ceremonial speeches is brevity: They are generally—although not always—fewer than five minutes long. This chapter describes six common types of ceremonial speeches given on special occasions: speeches of welcome, introduction, nomination, recognition, acceptance, and tribute. For each speech type, we describe the typical expectations to keep in mind as you prepare.

15-1 SPEECHES OF WELCOME

A **speech of welcome** greets and expresses pleasure for the presence of a person, group, or organization. You can welcome someone on your own, but you will usually give a speech of welcome as the representative of a group. You must be familiar with the group you are representing and the occasion. As you prepare your welcome, you may need to do some research so you can accurately describe the group, circumstances, and occasion to the person or people you are welcoming. A speech of welcome is generally not more than two to four minutes long.

A speech of welcome invites listeners to agree that the occasion is friendly and their attendance is appreciated. Do this by respectfully catching their attention, and after expressing appreciation on behalf of your group for their presence, provide a brief description of the group and setting to which they are being welcomed. The conclusion should briefly express your hope for the outcome of the visit, event, or relationship. A typical speech of welcome might be as simple as this:

> *Today, I want to welcome John Sheldon, who is joining us from the North Thurston Club. John, as you are aware, we are a newer club, having been established in 2007. At that time, we had only ten members. But we had big hopes. Today, we are 127 members strong, and we raised more than $250,000 last year to support local children's organizations. We hope our talks today will lead to closer cooperation between the North Thurston Club and ours here in Yelm.*

On some occasions, you may be asked to serve as **master of ceremonies**, an individual designated to welcome guests, set the mood for the program, introduce participants, and keep the program moving. (Either a woman or a man can be referred to as a master of ceremonies.) Year-end honorary banquets, corporate dinner meetings, and local charity events typically use someone in this role. As master of ceremonies, you might actually be asked to give a speech that both welcomes and introduces a speaker. When this is the case, the speech can be a bit longer and should also include the type of information described in the next section.

speech of welcome: a brief, ceremonial address that greets and expresses pleasure for the presence of a person or an organization

master of ceremonies: an individual designated to set the mood of the program, introduce participants, and keep the program moving

15-2 SPEECHES OF INTRODUCTION

A **speech of introduction** introduces the main speaker by establishing a supportive climate, highlighting pertinent biographical information, and generating enthusiasm for listening to the speech. At times, you will be given a résumé or brief biography of the speaker; at other times, you may need to research the speaker's background yourself. Regardless of what you learn, you should also try to contact the speaker and ask what points in the biography the speaker would like you to emphasize. Generally, a speech of introduction is not more than three to five minutes long.

The beginning of the speech of introduction should quickly establish the nature of the occasion, the body of the speech should focus on three or four things the audience ought to know about the person being introduced, and the conclusion should mention the speaker by name and briefly identify the topic and title of the speech. If the person is well known, you might simply say something like, "Ladies and gentlemen, the president of the United States." If the person is less well known, however, then mentioning his or her name specifically during the speech of introduction and especially at the end is imperative.

Speeches of introduction should honestly represent the person being introduced. Do not hype a speaker's credentials or overpraise the speaker. If you set the audience's expectations too high, even a good speaker may have trouble living up to them. For instance, an overzealous introducer can doom a competent speaker by saying, "This man [woman] is undoubtedly one of the greatest speakers of our time. I have no doubt that what you are about to hear will change your thinking." Although this introduction is meant to be complimentary, it does the speaker a grave disservice. A typical speech of introduction might look like the following:

> Today, it is my pleasure to introduce our speaker, Ms. Susan Wong, the new president of the finance club. I've worked with Susan for three years and have found her to have a gift for organization, insight into the financial markets, and an interest in aligning student organizations with leaders in our community. Susan, as you may not know, has spent the past two summers working as an intern at Salomon Smith Barney and has now laid the groundwork for more college internships for students from our university. She is a finance major, with a minor in international business. Today, she is going to talk with us about the benefits of summer internships. Let's give a warm welcome to Susan Wong!

15-3 SPEECHES OF NOMINATION

A **speech of nomination** proposes a nominee for an elected office, honor, position, or award. Every four years, the Democratic and Republican parties have speeches of nomination at their national conventions. Those speeches are rather long, but most speeches of nomination are brief, lasting only about two to four minutes.

The goal of a speech of nomination is to highlight the qualities that make this person the most credible candidate (Photo 15.1). To do so, first clarify the importance of the position, honor, or award by describing the responsibilities involved, related challenges or issues, and the characteristics needed to fulfill it. Second, list the candidate's personal and professional qualifications that meet those criteria. Doing so links the candidate with the position, honor, or award in ways that make him or her appear to be a natural choice. Finally, formally place the candidate's name in nomination, creating a dramatic climax to clinch your speech. A speech of nomination could be as simple and brief as this:

> I am very proud to place in nomination for president of our association the name of one of our most active members, Ms. Adrienne Lamb.

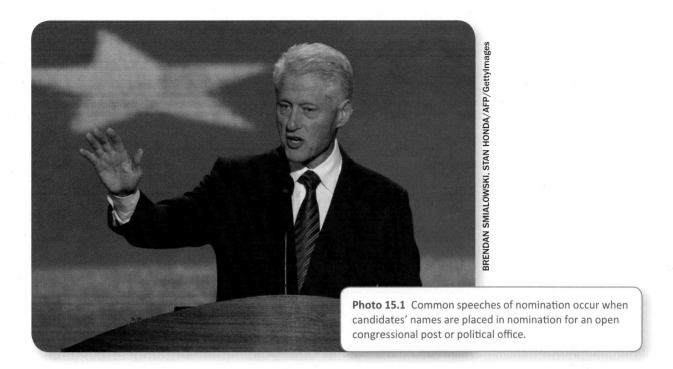

Photo 15.1 Common speeches of nomination occur when candidates' names are placed in nomination for an open congressional post or political office.

We all realize the demands of this particular post. It requires leadership. It requires vision. It requires enthusiasm and motivation. And, most of all, it requires a sincere love for our group and its mission.

Adrienne Lamb meets and exceeds each one of these demands. It was Adrienne Lamb who chaired our visioning task force. She led us to articulate the mission statement we abide by today. It was Adrienne Lamb who chaired the fund-raising committee last year when we enjoyed a record drive. And it was Adrienne Lamb who acted as mentor to so many of us, myself included, when we were trying to find our place in this association and this community. This association and its members have reaped the benefits of Adrienne Lamb's love and leadership so many times and in so many ways. We now have the opportunity to benefit in even greater ways.

It is truly an honor and a privilege to place in nomination for president of our association Ms. Adrienne Lamb!

speech of nomination: a ceremonial speech that proposes a nominee for an elected office, honor, position, or award

15-4 SPEECHES OF RECOGNITION

A **speech of recognition** acknowledges someone and usually presents an award, a prize, or a gift to the individual or a representative of a group. You have probably watched speeches of recognition given as lifetime achievement awards on the Academy Awards, the Grammys, or the Golden Globes. Speeches of recognition may be a bit longer depending on the prestigious nature of the award, but are more commonly quite brief (fewer than three minutes long).

Because the audience wants to know why the recipient is being recognized, you must recount the nature and history of the award, as well as the recognition criteria and how the recipient met them (Photo 15.2). If the recognition is based on a competition, this might include the number of contestants and the way the contest was judged. If the person earned the award through years of achievement, you will want to describe the specific milestones that the person passed.

speech of recognition: a ceremonial speech that acknowledges someone and usually presents an award, a prize, or a gift to the individual or a representative of a group

Photo 15.2 When presenting an award, discuss the nature of the award and the recipient's accomplishments.

David Young-Wolff/Alamy

speech of acceptance: a ceremonial speech given to acknowledge receipt of an honor or award

speech of tribute: a ceremonial speech that praises or celebrates a person, a group, or an event

toast: a ceremonial speech offered at the start of a reception or meal that pays tribute to the occasion or to a person

roast: an event where guests provide short speeches of tribute about the featured guests that are developed with humorous stories and anecdotes

Ordinarily, the speech begins by describing what the recognition is for, then states the criteria for winning or achieving the recognition, and finally describes how the person being recognized won or achieved the award. In some cases, the recognition is meant to be a surprise, so you will deliberately omit the name of the recipient in what you say, building to a climax when the name is announced.

Keep two special considerations in mind when you prepare a speech of recognition. First, refrain from overpraising; do not explain everything in superlatives that make the presentation seem to lack sincerity and honesty. Second, in the United States, it is traditional to shake hands with recipients as awards are received. So, if you have a certificate or other tangible award to hand to the recipient, be careful to hold it in your left hand and present it to the recipient's left hand. That way, you will be able to shake the right hand in congratulations. A typical speech of recognition may look like this:

I'm honored to present this year's Idea of the Year Award to Ryan Goldbloom from the installation department. As you may remember, we have been giving this award since 1985 to the employee who has submitted an idea that resulted in the largest first-year cost savings for the company. Ryan's idea to equip all installation trucks with prepackaged kits for each type of job has resulted in a $10,458 savings in the first twelve months. And in recognition of this contribution to our bottom line, I am pleased to share our savings with Ryan in the form of a check for $2,091.60, one-fifth of what he has saved us. Good work, Ryan.

15-5 SPEECHES OF ACCEPTANCE

A **speech of acceptance** acknowledges receipt of an honor or award. The goal is to sincerely convey your appreciation for the honor. You should briefly thank the person or group bestowing the honor, acknowledge the competition, express gratitude about receiving the award, and thank those who contributed to your success. To be effective, the speech should be brief, humble, and gracious. Remember that your goal is to convey appreciation in a way that makes the audience feel good about you receiving the award. Rarely, as in the case of a politician accepting a nomination, a professional accepting the presidency of a national organization, or a person receiving a prestigious award that is the focus of the gathering, an audience will expect a longer speech. Generally, however, acceptance speeches are no longer than one to two minutes.

Acceptance speeches that don't adhere to expectations often have disastrous results. If you have ever watched award programs such as the Academy Awards, MTV Music Awards, the People's Choice Awards, or Grammys, you no doubt have observed an award winner who gave an overly long or otherwise inappropriate acceptance speech. Some of the most famous of them, for instance, were when in 1985 Sally Field chose to say "you like me, right now, you really like me" rather than to humbly and graciously thank the academy for honoring her, and when in 2003 Michael Moore used the occasion to chastise the U.S. president by saying "shame on you Mr. Bush, shame on you" rather than to focus on humbly and graciously thanking the academy and when in 2011 Melissa Leo said "it looked so F—kin' easy" in her speech rather than graciously saying her thank you (which became all anyone ended up remembering from it). So, when you have the opportunity to give an acceptance speech, focus your remarks on the recognition you have been given or on the position you are accepting. It is inappropriate to use an acceptance speech to advocate for an unrelated cause. The following is an example of an appropriate speech of acceptance:

> I would like to thank the hospital for hosting this beautiful luncheon today. It is absolutely lovely! Thank you, too, to the chef, cooks, and wait staff. You have really made this event memorable in so many ways. In all honesty, I must admit I am a bit stunned and also truly honored to be recognized today as this year's Volunteer of the Year. As I look out at all of you here today, I am humbled to think of the countless hours you all spend giving freely of your time, and your love for the hurting children in our community. I am grateful to count myself among such amazing, selfless servant leaders. Each one of you deserves this trophy. I want to also thank my husband, Terry, for encouraging me to join Big Hearts, Big Hands and for supporting me when I became involved as a volunteer. You are my rock and I love you! Thank you, again, for this award. I will treasure it forever.

To see an example of an acceptance speech at a formal occasion, go to **Web Link 15.1, Martin Luther King's Nobel Prize Acceptance Speech,** on your MindTap for *Challenge.*

 MindTap™

eulogy: a ceremonial speech of tribute during a funeral or memorial service that praises someone's life and accomplishments

Reflect on Ethics

LANGUAGE OKAY FOR THE OCCASION?

On January 6, 2010, actor and comedian Steve Carell won the People's Choice Award for favorite TV comedy actor. His acceptance speech was filled with sexual innuendos. For example, he said, "Wow! I can't believe it. This is much *bigger* than I thought it would be," and "I'm going to go home, and I'm going to find a special place to *put* this," and "I'm glad I *came.*" You can search for and watch Carell's speech on YouTube.

1. What, if any, expectations for an acceptance speech did Carell violate?

2. What, if any, ethical communication principles did Carell violate?

3. Do you think his speech offended any members in the live or television audience? Explain.

4. Based on your answers to questions 1, 2, and 3, do you think his speech was appropriate? Effective? Why or why not?

commencement address:
a speech of tribute praising
graduating students and
inspiring them to reach for
their goals

commemorative address:
a speech of tribute that
celebrates national
holidays or anniversaries
of important events

SPEECH SNIPPET

Connecting Virtually

Tim wasn't able to travel so far to attend the milestone birthday roast for his longtime buddy, Tom. He wasn't the only one. He, and several other longtime friends, used Adobe® Connect to participate virtually. That way, Tim still got to share his own stories about Tom, and he got to laugh along with the others who were attending the roast in person.

IMPROMPTU SPEECH CHALLENGE

Prepare a two- to three-minute roast speech. Criteria for evaluation include how well you identify and develop the person's laudable characteristics and accomplishments in the form of good-natured humorous anecdotes, stories, and examples.

15-6 SPEECHES OF TRIBUTE

A **speech of tribute** praises or celebrates a person, a group, or an event. You might be asked to pay tribute to a person or persons on the occasion of their birthday, wedding, anniversary, oath of office, retirement, or funeral. There are a variety of special types based on the specific special occasion they are meant for. The goal in any of them, however, is to invite listeners to truly appreciate the person, group, or event by arousing their sentiments. This is achieved by focusing on the most notable characteristics or achievements of the person, group, or event with vivid stories, examples, and language that arouses sentiments. Speeches of tribute can vary in length from very brief to lengthy depending on the nature of the occasion. Let's take a closer look at three types of tribute that you are likely to be asked to give at some point in your life.

15-6a Toasts

A **toast**, usually offered at the start of a reception or meal, pays tribute to the occasion or to a person. On most occasions, a toast is expected to be very brief (lasting less than a minute), consisting of only a few sentences, and focusing on a single characteristic of the person or occasion. Usually, a short example is used to support or illustrate the characteristic. Wedding toasts, given at a rehearsal dinner or reception by a family member or member of the wedding party, are generally longer speeches (three to four minutes) that may use humor but should not embarrass the persons at whom they are directed.

A toast should be sincere and express a sentiment that is likely to be widely shared by those in attendance. Generally, the person giving the toast and all other attendees have a drink in hand, which they raise and sip from at the conclusion of the toast (Photo 15.3). So, before offering a toast, it is customary to make sure that drinks are refreshed so that all can participate. If particular people are being toasted, the toast is drunk in their honor, so they do not drink. A typical toast by a daughter given to honor her mother's college graduation might be:

> *Tonight, I'd like to offer a toast to a woman I admire, respect, and love. My mom has always supported my brother and me. So, when she told me that she wanted to go back and finish college, I was worried about how we'd all manage. But I shouldn't have worried. Mom not only finished her degree in less than two years, but she also continued to work full time, and, what's more, she's even had time to coach my brother's Little League team. Here's to you, Mom—you're amazing!*

15-6b Roasts

One unique type of tribute speech is given as part of a **roast**, which is an event where family and friends share short speeches in honor of one person. In these short speeches, guests might offer good-natured insults or anecdotes, heartwarming or outlandish personal stories, or uplifting accolades. Roasts became mainstream in popular

speech assignment

Toast

Prepare a one-minute toast to a specific person or persons on a specific occasion. Criteria for evaluation include how well you illustrate a quality or behavior of the person you are celebrating.

Photo 15.3 Special occasions such as weddings, birthdays, and retirements often call for a toast to pay tribute to the occasion or honored person(s).

image 100/Alamy

culture when Dean Martin hosted a series of celebrity roasts on television during the 1970s. Some of the most famous celebrity roasts have been of William Shatner, Pamela Anderson, Frank Sinatra, Hugh Hefner, Johnny Carson, and Muhammad Ali. The key when offering a speech of tribute during a roast is to demonstrate the ethical communication principles of respect and integrity by offering only jokes, stories, and anecdotes that do not offend the featured guest (Photo 15.4). The point, after all, is to honor and laud the guest.

15-6c Eulogies

A **eulogy** is a ceremonial speech of tribute presented at a funeral or memorial service that praises someone's life and accomplishments. You might recall that Ben from our opening scenario was preparing a eulogy for his grandfather (Photo 15.5). Your goal is to comfort the mourners by focusing on positive memories of the deceased person. Based on what you know about the person, select three or four positive personal characteristics of the person to use as the main points, and then use personal stories about the person to develop each of them. Your audience will enjoy hearing new stories that exemplify the characteristics as well as revisiting widely shared stories. Incidents that reveal how a personal characteristic helped the person overcome adversity will be especially powerful. To see an example of a eulogy, go to your MindTap for *Challenge* to access the Interactive Video Activities for Chapter 15. Oprah Winfrey's eulogy for civil rights activist Rosa Parks. Also access **Web Link**

Michael Tran/FilmMagic/Getty Images

Photo 15.4 Ethical communicators offer only good-natured jokes and stories that respect the individual being honored and do not offend others.

Giving a Eulogy

In the eulogy for his grandfather, "Gramps," Ben highlighted three character traits in Gramps that he admired. One trait was Gramps's patience, which Ben highlighted by telling stories of how Gramps had handled Ben's mistakes during three different incidents: when he tipped the fishing boat at four years old, when he wandered away at the state fair at eight, and when he pouted about a Christmas gift at thirteen. In each instance, Gramps had taught Ben a life lesson by sharing a story from his own boyhood rather than reprimanding him.

keynote address: ceremonial speech that both sets the tone and generates enthusiasm for the topic of a conference or convention

dedication: a speech of tribute that honors a worthy person or group by naming a structure, monument, or park after them

farewell: a speech of tribute honoring someone who is leaving an organization

speech to entertain: a humorous speech that makes a serious point

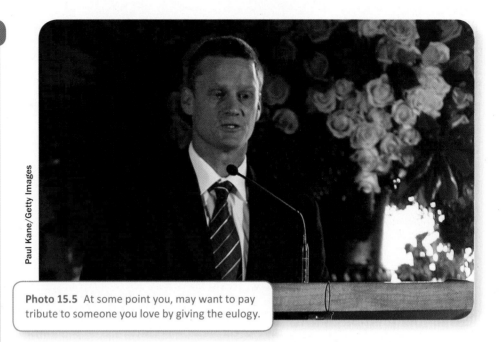

Paul Kane/Getty Images

Photo 15.5 At some point you, may want to pay tribute to someone you love by giving the eulogy.

15.2, Bob Costas's Eulogy for Mickey Mantle, on your MindTap for *Challenge*. This popular tribute speech uses language that enables audiences to understand Mantle's impact, regardless of their knowledge of baseball.

15-7 OTHER CEREMONIAL SPEECHES

Other occasions that call for ceremonial speeches include graduations, holidays, anniversaries of major events, and special events. A **commencement address**, for example, is a speech of tribute praising graduating students and inspiring them to reach for their goals. A **commemorative address** is a ceremonial speech of tribute that celebrates national holidays or anniversaries of important events. A **keynote address** is a ceremonial speech that both sets the tone and generates enthusiasm for the topic of a conference or convention. A **dedication** is a speech of tribute that honors a worthy person or group by naming a structure such as a building, monument, or park after the honoree. A **farewell** is a ceremonial speech of tribute honoring someone who is leaving an organization. A **speech to entertain** is a humorous speech that makes a serious point. To learn more about each of these types of ceremonial speeches, go to your MindTap for *Challenge* to access "Other Ceremonial Speeches" under the Chapter 15 resources.

🔇 speech assignment

Eulogy

Prepare a four- to six-minute eulogy for an important person in your life (e.g., family member, friend, mentor, teacher, coach). Criteria for evaluation include how well you identify and develop the person's laudable characteristics and accomplishments.

PUBLIC SPEAKING IN THE REAL WORLD

10 Things Kristen Stewart Can Teach Us about Public Speaking

© Flanigan/wire image/Getty Images

By now you know that effective public speaking is a skill that anyone can learn and improve with practice. Quite frankly, even those who have an aptitude for performing in front of audiences can't just "wing it" and expect to be effective public speakers. Just ask *Twilight* motion picture star, Kristen Stewart. As writer of *The Grindstone*, Kelsey Manning, points out, "K-Stew is the epitome of what not to do when public speaking" based on her many public speaking fiascos. Here they are:

1. Don't act like those you are speaking to are beneath you. No one wants to listen to someone who acts like she has better places to be.

2. Don't excessively touch your face. Classic Kristen Stewart move. Even if you're nervous, don't do this unless you're about to sneeze on someone.

3. Don't bite your lip. Another classic. It's not cute, coy, or sexy; you just look like you're a little kid trying to tell his mom he broke a vase.

4. Avoid "like," "um," "uh," or any other interjection that means nothing. The best thing to do is to try to eliminate that word in all conversation, which will make it easier to avoid using when giving speeches too.

5. Don't trail off at the end of sentences.

6. Don't turn declarative sentences into questions.

7. Look at the person you're speaking to (not at the floor).

8. Avoid long pauses.

9. Don't curse or make jokes that will make people feel awkward. Throwing in a curse word does not make you sound more casual and curse words are particularly jarring in speeches.

10. Don't end speeches with "So. . . there you go," "So. . . yeah," "Kay, bye," or any derivative thereof. These are actual quotes from the ends of some of Kristen Stewart's speeches. Just don't.[1]

If you've ever heard Ms. Stewart introduce or accept an award, you'll probably agree with Manning, we can learn a lot about what *not* to do when giving speeches from Kristen Stewart.

Reflection and Assessment

In addition to informative and persuasive speeches, you are likely to have occasion to give speeches to welcome, introduce, nominate, recognize, accept, and tribute. To assess how well you've learned what we've discussed in this chapter, answer the following questions. If you have trouble answering any of them, go back and review that material. Once you can answer each question accurately, you are ready to move ahead to read the next chapter.

1. What should you include in a speech of welcome?
2. Why should a speech of introduction be brief?
3. What is your goal in a speech of nomination?
4. When might you be expected to give a speech of recognition?
5. What are the key elements of an effective acceptance speech?
6. What are some common types of speeches of tribute?
7. What are some other types of ceremonial speeches?

 MindTap

Challenge Resource and Assessment Center

Now that you have read Chapter 15, go to your MIndTap for *The Challenge of Effective Speaking in a Digital Age* for quick access to the electronic resources that accompany this text. These resources include the following:

- **Study tools** that will help you assess your learning and prepare for exams (*digital glossary, key term flash cards, review quizzes*).
- **Activities and assignments** that will help you hone your knowledge and build your public speaking skills throughout the course (Practice, Do). Many of these activities allow you to compare your answers with those provided by the authors and, if requested, submit your answers to your instructor.
- **Media resources**—all of which are available on your MindTap for *Challenge*— will help you explore communication concepts online (Practice), develop your speech outlines (Do), watch and critique videos of sample speeches (Do), and upload your speech videos for instructor feedback and critique other students' speeches. (Do)
- **Web Links that provide you with additional information or resources related to the topics discussed in this chapter.**

  15.1 Martin Luther King's Nobel Prize Acceptance Speech (p. 321)

  15.2 Bob Costas's Eulogy for Mickey Mantle (p. 324)

- **Video resource allows you to see other students giving speeches and record your own speech.**

  1. Other students' ceremonial speeches. Or go to the Practice and Present section of MindTap and record a speech you're working on, upload it, and ask your peers for their feedback. What feedback could you use to fine-tune your ceremonial speech before you give it in class?

Applying What You've Learned

1. **Impromptu Speech Activity:** Consider what you would like people to remember or know about you if you were to die tomorrow. Prepare a two- to three-minute impromptu speech eulogy based on the expectations detailed in this chapter.
2. **Assessment Activity A:** Watch the opening segment to a popular late-night television program such as *Saturday Night Live, The Tonight Show,* or *Late Night with David Letterman,* or talk show such as *Ellen DeGeneres* or *The View*. Consider the

guidelines for a speech of welcome as described in this chapter. In what ways does the speaker follow or not follow the guidelines suggested in this chapter? How effective do you believe the speaker to be and why? Write up your assessment in the form of a one- to two-page reflection paper.

3. **Assessment Activity B:** Attend a professional public speaking event on campus or in your community. Assess the ways in which the master of ceremonies follows or does not follow the guidelines for a speech of introduction as described in this chapter. Do you believe the speech of introduction was effective in meeting the goals described in this chapter? Why or why not?

16 "group communication and presentations"

© iStockphoto.com/svetikd

WHAT'S THE POINT?
WHEN YOU'VE FINISHED THIS CHAPTER, YOU'LL BE ABLE TO:

16-1 Share leadership responsibilities when working in groups

16-2 Manage conflict among group members

16-3 Engage in the steps of the systematic problem-solving process

16-4 Communicate more in virtual groups

16-5 Present your group findings in different formats

16-6 Evaluate group dynamics and presentations

MindTap™

Review the chapter **Learning Objectives** and **Start** with quick warm up activity.

Ethical communicators demonstrate respect for other group members by resolving interpersonal conflict through collaboration, encouraging input, and acknowledging all sides of an issue.

WORK SESSION 1: Julio, Kristi, Luke, Bryn, and Nick have been asked to work as a small group to prepare a persuasive presentation that will count for one-third of the grade in the course. As the other members see it, Nick is a troublemaker because he has contradicted the instructor several times during previous class sessions. Nick has also been absent several times and seems less than fully committed to earning a good grade. In short, the other members are worried that Nick will cause them to earn a lower grade than they would earn without him in their group.

WORK SESSION 2: After the instructor refused to move Nick to another group, Julio, Kristi, Luke, and Bryn decide to restrict Nick's participation by not asking him for substantive help even though that means he'll get a better grade than he deserves. As the full group begins discussing their topic—gun control—Nick explains that he has a lot of material on it since he is a fairly vocal opponent of this proposal. Kristi, Julio, and Luke become disgruntled because they plan to argue in support of the proposal, and as they suspected, Nick opposes it. Kristi asks Bryn: "How do YOU feel about this conflict?" Much to Kristi's surprise, Bryn replies, "Actually, I'd like to hear more from Nick before I decide. Nick, tell us more." Nick goes on to share highly relevant information that would eventually be used to strengthen the group's speech. The group soon realizes the hastiness of their judgments about Nick.

> *"Nick goes on to share highly relevant information...The group soon realizes the hastiness of their judgments about Nick."*

Perhaps you have already been part of a group whose task was to prepare a joint presentation. If so, the opening scenario might sound familiar. In fact, when asked to work in small groups on a class or work project, many people respond—as Julio, Kristi, Luke, and Bryn did—with resistance. Their reasons usually focus on concerns that a few members will end up doing most of the work, that the group process will slow them down, that they'll earn a lower grade than if they worked alone, or that they will be forced to work on a topic that they aren't interested in or take a position they don't agree with.

Although working in a group to develop and deliver a presentation has its disadvantages, it is the preferred approach in business and industry.[1] These **problem-solving groups** (usually composed of five to seven people) are formed to carry out a specific task or solve a particular problem. Whether you want to or not, you can expect to work in a problem-solving group or team in your professional life, sometimes in face-to-face settings and often in virtual settings through e-mail, chat rooms, discussion boards, and video conferences.[2] Leaders in business and industry have come to realize that the advantages (e.g., deeper analysis of problems, greater breadth of ideas and of potential solutions, improved group morale, increased productivity) far outweigh the disadvantages.

We include a chapter on problem-solving groups in this book because these groups typically present their findings in formal presentations, for example, as progress reports, sales presentations, proposals, or staff reports.[3] So it makes sense to learn how to work effectively in groups and then how to present your group findings. In this chapter, we begin by talking about effective leadership and the responsibilities of group members in achieving it, as well as managing conflict among members. Then we explain an effective problem-solving method first described by educational philosopher John Dewey. From there, we turn our attention to particular strategies for effective communication in virtual groups. Finally, we describe several formats for communicating your findings publically and evaluating group effectiveness both in terms of group dynamics and presentations.

problem-solving groups: five to seven people who work together to complete a specific task or solve a particular problem

Photo 16.1 Procedural leaders are good at making logistical arrangements and keeping track of group decisions and accomplishments.

16-1 LEADERSHIP

Leadership is a process "whereby an individual influences a group of individuals to achieve a common goal."[4] When we think of leadership, we often think of a person who is *in charge*.[5] In fact, scholars once thought leaders were "born"—that some people inherited traits that made them naturally suited to be leaders. This trait theory approach was called "The Great Man Theory of Leadership."[6] Later, scholars believed that different leadership styles were more or less effective based on the goal and situation. These classic theories suggest that *leadership* is enacted by one person. Today, however, we understand leadership as a set of communication functions performed by different group members at various times based on each person's unique strengths and expertise.[7][8] So, although a group may have a **formal leader** (a person designated or elected to oversee the group process), a series of **informal leaders** (members who help lead the group to achieve different leadership functions) make for the most effective leadership in groups.

Shared leadership functions are the sets of roles you and other members perform to facilitate the work of the group and to help maintain harmonious relations among members. A **role** is a specific communication behavior group members perform to address the needs of the group at any given point in time. When these roles are performed effectively, the group functions smoothly. Shared leadership functions may be categorized as task, procedural, and maintenance roles.

1. **Task leadership roles** help the group acquire, process, or apply information that contributes directly to completing a task or goal. Task leaders are good at finding pertinent research related to the goal and sharing it with the group. They may also be good at summarizing group discussions in ways that pull them together toward the group goal.

2. **Procedural leadership roles** provide logistical support and record the group's decisions and accomplishments (Photo 16.1). Procedural leaders are usually good at arranging a time and place for face-to-face meetings or setting up links for access to teleconferences or videoconferences. They may also be good at taking notes and keeping track of group decisions.

3. **Maintenance leadership roles** help the group to develop and maintain cohesion, commitment, and positive working relationships. Maintenance leaders are good at encouraging others to share ideas and praising them for sharing, as well as intervening when conflict is threatening to harm the group process.

When problem-solving groups work well, the product is better than what any one member could have accomplished alone. This is known as **synergy**. We believe small groups usually fail when members do not engage in shared leadership in ways that adhere to the ethical responsibilities shown in Exhibit 16.1. When met by all members, these five responsibilities result in shared leadership where every member and his or her contributions are valued and synergy can occur.

1. **Be committed to the group goal.** Being committed to the group goal means finding a way to align your expertise with the agreed-upon goal of the group.

---

leadership: a process whereby an individual influences a group of individuals to achieve a common goal

formal leader: a person designated or elected to oversee the group process

informal leaders: members who help lead the group to achieve different leadership functions

shared leadership functions: the sets of roles you and other members perform to facilitate the work of the group and to help maintain harmonious relations among members

role: a specific communication behavior group members perform to address the needs of the group at any given point in time

task leadership roles: help the group acquire, process, or apply information that contributes directly to completing a task or goal

Exhibit (16.1) **Responsibilities of Group Members**

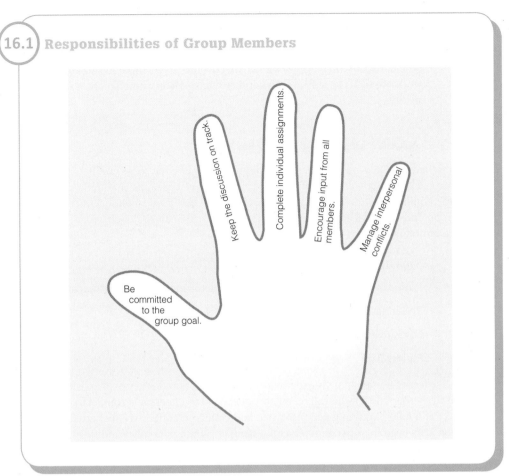

Keep the discussion on track.

Complete individual assignments.

Encourage input from all members.

Manage interpersonal conflicts.

Be committed to the group goal.

In addition to demonstrating responsibility, doing so also conveys both integrity and respect. So, for a class project, this might mean working together on a topic that wasn't your first choice. Once the decision has been agreed upon, however, it is no longer appropriate to dredge up old issues that have already been settled.

2. **Keep discussions on track.** It is every member's responsibility to keep the discussion on track by offering only comments that are relevant and by gently reminding others to stay focused if the discussion starts to get off track. It is unproductive to talk about personal issues during the team's work time. Moreover, it is unethical to try to get the discussion off track because you disagree with what is being said.

3. **Complete individual assignments on time.** One potential advantage of group work is that tasks can be divided among members. However, each member is responsible for completing his or her tasks thoroughly and on time.

4. **Encourage input from all members.** All too often, extroverts overshadow quiet group members. Sometimes, outspoken members interpret this silence as having nothing to contribute or not wanting to contribute. On the contrary, all members have valuable perspectives. If you are an extrovert, you have a special responsibility to refrain from dominating the discussion and to ask others for their opinions. Likewise, if you tend to be an introvert, make a conscious effort to express yourself. You might write down what you want to share or even raise your hand to get the attention of other members in an unobtrusive way.

5. **Manage conflict among members.** All small groups experience some **conflict**— disagreement or clash among ideas, principles, or people. If managed appropriately, conflict can actually be beneficial to the group goal by stimulating

procedural leadership roles: provide logistical support and record the group's decisions and accomplishments

SPEECH SNIPPET

Keeping the Discussion on Track

When Luke and Kristi began talking about attending the upcoming football game during the group work session, Bryn gently reminded them that the group had only thirty minutes to figure out how to proceed and assign tasks for the speech that would be due next week.

Glossary (margin)

maintenance leadership roles: help the group to develop and maintain cohesion, commitment, and positive working relationships

synergy: when the result of group work is better than what one member could achieve alone

conflict: disagreement or clash among ideas, principles, or people

groupthink: when group members accept information and ideas without subjecting them to critical analysis

pseudo-conflict: occurs when group members who actually agree about something believe they disagree due to poor communication

thinking, fostering open communication, encouraging diverse opinions, and enlarging members' understanding of the issues.[4] Doing your part to manage conflict demonstrates the ethical principles of responsibility and respect for others. Because managing conflict effectively is so essential to successful group work, we focus specifically on conflict management and resolution in the next section.

16-2 CONFLICT IN GROUPS

As we have already mentioned, all small groups experience some conflict, and, when managed effectively, conflict enhances synergy. In fact, groups that *don't* experience some conflict risk the problem of **groupthink**—when group members accept information and ideas without subjecting them to critical analysis.[10] Behaviors that signal groupthink include:

- Avoiding conflict to prevent hurting someone's feelings.
- Pressuring members who do not agree with the majority of the group to conform.
- Reaching "consensus" without the support of all members.
- Discouraging or ignoring disagreements.
- Rationalizing a decision without testing it.

If effective groups actually experience conflict, then how do they manage it effectively? Effective groups do so when all members understand their personal conflict management styles and follow certain guidelines when addressing potentially conflict-arousing situations. Let's begin by discussing several potential sources of conflict and then five of the most common conflict management styles as they function in groups.

16-2a Sources of Conflict

1. **Pseudo-conflict** occurs when group members who actually agree about something believe they disagree due to poor communication. Since *pseudo* means *fake*, the perceived conflict is actually a misperception.

2. **Issue-related conflict** occurs when two or more group members' goals, ideas, or opinions about the topic are incompatible. Issue-related conflict can be a good thing when handled effectively because, without it, groupthink is far more likely to occur.

3. **Personality-related conflict** occurs when two or more group members become defensive because they feel as though they are being attacked. Typically, personality-related conflicts are rooted in a power struggle.[11]

4. **Culture-related conflict** occurs when the communication norms of group members are incongruent. For example, people who identify with individualistic cultural norms tend to use direct communication to manage conflict whereas those who identify with collectivist norms tend to use indirect nonverbal means for doing so.[12]

5. **Virtual group-related conflict** arises as a result of meeting through this technology-enhanced channel. For example, most technology channels reduce our ability to send and receive subtle nonverbal messages, particularly those related to emotions and relational issues. Most of us use emoticons and emojis to represent missing nonverbal cues; however, a smiley face can be offered sincerely or sarcastically and it can be difficult for the receiver to ascertain the difference. Unfortunately, conflict often goes unresolved in virtual groups because we cannot see the nonverbal reactions of frustration that are visible

when interacting in person.[13] When communication is effective, however, the bonds among members of virtual groups can be even stronger than those in face-to-face ones.[14] [15] Effective members of virtual groups make a conscious effort to communicate both what they *think* and how they *feel* about a topic.

We can deal with these sorts of conflict in several ways. We can manage disagreements by separating the issues from the people involved, keeping our emotions in check, and phrasing our comments descriptively, not judgmentally (Photo 16.2). Rather than calling a particular idea stupid, for example, ask for clarification about why people think or feel the way they do. Seek first to understand.

We can also employ perception checking or paraphrasing, using "I language" that phrases our interpretations and opinions as our own rather than as defense-arousing "you language."[16] In other words, our language needs to reflect the fact that we are responsible for our feelings.[17] We can also diffuse potential conflicts by using "we" language. Exhibit 16.2 shows some examples of how to change a "you" statement into "I" and "we" statements.

Photo 16.2 Group members demonstrate ethical communication behavior by managing conflict, collaborating, perception-checking, and paraphrasing.

Steve Chenn/CORBIS

Perception checking is a verbal statement that reflects your understanding of another's behavior. It is a process of describing what you have seen and heard and then asking for feedback. A perception check statement consists of three parts: (1) In a non-evaluative way, describe what you observed or sensed from someone's behavior. (2) Offer two possible interpretations. (3) Ask for clarification. **Paraphrasing** is putting your understanding of another person's verbal message into words. It is a four-step process: (1) Listen carefully to the message; (2) notice what images, ideas, and feelings you experience from the message; (3) determine what the message means to you; (4) share your interpretation and ask for confirmation that you did so correctly. Exhibit 16.3 provides examples of perception checking and paraphrasing as they may be applied to avoid personality conflict.

issue-related conflict: occurs when two or more group members' goals, ideas, or opinions about the topic are incompatible

personality-related conflict: occurs when two or more group members become defensive because they feel as though they are being attacked

culture-related conflict: occurs when the communication norms of group members are incongruent

virtual group-related conflict: arises as a result of meeting through this technology-enhanced channel

perception checking: a verbal statement that reflects your understanding of another's behavior

Exhibit (16.2) Reframing "You" Statements into "I" and "We" Statements

"You" Statement	"I" Statement
"You hurt my feelings."	"I feel hurt when you don't acknowledge what I say."
"You're so irresponsible."	"I feel my efforts don't matter when you come to the meeting unprepared."
"Don't be so critical."	"I feel disrespected when you say my opinion is stupid."
"I can't believe you said that!"	"I feel humiliated when you mention my problems in front of others."

Situation	Perception Check	Paraphrase
As you are offering your idea about who the group might interview to get more information on your topic, you notice that Tomika, who you see as uncommitted to the group, says, "Whatever. . ." and begins reading a message on her cell phone.	Tomika, when you give a dismissive response to my ideas and then start checking your messages, I sense that you don't like my suggestion. Is that an accurate read, or are you just expecting an important message, or is it something else?	From your "whatever" response, I sense that either you don't really agree with my suggestion, you aren't really committed to the project, or you just don't respect me. Or is it something else?
Over the term, Jose has been quick to volunteer for the easiest assignments and has never taken on a difficult piece of work. Today the group was finalizing who would deliver which part of the group presentation and Jose quickly volunteered, saying: "I'll be the master of ceremonies and introduce our topic and each speaker."	Jose, I have been noticing that you have been quick to volunteer and you usually choose the least time consuming and simplest tasks, and now you're offering to take a role in the presentation that will again require little effort. Are you really overextended in your other classes or trying to take the easy way out, or is there some other explanation?	Jose, it seems to me like you are again volunteering to do the part of the presentation that will be the least amount of work. Are you really overextended with other courses or not committed to doing your share? Or is there some other reason that you want to be the master of ceremonies?
Today is the day that Madison is supposed to lead the group's discussion, as she was responsible for the research on this part of the group's project. As the group waits for her to begin, she avoids eye contact and rummages through her backpack, finally looking up and saying, "Well, I guess that you all are going to be kind of mad at me."	Madison, I'm noticing you don't seem like you want to get the meeting started, are avoiding eye contact, and have been rummaging around in your bag. I get the sense that you haven't done your homework or lost it. Am I on target, or is it something else?	Madison, from what you said, I understand that you are not prepared to lead the meeting. I'm wondering if you did your homework and lost it. Or is there something else?

16-2b Conflict Management Styles

paraphrasing: a verbal statement that conveys your understanding of another person's verbal message

Perception checking and paraphrasing are useful strategies for resolving conflict. Members also can be effective at resolving conflicts when they understand conflict management styles and employ the most effective ones when working in groups. Research has revealed five common conflict management styles. These are avoiding, accommodating, competing, compromising, and collaborating.[18]

avoiding: involves physically or psychologically removing yourself from the conflict

Avoiding involves physically or psychologically removing yourself from the conflict. For instance, in our opening scenario, if Nick decided to leave the first group session and then not show up at others because he perceived other members didn't agree with him, he would be managing conflict by avoiding. Similarly, if he would attend the work sessions, but not share his input, he would also be avoiding. When a group member engages in avoiding as a conflict management style, the whole group suffers because everyone is not committed to the group goal and every member's input is not being considered. Researchers describe this as a lose-lose conflict management style.

Accommodating is accepting others' ideas and opinions while neglecting our own, even when we disagree with their views. If we continue with the example of Nick and his group members, we could say that Nick is engaging in accommodating style if he goes along with Kristi, Julio, and Luke, who want to support increased gun control, even though he personally opposes that view. When a group member engages in accommodating as a conflict management style, the whole group suffers because not all potential ideas are being weighed in the discussion. Researchers describe this as a lose-win conflict management style.

accommodating: a conflict management style that involves accepting others' ideas while neglecting your own, even when you disagree with their views

Competing is satisfying our own needs without concern for the needs of others or for the harm it does to the group dynamics or problem-solving process. When one member dominates the group discussion by forcing his or her opinions without considering other views or even allowing them to be expressed, the whole group suffers because input from all group members is not being heard. If two or more members engage in competing conflict styles, the whole group suffers, not only because all ideas are not being heard, but also because the discussion gets off track, interpersonal conflicts are not being managed, and the arguments may even impede the completion of individual assignments. If Nick and Luke engage in competing behavior over the gun control issue, other input is squelched and the group process comes to a halt. Researchers describe this as a lose-lose conflict management style.

competing: a conflict management style that involves satisfying our own needs with no concern for the needs of the others and no concern for the harm it does to the group dynamics or problem-solving process

Compromising occurs when individuals give up part of what they want to provide at least some satisfaction to other opinions. If the group members can't find an ideal time to meet outside of class because they all have busy schedules, they might compromise on a time to meet that isn't particularly ideal for any of them or decide to meet virtually by posting to a blog. In terms of coming to a solution, one drawback of this

compromising: a conflict management style that involves individuals giving up part of what they want in order to provide at least some satisfaction to other opinions

Reflect on Ethics

WHAT WOULD *YOU* DO?

MODELING GROUP DYNAMICS ON TV TALK SHOWS

ABC's *The View* is among the most popular daytime talk shows today. The program has garnered numerous daytime Emmy Awards since it first aired in 1997. It features a team of four female cohosts of different ages and backgrounds, who discuss and debate current events and issues. What do *The View* and similar programs convey to viewers about engaging in group discussion? We can begin to answer this question by observing comments bloggers have posted to the show's website:

- KellyKKelly wrote: "I realized that every time I catch excerpts from the thing, I wind up with a headache. They talk over each other, Whoopi yells (especially at Sherri who she thinks is a ditz but then overcompensates by ... giving her time to finish her sentence)."

- And Sanbur posted this comment: "I am all for free speech, ... I want to hear all opinions, but I expect them

to be informed, to be respectful, and to be open to the FACT that there are always two sides to a story."[19]

If you haven't seen *The View*, watch an episode of it, and then answer the following questions:

1. In what ways, if any, does this program violate the guidelines for effective group dynamics discussed in this chapter?

2. What, if any, ethical communication principles do the cohosts of this program violate?

3. What are the possible implications of this sort of modeling on viewers with regard to communicating with others in groups?

4. What would you do if you found yourself interacting in a group functioning as these cohosts do?

Chapter 16 | Group Communication and Presentations | 335

Exhibit (16.4) Collaborative Conflict Management Tips

Initiating Collaboration	Responding Collaboratively
1. Identify the problem as your own using "I language." "I could really use your help here."	1. Disengage to avoid a defensive response.
2. Describe the behavior in terms of behavior, consequences, and feelings. "When I see you checking your e-mail, I feel we're missing out on your ideas for the project, and I get frustrated."	2. Respond empathically with genuine interest and concern by first describing the behavior you observe. "I see you checking your e-mail, and I wonder if you're angry or frustrated with something."
3. Refrain from blaming or accusing.	3. Paraphrase your understanding of the problem and ask questions to clarify issues. "Is there something bothering you or something we're overlooking?"
4. Find common ground. "Figuring this out is really tough. I know I feel overwhelmed about it sometimes."	4. Seek common ground. "I know that trying to come to one goal and solution seems impossible at times."
5. Mentally rehearse so you can state your request briefly.	5. Ask the other person to suggest alternative solutions. "What other ideas do you have that we might consider?"

style is that the quality of the decision is probably affected when someone "trades away" a better solution to reach a compromise. Researchers describe this as a partial lose-lose conflict management style.

collaborating: a conflict management style that involves discussing the issues, describing feelings, and identifying the characteristics of an effective solution before deciding what the ultimate solution will be

Collaborating occurs when people work through the problem together to discover a mutually acceptable solution. Researchers describe this as a win-win conflict management style. A win-win solution occurs when input from all members is heard, valued, and evaluated honestly and fairly until the group reaches consensus about how to proceed. Consider the tips in Exhibit 16.4 to achieve effective collaborative conflict management.

16-3 SYSTEMATIC PROBLEM SOLVING

When you meet with your classmates, coworkers, or community members to work on a project, you will be trying to solve a problem. To be effective, your group will need to follow a concrete process for analyzing the problem and coming up with a productive solution in a short amount of time. One effective means for doing this is the **systematic problem-solving method.**[20] This six-step process, first described by John Dewey in 1933 and since revised by others, remains a tried and true method for individual and group problem solving.[21]

systematic problem-solving method: an efficient six-step method for finding an effective solution to a problem

1. **Identify and define the problem.** The first step is to identify the problem and define it in a way all group members understand and agree with. Groups might begin by coming up with a number of problems and then narrow them to a particular one. So your class project group might identify the problems as

- What are the symptoms of this problem?
- What are the causes of this problem?
- Can this problem be subdivided into several smaller problems that each may have individual solutions?
- What have others who have faced this problem done?
- How successful have they been with the solutions they attempted?
- How is our situation similar and different from theirs?
- Does this problem consist of several smaller problems? If so, what are their symptoms, causes, previously tried solutions, and so forth?
- What would be the consequences of doing nothing?
- What would be the consequences of trying something and having it fail?

developing an effective group presentation, identifying a topic for the presentation, fairly sharing the workload, etc. By posing questions, you can also identify and define a problem: What is the problem? What is its history? Who is affected by it, and how does it affect them? How many people are affected, in what ways, and to what degree? These questions help a group realize what kinds of information must be gathered to help define the problem. To ensure that your group is focusing on the problem itself and not just the symptoms of the problem, don't rush through this step.

2. **Analyze the problem.** To analyze the problem, you must find out as much as possible about it. Most groups begin with each member sharing information he or she already knows about the problem. Then the group needs to determine what additional questions they need to answer and search for additional information to answer them. You might consider questions such as those in Exhibit 16.5.

3. **Determine criteria for judging solutions. Criteria** are standards used for judging the merits of proposed solutions—a blueprint for evaluating them. Research suggests that when groups develop criteria before they think about specific solutions, they are more likely to come to a decision that all members can accept.[22] Without clear criteria, group members may argue for their preferred solution without thoughtfully considering whether it will adequately address the problem or whether it is truly feasible. Exhibit 16.6 poses questions that can help groups think about the types of criteria a solution might need to meet.

criteria: standards used for judging the merits of proposed solutions

- What are the quantitative and qualitative measures of success that a solution must be able to demonstrate?
- Are there resource constraints that a good solution must meet (costs, time, manpower)?
- Is solution simplicity a factor?
- What risks are unacceptable?
- Is ease of implementation a consideration?
- Is it important that no constituency be unfairly harmed or advantaged by a solution?

brainstorming: an uncritical, nonevaluative process of generating alternatives by being creative, suspending judgment, and combining or adapting the ideas of others

virtual groups: groups that convene using telephone or computer technology

asynchronous virtual groups: those whose members can post and respond to messages at any time, although usually within a few days

4. **Generate a host of solutions.** Arriving at a good solution depends on having a wide variety of possible solutions to choose from. Many groups fail at generating a variety of possible solutions because they criticize the first ideas expressed, which discourages members from taking the risk to put their ideas out there for the group to consider. One way to encourage input is to use the brainstorming technique. **Brainstorming,** you'll recall, is an uncritical, non-evaluative process of generating alternatives by being creative, suspending judgment, and combining or adapting the ideas of others. It involves verbalizing your ideas as they come to mind without stopping to evaluate their merits. At least one member should record all solutions as they are suggested. To ensure that creativity is not stifled, no solution should be ignored, and members should build on the ideas presented by others. You might come up with twenty or more solutions. As a minimum, try to come up with eight to ten solutions before moving to the next step. For more on brainstorming, go to your MindTap for *Challenge* to access **Web Link 16.1: Rules for Brainstorming**.

5. **Evaluate solutions based on the criteria and select one.** Here you need to evaluate the merits of each potential solution based on the criteria established by the group. Consider each solution as it meets the criteria, and eliminate solutions that do not meet them adequately. In addition to applying the criteria, the group might also ask questions such as the following: How will the solution solve the problem? How difficult will it be to implement? What problems might be caused as a result of implementing the solution? Once each potential solution has been thoroughly evaluated based on the criteria, the group must select the best one(s). For more resources on evaluating solutions and making decisions, go to **Web Link 16.2, Decision Making Methods,** on your MindTap for *Challenge*.

6. **Implement the agreed-upon solution and assess it.** Finally, the group implements the agreed-upon solution or, if the group is presenting the solution to others for implementation, makes recommendations for how the solution should be implemented. The group has already considered implementation in terms of selecting a solution but now must fill in the details. What tasks are required by the solution(s)? Who will carry out these tasks? What is a reasonable time frame for implementation generally and for each of the tasks specifically? Because the agreed-upon solution may or may not prove effective, the group should determine a point at which they will revisit and assess its success. Doing so builds in an opportunity to revise or replace the solution if warranted.

16-4 COMMUNICATING EFFECTIVELY IN VIRTUAL GROUPS

Virtual groups that convene using telephone or computer technology are becoming increasingly popular for many reasons (Photo 16.3). First, members need not be physically present. Before these technologies became available, groups had to meet face-to-face to exchange information, solve problems, and make decisions. But today, group members can interact while in different cities, states, and countries. Second, **asynchronous virtual groups**—those whose members can post and respond to messages at any time, although usually within a few days—allow people to participate across time. Busy people often struggle to find a meeting time that works with everyone's schedule. So a group can "meet" via a threaded discussion instead. Third, virtual meetings can save money. Before these technologies, people often had to travel to a meeting site. That often also meant paying for travel, accommodations, meals, parking, and even meeting space rental. Because virtual meetings can be conducted over the phone or Internet, meeting costs can be reduced for both participants and hosts.

These benefits can also come with potential costs. For example, research has found that communication problems can impact both task and relational outcomes.[23] Face-to-face groups are often more dedicated to completing the task,[24] to fostering positive relationships among members,[25] and to building cohesion[26] than virtual groups. Thus, we offer a few guidelines to follow for effective communication when working in a virtual group.

1. **Train members to use the technology.** Do not assume everyone is adept at using the technology needed to conduct the work session. Provide training if needed.

2. **Create ice-breaker and team-building opportunities.** Just as face-to-face groups benefit from getting to know and trust one another, so do members of virtual groups. You can do so, for example, by encouraging members to share personal websites, photos, and self-introduction narratives. Members can also become Facebook friends and follow one another on Twitter accounts.

3. **Develop group ground rules.** Just as rules need to be clarified for face-to-face groups, so do they need to be articulated for virtual groups. For example, set rules regarding how quickly members should respond to messages, turn-taking, and **netiquette** (etiquette rules when communicating over computer networks). Netiquette rules include such things as being courteous and respectful, using emoticons and imogees, keeping messages short, refraining from the use of all capital letters, thinking before posting, being patient with new users, obeying copyright laws, and keeping personal information private.[27]

Photo 16.3 As virtual groups become more prevalent, we must take care to adhere to effective communication practices in them.

Monty Rakusen/Newscom

netiquette: etiquette rules when communicating over computer networks

4. **Provide clear structure.** Virtual groups perform best when a clear structure is provided. A formal task leader ought to clearly lay out not only the goal but also the systematic process the group will follow to achieve it.

5. **Use synchronous technology if possible.** Although threaded discussions allow people to interact at their own convenience, these formats offer limited means for conveying nonverbal, emotional, and social cues. So, whenever possible, use regularly scheduled synchronous teleconference or videoconference meetings.

6. **Create opportunities to meet outside the virtual environment.** Members of virtual groups can feel closer if they can also have side conversations. One way to accomplish this is to set up an instant messaging system that allows members to contact each other for short conversations during and between meetings.

7. **Schedule regular opportunities to assess the pros and cons of the technology and make adjustments as warranted.** Survey the group regularly to discover emerging problems and work together to correct them before they undermine the quality of the group's work.

Obviously, group communication in virtual settings poses an additional set of challenges to ensure an effective outcome. As more and more people opt to engage in virtual groups, it is critical to continuing developing and engaging in communication strategies that will promote effective outcomes.

16-5 GROUP PRESENTATION FORMATS

Once a group has completed its deliberations, it is usually expected to communicate its results. **Deliverables** are products of your work you provide to someone else. Although some deliverables are objects, typically the deliverables from problem-solving groups come in the form of communicating the information, analyses, and recommendations of the group. These deliverables can be communicated in written formats, oral formats, or virtual formats.

deliverables: products of your work that must be provided to someone else

16-5a Written Formats

written brief: a very short document that describes the problem, background, process, decision, and rationale so that the reader can quickly understand and evaluate the group's product

1. A **written brief** is a very short document that describes the problem, background, process, decision, and rationale so that the reader can quickly understand and evaluate the group's product. Most briefs are one or two pages long. When preparing a brief, begin by describing your group's task. What problem were you attempting to solve and why? Then briefly provide the background information the reader will need to evaluate whether the group has adequately studied the problem. Present solution steps and timelines for implementation as bullet points so that the reader can quickly understand what is being proposed. Close with a sentence or very short paragraph that describes how the recommendation will solve the problem, as well as any potential side effects.

comprehensive report: a written document that provides a detailed review of the problem-solving process used to arrive at the recommendation

2. A **comprehensive report** is a written document that provides a detailed review of the problem-solving process used to arrive at the recommendation. A comprehensive report is usually organized into sections that parallel the problem-solving process.

Because comprehensive reports can be very long, they usually include an executive summary. An **executive summary** is a one-page synopsis of the report. This summary contains enough information to acquaint readers with the highlights of the full document without reading it. Usually, it contains a statement of the problem, some background information, a description of any alternatives, and the major conclusions.

executive summary: a one-page synopsis of the report

16-5b Oral Formats

oral brief: essentially a summary of a written brief delivered to an audience by a group member

1. An **oral brief** is essentially a summary of a written brief delivered to an audience by a group member. Typically, an oral brief can be delivered in less than 10 minutes.

oral report: similar to a comprehensive report

2. An **oral report** is similar to a comprehensive report. It provides a more detailed review of a group's problem-solving process. Oral reports can range from 30 to 60 minutes.

panel discussion: a problem-solving discussion in front of an audience

3. A **panel discussion** is a structured problem-solving discussion held by a group in front of an audience. One member serves as moderator, introducing the topic and providing structure by asking a series of planned questions that panelists answer. Their answers and the interaction among them provide the supporting evidence. A well-planned panel discussion seems spontaneous and interactive but requires careful planning and rehearsal to ensure that all relevant information is presented and that all speakers are afforded equal speaking time. After the formal discussion, the audience is often encouraged to question the participants. Perhaps you've seen or heard a panel of experts discuss a topic on a radio or television talk show like *Sports Center, Meet the Press,* or *The Doctors.*

symposium: a set of prepared oral reports delivered sequentially by group members.

4. A **symposium** is a set of prepared oral reports delivered sequentially by group members before a gathering of people who are interested in the work of the group. A symposium may be organized so that each person's speech focuses on one step of the problem-solving process, or it may be organized so that each speaker covers all of the steps in the problem-solving process as they relate to one of several issues or recommendations that the group worked on or made. In a symposium, the speakers usually sit together at the front of the room. One member acts as moderator, offering the introductory and concluding remarks and providing transitions between speakers. When introduced by the moderator, each speaker may stand and walk to a central spot, usually a lectern. Speakers who use a computerized slideshow should coordinate their slides so that there are seamless transitions between speakers. Symposiums often conclude with a question-and-answer session facilitated by the moderator, who directs one or more of the members to answer based on their expertise. Questions can be directed to individuals or to the group as a whole.

Exhibit (16.7) **Example of a Slide in a Remote Access Report**

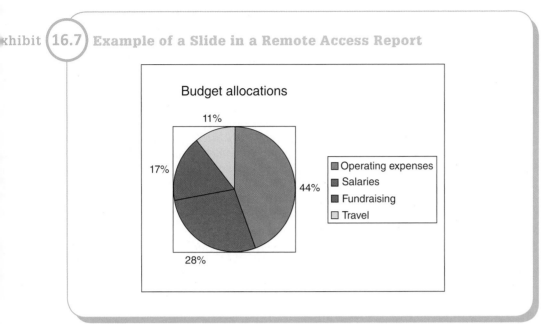

16-5c Virtual Formats

1. A **remote access report (RAR)** is a computer-mediated audiovisual presentation of the group's process and outcome that others can receive through e-mail, Web posting, and so forth. Prepared by one or more members of the group, the RAR is prepared using PowerPoint or some other computer slideshow software and provides a visual overview of the group's process, decisions, and recommendations. Effective RARs typically consist of no more than 15 to 20 slides. Slides are titled and content is presented in outline or bullet-point phrases or key words (rather than complete sentences or paragraphs), as well as through visual representations of important information. For example, a budget task force might have a slide with a pie chart depicting the portions of the proposed budget that are allocated to operating expenses, salaries, fundraising, and travel (see Exhibit 16.7). RARs may be self-running so that the slides automatically forward after a certain number of seconds, but it is better to let the viewer choose the pace and control when the next slide appears. RARs can be silent or narrated. When narrated, a voice-over accompanies each slide, providing additional or explanatory information.

   remote access report (RAR): a computer-mediated audiovisual presentation of the group's process and outcome that others can receive through e-mail, Web posting, and so forth

2. A **streaming video** is a recording that is sent in compressed form over the Internet. You are probably familiar with streaming video from popular websites such as YouTube. Streaming videos are a great way to distribute oral briefs, but they also can be used to distribute recordings of oral reports, symposiums, or panel presentations. Streaming videos are useful when it is inconvenient for some or all the people who need to know the results of the group's work to meet at one time or in one place.

   streaming video: a prerecording that is sent in compressed form over the Internet

16-6 EVALUATING GROUP EFFECTIVENESS

Just as preparing and presenting are a bit different for group speeches than for individual speeches, so is the process of evaluating effectiveness. Evaluations should focus on group dynamics during the preparation process as well as on the effectiveness of the actual presentation.

16-6a Group Dynamics

To be effective, groups must work together as they define and analyze a problem, generate solutions, and select a course of action. They also need to work together as they prepare their written report, as well as prepare and practice, their oral presentation if warranted. These communication interactions among members to achieve a goal are known as **group dynamics**.

group dynamics: how individuals work together as a team toward a common goal

You can evaluate group dynamics by judging the merit of each member's efforts in terms of the five group member responsibilities discussed earlier in this chapter. In addition, each group member could prepare a "reflective thinking process paper," which details in paragraph form what each member did well and could improve upon in terms of the five member responsibilities. In the final paragraph of the paper, each member should provide a self-evaluation of what he or she did and what he or she could do to improve the group process in future sessions. To complete a reflective thinking process paper online, go to **Web Link 16.3, Reflective Thinking Process Paper,** on your MindTap for *Challenge*.

Like the evaluations business managers make of employees, these evaluations serve to document the efforts of group members. They can be submitted to the instructor, just as they would be submitted to a supervisor. In business, these documents provide a basis for determining promotion, merit pay, and salary adjustments. In the classroom, they can provide a basis for determining one portion of each member's grade.

16-6b Group Presentations

Effective group presentations depend on quality individual presentations as well as quality overall group performance. So evaluations of group presentations should consist of both an individual and a group component. Exhibit 16.8 shows a form you can use to evaluate the effectiveness of a group presentation.

Evaluating Your Effectiveness

Effective group presentations depend on the combined efforts of individuals. So it's also a good idea to conduct a self-evaluation to determine whether you could be doing something better during the group problem-solving process, while preparing the group presentation, and when giving your portion of the group speech. Exhibit 16.9 is an example of a form used to evaluate your own efforts.

speech assignment

Public Group Presentation

Following your instructor's directions, form groups of four to six members. Each group will prepare a symposium or a panel discussion of a topic. Groups will use the problem-solving process to guide their work. Each group member must help identify an appropriate issue, participate in the problem-solving process, and take part in the presentation. Your instructor will provide more details of the expectations for this assignment.

Group Member Name: _____

Critic (your name): _____

Directions: Evaluate the effectiveness of each group member according to each of the following criteria for effective presentations individually and as a group.

Rating Scale:

1	2	3	4	5	6	7
(poor)						(excellent)

INDIVIDUAL PERFORMANCE CRITIQUE

_____ **Content** (Breadth and depth and listener relevance)

(rating) Critique (Provide a rationale for the rating you gave):

_____ **Structure** (Macrostructure and microstructure/language)

(rating) Critique (Provide a rationale for the rating you gave):

_____ **Delivery** (Use of voice and use of body)

(rating) Critique (Provide a rationale for the rating you gave):

GROUP PERFORMANCE CRITIQUE

_____ **Content** (Thematic? Focused? Thorough? Construction of presentational aids?)

(rating) Critique (Provide a rationale for the rating you gave):

_____ **Structure** (Balanced? Transitions? Flow? Attn/Clincher?)

(rating) Critique (Provide a rationale for the rating you gave):

_____ **Delivery** (Teamwork? Cooperation? Fluency? Use of aids?)

(rating) Critique (Provide a rationale for the rating you gave):

Overall Comments:
_____

Directions: Complete the items below with regard to your presentation in the group symposium.

1. If I could do my portion of the oral presentation over again, I would do the following things differently:
   a.
   b.

2. In terms of content, I did the following things well in my oral presentation:
   a.
   b.

3. In terms of structure, I did the following things well in my oral presentation:
   a.
   b.

4. In terms of delivery, I did the following things well in my oral presentation:
   a.
   b.
   c.

5. In terms of my role as a group member, I am most proud of how I:

6. In terms of my role as a group member, I am least proud of how I:

7. Overall, I would give myself a grade of _____ for the group speech because:

Reflection and Assessment

Today, working and speaking in groups is popular not only in the classroom but also in business and industry. Effective problem-solving groups produce better products than individuals can do on their own. To assess how well you've learned what we've discussed in this chapter, answer the following questions. If you have trouble answering any of them, go back and review that material. Once you can answer each question accurately, you will have a basic understanding of how to master the challenge of effective speaking in a digital age.

1. Why is shared leadership so critical when working in groups?
2. What can you do to manage conflict effectively in groups?
3. What are the steps in the systematic problem-solving method?
4. What are some special guidelines to follow when communicating in virtual groups?
5. What are some formats for group presentations?
6. How can you evaluate group dynamics and presentations?

Challenge Resource and Assessment Center

Now that you have read Chapter 16, go to your MIndTap for *The Challenge of Effective Speaking in a Digital Age* for quick access to the electronic resources that accompany this text. These resources include the following:

- **Study tools** that will help you assess your learning and prepare for exams (*digital glossary, key term flash cards, review quizzes*).

- **Activities and assignments** that will help you hone your knowledge and build your public speaking skills throughout the course (Practice, Do). Many of these activities allow you to compare your answers with those provided by the authors and, if requested, submit your answers to your instructor.

- **Media resources**—all of which are available on your MindTap for *Challenge*—will help you explore communication concepts online (Practice), develop your speech outlines (Do), watch and critique videos of sample speeches (Do), and upload your speech videos for instructor feedback and critique other students' speeches (Do).

- **Web Links that provide you with additional information or resources related to the topics discussed in this chapter.**
  16.1: Rules for Brainstorming (p. 338)
  16.2: Decision Making Methods (p. 338)
  16.3: Reflective Thinking Process Paper (p. 342)

- **Video resources allow you to see other students giving speeches and record your own speech.**
  1. Use your Interactive Video Activities to watch, analyze, and see the transcript and outlines for the group speech "The Dirty Truth about Antibacterial Products."
  2. View group speeches given in other classes. Or go to the Practice and Present section of MindTap and record a speech your group is working on, upload it to Speech Studio, and ask your peers for their feedback. What feedback could you use to fine-tune your group speech before you give it in class?

Applying What You've Learned

1. **Impromptu Speech Activity:** Each group should brainstorm a list of at least ten topic ideas for their group presentation. Then, each member of the group should select one of the topics (no duplicates allowed) and quickly prepare a two- to three-minute impromptu speech whose goal is to convince the other group members that his or her topic should be the one the group selects for the group's panel or symposium. After members have presented their speeches to the other group members, each member should rank order his or her preference for each topic. Groups should compile these results and use them as they decide on a topic.

2. **Assessment Activity A:** Watch a television talk show program that is presented as a panel discussion, for example, *The View, SportsCenter, Fox and Friends*, or *Morning Joe*. Evaluate the group dynamics process based on the five responsibilities of group members described in this chapter. Be sure to offer specific examples supporting your evaluation as to how each member of the panel performed and what he or she could do to improve. Then prepare a one- to two-page reflection paper as described in **Web Link 16.3**.

3. **Assessment Activity B:** Assess how well your group functioned for this project by completing a one- to two-page reflection paper as described in **Web Link 16.3**. Indicate what each member did well according to the five responsibilities and why, what each member could do to improve and why, and what your role is in that process. Also assess how well you performed according to each of the five responsibilities and why, as well as what you could do to improve, why, and how.

notes

Chapter 1 Foundations of Public Speaking

1. Morreale, S., Hugenberg, L., & Worley, D. (2006). The basic communication course at U.S. colleges and universities in the 21st century: Study VII. *Communication Education, 55*(4), 415–437.

2. Ankita. (2012). 9 most essential civic rights enjoyed by a citizen. *Preserve Articles.* Retrieved from: http://www.preservearticles.com/201106248527/9-most-essential-civic-rights-enjoyed-by-a-citizen.html

3. Cooper, L. (1932). *The rhetoric of Aristotle.* Englewood Cliffs, NJ: Prentice-Hall.

4. Koncz, A. (2008). *Job outlook 2009.* Bethlehem, PA: National Association of Colleges and Employers.

5. Hansen, R. S., & Hansen, K. (n.d.). What do employers *really* want? Top skills and values employers seek from job-seekers. Retrieved from http://www.quintcareers.com/job_skills_values.html

6. Taylor, P., Parker, K., Lenhart, A., & Patten, E. (2011, August 28). The digital revolution and higher education: College presidents, public differ on value of online learning. Washington, D.C.: Pew Research Center.

7. What is plagiarism? (n.d.). Retrieved from http://www.plagiarism.org/learning_center/what_is_plagiarism.html

8. McCullen, C. (2003, November–December). Tactics and resources to help students avoid plagiarism. *Multimedia Schools,* 40–43.

9. Littlejohn, S. W., & Foss, K. A. (2008). *Theories of human communication* (9th ed.). Boston, MA: Wadsworth/Cengage.

10. Cragen, J. F., & Shields, D. C. (1998). *Understanding communication theory: The communicative forces for human action.* Boston, MA: Allyn & Bacon.

11. Frey, L. R., Botan, C. H., & Kreps, G. L. (2000). *Investigating communication: An introduction to research methods.* (2nd ed.). Needham Heights, MA: Allyn & Bacon.

12. Littlejohn, S. W., & Foss, K. A. (2011). *Theories of human communication* (10th ed.). Longrove, IL: Waveland.

13. Kellerman, K. (1992). Communication: Inherently strategic and primarily automatic. *Communication Monographs, 59,* 288–300.

14. Ibid.

15. Knapp, M., & Daly, J. (2002). *Handbook of interpersonal communication.* Thousand Oaks, CA: Sage.

16. Poole, M. S. (1998). The small group should be the fundamental unit of communication research. In J. Trent (Ed.), *Communication: Views from the helm for the twenty-first century* (p. 94). Needham Heights, MA: Allyn & Bacon.

17. Beebe, S., & Masterson, J. (2006). *Communicating in groups: Principles and practice* (8th ed.). Boston: Pearson.

18. Hirokawa, R., Cathcart, R., Samovar, I., & Henman, I. (Eds.). (2003). *Small group communication theory and practice* (8th ed.). Los Angeles, Roxbury.

19. Devine, D. J., Clayton, L. D., Phillips, J. L., Dunford, B. B., & Melner, S. B. (1999). Teams in organizations: Prevalence, characteristics, and effectiveness. *Small Group Research, 30,* 678–711.

20. Forsythe, D. R., & Burnette, J. L. (2005). The history of group research. In S. A. Wheelen (Ed.). *The handbook of group research and practice.* Thousand Oaks, CA: Sage.

21. Knapp, M. L., & Daly, J. A. (Eds.). (2011). *The SAGE handbook of interpersonal communication* (4th ed.). Thousand Oaks, CA: Sage.

22. Wazlawick, P., Bavelas, J., & Jackson, D. (1967). *Pragmatics of human communication: A study of interactional patterns, pathologies, and paradoxes.* New York: Norton.

23. Bitzer, L. F. (1995). The rhetorical situation. In Covino, W. A., Jolliffe, D. A. (Eds.), *Rhetoric: Concepts, definitions, boundaries.* Boston, MA: Allyn & Bacon.

24. Ibid.

25. Exigence. (2009). In *Microsoft Encarta world English dictionary* (North American edition). Retrieved from http://encarta.msn.com/dictionary_1861609760/exigency.html

26. Cooper, *Rhetoric.*

27. The Stuttering Foundation. (1991–2012). *Famous people.* Retrieved from www.stutteringhelp.org/famous-people

28. Jensen, V. (1985). Teaching ethics in speech communication. *Communication Education, 34,* 324–330.

29. Decker, B. (1992). *You've got to be believed to be heard.* New York, NY: St. Martin's Press.

30. Treinen, K. Unpublished manuscript, delivered in speech class, North Dakota State University.

31. The Stuttering Foundation.

32. Ibid.

Chapter 2 Your First Speech

1. Hahner, J. C., Sokoloff, M. A., & Salisch, S. L. (2001). *Speaking clearly: Improving voice and diction* (6th ed.). New York, NY: McGraw-Hill.

2. Richmond, V. P., & McCroskey, J. C. (2000). *Communication apprehension, avoidance, and effectiveness* (5th ed.). Scottsdale, AZ: Gorsuch Scarisbrick.

3. Phillips, G. M. (1977). Rhetoritherapy versus the medical model: Dealing with reticence. *Communication Education, 26,* 37.

4. Motley, M. (1997). COM therapy. In J. A. Daly, J. C. McCroskey, J. Ayres, T. Hopf, & D. M. Ayres (Eds.), *Avoiding communication: Shyness, reticence, and communication apprehension* (2nd ed., p. 382). Cresskill, NJ: Hampton Press.

5. Phillips, Rhetoritherapy, 37.

6. Richmond & McCroskey, *Communication.*

7. Behnke, R. R., & Carlile, L. W. (1971). Heart rate as an index of speech anxiety. *Speech Monographs, 38,* 66.

8. Beatty, M. J., & Behnke, R. R. (1991). Effects of public speaking trait anxiety and intensity of speaking task on heart rate during performance. *Human Communication Research, 18,* 147–176.

9. Richmond & McCroskey, *Communication.*

10. Beatty, M. J., McCroskey, J. C., & Heisner, A. D. (1998, September). Communication apprehension as temperamental expression: A communibiological paradigm. *Communication Monographs, 65,* 200.

11. Richmond & McCroskey, *Communication.*

12. Bandura, A. (1973). *Social learning theory.* Englewood Cliffs, NJ: Prentice Hall.

13. Daly, J. A., Caughlin, J. P. & Stafford, L. (1997). Correlates and consequences of social-communicative anxiety. In J. A. Daly, J. C. McCroskey, J. Ayres, T. Hopf, & D. M. Ayres (Eds.), *Avoiding communication: Shyness, reticence, and communication apprehension* (2nd ed., p. 27). Cresskill, NJ: Hampton Press.

14. Dunn, J. (2008, April). Tina Fey: Funny girl. *Reader's Digest Magazine* [online]. Retrieved from: http://www.rd.com/advice/tina-fey-interview/

15. Motley, COM therapy, 382.

16. Ibid., 380.

17. Ayres, J., & Hopf, T. S. (1990, January). The long-term effect of visualization in the classroom: A brief research report. *Communication Education, 39,* 77.

18. Scott, P. (1997, January–February). Mind of a champion. *Natural Health, 27,* 99.

19. Bourne, E. J. (1990). *The anxiety and phobia workbook.* Oakland, CA: New Harbinger Publications.

20. Friedrich, G., & Goss, B. (1984). Systematic desensitization. In J. A. Daly & J. C. McCroskey (Eds.), *Avoiding communication.* Beverly Hills, CA: Sage.

21. Davis, M., Echelon, E., & McKay, M. (1988). *The relaxation and stress workbook.* Oakland, CA: New Harbinger Publications.

22. Richmond & McCroskey, *Communication.*

23. Ibid.

24. Griffin, K. (1995, July). Beating performance anxiety. *Working Woman,* 62–65, 76.

25. Dwyer, K. K. (2000, January). The multidimensional model: Teaching students to self-manage high communication apprehension by self-selecting treatments. *Communication Education, 49,* 79.

26. Thomas, B. (2000, February 28). In normal conversation. Associated Press.

27. Bailey, E. (2008, August 7). Celebrities with anxiety: Harrison Ford: Fear of Public Speaking. *Health Central.* Retrieved from: http://www.healthcentral.com/anxiety/c/22705/36519/celebrities-public

28. Ford, H. (IMDb). Biography for Harrison Ford. Retrieved from: http://www.imdb.com/name/nm0000148/bio

29. Richmond & McCroskey, *Communication.*

30. Study shows how sleep improves memory. (2005, June 29). *Science Daily.* Retrieved from http:// www.sciencedaily.com/releases/2005/06/050629070337.htm

31. *Rhetorica ad herennium.* (1954, H. Caplan, Trans.). Cambridge, MA: Harvard University Press.

32. Bitzer, L. (1968). The rhetorical situation. *Philosophy and Rhetoric, 1*(1), 1–14.

33. Aristotle. (1960). *On rhetoric.* (L. Cooper, Trans.). New York: Appleton-Century-Crofts.

34. Associated Press. (14 December 2001). O'Leary out at Notre Dame after one week. *Sports Illustrated.* Retrieved online at: http://sportsillustrated.cnn.com/football/college/news/2001/12/14/oleary_notredame/

Chapter 3 Listening

1. Donaghue, P. J., & Seigal, M. E. (2005). *Are you really listening? Keys to successful communication.* Notre Dame, IN: Sorin Books.

2. International Listening Association. (1996). Retrieved from http://www.listen.org/

3. Janusik, L. A., & Wolvin, A. D. (2006). *24 hours in a day: A listening update to the time studies.* Paper presented at the meeting of the International Listening Association, Salem, OR.

4. International Listening Association. (2003). *Listening factoid.* Retrieved from http://www.listen.org/pages/factoids/html

5. DeWine, S., & Daniels, T. Beyond the snapshot: Setting a research agenda in organizational communication. In S. A. Deetz (Ed.), *Communication yearbook 16* (pp. 252–230). Thousand Oaks, CA: Sage.

6. Salopek, J. J. (1999). Is anyone listening? *Training and Development, 53*(9), 58–60.

7. Brownell, J. (2006). *Listening: Attitudes, principles, and skills* (3rd ed.). Boston: Allyn & Bacon.

8. Watson, K. W., Barker, L. L., & Weaver, J. B. III. (1995). The listening styles profile (LSP-16): Development and validation of an instrument to assess four listening styles. *International Journal of Listening, 9,* 1–13.

9. Weaver, J. B. III, & Kirtley, M. D. (1995). Listening styles and empathy. *The Southern Communication Journal, 60*(2), 131–140.

10. O'Shaughnessy, B. (2003). Active attending or a theory of mental action. *Consciousness and the World, 29,* 379–407.

11. Wolvin, A., & Coakley, C. G. (1996). *Listening* (5th ed.). New York, NY: McGraw-Hill.

12. Stephens, M. (1999). The new TV: Stop making sense. In Ray E. Hiebert (Ed.), *Impact of mass media: Current issues* (4th ed., pp. 16–22). White Plains, NY: Longman.

13. Dukette, D., & Cornish, D. (2009). *The essential 20: Twenty components of an excellent health care team* (pp. 72–73). RoseDog Books; Turning into digital goldfish. (2002, February 22). *BBC News.* Retrieved from http://news.bbc.co.uk/2/hi/science/nature/1834682.stm

14. Sharpening your listening skills. (2002, October). *Teller Vision* 0895-1039, 7.

15. Bonaguro, A. (2009, September 13). Kanye West steals Taylor Swift's thunder at MTV Video Music Awards. Retrieved from http://blog.cmt.com/2009-09-13/kanye-west-steals-taylor-swifts-thunder-at-mtv-video-music-awards/

16. Melas, C. (2012, August 30). Kanye West Will Not Apologize to Taylor Swift at VMAs. *Hollywood Life.* Retrieved from http://hollywoodlife.com/2012/08/30/kanye-west-taylor-swift-vmas-video/

17. Estes, W. K. (1989). Learning theory. In A Lesgold & R. Glaser (Eds.). *Foundations for a psychology of education* (pp. 1–49). Hillsdale, NJ: Erlbaum.

18. Wolvin & Coakley, *Listening.*

19. Dunkel, P., & Pialorsi, F. (2005). *Advanced listening comprehension: Developing aural and notetaking skills.* Boston, MA: Thomson Heinle.

20. Carnegie, D. (1936). *How to win friends and influence people.* New York: Simon and Schuster. Dale Carnegie Training. [website] Retrieved June 20. 2013 at www.dalecarnegie.com

21. *BBC Presents Warren Buffet on Dale Carnegie—Dale Carnegie Training.* YouTube video retrieved on June 20, 2013 at http://www.youtube.com/watch?feature=player_embedded&v=k7gXaPY5241

Chapter 4 Determining an Appropriate Speech Goal

1. Sorkin, A. (2012, July 16). Aaron Sorkin: The Writer Behind "The Newsroom." Interview by Terry Gross. Philadelphia, PA: National Public Radio. Retrieved from: http://www.npr.org/2012/07/16/156841165/aaron-sorkin-the-writer-behind-the-newsroom

2. Berger, C. R. (1988). Uncertainty reduction and information exchange in developing relationships. In S. Duck, D. Hay, S. Hobfoll, W. Ickes, & B. Montgomery (Eds.), *Handbook of interpersonal relationships: Theory, research, and interventions* (pp. 239–255). New York, NY: Wiley.

3. Callison, D. (2001). Concept mapping. *School Library Media Activities Monthly, 17*(10), 30–32.

4. Edwards, A. (2012, July 25). Once blocked, boy's appeal for gays to wed gets Council audience. *New York Times.* Retrieved from: http://www.nytimes.com/2012/07/26/nyregion/kameron-slades-appeal-for-gay-marriage-once-blocked-at-school-gets-council-audience.html?_r=0

Chapter 5 Adapting to Audiences

1. Blumer, H. (1969). *Symbolic interactionism.* Englewood Cliffs, NJ: Prentice-Hall.

2. Thamel, P. (2012, October 1). The full manti. *Sports Illustrated.* Retrieved from http://sportsillustrated.cnn.com/vault/article/magazine/MAG1206734/index.htm?eref=sisf

3. The Faces of Wealth. (2012, September 12). *Forbes.* Retrieved from http://www.forbes.com/forbes-400/

4. Celebrity Lessons in Selling. (2010). *Inc.* New York: Mansueto Ventures. Retrieved from http://www.inc.com/ss/celebrity-lessons-selling#0

5. Tannen, D. (1998, June 8). Oprah Winfrey: The TV host. *Time.* Retrieved from http://www.time.com/time/magazine/article/0,9171,988512-2,00.html

6. Barbe, W., & Swassing, R. H. (1979). *The Swassing-Barbe Modality Index.* Columbus, OH: Waner-Bloser; Canfield, A. A. (1980). *Learning styles inventory manual.* Ann Arbor, MI: Humanics Inc.; Dunn, R., Dunn, K., & Price, G. E. (1975). *Learning styles inventory.* Lawrence, KS: Price Systems; Gardner, H. (1983). *Frames of mind: The theory of multiple intelligences.* New York, NY: Basic Books; Kolb, D. (1984). *Experiential learning: Experience as the source of learning and development.* Englewood Cliffs, NJ: Prentice Hall.

7. Kolb, D. A. (1984). *Experiential learning: Experience as the source of learning and development.* Upper Saddle River, NJ: Prentice-Hall.

8. Dewey, J. (1938/1997) *Experience and education.* New York, NY: Macmillan.

9. Ibid.

10. *The world almanac and book of facts* (pp. 798, 850). (2004). New York, NY: World Almanac Books.

Chapter 6 Topic Development

1. Pistor, N. J. C. (2012, November 16). "Lincoln" actor Daniel Day-Lewis studied role "under the radar" in Springfield, *St. Louis Post-Dispatch.* Retrieved from http://www.stltoday.com/news/local/illinois/lincoln-actor-daniel-day-lewis-studied-role-under-the-radar/article_7bdaa148-fe4c-5756-ae8b-06e0e740c05d.html

2. Lowman, R. (2012, December 3). Sally Field fought a long campaign to be first lady in "Lincoln." *Denver Post,* Retrieved from http://www.denverpost.com/entertainment/ci_22105071

3. Munger, D., Anderson, D., Benjamin, B., Busiel, C., & Pardes-Holt, B. (2000). *Researching online* (3rd ed.). New York, NY: Longman.

4. Tengler, C., & Jablin, F. M. (1983). Effects of question type, orientation, and sequencing in the employment screening interview. *Communication Monographs, 50,* 261.

5. Biagi, S. *Interviews that work: A practical guide for journalists* (2nd ed., p. 94). Belmont, CA: Wadsworth.

6. Frances, P. (1994). Lies, damned lies. *American Demographics, 16,* 2.

7. Ibid.

8. Ahladas, J. (1989, April 1). Global warming. *Vital Speeches,* 382.

9. Shalala, D. (1994, May 15). Domestic terrorism: An unacknowledged epidemic. *Vital Speeches,* 451.

10. Howard, J. A. (2000, August 1). Principles in default: Rediscovered and reapplied. *Vital Speeches,* 618.

11. Nelson, J. C. (2006). *Leadership.* Utah School Boards Assocaition 83rd Annual Conference, Salt Lake City, Utah. Retrieved from http://www.ama-assn.org/ama/pub/category/15860.html.

12. Durst, G. M. (1989, March 1). The manager as a developer. *Vital Speeches,* 309–310.

13. Becherer, H. (2000, September 15). Enduring values for a secular age: Faith, hope and love. *Vital Speeches,* 732.

14. Opheim, C. (2000, November 1). Making democracy work: Your responsibility to society. *Vital Speeches,* 60.

15. Kreps, D. (2009, September 16). Satriani's "Viva La Vida" copyright suit against Coldplay dismissed. *Rolling Stone.* Retrieved from http://www.rollingstone.com/rockdaily/inde.php/2009/09/16satrianis-viva-la-vida-copyright-suit-against-coldplay-dismissed/

Chapter 7 Organizing and Outlining the Speech Body

1. Barribeau, T. (2012, March 26). Fortune names Steve Jobs "greatest entrepreneur *of our time.*" *Fortune.* Retrieved from http://archive.is/20120916/http://www.everythingicafe.com/fortune-names-steve-jobs-greatest-entrepreneur-of-our-time/2012/03/26/

2. Barber, C. (2010, September 29). Steve Jobs: Chunk structure helps engage Stanford audience. Vivid Learning. Retrieved from http://vividmethod.com/a-good-structure-helps-steve-jobs/

3. Fisher, W. (1987). *Human communication as narration: Toward a philosophy of reason, value, and action.* Columbia, SC: University of South Carolina Press.

4. Kids book gets pulled. (2006, January 31). *Associated Press.* Retrieved from http://www.canada.com/topics/entertainment/story.html?id=45761b54-245c-4c76-9618-212c645f9800&k=23104

5. Deahl, R. (2006, January 31). Blue Apple to cancel book. *Publishers Weekly.* Retrieved from http://www.publishersweekly.com/article/CA6303375.html

Chapter 8 The Introduction and Conclusion

1. Trenholm, S. (1989). *Persuasion and social influence.* New Jersey: Prentice-Hall; Crano, W. D. (1977). Primacy versus recency in retention of information and opinion change. *The Journal of Social Psychology, 101,* 87–96.

2. Mackay, H. (2009, July). Changing the world: Your future is a work in progress. *Vital Speeches,* 319–323.

3. Gupta, Y. (2010, February). Beyond wisdom: Business dimensions of an aging America. *Vital Speeches,* 69–75.

4. Humes, J. C. (1988). *Standing ovation: How to be an effective speaker and communicator.* New York: Harper & Row,.

5. Olsteen, J. (2012). Best jokes of Joel Olsteen. *Better Days TV.* Retrieved from http://www.betterdaystv.net/play.php?vid=247

6. Mason, S. (2007, April). Equality will someday come. *Vital Speeches,* 159–163.

7. Bitzer, L. F. (1995). The Rhetorical Situation. In W. A. Covino & D. A. Jolliffe (Eds.), *Rhetoric: Concepts, Definitions, Boundaries.* Boston, MA: Allyn and Bacon.

8. Cieply, M., & Barnes, B. (2013, February 25). Academy award show raises ratings and hackles. New York Times. Retrieved from http://www.nytimes.com/2013/02/25/movies/awardsseason/higher-ratings-and-controversy-for-seth-macfarlane-at-oscars.html?pagewanted=all&_r=0

9. Ravitz, J. (2013, February 24). Seth MacFarlane jokes about Rihanna, Chris Brown "Violence" in Oscars opening monologue. Us Weekly, Retrieved from http://www.usmagazine.com/celebrity-news/news/seth-macfarlane-jokes-about-rihanna-chris-brown-violence-in-oscars-opening-monologue-2013242

10. Chen, J. (2013, February 26). Seth MacFarlane says there's "no way" he'll host the Oscars again. Us Weekly, Retrieved from http://www.usmagazine.com/celebrity-news/news/seth-macfarlane-says-theres-no-way-hell-host-the-oscars-again-2013262

11. Aristotle. (1954). *Rhetoric* (W. Rhys Roberts, Trans.). New York: Modern Library.

12. Mariano, C. (2010, January). Unity, quality, responsibility: The real meaning of the words. *Vital Speeches,* 20–22.

13. Jobs, S. (2005, 15 June). You've got to find what you love. *Stanford University News*. Retrieved from http://news.stanford.edu/news/2005/june15/jobs-061505.html

14. Cossolotto, M. (2009, December). An urgent call to action for study abroad alumni to help reduce our global awareness deficit. *Vital Speeches*, 564–568.

15. Avery, R. (2013, February 6). 9 lessons learned from Lady Gaga. AveryToday. [blog post] Retrieved from http://averytoday.com/9-public-speaking-lessons-learned-from-lady-gaga/

Chapter 9 Presentational Aids

1. Muren, D. (2009). *Humblefacturing a sustainable electronic future*. Presentation at Ignite Seattle 6. Retrieved from http://www.youtube.com/watch?v=FIoU1pemi18

2. Tversky, B. (1997). Memory for pictures, maps, environments, and graphs. In D. G. Payne & F. G. Conrad (Eds.), *Intersections in basic and applied memory research* (pp. 257–277). Hillsdale, NJ: Erlbaum.

3. Kolb, D. (1984). *Experiential learning: Experience as the source of learning and development*. Englewood Cliffs, NJ: Prentice Hall; Gallo, C. (2006, December 5). Presentations with something for everyone. *Business Week Online*. Retrieved from http://www.businessweek.com/smallbiz/content/dec2006/sb20061205_454055.htm

4. Hanke, J. (1998). The psychology of presentation visuals. *Presentations, 12*(5), 42–47.

5. Ayers, J. (1991). Using visual aids to reduce speech anxiety. *Communication Research Reports*, 73–79; Dwyer, K. (1991). *Conquer your speechfright*. Orlando, FL: Harcourt Brace.

6. International Charter. (1997–2012). EAS-405: Ethical advertising standard. Retrieved from http://www.icharter.org/standards/eas405/index.html

7. Booher, D. D. (2003). *Speak with confidence [electronic resources]: Powerful presentations that inform, inspire, and persuade*. New York, NY: McGraw-Hill.

8. Kolb, *Experiential Learning*; Long, K. (1997). *Visual-Aids and Learning*, University of Portsmouth, Retrieved from http://www.mech.port.ac.uk/av/AVInfo.htm

9. Ristor, A. (2012, October 31). What is an ignite presentation and why should you try it? Six Minutes: Speaking and Presentation Skills [Blog post]. Retrieved from http://sixminutes.dlugan.com/ignite-presentations/

10. VanGrove, J. (2010, March 1). 10 reasons you should attend or watch a Global Ignite Week event. Mashable, Inc.. Retrieved from http://mashable.com/2010/03/01/global-ignite-week/

11. Connecting Veterans to Career Opportunities (2013). Boots to Suits website. Retrieved from http://boots-to-suits.com/

12. Forrest, B. (2009). Speaker confessions. True tales from a veteran public speaker. O'Reilly Media, Inc. Retrieved from http://www.speakerconfessions.com/press/

Chapter 10 Language and Oral Style

1. Weeks, L. (2009, February 11). The art of language, Obama style? National Public Radio. Retrieved from http://www.npr.org/templates/story/story.php?storyId=100525275

2. Hart, R., & Jamieson, K. H. (2012). Campaign mapping project. The Annette Strauss Institute for Civic Life at the University of Austin Texas. [Funding support from the Ford Foundation and Carnegie Foundation of New York]. Retrieved from http://communication.utexas.edu/strauss/campaign-mapping-project

3. Leith, S. (2013, January 21). Barack Obama inauguration speech: A greatest hits of rhetorical tricks. *The Guardian*. Retrieved from http://www.guardian.co.uk/world/2013/jan/21/barack-obama-speech-greatest-hits-rhetoric

4. Ibid.

5. Witt, P. L., Wheeless, L. R., & Allen, M. (2007, May). A meta-analytical review of the relationship between teacher immediacy and student learning. Paper presented at the annual meeting of the International Communication Association, San Diego. Retrieved from http://www.allacademic.com/meta/p112238_index.html

6. Edwards, C. C. (2002). Verbal immediacy and androgyny: An examination of student perceptions of college instructors. *Academic Exchange Quarterly*,6, 180–185; Gorham, J. (1998). The relationship between teacher verbal immediacy behaviors and student learning. *Communication Education*, 37, 40–53; Powell R. G., & Harville, B. (1990). The effects of teacher immediacy and clarity on instructional outcomes: An intercultural assessment. *Communication Education*, 39, 369–379.

7. Braithwaite D., & Braithwaite, C. (1997). Viewing persons with disabilities as a culture. In L. Samovar & R. Porter (Eds.), *Intercultural communication: A reader* (8th ed., pp. 154–164). Belmont, CA: Wadsworth; Treinen, K., & Warren, J. (2001). Antiracist pedagogy in the basic course: Teaching cultural communication as if whiteness matters. *Basic Communication Course Annual,*13, 46–75.

8. Stewart, L. P., Cooper, P. J., Stewart, A. D., & Friedley, S. A. (2003). *Communication and gender* (4th ed., p. 63). Boston, MA: Allyn & Bacon.

9. Gastil, J. (1990). Generic pronouns and sexist language: The oxymoronic character of masculine generics. *Sex Roles*, 23, 629–643; Hamilton, M. C. (1991). Masculine bias in the attribution of personhood: People = male, male = people. *Psychology of Women Quarterly*, 15, 393–402; Switzer, J. W. (1990). The impact of generic word choices: An empirical investigation of age- and sex-related differences. *Sex Roles,* 22, 69–82.

10. Treinen and Warren, Antiracist pedagogy in the basic course.

11. DuFrene D. D., & Lehman, C. M. (2002, March). Persuasive appeal for clean language. *Business Quarterly*, 65, 48.

12. O'Connor, J. V. (2000). FAQs #1 Cuss Control Academy. Retrieved from http://www.cusscontrol.com/faqs.html

13. Gudykunst, W. B., & Matsumoto, Y. (1996). Cross-cultural variability of communication in personal relationships. In W. B. Gudykunst, S. Ting-Toomey, & T. Nishida (Eds.), *Communication in personal relationships across cultures* (p. 21). Thousand Oaks, CA: Sage.

14. Levine, D. (1985). *The flight from ambiguity* (p. 28). Chicago, IL: University of Chicago Press.

15. Anti-Defamation League: National Security Adviser Jones told "inappropriate, stereotypic" joke about Jewish merchant (2010, April 26). ABCNews.com. Retrieved from http://blogs.abcnews.com/politicalpunch/2010/04/antidefamation-league-national-security-adviser-jones-told-inappropriate-stereotypic-joke-about-jewi.html

16. Duck, S. W. (1994). *Meaningful relationships*. Thousand Oaks, CA: Sage. See also Shotter, J. (1993). *Conversational realities: The construction of life through language*. Newbury Park, CA: Sage.

17. Richards, I. A., & Ogden, C. K. (1923). *The meaning of meaning: A study of the influence of language upon thought and the science of symbolism*. Orlando, FL: Harcourt.

18. Ibid.

19. O'Grady, W., Archibald, J., Aronoff, M., & Rees-Miller, J. (2001). *Contemporary linguistics* (4th ed.). Boston: Bedford/St. Martin's.

20. Fought, C. (2003). *Chicano English in context* (pp. 64–78). New York, NY: Pallgrave MacMillan.

21. Glenn, C., & Gray, L. (2013). *Hodges Harbrace handbook* (18th ed.) Boston MA: Wadsworth, Cengage Learning.

22. Princeton Review (2012). *Word smart: How to build a more educated vocabulary* (5th ed.) Princeton, NJ: Princeton Review, Inc.

23. Rader, W. (2007). The online slang dictionary. Retrieved from http://www.ocf.berkeley.edu/~wrader/slang/b.html

24. Hensley, C. W. (1995, September 1). Speak with style and watch the impact. *Vital Speeches of the Day*, p. 703.

25. Schertz, R. H. (1977, November 1). Deregulation: After the airlines, is trucking next? *Vital Speeches*, p. 40.

Chapter 11 Delivery

1. Decker, B. (1992). *You've got to be believed to be heard.* New York, NY: St. Martin's Press.

2. Watzlawick, P., Bavelas, J. B., & Jackson, D. D. (1967). *Pragmatics of human communication.* New York, NY: Norton.

3. Bates, B. (1992). *Communication and the Sexes.* Prospect Heights, IL: Waveland Press; Cherulnik, P. D. (1989). *Physical attractiveness and judged suitability for leadership,* Report No. CG 021 893. Paper presented at the Annual Meeting of the Midwestern Psychological Association, Chicago, IL (ERIC Document Services No. ED 310 317); Lawrence S. G., & Watson, M. (1991). Getting others to help: The effectiveness of professional uniforms in charitable fund raising. *Journal of Applied Communication Research, 19,* 170–185; Malloy, J. T. (1975). *Dress for Success.* New York, NY: Warner; and Temple, L. E., & Loewen, K. R. (1993). Perceptions of power: First impressions of a woman wearing a jacket. *Perceptual and Motor Skills, 76,* 339–348.

4. Phillips P. A., & Smith, L. R. (1992). *The effects of teacher dress on student perceptions,* Report No. SP 033 944. (ERIC Document Services No. ED 347 151).

5. Morris, T. L., Gorham, J., Cohen, S. H., & Huffman, D. (1996). Fashion in the classroom: Effects of attire on student perceptions of instructors in college classes. *Communication Education, 45,* 135–148.

6. Burgoon, J. K., Coker, D. A., & Coker, R. A. (1986). Communicative effects of gaze behavior: A test of two contrasting explanations. *Human Communication Research, 12,* 495–524.

7. Chiang, L. H. (1993). *Beyond the language: Native Americans' nonverbal communication.* Paper presented at the Annual Meeting of the Midwest Association of Teachers of Educational Psychology, Anderson, IN (ERIC Document Services No. ED 368540).

8. Boardman, M. (2013, February 26). Anne Hathaway acceptance speech: Best supporting actress winner practiced a lot. Huffington Post, Retrieved from http://www.huffingtonpost.com/2013/02/26/anne-hathaway-acceptance-speech-best-supporting-actress_n_2767270.html

9. Exclusive: Anne Hathaway practiced her Oscar speech a lot to be more likable. (2013, February 26). UsWeekly. Retrieved from http://www.usmagazine.com/celebrity-news/news/anne-hathaway-practiced-her-oscar-speech-a-lot-to-be-more-likable-2013262

10. Menzel, K. E., & Carrell, L. J. (1994). The relationship between preparation and performance in public speaking. *Communication Education, 43,* 23.

11. Palin's "cheat sheet" on hand. *CNN.com.* Retrieved from http://www.cnn.com/video/#/video/politics/2010/02/08/lemon.palin.cheat.sheet.cnn?iref=allsearch

12. Mankowski, D., & Jose, R. (2012). MBC flashback: The 70th anniversary of FDR's fireside chats. *The Museum of Broadcast Communications.* Retrieved from http://www.museum.tv/exhibitionssection.php?page=79

13. Obama, B. (n.d.). Your weekly address. *The White House.* Retrieved from http://www.whitehouse.gov/briefing-room/weekly-address/

14. Thomas, W. G. (2004). Television news and the civil rights struggle: The views in Virginia and Mississippi. *Southern Spaces.* Retrieved from http://southernspaces.org/2004/television-news-and-civil-rights-struggle-views-virginia-and-mississippi

15. Camia, C. (2011, October 31). Rick Perry's speech video goes viral. *USA Today.* Retrieved from http://content.usatoday.com/communities/onpolitics/post/2011/10/rick-perry-viral-video-new-hampshire-/1#.UXvsbIJOmcY

16. Used with permission of Alyssa Grace Millner.

Chapter 12 Informative Speaking

1. Otzi, the ice man. (n.d.). *Dig: The archaeology magazine for kids.* Retrieved from http://www.digonsite.com/drdig/mummy/22.html

2. Dote, L., Cramer, K., Dietz, N., & Grimm, R. Jr. (2006). *College students helping America.* Washington, DC: Corporation for National and Community Service. Vegan Society website. Retrieved from http://www.vegansociety.com

3. Based on "Narrative" by Baerwald, D., & Northshore School District. Retrieved from http://ccweb.norshore.wednet.edu/writingcorner/narrative.html

4. Needleman, R. (Host). (2010, May 7). Reporters' roundtable: Ethics in online journalism. *CNET News.* [Audio podcast]. Retrieved from http://www.cnet.com/8301-30976_1-20004497-10348864.html

5. Sandoval, G. (2010, April 20). How Gizmodo got its iPhone scoop. *CNET News.* Retrieved from http://news.cnet.com/8301-31001_3-20002975-261.html?tag=mncol;txt

6. Bilton, Nik. "Two charged in missing iPhone Prototype case." Retrieved from http://bits.blogs.nytimes.com/2011/08/10/2-charged-in-missing-prototype-iphone-4-case/. *New York Times: Bits,* August 10, 2011.

7. Used with permission of Logan Hurley.

Chapter 13 Persuasive Messages

1. Kang, C. (2010, April 24). Undercover persuasion by tech industry lobbyists. *The Washington Post.* Retrieved from http://www.washingtonpost.com/wp-dyn/content/article/2010/04/23/AR2010042305249.html

2. Perloff, R. M. (1993). *The dynamics of persuasion.* Hillsdale, NJ: Erlbaum.

3. Kennedy, G. A. (1980). *Classical rhetoric and its Christian and secular tradition from ancient to modern times.* Chapel Hill, NC: The University of North Carolina Press.

4. Toulmin, S. (1958). *The uses of argument.* Cambridge, England: Cambridge University Press.

5. Theron Tackles Public Speaking Fears in New Film. (2005, October 26). Contact Music.com. Retrieved from http://www.contactmusic.com/news-article/theron-tackles-public-speaking-fears-in-new-film

6. Hall, K. (2009, September 17). Charlize Theron: I won't get married until my gay friends can. *Huffington Post.* Retrieved from http://www.huffingtonpost.com/2009/09/17/charlize-theron-i-wont-ge_n_290073.html

7. Messengers of Peace (n.d.). United Nations. Retrieved from http://www.un.org/sg/mop/theron.shtml

8. Retrieved from http://www.nia.nih.gov/Alzheimers/Publications/ADProgress2005_2006/Part1/looming.htm

9. Labor, R. (1998). Shaken baby syndrome: The silent epidemic. In *Winning orations* (pp. 70–72). Mankato, MN: Interstate Oratorical Association.

10. James, J. (2007, January). No time for complacency. *Vital Speeches of the Day, 73,* 26–29.

11. Ibid.

12. Ibid.

13. Stewart, R. (1994). Perceptions of a speaker's initial credibility as a function of religious involvement and religious disclosiveness. *Communication Research Reports, 11,* 169–176.

14. Morris, T. L., Gorham, J., Cohen, S. H., & Huffman, D. (1996). Fashion in the classroom: Effects of attire on student perceptions of instructors in college classes. *Communication Education, 45,* 135–148; Treinen, K. (1998). *The effects of gender and physical attractiveness on peer critiques of a persuasive speech.* Unpublished master's thesis, North Dakota State University, Fargo, ND.

15. Perloff, *Dynamics of persuasion.*

16. Petri, H. L., & Govern, J. M. (2004). *Motivation: Theory, research, and application* (5th ed., p. 376). Belmont, CA: Wadsworth.

17. Nabi, R. L. (2002). Discrete emotions and persuasion. In J. P. Dillard & M. Pfau (Eds.), *The persuasion handbook: Developments in theory and practice* (pp. 291–299). Thousand Oaks, CA: Sage.

18. Megan's law. Retrieved from http://www.accessmylibrary.com/coms2/summary_0286-6368573_ITM

19. Slator, D. (1998). Sharing life. In *Winning orations* (pp. 63–66). Mankato, MN: Interstate Oratorical Association.

20. Labor, Shaken baby syndrome.

21. Ibid.

Chapter 14 Persuasive Speaking

1. Petty, R. E., & Cacioppo, J. (1996). *Attitudes and persuasion: Classic and contemporary approaches* (p. 7). Boulder, CO: Westview.

2. Cheadle, D., & Prendergast, J. (2007). *Not on our watch: The mission to end genocide in Darfur and beyond.* New York: Hyperion.

3. Pitt, B. (n.d.) Brad Pitt quotes with pictures. *QuotesPapa.* Retrieved from http://www.quotespapa.com/authors/brad-pitt-quotes.html

4. Hill, B., & Leeman, R. W. (1997). *The art and practice of argumentation and debate* (p. 135). Mountain View, CA: Mayfield.

5. Ziegelmueller, G. W., Kay, J., & Dause, C. A. (1990). *Argumentation: Inquiry and advocacy* (2nd ed., p. 186). Englewood Cliffs, NJ: Prentice Hall.

6. Molly Reynolds, University of Kentucky.

7. Used with permission.

8. Benbow, J. (2013, April 21). David Ortiz's speech caps emotional ceremony. *Boston Globe,* Retrieved from http://www.bostonglobe.com/sports/2013/04/20/david-ortiz-impassioned-speech-caps-emotional-red-sox-pregame-ceremony/Ushx2LJ6b8ozPsz1u71cPM/story.html

9. Perry, D. (2013, April 20). The FCC has no problem with David Ortiz's speech. *CBSSports.com.* Retrieved from http://www.cbssports.com/mlb/blog/eye-on-baseball/22111863/the-fcc-has-no-problem-with-david-ortizs-speech

10. Ibid.

11. Schwartz, N. (2013, April 21). FCC overlooks Ortiz's passionate, profane speech to Red Sox fans. *USA Today,* Retrieved from http://usatoday.com/story/gameon/2013/04/20/david-ortiz-boston-red-sox-speech-fcc/2100051/

Chapter 15 Ceremonial Speaking

1. Manning, K. (2012, June 4). 10 things we can learn about public speaking from Kristen Stewart (because she is the worst). *The Grindstone.* Retrieved from http://www.thegrindstone.com/2012/06/04/career-management/dos-and-donts-strategy/10-things-we-can-learn-about-public-speaking-from-kristen-stewart-597/

Chapter 16 Group Communication and Presentations

1. O'Hair, D., O'Rourke, J., & O'Hair, M. (2001). *Business communication: A framework for success.* Cincinnati, OH: South-Western; Snyder, B. (2004). Differing views cultivate better decisions. *Stanford Business.* Retrieved from http://www.gsb.stanford.edu/NEWS/bmag/sbsm0405/feature_workteams_gruenfeld.shtml; Teams that succeed. (2004). *Harvard Business Review.* Boston: Harvard Business School Press.

2. Tullar, W., & Kaiser, P. (2000). The effect of process training on process and outcomes in virtual groups. *Journal of Business Communication, 37,* 408–427.

3. Lesikar, R., Pettit Jr., J., & Flately, M. (1999). *Basic business communication* (8th ed.). New York, NY: McGraw-Hill.

4. Northouse, G. (2007). *Leadership theory and practice* (4th ed.). Thousand Oaks, CA: Sage.

5. Gardner, H. (2011). *Leading minds: An anatomy of leadership.* New York: Basic Books.

6. Kippenberger, T. (2002). *Leadership styles.* New York: John Wiley and Sons.

7. Fairhurst, G. T. (2001). Dualism in leadership. In F. M. Jablin & L. M. Putnam (Eds.), *The new handbook of organizational communication* (pp. 379–439). Thousand Oaks, CA: Sage.

8. Frey, L., & Sunwulf. (2005). The communication perspective on group life. In S. A Wheelen (Ed.). *The handbook of group research and practice* (pp. 159–186). Thousand Oaks, CA: Sage.

9. Rahim, M. A. (2001). *Managing conflict in organizations* (3rd ed.). Westport, CT: Greenwood Press.

10. Janis, I. L. (1982). *Groupthink: Psychological studies of policy decision and fiascos* (2nd ed.). Boston, MA: Houghton Mifflin.

11. Sell, J., Lovaglia, M. J., Mannix, E. A., Samuelson, C. D., & Wilson, R. K. (2004). Investigating conflict, power, and status within and among groups. *Small Group Research, 35,* 44–72.

12. Ting-Toomey, S., & Oetzel, J. (2003). Cross-cultural face concerns and conflict styles: Current status and future directions. In W. B. Gudykunst and W. B. Mody (Eds.). *Handbook of international and intercultural communication* (2nd ed.; pp. 143–163). Thousand Oaks, CA: Sage.

13. Bordia, P., DiFonzo, N., & Change, A. (1999). Rumor as group problem-solving: Development patterns in informal computer-mediated groups. *Small Group Research, 30,* 8–28.

14. Jiang, L., Bazarova, N. N., & Hancock, J. T. (2011). The disclosure-intimacy link in computer-mediated communication: An attributional extension of the hyperpersonal model. *Human Communication Research, 37,* 58–77.

15. Wang, Z., Walther, J. B., & Hancock, J. T. (2009). Social identification and interpersonal communication in computer mediated communication: What you do versus who you are in virtual groups. *Human Communication Research, 35,* 59–85.

16. Godamer, H. (1989). *Truth and method* (2nd ed., J. Weinsheimer & D. G. Marshall, Trans.). New York, NY: Crossroad.

17. Braithwaite, D. O., & Eckstein, N. (2003). Reconceptualizing supportive interactions: How persons with disabilities communicatively manages assistance. *Journal of Applied Communication Research, 31,* 1–26.

18. Conrad, C. (1997). *Strategic organizational communication: Toward the 21st century.* Harcourt Brace.

19. *The View on TV.com.* Retrieved from http://www.tv.com/the-view/show/1676/summary.html

20. Dewey, J. (1933). *How we think.* Boston: Heath.

21. Duch, B. J., Groh, S. E., & Allen, D. E. (Eds.). (2001). *The power of problem-based learning.* Sterling, VA: Stylus; Edens, K. M. (2000). Preparing problem solvers for the 21st century through problem-based learning. *College Teaching,48*(2), 55–60; Levin, B. B. (Ed.). (2001). *Energizing teacher education and professional development with problem-based learning.* Alexandria, MN: Association for Supervision and Curriculum Development.

22. Young, K. S., Wood, J. T., Phillips, G. M., & Pedersen, D. J. (2007). Group discussion: A practical guide to participation and leadership (4th ed). Long Grove, IL: Waveland Press.

23. Andres, H. P. (2002). A comparison of face-to-face and virtual software development teams. Team Performance managements: An International Journal, 8–1/2, 39–48.

24. Olson, J., & Teasley, S. (1996). Groupware in the wild: Lessons learned from a year of virtual collocation. In Proceedings of the ACM Conference, Denver, CO, USA, pp. 419–427.

25. Warkentin, M. E., Sayeed, L., & Hightower, R. (1997). Virtual teams versus face-to-face teams: An exploratory study of a Web-based conference system. Decision Sciences, 28(4), 957–996.

26. Huang, W. W., Wei, K. K., Watson, R. T., & Tan, B. C. Y. (2003). Supporting virtual team-building with a GSS: An empirical investigation. *Decision Support Systems, 34,* 359–367.

27. Shoemaker-Galloway, J. (2007, August 6). Top 10 netiquette guidelines. *Suite 101,* Retrieved from http://suite101.com/article/netiquette-guidelines-a26615

glossary

abstract a short paragraph summarizing the research findings

accent the inflection, tone, and speech habits typical of native speakers of a language

accommodating a conflict management style that involves accepting others' ideas while neglecting your own, even when you disagree with their views

accurate language words that convey your meaning precisely

accurate sources attempt to present unbiased information and often include a balanced discussion of controversial topics

action an attention-getting act designed to arouse interest in your topic

the action appeal step the conclusion

action-oriented listeners listeners who focus on the ultimate point the speaker is trying to make

active listening the deliberate and conscious process of attending to, understanding, remembering, evaluating, and responding to messages

actual object an inanimate or animate sample of the idea you are communicating

ad hominem a fallacy that occurs when a speaker attacks or praises a person making an argument rather than addressing the argument itself

adaptation phase the period during which your anxiety level gradually decreases

alliteration repetition of consonant sounds at the beginning of words that are near one another

analogy an extended metaphor

anecdotes brief, often amusing stories

anger feeling when we are faced with an obstacle in the way of something we want

animated delivery that is lively, and dynamic

annotated bibliography a preliminary record of the relevant sources you find pertaining to your topic

anticipation phase the anxiety you experience prior to giving the speech

antithesis combining contrasting ideas in the same sentence

antonym a word that is directly opposite in meaning

apathetic the audience is uninterested in, unconcerned about, or indifferent toward your topic

appeal to action a statement that describes the behavior you want your listeners to follow after they have heard your arguments

appearance the way you look to others

argue from analogy to support a claim with a single comparable example that is significantly similar to the subject of the claim

argue from causation to support a claim by citing events that have occurred that result in the claim

argue from example to support your claim by providing one or more individual examples

argue from sign to support a claim by citing events, characteristics, or situations that signal the claim information that signals the claim

argument articulating a position with the support of logos, ethos, and pathos

articulation using the tongue, palate, teeth, jaw movement, and lips to shape vocalized sounds that combine to produce a word

assonance repetition of vowel sounds in a phrase or phrases

asynchronous virtual groups those whose members can post and respond to messages at any time, although usually within a few days

attend paying attention to what the speaker is saying regardless of extraneous interference

the attention step the introduction

attitude a general or enduring positive or negative feeling about some person, object, or issue

audience the specific group of people to whom the speech is directed

audience adaptation the process of tailoring your speech's information to the needs, interests, and expectations of your listeners

audience analysis a study made to learn about the diverse characteristics of audience members and then, based on these characteristics, to predict how audience members are apt to listen to, understand, and be motivated to act on your speech

audience contact creating a sense of looking listeners in the eye when speaking to large audiences

audience diversity the range of demographic and subject-related differences represented in an audience

audio aid a presentational aid that enhances the speaker's verbal message with additional sound

audiovisual aid a presentational aid that enhances the speech using a combination of sight and sound

avoiding involves physically or psychologically removing yourself from the conflict

bar graph uses vertical or horizontal bars to show relationships between or among two or more variables

blogs websites that provide personal viewpoints of their author

brainstorming an uncritical, nonevaluative process of generating alternatives by being creative, suspending judgment, and combining or adapting the ideas of others

canons of rhetoric five general rules for effective public speeches

channels both the route traveled by a message and the means of transportation

chart a graphic representation that distills a lot of information and presents it in an easily interpreted visual format

chronological following an order that moves from first to last

civic rights the essential conditions for individuals to live happy and successful lives

claim (C) the proposition or conclusion to be proven

clincher a one- or two-sentence statement that provides a sense of closure by driving home the importance of your speech in a memorable way

closed questions narrowly focused questions that require only very brief answers

cognitive restructuring a process designed to help you systematically change your intrapersonal communication (self-talk) about public speaking

collaborating a conflict management style that involves discussing the issues, describing feelings, and identifying the characteristics of an effective solution before deciding what the ultimate solution will be

commemorative address a speech of tribute that celebrates national holidays or anniversaries of important events

commencement address a speech of tribute praising graduating students and inspiring them to reach for their goals

common ground the background, knowledge, attitudes, experiences, and philosophies audience members and the speaker share

communication context the environment in which communication occurs

communication orientation motivation (COM) methods designed to reduce anxiety by helping the speaker adopt a "communication" rather than a "performance" orientation toward the speech

communication orientation viewing a speech as just an opportunity to talk with a number of people about an important topic

comparative advantages an organization that shows that a proposed change has more value than any of the alternatives.

comparison and contrast a method of informing that explains something by focusing on how it is similar to and different from other things

comparison illuminating a point by showing similarities

compassion feeling of selfless concern for the suffering of another

competing a conflict management style that involves satisfying our own needs with no concern for the needs of the others and no concern for the harm it does to the group dynamics or problem-solving process

comprehensive report a written document that provides a detailed review of the problem-solving process used to arrive at the recommendation

compromising a conflict management style that involves individuals giving up part of what they want in order to provide at least some satisfaction to other opinions

concept mapping a visual means of exploring connections between a subject and related ideas

conflict disagreement or clash among ideas, principles, or people

confrontation phase the surge of anxiety you feel as you begin delivering your speech

connotation the positive, neutral, or negative feelings or evaluations we associate with a word

constructive critique an analysis of a speech or presentation that evaluates how well a speaker meets a specific speaking goal while following the norms for good speaking and that recommends how the presentation could be improved

content-oriented listeners listeners who focus on and evaluate the facts and evidence

content the information and ideas you present

context the position of a word in a sentence and its relationship to the words around it

contrast illuminating a point by highlighting differences

conversational delivery that seems spontaneous, as though one is talking with an audience

creating suspense wording an attention getter so that what is described generates initial uncertainty or mystery and excites the audience

creative the ability to produce original, innovative ideas

credentials your experiences or education that qualifies you to speak with authority on a specific subject

credibility the perception that you are knowledgeable, trustworthy, and personable

criteria satisfaction an indirect organization that seeks audience agreement on criteria that should be considered when evaluating a particular proposition and then shows how the proposition satisfies those criteria

criteria standards used for judging the merits of proposed solutions

culture-related conflict occurs when the communication norms of group members are incongruent

decoding the process of interpreting the verbal and nonverbal messages sent by others

dedication a speech of tribute that honors a worthy person or group by naming a structure, monument, or park after them

deductive reasoning arriving at a conclusion based on a major premise and minor premise

definition a statement that clarifies the meaning of a word or phrase

deliverables products of your work that must be provided to someone else

delivery how a message is communicated through the use of voice and body

demonstration a method of informing that shows how something is done, displays the stages of a process, or depicts how something works

denotation the explicit dictionary definition of a word

derived credibility strategies employed throughout the speech that signal a speaker's expertise

description the informative method used to create an accurate, vivid, verbal picture of an object, geographic feature, setting, or image

diagram a type of drawing that shows the whole and its parts

dialect a regional variety of a language

direct question a question that seeks an overt response from the audience, usually by a show of hands

either/or a fallacy that argues there are only two alternatives when, in fact, there are many

emotions the buildup of action-specific energy

empathy the ability to see the world through the eyes of someone else

encoding the process of putting our thoughts and feelings into words and nonverbal behaviors

ethics moral principles that a society, group, or individual hold that differentiate right from wrong

ethnography a form of primary research based on fieldwork observations

ethos arguments based on competence, credibility, and good character

eulogy a ceremonial speech of tribute during a funeral or memorial service that praises someone's life and accomplishments

evaluating critically analyzing what is said to determine its truthfulness, utility, and trustworthiness

evidence any information that clarifies, explains, or otherwise adds depth or breadth to a topic

examples specific instances that illustrate or explain a general factual statement

executive summary a one-page synopsis of the report

expert opinions interpretations and judgments made by authorities in a particular subject area

expert a person recognized as having mastered a specific subject, usually through long-term study

expository speech an informative presentation that provides carefully researched in-depth knowledge about a complex topic

extemporaneous speech researched and planned ahead of time, but the exact wording is not scripted and will vary from presentation to presentation

eye contact looking at the people to whom you are speaking

facial expressions eye and mouth movements that convey emotions

facts statements whose accuracy can be verified as true

factual statements information that can be verified

false cause a fallacy that occurs when the alleged cause fails to be related to, or to produce, the effect

farewell a speech of tribute honoring someone who is leaving an organization

fear perceiving no control over a situation that threatens us

feedback the reactions and responses to messages that indicate whether and how a message was heard, seen, and interpreted

flipchart a pad of paper mounted on an easel

flowchart diagrams a sequence of steps through a complicated process

formal leader a person designated or elected to oversee the group process

formal outline a full sentence outline of your speech that includes internal references and a reference list

formal speech outline a sentence representation of the hierarchical and sequential relationships among the ideas presented in the speech

general goal the overall intent of the speech

generic language language that uses words that apply only to one sex, race, or other group as though they represent everyone

gestures movements of hands, arms, and fingers

goodwill a perception the audience forms of a speaker who they believe understands them, empathizes with them, and is responsive to them

graph presents numerical comparisons in visual form

group dynamics how individuals work together as a team toward a common goal

groupthink when group members accept information and ideas without subjecting them to critical analysis

guilt feeling when we personally violate a moral, ethical, or religious code that we hold dear

handout material printed on sheets of paper

happiness or joy the buildup of positive energy

hasty generalization a fallacy that presents a generalization that is either not supported with evidence or is supported with only one weak example

hearing the biological process that occurs when the brain detects sound waves

hope emotional energy that stems from believing something desirable is likely to happen

hypothesis an educated guess about a cause-and-effect relationship between two or more things

hypothetical examples specific instances based on reflections about future events

impromptu speech delivered with only seconds or minutes of advance notice for preparation and is usually presented without referring to notes of any kind

incremental change attempting to move your audience only a small degree in your direction

inductive reasoning arriving at a conclusion based on a series of pieces of evidence

inferences assertions based on the facts presented

informal leaders members who help lead the group to achieve different leadership functions

informative speech a speech whose goal is to explain or describe facts, truths, and principles in a way that stimulates interest, facilitates understanding, and increases the likelihood of remembering

initial audience disposition the knowledge of and opinions about your topic that your listeners have before they hear you speak

initial credibility perception of a speaker's expertise at the beginning of the speech

intellectually stimulating information that is new to audience members and is explained in a way that piques their curiosity

intelligible capable of being understood

interference/noise any stimulus that interferes with the process of sharing meaning

interpersonal communication communication between two people

interview protocol the list of questions you plan to ask

interview a planned, structured conversation where one person asks questions and another answers them

intrapersonal communication communicating with yourself (a.k.a. self-talk)

irrelevant association emphasizing one person's relationship to another when that relationship is irrelevant to the point

issue-related conflict occurs when two or more group members' goals, ideas, or opinions about the topic are incompatible

jargon the unique technical terminology of a trade or profession

joke an anecdote or a piece of wordplay designed to make people laugh

keynote address ceremonial speech that both sets the tone and generates enthusiasm for the topic of a conference or convention

knowledge and expertise how well you convince your audience that you are qualified to speak on the topic

leadership a process whereby an individual influences a group of individuals to achieve a common goal

leading questions questions phrased in a way that suggests the interviewer has a preferred answer

learning style a person's preferred way of receiving information

line graph indicates changes in one or more variables over time

listener relevance link a statement alerting listeners about how a main point or subpoint relates to them or why they should care about it

listening apprehension the anxiety we feel about listening

listening style the favored and usually unconscious approach to listening

listening the process of receiving, attending to, constructing meaning from, and responding to spoken or nonverbal messages

logical reasons order organizing the main points of a persuasive speech by the reasons that support the speech goal

logos everything you say and do to appeal to logic and sound reasoning

macrostructure the overall organizational framework you use to present your speech content

main points complete sentence statements of the two to four central ideas the audience needs to understand for your speech goal to be realized

maintenance leadership roles help the group to develop and maintain cohesion, commitment, and positive working relationships

major premise a general principle that most people agree upon

marginalizing ignoring the values, needs, and interests of certain audience members, leaving them feeling excluded from the speaking situation

marking the addition of sex, race, age, or other group designations to a description

mass communication communication produced and transmitted via media to large audiences

master of ceremonies an individual designated to set the mood of the program, introduce participants, and keep the program moving

mediated channels technology-enhanced auditory and visual channels

messages the verbal utterances and nonverbal behaviors to which meaning is attributed during communication

metaphor an implied comparison between two unlike things without using *like* or *as*

microstructure the specific language and style choices you use as you frame your ideas and verbalize them to your audience

minor premise a specific point that fits within the major premise

mnemonic device associates a special word or very short statement with new and longer information

model a three-dimensional scaled-down or scaled-up version of an actual object

modeling learning by observing and then imitating those you admire or are close to

monotone a voice in which the pitch, volume, and rate remain constant, with no word, idea, or sentence differing significantly from any other

motivated movement movement with a specific purpose

motivated sequence a persuasive organization that combines a problem-solution pattern with explicit appeals designed to motivate the audience to act.

movement changing the position or location of the entire body

multiple-response items survey items that give the respondent several alternative answers from which to choose

narration a method of informing that explains something by recounting events

narrative order organizing the main points as a story or series of stories

narratives accounts, personal experiences, tales, or lengthier stories

the need step explores the nature of the problem

negative emotions disquieting feelings people experience

netiquette etiquette rules when communicating over computer networks

neutral the audience has some information about a topic but does not really understand why one position is preferred and so still has no opinion

neutral questions questions phrased in ways that do not direct a person's answers

nonparallelism when terms are changed because of the sex, race, or other group characteristics of the individual

nonverbal communication all speech elements other than the words themselves

nonverbal immediacy a perception of being personable and likeable

occasion the expected purpose and setting for the speech

online social networks websites where communities of people interact with one another over the Internet

onomatopoeia words that sound like the things they stand for

open questions broadbased questions that ask the interviewee to provide perspective, ideas, information, or opinions

open-ended items survey items that encourage respondents to elaborate on their opinions without forcing them to answer in a predetermined way

oral brief essentially a summary of a written brief delivered to an audience by a group member

oral footnote reference to an original source, made at the point in the speech where information from that source is presented

oral report similar to a comprehensive report

oral style how one conveys messages through the spoken word

organizational chart shows the structure of an organization in terms of rank and chain of command

organizing the process of arranging your speech material, guided by what you learned from your audience analysis

other sensory aid a presentational aid that enhances the speech by appealing to smell, taste, or touch

panel discussion a problem-solving discussion in front of an audience

parallel structure when the main points follow the same structural pattern, often using the same introductory words

paraphrase putting into your own words the meaning you have assigned to a message

paraphrasing a verbal statement that conveys your understanding of another person's verbal message

participants the individuals who assume the roles of senders and receivers during an interaction

passive listening the habitual and unconscious process of receiving messages

pathos arguments that appeal to the emotions

pauses moments of silence strategically placed to enhance meaning

people-oriented listeners listeners who focus on the feelings their conversational partners may have about what they are saying

perception checking a verbal statement that reflects your understanding of another's behavior

performance orientation viewing public speaking as a situation demanding special delivery techniques to impress an audience

periodicals magazines and journals that appear at fixed periods

personableness the extent to which you project an agreeable or pleasing personality

personal pronouns "we," "us," and "our"—pronouns that directly link the speaker to members of the audience

personal reference a brief account about something that happened to you or a hypothetical situation that listeners can imagine themselves in

personality-related conflict occurs when two or more group members become defensive because they feel as though they are being attacked

personification attributing human qualities to a concept or an inanimate object

persuasion the process of influencing people's attitudes, beliefs, values, or behaviors

persuasive speaking the process of influencing people's attitudes, beliefs, values, or behaviors in a public speech

pie chart shows the relationships among parts of a single unit

pitch the highness or lowness of the sounds produced in your larynx

plagiarism the unethical act of representing another person's work as your own

plagiarize to pass off the ideas, words, or created works of another as one's own by failing to credit the source

poise the graceful and controlled use of the body that gives the impression

positive emotions feelings that people enjoy experiencing

posture the position or bearing of the body

preparation outline provides a starting point of main points but doesn't specify clearly how each main point is related to the goal

presentational aid any visual, audio, audiovisual, or other sensory material used in a speech

pride feeling of self-satisfaction as the result of an accomplishment

primacy-recency effect the tendency to remember the first and last items conveyed orally in a series

primary questions introductory questions about each major interview topic

primary research the process of conducting your own study to acquire the information you need

problem-cause-solution a form of persuasive organization that examines a problem, its cause(s), and solutions designed to eliminate or alleviate the underlying cause(s)

problem-solution a persuasive organizational pattern that reveals the nature of a problem and proposes a solution to it

problem-solving groups five to seven people who work together to complete a specific task or solve a particular problem

procedural leadership roles provide logistical support and record the group's decisions and accomplishments

process speech a speech that explains and shows how something is done, is made, or works

productive thinking to contemplate something from a variety of perspectives

pronunciation the form and accent of various syllables of a word

proposition a declarative sentence that clearly indicates the position the speaker will advocate

proposition of fact a statement designed to convince the audience that something did or did not exist or occur, is or is not true, or will or will not occur

proposition of policy a statement designed to convince the audience that they should take a specific course of action

proposition of value a statement designed to convince the audience that something is good, bad, desirable, undesirable, fair, unfair, moral, immoral, sound, unsound, beneficial, harmful, important, or unimportant

proximity the relevance of information to personal space

pseudo-conflict occurs when group members who actually agree about something believe they disagree due to poor communication

public communication communication that occurs among more than ten people where one message is presented to the participants who function as receivers whose own messages are limited to feedback

public speaking apprehension the level of fear a person experiences when anticipating or actually speaking to an audience

public speaking a sustained formal presentation by a speaker to an audience

quality the tone, timbre, or sound of your voice

question a statement designed to clarify information or get additional details

quotation a comment made by and attributed to someone other than the speaker

rapport-building questions nonthreatening questions designed to put the interviewee at ease and demonstrate your respect for them

rate the speed at which you talk

reasoning fallacies errors in reasoning

receivers participants who interpret the messages sent by others

refutative an organization that persuades by both challenging the opposing position and bolstering one's own

rehearsing the iterative process of practicing your speech aloud

reinforcement learning from personal experiences and past responses to our behavior

relaxation exercises breathing techniques and progressive muscle relaxation exercises that help reduce anxiety

relevance adapting the information in a speech so that audience members view it as important to them

reliable sources are those that have a history of presenting valid and accurate information

relief feeling when a threatening situation has been alleviated

remote access report (RAR) a computer-mediated audiovisual presentation of the group's process and outcome that others can receive through e-mail, Web posting, and so forth

repetition restating words, phrases, or sentences for emphasis

research cards are individual index cards or electronic facsimiles that identify (a) one piece of information relevant to your speech, (b) a key word or theme the information represents, and (c) the bibliographic data identifying where you found it

responding providing feedback to the speaker about what is being said; usually occurs in the form of nonverbal behaviors

responsive when speakers show that they care about the audience by acknowledging feedback, especially subtle negative cues

rhetorical figures of speech phrases that make striking comparisons between things that are not obviously alike

rhetorical questions questions phrased to stimulate a mental response rather than an actual spoken response from the audience

rhetorical situation the composite of the occasion, speaker, and the audience that influences the speech that is given.

rhetorical structures of speech phrases that combine ideas in a particular way

roast an event where guests provide short speeches of tribute about the featured guests that are developed with humorous stories and anecdotes

role a specific communication behavior group members perform to address the needs of the group at any given point in time

sadness feeling when we fail to achieve a goal or experience a loss or separation

the satisfaction step explains the proposed solution to the problem

scaled items survey items that measure the direction and/or intensity of an audience member's feeling or attitude toward something

scripted speech prepared by creating a complete written manuscript and delivered by reading from or memorizing a printed copy

secondary questions questions designed to probe the answers given to primary questions

secondary research the process of locating information that has been discovered by other people

section transitions complete sentences that show the relationship between, or bridge, major parts of a speech

self-talk intrapersonal communication regarding success or failure in a particular situation

senders participants who form and transmit messages using verbal symbols and nonverbal behaviors

sensory language appeals to the senses of seeing, hearing, tasting, smelling, and feeling

setting the location where the speech will be given

shame feeling when we have violated a moral code and it is revealed to someone we think highly of

shared leadership functions the sets of roles you and other members perform to facilitate the work of the group and to help maintain harmonious relations among members

signposts words or phrases that connect pieces of supporting material to the main point or subpoint they address

simile a direct comparison of dissimilar things using like or as

skimming a method of rapidly going through a work to determine what is covered and how

slang informal, nonstandard vocabulary and definitions assigned to words by a social group or co-culture

small group communication the interaction that occurs in a group of approximately three to ten people

speaker the source or originator of the speech

speaking appropriately using language that adapts to the needs, interests, knowledge, and attitudes of the listener and avoiding language that alienates audience members

speaking notes a keyword outline of your speech, plus hard-to- remember information and delivery cues

specific goal a single statement that identifies the exact response the speaker wants from the audience

specific language words that clarify meaning by narrowing what is understood from a general category to a particular item or group within that category

speech communities a group of people who speak a common dialect

speech goal a specific statement of what you want your listeners to know, believe, or do

speech of acceptance a ceremonial speech given to acknowledge receipt of an honor or award

speech of introduction a brief ceremonial speech that establishes a supportive climate for the main speaker, highlights the speaker's credibility by familiarizing the audience with pertinent biographical information, and generates enthusiasm for listening to the speaker and topic

speech of nomination a ceremonial speech that proposes a nominee for an elected office, honor, position, or award

speech of recognition a ceremonial speech that acknowledges someone and usually presents an award, a prize, or a gift to the individual or a representative of a group

speech of tribute a ceremonial speech that praises or celebrates a person, a group, or an event

speech of welcome a brief, ceremonial address that greets and expresses pleasure for the presence of a person or an organization

speech plan a strategy for achieving your goal

speech to actuate a speech designed to incite action

speech to convince a speech designed to seek agreement about a belief, value, or attitude

speech to entertain a humorous speech that makes a serious point

spontaneity a sounding natural no matter how many times one has practiced

stance An author's attitude, perspective or viewpoint on a topic

Standard English form of English described in an English grammar handbook

startling statement a sentence or two that grabs your listeners' attention by shocking them in some way

statement of reasons a straightforward organization in which you present your best-supported reasons in a meaningful order

statistics numerical facts

stereotyping assuming all members of a group have similar behaviors or beliefs simply because they belong to the group

story an account of something that has happened (actual) or could happen (hypothetical)

straw man a fallacy that occurs when a speaker weakens the opposing position by misrepresenting it and then attacks that weaker position

streaming video a prerecording that is sent in compressed form over the Internet

stress emphasis placed on certain words by speaking them more loudly than the rest of the sentence

structure the framework you use to organize your speech content

subject a broad area of expertise, such as movies, renewable energy, computer technology, or the Middle East

subpoints statements that elaborate on a main point

support (S) the evidence the speaker offers as the grounds for accepting the conclusion

supporting material developmental material, including personal experiences, examples, illustrations, anecdotes, statistics, and quotations

survey a canvassing of people to get information about their ideas and opinions,

syllogism the three-part form of deductive reasoning

symposium a set of prepared oral reports delivered sequentially by group members.

synergy when the result of group work is better than what one member could achieve alone

synonym a word that has the same or a similar meaning

systematic desensitization a method that reduces apprehension by gradually having people visualize and perform increasingly more frightening events while remaining in a relaxed state

systematic problem-solving method an efficient six-step method for finding an effective solution to a problem

target audience the group of people you most want to persuade

task leadership roles help the group acquire, process, or apply information that contributes directly to completing a task or goal

terminal credibility perception of a speaker's expertise at the end of the speech

thesis statement a one- or two-sentence summary of the speech that incorporates the general and specific goals and previews the main points

time order organizing the main points in sequence or by steps in a process

time-oriented listeners listeners who prefer brief and hurried conversations

timeliness showing how information is useful now or in the near future

toast a ceremonial speech offered at the start of a reception or meal that pays tribute to the occasion or to a person

topic some specific aspect of a subject

topical following an order of interest

topical order organizing the main points of the speech by categories or divisions of a subject

transcribe translating responses word for word into written form

transition a sentence or two that summarizes one main point and introduces the next one

trustworthiness the extent to which the audience can believe that what you say is accurate, true, and in their best interests

two-sided items survey items that force the respondent to choose between two answers, such as yes/no, for/against, or pro/con

understand assigning accurate meaning to what is said

uninformed the audience doesn't know enough about a topic to have formed an opinion

valid sources report factual information that can be counted on to be true

verbal immediacy language that reduces the psychological distance between you and your audience

virtual group-related conflict arises as a result of meeting through this technology-enhanced channel

virtual groups groups that convene using telephone or computer technology

virtual presence simulated presence made possible through the use of digital technology

visual aid a presentational aid that allows the audience to see what the speaker is describing or explaining

visualization a method that reduces apprehension by helping speakers develop a mental picture of themselves giving a masterful speech

the visualization step asks the audience to imagine what will happen if your proposal is implemented and is successful and/or not implemented.

vivid language language that is full of life—vigorous, bright, and intense

vocal expression variety you create in your voice through changing pitch, volume, and rate, as well as stressing certain words and using pauses

vocalized pauses unnecessary words interjected into sentences to fill moments of silence

voice the sound you produce using your vocal organs

volume how loudly or softly you speak

warrant (W) the reasoning process that connects the support to the claim

words arbitrary symbols used to represent things

written brief a very short document that describes the problem, background, process, decision, and rationale so that the reader can quickly understand and evaluate the group's product

index

A

Abbreviations, overusing, 192
Abdominal breathing, 26
Abstract, 102, 187
Accent, 201–202
Acceptance speech, 320–321
Accommodating, conflict management style, 335
Accurate language
    abstractness of, 187
    arbitrariness of, 187
    challenges of using, 187–188
    changeability of, 188
    connotation and, 188–189
    denotation and, 188
    dialect and, 189
Accurate sources, 102
Acrobat®, 164
Acronyms
    as memory prompt, 232
    overusing, 192
Action, 144
    appeal to, 149–150
    perform/motivate, 144
Action-oriented listeners, 43
Active listening, 44
Actual objects, 164
Actuation speech. See Speeches to actuate
Adaptation phase, 22
Adaptation plan. See also Audience adaptation
    for expository speech, 250
    for informative speech, 220
    for process speech, 239
    for speeches to actuate, 305
    for speeches to convince, 289
Ad hominem fallacy, 269
Adobe®, 164
Advertising, ethical standards in, 170
Age description, 233
Alliteration, 194
American Psychological Association (APA), 152
Analogy, 194, 266
Anecdotes, 111–112, 232
Anger, 273–274
Animated delivery, 200
Annotated bibliography, 113–114
Anthony, Katie, 156–159
Anticipation phase, 22
Antithesis, 195
Antonym, 234
APA. See American Psychological Association (APA)

Apathetic audience, 281, 282–283
Appeal to action, 149–150
Appearance, 203–204
Appreciative listening, 42
Apprehension, listening, 42–43
Apprehension, public speaking
    biologically based temperament and, 23
    causes of, 23–24
    cognitive restructuring and, 26–27
    communication orientation motivation (COM) methods and, 24–25
    defined, 21
    managing, 24–29
    measuring, 22–23
    personal report of (score sheet), 23
    phases of (illustrated), 22
    previous experience and, 23–24
    relaxation exercises for, 25–26
    skills level and, 24
    speech plan for reducing, 29–33
    symptoms of, 22–23
    systematic desensitization for, 26
    techniques, general, for managing, 24–27
    techniques, specific, for managing, 28–29
    visualization for reducing, 25
Arbitrary, 187
Arguments
    from analogy, 266
    from causation, 266–267
    combining, 267–268
    defined, 262
    from example, 265–266
    from sign, 264–265
    types/tests of, 264–268
Aristotle, 9–10, 216
Articles, 99–100, 117, 153
Articulation, 201
Assignments, speech
    actuation speech, 303
    constructive critique, 52
    convince, speech to, 287
    eulogies, 324
    expository speech, 248
    informative speech with presentational aids, 218
    process speech, 237
    public group presentation, 342
    self-introduction speech, 14, 34
    toast, 322
Assonance, 194
Asynchronous virtual groups, 338–339
Attending, 44–45

Attention, getting, in introduction, 141
    ask a question for, 142
    create suspense for, 144
    perform/motivate action for, 144
    personal reference for, 143
    quotation used for, 144
    with startling statement, 142
    tell joke for, 143
    tell story for, 142–143
Attention span, for adults, 45
Attitude, of audience, 63–64, 281
Audience
    in ancient Greece, 9–10
    defined, 11
    unintended, 217
Audience adaptation, 80. See also Adaptation plan
    common experiences and, 82–83
    common ground and, 82–83
    comparing unfamiliar with familiar idea, 89–90
    comprehension aids and, 87–90
    credibility of speaker and, 84–87
    cultural differences and, 91, 185–186
    defined, 11, 31, 58
    initial audience disposition and, 81
    knowledge/expertise and, 84–85
    language, familiar/specific/vivid, 88–89
    learning styles awareness and, 87–88
    opportunity recognition for, 92, 93
    personableness and, 85–87
    personal impact and, 84
    personal pronoun use and, 82
    planning and, 31–32
    planning for, 91
    proximity and, 84
    relevance and, 83–84
    retention aids and, 87–90
    rhetorical questions and, 82
    sample plan, 220
    second language regarding, 90
    timeliness and, 83
    transition use and, 88
    trustworthiness and, 85
    for virtual audiences, 216–217
    while delivering speech, 214–216
Audience analysis
    attitudes and, 63–64, 281–283
    contact person questioning for, 65
    data ethics regarding, 66
    data-gathering methods for, 64–66
    data needed in, 59–61, 63–64
    defined, 11, 57–58

of speaker, audience adaptation and, 84–87, 91, 220

types of, 271–272

Criteria, 337

Criteria satisfaction pattern, 286

Critical listening, 42

Critical thinking, 4

Critiques. *See* Constructive critiques

Cultural diversity
audience adaptation and, 91
in speaking appropriately, 185–186

Cultural perspectives, information sources and, 113

Culture-related conflict, 332

Currency, 102

Cycle of learning, 87

D

Daly, Sean, 236

Data-gathering methods, for audience analysis, 64–66

Decoding, 8

Dedication speech, 324

Deductive reasoning, 264

Definition, 111, 233–234

Deliverables, 339

Delivery, 198
adapting while delivering, 214–216
animated, 200
body, use of, 203–207
conversational, 199
defined, 13–14, 199
effective, characteristics of, 199–200
methods of, 207–209
nonverbal, 272, 277
planning and, 33
presentational aids and, 211–213
rehearsal, 209–214
speaking notes (outline) with, 209–211
speech evaluation checklist, 218–219
spontaneous, 199
style of, and speech plan, 33
virtual audience, adapting speech for, 216–217
voice, use of, 200–203

Delivery critique statements, 50–51

Democracy, 4–5

Demographic audience data, 59–60, 61, 67, 68–69

Demographic diversity, 59, 63

Demonstration, 235–236

Denotation, 188

Denton, Nick, 246

Depth, 13

Derived credibility, 271

Description, 232–233

Diagrams, 165, 166

Dialect, 189

Direct question, 142

Discriminative listening, 42

Diversity, 91, 185–186

Document cameras, 174

Dogpile, 98

Drawings, 165

DVD players, 174–175

E

EBSCOhost, 98

Economics, expository speech and, 245

Educated guesses, 66

Either/or fallacy, 268–269

Elaboration Likelihood Model (ELM), 262–263

Elaborations
anecdotes/narratives as, 111–112
comparisons/contrasts as, 112
quotations as, 112

ELM. *See* Elaboration Likelihood Model (ELM)

Emotion, 12. *See also* Pathos; *specific emotions*
guidelines for appealing to, 275–277
memorable speech and, 232
negative, 272–274
positive, 274–275
strategy of pathos and, 272–277

Emotional symptoms, of public speaking apprehension, 22

Empathic listening, 42

Empathy, 270–271

Empowerment, 5

Encoding, 8

Encyclopedias
online, 98
for secondary research, 99

Entertainment speeches, 324

Ethics. *See also* Reflect on Ethics
audience data and, 66
defined, 5
expository speech and, 245
in persuasive speeches, guidelines for, 313
as responsibility of speakers, 5–6

Ethnography, 103

Ethos
competence/credibility and, 271–272
defined, 12, 262
empathy and, 270–271
eye contact and, 204
good character and, 270–271
goodwill and, 270
in introduction, 146
responsiveness and, 271
strategy of persuasion and, 270–272

Eulogy, 16–17, 323–324

Evaluating, 48

Evaluation checklists
for critiquing a speech, 53
for delivery, 218–219
for expository speech, 249
general criteria, 15, 34–35
for group presentations, 343
for process speech, 238

for self-introduction speech, 34–35
for speeches to actuate, 304
for speech to convince, 288

Evidence, 97

Example, arguing from, 265–266

Examples, 110

Executive summary, 340

Exigence, 10, 11, 12, 44, 58, 66

Experience
common, drawing from, 82–83
as evidence, 97

Experiments, 107, 108

Expertise, articulating, 84–85

Expert opinions, 111

Expository speeches
adaptation plan for, 250
analysis of, 255–257
assignment of, 248
of a creative work, 247–248
defined, 245
evaluation checklist for, 249
goal of, 245
of historical events/forces, 246
outline for, 250–254
overview, 245
of political/economic/social/religious/ethical issues, 245
sample, 250–254
of a theory/principle/law, 247

Expressiveness, 14

Extemporaneous speeches, 208–209

Eye contact, 13–14, 33, 204–205

F

Facebook pages, 9, 99, 103

Facial expressions, 205, 277

Facts, 48

Factual statements, 107–108, 110–111

Fallacies, in reasoning, 268–269

False cause fallacy, 268

Farewell speech, 324

Fear
cognitive restructuring and, 26–27
negative emotion/pathos and, 272–273

Federal Communications Commission (FCC), 262, 313

Feedback, 8, 214

Fey, Tina, 24

Field, Sally, 101

Fieldwork observations, 103

Figures of speech, 193

Flipcharts, 174

Flowchart, 165, 167

Footnotes, oral, 116

Ford, Harrison, 27

Formal leader, 330

Formal outline, 152–159, 220–223

Formal presentation, 9

S